**by
kalton c. lahue**

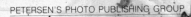

1

Photography— What It's All About

The nation's most popular hobby? It may very well be photography, which certainly enjoys the attention of countless millions. From those who still cling to their ancient box cameras to the dedicated hobbyist who counts that expensive camera and equipment among his most prized possessions, Americans continue to click their shutters with ever-increasing frequency. And by those clicks, we now count photography as an industry whose value exceeds five billion dollars a year, and one that continues to grow by leaps and bounds. Why? What's it all about? How does it work?

To address ourselves to the first question, there are many reasons why photography captivates the imagination of so many of us. Here are a few:

1—It still has a sense of magic about it, despite the fact that we can create finished pictures on the spot—almost as quickly as the so-called "instant" cameras can spit them out.

2—It's an ideal means of self-expression, allowing artistic creation on virtually any level of visual literacy. We can't all be singers, movie stars or writers, but we can all take pictures.

3—Mastering certain of its skills can gain desired approval from our peers and appreciation for our efforts—things that our vocation may not provide as readily.

4—It provides a common denominator for communication between individuals—from "shop talk" to the serious discussion of photography's merit as an art form, it's a great conversational ice-breaker.

5—It holds forth the possibility of income and offers the promise of a career to those who can qualify; rare is the amateur who has not entertained

the thought at one time or another of becoming a full-time professional, with all the attendant glamour attached to photography as a career.

With all these factors (and others not mentioned) working for it, there's little wonder that we're fascinated with the possibilities and potentials of photography, and that's what this book is all about. In its pages, I'm going to carry you through several levels, from an understanding of the fundamentals through the acquisition of a camera and equipment, showing you how to take good pictures and what to do with them. We'll look at techniques and how you can improve yours both in and out of the darkroom. And as a bonus, I'll even introduce you to the fascination of photography's history with a look at collecting photographica, the newest aspect of photography as a hobby.

To understand what photography is all about, we must look at how it works. To create a picture, we need a lighttight box (camera) to hold a piece of light-sensitive material (film) and a means of transmitting the image of the subject we wish to photograph (light). Thus, a camera, film and light are basic to photography.

THE PINHOLE CAMERA

The simplest form of camera is nothing more than a lighttight box with a sheet of film positioned at one end so that it is as flat as possible, and a very tiny hole in the other end through which light can pass. This is called a pinhole camera and is often used in basic photo classes to teach the fundamentals. As light rays always travel in a straight line, those reflected from the subject will enter the pinhole and strike the film in tiny points, creating an invisible or latent image which will become visible and permanent only after the film is treated chemically. While Figure A shows only three rays of light (for the sake of diagrammatic simplicity), every part of the subject will reflect light rays, each of which passes through the pinhole and strikes the film in a tiny point to form a continuous image or reproduction of the subject.

A pinhole camera will take good, sharp pictures, but it has several limitations. Because of the size of the passageway through which the light must pass to reach the film, it takes a comparatively long time for sufficient light reflected from the subject to create a suitable image. But suppose we enlarge the size of that pinhole entrance to let more light pass more quickly? This creates another problem, as the

light rays no longer reach the film as a series of tiny points—they're now larger circles or cones which tend to overlap each other, resulting in a blurry image as in Figure B.

In order to solve the problem and turn our pinhole camera into a useful instrument for taking pictures under a variety of conditions, we must add a lens. Now light rays reflected from the subject as a series of points can travel as cones, but when they reach the lens, it will bend them in such a manner as to reform the light cones back into points when they strike the film. By this process of bending and reforming light rays, the lens can create a sharp image of the subject, regardless of how wide its opening is (Figure C). This reduces the length of time required to form a suitable image on the film, but now we must have some means of controlling the passage of light to the film. To accomplish this, we'll add two devices—an aperture to our lens and also a shutter to our lighttight box.

THE APERTURE AND HOW IT WORKS

Also known as an iris or diaphragm, the aperture is almost always built into the lens in modern cameras, and acts in a manner similar to that of the iris in the human eye. In all but the simplest (nonadjustable) cameras, it can be opened to allow more light to pass, or closed to restrict the passage of light (Figure D). Each aperture is designed to operate at a variety of settings or f-stops which are designated by a number on a scale (Figure E). This number indicates the relative amount of light which is passed to the film at that particular setting. The *smaller* the numerical designation, the *greater* the amount of light it passes through the lens to the film; *larger* numerical designations permit *less* light to reach the film. The *smallest* aperture is also the *maximum* speed of the lens; that is, it is the setting at which the greatest amount of light the lens is capable of transmitting to the film will be passed.

Generally speaking, each aperture setting is designed to double or halve the amount of light passed, depending upon the direction of its operation. To increase the amount of light, we "open up" the aperture, or increase the size of its opening. To decrease the amount

Hank Harris' delightful interpretation of a boy and his first camera strikes a responsive chord for many of us, bringing back memories of our very first encounter with photography.

of light it passes, we close or "stop down" the aperture. To see how this works, suppose that we set the aperture indicator at the setting marked "4" (called f/4) on the scale. It will now allow *twice* as much light to pass as will the setting marked 5.6 (f/5.6). In the same manner, closing down the aperture from f/4 to f/5.6 will cut the light by one half (Figure E). Thus, it's necessary that you remember the following—the smaller the aperture number used, the greater the amount of light passed.

At this point, we are now able to exercise control over the amount of light reaching the film by adjusting the size of the aperture opening in the lens through which the light passes. But the degree of control afforded by the aperture is often insufficient for the kind of pictures we wish to take, and so further control is necessary in the form of a shutter.

THE SHUTTER

The function of the shutter is also very simple—it opens and closes to regulate the amount of light passing to the film. The quantity of light passed to the film by a shutter is measured in terms of "shutter speed" and is expressed in fractions of a second. Non-adjustable cameras use a shutter that operates at a constant, fixed speed; adjustable cameras will have a control mechanism in the form of a lever/scale or a dial containing some or all of the following series of numbers: 1, 2, 4, 8, 15, 30, 60, 125, 250, 500 and 1000. Except for the first number (1), all the rest represent fractions of a second, from ½ to 1/1000 second. When you set the lever/scale or dial to 1, you are

allowing light to pass through the aperture of the lens for one full second; set it to 500 and light will pass for only 1/500 second.

The important point here is that the shutter speed numbers relate to the amount of light reaching the film in terms of *duration,* while f-stop numbers refer to the amount of light in terms of quantity. It's a case of one standard of measurement reference versus the other, because both aperture and shutter accomplish the same thing—they permit more or less light to strike the film.

Too much light reaching the film will *overexpose* it and the image formed will become so dark that all detail is blocked out. Too little exposure will *underexpose* the film, preventing the desired detail from registering on the film. Somewhere between these extreme is the correct exposure, which will allow the image to register sufficiently to reproduce the majority of details seen in the original scene. Thus the aperture and shutter speed must be coordinated in such a way as to produce the exposure desired. We'll discuss how this is arrived at later.

As we've seen, f-stops are designed in increments to double or halve the amount of light passed. Shutter speeds are also designed in the same way. Setting the dial at 1/125 second will allow twice as much light to enter the camera as will 1/250 second, while a setting of 1/500 second will permit only half that amount of light to pass. By now, you should begin to see a correlation between shutter speeds and f-stops to control passage of light.

Suppose that the correct exposure for a given situation is determined to be 1/125 second at f/8. If you set the shutter to 1/250 second, you've cut the light in half, but open the lens from f/8 to f/5.6 (one f-stop) and you've restored the balance by doubling the amount of light again. Thus, an exposure of 1/250 second at f/5.6 will transmit *exactly* the same amount of light as an exposure setting of 1/125 at f/8. So why do we need both?

Depth of field and subject motion are the two reasons an adjustable camera requires control over both quantity and duration of light passage to the film. By using the various f-stops and shutter speeds in conjunction, we can correctly expose any given film under a wide variety of lighting and subject conditions. Let's see how it works.

DEPTH OF FIELD

Depth of field can be defined for our purposes here as the distance range

1-2. Photography means different things to different people. While some see it primarily as a means of recording the growth of their family, others use it as a tool in documenting and interpreting the society around us. (Hank Harris.)

between your camera and infinity in which objects within your picture will appear to be sharp (Figure F). The smaller the aperture setting used (f/22), the greater this range; the larger the aperture (f/1.8), the smaller the range. Every picture you take will require a certain exposure, depending upon the lighting conditions, the subject and the film used. If the correct exposure happens to be 1/250 at f/8 and you wish to increase the sharpness range, you will stop down the

lens to a smaller aperture, but to retain the correct exposure, you must also adjust the shutter speed to keep your exposure in balance or equivalent to 1/250 at f/8. So if you select f/16 under these conditions, you've closed the aperture down two f-stops (f/8 to f/11 to f/16) and must therefore allow the light to pass to the film for a longer duration of time as compensation for the reduction in quantity. To regain an equivalent exposure, the shutter should be slowed by two speeds (1/250 to 1/125 to 1/60); thus 1/60 at f/16 will produce exactly the same amount of light on the film as will 1/250 at f/8.

Depth of field can be used as a means of creative control. An unsharp background will emphasize your sub-ject in pictures taken at close distance from the camera. By using a large aperture, you will produce a limited depth of field, throwing the background into a blur. Should you want everything from foreground to background as sharp as possible, as in a landscape, the use of a small aperture size will produce the greatest range of sharpness. Depth of field is also dependent upon the point at which your lens is focused—but we'll get to that in a moment.

STOPPING MOTION

Now that we understand the practical value of an adjustable aperture beyond its ability to control the quantity of light passed to the film, let's con-sider a practical reason for the adjust-able shutter speed. If every subject which you photographed would stand as still as a statue during the exposure, you would require the use of only one shutter speed. But in many cases, sub-jects move—they talk, walk, run, jump, etc. The faster the shutter speed, the shorter duration or length of time that light is allowed to pass to the film. Shorter durations also have the capa-bility of stopping action to give you a sharp image even though your subject is moving. The action-stopping ability of any shutter speed depends upon the speed of the subject and the direction in which it is moving in front of the camera. Figure G shows this relation-ship for various common subjects.

Obviously, there are occasions when

compromises have to be made. Because of variations in film, subject and lighting conditions, it is not always possible to use a high shutter speed to stop movement while using a small aperture to retain the greatest possible sharpness range. For this reason, the photographer must understand the interrelationship between shutter speeds and apertures in order to make the most appropriate compromise which will allow him to record the subject image in a satisfactory manner.

TIME EXPOSURES

There are also times when none of the marked shutter speeds will produce an adequate exposure with the desired aperture. Thus if you refer back to the shutter speed dial or lever/scale on the camera, you'll find a setting marked "B," and on some cameras, one marked "T." These stand for *Bulb* and *Time* respectively, exposure designations that date back to the days when all exposures were made by means of a bulb and tube connected to the camera, instead of today's modern shutter release button integrated into the camera body's design.

When the shutter is set at the T or Time position and released, it will remain open indefinitely, and close only when the release is tripped a second time. If used on the B or Bulb setting, the shutter will open when released and remain open only so long as the release is held depressed. When pressure on it is released, the shutter will close. By means of a cable release with a thumbscrew lock, the B setting can be made to function in the same way that the T does. Once the cable release has been depressed and the shutter opens, the thumbscrew is tightened to hold the release plunger depressed. Release the thumbscrew when the exposure is complete and the plunger returns to the cable release, allowing the shutter to close. These two special shutter settings are designed to permit exposures greater than one second in duration, and are useful under certain circumstances, such as night exposures of stationary objects.

FOCUSING AND DEPTH OF FIELD

To return to the lens for a moment, depth of field is not the primary tool for controlling image sharpness. With adjustable cameras, this is accomplished by focusing the lens. As we've seen, when light passes through a lens, the conical rays are bent and reshaped to come to tiny points, where they create a sharp image. Thus if the picture is to

1-2. For the artistic, photography can be a means of self-expression through experimentation. (Shirley I. Fisher.)

be sharp, the film must be located at the same place where the reshaped light rays strike to form a sharp image.

The optical rules involved become overly complicated for our purpose at this time, so let's keep things simple by just stating a fact—as the distance between the lens and subject increases, the distance between the lens and film must decrease for a sharp image to form. This can be stated in another way—as the distance between the lens and subject decreases, the distance between the lens and film must increase. A bellows-type camera provides the most striking visual example of this—with the focus set at a point of infinity, the bellows will be very short when the subject is in sharp focus. Move your attention to a nearby object and bring it into sharp focus; you'll find that to do so will require a considerable bellows extension due to the nec-essary increase in lens-to-film distance (Figure H).

To assure a sharp image, the camera is first focused on the subject. The range of apparent sharpness is then determined by the choice of lens aperture. Whatever falls within this range will seem sharp when viewed by the eye, although optimum sharpness will occur only at the point at which the lens has been focused. Whatever falls outside the near and far limits of depth of field will be unsharp. At either the near or far limits of depth of field, sharpness falls off gradually; there are no abrupt or absolute changes between the sharp and unsharp areas in a picture.

To determine depth of field, you must know both the aperture to be used and the exact distance at which the lens will be focused. Using these two variables, you can find the near and far limits of the sharpness range by using a depth of field table for the particular focal length lens on your

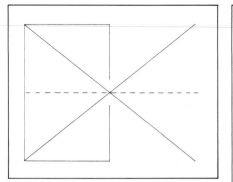
FIGURE A

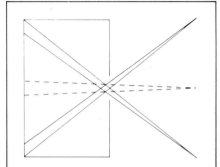
FIGURE B

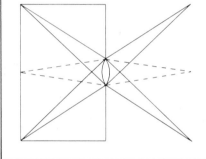
FIGURE C

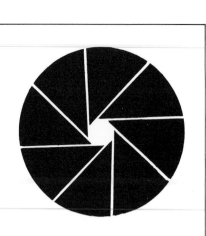

FIGURE D

F-Stop	Exposure Increase
1.4	1
2	2
2.8	4
4	8
5.6	16
8	32
11	64
16	128
22	256

Full stop aperture openings offer a 100% difference in the amount of light passed to the film. Opening the lens one f-stop doubles the amount of light; closing it one stop halves the amount.

FIGURE E

The camera's shutter speed dial can be set to regulate the duration of time light is allowed to reach the film.

camera (Figure I). These are calculated mathematically and can be used with a high degree of precision.

For most situations, the camera's depth-of-field indicator will prove adequate. This may be a table similar to that of Figure I attached to the side of a press/view camera, or it may be combined with the focusing scale on the lens barrel of most modern cameras (Figure J). To determine the *approximate* depth of field with any depth-of-field indicator, you first set the lens to a given point of focus. On each side of the focusing indicator or index line, note the lens aperture scale, which is reproduced with an index line for each aperture setting. Locate the index mark on each side of the focus index mark which corresponds to the aperture in use and then read the distances on the focusing scale to which the aperture index lines point. These will provide you with the near and far points of acceptable sharpness or depth of field, which will change if you (a) select another aperture for use or (b) focus at a different distance from the camera.

As I mentioned, this type of depth-of-field scale or indicator provides only an *approximate* indication, as focusing scales are not divided into precise increments, and at close distances it is possible that several different apertures will fall within the space between a one-foot range on the focusing scale. For precise determination of depth of field, the more comprehensive table shown in Figure I should be consulted.

BACK TO THE PINHOLE

Let's stop for a moment and think about all that we've added to and learned about what makes our pinhole camera tick. At this point, it shouldn't be too difficult to understand why the pinhole camera is inadquate for more than experimental photography—it simply isn't versatile enough. As it will only take a single picture at a time, such a camera is limited in its usefulness. To load, unload or to change film, it must be taken into a darkroom, but for *our* camera, we need some way in which we can store sufficient film in it to make several pictures at one time. To do this, there must be some means of moving the exposed film and replacing it with unexposed film for the next shot. Let's see how this can be accomplished.

FILM TRANSPORT

This can be done in various ways, depending upon the type and design of the camera. With a press or view camera (which is the nearest useful approximation to a pinhole camera) a special back accepts sheets of film in individual holders. To load the camera with film, a holder containing an unexposed piece of film is inserted in this back and a dark slide (used to protect the film in the holder from light) is removed from the holder. Light can now pass directly from the lens to the film for the exposure.

After taking the picture, the dark slide is replaced and the holder withdrawn from the back of the camera. If the holder is a standard unit, it will contain two sheets of film back-to-back but separated by a divider inside the holder. With this type of holder design, the holder can be turned over and replaced in the camera to make a second exposure on the remaining piece of film. Each side of the holder is fitted with its own separate dark slide for protection. But some holders are designed to accommodate only a single sheet of film, and with these, a fresh holder must be used for each picture. Despite such advantages as allowing you to take different pictures with different types of film at the same time, carrying all of the holders necessary for a day's shooting can be a tiresome task, and they must also be unloaded and reloaded in a darkroom.

Roll film is another way to solve the problem of taking several pictures at one time without changing film in a darkroom after each exposure. A length of film is rolled on a spool and protected from light by a somewhat longer length of opaque paper. The film is wound inside this paper backing

FIGURE F

and attached to it at one end. The back of the camera inside is designed to accept a full roll of film on one side and an empty spool on the other. To use, the paper end of the full spool must be "threaded" or connected to the empty spool on the opposite side. Turning a geared knob or handle on the outside of the camera body moves the film in its proper path (called the film plane) at the back of the camera.

To position the film for each succeeding exposure, the camera may use a small colored window on the back through which individual numbers stamped on the backing paper can be seen and thus centered as the film wind knob or lever is operated. Once very popular with roll-film cameras, this system is now considered quite primitive and has been replaced in the modern roll film camera by an exposure counter dial and gearing which allows the film to move sufficiently for a new picture and then stops it automatically when the film has been repositioned, indicating the exposure number on the exposure counter dial.

Many people have found roll film difficult to use, as it is possible that the film on the roll will loosen sufficiently while you are connecting the paper backing to the empty spool to allow light to leak in under the backing and "fog" or expose the edges of the film. And every once in a while, the fumble-fingered would fail to secure the roll in place and it would pop out and unspool while being loaded or unloaded.

To overcome these objections to roll-film camera loading, manufacturers devised the drop-in cartridge.

Essentially, this contains a roll of film complete with numbered paper backing. As it is designed to fit into the back of the appropriate camera in one way only, there can be no mistake about how to insert it. You simply open the back, drop the cartridge in place and press down to make certain that it

1

2

3

1-3 Motion can be treated in various ways. A fast shutter speed can "freeze" the subject in time and space. It may be desirable to use a shutter speed which will not freeze the subject, but permit a slight blur to visually indicate motion. For a feeling of tremendous speed, move or pan the camera with the subject to blur the background. This technique permits the use of slower speeds than would be required to freeze the action. Understanding the relationship between shutter and aperture allows the photographer to treat his subject as desired. (Ron Berkenblitt.)

USE THESE SHUTTER SPEEDS TO STOP MOTION

Subject At 25'		Line Of Motion	
Normal Walking	1/30	1/60	1/125
Child Playing	1/60	1/125	1/250
Street Activity	1/60	1/125	1/250
Swimmers, Skaters	1/60	1/125	1/250
Vehicles at 20 mph	1/125	1/250	1/500
Football & Running	1/125	1/250	1/500
Vehicles at 40 mph	1/250	1/500	1/1000
Tennis	1/250	1/500	1/1000
Horse Racing	1/500	1/1000	1/2000
Airplanes, Race Cars	1/500	1/1000	1/2000

FIGURE G

engages, then close the camera back and operate the film transport device to move the film into position until it stops. The film transport mechanism will not allow you to wind the film too much, and slots in the back of the cartridge and camera back permit you to use the numbers on the paper backing instead of an exposure counter dial to determine how many pictures you have taken and/or remain to be used.

While the drop-in cartridge is used mainly with inexpensive and uncomplicated cameras, the most common solution to our problem of multiple pictures is the 35mm cartridge or cassette. This contains a length of film 35mm wide (hence its name) sufficient for 20 or 36 exposures, and has evenly spaced perforations (called sprocket holes) along each edge. The cartridge is placed in the camera, the film which sticks out of the cartridge (called leader) is withdrawn far enough to connect it securely to the take-up spool on the opposite side of the camera body, and the film is positioned and transported by one or two sprockets containing a number of teeth which engage the perforations along the edge of the film.

Once the specified number of pictures has been taken, the film must be rewound back into the original cartridge before the camera back can be opened and the film replaced by a fresh cartridge. To do this, there is a rewind device built into the camera's transport system. When activated, it disengages the transport mechanism in the same way that shifting a car's transmission into neutral disengages the transmission from the engine. This allows the film to be pulled back into the cartridge by turning a small rewind crank provided for the purpose.

Having explored the theory behind the pinhole camera and how it works to take a picture, it's time to move into the realm of specifics. Cameras come in various shapes and sizes, and use several different types of designs to solve basic problems of viewing, focusing, etc. So let's turn our attention from our modified pinhole camera and take a look at the basic features as used in different types of cameras, and how they work.

VIEWING/FOCUSING SYSTEMS

Basically, there are three types of viewing and focusing systems used by modern cameras. The most popular design at the present is the single-lens reflex (Figure K) which diverts the light passing through the lens on its way to the film to form its image on a focusing screen via a mirror. This image may be viewed from a waist-level position, but it will be reversed left-to-right. For eye-level viewing, the image is directed through the focusing screen and into a pentaprism, which reverses the image so that when seen by the eye, it reproduces the original scene before the camera in all respects. At the moment of exposure, the mirror swings up and out of the way to allow the light to reach the film, returning to a viewing position after the shutter closes. In the large-format or roll-film SLR designs (Figure L), the mirror does not return to a viewing position until the film is transported to its next frame.

The SLR design comes the closest to providing the user with a true idea of how the image will appear on the film. Because you are viewing the image as formed by the camera lens at its maximum aperture, the brightness of the image on the focusing screen will depend upon the size of that maximum aperture. A scene viewed through an f/1.2 lens will be far brighter on the focusing screen than when a telephoto lens with a maximum aperture of f/8 has been used.

Viewing the image formed by the lens provides another advantage in that you can focus at maximum aperture and then check your depth of field by stopping the lens to the aperture at which the picture will be taken. If depth of field is insufficient at that aperture, you can select another exposure combination which will allow you to use an aperture setting with sufficient depth of field. To make this process easy, most SLR camera lenses are fitted with a depth-of-field preview lever or button which stops the lens down to its preselected aperture; this can be activated without removing the camera from your eye.

You should be aware that most SLR cameras do not show you the *exact* image, but one that is slightly smaller than the film will register. This is done for a good reason. It provides a safety measure in composing your picture. As you get a hair more than you see in the viewfinder, it offers insurance against composing so close to the edge of the frame that you inadvertently cut off a part of the subject. And as color slide mounts generally intrude slightly into the picture area, it prevents composing so close to the frame edge that part of the subject will be cropped out when the transparency is mounted for projection.

A variation of this design, the twin-lens reflex or TLR camera uses two lenses arranged vertically, one to take the picture and the other for viewing purposes only (Figure M). The TLR image on the viewing screen is the same size as the negative and reversed left-to-right. Screen brightness depends

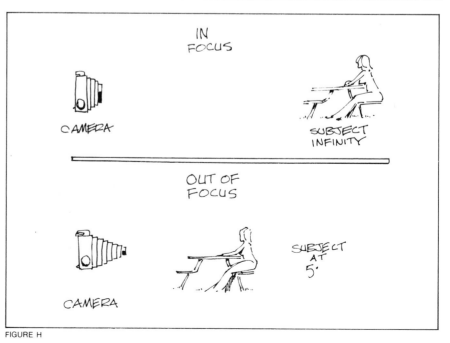

FIGURE H

FIGURE J

upon the maximum aperture of the viewing lens, which is usually close in speed to that of the taking lens. As the viewing lens contains no aperture, it is not possible to check the effect of depth of field.

Because of the difference in position of the taking and viewing lenses, subjects photographed at close distances (three feet and less) will be subject to parallax, which results from the discrepancy in viewpoint. Put simply, what you see through the viewing lens will not be the same as what the film sees through the taking lens at close distances (Figure N). Unless you compensate for this discrepancy, you'll cut off the top of your subject on the negative, even though everything looked fine in the viewfinder.

Viewing/focusing is usually done from a waist-level position, but accessory prisms are available for eye-level viewing. Very popular in the 1930s and 1940s, the TLR design has all but passed from the scene, with only three manufacturers currently offering the TLR models.

The third design uses an eye-level optical finder containing a rangefinder device as a focusing aid (Figure O). The rangefinder may provide a split image in the center of the viewfinder, or it may use a superimposed or out-of-register image (Figure P). The rangefinder works by providing two views of the subject from slightly different viewpoints. One is a direct line-of-sight view while the other passes through a semitransparent prism or mirror set at an angle 45 degrees to the axis. As the rangefinder is mechanically coupled or linked to the camera lens, focusing the lens on a given distance will align the broken lines or cause the out-of-register images to form as one. One of the two images in the range-

Object Distance (ft)	f/1.4	f/2	f/2.8	f/4	f/5.6	f/8	f/11	f/16
∞	187' / —∞	131' / —∞	93'7" / —∞	65'6" / —∞	46'10" / —∞	32'9" / —∞	23'10" / —∞	16'5" / —∞
30	25'11" / —35'8"	24'6" / —38'9"	22'10" / —43'11"	20'8" / —54'10"	18'5" / —81'11"	15'9" / —321'	13'5" / —∞	10'9" / —∞
15	13'11" / —16'3"	13'6" / —16'11"	13' / —17'9"	12'3" / —19'4"	11'5" / —21'10"	10'5" / —27'1"	9'3-7/8" / —39'	7'11-1/2" / —146'
10	9'6-1/8" / —10'6"	9'3-7/8" / —10'9"	9'7/8" / —11'2"	8'8-3/4" / —11'9"	8'3-5/8" / —12'7"	7'8-7/8" / —14'2"	7'1-3/4" / —16'9"	6'3-7/8" / —24'4"
7	6'9-1/8" / —7'3-1/8"	6'8" / —7'4-1/2"	6'6-1/2" / —7'6-3/8"	6'4-3/8" / —7'9-3/8"	6'1-5/8" / —8'1-3/4"	5'10" / —8'9-1/4"	5'5-7/8" / —9'8-3/8"	5' / —11'9"
5	4'10-5/8" / —5'1-1/2"	4'10" / —5'2-1/8"	4'9-1/4" / —5'3-1/8"	4'8-1/8" / —5'4-1/2"	4'6-5/8" / —5'6-1/2"	4'4-5/8" / —5'9-3/4"	4'2-3/8" / —6'2-3/8"	3'11" / —6'11-1/2"
4	3'11-1/8" / —4'7/8"	3'10-3/4" / —4'1-3/8"	3'10-1/4" / —4'1-7/8"	3'9-1/2" / —4'2-3/4"	3'8-5/8" / —4'4"	3'7-1/4" / —4'5-7/8"	3'5-3/4" / —4'8-1/2"	3'3-1/2" / —5'1-1/2"
3.5	3'5-3/8" / —3'6-3/4"	3'5" / —3'7"	3'4-5/8" / —3'7-3/8"	3'4-1/8" / —3'8-1/8"	3'3-3/8" / —3'9"	3'2-3/8" / —3'10-3/8"	3'1-1/4" / —4'1-1/4"	2'11-3/8" / —4'3-7/8"
3	2'11-1/2" / —3'1/2"	2'11-1/4" / —3'3/4"	2'11" / —3'1"	2'10-5/8" / —3'1-1/2"	2'10-1/8" / —3'2-1/8"	2'9-3/8" / —3'3-1/8"	2'8-1/2" / —3'4-3/8"	2'7-1/8" / —3'6-3/4"
2.5	2'5-5/8" / —2'6-3/8"	2'5-1/2" / —2'6-1/2"	2'5-3/8" / —2'6-5/8"	2'5-1/8" / —2'7"	2'4-3/4" / —2'7-3/8"	2'4-1/4" / —2'8"	2'3-5/8" / —2'8-7/8"	2'2-5/8" / —2'10-3/8"
2	1'11-3/4" / —2'1/4"	1'11-3/4" / —2'1/4"	1'11-5/8" / —2'3/8"	1'11-3/8" / —2'5/8"	1'11-1/4" / —2'7/8"	1'10-7/8" / —2'1-1/4"	1'10-1/2" / —2'1-3/4"	1'9-7/8" / —2'2-5/8"

FIGURE I

1-2 Depth of field or the range of apparent sharpness is determined by two factors— the point at which the lens is focused and the aperture used. Background/foreground control is demonstrated here; both pictures were taken at the same aperture, but the focal point of the lens was changed between shots.

finder is usually tinted a contrasting color to assist in focusing.

Rangefinder focusing is considered to be faster in use and more accurate under low light conditions, but as viewing is not done through the lens, it is not possible to check depth of field, or to avoid parallax at close distances. Some rangefinder cameras use a viewfinder with a projected bright frame as an aid in composing your picture. Such bright-frame viewfinders usually include parallax compensation marks to help guide you in accurate framing of your subject at close distances (Figure Q).

Variations of the optical viewfinder without a rangefinder are used in less-expensive cameras, most 110 pocket cameras and the Kodak/Polaroid instant cameras. Such viewfinders may

contain data displays of exposure information, bright frame lines with parallax marks, center framing circles or absolutely nothing. Cameras using such viewfinders either have fixed-focus lenses, or are focused by scale—that is, aligning the focusing ring on the lens to an index mark after estimating the distance visually.

AUTOMATIC EXPOSURE CONTROL

Automatic exposure control may be either the shutter-preferred or aperture-preferred type, depending upon the philosophy of exposure adopted by the manufacturer of a given camera. Both are quite simple in their operation and can be easily used.

To use a shutter-preferred camera, you select and set the shutter speed desired and the metering system will pick the correct aperture to provide proper exposure as it determines the requirements of the scene. With an aperture-preferred model, you choose and set the aperture and the meter adjusts the shutter speed accordingly.

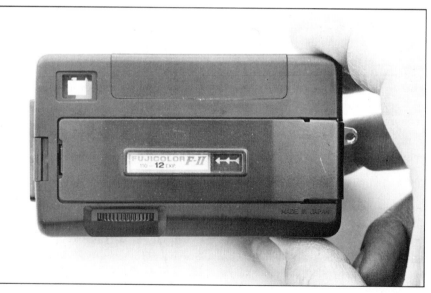

Proponents of each system condemn the other as follows—those in favor of shutter-preferred cameras complain that the aperture-preferred model may select a shutter speed too slow to capture the subject without blurring it. Aperture-preferred fans claim that the shutter-preferred models do not make proper allowances for a desired depth of field—the camera may select an aperture too large or too small to provide the effect wanted. Both viewpoints are narrow-minded and exhibit a lack of basic understanding on the part of those who repeat them.

Either type of exposure automation can be used without penalty. The aperture-preferred camera will indicate the shutter speed selected, and if the user feels it is not sufficiently fast, all he need do is adjust the aperture ring until the camera indicates a more suitable speed. In essence, the aperture ring is used to regulate and control the shutter speed.

By the same token, users of shutter-preferred cameras who are not in agreement with the aperture selected by the metering system have only to turn the shutter speed dial to another setting and the aperture will change. While it's true that a compromise has been made in either case, every photographer should realize that he is

dealing with a series of compromises all along the line whenever he sets out to take a picture. For every advantage or convenience, there's an accompanying disadvantage or inconvenience to be considered.

One type of metering system is no better than the other in terms of convenience; it's now you make use of it that really counts, and for this reason, a manual override on the automation is provided on most automatic-exposure models. This allows you either to compensate in the exposure chosen by the

camera, or return its operation to a match-needle (semiautomatic) mode whenever you wish to allow for special conditions, such as backlighting.

CAMERA SHUTTERS

The two major shutter designs used in modern cameras are improved versions of shutters which date back to the turn of the century. While a large number of refinements characterize today's versions, they operate essentially as did their predecessors.

LEAF SHUTTERS—These use a series

3

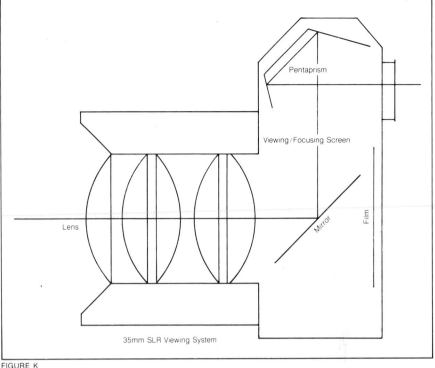

FIGURE K

35mm SLR Viewing System

1. The drop-in cartridge-loading camera has greatly simplified photography for millions of users.

2. Convenience has been a key factor in popularizing photography. With the cartridge camera, there's never any doubt about which type of film is being used, how many exposures it contains or when all the film has been exposed.

3. Film comes in different forms, depending upon the camera with which it is intended to be used.

of metal blades shaped like pie wedges which converge to form a whole. When the shutter is released, the blades pivot out of the aperture's way for the duration of the exposure, then return. Shutter speeds are controlled by escapement-retard or gear-detent systems in which a series of cams, gears and springs are used.

The leaf shutter is relatively simple, can be adjusted with great precision and will maintain such adjustment as long as undue tension is not placed on the springs for long periods of time. Because of blade bounce at high shutter speeds, the leaf shutter is limited to a top speed of 1/500 second, although the epitome of its design was reached some years ago with the Kodak Synchro-Rapid 800 shutter. Although no longer available, this shutter had a top speed of 1/800 second and is highly prized on the used market now.

FOCAL-PLANE SHUTTERS—The most commonly used shutter today is the horizontal-traveling focal plane (Figure R). In its simplest form, the typical focal-plane shutter consists of a length of rubberized cloth or metal on rollers and uses a pair of opaque flexible ''blinds'' that traverse the film plane from right to left. Releasing the shutter rolls the curtain across the focal plane and the second blind follows the first a fraction of a second later, creating a slit which exposes the film one portion at a time as it travels. This can cause elongation or compression of moving objects under certain conditions, leading to unusual effects when photo-

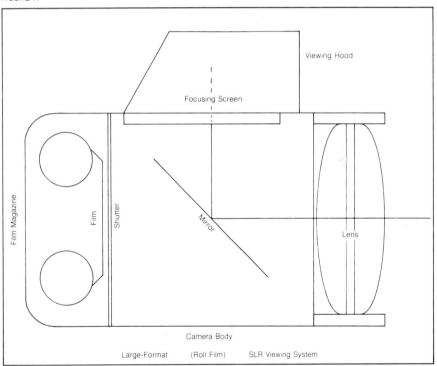

FIGURE L

Large-Format   (Roll Film)   SLR Viewing System

graphing such subjects as race cars.

Three methods are used to determine how much light will strike the film: a fixed speed of travel with a variable slit, a variable speed of travel with a fixed slit, or both variable speed and variable slit. The curtain must be rewound after each exposure, an operation which is usually coupled to the film advance. Focal-plane shutters are relatively easy to design, manufacture and maintain, and today's versions are both accurate and rugged, qualities not always attributed to the focal-plane design in the past. Generally speaking,

the horizontal focal-plane shutter can deliver higher speeds (to 1/2000 second), tends to develop problems with the slower speeds (below 1/30 second) first, and can usually be synchronized for flash only at speeds of 1/60 second and below.

Recent variations in focal-plane shutter design use vertical traveling metal blades (Figure R). Because it must traverse a shorter distance than the horizontal type, these shutters can be flash synchronized at speeds to 1/90 second (Copal Leitz shutter) or 1/125 second (Copal Square).

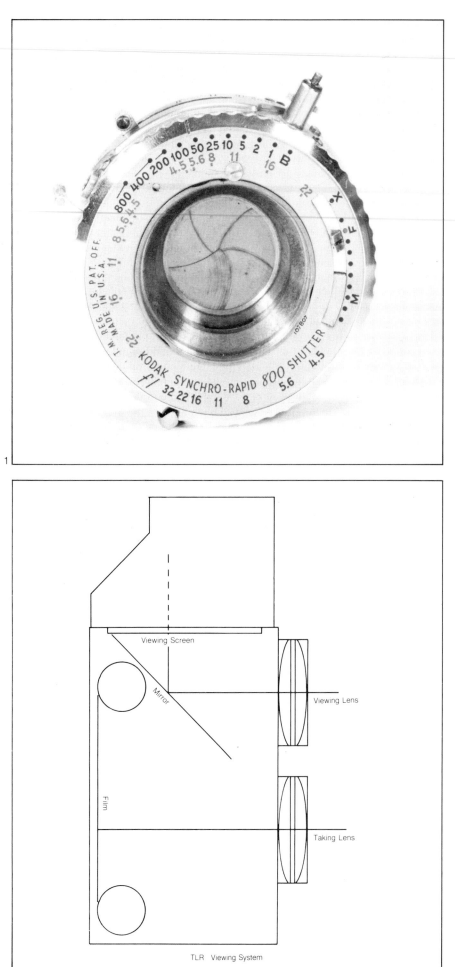

FIGURE M

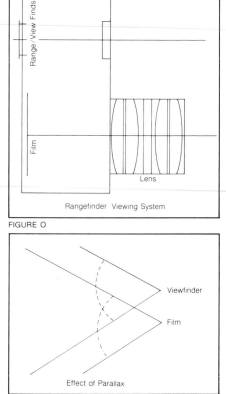

Rangefinder Viewing System

FIGURE O

Viewfinder

Film

Effect of Parallax

FIGURE N

BLADE-TYPE SHUTTERS

Brought to prominence by Polaroid in its Color Pack Automatic 100 of 1963, blade shutters are usually mechanically cocked and electromagnetically governed. Variations of this type shutter abound in the 110 pocket camera and instant camera designs because of its compactness. While some use a separate aperture device, the recent trend has been to form an aperture of the desired size by controlling blade movement in a semi-circular motion (Figure S) rather than the horizontal motion as shown in Figure T.

Generally speaking, blade-type shutters operate in the following manner. Tripping the shutter release button after the shutter is cocked lets the first blade move, allowing light to pass through the aperture to the film. The shutter's transistorized circuitry monitors this light, while an energized electromagnet holds back the second or closing blade. With the release of the opening blade, the timing switch also opens, allowing its circuit capacitors to draw and store electrical current from the battery and passed by the CdS photocell.

Current builds up at the base of a timing circuit transistor at a rate controlled by the light intensity as read by the photocell and the combination of capacitors selected by the aperture wheel. When this current reaches a predetermined triggering level, the tim-

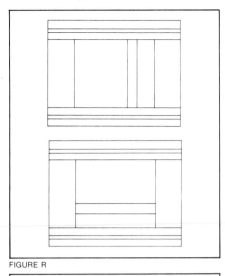

FIGURE R

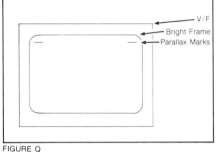

FIGURE Q

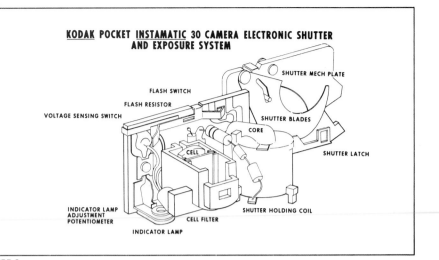

FIGURE S

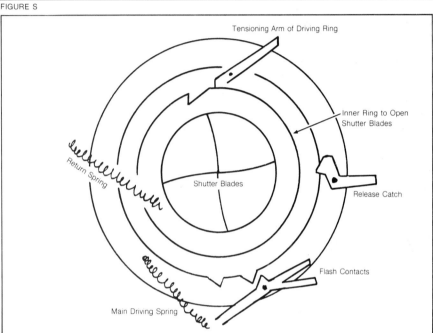

FIGURE P

ing circuit transistor begins to conduct, drawing energy from the electromagnet hold-on circuit. This in turn de-energizes the electromagnet, which then releases the closing blade to automatically complete the exposure. Electronically governed blade shutters can be designed to operate efficiently at speeds between 10 seconds and 1/1200 second or even faster, although the speed of most seldom exceeds 1/450 second because of the camera's exposure control programming system.

SHUTTER-GOVERNING DEVICES

Until the early 1970s, all leaf and focal-plane shutters were mechanically operated and governed with specific predetermined mechanical speed settings. Some older leaf shutter designs allowed the user to split the difference between designated settings by placing the speed dial in the middle of two settings. But the only mechanical means of varying focal-plane shutter speeds remained the size of the slit and speed of travel, until Asahi introduced its Pentax ES with an electrically governed focal-plane shutter in 1971.

Mechanically governed shutters operate on a step basis; that is, each shutter speed gives 50 percent less exposure (starting from one second) than the preceding speed. By adding an electronic governor to the focal-plane shutter, it became possible to produce a stepless shutter in which speeds are infinitely variable, and chosen according to the requirements specified by the camera's metering system. This means that instead of calculating exposure in terms of the required aperture, as set by the user, and a corresponding mechanical shutter-speed block

1. The Kodak Synchro-Rapid 800 shutter exemplifies leaf shutter design.
2. This simplified operational diagram of a four-blade leaf shutter shows the reliance on springs, gears and cams to regulate its operation.

(1/60, 1/125, 1/250 second, etc.), this new form of control allowed the shutter to open and close at any speed it was told to—1/47, 1/85, 1/167, 1/381 second, or whatever precise speed is determined by the meter as being optimum for the subject/light conditions at hand.

At the present time, leaf shutters continue to be mechanically governed, and probably always will be. The focal-plane shutter used in shutter-priority cameras relies on traditional mechanical gearing and linkage for its operation, while those used with aperture-priority cameras, as well as the less sophisticated blade shutters are electronically controlled.

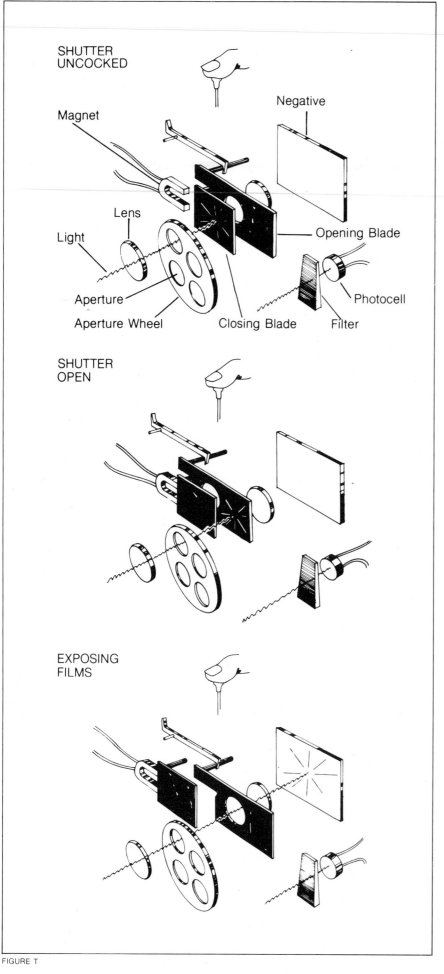

SHUTTER
UNCOCKED

Magnet

Negative

Lens

Light

Aperture

Opening Blade

Aperture Wheel

Closing Blade

Photocell

Filter

SHUTTER
OPEN

EXPOSING
FILMS

FIGURE T

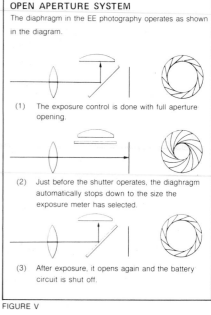

OPEN APERTURE SYSTEM

The diaphragm in the EE photography operates as shown in the diagram.

(1)   The exposure control is done with full aperture opening.

(2)   Just before the shutter operates, the diaphragm automatically stops down to the size the exposure meter has selected.

(3)   After exposure, it opens again and the battery circuit is shut off.

FIGURE V

The convertible front element design affords the option of various lenses for what is essentially a fixed lens camera. Kodak has used this system several times, although none are currently being made.

LENSES

With many cameras, it's possible to remove the lens from the camera body and replace it with one of a longer (telephoto) or shorter (wide-angle) focal length to change both the size of the image and its relationship to its surroundings as recorded on the film. Virtually all SLR cameras fall into this "interchangeable lens" category, but only one TLR (Mamiya) and one range-finder model (Leica) manufactured today will interchange lenses.

Cameras whose lenses are not removable can often be fitted with auxiliary or converter lenses which provide a limited telephoto or wide-angle effect, or they may be designed to interchange just the front element (convertible lens design) to achieve a somewhat greater degree of effect. No convertible designs are currently offered, but older examples of this type are the Zeiss Contaflex, Kodak Retina Reflex and the Retina IIIc/IIIC series—all cameras still used by many owners and desirable as second cameras for those who wish an inexpensive but quality camera which they can carry around without worrying too much about theft/damage/etc.

LENS MOUNT SYSTEMS—Interchangeable lenses are available in bayonet or threaded mounts according to the requirementsof the camera body to which they will be fitted. A few years back, the 42mm screw thread design

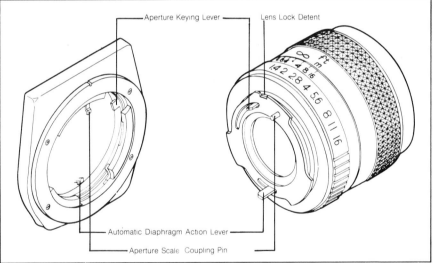

FIGURE U

(known as the Practica/Pentax thread because it fitted those cameras) was extremely popular and lenses bought for one camera body could be used with that of a different manufacturer without difficulty. This compatibility was appreciated by many owners, since they could use any one of the many hundreds of different optics offered.

But with the increasing complexity of automation built into the lens and camera body unit for metering and automatic diaphragm operation, manufacturers gradually designed their camera bodies to accept only their own lenses, and to achieve this, each used a slightly different type of mount, usually of bayonet design. By simply aligning an index mark on the lens mount with that on the camera body and turning the lens approximately one-quarter turn, the lens could be interchanged and locked in place much easier and faster than those with a screw thread, but the compatibility was gone between brands.

The latest Yashica mount used with its new Contax RTS, Yashica FX-1 and FR cameras, and shown in Figure U, is typical of the bayonet design. Note that the mount contains a corresponding pin and lever to couple with those of the lens and transfer automatic diaphragm and aperture functions regardless of the optics being used. Thus, an extreme wide-angle lens or a long telephoto will operate with the same de-

gree of automation as the camera's normal lens.

ADAPTERS—Most independent lens manufacturers offer their optics either in fixed mounts to fit a particular camera body, or in one of the "T" systems (TX, T4, T2), which use an adapter to attach the lens to the camera body. By means of various "T" adapters, the same lens can be used with a variety of different bodies. In some cases, the automatic diaphragm/automatic exposure capability may not function when an adapter is used to couple the lens and body; in other cases, full automation may be retained. It depends upon the manufacturer and the complexity of adapter design.

The primary difference between the TX, T4 and T2 adapter systems is one of automation. The T2 adapter simply allows you to connect the lens properly to different camera bodies. The T4 adapter transfers the automatic diaphragm operation and automatic exposure control from one body to another, but will not work with open-aperture metering; Vivitar's TX system does. In addition to the universal adapter systems mentioned thus far, a handful of independent lens houses have designed their own adapter system which can only be used with their lenses.

METERING SYSTEMS

We'll delve more deeply into these in later chapters; at this point, you should

1

2

1-2. Whether used for personal enjoyment or creative expression, photography holds a great fascination for all who come in contact with it. (Photo [1] Hank Harris and [2] Ron Berkenblitt.)

be aware of the differences between stop-down and open-aperture metering. Cameras equipped for stop-down metering require that you adjust the camera's exposure at the aperture to be used for taking the picture. This can be a disadvantage on bright days, as the viewfinder image darkens according to the amount of light passing through the lens and properly metering a subject at f/16 is just not as easy as metering it at f/1.8 because of the dim image. Once metering is completed, the lens can be opened to its maximum aperture for focusing and composing the picture, and when the shutter is released, the automatic diaphragm will stop the lens down to the shooting aperture just before the picture is taken. And if the lighting conditions haven't changed from the time you metered the subject to the time you actually release the shutter, you're all right.

Since about 1971, manufacturers have switched their designs over to open-aperture metering (Figure V) in which exposure is adjusted with the lens at maximum aperture and when the shutter is released, the lens stops down to the shooting aperture, just as it did with the stop-down metering system. Open-aperture metering possesses two big advantages—the ease and convenience of exposure adjustment with the bright image provided by the maximum aperture, and the ability to make necessary changes in expo-

sure right up to the moment of actually taking the picture without having to switch the aperture back and forth to make certain that you're still O.K.

FILM SUPPLY SYSTEMS

Earlier in this chapter, we discussed film transport as one of the limitations of our pinhole camera, and briefly explored ways and means of equipping it to take more than a single picture without returning to the darkroom to unload the exposed piece of film and reloading the camera with another fresh piece good for another single picture.

Various types of cameras utilize different answers to this problem. As we've seen, the basic film supply of press/view cameras is the sheet-film holder, which contains two single sheets of film separated within the holder by a divider and protected from exposure by a dark slide which is removed once the holder is positioned within the camera's back.

All large-format (6x4.5, 6x6 and 6x7cm) cameras use 120 roll film, taking 15, 12 and 10 pictures, respectively, on a roll—double that if 220 roll film is used. Many of these cameras like the Hasselblad are also designed for use with interchangeable film magazines—self-contained units which are loaded with a roll of film, fastened to the camera body and with the removal of a dark slide, allow the photographer to work rapidly without having to stop and change film. He simply inserts the dark slide, removes the magazine and replaces it with another preloaded magazine, pulling out the slide and returning to work within a matter of seconds. The interchange-

able magazine also permits the use of a variety of different film types including Polaroid materials during a picture session without the need of several camera bodies, or much down-time while one film is removed and another is loaded.

Interchangeable backs are available for press/view cameras which permit the use of roll film, film packs, Polaroid 4x5 Land sheets or Polaroid Land pack films. These simply slip into the camera back as would a film holder and provide multiple exposure capability, as well as giving the large-format us a wider variety of film types from which to choose. The Polaroid Land backs permit the use of Polaroid films for special effects, or for checking exposure/lighting/composition before committing the shot to 4x5, 5x7 or 8x10 film.

All current 35mm cameras, whether SLR or rangefinder design, use a self-contained film supply in the form of the daylight-loading cartridge housed within the camera. Interchangeable backs have been offered at various times, but the cameras for which they were made never sold sufficiently well to keep them in production, although the prototype of a new design using interchangeable backs was seen at the last two Photokina trade shows in Cologne, Germany.

The sole exceptions to my statement above are the bulk film magazines which replace the camera back of certain models and hold sufficient film for 250 exposures for use with motor drives, but these are hardly general-purpose magazines, falling into the category of specialized accessories.

The 110 pocket and 126 easy-loading cameras use the drop-in cartridges described earlier, which amount to prethreaded roll film housed in a light-tight container. Subminiature cameras like the Minox and Yashica Atoron also use drop-in cartridges, but these are not completely self-contained, as are the 110/126 cartridges.

IN SUMMARY

Having a smattering of knowledge about the principles of photography certainly will not turn you into a photographer overnight—you must master the camera and its use. To help you do so, it's time to move along and give you a better understanding of the nature of light and how it functions to make photography possible, leading us into a thorough discussion of proper exposure and how it is determined for the film you're using. □

2

The Chemistry Of Light

For most of us, the world in which we live is one of light. Light is the photographer's medium; without it, he could put no pictures on film. Yet far too few of us understand light and how it works, what it does and why. In fact, most of us do not *see* light; we merely see its reflection from objects around us, without even thinking of its source—unless the weather is bad, the illumination poor or its color rendition unusual.

How many times have you photographed something because it was striking or dramatic to the eye, only to find that the finished print contained far less than you saw—that your picture was really dull and lifeless compared to the scene which moved you to use your camera? In many such cases, the drama was there when you took the picture, but you failed to analyze what was happening, both in front of your camera and in your mind's eye—the brain.

You see, our eyes are selective. Many times they see what they want to see, and our mental process embellishes the three-dimensional quality which they transmit to the brain. It's an unconscious process of which we are seldom aware, but the camera has no such ability to compensate or alter—it simply records exactly what it sees in front of it, reducing the three-dimensional posture of our subject to a flat reproduction. It's unfortunate, but the picture can easily lose something in the transmission from reality to image (and often does), and that something is all too often what motivated us to take the picture in the first place.

THE THREE LEVELS OF RESPONSE

The great majority of camera users see their subject and nothing more—they take bushels of pictures every year and getting an image that's fairly sharp and a reasonably faithful copy of the original object or subject is about all they ask from their camera. Another smaller group not only see their subjects, they also instinctively see and understand the light which illuminates the objects before them, but are unable to project themselves further. They tend to use their camera in a gut-level fashion, as they're not sophisticated enough in how the chemistry of light works to think, "If I change my camera position, the change in lighting will cause a change in my interpretation of this subject and I'll get a better/worse picture as a result," or, "This isn't quite right. I should wait for awhile until the lighting changes for the better (or should I change the lighting myself?)." Their action is simply one of reaction—they do without knowing why they do it.

The truly knowledgeable photographer is the one who sees his subject and the light, understands what is going on and reacts to the situation in a positive, thinking manner. While many such photographers are professionals, there's a healthy number of amateurs who possess this thinking approach rather than relying upon instinct. If you can see yourself fitting into one of these groupings, then you know how far you have to travel if you want to conquer and master light, making it your medium.

Ask any three people to define light, and you'll get three different

1. Texture, form and depth are added to the sand dunes by the photographer's choice of lighting, which should be instinctive with such subjects. (Photo taken by Shirley I. Fisher.)
2. Those who intend to work with photography as a means of self-expression must be keenly aware of all aspects of light if they wish to create blends like this. When more than one negative is used to make a print, the direction of lighting must be appropriate in all. (Shirley I. Fisher.)

responses—light means different things to different people. To the scientist, it is a phenomenon; to the blind, something very precious of which they have been deprived; to the man in the street, it's the signal to get out of bed and go to work, or to leave work and return home. A scientific explanation of light to the photographer is more or less irrelevant, beyond the few facts I am about to provide. It's far more important to understand the practical aspects of light and how to put them to work for you.

WHAT IS LIGHT!—SCIENTIFIC TIDBITS OF INTEREST

Light is radiant energy, measurable in quality and quantity, which travels in waves whose intensity diminishes in an orderly progression as the distance it must travel increases. This is the *inverse square law*, to which we'll return later. Each wavelength generates a particular color and although we perceive light as being "white," it really isn't. What we call "white" light is actually a mixture of varying wave lengths which combine to produce the

appearance of white light—a fact proven countless times over in high school physics classes with the aid of a prism.

When so-called white light is directed through a prism, it is refracted or shattered into its individual components or colors. Taken together, these form a *spectrum* or visible display of the different wavelengths. Physicists consider white light to be composed of three additive primary colors: blue (short wavelengths), green (medium wavelengths) and red (long wavelengths). All other colors are produced by combining red, green and/or blue wavelengths in varying amounts. Pairs of these three additive primary colors form three complementary colors: yellow, cyan and magenta. These are also called subtractive primary colors, because they are formed by subtracting one of the additive primaries from white light.

Figure A shows the traditional color wheel—a graphic representation of the primary and complementary colors. By means of this device, we can quickly determine that red and cyan are complementary colors because when they are combined, they contain all three additive primary colors to produce white light. Green and magenta are complementary, as are blue and yellow, and for the same reason—they produce white light when combined.

As white light is considered to be the sum of the additive primary colors, black is the *absence* of *all* color and occurs when no wavelengths of the visible spectrum are present. Gray is found when all wavelengths are present in equal amounts, but in small quantities. At each end of the visible spectrum, wavelengths exist to which the human eye is not sensitive. At the long wavelength end is infrared radiation, a form of heat rather than light. Ultraviolet radiation is found just below the blue end of the spectrum, and like infrared, these shorter wavelengths are not light rays per se, but radiation.

Color is not inherent in any object—it is the result of which wavelengths are reflected and which are not, which in turn depends upon the reflective properties of the object in question, as well as the wavelength properties of the illuminating source. All light sources are not white in nature; in fact, only a very few give off what we could call white light. But our eyes possess the marvelous ability to adapt to various wavelengths as well as various levels of light, becoming more sensitive to blue light when objects are illuminated by yellowish-red or tungsten lamps, and

less sensitive to blue when a light source contains more blue, such as daylight.

Whether color or black-and-white, photographic film also has a sensitivity to color which can be described, but it does not have the ability to compensate for various intensities or wavelength mixtures. A given exposure to light is necessary to produce an image on film; if it receives less (say 1/100) of that amount, it will not record an image, despite the fact that our eye can still discern the object.

Color film is "balanced" by its manufacturer to "see" certain colors under specific conditions; one balanced to see objects illuminated by daylight as normal will see the same objects as being too yellow/red under tungsten lighting. A color film balanced to see objects as normal under tungsten illumination can only see them as too bluish in daylight. Black-and-white films also have a spectral sensitivity. While ordinary silver bromide, which constitutes the basic light-sensitive element in black-and-white film emulsions, is sensitive only to blue and ultraviolet radiation, it can be optically sensitized by the use of certain dyes which absorb radiations of longer wavelengths. In this way, it is possible to expand the sensitivity of the emulsion through the green (orthochromatic), through green and red (panchromatic) and into the infrared wavelengths.

This color or spectral sensitivity of black-and-white film is most important when selecting a particular film for a specific use, as it determines how objects which reflect certain colors will photograph in gray tones (the basis of black-and-white photography), the types of filters which can be used to

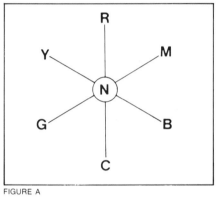

FIGURE A

1-3. As light means different things to different people, photographers use it differently. It reveals texture in (1), form in (2) and shape in (3). (Photo [2] by Shirley I. Fisher and [3] by Ron Berkenblitt.)

alter this tonal scale, and the manner in which the film is handled when processed. We'll delve deeper into this when we reach the chapter dealing with films.

At this point, we can briefly summarize the scientific tidbits we need to know and then move on to a more practical consideration of light.

1—Light travels in waves whose lengths determine its color.

2—When combined, the three additive primary colors—red, blue and green—form white light.

3—Blue light waves are the shortest in length; red waves are the longest.

4—As white is the sum of all colors, so black is their absence.

5—Objects by themselves do not possess color—they reflect certain portions of the visible spectrum and thus appear to have color.

6—Light sources vary in the make-up of the light which they give off. Daylight contains a relatively high percentage of blue; tungsten or artificial light

2

is generally composed of yellow/red wavelengths.

7—Photographic film is sensitive to light in a manner predetermined by its manufacturer. Color film is balanced to "see correctly" in either daylight or tungsten illumination, but not both. Black-and-white film is basically sensitive to blue, but can be sensitized to red and to green wavelengths, depending upon its usage.

We now understand enough of the basic chemistry of light and its application in photography to consider its effects. As this knowledge is fundamental for an understanding of exposure, film and filtration, you'll find brief recaps where necessary in those chapters, but I promise that we've exhausted our interest in the technical aspects of the subject.

THE EFFECT OF NATURAL LIGHT

It is the effect of light on the photographic film that makes it possible to take pictures. For this reason, the way in which illumination is applied controls the appearance of your subject and the way in which you manipulate the lighting and/or subject determines the end result. At the present, we'll confine our discussion to natural or outdoor illumination, as provided by sunlight. Light has four important and distinctive characteristics which the photographer must learn to see, evaluate and control, when necessary.

QUALITY—Light changes constantly, in both its color content and brightness level. Subconsciously, we may take notice of this, especially where the level of illumination is concerned, but all too often we neglect to consider the alteration in color—white is white, right? Wrong. Watch the sun as it winds its way through our timespan known as a day. As dawn breaks, the edge of its bright disk peeks over the horizon line and its rays travel practically parallel to the earth's surface. Because of this angle, the atmospheric dust and water vapor scatter the bluish portion of the

3

light. What is left to reach the earth's surface has a warm, almost reddish hue and is less intense (Figure B).

But as the sun climbs higher in the sky, the angle which its rays must travel changes, and so they pass through a decreasing amount of atmospheric "garbage." This results in the passage of an increasing quantity of blue light and a greater overall intensity. This increase continues to occur until noon, when the sun reaches its highest point. After this, as the angle decreases, the blue content diminishes until sunset, when the rays are again parallel to the earth's surface and the red content

again exceeds the blue. This process occurs every day, whether the sky is clear, spotted with clouds or is completely overcast.

On overcast or rainy days, the light is diffused considerably, and it's not as easy to visually distinguish the "warmth" from the "cold," but the ratio of red, blue and green wavelengths which compose the white light has not changed. Above the cloud or overcast cover in the atmosphere, the sunlight remains true to its formula and content; it's the cloud or overcast condition which acts as a filter to slightly alter the composition of white light

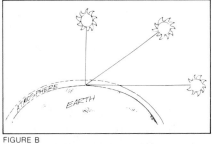

FIGURE B

reaching the earth's surface.

There is, however, a seasonal difference in the quality of sunlight, caused by the earth's tilting on its axis. This results in the sun's rays striking the earth at differing angles each season—more sharply during summer months and less acutely during the winter. Intensity does not vary per se, but sunlight reaching the earth at less acute angles has a softer quality (less contrast), creating shadows that are not as harsh as those found during summer.

QUANTITY (INTENSITY)—The amount of light *available* to take a picture has a very distinct bearing on the end result. In the first place, the amount required for the picture will depend upon the speed of the film you use—how sensitive it is to light. A "slow" film will require more exposure than a "fast" film. But suppose that you have too much light available for a given film and you use it all. The film will be *overexposed*, with a washed-out, light picture resulting. If you have too little light present for the film, the picture will be *underexposed*, with a dark, muddy appearance. Using the right amount of light results in a good picture, with detail visible in both the light (highlight) and dark (shadow) areas. This is the reason an adjustable camera provides control over the aperture and shutter—to allow the photographer to select and use only the right amount of light.

One fallacy to which many photogra-

1. When light passes from one medium to another, its quality and intensity change considerably.

2. Cloudy days cause lowered contrast, which can result in lighting that's far too flat to produce visual punch.

3. As fog alters the quality of light considerably, it can often be used to provide atmosphere for what might otherwise be a mundane subject. (Hal Stoelzle.)

phers fall victim is the idea that the sunlight in tropical areas is more intense than that of temperate regions. While physical measurements have proven this to be incorrect, it is easy to visually accept. Sunlight in tropic zones reaches the earth at sharper angles through clear atmospheric conditions. This results in strong top lighting with a high lighting contrast.

Should the light available exceed that required for a correct exposure, and the use of the aperture and shut-

ter controls cannot reduce the amount received by the film sufficiently for a correct exposure, changing to a slower film provides another form of control. If this is neither possible nor desirable, the amount of light striking the film can be brought to manageable levels by filtration, in the form of either a contrast filter (black-and-white only) or a neutral density filter (black-and-white/color photography).

When there is insufficient light available for a proper exposure, the aperture can be opened to its maximum and the shutter used for a time exposure, providing the subject matter and other conditions permit. When this is not practical, the use of a faster film can be substituted, or additional light can be added to the scene in the form of floodlamps, flash bulbs or electronic flash. If both of these solutions are out of the question, there are techniques of film processing (or "pushing") which may be used to build a minimal exposure to a level sufficient to extract a print, although the end results may

be less than satisfactory.

Except under extreme circumstances then, the amount of light falling upon a particular object will not restrict photographic activities. As it's the amount of light *reaching the film* rather than the amount *striking the subject* that determines a correctly exposed picture, the photographer has a variety of tools and techniques with which to work, one of which will generally solve the problem.

CONTRAST—Image quality is dependent upon contrast, or the difference in tonal quality between different areas of the picture. Insufficient contrast results in muddy tones, with no clean white or dark areas distinguishable in the picture. Excessive contrast results in a print in which detail is obstructed or blocked up in both highlight and shadow areas.

Two major factors control contrast—subject tone and illumination. You can determine the contrast within a picture by changing the subject's tones or controlling the intensity and direction

of the light. Filtration will alter the reproduction of the subject tones on the film; reflectors or fill-flash will balance differences in light intensity; a different camera or subject position will change the direction of illumination.

Contrast is related to image darkness; a contrast level equivalent to that of the subject in real life should be sought, unless you desire a special effect. Generally speaking, medium contrast with a wide tonal scale will produce the best prints. Unfortunately, this is not always easily obtained—it depends upon the subject, the direction of light, and the photographer's knowledge of the controls at his disposal.

DIRECTION—In many ways, the direction from which the light falls upon the subject in relation to the camera position is far more important to us than either the quality or quantity of illumination available. There are three major types of outdoor illumination, usually discussed in terms of their direction:

1—Frontal Lighting. If we place our

camera so that the sun is somewhere behind the photographer, the result will be fairly even illumination of the entire subject by lighting that is comparatively flat in nature. Those subjects falling primarily in the same plane before the camera will exhibit tone contrast, while those with dimension will contain shadows created by the dimensional shape. Should the sun be directly behind the camera (a rare instance), there will be virtually no shadow areas in the subject. Under most circumstances, however, the sun will usually be high enough in the sky to produce shadows to some degree.

A variation of flat, frontal lighting is found during cloudy or overcast days, or when you photograph a subject in the shade. Under these conditions, the light is soft and diffused, far less directional in nature, with the degree and density of shadow areas more dependent upon the intensity than the direction of the light. Such flat lighting, characteristic of overcast days or open shade, is ideal for outdoor portraits, as

2

3

4

1. Where the amount of light available is both limited and excessive at the same time, you must be able to balance the two to achieve the effect you desire. (Hank Harris.)

2. When the level of illumination is too low, a time exposure can be used. M. Jeffery photographed Toronto's City Hall on Ilford FP4 with a two-second exposure through illuminated concrete arches.

3-4. Light produces contrast—a necessary ingredient of successful black-and-white photography. In (4), it's used to create contrast directly by photographing translucent roof panels and in (3), indirectly by use of subject tones.

it does not create deep, ugly shadows with which the photographer must cope, nor does it cause the person being photographed the discomfort of squinting in bright sunlight. When a fill-in light is necessary, a reflector is generally sufficient. The end result is a far more natural, pleasing picture, though generally one of lower contrast. If an increase in subject contrast is desirable when shooting black-and-white film on an overcast day, try underexposing the film by one f-stop and then overdevelop by 40 percent, as this will raise the contrast level.

2—Sidelighting. When sunlight is directional from one side or the other, part of the subject will be lighted and the rest will be in shadow. This results in much greater contrast, as the brightness range between shadow and highlight areas increases considerably. If the intensity is great enough, the difference between light and dark areas may be too great for the film to handle while providing adequate detail in both. This type of lighting works well with many subjects.

3—Backlighting. Sunlight illuminating the subject from behind gives the most contast in outdoor pictures and if used correctly, will produce the most sparkling results. The problem most amateurs face in working with backlight is one of correct exposure. If a meter reading is followed without modification, the subject will generally acquire the characteristics of a silhouette in a normal print, possessing only shape, with little form and no detail. Obviously, an increase in exposure is required, and this is where most of us fall down. Too much of an increase will destroy the backlight effect while too little will not provide the balance necessary to adequately illuminate the shadow detail. Such situations outdoors can be very tricky to handle, especially if no source of fill light is readily available.

WHERE IT COMES FROM

It's pretty obvious, isn't it? Light comes from a direction opposite to the shadows found within the subject. That sounds reasonable enough, but if you think about it for a moment, you'll see

that it isn't necessarily so. Remember, the photographer doesn't see the light itself; he sees only its effects, and the variations are countless—they seldom repeat themselves. Each outdoor picture situation is different; similar to others with which you've dealt, perhaps, but never identical. And how well your pictures turn out will depend upon how well you are able to recognize and deal with these variations. Here are some things to consider.

Light does not always strike the subject directly. In some cases, it illuminates the general area, reflecting on our subject from other objects in the same general area. In essence, the source has changed from direct sunlight to the object surface from which it's reflected. As such surfaces will modify and alter the light's quality and quantity, it's important to consider what is happening before your camera and how it affects your picture.

Light that reflects from an object will change in various but often predictable ways, both in direction and in quality. The reflective surface will not only affect the direction, it will alter the characteristics. The following examples will provide food for thought. Light striking a single colored surface will pick up or acquire some of the color of the surface when it is reflected. A light surface will reflect a higher percentage than a dark one. Smooth surfaces will reflect light in a directional manner, while rough or uneven ones will scatter the light before reflecting it. All of which serves to introduce another important consideration in the basics of using light—the subject.

CONSIDER THE SUBJECT

Like sunlight, every object has certain characteristics standard to photographic situations. If you consider light as an entity unto itself and disregard the effect which the subject and its reflective surface have, you're missing half of the equation and cannot hope to "see" how the subject will appear to the camera.

Regardless of the subject's nature—box, body, tree or building—each possesses three important characteristics: form, surface and tone. It's the interaction of these characteristics with those of sunlight (direction, contrast, quantity and quality) that determines the success or failure of your picture. Ignore them and your pictures will remain snapshots—no more, no less—but learn to see, think about and respond to them and you're on your way to some truly marvelous results.

FORM—An object's form is composed of surfaces and lines, which may be straight or irregular. Form can be used to introduce dimension to an object according to how it's lighted. If a light-colored cube is photographed against a dark background using frontal lighting, it will appear virtually nondimensional. Change the direction of the light so that it strikes the cube from one side, and the other side of the cube will be dark. This contrast between the light and dark sides of the cube produces an apparent dimensional quality. If we then change to backlighting, the form of the cube will continue to remain dimensional, but the relationship between light and dark changes, with the front two sides of the cube becoming darker and the background lightening up (Figure C).

SURFACE—In addition to its gross shape or outline, an object possesses a surface finish or texture. Such form variations can range from perfectly smooth to rough, with the degree of texture emphasized by the direction of lighting. Texture can usually be detect-

ed to some degree in front-lighted subjects, but its appearance increases considerably, as does its considerable power to suggest a dimensional quality or illusion of depth in the object, as the lighting angle becomes sharper. A determination of the best angle to emphasize the surface texture is usually dependent upon the effect desired and the texture itself.

TONE—Variations in the tone of an object are not affected when the direction of lighting changes. The tone will depend upon how the object reflects light and its reproduction on the film is relative to the amount of light reflected. Tonal differentiation can be achieved by the correct choice of filters according to the tonal changes desired.

LIGHT CONTROL OUTDOORS

Unfortunately, the majority of pho-

1. The soft, diffused illumination provided by overcast days can be ideal for outdoor portraits, as long as you determine its direction and face your subject accordingly for the most pleasing results.

2. Frontal lighting and open shade combine to provide even illumination without harsh shadows, while creating an overexposed background to set off the young subject. (Hank Harris.)

3. Sidelighting produces considerable contrast while adding form to a subject. As the brightness range here was far too great for the film to handle, Dave Neibel posed his model in contrasting attire and deliberately threw the background out of focus for the effect he desired.

tographers practice light control only in the form of determining exposure, paying little or no attention to light and shadows as such, even if they're aware of the qualities of light and subjects which we have just discussed. Under such circumstances, it's not surprising that their pictures are most often ineffective and sterile at best.

If you really want to take *good* pictures that exploit the potential inherent in the subject, you must be able to exercise a certain discrimination in your approach to a subject. When the lighting is not right—if it's too soft or too harsh, should its direction be unsuited for the desired effect, if shadows obscure subject detail, are harsh or unpleasant in their design—you might just as well ignore the picture and save yourself the effort if you're unwilling or unable to respond in a positive manner.

Unless the subject is a once-in-a-lifetime grab-type shot (in which case you should grab it), it will pay to wait until conditions are more favorable.

This may mean a return to the location when the lighting is more suitable for the right effect, or it may require moving the subject when and where possible. If changing the subject's position is out of the question, the answer may be supplemental lighting in the form of a fill-in light or reflector.

Whatever the situation, if the photographer studies the lighting and its effect on the subject, and then responds accordingly, he will come away with a far better and more effective picture than those who simply shrug their shoulders and shoot anyway. The key in utilizing the chemistry of light is a willingness to put into a picture at least as much as you hope to take out.

ARTIFICIAL LIGHT AND ITS EFFECT

Sunlight is a richly varied, constantly changing and highly unpredictable source of illumination for the photographer; working indoors he will use artificial lighting, which possesses the opposite characteristics. It is uniform, predictable, highly stable and controllable—and it also causes photographers much unnecessary difficulty in its proper handling. With the correct choice of artificial light, the experienced photographer can exercise a high degree of control that is lacking when working with sunlight.

In theory at least, there's very little difference between indoor and outdoor lighting—you simply manipulate different parts of the equation to arrive at the same effect. Working with artificial illumination requires that you manipulate your light sources; outdoors you must rely in most cases on manipulating the subject, as the sun does not lend itself as easily to the photographer's control, although the picture can be postponed until the light changes to a position or type that's more agreeable with your requirements. But this does not really amount to manipulation of outdoor lighting.

Yet virtually all the effects of sunlight can be duplicated indoors by the proper use of lights—harsh or contrasty, soft or diffused—the choice is yours. To exercise the available options, you must understand both the hardware and its use to achieve the results you desire. You must be familiar with a variety of photographic lamps, diffusers, reflectors of varying sizes, lamp placement, subject-to-light distances, directional lighting control and the mixture of two or more light sources and how they interact with each other. Unfortunately, all this appears overwhelming to many and their confusion is further

complicated by less than satisfactory results—often to the point where they simply fit an electronic flash to the camera's hot shoe and fire away, accepting the rather bland results as their lot in life, however unhappily.

ARTIFICIAL LIGHT VS. SUNLIGHT

DIRECTIONAL LIGHTING—Spotlights and floods offer light that's equivalent to direct sunlight on a bright, cloudless day; used primarily for overall lighting or as a general source of illumination, they possess the same advantages/disadvantages as direct sunlight, and

must be supplemented by other forms of lighting for proper results.

DIFFUSED LIGHTING—Flash bulbs, electronic flash and reflector floods produce light equal to that of the sun on a hazy or slightly overcast day. Possessing moderate contrast and a crispness rather than the harshness of directional lighting, they create well-defined shadow areas but do not block up detail, and are thus used as either a main or fill light source.

OTHER FORMS OF DIFFUSED LIGHTING—By using electronic flash with a reflecting umbrella, or photofloods in large reflectors in conjunction with diffusers, it's possible to duplicate the effect of daylight on an overcast day. Useful for either general or fill-in illumination, this type of indoor lighting is soft and nearly shadowless.

The use of a light tent or ringlight flash will produce a totally diffused form of lighting with virtually no shadows, as it surrounds the subject in a uniform manner that prevents the formation of shadow areas. Outdoor lighting has no equivalent and this type of diffused artificial light is useful primarily for highly specialized purposes, such as scientific photography or product illustration where the control of reflections is of paramount concern.

WHICH TYPE OF ARTIFICIAL LIGHT?

The question most often faced by photographers interested in working with artificial illumination is which type they should use—the continuous light emitted by photoflood, spots, etc., or the intermittent light provided by flash bulbs and electronic flash.

Until the mid-1950s, continuous illumination was very popular with the amateur by virtue of its low cost relative to flash bulbs. But with the appearance of electronic flash units, continuous lighting (which few amateurs really handle well anyway), passed into the province of the professional and those serious amateurs who emulated the pro on a part-time basis. Even the venerable flash bulb could not withstand the tide of electronics, and while they are still with us today in the form of flashcubes and Flipflash, they are far less popular than in the past.

I still remember the considerable elation I experienced in the mid-'50s with the purchase of my first electronic flash, a Pho-Tak Thrift-Light II. I immediately threw my entire box of photoflood lamps, reflectors and stands into the garbage, breathed a deep sigh of relief and declared my independence. A large, 24-ounce ''potato masher'' type of unit which dwarfed my 35mm camera, this early EF was powered by AC only and required the acquisition of a long extension cord if one were to be fully prepared and mobile in relation to the location of the nearest AC outlet. But like many other amateurs of that era, I had tired of fussing with the low light output, fuming at the high heat of photofloods, and the always present blown fuse because of a circuit overload whenever a household appliance like the refrigerator decided

2

1

3

1-3. Sidelighting can pose problems, such as deep shadows and a partial squinting of the eyes (1). Having the subject turn slightly to one side eliminates the closed-eye effect (2) and moving the camera position slightly takes care of the shadows, while still retaining the light's modeling effect (3).
4. Sidelighting is far more effective in establishing a mood and defining a subject's personality than frontal lighting. (Hank Harris.)

to do its thing. The necessity of using an extension cord with the electronic flash unit was an even trade-off with the extension cords required to tie in the photoflood setup.

Of course, those of us who went to electronic flash gave up the ability to see the effect of our artificial lighting arrangement, to measure its brightness and contrast range with a meter, and to rearrange the lamps as necessary to suit our needs. We gave up the 25-cent photoflood bulbs for $25 flash-tubes, but the limitations of the future seemed minor when compared to the frustrations of the past.

While the light produced by EF units possessed a considerable ability to stop moving objects in their tracks (a far cry from the days of the gas-filled SM/SF flash bulbs), and over the years, refinements in circuitry and battery supply have greatly increased both its mobility and portability, we gradually discovered the EF had its own set of drawbacks and limitations, which have continued to the present.

The primary disadvantages to EF are two-fold—you can't see the effect of the light on your subject before taking the picture, nor can you measure either its intensity or contrast range

unless you have a special and quite expensive flash meter, for which few amateurs can really justify the purchase. But EF units have proliferated and as we'll see when we reach that chapter, are virtually foolproof in accomplishing certain tasks.

They still retain many of the drawbacks they've shared with flash bulbs for years, such as flat lighting when used close to or on-camera, and a dark background beyond their limited reach. Slowly but surely, the pendulum has started to swing back and today's young photographers are rediscovering the virtues of continuous lighting in its modern form. As many of us have known right along (but refused to admit), both types of artificial lighting have a place in the amateur photographer's repertoire.

ARTIFICIAL LIGHT SOURCES

As electronic flash is so popular these days, a later chapter is devoted entirely to its selection and use. For this reason, our concern here is with the various forms of continuous lighting, many of which the reader may be totally unfamiliar with or even unaware of. While the hardware configuration differs from one manufacturer to another, all are basically similar in the way in which they are used, and most can be divided into three major components—a source of light, a reflector and a support unit—augmented for special purposes by auxiliary devices such as diffusers.

4

THE LIGHT SOURCE

A considerable variety of different lamps with specific characteristics useful for particular photographic applications is currently available. None of them present any difficulties when used with black-and-white film, but you should remember that their use with color emulsions is restricted to either a film balanced for their color temperature, or one used with the appropriate conversion filter.

PHOTOFLOOD LAMPS—Commonly designated as #1 (250 watts) or #2 (500 watts), these look much like over-sized household light bulbs, but deliver a good deal more light per watt. Consequently, their life span is fairly short (3-6 hours) and their color temperature of 3400°K. (Type A film) changes as their life grows shorter. Photoflood lamps produce light that is diffused in nature and the bulbs must be used in appropriate metal reflectors.

A blue-coated photoflood lamp with a color temperature ranging between 4800-5400°K. (depending upon manufacturer) is also available and should be used mainly for filling shadows or supplementing daylight in interiors where sunlight provides the main source of illumination. If used as the sole light source with daylight color film, they will cause your slides to take on a warmer, yellowish tone, as the color temperature of blue-coated bulbs is not perfectly matched with that of the film.

REFLECTOR FLOODS—Similar to photoflood bulbs but containing their own high-efficiency reflector, these 3400°K. (Type A film) lamps are available in two strengths—250 or 500 watts—and

have a life expectancy of 4-6 hours. Their light output is semi-diffused and separate reflectors are not required. Like photoflood lamps, their color temperature tends to change with extended use, and slight filtration may be required to retain normal color balance as they grow older.

TUNGSTEN-HALOGEN LAMPS—Also known as quartz-iodine lamps, these use a tungsten filament inside a quartz tube containing iodine or bromine gas. This prevents darkening of the lamp with use and results in an artificial light source that retains its original color temperature and light output throughout a life expectancy of 25-30 hours. Intensely brilliant, these have their own high-efficiency reflector built in, can be powered by either AC or battery current, and are thus more versatile in use. Two types are available, 3200°K. (for Type B film) and 3400°K. (for Type A film).

1. Backlighting produces highly dramatic effects when exposure is carefully calculated. (Hal Stoelzle.)

2. Backlighting can be utilized in many different ways. Ron Berkenblitt used it here to create a semisilhouette effect, with a polarizing filter to deepen the intensity of the sky.

3. The combination of maximum aperture, fast film and backlighting was used by Hank Harris in establishing form and delineating texture. Frontal lighting of this subject would have been far too flat to be effective.

4. Aerial photography requires lighting contrast to produce the necessary dimensional effect. (Hank Harris.)

TUNGSTEN LAMPS—Until the advent of tungsten-halogen lamps, these dominated the professional's lighting kit. Available in a wide variety of sizes and outputs, they are balanced for use with Type B film and, like photoflood bulbs, require the use of an appropriate reflector. Their color temperature changes rapidly with changes in voltage; for each increase of one volt, the color temperature of a tungsten lamp rated at 115 volts will increase by 10°K. Line-voltage fluctuations are quite common but unnoticed by the human eye. For this reason, an adjustable variable transformer is required for serious work with tungsten lamps.

PROJECTION LAMPS—Used primarily with spotlights, these contain high-intensity tungsten filaments, come in various sizes and outputs from 150 to 1000 watts, and generally have a color temperature of 3200°K. for use with Type B film.

FLUORESCENT LIGHTS—Generally unsuitable for use with color film because of a discontinuous spectrum, the wide use of fluorescents in homes, offices and industrial applications makes them unavoidable in many circumstances. Under such conditions, appropriate filtration should be used (see the chapter on filters and lens attachments) if color film is involved. With black-and-white films, fluorescent lighting can be formed in banks to produce soft, diffused light and many photographers build units to use this type of bulb.

REFLECTORS

Two types of reflectors are used—one type forms part of the lighting system and works in conjunction with a lamp, while the other is more appropriately referred to as a reflector panel, as it is used to catch and bounce light.

LIGHTING SYSTEM OR LAMP REFLECTORS—The efficiency of any photographic lamp is dependent upon the reflecting surface behind or surrounding it. Such a surface is necessary to direct the light where it is required, to prevent unnecessary loss of light to the side or behind the lamp, and to keep such "spill" light from causing lens reflections and flare.

Photo lamp reflectors come in three different shapes—spherical, parabolic and elliptical (Figure D). Of the three, spherical reflectors are the type generally used for indoor lighting, as they distribute the light from the lamp most evenly. The larger the reflector size, the greater the amount of diffusion and the softer the shadows will be. Polished surfaces produce light with more contrast and sharper shadows than do satin or matte finishes.

REFLECTOR PANELS—A great variety of things can constitute this type of reflector—it may be of stiff white cardboard, a thin plywood sheet painted

3

4

1

white, a sheet of crinkled aluminum foil, or one of the umbrella reflectors so popular with electronic flash users. Whatever the material and construction, the purpose of a reflector panel is to reduce the lighting contrast ratio of the primary illumination to a level more appropriate to the film's contrast range by lightening or filling in shadow areas.

To be effective, the reflector panel should be as large as the area to be lightened, and its surface should be kept clean and free from blemishes. The use of mirrors, ferrotype plates and other highly reflective surfaces will produce specular fill light with the same directional characteristics as the primary light which it reflects. If higher reflectance is required than that provided by a white finish, aluminum foil that has been crinkled and straightened out is recommended.

SUPPORT UNITS

A lamp and reflector are useless to the photographer unless he has some means of holding and positioning it. For this job, an appropriate support unit is necessary.

LIGHT STANDS—Rigid or collapsible, these come in all shapes, sizes and descriptions. Many of the less-expensive models should be avoided, as they are so light in weight and poorly constructed that they become more of a hindrance than a help. To be suitable for your purposes, the light stand should be solid, stable and sufficiently heavy to balance the light unit in a variety of positions without tipping.

Should you wish to use overhead lighting, you'll need a boomlight. This is a counterbalanced arm attached to the light stand which holds a light source at one end; the other end is manipulated to position the light as desired over the subject. A boomlight can come in very handy, as ordinary light stands will not allow light placement from above.

SPRING CLAMPS—For photographers on the go, spring clamps attached to the lamp socket can be used instead of adjustable light stands. These can be clamped to any suitable support and adjusted to position the light as required. The types with toothed jaws are far more secure in their mounting than those with rubber-covered gripping surfaces, and can support heavier lamps. As the toothed-jaw design is not gentle to the back of a chair, the edge of a shelf or a table leg—common mounting surfaces used by amateurs—a heavy cloth should be placed on the surface to prevent damage. The

2

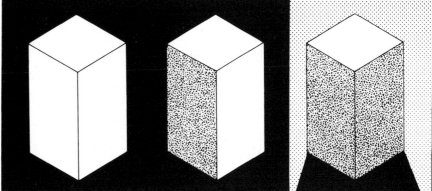

FIGURE C

major disadvantage to the spring clamp design lies in locating a potential support of the proper size and height to achieve the desired lighting.

AUXILIARY DEVICES

The following units are used when

1. **Watching two men load hay, Hal Stoelzle combined the characteristics of his subject with those of the lighting to add dramatic punch.**

2. **As there are few shadows in the Moscow subway, Hal Stoelzle relied upon tonal variations to create contrast.**

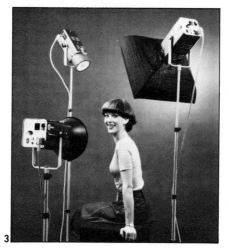

1

4

2

3

you wish to alter or modify the light to suit a specific purpose.

DIFFUSION AIDS—In addition to the reflector panels discussed earlier, screens are available that clip over the outside of a reflector to further soften the light. The most efficient ones are those that mount sufficiently in front of the reflector to permit their complete illumination by the lamp.

RESTRICTION AIDS—There may be times when it is essential to restrict the light from a photographic lamp in order to contain it to a specific area of the subject. Hinged flaps called *barndoors* can be attached to the reflector for this purpose. In an emergency, pieces of poster board can be taped to the reflector to serve the same purpose.

When lights are used at certain angles to the lens, stray rays may strike the lens, causing flare. To prevent this, a stiff black card called a *gobo* can be placed between the camera and the light source. The size and shape will differ according to the need, but these are usually rectangular and supported by some kind of stand.

GELS—Short for gelatin, the gel is a transparent colored sheet placed in front of the light source. It is used either to add a specific tint for effect, or to provide filtration for balancing the light to the film. The latter use has fallen out of favor with most photographers, as a gel or filter placed over the lens accomplishes the same purpose with far less difficulty.

Now that you're familiar with the various types and pieces of equipment necessary to duplicate the effect of sunlight indoors, let's look at some of the basics behind their use.

THE INVERSE SQUARE LAW

This fundamental rule governing the application of artificial illumination describes what happens to the amount of light reaching a subject when the dis-

tance between the light source and subject is changed. Stripping away the complications of textbook definitions, we can regard it this way: As you increase the distance between the two, the intensity of illumination decreases by the square of that number, as shown in Figure E.

Suppose we begin with our light source one foot from our subject and then double the distance by moving it to a position two feet from the subject. Quick mental math might lead you to believe that we halved the light intensity by doubling the distance, but this is not so because of the inverse square law. By doubling the distance, we've actually reduced the intensity by four times ($2^2 = 4$).

Now let's increase the subject to light distance to three feet and we'll find that we've decreased the illumina-

tion level to 1/9 of its original intensity ($3^2 = 9$). If we move the light back still another foot, the intensity striking the subject becomes but 1/16 of the original ($4^2 = 16$). In theoretical terms, the inverse square law tells us that whenever we double the light-to-subject distance, we have not simply doubled (one f-stop) the amount of exposure necessary, we've quadrupled it (two f-stops). In practical terms, doubling the distance between light source and subject will cause the light intensity to fall off somewhat less than the inverse square law states. This is especially true with small-area lights, such as spots. Thus, any lighting pattern should be set up with the help of an exposure meter, not a yardstick or tape measure. While theory tells us that either device should produce the same results, they do not.

LIGHTING RATIO

In any lighting scheme, the brightest highlight areas will receive X amount of light, and the darkest shadow areas Y amount. The difference between X and Y constitutes the lighting ratio. To demonstrate how this works, suppose you wish to copy a flat object containing no depth, such as a painting or a page from a book. To do this with satisfactory results, the lighting must be evenly

1. **Strong sidelighting increases shadow areas, displaying form and texture to far better advantage in this interpretation of the ruins of Machu Picchu, Peru. (Dave Neibel.)**

2. **Very popular with pros and serious amateurs these days, electronic flash rules studio lighting at the present. Units are available in all price brackets. This sampling from Ascor shows some of the many types available.**

3. **A typical electronic flash lighting arrangement is shown here using Multiblitz® equipment.**

4. **For totally diffused lighting without shadows, a ringlight can be mounted on the camera lens to light the subject in a uniform manner.**

5. **Balancing indoor illumination with that from an external source may require the use of a reflector, but the skilled photographer can often produce an effective picture without one. (Hank Harris.)**

5

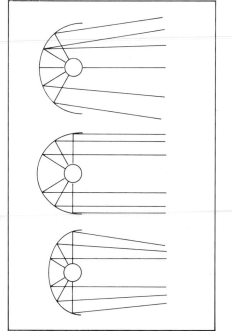

FIGURE D

the fill is moved as close as possible to the camera-subject axis, as in Figure G. In this lighting scheme, the areas of our subject receiving light from both lamps (highlights) will be twice as bright as those affected by only one lamp (shadows), giving us a 2:1 lighting ratio.

Moving the fill light back from the subject until it is twice as far as the main light (Figure H) will reduce its intensity to one-quarter that of the main light. This means that the highlights will now receive five times as much light as the shadows, or a lighting ratio of 5:1.

WHAT'S ACCEPTABLE?

Which lighting ratio you use will depend upon the subject, the effect you desire, and your own personal preference. With black-and-white film, we usually do not exceed a 5:1 ratio unless the subject is of less than average contrast. Color film is far more restrictive and the maximum lighting ratio permissible is generally 3:1 if color prints are to be made. When the subject's reflectance range is low (all colors in the subject are either relatively light or uniformly dark), a ratio of 4:1 can be used.

When transparency film is used and the slides will be viewed only by projection, it's possible to raise the lighting ratio as high as 6:1, as a transparency will hold a far greater range of tonal values than a print viewed by reflected light. For special effects, as often used in advertising work, a ratio as high as 10:1 may be used, but such extremes in lighting require a good deal of experience to achieve the desired effect.

distributed across the surface of the object to be copied.

To achieve even illumination, you would place two identical lights at the same distance from the object, but one on each side of the camera at a 45-degree angle to the object-camera axis, as in Figure F. To assure that the lighting is evenly distributed across the surface, you hold a neutral gray test card (see the chapter on exposure) against the center and each corner of the object and take a reflected light reading with your meter. If the illumina-tion is even, all five readings will be identical; if not, adjust the lights until all readings are the same. Once the light reaching all areas of the object is equal, you have achieved a lighting ratio of 1:1.

Now, let's replace our flat object with a dimensional one—a person. Again, we'll use the same two identical lights placed at equal distances from our subject. But this time, we'll use one as a main light and the other as a fill light. The main light remains on the 45-degree camera-subject axis, while

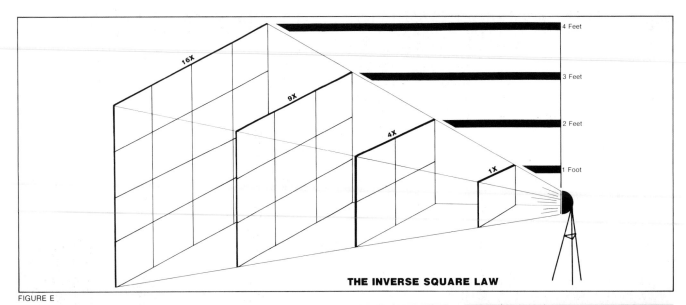

THE INVERSE SQUARE LAW

4 Feet
3 Feet
2 Feet
1 Foot

16X 9X 4X 1X

FIGURE E

UTILIZING THE CHEMISTRY OF LIGHT INDOORS

It's not uncommon for an amateur photographer to wrestle with indoor lighting problems but never quite come to grips with their solution. After a few such stints, he gives up this aspect of his hobby completely, or resorts to the old reliable electronic flash on-camera, with flat, chalky lighting as his reward. Somewhere along the line, he has overly complicated the whole matter and so sinks in a tangled web of extension cords. What has he missed?

Ask any successful pro about his lighting technique, and invariably the answer comes back, ''Keep the lighting simple.'' The more lights you add to a setup, the more complex the factors become, and the more easily you lose control of the situation. If it seems to have gotten out of hand and you're having difficulty controlling shadows, backgrounds, etc., the solution is generally *less* lights rather than more. Unfortunately, the basic response by an amateur is to increase the number of lights when he should *decrease* them.

To build a basic lighting setup correctly, you should begin with the dominant light source or main light. If more than one prominent light source is used, the result will be disturbing to the viewer, unless a special effect is definitely intended. We are accustomed to seeing only *one* shadow cast by an object; when two or more distinct shadows are visible, we instinctively know that something is wrong.

Once the main light has been positioned, the fill light should be added and adjusted in position and intensity to keep the shadow detail visible without creating objectionable secondary shadows. It's at this point that most of us go off the deep end. Incorrect

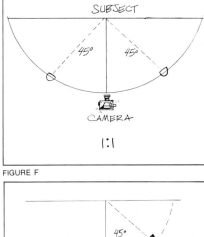

FIGURE F

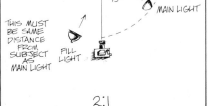

FIGURE G

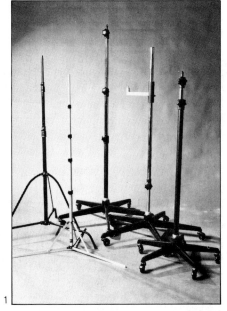

FIGURE H

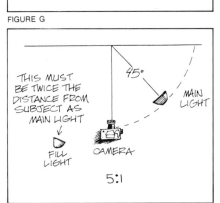

1. Lighting stands such as these from Multiblitz® are available in a wide range of types, and may be rigid or collapsible.
2. Existing-light photography requires that you make the type and direction of lighting work for you by your choice of camera position.
3. Artificial illumination affords far greater flexibility in allowing the photographer to interpret his subject. (Ron Berkenblitt.)

placement of the fill results in more shadows and to correct the problem, a third light may be added. This is followed by further adjustment of the lamps, which only serves to aggravate the problem.

The situation is also complicated by

another factor—shadows in a picture generally reproduce darker on the film than the untrained eye sees them. This is another of nature's tricks the eye is capable of playing—we see a shadow as being more translucent than it really is, or at least than the camera sees it.

This visual double-see is sometimes called ''brightness consistency,'' and can be explained by the fact that the film has a fixed degree of sensitivity while the eye does not. As our eyes roam over a scene, from foreground to background, from highlight to shadow,

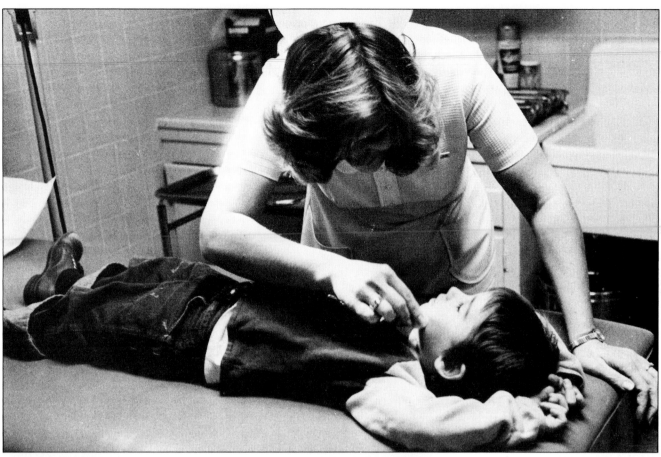

2

3

mass production. The background is standardized, the poses are rarely varied, and the lighting is uniform—or is it? Watch him carefully between sittings and you'll see that although he holds to a basic lighting pattern, he also makes separate and individual adjustments (however slight) as each new subject faces his camera. If the experts' lighting diagrams were correct, this wouldn't be necessary—he'd just run the people by the camera as they do at the motor vehicle department when they photograph you for a driving license (and he'd get the same results as they do).

I don't want to leave you with the idea that all lighting diagrams are bunk—you *should* learn the basic lighting setups as a point of departure. But if you want to use light effectively, I'd suggest that you forget about the mechanics and study the effects instead. Experience is the best teacher in photography, and no diagram can adequately substitute for practice—the essence of mastering the use of artificial light sources.

Now that you've been exposed (no pun intended) to the basics of light, it's time to look at the other parts of the photographic equation—film and exposure. And after that, we'll take a second look at light and I'll show you how to use it simply and effectively. □

they tend to accept the differences as being less than they really are. Incidentally, the larger the area in question, the more important this factor becomes, as the increased size provides the eye with its greatest opportunity to fool us.

SHOULD YOU FOLLOW THE RULES?

Wherever you look, you'll find rules of lighting which have been formulated by different ''experts,'' and concentration on following these so-called ''rules'' can quickly make you wish that you had never undertaken indoor photography. We know that every sub-

ject appears different under the lights, and so it's reasonable to assume that what seems to work for one may not work for the other. ''Expert'' lighting diagrams are attempts at devising a foolproof formula of lighting so that you can knock out pictures one after the other with no problems, but invariably they fail to do the job properly.

To see just how wrong the concept of formula lighting is, pay a visit to a nearby department store or supermarket the next time one holds its 99 cent or $1.49 special picture offer and watch the photographer at work. His entire operation has to be geared to

3

Film— The Photographer's Canvas

As light is the photographer's medium, film is his canvas. To create as he will, the photographer must understand the basic characteristics of film—what it is, why it acts as it does, how to control it and select the one most appropriate for his particular requirements. To that end, this chapter has been divided into two parts, the first of which will deal with black-and-white photography.

BLACK-AND-WHITE FILM

Photography is made possible by coating a stable base with an emulsion or gelatin substance containing light-sensitive silver particles. The base itself can be, and has been a variety of materials over the years, as long as it's transparent; glass plates were used for years until the development of a flexible base, most recently cellulose acetate and/or polyester. Exposure of the light-sensitive emulsion to light creates an invisible or latent image of the subject. To see this image, the emulsion must be treated with certain chemicals that transform the gelatin-suspended silver particles, making them visible and permanent.

The image created in this manner is called a *negative,* as it is the reverse of the original subject. The greater the amount of light which strikes the film, the darker the corresponding area on the film will be; those areas receiving less light will be lighter. By passing light through the negative (this is why the film base must be transparent) to a sheet of paper coated with a similar light-sensitive emulsion, we create the final print or *positive,* in which the negative values are reversed back to those originally seen in the subject.

Here is Ralph Merzlak's rendition of drought-stricken Nicasio, California.

At this point, let's recap the process, using what we've learned about cameras and light thus far. The camera body serves to hold the light-sensitive film in place behind the lens and keep light other than that which passes through the lens from striking the film. Moving the camera lens back and forth relative to the film focuses a sharp im-

age of the subject on the film. By adjusting the camera's shutter speed and the aperture of the lens, we can allow just the right amount of light to strike the film, producing an invisible image on it. We now have a correctly exposed piece of film which contains a latent image of our subject. After subjecting the film to development and fixing, we now have a negative.

The negative is an image of our sub-

ject, but a reversed one—bright objects appear dark and dark objects appear light. Why? Light striking the film's emulsion exposes it. The more light that hits the film, the more the film is exposed, and the more the film is exposed, the darker it will become when subjected to development. As the brightest subject areas reflect the most light, they produce the greatest exposure on the film, and the darkest

(densest) areas on the negative. The darkest areas of the subject reflect the least light, so they produce the least exposure on the film, and the lightest (thinnest) areas on the negative.

By passing light through this negative onto a sheet of photographic paper that has been coated with an emulsion similar to that of the film, we can reverse the negative values to create a positive print. This happens be-

cause the dark areas on the negative (bright areas of the subject) allow little light to reach the paper, resulting in light areas on the print when it is developed. The light areas of the negative (dark areas of the subject) permit more light to reach the paper, resulting in dark areas on the print.

Should too much light reach the film, it will turn completely dark when developed and there will be little or no im-

age visible. Similarly, too little light striking the film will fail to form a latent image and nothing will appear when the film is developed. To get a good negative, we must allow just the right amount of light through the lens to the film, but this is the subject of the next chapter. Right now, let's look at those characteristics common to all black-and-white photographic films.

FILM CHARACTERISTICS

Regardless of who makes the film, there are several characteristics of any photographic emulsion that govern the results you'll get: speed, grain structure, acutance and latitude. Of course, external factors such as exposure and development, as well as the choice of subject and lighting used, will also affect the quality of your final picture. But different types of film are manufactured to do different jobs.

Films used for ordinary photographs are known as continuous-tone emulsions, as they must reproduce the full range of black, gray and white tones found in the subject. As line drawings, diagrams, documents and other such copy work contain no intermediate tones, a high-contrast film is used for such copy work. These films have a limited amount of latitude and must be precisely exposed if a good reproduction is to be obtained. Other materials to be copied such as etchings, pencil drawings, and the like contain intermediate tones and a special high-contrast continuous-tone film is best suited for this work. As you can see, selecting the right emulsion for the occasion is a necessary first step which depends

upon a basic understanding of these characteristics.

SPEED/SENSITIVITY

Whenever you talk about the "speed" of a film, or how "fast" it is, you're referring to its sensitivity to light. Light sensitivity is most often expressed in the United States by an ASA rating or number; in Europe, the system used is called DIN. In recent years, the ASA system has been supplemented by the Exposure Index or EI rating. To clear up any confusion about the two, when a film is exposed at a speed other than its rated ASA designation, you are not exposing at a higher/lower ASA but at a different EI. Insofar as exposure determination is concerned, the practical result of using an EI value instead of an ASA rating is the same, as the higher/lower EI is set on the camera's dial marked ASA.

The faster or more sensitive the film is to light, the higher the ASA or DIN number. Such a rating system gives you some basis for comparison between films. All other factors in a given situation remaining constant, a film rated at ASA 125 is twice as fast or sensitive to light as one designated ASA 64. These ASA speed designations are arithmetic in nature—they refer directly to the relative sensitivity of various films to light. Since a fast film needs less exposure than a slow one to deliver the same negative qualities, the higher-speed film will extend your picture-taking capability considerably, but it usually extracts payment in the form of increased grain structure and lessened acutance.

1. While most people strive for minimal grain effect, granularity in a print can add visual emphasis. Hal Stoelzle's sunrise over smog-filled San Bernardino Valley (California), helps achieve the visual effect desired. Compare granularity in this photo with one on previous page—both shot with ASA 400 film.
2. Film is the photographer's canvas, and light is his paint. Whether you take pictures for fun, or to be creative, you must understand both if your work is to be effective. (Shirley I Fisher.)

The film speed rating system will deliver the minimum exposure necessary under most circumstances to produce negatives of optimum quality. But film speeds are devised by a sensitometric procedure that is highly standardized, and exposure/development procedures which differ materially from those used to determine the rated speed in the laboratory may result in a different effective speed. In such cases, it may be necessary to use a higher/lower speed number or exposure index if optimum exposure is to be obtained under the differing conditions you impose upon the film's use.

One good example is found in the elimination of a tungsten speed rating. Although film manufacturers no longer differentiate between tungsten and daylight illumination when assigning film speeds, you'll find that most black-and-white emulsions are slightly slower in speed when used under tungsten lighting conditions. When shooting under the lights or by existing light indoors, it's a good idea to open the lens an extra one-half to one f-stop from that suggested by the meter or you're likely to end up with a case of underexposure.

1-2. Blue-sensitive litho film (1) is used to drop intermediate tones that a normal panchromatic emulsion (2) would deliver. (Shirley I. Fisher.)
3-4. High-contrast effects similar to those provided by litho film can also be achieved in-camera with ASA 32 (3) or ASA 400 (4) films. The key lies in development and choice of printing paper. (Photo [3] Michael Parrish and [4] Hank Harris.)

Film speeds differ according to the nature of the emulsion's sensitivity to light. As we learned in the last chapter, the spectral sensitivity of an emulsion refers to its response to different wavelengths in the invisible/visible spectrum. Basically, there are four sensitizing classes:

BLUE SENSITIVE—Emulsions containing only the blue/ultraviolet sensitivity basic to the silver used, these are very slow in speed and their use is restricted to applications where red/green sensitivity is not required, as in copy work, black-and-white transparencies, or the like.

BLUE/GREEN SENSITIVE—Known as "ortho" or orthochromatic emulsions, these react to blue/ultraviolet and green wavelengths. Once very popular with amateurs as their lack of red sensitivity made processing under a red light possible, ortho emulsions are primarily available today in sheet film sizes and are used for portraiture,

copy work and other applications where red sensitivity is not necessary. Ortho films are generally slow to moderately slow in speed.

RED/BLUE/GREEN SENSITIVE—The vast majority of today's amateur films fall into this class known as "pan" or panchromatic emulsions. These possess a fairly well-balanced sensitivity to the additive primary colors—red, blue/UV and green wavelength—and can be manufactured in a wide range of speeds. Because of their balanced sensitivity, processing in total darkness is recommended, although a faint green safelight can be used if kept a specified distance from the film.

INFRARED SENSITIVE—Special emulsions coated for sensitivity to blue/UV, red and infrared radiation, the latter not visible to the human eye, these are not general-purpose films. As similar light levels may contain varying amounts of infrared radiation, it is not possible to assign definite speed rat-

ings, and exposure meters are calibrated only for use with the visible spectrum of light.

Used primarily for scientific and medical purposes, infrared-sensitive films are also useful in aerial work and where haze penetration is necessary in outdoor scenics. As infrared film is used with a variety of filters, exposure index values suggested by the manufacturer will differ considerably depending upon the filter used.

GRAIN, GRANULARITY AND GRAININESS

We hear more about grain than any other characteristic of film. Every respectable photo book of the 1930s that dealt with film and developing invariably contained a section of formulas for mixing your own fine-grain developer. Each such formula claimed to provide some advantage in terms of minimizing the effect of grain structure.

Thankfully, those days are gone forever. Advances in photographic research have led to emulsion improvements without materially increasing the size of the silver crystals which are used. The term "grain" refers to the physical size of the silver particles which form the developed silver image. To achieve its greater speed, a modern fast or highly sensitive emulsion depends upon further sensitizing the silver with salts of rare metals, such as palladium or gold, and by evolving better sensitizing dyes which produce more efficient use of the light energy reaching the film during exposure.

As "grain" has fallen into the public domain—every photographer is his own expert on the subject—the term has come to be used rather loosely in several contexts. Properly, it should be used only in reference to the sizes of the emulsion crystals or silver in an image. To describe those variations in density which occur in uniform tonal areas of a negative, the term "granularity" is more appropriate. The amount of exposure received by a film affects granularity, not grain, and the greater the exposure, the greater granularity.

Once a print has been made, the result of grain and granularity is seen in the form of a mealiness in the image, which visually detracts from image quality—this is more properly called "graininess." In theory, an emulsion composed of fine grain crystals should produce negatives containing a low degree of granularity, resulting in a minimum amount of graininess in the final enlargement. We'll delve deeper into this relationship in the chapter on film developing—all you need at this point is to understand the differentiation between the three terms, which most photographers tend to lump together as "grain."

Generally speaking, the grain size of an emulsion is related to its speed. The slower the speed, the finer the grain pattern. Increases in film speed are related to the size of the silver crystals which compose the emulsion, as well as their spacing—larger crystals are spaced further apart. This results in negatives from fast films whose granularity is far more pronounced than that of slower, fine-grained emulsions.

As this negative is enlarged during the printing process, the graininess becomes very apparent and at very high degrees of enlargement, can result in an apparent loss of image sharpness when viewed at close range. Thus, for any subject which requires very large reproductions or extremely fine definition, a slower film is by far a more practical choice.

The degree to which negative granularity reproduces as graininess in the

final print is also dependent upon the subject to some extent. Portraits which contain large areas of very smooth skin tones, and landscapes/scenics with a considerable amount of uniform sky area will exhibit much more graininess than those subjects containing smaller areas of tonal uniformity and more fine detail. At the same time, graininess in a razor-sharp image is far less noticeable than in an image whose sharpness is borderline. Beginners have been known to remark that one of their lenses produced much less grain than another, and while such a remark is bound to draw loud laughter from most photographers, there's a round-about ring of truth to their mistaken analysis—graininess *will* be less evident in images made with a critically sharp

lens than with one less capable of producing a finely honed image. Because grain plays such a fabled role in photography, I'll come back to it shortly with some hints and suggestions, but right now, let's continue with the characteristics of an emulsion.

ACUTANCE

Grain was long considered to be the chief culprit in determining image sharpness, but in recent years, photographic scientists have concluded that another characteristic known as acutance or edge sharpness is of greater concern. This can be defined as a combined quality of chemical and physical sharpness found in a picture with crisp details. In such pictures, each image-forming grain of silver has a sharp edge rather than a blurry or fuzzy edge.

Acutance also refers to the degree to which one tonal area visually blends into another, and thus it appears to be psychologically more important than grain in determining the degree of visual sharpness seen in a print. You can easily visualize acutance by photographing a white circle against a black background. Films with poor acutance qualities will deliver a fuzzy separation between the two highly contrasting densities, as light diffusion within the emulsion causes the areas of high density to intrude upon those of lower density. For this reason, modern films are coated on the back of the base with an antihalation or light-absorbing dye. Films with good acutance will show far more of a distinct break between the tonal masses described above. As depth of field is the the lens's range of apparent sharpness, so acutance is the corresponding range of a film's sharpness.

Acutance and grain are interrelated and interdependent to a degree in producing apparent sharpness in an image. Like grain, acutance is partially the result of correct exposure and development of the film. Some developers will enhance the acutance quality of a film, while others affect it adversely. Acutance is also related to the type and thickness of both the emulsion and the film base—excellent reasons why the newer fine-grained emulsions are all thinner and use a thinner film base than did comparable films of only a few years back.

EXPOSURE LATITUDE

Most professionals live by the dictum that the best quality negative is one which has received the least exposure necessary to produce an adequate amount of shadow detail, and so they expose their film accordingly. Exposure latitude is simply the amount of deviation permissible from the optimum exposure which will still produce a satisfactory negative. If exposed at a minimum value, as stated for the best negative quality, the film's tolerance for further reductions in exposure is minimal. In such cases, latitude is primarily in the direction of overexposure. Excessive exposure will yield a printable negative, but as density increases, so does granularity in the negative and graininess in the print.

Latitude is not necessarily a constant factor; it varies according to the brightness ratio of the subject. While the ratio between highlight and shadow

areas of an average subject in bright sunlight may range as high as 125:1 or 130:1, subjects with few shadow areas of importance may have a ratio no greater than 30:1. For this reason, contrasty subjects permit less deviation from an optimum exposure than do flat subjects with few shadow areas.

GETTING AROUND GRAIN

The "grain" syndrome came into vogue with the development of the 35mm camera in the mid-'20s. Prior to that time, large format cameras and film were used almost exclusively, and contact prints (same size) of negatives were more common than enlargements. But when the "candid" craze struck in the 1930s, darkroom technique became an end in itself, as photographers tried to outdo each other in the size of enlargement which they could coax from the comparatively tiny 1x1½-inch negative. This gradually evolved to the opposite extreme in which print graininess became the ultimate end to which the creative strived. How should *you* regard grain?

Serious photographers who are concerned about sharp detail and smooth tonal gradation work with large format

1-2. The Egyptian architecture shown in (1) falls short of being visually impressive, but Shirley I. Fisher's choice of infrared film with a red filter (2) provides a striking tonal reverse of sky and foliage for visual impact.

cameras and films—it's that simple. The recent boom in view camera sales and usage is an indication that more and more amateurs are becoming fascinated with the potential offered by the larger negatives. The same degree of enlargement required to make an 8x10 print from a 35mm negative will give the 4x5 user a 30x40 enlargement. Provided that the same emulsion is used in both cases, theory tells us that the 30x40 print will exhibit the same degree of graininess as the 8x10—no more, no less—but when the two prints are viewed at their proper distances, the graininess will be far less apparent in the 30x40 print.

Those 35mm users who practice good exposure and darkroom techniques can produce a print from a fast emulsion (ASA 400) in which graininess is not noticeable from a normal viewing distance—it's there, but you have to hunt for it. And working with one of the moderate 35mm emulsions

2

(ASA 125), those with good technique need not worry about the problem.

To get around grain, it's essential that you select the right film for the subject at hand. For example, there's no good reason to use an ASA 400 film when photographing landscapes or scenics. You'll just lose distant detail completely, and the fine lines and shapes of objects nearer the camera will be shattered by the negative's gran-ularity. Smooth mid-tones such as sky and water areas will end up with uneven gradation. Thus, a medium speed (ASA 125) film makes far more sense when photographing such subjects, and if you want genuine exhibition quality, go to the slower emulsions (ASA 32-64).

Beginners are usually advised to stick with a medium-speed film for general purposes. The theory is that such an emulsion is adequate in speed for any ordinary subject or situation he'll encounter, and the tonal range and image sharpness will be sufficient. Unfortunately, giving such advice does him no favor, as it's a compromise designed solely for convenience. While it's true that I told you earlier that photography is a series of compromises at best, the necessity to compromise should be minimized whenever the op-

tion exists, if you want the best results.

One problem is that many of us are not really as interested in obtaining the best results as we are in the convenience factor. Liquid concentrate developers are sold at a far higher unit cost to those who don't want to take the time and effort to mix up a less-expensive powdered solution. In the same way, we standardize on a medium-speed film because it can deal capabably with many subjects and is adequate to handle the others—not because it's the best. And there are even some who settle for a fast film simply because it gives them the potential ability to work in lower light levels, without using a flash unit or tripod. Whether or not they actually do so isn't of prime importance to them; it's the idea that they *can* if they want to.

Large-format cameras using single sheets of film for each exposure provide their user with the luxury of developing each individual picture taken according to the specific requirements of the subject. They also permit choosing a particular emulsion for a given subject or lighting, but roll film and 35mm users are stuck with 12 to 36 exposures on a continuous roll, which usually ends up containing a variety of subjects photographed under varying lighting conditions. For them, development becomes a matter of compromise, and contrast is controlled by manipulation of the enlarging paper, either by using different grades or printing filters.

If you were to watch a professional photographer at work, you might be surprised to see him shoot an entire roll or cartridge on a single subject, or to remove a half-exposed roll from the camera and replace it with a fresh load of a different emulsion when his subject or lighting changes. This is done to allow processing of the film to suit the subject and exposure given. After all, film is a very inexpensive commodity if you place any value whatsoever on the picture that is to result, and using up that last 10-12 frames is not that important to him. If you want to make grain work for you, and thus tailor your film choice to your subject, it should not be that important to you.

In addition to exposing an entire cartridge on a given subject, or removing one that is only partially exposed, 35mm users have a third and less-expensive alternative to consider—bulk-

Ron Berkenblitt took advantage of the speed and gobs of grain offered by Kodak 2475 Recording Film to provide atmosphere in this motorcycle race scene.

loading their own cartridges with shorter lengths of film than provided by the standard 20- or 36-exposure factory loads. A mere 18 inches of film will provide for 10 exposures, including the leader, and with this technique, you can have a fine-grain film available for landscape and detail work, a medium-speed film at your fingertips for candids and average subjects, and a fast emulsion for use whenever the lighting or subject requires it. This will allow you to take a number of pictures of a given subject using the right film and adjusting both exposure and development accordingly, without fear of compromising any other pictures on the same film.

SHORT ENDS AND ODD LOTS

Not only will loading your own 35mm cartridges save you money while letting you tailor your film needs to each subject exactly, there's another advantage. Certain film emulsions are available only in bulk lengths and should you want to use these particular films, bulk loading is necessary anyway. Virtually every popular 35mm emulsion, black-and-white or color, is available in one of three lengths—generally 27½-, 50- or 100-foot rolls, although a few are offered in 25-, 55- or 97-foot quantities. This film comes wound on a plastic core, wrapped in opaque paper and sealed in small metal cans. To use, the can is opened in a darkroom, the paper unwrapped and a length of film cut from the roll.

Special reloadable cartridges are available and their use is recommended instead of attempting to reload factory cartridges. These come apart quite easily for attaching the cut length of film to the spool with a small piece of masking tape and then rolling it up. The wound spool of film is then replaced inside the cartridge with a 2-3-inch length sticking out through its light trap and the end resealed. The short length of film is then trimmed with a tongue so that it can be easily attached to the camera's take-up spool, and that's all there is to it.

EQUIPMENT FOR BULK LOADING

While the procedure as outlined above is quick and simple, it does require that all work be done in absolute darkness, and many find the use of a daylight film loader desirable. Offered in various styles and designs, these all essentially serve the same purpose—once loaded in the dark with the roll of

Shirley I. Fisher chose a slow emulsion for both negatives used to make this blend of daybreak over the edge of a lake.

bulk film, they can be used to spool cartridges in daylight.

Most often, the differences in bulk film loaders center primarily around how convenient they are to use. The more expensive ones will have exposure counters or footage counters to tell at a glance how much film you've used from the roll, or how many frames you've wound onto a given spool, etc. The one crucial difference between loaders is whether the bulk film passes from its compartment to that of the cartridge through a felted or feltless light trap.

The fewer times the film is touched on either side, the less the possibility of scratches occurring during the loading process. The felted light trap loader design works very well, just as long as you treat it with care and follow certain precautions. The felt must be kept extremely clean and so must the interior of the loader. The nonfelted trap design eliminates this problem, as it opens during the loading process and the film isn't touched at all as it's wound from bulk roll to cartridge spool.

The reloadable cartridge is another critical link in the chain. Cartridges suffer from metal fatigue at each end, and "felt failure." Metal fatigue results from the continual popping on/off of the cartridge ends to load and unload film. This repeated removal/replacement may cause the ends to leak light after a few uses, or the ends may become loose enough to pop off under impact.

Felt fatigue is less obvious, but can cause film scratching and localized fogging. This is related to the removal/replacement of the ends, since repeated use may cause the ends to lose their ability to hold the felt-lined cartridge lips through which the film passes adequately close together. In addition, dust and dirt can accumulate on the lips and work their way into the felt, where they become imbedded and cause fine scratches each time the film passes through the lips. This is especially likely to happen rather quickly if you carry reloaded cartridges around in your pocket or gadget bag without benefit of the dustproof containers such as factory-loaded film comes in.

One solution to these problems is to buy the reloadable cartridges of plastic, as these are fitted with screw-on ends instead of the snap-together metal ones. Although they are more delicate in terms of impact resistance, the improved security of the screw-on type end is worth considering, as well as the ease in removing the film for development. Since bulk film is so inexpen-

sive, it's still more economical to load your own and treat the cartridges as being expendable—one or two uses before replacement with new cartridges—than it is to buy factory fresh loads.

The final item which you may or may not feel to be necessary is a metal template used to tailor the leader tongue correctly. A variety of these are available in different styles, but all are only a couple dollars in cost. The advantage of a template to trim leader tongues is simply the uniformity it provides—you can get along quite nicely without one, but it is a neat really convenience.

COLOR FILM

Color films are generally classified in one of two types—reversal or negative—depending upon the end result of exposure and development. Reversal color films produce a positive image; as this image is designed for viewing by transmitted light, they are often called transparency or slide films. Negative or color print emulsions produce a negative which must be printed on either paper or film to obtain a positive image. In addition to the characteristics already described for black-and-white films, color films have two more which are separate and distinct: light balance and multilayered emulsions. emulsions are balanced

LIGHT BALANCE—Color emulsions are balanced to provide their most accurate color rendition with a specific light source. Offered by all color film manufacturers, daylight reversal color films are balanced for 5500-6000°K. Indoor or tungsten color films are generally balanced either for use with 3400°K. lights (Type A) or 3200°K. lights (Type B). As this is being written, Kodak has announced that it is phasing out its Type A emulsions completely, leaving Type B as the only tungsten-balanced color films on the market. Of course, it's possible to use daylight emulsions under tungsten illumination, providing that the proper filtration is used (see the chapter on Filters), but this reduces the film speed considerably.

Color negative films are designed for exposure by daylight, electronic flash or blue flash bulbs. When used with tungsten illumination, an 80B filter is generally recommended, but as the processor uses corrective filtration when printing, you may not find the somewhat warmish tint of indoor pictures taken without the use of a filter to be overly objectionable.

EMULSION STRUCTURE—Color emulsions are multilayered. Each layer is sensitive to one of the additive primary colors and filter layers between the image-forming layers hold back the appropriate wavelengths to assist in correct layer exposure. Emulsion designs vary from one manufacturer to another, but all work in essentially the same manner. Figure A shows the structure of Fujicolor F-II, Agfacolor CNS and Agfacolor CNPS emulsions; reversal films have a cross section which is similar in appearance and design.

In general, the thicker the overall total of the different emulsion layers, the lower the image sharpness will be, as the diffusion of light by the layers causes image clouding. Reducing the total thickness by reducing the thickness of the emulsion coating will also reduce the maximum density and exposure scale of the image, resulting in a narrower latitude. For this reason, thinner emulsions are usually achieved by reducing only the gelatin in the emulsion layers.

WHERE DOES THE COLOR COME FROM?

Except for films of the Kodachrome family, all reversal color emulsions contain color couplers in each emulsion layer, which form dye images during processing. A single color developer produces the dye images in each of the three emulsion layers simultaneously. Such color films can be processed by the user at home or by a commercial lab service.

Kodachrome films do not have the couplers in the emulsion, but use separate color developer solutions to produce the color dyes in each of the three layers. Thus, Kodachrome processing is far more complex and requires precise controls and equipment not available outside of a professional processing lab.

Most amateur negative color films contain the color couplers within the emulsion layers and unused couplers which remain in the film after development produce an automatic mask for color correction during printing. These can be processed at home.

COLOR FILM SPEEDS

Compared to black-and-white, far fewer color emulsions are available, and most fall into the moderate-speed category (ASA 64), with only three reversal films currently rated faster than ASA 100. Until very recently, ASA 100 was also the upper limit for color negative films, but the recent arrival of Fujicolor F-II 400 and Kodacolor 400 indicates a breakthrough in film speed.

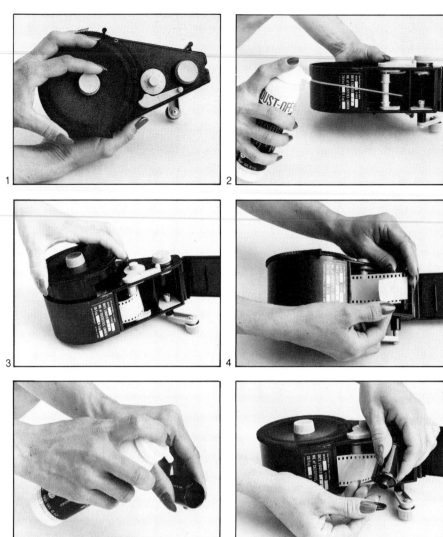

LATITUDE

Many photographers in doubt about the correct exposure tend to give black-and-white film "a little more" just to be on the safe side. This is understandable, as nothing will add shadow detail to a black-and-white negative if it isn't there to begin with, and black-and-white film's latitude is greater on the overexposure or "too much" side of normal.

But the exposure latitude of color film is much more limited than with black-and-white emulsions. Deviations from correct exposure with reversal color films can have a devastating effect on the resulting transparency. The lighter values will lose what little color saturation they possess, highlights will lose detail and separation, and with sufficient overexposure, they'll turn perfectly clear. Depending upon the subject in question, this can happen with as little as ½ f-stop over normal, and highlight detail lost in this way cannot be restored by copying the transparency or by making a print—if

1. **To use a bulk film loader, turn the center knob on the film compartment and remove its cover.**
2. **Make certain that the loader compartments are clean and dustfree.**
3. **Drop the bulk film into the compartment and thread the end of it through the light trap. Replace the cover and lock it in place. This and the following four steps should be done in total darkness.**
4. **Attach the end of the film to the cartridge spool with a short length of masking tape.**
5. **Blow out the interior of the cartridge, paying particular attention to the felt trap. Dust and dirt caught here will scratch every frame twice—as you wind and as you rewind the film.**
6. **Slide the film and spool into the car-**

the detail is washed out in a positive, it's gone for good.

Underexposure is not quite as serious, especially if the slide is to be used for reproduction since the photoengraver can correct it somewhat. While slight underexposure increases color saturation, such slides possessing sufficient highlight color and detail can often be corrected to an acceptable degree by copying, and may even

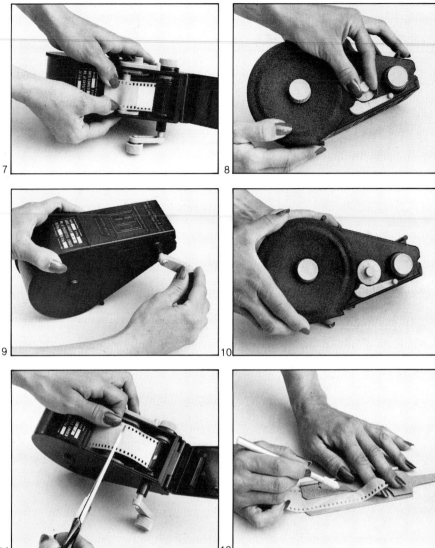

7

8

9

10

11

12

tridge and secure the end cap.
7. Make certain that the film's sprocket holes engage the sprocket teeth in the loader before closing and locking the cover in place.
8. Turn on the room lights and set the exposure counter.
9. Rotate the handle with a slow and steady motion until the exposure counter indicates that you've loaded the desired number of exposures.
10. Rotate the cover to close the light trap inside the loader.
11. Open the back and cut the film as shown, then remove the loaded cartridge.
12. Pull a short length of film from the cartridge and trim it to form a leader. The Prinz template shown here is typical of those available to do a neat job.

make an acceptable color print. But near-correct exposure is also highly desirable; more than a ½-stop either way can make the difference between a useful or useless slide, unless a deliberate departure from normal color rendition is sought.

The situation with negative color films is just the opposite. In general, an underexposure of one-half f-stop is about as great as you can get away

with before image quality begins to deterioriate considerably. But overexposure up to 1½-2 stops can be tolerated with very good prints resulting before highlight detail begins to disappear. Slight errors in exposure of color negative emulsions can usually be compensated for during printing.

RECIPROCITY FAILURE

There's a straight-line relationship between negative density and duration of exposure—the effect of exposure relative to density is the same, no matter if the film is exposed for 100 seconds at one foot-candle (a measurement of light), or one second at 100 foot-candles. The results will theoretically be the same; this is known as the law of reciprocity and pertains to both black-and-white and color films. But when the duration of exposure becomes abnormally long (a time exposure) or abnormally brief (electronic flash duration), the straight-line relationship breaks down and reciprocity failure occurs.

Basically, this means a loss of film speed—a 10-second exposure at f/2.8 does not provide sufficient exposure for the subject despite the fact that the light meter tells us it is correct. Reciprocity failure is often encountered in extreme close-up work, where the magnification ratio may be so great that the increase in lens-to-film-plane distance requires an abnormal increase in exposure by way of compensation. Despite what our meters and tables tell us, their recommended exposure falls short of producing a properly exposed image. Reciprocity failure is far more important when working in color than black-and-white, as it affects not only density but also the film's color balance, causing a shift which requires the use of a color compensating or CC filter to restore proper balance.

For most color films, the "safe" exposure range is between 1/10 and 1/1000 second. Since different color films as well as different emulsion batches are affected differently by the law of reciprocity, shooting an emulsion test is recommended for critical work where exact color balance is desired. Buy several rolls of the same emulsion number (this is printed on the film box near the expiration date) and expose a roll under conditions identical to those you'll be using for your critical work. Follow the manufacturer's recommendation for filtration with that particular emulsion—this is included on the data sheet accompanying the film.

After processing, analyze the pictures for both color balance and exposure. If the color balance seems to be off and you can't tell in which direction, look at the pictures through various CC filters—the one that makes them look best is the one you want to use. Repeat the procedure with a second roll and the new filtration and check the results again. Once you've established both the correct exposure and filtration, you can proceed with shooting the critical work.

A TECHNOLOGICAL LAG?

Since the introduction of the first Ektachrome emulsions by Kodak in the late 1940s, the push in color emulsion technology has been a considerable one; those primarily interested in black-and-white work continually complain that color has received more than its share of research attention, and the latest developments in color films would appear to bear out their complaints of unequal emphasis. But, it must be remembered that approximately 90 percent of all amateur film presently sold in the United States is color, with black-and-white taking the other 10 percent (this does not include instant camera films). Naturally, manufacturers can be expected to put their research dollars where the greatest return lies. And it must also be remembered that while no quantum leaps have been made in black-and-white film technology recently, there have been numerous and continuing improvements quietly introduced by manufacturers over recent years. By comparison with the color film user, black-and-white addicts are not as bad off as they might think.

For example, existing-light photography has been possible with black-and-white materials for many years, and the days of extreme graininess, low resolution and high fog levels are long gone. But most color enthusiasts have not had the same opportunity until now. Using an ASA 80-100 film for available-light work and pulling decent prints from the negatives has been very difficult. There is one fast reversal film on the market, but its graininess has been a marked feature holding back its general popularity, and most who use color have labored under overwhelming difficulties in working without supplemental lighting under the same conditions where the black-and-white user would not hesitate to shoot and then push the film in development 2-3 stops beyond its rated speed.

FUJICOLOR F-II 400

With the announcement of its ASA 400 color negative emulsion at Photokina '76, Fuji Photo Film caught the industry completely off guard. Abundant rumors over the past few years that Kodak's introduction of such a fast color negative film was imminent had led most observers to believe that Kodak would indeed break the negative color speed barrier first.

An even greater surprise awaited the skeptics when they used their first cartridges of the fast new color print film. It had been expected that the new film's color rendition would not be very great and that noticeable graininess would be evident in the prints made from ASA 400 negatives. But the skeptics were wrong on both counts, and because they were wrong, the new Fuji color negative film will probably have a greater impact on color photography than any development in the color field since the original Kodachrome was introduced in 1934. Here's why:

Incorporating 14 separate layers, the emulsion of Fujicolor F-II 400 is no

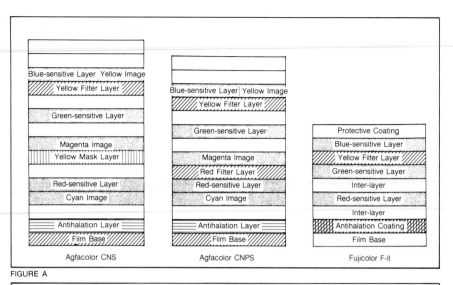

FIGURE A

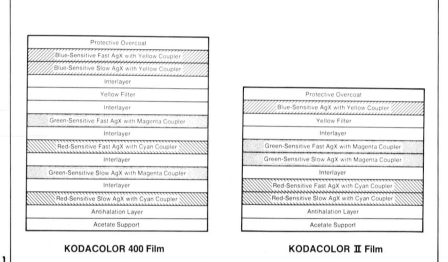

FIGURE B

thicker than the 11-layer emulsion of Fujicolor F-II 100 film—which certainly indicates advances few had thought were possible at this point in the state of the art. The new film is fully compatible with the current C-41 processing chemistry, another considerable advantage. As it has virtually no sensitivity to ultraviolet, the film sees in much the same way as does the human eye. Its spectral sensitivity is so designed that the film can be used under ordinary household or even fluorescent illumination with more than satisfactory results, and no shift in speed is necessary unless a color correction filter is used. For the greatest fidelity in color rendition under illumination other than daylight, the use of an 80A filter is recommended, along with a film speed drop to ASA 125, but I suspect that most users will prefer the slightly warm but pleasing results of exposure without a filter rather than give up the extra speed for a shade cooler picture.

The reproduction of skin tones, tonal gradation and color fidelity are all very similar to Fujicolor F-II 100, as are im-

1. The major improvement in Kodacolor 400 is its two-stop speed increase, accomplished by new high speed silver halide emulsions and inverting the fast red-sensitive/slow green-sensitive layers relative to Kodacolor II film. Kodacolor 400 film also responds well under a variety of lighting conditions, including fluorescent lights.
2. John Guarante puts the grain structure of Kodak 2475 Recording film to work in subtle ways.

age sharpness, latent-image stability, exposure latitude and storage qualities. Prints made from negatives of both films simultaneously exposed of the same subject appear virtually identical in all respects, except for the two f-stop or two shutter speed setting difference. Outdoors in bright sunlight, the extra speed permits greater manipulation of depth of field and/or action stopping ability by virtue of the higher shutter speed possible.

KODAK KODACOLOR 400

A high-speed color negative film available in both 110 and 35mm sizes, Kodacolor 400 is balanced for daylight, blue flash and electronic flash sources. The new film exhibits somewhat more grain and slightly greater contrast than Kodacolor II, which remains available and now carries an ASA index of 100. Its major improvement over Kodacolor II is, of course, the two-stop speed increase. This was achieved by incorporating new, high-speed silver halide emulsions and inverting the fast red-sensitive layer and slow green-sensitive layer relative to their use in Kodacolor II (Figure B).

The spectral sensitivity of Kodacolor 400 has been "fine-tuned" to minimize the sensitivity at the ends of each primary color's spectrum where daylight and incandescent illuminants vary, and by tailoring the relative sensitivities within the visible region to respond more naturally to common fluorescent lighting. By reducing the exaggerated response to variations in illumination, the remaining color variation to which the human eye normally adapts is taken care of by color corrections in printing. The end result is that color pictures which appear visually pleasing can be taken under a wider range of lighting conditions with Kodacolor 400.

WHAT'S AHEAD?

Agfa has demonstrated an ASA 400 color negative film, 3M offers one and Sakuracolor is being sold under private labels, with others certain to follow. It appears that a large-scale battle is about to be fought, which can only benefit the consumer, as further advances in film technology cannot be far behind,

ADVANCES IN REVERSAL FILM TECHNOLOGY

While Fuji was popping eyes with its ASA 400 color negative stock, Kodak quietly retired the E-4 process and replaced it with a new one designated E-6. Also long-rumored, the advent of E-6 meant the discontinuance of Ektachrome-X and High Speed Ektachrome in favor of the new Ektachrome Professional films, which were soon followed by comparable emulsions designated specifically for the consumer or amateur market—Ektachrome 64, Ektachrome 160 (tungsten) and 200 (daylight). Before we examine the differences between the two, let's take a quick look at the new E-6 films and how they compare with their predecessors, as they will be around for quite some time.

THE E-6 EKTACHROMES

For openers, the E-6 Ektachromes are represented by Kodak as having better color qualities than the emul-

2

sions they've replaced, they require a shorter processing time with chemicals said to be less polluting, and carry slightly higher ASA ratings. As of this writing, each package of the professional emulsions is provided with an indication of any deviation from the rated speed—something which happens with different emulsion batches of every color film, but information not generally provided to the user in the past.

As both the professional and consumer films are so very new, it's virtually impossible to provide any definitive evaluations. To do so takes several months after a new color film is marketed before all the minor variations which inevitably occur in the manufacturing process are noted and account-

ed for. Early test results amount to just that—early test results—which may well change as time passes and more experience is gained.

Yet it is possible to make a few general observations based on early looks at the new Ektachromes. Image definition is sharper, but the difference is subtle to the eye. This greater acuity and reduced granularity are the result of a reduction in the silver content of the emulsion, which has the undesirable side effect of increasing contrast somewhat, especially noticeable when the films are used in bright sunlight. Contrast does not increase as greatly when used under conditions of diffused or indirect lighting. Shadow and highlight details are generally better, with a

1

1. Your choice of film will have a good deal to do with how you use light. Anna Lee Cutrone finds an ASA 400 emulsion ideal for grab shots like this under a variety of lighting conditions.
2. Glenn Cooper pushed his ASA 400 film two stops for this shot of L.A. Dodger pitcher Don Sutton preparing to work.
3. Michael Parrish used the lower contrast and greater grain of an ASA 400 emulsion in preference over a slower film for this visual interpretation of a castle in Segovia, Spain.

wider density range which slightly extends latitude in each direction from normal by about ¼-½ f-stop.

Modifications in emulsion structure and changes in dye content provide slightly different color rendition from that of the older Ektachromes, along with more purity in whites. The new processing chemistry functions at a much higher temperature than did E-4 (100° vs. 85°). This 15°F. increase allows a reduction in developing time by 50 percent and results in greater color saturation, as well as helping to extend the detail range in shadow areas. All in all, the E-6 Ektachromes represent a significant advance in reversal color film technology.

But are the new films *really* better? That will depend upon you and other photographers, and how you react to the slight changes in color rendition. If you were pleased with the old Ektachromes, you may very well not care for the new E-6 versions; those displeased with the old films will probably welcome the newcomers; if you're new to photography, you won't know the difference anyway.

2

PROFESSIONAL VS. NON-PROFESSIONAL EKTACHROMES

There's only one significant difference between the E-6 Ektachrome films designated as "professional" and the so-called amateur versions—aging. All sensitized materials are perishable by nature and color emulsions are no exceptions—they change constantly from the date of manufacture until they're exposed and processed. Like meat, cheese and fine wine, a freshly coated emulsion is "green," that is, it must be aged to a certain degree be-

fore its color rendition will equal the theoretical "aim point" at which the colors will reproduce as the manufacturer intends they should.

But the distribution process between the film's manufacture and its ultimate use is a long and sometimes tedious road; film enters the distribution pipeline and ends up in all kinds and types of storage in warehouses, drug stores, supermarkets, photo stores, etc. where it may or may not be sold immediately. Along the way, it has most likely been subjected to at least some variations if not extremes in temperature, and even if the process moves quickly from manufacture to point of sale, there's no guarantee that the consumer will use the film right after buying it. He may load his camera, take a few shots at the beach during his summer vacation and not finish off the roll until the Christmas season.

Because of the many vagaries and uncertainties of this distribution process, color film has traditionally been marketed while still "green," with the expectation that it will be close to its optimum when finally used. The significant difference mentioned above is simply that the "professional" packaging is aged before the film is released to the market; thus it's very close to its "aim point." The other packaging is released "green" as before and allowed to shift to its aim point as in the past. This pre-aging of the E-6 professional films means that if you do not plan on using the film immediately after purchase, it should be refrigerated to prevent a shift away from the optimum point. And regardless of whether you shoot it at once, or refrigerate and use it later, the film should be processed as quickly as possible after exposure.

Knowledgeable readers are probably mumbling to themselves that this isn't really a new procedure—manufacturers have long recommended that film be refrigerated until use and processed promptly—and for the most part, the average photographer has paid little attention to either admonishment. Why then, you might well ask, go to the trouble of packaging what is essentially the same film in two different ways? Well, this marketing approach puts serious amateurs and professional users on notice—if they want optimum color without going to the trouble of making an emulsion test, they now have both the films and the means to get it.

SPECIAL-PURPOSE FILMS

There are a number of black-and-white and color films which have been

3

and grainy. Add a little diffusion, enlarge a tiny portion of the negative and the effect is sensational. For general high-speed existing-light photography, this emulsion can produce results superior to the more typical high-speed emulsions pushed three or four stops, with the additional benefit that the increase in sensitivity is a true increase in film speed. For general use, Kodak recommends D-76 development; for pushing the film with low-contrast subject matter, D-19.

KODAK HIGH CONTRAST COPY FILM 5069—Rated at ASA 64, this high-contrast negative film reproduces well when you need very good black-and-white transparencies from black-and-white negatives. Bracket exposures and process in Kodak D-19 developer for 11 minutes at 68°F. The black-and-white brightness ratio that the eye can see in a print is around 1:50; by using this film for transparencies, you can increase that ratio to around 1:1000, an ideal way to put together a super black-and-white portfolio. Its extreme fine grain and very high resolving power make this film ideal for copying line material and reducing the size of line copy originals while holding excellent detail.

KODALITH ORTHO FILM 6556, TYPE 3—An extremely high-contrast orthochromatic film (can be handled under a red safelight in the darkroom), this film delivers top-quality line and halftone negatives and positives. Rated at ASA 10 and available only in bulk rolls of 100 feet (load it yourself), it requires use of the special Kodalith A&B developer. As Kodalith has an exceptionally wide exposure/development latitude, you should bracket your exposures. Kodalith can be sandwiched with a straight color transparency, or used as an aid in making posterizations.

KODAK DIRECT POSITIVE PAN FILM, 5246—The use of this film permits black-and-white transparencies without going through the negative-to-positive process. Used directly in the camera to produce transparencies, it's rated at ASA 80. Uses for this emulsion are creative, bounded only by the limits of your imagination. A Direct Positive film developing kit is required for processing and contains all the chemistry necessary to do the job.

KODAK FINE GRAIN POSITIVE FILM, 5302—Unlike the Direct Positive emulsion, this film can be used in a darkroom illuminated by a greenish-yellow or red safelight, as it is blue-sensitive only. Its basic use is to produce

designed for special photographic purposes, but which are also of interest to the creative photographer, as their use permits certain effects not obtainable in any other way. The following capsule descriptions will serve to introduce you to some of these more exotic emulsions.

KODAK 2475 RECORDING FILM—Originally designed for low-light illumination or short-duration exposures such as found in surveillance work, this film is a very fast emulsion (EI 1000) with a high degree of sensitivity to the red end of the spectrum, and can be pushed to EI 6400. There's no way to avoid graininess when using 2475, but it's a great film to experiment with using various developers and development times. And once you've settled upon a developer, devel-

opment time and speed rating that suit your taste, you'll find a new fascination in existing-light photography.

KODAK 2484 PAN FILM—Like its cousin, 2475 Recording Film, this emulsion is a high-speed concoction, and with varying degrees of forced development, can be pushed way up into the same EI range as 2475, should you feel the need to do so. Many photographers feel that 2484 is sharper and finer in gradation and granularity than 2475. Developed in Kodak D-76 or similar developers, it yields negatives of beautifully soft tonal quality, very reminiscent of the tones obtained by pictorial photographers at the early part of this century. While this film won't duplicate antique printing techniques right out of the box, it leads in the direction by providing an initial image that's soft

1

black-and-white transparencies by contact printing with the desired negatives. Try using it with color slides as your original and develop in Kodak D-76 for low contrast, Kodak Dektol for moderate contrast and Kodak D-11 for high contrast.

KODAK HIGH SPEED INFRARED FILM—This high-speed, infrared-sensitive emulsion has a fairly high contrast level, is ideal for haze penetration when used with the appropriate filter, and produces special effects in commercial and architectural photography. Dark skies, fleecy white clouds, light-colored foliage and translucent skin tones are characteristic and experimentation is the key word. As nor-

mal speed values are not applicable because of the infrared sensitivity, you should make trial exposures under typical conditions, using a meter setting of ASA 50 with a No. 25 (A) red filter over the lens for a starting point. Regardless of the exposure index on which you settle, bracket your exposure whenever you use this film, as infrared levels do vary somewhat from scene to scene, and will be more prominent in distant landscapes than in nearby scenics.

KODAK EKTACHROME INFRARED FILM—This modified-color, infrared-sensitive transparency film was originally designed for scientific work, but its emulsion produces beautiful pictorial

effects when used with appropriate color filters. The modified color sensitizing produces a yellow positive image in the green-sensitive layer, a magenta image in the red-sensitive layer, and a cyan image in the infrared-sensitive layer. Because of the infrared sensitivity, ordinary film speed ratings do not apply and the usable exposure indexes vary according to the type and density of filter used.

KODAK PHOTOMICROGRAPHY COLOR FILM 2483—This is a high-definition, high-contrast, slow-speed (ASA 16) color transparency film with extremely fine grain and very high resolving power. The camera should be loaded and unloaded in subdued light, with

1. While the use of litho film has been greatly overdone in recent years, some subjects like this picture by Jeff Blackwell lend themselves well to the high-contrast technique.
2. Don't know what to do with all those color negatives lying around? Michael Parrish prints his on a hard grade of black-and-white paper to come up with unusual effects like this.

the film rewound completely into the cartridge before opening the camera back. Excellent for brilliant copy work, the high contrast level of 2483 makes it an ideal emulsion for special effects and contrast build-up in slide duplicating operations.

Kodak 2483 can also be processed to a negative using Kodak C-22 chemistry. If you use this special development, rate the film at ASA 100 and bracket your exposures in half-stop increments. Colors will be complementary, that is, black letters on a white background when photographed with a yellow filter will become white letters on a blue background, etc.

EASTMAN COLOR NEGATIVE FILM

5254 AND 5257—High-speed (ASA 100) color negative films characterized by accurate tonal reproduction, good image structure and a wide exposure latitude, these are motion picture stock and have been promoted into big business by reloaders. Available only in bulk, 5254/5257 are bought by companies who respool the films into camera-length cartridges and then sell them as a "universal" color film. You are told to use them indoors or outdoors and the respooler will process it in his lab, making any necessary color corrections and returning the negatives along with a complete set of prints *and* color slides to you. Actually, Kodak recommends the use of an 85 filter

when the 3200°K. film is exposed outdoors, and this drops the film speed to ASA 64.

On the whole, it sounds great, but 5254/5257 are not quite as fantastic as they sound. Type 5254 uses a remjet black backing which should be removed mechanically by commercial processors; try it yourself and you may well end up with a mess and emulsion damage to boot. If the processor uses chemical solutions other than those intended for the film, color distortions will occur which cannot be compensated for in printing—and some labs use a C-22 process rather than the motion picture chemicals.

Obviously, these are not films which you would work with in your own darkroom on other than an experimental basis, and if you rely upon a commercial lab which sells the reloads (Kodak will neither process nor print from 5254/5257), you can expect considerable variations in the quality of work, color rendition, overall cost and how long the lab takes to return the results to you.

Now that you've added another limb to your tree of knowledge, it's time to start pulling the odd pieces together. To do this, we'll take up the subject of determining correct exposure next, and show you how to use light and film to create an image that's suitable for framing. □

4

1/125 At f/8—How Exposure Is Determined

Correct exposure leads to good photographic quality in a negative or transparency. In order to achieve good quality in the image we produce, a specific amount of light reflected from the subject must strike the film. Too much light reaching the film results in overexposure; too little causes underexposure. We know, for example, that when X amount of light is allowed to strike the film for Y length of time, a properly exposed image will be formed. We know that the speed or sensitivity of the film's emulsion to light is a major factor in determining what that correct exposure should be.

We also know that both the aperture size and shutter speed of an adjustable camera can be manipulated to provide varying combinations which will give a correct exposure. These various combinations allow us to take two other factors into account—the apparent range of sharpness in the picture, and the ability to stop subject motion. The use of a large aperture will limit the range of sharpness in the picture, while a small one will extend it—a fast shutter speed will "freeze" or stop action, while a slow speed may cause a moving subject to blur as it forms its image on the film.

WHAT IS CORRECT EXPOSURE?

The amount of metallic silver in a processed negative is regarded as a measure of the negative's "density." The more light that is passed through the dark areas of the negative, the less dense or "thinner" the negative; the less light transmitted through these areas, the more dense the negative is. Looking at very light areas on a cor-

You must carefully determine the ratio between shadow and highlight areas and expose accordingly if you wish to retain texture, tone and shape to the greatest degree. (Shirley I. Fisher.)

rectly exposed print, we know that the corresponding areas on the negative are very dense, as they blocked light from passing through the negative during the printing exposure. Sections which appear very dark on the print

represent a thin negative area, as much more light was passed through the negative at these points.

When the final print exhibits a complete lack of white areas—the highlight areas are gray or black instead—the metallic silver constituting those areas was not dense enough to hold back sufficient light during printing and so we say that the negative in question is too "thin" or underexposed. Just the

opposite is true with overexposed negatives—when the darkest subject areas or shadows are too light on the print, and areas which should have reproduced as gray are really white, the metallic silver content in the negative is excessive (too dense) and holds back too much light.

At a point somewhere between these two extremes is a negative of medium density which yields black, white and gray areas in the same relative proportion as that of the subject when printed. A long-used and fairly dependable test for such a negative is to place it flat on the surface of a white page which contains black lettering, such as this one. Hold the combination under a bright light and examine the highlight areas—those which are darkest in the negative. You should be able to read the type through the silver density; if not, the negative is overexposed.

Do the same with the shadow or lightest areas of the negative, comparing them to the completely transparent area between two frames on the negative strip. The page underneath the negative should appear slightly darker when seen through the clear areas of the negative than it does when viewed through the space between two frames; if not, your negative is un-

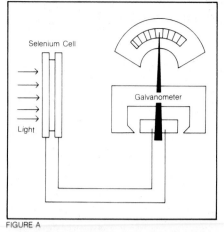

FIGURE A

1-2. Anna Lee Cutrone demonstrates two different approaches to mixing daylight with indoor ilumination. In (1), dark areas are used to frame the subject and exposure based on the flesh tones; (2) splits the tonal scale in half, with highlight areas concentrated on the left and shadows to the right.

3. Photographers have relied on a variety of devices to help determine correct exposure. This sampling of prewar tools includes left-to-right the Watkins, which exposed light-sensitive paper and then compared the results to a known value; the original GE and Weston photoelectric meters; the Univex extinction meter containing a numbered graduated wedge. The last visible number was the key, but most people saw them all. The Ansco was similar to the Watkins, while the Relio was but one of the many charts/scales used.

derexposed. A negative which passes both tests is most likely properly exposed, and when printed should deliver a full range of black, white and gray tones, with visible detail in both shadow and highlight areas. This kind of negative quality depends upon an accurate measurement of the light reflected from your subject that is translated into the proper combination of aperture and shutter speed required to achieve the effect you want. To do this, we measure light with a photoelectric light meter.

PHOTOELECTRIC LIGHT METERS

Until the mid-'30s, photographers had no consistently reliable way in which to determine proper exposure. Measuring light was primarily a matter of educated guesswork, sometimes based on the use of charts, tables and visual metering devices called extinction meters. But the accuracy of the end result was always highly dependent upon the photographer's experience based on trail and error. Rapid developments in the modern light meter since World War II have taken much of the guesswork out of the process of determining correct exposure, and the real key in exposure determination today lies in perfecting

your understanding of the light meter and how to use it properly.

As with film, the principle behind the operation of the photoelectric light meter is based on the photosensitive properties of certain minerals. All light meters use a light-sensitive cell wired to the circuit of an indicator gauge. At the present, there are four different types of cells which are used to con-

vert light intensity into electric current—selenium, cadmium sulphide (CdS), silicon blue and gallenium-arsenide cells.

SELENIUM—The electrical resistance property of selenium varies with the amount of light that reaches it. Placing a flat disc of selenium between a translucent metal surface and an iron disc causes an electrical current to be

generated when light strikes it. This current is fed to an instrument that measures electrical current, called a galvanometer. The galvanometer indicates the amount of electricity generated by the cell by moving a needle on a dial marked in light values (Figure A). The value is then transferred to a calculator scale on the meter by the user to determine the various combinations of aperture and shutter speed usable under the prevailing light conditions.

Selenium-cell light meters are characterized by quick and accurate response to all but low light levels. The color response of selenium is fairly close to that of the human eye and a good indication of a filter's factor can be obtained by placing the filter in front of the meter's cell.

CADMIUM-SULPHIDE (CdS)—A CdS cell does not generate its own electrical current. The cell is wired into the circuit of a meter gauge operated by a small battery and basically functions as a resistor, "blocking" the flow of current between the battery and the measuring meter. When light strikes the CdS cell, its resistance decreases and the resulting current flow activates the indicator needle on the gauge. The greater the light intensity, the lower the cell's resistance. This enables more current to pass and results in a higher light value indication on the meter's gauge (Figure B).

The CdS cell has a high degree of sensitivity to low light levels—its pri-

mary advantage over selenium. but its spectral sensitivity is not as accurate, being biased in favor of red. Placing a deep red filter over the cell will hardly cause a reaction, but a green filter elicits the opposite response. Measuring a red and green subject of approximately equal reflectances will result in the CdS cell giving a higher than necessary reading because of its bias. Manufacturers compensate for this somewhat by interposing corrective filtration with the cell.

Cadmium-sulphide also has a "memory" factor, requiring a respite from exposure to very bright light levels before it can accurately read a very low level of illumination. Because the CdS cell depends upon a battery which does not deteriorate quickly, it will perform in a uniform manner over a long period of time, but when battery voltage begins to drop, it does so rapidly—one minute the meter functions properly and the next, it doesn't function at all. As the CdS cell is dependent upon a battery for its operation, it is also affected by temperature changes.

SILICON BLUE CELL—One answer to many of the CdS cell's imperfections, silicon blue cells provide a better overall response to all wavelengths of light (but not as good as selenium) and can indicate peak response in a fraction of a second—a definite advantage when you consider that a CdS cell requires between 12 and 60 seconds to respond and indicate *peak* response. As

the silicon blue cell has no "memory" factor, it can switch from extremes in illumination levels with virtually no lag, while providing a true reading at each extreme.

GALLENIUM-ARSENIDECELL—Developed by the Nippon Electric Company, the GAP cell is a combination of gallenium, arsenic and phosphorous, a mixture of compounds designed to overcome the shortcomings of both CdS and silicon blue cells. Manufactured on a linear integrated circuit (IC) chip, the GAP cell is not overly red-sensitive, thus requires no dampening with overlaid filtration to compensate, as does the CdS cell. Spectral sensitivity of the GAP cell closely matches that of the human eye and its response to light changes is instantaneous. Although slightly temperature-sensitive, there's far less deviation in the accuracy of GAP caused by ambient weather changes.

WHICH IS BEST?—While I've described the four types of light sensors used in photoelectric metering systems along with their limitations, I've done so primarily to help you differentiate between them, not to cast aspersions on one type as being *less useful* or *better* than another. All produce accurate results and their limitations rarely interfere with their use under normal circumstances. By and large, you'll seldom encounter problems with any one type, and only in very specialized situations will their inherent limitations interfere

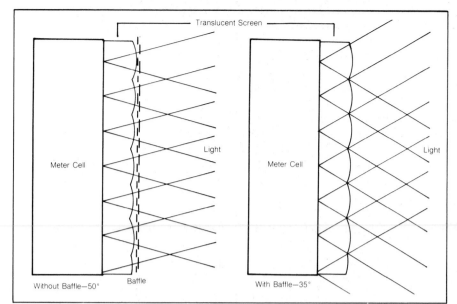

Translucent Screen

Meter Cell

Light

Meter Cell

Light

Without Baffle—50°   Baffle

With Baffle—35°

FIGURE C

1. Seen through the camera's viewfinder, this scenic had plenty of visual punch, none of which found its way to the film. While composition is questionable, the primary problem is one of lighting, and photographers take thousands of such pictures without realizing what's wrong.

with the exposure you choose.

For example, if you do not work in low light levels at all, there's no reason why the less-sensitive (and less expensive) selenium meter will not prove entirely suitable for your purposes. But if you do much photography at rock concerts and in other such limited-light situations, the selenium meter is obviously a poor choice—you need a meter cell that will respond swiftly and accurately to constantly changing illumination levels and without a red bias. In between the two extremes of average and extremely low light levels, one of the four sensor systems available will be satisfactory for your use.

OTHER FEATURES—As we've seen, a photoelectric exposure meter is basically a light-sensitive cell which measures the intensity of light. The value of the light as indicated by the meter cell is translated into aperture/shutter speed combinations by means of a calculator device attached to the meter body. By setting the calculator dial according to the ASA index of the film, and transferring the light value from the meter scale to the calculator, its scale will provide all possible aperture/shutter speed combinations at a glance. The latest and most expensive light meters feature a light-emitting diode (LED) digital readout of exposure settings.

Meters may use two series of light values on a single scale, or have separate high/low scales. When the light is

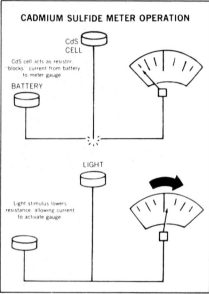

CADMIUM SULFIDE METER OPERATION

CdS CELL

CdS cell acts as resistor, "blocks" current from battery to meter gauge

BATTERY

LIGHT

Light stimulus lowers resistance, allowing current to activate gauge

FIGURE B

very intense, the needle will move off the lower value scale. A baffle of some type is then introduced over the meter cell to restrict the light level, allowing values to be read on the higher scale. Under less bright illumination, the baffle is removed and the meter needle will again indicate a value on the lower value scale.

Should you find that the reading is not the same when changing from one scale to the other, the meter itself is not at fault. This is caused by the baffle, which may change the meter cell's angle of acceptance or angle of view slightly as a means of reducing light intensity (Figure C). Most meter cells are provided with an angle of view of approximately 50 degrees, or slightly greater than the angle seen by the camera lens. If your meter provides slightly different readings when you change from one scale to the other, this variation can be compensated for

by moving the meter's position farther from the subject whenever the baffle is in place.

INCIDENT VS. REFLECTED

While meters differ very little in the basic principles of their internal operation, there is considerable variation in the ways in which they are actually used to measure brightness of a scene. The most fundamental distinction depends upon whether a meter is used to measure the amount of incident light falling directly on the subject, or the amount of light reflected from it (Figure D).

The brightness of an object depends upon two primary factors—the amount of light striking it and the absorption characteristics of the object's surface. When we disregard the absorption characteristics and measure only the intensity of the light falling on the object, we are taking an "incident light" reading. The type of meter used for this purpose is referred to as an incident-light meter.

The most outstanding physical feature of the incident meter is its translucent light collector or diffuser. This may be built into the meter or available as an attachment, but usually takes the form of a hemispherical plastic cap which is positioned in front of the meter's photoelectric cell. When the meter is held near the subject and facing the camera position, the light falling on it is diffused through the plastic cap and distributed evenly over the cell's surface. The resultant reading tells you how much light is actually incident upon that position. It may seem a bit unusual to find that an accurate reading can be obtained without consideration of the subject's absorption characteristics, but we'll get to the reason for it shortly.

A reflected-light meter is used to measure the light reflecting from the subject. While the photoelectric cell of the incident meter is pointed toward the camera when a reading is made, the reflected-light meter's cell must be aimed directly at the subject. The reading thus obtained provides a direct measurement of the subject's brightness. Both incident- and reflected-light meters are available as small, hand-held units, but as the reflected type requires that it be aimed at the subject, it is also the type used in cameras featuring built-in metering systems, which we'll discuss later.

THE WORLD IS 18-PERCENT GRAY

A photoelectric light meter is a mechanical device—nothing more. As

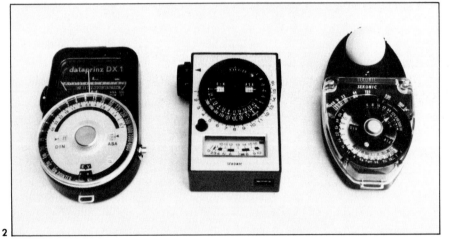

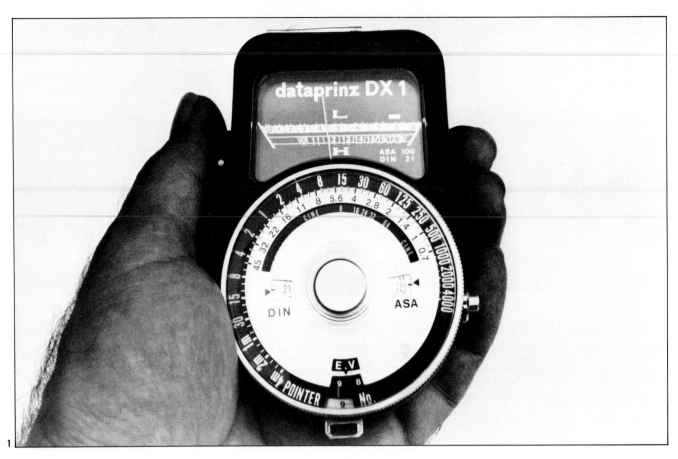

such, it has no brain and it cannot think; it can only interpret the information it is programmed to record. To use a light meter effectively, you must first translate the information it provides into useful exposure data. To do this, it's necessary that you know and understand what the meter's information means, as it's hardly a foolproof instrument—a light meter will lie through its baffle, if used without thought and understanding. Unfortunately, many do not really understand how a meter works or what it is telling them. For this reason, the meter takes the blame when the finished picture does not turn out as envisioned.

Regardless of its type—reflected, incident, hand-held or built-in—every light meter is calibrated to "see" one shade of brightness: middle gray. This means that no matter what the absorption characteristics of the subject are, or how much light falls on it, the light value as determined by the meter and transferred to your camera will produce a picture whose average tone is that of a neutral gray card which reflects 18 percent of the light.

To put it another way, if you take a reflected-light reading from such a card and then expose a negative according to that reading, your picture will match the tone of the gray card perfectly. Now suppose you do the same with a deep black card—your picture will again match the tone of the gray card, not the black one, as the meter is calibrated to "see" everything as gray. Take a reading from a perfectly white card and the meter will once more reduce the white tone to that of middle gray.

Here's an interesting experiment which will prove this, while helping you to understand how the meter sees your subject. Place the black, neutral gray and white cards side by side to photograph them simultaneously. If you base your exposure setting on a reflected reading taken from the black card's surface, your picture will reproduce the black as gray and the gray card as white. Taking your reading from the white card will produce the opposite effect—the white card will reproduce as gray and the gray card will reproduce as black (Figure E).

What you are demonstrating is the phenomenon of overexposure and underexposure. In taking a reading from the black surface, the meter "raises" the black tone to that of middle gray and at the same time, the original tone of the gray card is also raised so that it reproduces as white. As a result, both are overexposed. When you base your exposure on the reading taken from the white card, the white is "lowered" to a middle gray, thus lowering the original gray card to black by underexposure. But if you take your reading from the gray card and base your exposure accordingly, all three cards will reproduce in their proper tonal relationships in the photo.

Now let's put this knowledge into actual practice photographing a building in bright sunlight. For our purposes here, we'll assume that the sunlight is striking the building from one side, causing a difference in brightness between that part which faces the sun—the highlight area—and the part which is in shadow. We'll also assume that the highlight and shadow areas are approximately equal in size as the scene is viewed through the camera.

Having established the situation, you now approach the building with your reflected-light meter and take a reading from the highlight area. If you follow the meter's recommendation religiously and set the camera at the exposure indicated, the details of the building on the shadow side will be lost by underexposure. What the meter has done is to reduce the bright highlights to a middle gray tone. At the same time, this reduces the amount of light from the shadow area as well.

But suppose that you approach the building and take a reading from the shadow area. This exposure recommendation raises the shadows to a middle gray tone and so shadow detail will reproduce very well, but at the same time, highlight details of the building will practically wash out due to overexposure. Neither method of determining the correct exposure for this particular subject will provide you with a properly exposed negative.

To get an accurate reading, you should step back to the camera position and aim the meter at the entire building. As the shadows and highlights are almost evenly divided in this case, the average reading you obtain from the meter will represent a tone (often called the keytone) that is exactly midway between the two extremes. Not surprisingly, a reading taken from a neutral gray card with 18-percent reflectance would provide the same exposure as the average reading.

In most situations, taking a reflected-light reading from the camera position will prove accurate, but where there are either dark or light tonal areas which predominate in a subject, they will weight the meter's average to one side or the other and result in an erroneous reading. Back to our building for a moment—had you composed the picture to include a large expanse of sky as well, the meter would not see an equal amount of highlight and shadow areas as it did when the building represented the entire picture. The

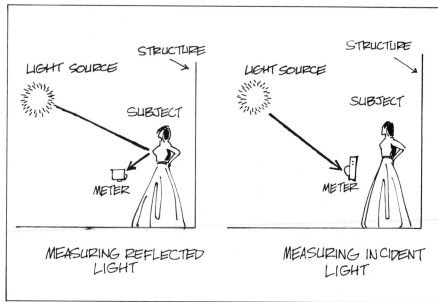

MEASURING REFLECTED LIGHT

MEASURING INCIDENT LIGHT

FIGURE D

1. Regardless of its type, the meter's calculator dial is set to the ASA/DIN rating of the film and reads in either corresponding f-stops and shutter speeds, or E.V. (exposure value) numbers. Note that the Prinz DX-1 uses separate high/low scales; other meters may combine the two into a single scale.
2. Meter configuration differs considerably depending upon manufacturer and intended use—these three are representative of the many. The Prinz DX-1 is a dual function meter for reflected or incident light use, the Sekonic 428 is a semispot meter which reads reflected light, and the Sekonic Studio Deluxe an incident light meter descended directly from the original Norwood Director.

large sky area would present a major addition to the picture's highlight area, and so the meter would deal with it by giving a reading heavily weighted in favor of the overall brightness. By setting the camera to that reading, you would lose detail in the shadow area of the building through underexposure.

When you encounter exposure situations such as this, you can reduce the influence of large background or foreground areas on the meter by shading the photocell from exposure to the undesired areas. Simply placing your hand in a horizontal position above the cell will prevent it from recording the additional brightness caused by the unwanted sky area. A hint—if you're working at the beach or in snow country, place your hand horizontally *under* the meter cell to reduce the influence of large masses of highly reflective sand or snow.

METERING TECHNIQUES

There are many times when you will not be able to deal so easily with the imbalance in a scene's distribution of highlight and shadow areas. You can't always expect to find the highlight/

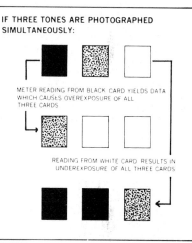

IF THREE TONES ARE PHOTOGRAPHED SIMULTANEOUSLY:

METER READING FROM BLACK CARD YIELDS DATA WHICH CAUSES OVEREXPOSURE OF ALL THREE CARDS

READING FROM WHITE CARD RESULTS IN UNDEREXPOSURE OF ALL THREE CARDS

FIGURE E

shadow areas in equal proportion, and when they're not equal, a reflected-light reading taken from the camera position will not be entirely accurate. If the subject contains mainly highlight areas, the meter will reduce them to its standard middle gray and you'll lose detail in the shadows as a result. Where shadow areas constitute a majority of the subject, highlight areas will wash out if you follow the meter's recommended exposure as given.

Perhaps the simplest technique of getting around such difficulties is the brightness range method of determining exposure. Using a reflected-light meter, you simply move in close to your subject, take a reading from the brightest highlight area and one from the deepest shadow area. Averaging the two readings will determine your final exposure setting. While it's true that distribution of highlight/shadow areas is not equal, these separate readings of the extremes will permit each to contribute equally to the final exposure. And as the final exposure in this case is exactly midway between

by five. This results in the white card acting as a false highlight, but subject highlights will coincide and other tones will record on the film as densities below this point, resulting in a picture you might have otherwise missed in trying to determine what a reasonably correct exposure should be when the meter won't answer your question.

From our discussion to this point, it should be quite obvious that subjects which fall outside the range we call average will require some thinking on the part of the photographer if a correct exposure is to be determined by use of a light meter. But before we apply such criteria to the meter's recommended exposure, we must be certain that we have recognized the subject for what it is—average or abnormal—and this is not always as cut-and-dried as it might appear on first thought. For example, suppose the subject is a pretty girl and we want a close-up of her against a darker background. To make certain that our exposure is correct, we approach her and take a close-up reading of her face with a reflected-light meter, taking care not to let other tones influence our reading. The result will be underexposure of our picture.

What went wrong? Simple, the model's face is the lightest tone in the picture area and we exposed accordingly. But remember that the meter treated the measured area—her fair complexion—as a medium gray instead of as a very light tone and so the exposure recommendation which we mistakenly followed was one designed to reproduce those lighter tones as medium. Handy hint: *Think* about your subject before you meter and when you take close-up readings of a selected area of your subject in such a situation; be certain that the area you meter is of *average* brightness or compensation will be required in applying the meter's recommended exposure.

INTERPRETING METER DATA

An example or two should prove useful in helping you to understand the necessity for correctly interpreting the subject in terms of the data provided by the light meter. Let's go back to our model to illustrate how this type of interpretation works. Our portrait shows important brightness differences between the tone of the face and hair, as well as the shade of the clothing. But these differences have little to do with the amount of light falling on any one particular area, as the lighting is quite evenly distributed to all areas. The reason for any apparent differences in

the shadow and highlight areas, you'll retain detail in both.

There are times, however, when using the brightness-range technique is not practical, especially when you are not able to move close enough to the subject to make such close-up readings. The average meter's angle of acceptance is far too great to let you select small portions of the two extremes from your camera position. Here's where a "spot" meter comes in very handy. These are much like any other reflected-light meter in use, but the meter cell's angle of acceptance is highly selective, say 1-3 degrees instead of the approximate 50 degrees of the standard meter. They also contain a viewfinder through which you aim the meter's cell at a specific area of the subject which you wish to meter. With such a meter, you can remain at your camera position and meter brightness range extremes in the subject from a distance with good accuracy.

Without a spot meter, the next best alternative is to introduce a gray tone to the picture area that represents an average of your shadow/highlight tones. Providing the light falling at your

camera position is equal in intensity to that falling on the subject, you can simply place an 18-percent reflectance neutral gray card in front of your camera and take your exposure reading directly from the card's surface. The resulting reading will be identical to that you would obtain by averaging the brightness-range readings.

In addition to the techniques already described, you might consider the use of an incident-light meter. Like the reflected-light meter, the incident type is programmed to provide exposure data which will reproduce the neutral gray tone of the 18-percent reflectance gray card. If you held the meter in front of the building we metered earlier, the reading would represent an average of the highlight/shadow brightnesses, making the incident meter an alternative to approaching the subject for close-up brightness-range readings.

Before leaving the subject of cards and metering for now, here's a handy hint for using a selenium-cell meter under low light levels when it's difficult to get the needle to register on the scale. Take a reading from a perfectly white card and multiply the indicated value

3

4

1. The difference between shadow and highlight areas of this building are minimal under overcast lighting, and a single meter reading gives accurate exposure.

2. But change the lighting and the exposure situation also changes. The same building photographed on a bright morning ·and metered for the shadows results in a loss of highlight detail.

3. Metering instead for the highlight detail will cause the shadow areas to go too dark, obscuring their detail.

4. The correct exposure is one which takes into account the difference between bright highlights and dark shadows, holding detail in both.

brightness is realted to the differing absorption characteristics; her clothing and hair appear darker than her skin as they absorb more light. Because the skin reflects more, it appears brighter.

In this case, it is necessary to first recognize that the basic exposure problem is one of rendering tones of the light and dark areas in their truest relationship to each other, with equal amounts of detail visible in both. As the predominant tone in the picture is darker than the model's face, an average reflected-light reading taken from the camera position would be overly

influenced by the overall darkness. Her hair, clothing and the background would appear as a middle gray in the final picture—containing ample detail—but the face would be washed out by overexposure.

Because of the latitude of modern film emulsions, this would probably not present a real problem, as the slight amount of overexposure could be compensated for when the negative is printed. But my purpose in this chapter is not to show you how to come away with a negative that's close to being a good one; I want you to come away with a perfect negative, and to do this we must override the influence of the dominant dark tonal areas in this case. To achieve this, let's try the brightness-range technique.

As the girl's face represents the brightest zone of the picture, a reflected-light reading should be taken of this area first. Setting the light meter to read for a film speed of ASA 125, our first reading will compute to an exposure of 1/125 second at f/8 on the exposure scale. Our second reading is taken from the darkest area of the model's hair and indicates a setting of

1/125 second at f/4. When these two readings are averaged, the final exposure is 1/125 second at f/5.6.

This shutter speed/aperture combination will provide sufficient depth of field for our subject to throw the background out of focus and concentrate attention on the subject herself. It will also provide a shutter speed fast enough to minimize any camera movement if a tripod is not used. Any other equivalent combination could be used if you required more depth of field or a higher shutter speed.

A portrait like this presents few real exposure problems as long as the exposure information provided by the meter is correctly applied. The soft, even illumination is ideal, and as the light and dark areas are fairly close in brightness (only two stops apart), the all-important facial detail can be rendered perfectly without sacrificing the detail which gives the dark background its texture. Thus translating the meter reading into actual exposure data to get the picture you want is relatively simple. But there are times when getting a full range of detail into a picture is not quite as easy and may be near-impossible. Look at the backlighted photos of the girl on the beach to see a more difficult situation.

The basic exposure problems in this case should be quite obvious. Again, there is an important difference in brightness caused by the relative amounts of light falling on the subject and on the background, but this difference is far more dramatic than our soft-lighted portrait. A brightness-range reading of this scene indicates the following exposure recommendations for a film rated at ASA 125—1/60 second at f/22 for the bright background and 1/60 second at f/4 for the subject's face. This scene actually has a brightness range of five full stops.

The difference between the bright and the dark ends of this range is called the scene's *contrast,* and with most modern films it's virtually impossible to render equal amounts of detail in both the bright and dark areas of a scene where contrast exceeds four f-stops, as this one does. The brightness-range method thus becomes a particularly valuable tool whenever contrast appears to be excessive. But even averaging the exposure readings from the dark and light areas will not turn the trick—1/60 second at f/13.5 will not provide sufficient exposure to reproduce all the details in the model, and much of the background details will be washed out through overexpo-

1

3

4

sure. In this case, the film is just not capable of handling both ends of the brightness range at the same time. Our only alternative here is to sacrifice detail at one end or the other.

The decisive factor will be the effect desired by the person behind the camera and how the meter's information is interpreted. Knowing that detail at one end of the brightness range will have to be sacrificed, there are two options for such a picture. The first is to establish the correct exposure for the model's face—this will result in severe overexposure of the background in the final shot. The second alternative is to disregard facial detail and expose only for the background, leaving the model in the foreground to appear as a dark, underexposed silhouette.

To achieve the silhouette effect, it is only necessary to take a reflected light reading of the general scene from the

2

camera position and expose accordingly. The large bright area of the background when combined with the darker shadowed area of the model will give a reading that is heavily weighted in favor of the highlights and thus provide adequate background detail.

But in order to record adequate detail in the subject's face, a different approach is necessary. As brightness-range readings of the face and hair would be tricky because of the strong

1. On occasion, the brightness range of some subjects may exceed the film's capability to record both ends adequately. In such situations, the photographer must determine which tonal areas are of most importance to him and then expose accordingly. (David Neibel.)

2. There are three ways to obtain the correct exposure for the building. You can use an incident light meter as shown, meter the brightness range with a reflected light meter and average the two readings, or you can meter a gray card from the camera position.

3. Newer meter designs such as the Minolta Auto Meter II utilize a silicon cell for extended range reading, and have a variety of modifying accessories available.

4. A spot meter can be very useful. These feature an SLR-type viewfinder and usually measure an area between one degree and ten degrees. The Minolta Auto-Spot II Digital shown here has a digital display of the proper exposure values—the center circle indicates the one degree spot being measured.

5. Another difficult exposure situation, this requires a balance between the outdoor illumination and the interior. An emulsion with a long tonal scale is best for such subjects. (Shirley I. Fisher.)

backlighting that could influence the results, the best method of determining a correct exposure of only the model's face would be to use the 18-percent reflectance gray card or an incident-light meter. Either method will provide an exposure recommendation in this case of 1/60 second at f/2.8, a setting that overexposes the background by a full six stops. But the important area of the picture—the model's face—will be correctly rendered.

WHEN YOU CAN'T INTERPRET

You must be prepared for those occasions when there isn't time to meticulously interpret meter readings. While experience is of great help in making such evaluations quickly and accurately, there are a few general rules that even a beginner can follow to prevent ''lost'' picture opportunities because of an inability to interpret exposure data rapidly.

Sudden changes in the highlight/shadow balance of a subject are a common cause of bad exposures but can be overcome with this rule of thumb: Given a correct shutter speed/aperture combination for a front-lighted subject, correct exposure with sidelight is maintained by opening the aprture by one f-stop and with backlight by opening the aperture by two f-stops.

As for gross exposure mistakes, we know that the best negatives are those created by the minimum exposure necessary to retain shadow detail. While this is the goal for which you should strive whenever possible, if your meter fails, or if you find yourself without it, remember that it is always preferable to over- rather than underexpose when in doubt about the correct exposure. While this will mean excessive silver density in the negative, it does insure that a minimum of detail will be recorded on the film.

In many such cases, you can compensate to a considerable degree for the increased density when you enlarge the negative, but no amount of corrective printing will conjure up details which were not recorded in the first place. This boils down to a choice between a less-than-perfect picture or no picture at all and in such cases, most of us will choose the less-than-perfect one over no picture.

USING FILM SPEED FOR CONTRAST CONTROL

Although overexposure is one of the ''safer'' mistakes you can make, you should not make a habit of it unless you have a definite purpose for doing so. One purpose many photographers

5

frequently exploit is the ability of over-exposure to compress a scene's contrast range. In the case of a backlighted portrait, it is possible to shorten the extreme brightness difference between the subject's face and the background by overexposing the face one stop from the meter's indicated reading. In effect, this means reducing the film speed by one-half from ASA 125 to ASA 64.

At this modified speed or exposure index, the film would need a considerable reduction in development time; developing for the full period of time would not compensate for the excess exposure. But by correctly reducing the length of development, the relatively thin density of exposed silver in the shadow areas would be fully developed while the much higher concentration of exposed crystals in the overexposed background would be only partially developed when the process was halted. As a result, the background's density would more closely match that of the shadow area, and the contrast between the two would be far less pronounced in the final print.

This technique is generally successful in lowering the contrast range, but

its opposite—the raising of the film's speed for low-light photography—possesses some grave restrictions. When you use a film at a higher exposure index than the ASA speed given it by the manufacturer, you are really underexposing. To compensate for this, you turn to an increase in developing time, but as we know, underexposure means a lack of detail in the picture's dark areas and you cannot develop detail that does not exist on the negative.

There are a number of special developing agents on the market sold to provide acceptable density with such underexposed negatives but the quality of the results will not be the best. Yet because it does increase contrast to some degree, pushing film in development can occasionally be used to improve the highlight brilliance in a relatively low-contrast situation, thus the technique does hold some value. It is also possible to exploit the considerably increased granularity of underexposed/overdeveloped negatives for striking special effects, but for general-purpose photography, it's better to use a higher speed film under low-light-level conditions than to attempt to push a slower emulsion

1

2

3

beyond the tolerances built in by the manufacturer.

Now that you're familiar with the basics of exposure determination and how to use a meter correctly in the majority of situations, it's time to back up just a bit and look at the metering systems built into the majority of today's automated cameras, especially the very popular 35mm SLR models.

CAMERA METERING SYSTEMS

Although a few cameras like the Argus CC and Contax IIIA incorporated uncoupled light meters as an integral part of the camera body, the photo-electric light meter was primarily a separate hand-held device from the introduction of the first Weston meter in the mid-'30s. But with the appearance of the Pentax Spotmatic and the Topcon in the mid-'60s, camera metering took a revolutionary turn—their metering systems were not only integrated inside the camera body and coupled to the aperture/shutter speed controls, but they read the light as it passed through the lens on its way to the film. By programming the film speed index into the camera and activating the metering system, the user could achieve a correct exposure determination by turning either the shutter speed dial or aperture ring until a moving needle in the viewfinder was aligned with a corresponding index notch. From the date these two cameras made their appearance, metering through the camera's optics became a design necessity for

1. Hal Stoelzle recorded this bridge collapse during construction at Pasadena, California with a single meter reading from the camera position. For such low-contrast subjects containing mostly mid-tones, a single camera-position reading is generally adequate.

2-3. While the semisilhouette is most effective from an artistic point, Ron Berkenblitt had two options in this situation—to expose for detail in his model or in his background. A polarizing filter was used in each case.

4. Exposing for our model's face in a situation like this will result in underexposure. Remember, her face is the lightest tone in the picture, but the meter sees it as a medium tone, and thus recommends its exposure accordingly. Meter both the lightest and darkest areas and split the reading for a correct exposure.

other camera manufacturers who wanted to stay in the 35mm SLR market.

A basic question was where best to read the light as it traveled through the lens to the film plane, and this was answered in a variety of ways, most of which are still with us today. The ideal place, of course, was the film plane, but as the film already occupied that spot, other locations were used. Topcon had placed its metering cells at the rear of the instant-return mirror and provided slits in the mirror to pass the light to them; others positioned one, two and even three cells at varying locations between the viewfinder eyepiece and focusing screen, all located in such a way as to read the light while circumventing locations already patented by others. Figure F shows the

arrangement used in the Petri FT EE.

Regardless of their location, each design contains certain optical characteristics which determine the metering system's sensitivity pattern. Unlike hand-held meters, which average the light received across the entire angle of acceptance, in-camera metering systems may be classified as averaging, center-weighted, bottom center-weighted, and narrow angle or spot. A few even combine two or more of these, giving the user a choice of metering pattern according to subject requirements. Figure G shows typical sensitivity patterns; while several camera manufacturers may use systems classified as averaging or center-weighted, the distribution of sensitivity takes slightly different forms so that Camera A's pattern is not identical to that of Camera B, despite the fact that both are classified as averaging.

None of these metering system classifications will give every user perfect exposures under all conceivable

types of light conditions. The camera manufacturer selects the classification and designs the sensitivity according to his philosophy of exposure. For example, the Pentax Spotmatic uses a full-averaging pattern despits its name; Nikon has rigidly adhered to its center-weighted pattern through its FTn, FT2, F2, EL and ELW models; Canon uses narrow angle (F-1, FTb), center-weighted (TLb, TX) and bottom center-weighted (EF).

While each classification has its supposed virtues and vices, all work sufficiently well under most circumstances, and if you're familiar with the eccentricities of the system used by your camera, you can reduce the possibility of exposure error and increase the percentage of well-exposed pictures in the process.

AVERAGING—The most common metering system used, the full-averaging type does quite well with "point-and-shoot" photography if the subject isn't too contrasty. When large expanses of

greatly varying tones are included in the picture, the primary subject of interest should be metered from a point close enough to exclude all else from the meter's view. If not, the meter will average the entire scene. This can present definite problems when using a full-frame fisheye lens, and it's a good idea to bracket your exposures in such cases just to be on the safe side. Bracketing means to shoot one picture at the indicated exposure, then take two more shots, one at one stop over and the other at one stop under (½ stop with color film) the exposure that is indicated.

CENTER-WEIGHTED—These systems consider the overall brightness of the entire area seen by the lens, but concentrate most of their sensitivity on the central area, with meter sensitivity diminishing sharply as it progresses from the center outward to the edges. This is especially accurate in situations where there's a marked difference in brightness between the primary subject and its surrounding area.

BOTTOM CENTER-WEIGHTED—A variation of the center-weighted pattern, this type places more emphasis on the lower part of the picture area to offset the influence of a bright sky or other such large tonal masses. This system works fine as long as the camera is held in the horizontal position, but turn it on its side for a vertical shot and the pattern becomes side center-weighted, right or left, depending upon how the camera is held. Many users overlook this change in the sensitivity pattern when taking vertical pictures, and end up with disappointing results without knowing exactly why.

NARROW ANGLE—Often referred to as "spot" metering, this type is *not* really a true spot metering system. While the meter's sensitivity pattern is usually indicated clearly on the focusing screen, the sensitivity tends to bleed along the edges of the marked area according to the focal length of the lens in use and the subject in question. Because of the nature of its pattern, this is not a "point-and-shoot" system. When using it, you should aim the center of the focusing screen at the tonal area of greatest importance and then compose your picture after setting the exposure as indicated by the important tones.

SELECTIVE METERING TECHNIQUES

Selective metering is often necessary with averaging or narrow angle metering systems, not as often required with center and bottom center-weighted types, but these techniques are handy to file away for possible use anyway. Your meter reading will be most reliable when you're careful in selecting the area to be metered. To do so, approach your subject until you can fill the metering area with that portion of the subject of primary importance, like skin tones. If you're physically unable to approach the subject that closely, try metering through a longer focal length lens, locate a similar object nearby that appears to have the same reflectance value, center the meter needle and return to your camera position to use the substitute reading for your original subject, or use a gray card as described earlier.

If you should happen to be without a gray card, you have an adequate substitute right in front of you—the palm of your hand. Once again, assuming that the light falling at your camera position is the same as that falling upon the subject, you can take a reading from your palm. Center the meter needle and then open up the aperture one full stop, or use the next slower shutter speed. Believe it or not, it really doesn't matter what color your hand is—black, green or blue—as long as it's free from grease and grime. Our palms are all pretty much the same color and reflect about twice as much light as does a gray card. So if you do use the palm of your hand as a basis for a meter reading, remember to give twice as much exposure as the meter indicates to avoid underexposure.

4

1. Looks can be deceiving—despite the appearance of fairly uniform tones, the amount of shadow area is far more than a casual glance at this new building on the University of Wisconsin's ground tells us. (Hal Stoelzle.)
2. Another difficult metering situation— how to retain subject detail within the car and outdoors for a near-normal appearance of both. Many would reach for a small electronic flash to punch detail in the shadows, but Jeff Blackwell worked out a far more acceptable compromise with natural lighting.
3. While Anna Lee Cutrone's exposure choice places emphasis on the subject, it also permits a sufficient amount of the background to record to establish both locale and the child's activity.
4. Backlighting can be used to destroy visually annoying backgrounds. By using an exposure of 1/250 at f/4, Hank Harris recorded ample detail on Tri-X while turning the background into a useful tonal mass which accentuates eye interest on his youthful subject.

BRACKETING

Mentioned briefly in connection with the averaging meter type, the technique of bracketing your exposures can be considered as both a safeguard against incorrect exposure and a creative tool. It's quite possible that an entire series of bracketed exposures will deliver acceptable pictures. Despite the fact that the subject matter remained the same, you may have created different moods or points of emphasis as you changed the exposure.

If you're working with color slide film, expose for the highlight areas of the subject, but with the somewhat wider latitude of color print film, expose for the shadows instead. Some professionals may not admit to following the practice, but any worth their salt will bracket their exposures whenever they work with color—the number of "insurance" shots being in direct proportion to the importance of the assignment. You may have heard the old adage, "Film is the least expensive part of photography," and it's true. Bracket and you'll at least have a choice between good and bad; don't bracket and you'll have to take what the meter gives you.

WHEN THE METER DOESN'T WORK

It's not terribly difficult to learn how to "eyeball" exposure—it just takes practice at evaluating a scene according to past experience. Some claim they are really good at it while others refuse to believe that it's more than a shot in the dark. It all really depends, of course, upon how experienced you really are, and how adept you are at "educated" guessing.

The secret to success is simple enough—it comes on that little sheet of paper that accompanies most packages of film. If you're caught with a dead battery or without a hand-held meter, try calculating your exposure

this way—with the lens set at f/16 on a bright, sunny day, set your shutter speed according to the reciprocal of the film's ASA rating. Working by this formula, you'd expose Kodak Plus-X or Ilford FP4 (ASA 125) at f/16 and the nearest shutter speed, 1/125 second; Kodak Tri-X, Ilford HP5 or Fujicolor F-II 400 (ASA 400) at f/16 and the shutter speed nearest to the reciprocal, (1/500) and so on.

Naturally, you're not locked into that particular combination—1/125 at f/16 is also equal to 1/250 at f/11 or 1/500 at f/8; 1/500 at f/16 equals 1/1000 at f/11, or 1/1000 at f/8 with a 2X ND filter, etc. And if you're working under hazy skies or open shade, open up the aperture one or two stops respectively from the basic exposure.

Now, how about those beautiful moon shots you've seen in so many magazines—how would you calculate exposure for a night shot of the moon? Well, it's a bright, sunny day on the moon, right? So with your aperture at f/16, your shutter speed again is the reciprocal of the film's ASA rating. And if you're using a slow film, there's absolutely nothing wrong with opening the aperture wider and using the corresponding shutter speed. And if you think that I'm putting you on with this formula, give it a try taking your own moon pictures—you'll be surprised at the results.

EXPOSE FOR EFFECT

When you're working in black-and-white and are uncertain of the correct exposure to use, too much exposure is

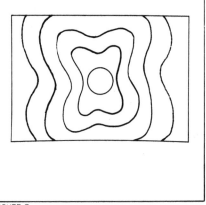

FIGURE G

always preferable to too little, as we've already seen. Working with color film, the situation is usually reversed. Over-exposure leads to washed-out slides with thin, pastel colors and a lack of detail—unless you specifically want what is known as a ''high-key'' effect. But you can achieve a dramatic effect by underexposing color slide film on bright sunlit days. A degree of underexposure leads to greater color sat-

uration and can serve to intensify a mood that you're trying to portray. Suppose that you're photographing stained glass windows. If you overexpose, the stained glass image will have a light, airy effect, but the deeper color saturation gained by underexposure will capture the eye's attention by adding mood and drama.

Sunsets are another excellent subject, both for bracketing and for deliberate underexposure. For the correct exposure, you should meter the sky, but not the sun. Then enhance the overall effect by underexposing one, two or even three stops. Incidentally, viewing the sun directly through your camera's viewfinder should be avoided, especially when using telephoto lenses, as it can lead to permanent eye damage which appears as a progressive deterioration in vision over a period of time. If you must photograph the sun directly while it's high in the sky, you should purchase a ''solar'' filter and

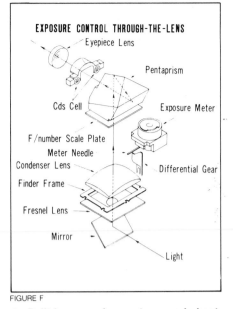

EXPOSURE CONTROL THROUGH-THE-LENS

- Eyepiece Lens
- Pentaprism
- Cds Cell
- Exposure Meter
- F/number Scale Plate
- Meter Needle
- Condenser Lens
- Differential Gear
- Finder Frame
- Fresnel Lens
- Mirror
- Light

FIGURE F

1. Built-in averaging meters work best with subjects that are fairly uniform in nature, as these stone carvings in Ottowa's Federal Parliament Building photographed by M. Jeffery.

2. You can often use exposure to establish, emphasize or heighten a mood. Exposing for detail in the structure would have caused the beach area to completely wash out.

3. Today's in-camera metering systems can all trace their lineage directly to the Contax IIIa of the late thirties, with its uncoupled selenium cell meter.

4. Built-in through-the-lens metering systems for rangefinder cameras appeared in the Leica CL and M5 models. Pressing the CL's shutter release swings the cell out of the way just before exposure; film advance swings it back in place.

5. To use a center-weighted metering system with this type of subject, center the viewfinder on the water and set the exposure, then recompose and shoot. (Ron Berkenblitt.)

use it. These are available from any well-equipped photo store.

There's a rule of thumb you can follow concerning sunsets and safely photographing the sun. Extend your arm and clench your fist so that it rests upon the horizon line; when the sun has dropped sufficiently in the sky to rest on top of your clenched fist positioned in this manner, you can safely photograph the sun. The opposite holds true for sunrises—you can shoot them safely until the sun has risen in the sky above your clenched fist.

AUTOMATIC EXPOSURE CONTROL

To this point, we've discussed the semiautomatic or "match-needle" form of in-camera metering. But full automation has now come into its own and each passing year sees more such cameras arriving to replace the older match-needle models. Konica broke the barrier in 1968 with its Autoreflex

5

design, which employed what we now call a shutter-priority system. After dialing in the correct film speed and setting the shutter speed as desired, the camera would select the appropriate aperture for a correct exposure—as the meter understood it.

If the chosen aperture did not meet with the user's needs, he simply selected a different shutter speed and the camera's meter readjusted the aperture accordingly. An aperture scale was provided in the viewfinder so that the user could read the aperture in use without removing the camera from his

eye. But the search for more perfect exposure continued as manufacturers developed variations on the Konica approach, each claiming that his system was more perfect. Late in 1971, the concept of aperture-priority appeared in the form of the Pentax ES with its electronically-governed shutter—you pick the aperture and the meter selects the appropriate shutter speed from an infinitely variable or stepless range.

We'll discuss both designs more fully in a later chapter; at this time, it's sufficient if you recall that the differences in design, as pointed out in the first

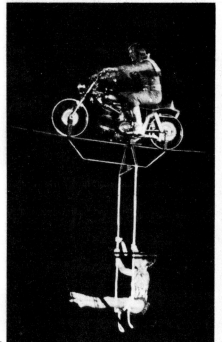

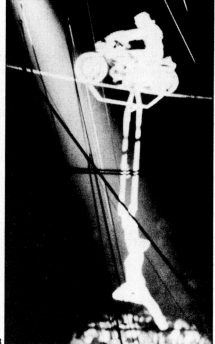

1. The built-in narrow angle meter type is useful in measuring highly selective areas and is best used to take several readings of different tonal areas which are then used to arrive at a compromise setting.

2-3. Exposure can also be used for creative effects. A normal exposure under the spotlights of the Barnum & Bailey and Ringling Brother's big top provides a routine shot of Elvin Bale's cycle act on Kodak 2475 Recording Film, but open up the aperture by three stops and the result is a ghostly image which changes the entire atmosphere.

4. The Olympus OM-2 utilizes the most innovative approach to in-camera metering yet seen—silicon blue cells read the light reflected from a computer-generated pattern imprinted on the shutter curtain.

5. A bottom-center-weighted metering system is ideal with subjects like this. The center-weighted and narrow angle (spot) systems will also handle this well, but the full-averaging would be overly influenced by the sky. (Hank Harris.)

ing capability for the camera's match-needle mode, as well as regulating the viewfinder display during the automatic mode to indicate the approximate shutter speed chosen by the silicon blue circuit. The revolutionary aspect of such a metering system has not been lost on the competition, who are hard at work attempting to equal or better this system.

Will the OM-2 really provide more accurate exposure? Yes, but in most cases, you won't know the difference. To use the camera to its fullest potential, you must be thoroughly conversant with the change in the metering sensitivity pattern at the various shutter speed levels and use the camera to reflect your knowledge. Under certain circumstances, such as a singer or dancer performing under constantly changing lighting, the OM-2 definitely has the edge in its ability to make alterations in the duration of exposure during exposure and photographers who work under such lighting conditions would notice a certain improvement in their negatives or slides.

But despite the sophisticated technology which makes such a metering system possible, the system itself is only as good as the person behind the camera is in using it. There is no metering system in existence that can think of its own accord (although many

chapter, are really immaterial in use. With the shutter-priority camera, the shutter-speed dial controls the aperture; with the aperture-priority models, the aperture ring on the lens controls the shutter speed. While the mode of operation differs, the metering systems themselves remain much as in the match-needle cameras, considering, of course, that each passing year finds more sophistication in design.

The most sophisticated approach to exposure determination to appear in recent years is embodied in the Olympus OM-2, which made its debut in 1976. The OM-2 takes a continuous reading throughout the actual moment of exposure. Two silicon blue cells are positioned to face in the direction of the film plane and read the light falling on both the shutter curtain and the film

itself. Should the level of illumination change once the exposure begins, the OM-2's automatic exposure control system calculates the amount of light reaching the film and correspondingly adjusts the exposure duration.

Meter readings at 1/60 second and faster are center-weighted, as the silicon blue cells read the light reflected from a computer-generated pattern imprinted on the shutter curtain. Between 1/60 and 1/15 second, the reading becomes a combination of center-weighted and averaging. During exposures of 1/15 second and slower, the system automatically switches to an averaging mode as the cells read the light reflected directly from the film's surface.

Two CdS cells placed above the instant-return mirror provide the meter-

5

might consider the OM-2 a giant step in that direction), and as long as that's true, proper exposure will continue to remain the province of the photographer in exercising control over the application to which the meter's information is put.

THE ZONE SYSTEM OF EXPOSURE DETERMINATION

A full-blown cult which exists within the ranks of serious photographers, the Zone System of exposure determination, as put forth by Ansel Adams and amplified by devotees, is not practically explained within these pages, as several full-length books have been written on the topic, and more will certainly be forthcoming.

Basically, the Zone System claims to offer complete tonal control regardless of the subject, lighting, etc., and is one of the few theoretical techniques in the field of photography sufficiently explosive to inspire heated debate and break up old friendships. If you're interested in exploring this topic, I suggest you check with your nearby photo book dealer and set aside several weeks for dedicated study.

NIGHT PHOTOGRAPHY WITHOUT METERING

There are numerous subjects offering dramatic photo possibilities at night, but whose brightness range cannot be easily measured with a light meter. If you use an aperture-priority

camera at wide open aperture, its electronic shutter will make the exposure determination for you. Otherwise, you'll find the following suggestions based on tables and experience by Kodak to be a practical way to find a base point for your exposure. A tripod or other steady support should be used, a cable release is helpful, and bracketing at full stop intervals is recommended.

The following suggestions are made for use with ASA 64 film—conversions for other film speeds can be easily made using the calculator dial of a hand-held meter.

1—Brightly illuminated street scenes—1/30 at f/2.

2—Brightly illuminated nightclub, theatre, Las Vegas-type scenes—1/30 at f/2.8.

3—Brightly illuminated interior scenes—1/30 at f/2-f/2.8.

4—Spotlighted acts at ice shows, circuses, etc.—1/60 at f/2.8.

5—Floodlighted buildings, monuments, fountains—4 sec. at f/5.6.

6—Fairs, amusement parks, etc.—1/15 at f/2.

7—Neon signs and other such displays—1/60 at f/5.6.

8—Racetracks, night ball games—1/30 at f/1.8.

9—Store windows and displays—1/30 at f/2.8.

10—Christmas lighting, indoor/outdoor—1/30 at f/1.8.

11—Campfire scenes—1/60 at f/4.

12—Fireworks, lightning bolts—set lens at f/8 (f/11 for lightning) and keep shutter open for one or more bursts/bolts.

WHICH METER TYPE IS BEST?

Those who do not yet own a meter or a camera with a built-in metering system are likely to wonder which type they should purchase—reflected or incident, hand-held or in-camera, averaging, center-weighted, etc. It's a decision the reader will have to make, but one made easier if you realize that *all* photoelectric light meters and metering systems will deliver approximately the same results if used properly.

I say approximately because you should also be aware that despite the manufacturers' claims for "absolute" accuracy, their tolerance level for acceptable performance is ⅓ f-stop over the entire range of response. At this point in the state of the art, it's virtually impossible to match photoelectric cells precisely on a mass-production basis.

I would suggest that you acquire a hand-held meter even if you use a camera with its metering system built in. Not only is one handy for back-up use in case your camera meter goes sour, it can expedite exposure measurement of subjects in situations where use of a camera meter is difficult. Whether you buy a reflected or incident meter is really immaterial; it's how you use it that counts! □

5

Choosing & Using A Camera

Using a camera is duck soup these days—it's choosing the one to use that's really difficult! But things weren't always this rough for the beginner. The photo industry used to change models only when a real innovation came along, or when a particular camera had completely lost its sales appeal. The classic example is the venerable Argus C-3, introduced in 1939 and discontinued in essentially the same form in the mid-1960s, some 3,000,000 cameras later.

Technology has now caught up with camera design and hardly a month goes by without some new improvement or innovation coming along, causing yesterday's new camera to become tomorrow's discontinued model. The feature-conscious purchaser who opted last year for a 35mm SLR with a silicon blue metering system (as the latest improvement over the older CdS cell) suddenly finds this year's hot new metering sensor is a GAP cell, and his new camera is less than a year old.

Hopefully, readers of this book are not caught up in the ''latest is the best'' syndrome which affects a fair share of the photo market these days. At the risk of offending many friends who sell cameras for a living, I would hope that if I leave you with any single impression from this chapter, it will be this—the latest camera design on the market *will not* improve your pictures! If you take lousy pictures with a CdS metering system or screw-thread lenses, you'll still take lousy pictures with a GAP meter or bayonet lenses.

Photo magazines periodically call in a working pro, hand him a snapshot camera and turn him loose with it for a few days. You've probably seen the resulting article which states that it's the

eye and mind behind the camera that count—and it's true! If you know and observe the fundamentals of photography as well as understand and work within the limits of your equipment, you can take just as good pictures with a $20 camera as can the next person with a $200 model.

The difference between the two cameras lies in the expanded capability of-

fered by the more expensive one. For example, the $200 camera will, as a matter of course take pictures from distances as close as 18 inches (closer with accessories), whereas the $20 camera is limited to a distance of 3-5 feet. This is the kind of versatility you get with the more expensive models, but for pictures in bright sunlight from a moderate camera-subject distance,

1. Before you select a camera, look the field over carefully. Find a salesman who will take both the time and patience to demonstrate those in which you're interested, as well as answer your questions.
2-3. The success of Canon's AE-1 drove home the point made several years before by the Olympus OM-1—there's a big market for compact 35mm SLR cameras, as the new Pentax ME has proven.
4-5. The trend toward smaller cameras resulted in the Mamiya 645 (shown with photo diode meter attached) and the Bronica ETR—compact contenders for sales in the medium-format roll film SLR camera market.

the photographer who knows how can make his $20 model perform just as well as the more expensive one.

NEW DESIGN TRENDS—A BIT OF BACKGROUND

Camera design in virtually every major category is presently undergoing a drastic revision in thought, which was brought about primarily by the success of the Olympus OM-1 since its introduction in 1972. For some time, it had been fashionable to complain about the gradual increase over the years in the size of the 35mm SLR camera. Those who did the complaining would think back fondly to the days of the Leica IIIc and its collapsible lens which could be carried very handily in a coat pock-et. When compared to the Leitz line of rangefinder 35mm cameras at the time, the IIIc certainly was diminutive, but it also possessed only a portion of the M-4's capability, a fact that has often been conveniently overlooked.

Those who took the 35mm SLR to task had apparently forgotten the size of the Contax D, the "granddaddy" of the pentaprism 35mm. But taking a cue from public opinion, Olympus brought forth its OM-1, some 30 percent smaller and lighter than the competition, with virtually the same features. After a rather slow start, the camera and its size caught on with the camera-conscious consumer—a fact which caused untold agony on the part of other camera manufacturers, most of whom were about to introduce new, even larger models, and were thus caught with their "pants" down.

The rush back to the drawing board became a stampede, and when Canon introduced its AE-1 in 1976, a second shock wave reverberated through the industry. Here was a small, completely automatic-exposure 35mm SLR containing a tiny silicon chip microcomputer programmed to cope with all control and operational functions—and at a reasonable price! Just as the OM-1 set the pace for miniaturization of the camera's size, the AE-1 provided the impetus toward electronic SLR design. To those manufacturers who had been dragging their feet between 1972 and 1975, it suddenly became crystal-clear that they must compete or step aside.

Miranda announced its compact dx-3, Konica its TC model, Cosina introduced prototypes of its CSL and CSR compacts, and Pentax, which had recently replaced its screw-thread series with a smaller K series utilizing bayonet-mounted lenses, brought forth its ME/MX models. Like the Canon AE-1, these were designed as electronic cameras in which as many mechanical parts as possible were replaced by electronic components. Even Nikon got into the act with a new compact model and redesigned lenses. More are on the way, and by the time you read this, there should be a complete selection of compact 35mm SLR cameras available from which to choose.

Similar things were happening in the large-format camera market. Some years ago, the Mamiya RB67 had made a big splash with its "ideal" format—6x7cm (2¼x2¾ inches). This provided a better negative-to-8x10 enlargement ratio than the traditional 6x6cm (2¼x2¼ inches). You no longer had to print an 8x8 or crop a healthy portion from the negative to end up with an 8x10. But in 1975, Mamiya introduced its 645 as a "mid-format" roll-film SLR with a negative area of 6x4.5cm (2¼x1⅝ inches). Hailed as the new wave which would combine a larger image quality with the handling ease of 35mm, the 645 was followed the next year by the Bronica ETR and the race was on to get new converts from all sides: 6x6cm, 6x7cm and 35mm users.

At the same time, the press/view camera market, which had virtually disappeared except for an occasional pro-

fessional, underwent a transformation unlike any it had enjoyed in a quarter-century. Students in hundreds of college photo courses across the country suddenly rediscovered the view camera as an ideal instrument with which to learn and practice the fundamentals of photography. They fell in love with the superior quality inherent in its large-format negative. At last report, the old, established and distinguished firm of L. F. Deardorff & Sons in Chicago was hard-pressed to keep up with orders for its basic wooden view camera, a situation typical of other manufacturers. Prices on the used market have shot up far out of proportion with their real worth. Even two Japanese manufacturers got into the U.S. view camera market with astounding success, and the only recently discontinued Graflex 4x5 press camera suddenly attained a new stature now that it was no longer available.

When Kodak introduced the 110 format and its pocket camera concept in 1972, it virtually wiped out the 126 camera market overnight. Rapidly reaching a level of sophistication never enjoyed by its larger cartridge-loading brother, the 110 swept the point-and-shoot market, while also reducing the demand for subminiature cameras (like the precision Minox) to practically nothing. With the introduction of its 110 Zoom SLR, Minolta pointed the direction for an entire new generation of sophisticated, tiny-format cameras.

No one knows where it will end. Smaller camera bodies mean smaller and more compact lenses, which puts an entirely new complexion on the market for optics. And in the midst of all this, consumer confusion reigns supreme; is large really better as we've been told for years, or is it small that's best? If you're in the market for a camera, these questions are most likely at the forefront of your considerations, and if you are one of the many with a rather sizable investment in the large (relatively speaking) camera body/lens design, you are probably wondering if you should rush out and trade the entire outfit before it loses the bulk of its trade-in value.

Whether you're shopping for your first camera, or wondering about the advisability of trading in your equipment for the latest, the decision is one you'll have to make yourself—no one can really make it for you. But let me point out that for many of us, there is really nothing wrong with the current SLR cameras, although they may be slightly larger than the newest models.

1. **To the surprise of many, view cameras are once again the rage. This 4x5 Deardorff view is typical of those offered in the medium price range.**
2. **While other format cameras are shrinking, the Minolta 110 Zoom SLR is indicative of larger pocket cameras.**
3. **Battery compartments are generally located on the camera's baseplate and require the use of a coin to open.**
4. **Most battery compartment caps will be marked to indicate the proper way to install the battery.**
5. **Virtually every modern camera runs on batteries, which vary widely in size and shape. Be sure to buy the right type, as some are almost identical except for power rating.**

I'm convinced that after a few years, the design will swing back in their direction, and so I'm not unloading my cameras and lenses. Those looking for their first camera of consequence will find some very good buys resting on dealer shelves and might well take that factor into consideration.

At the same time, a good case can be made for the smaller camera designs, and we can expect to see a considerable number of new ones before the trend abates. If you're involved in camping, backpacking or other activities where your camera is also your constant companion, the smaller and lighter SLR may be just your cup of

tea. But before you buy, study the market very carefully, making certain that the camera you buy has *all* the features you want and expect to want from it. Settle for nothing less. Today's market is so wide and varied that everyone should be able to find *their* camera once they've cut through the confusion of claim and counterclaim.

CAMERAS RUN ON BATTERIES

That's right. Today's camera is a battery-powered device and in order to power its metering system, as well as the shutter and film advance on some models, it must have fresh batteries of the correct size and voltage installed before you can use it. The most common battery installation is a circular compartment located on the camera base; it can be identified by the slotted screw-in or bayonet locking cap. Using a coin to avoid damaging the slot, turn the cover counterclockwise, or in the direction indicated if a directional arrow is provided, until the cover pops off. Taking care not to touch the surface of the battery or the cover, drop the battery into the compartment with the side marked "+" facing up toward you. Then replace the cap, and turn it in the opposite direction until it locks tightly.

Some cameras will require two or more batteries; these may be installed one on top of the other or side by side, depending upon the battery compartment design. Other cameras use a special type of battery compartment—the Nikkormat EL and ELW are good examples. To install the battery in these, you must remove the lens, lock up the mirror and slide the tabbed battery compartment cover to the left. The spring-loaded cover will then pop up, exposing the battery chamber.

Almost every camera has a battery-check device of some sort; you either push a button and a light comes on somewhere, or the meter needle inside the viewfinder will deflect to a specified position to indicate relative battery strength. This is a good place to stop and admonish you to read, yea, *study* the instruction manual that comes with the camera before you attempt to carry out these procedures. With the rapid advances being made in metering circuitry, power sources and operational design, you should *know* what you're doing before attempting to use a camera with which you're not familiar.

As for the battery itself, each one has a voltage rating and code assigned by the manufacturer. Although several different batteries may *look* alike in size and design, only the one specified by the camera manufacturer will properly operate his camera, and substitutions in code number or voltage rating should never be made. Always carry a spare battery or set of batteries with you; this is especially important with several of the fully automatic cameras on the market today, as they will *not function at all* if the batteries die.

Once the battery is properly installed, the metering circuit will function. With the film-speed dial set to the speed of the film you've loaded into the camera, you can now operate the metering circuit in anticipation of taking

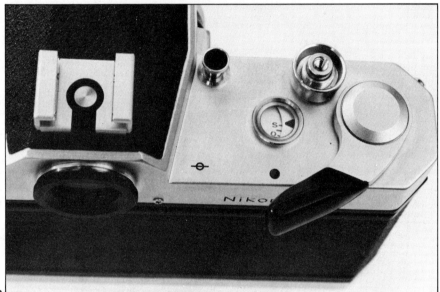

a picture. To activate the meter, you must (a) turn on a switch, (b) move the film-advance lever away from the body or (c) slightly depress the shutter button—the method is dependent upon the camera.

HERE COMES HELP!

The primary question to settle is one of format; once that has been decided upon, you can then go about determining which specific model provides the features you desire at the price you can afford. To help you with the format problem, here are a few thoughts on each major camera type.

VIEW CAMERAS

A basic box composed of a lens board at one end and a film back at the other, and connected by a flexible bellows, the view camera dates to the murky antiquity of photography. Although slow and somewhat cumbersome to use, this tripod-mounted camera is unsurpassed in its ability to deal with perspective distortion and control of focus because its front and back can be moved horizontally or vertically, in the same or in opposite directions. Primarily useful with subjects that do not move, the upside-down image produced by the lens on the ground-glass focusing screen is an ideal and disciplined tool with which to learn the elements of composition.

View cameras are as individual as those who use them, but there are certain things you should definitely look for. To begin with, it will be necessary to settle upon the film size or format—4x5, 5x7 or 8x10. While many feel that the larger the negative, the better the quality of the final print, there's no reason why a 4x5 shouldn't prove quite satisfactory in terms of quality, and from a financial standpoint, it's the most practical. The difference in film costs is really minor, but the savings

3

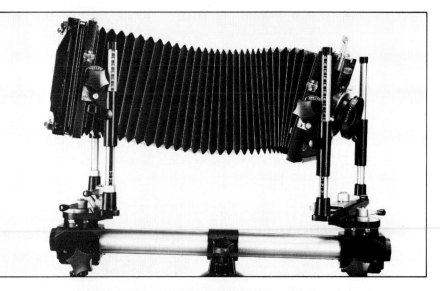

4

1. A battery check is almost a necessity. Depressing the tiny white button on the Nikkormat EL/ELW will cause the tiny lamp beside it to light if the battery has sufficient voltage. Other designs may use a deflection of the meter needle in the viewfinder to indicate battery condition.

2-3. Activating the metering system may be done by simply moving the film advance lever back slightly, or by turning on a specific control switch. A few 35mm SLR cameras use a metering system which is always on, and depend upon the lens cap to prolong battery life. Other metering systems come on when the shutter button is depressed slightly.

4-5. The Prinz view and Plaubel Mark II view cameras represent opposite ends of the view-camera spectrum in terms of price, features and sophistication. While the Prinz is the "Pinto" of the view-camera field, it's also an ideal camera for the beginner on a budget.

5

on lenses alone can pay for the camera several times over.

Having decided upon the film size with which you wish to work, the models you consider should have a full complement of movements—the rising/falling/tilting/sliding front, vertical and horizontal back swings, and front/rear focusing, although this latter feature will be found only on the more expensive in the line. These are mandatory features necessary to make a view camera useful to you; the remaining ones below are features that will make your photography easier.

Look for a revolving back to provide quick alignment of the format without having to move the camera. It should have at least 180-degree and preferably 360-degree movement. Click stops to indicate precise horizontal and vertical positioning are a decided advantage to you.

You'll want sufficient bellows extension to accommodate the variety of lenses for which you anticipate a use. Ordinarily, you'll find a double-extension bellows of 15-16 inches to be adequate; a longer one often comes in handy if you're working with close-ups,

since it permits moving in very close to your subject for a larger image.

The tripod block should be adjustable. This lets you position the camera for precise balance without moving the tripod, and is especially desirable whenever you're using extreme up or down angles.

The use of some sort of leveling device is almost essential for speed and accuracy of operation. Horizontal/vertical levels atop the camera provide

quick alignment of the back, even when used on terrain requiring an uneven adjustment of the tripod legs. The use of a level can prevent distortion in the negative that you were not able to detect on the ground glass and if the camera you select does not have the built-in variety, purchase a small carpenter's level for such use.

The fine-grain ground glass on which you focus should be of good quality and scribed with both horizontal and

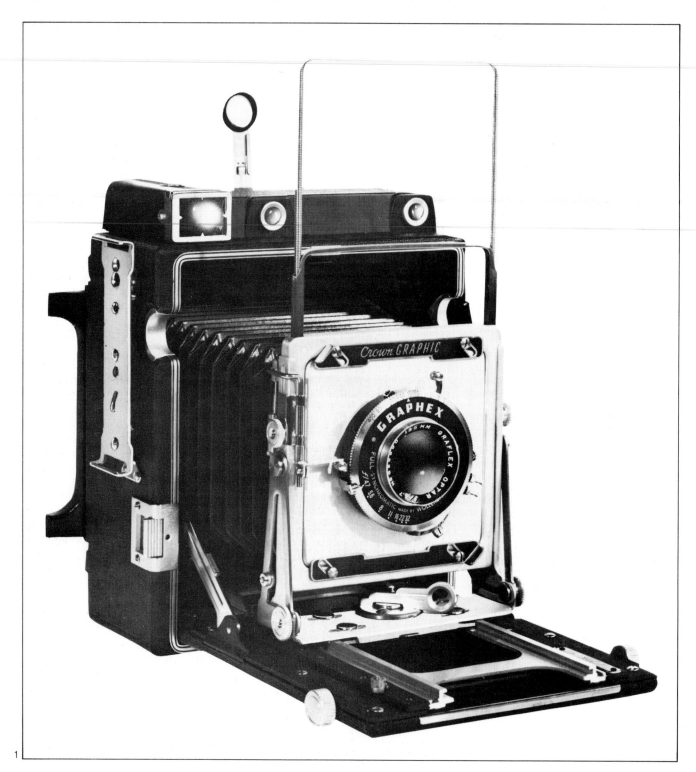

1

vertical dimensions as an aid in composition. A film-release lever on the camera back will relieve tension and permit film holders to be inserted without jarring the camera out of position. Positive locks on focusing drives and camera movements can save a lot of lost time for the fumble-fingered among us. In fact, all controls should be either easy to reach or oversize for convenience in use.

Those who find it helpful to combine the movements of a view camera with the versatility of a hand-held camera will do well to consider a press type

model, like the older Graflex and Busch Pressman cameras. Of the press cameras still manufactured, some like the Horseman Technical possess the same capabilities while others like the Mamiya and Rapid Omega do not possess them.

LARGE-FORMAT HAND CAMERAS

For the sake of convenience, I place all roll-film cameras—6x4.5 SLR, 6x6 SLR, 6x6 TLR and 6x7 SLR—in this category, despite the obvious disparity in negative sizes between the so-called ''medium'' format 6x4.5cm and the

much larger 6x7cm. Of the four types, the 6x6 TLR is probably the most limited in versatility, as only the Mamiya models possess lens interchangeability, although a Tele-Rolleiflex was once offered and is still in ample supply on the used market. The 135mm f/4 lens fitted to the Tele-Rollei is roughly equivalent in its field of view to that of a 90mm telephoto lens used on a 35mm camera. The TLR is also the lightest, it's hand-holdable, and some models feature semi-automatic (match needle) exposure automation, but at a list price approaching $1000. It's also

difficult to see this type of camera evolving into anything more sophisticated than it is already—now watch some manufacturer make a liar of me!

The newest of the 6x6, 6x7 and 6x4.5 SLR models feature electronically governed shutters, metering through the lens, a wide choice of optional lenses and interchangeable backs/magazines, but at a price of even greater expense, weight and bulk than that of the TLR. Of the three formats, the 6x4.5cm is likely to prove the most popular for this very reason.

COMPACT 35MM CAMERAS

Most of these cameras use some form of exposure control or programming that makes adjustments by the user unnecessary, and in many cases, impossible. All such cameras utilize a built-in light meter cell coupled to the lens and shutter, which are in turn cross-coupled in a preselected manner over which the user has no control.

1. Once extremely popular but now discontinued, press cameras like the Crown Graphic are again in demand—this time by view camera addicts seeking mobility with view camera movements.
2. Representative of a vanishing breed, the Mamiya C330 TLR is the only camera of its format to feature interchangeable lenses.
3-4. Rollei once offered its Tele-Rolleiflex (3), a special version of its popular Rolleiflex TLR (4), but fitted with a permanently mounted 135mm viewing/taking optic. These are still plentiful on the used camera market.

While two different camera brands may be equipped with the same aperture and shutter speed range, this does not mean that both would necessarily use the same combination of aperture and shutter speed under identical lighting

conditions. The manner in which the exposure system functions in a given camera model depends upon its manufacturer and his choice of exposure program used.

To illustrate this, let's consider the case of Camera X and Camera Y—both fitted with an f/2.8 lens which stops down to f/16 and a shutter speed range from ½ to 1/500 second. Under conditions of bright sunlight, Camera X uses a shutter speed of 1/300 second and an aperture of f/16 with a given film. As the light level diminishes, the shutter speed is reduced until it reaches 1/60 second. At this point, the shutter stabilizes and the aperture begins to open up as the light level continues to drop. Once the lens reaches its maximum aperture, the shutter drops in increments until it reaches its maximum exposure of ½ second.

On the other hand, Camera Y begins with a top shutter speed of 1/300 second and an aperture of f/16 under the same bright lighting/film speed conditions. But as the light level drops, the lens opens up progressively until it reaches its maximum aperture of f/2.8. Any further reduction in the level of illumination will now cause the shutter speed to slow down until it reaches its maximum exposure of ½ second.

What is our point of interest in this comparison? Although photographing the same subject with the same type of film at a given level of illumination, Camera X will take the picture at an exposure of 1/60 second at f/8, while Camera Y exposes the picture at 1/250 second at f/4—and neither camera tells you the combination it is using. Thus both produce an equally exposed negative, but the action-stopping ability of one camera is limited, while the range of sharpness surrounding the subject is narrow with the other.

The most compact of these cameras, the Rollei 35/35S uses a match-needle exposure system cross-coupled to the aperture and shutter, while a less expensive Rollei 35B contains a built-in meter not coupled to the lens. With any of these three, the user has total control over his choice of exposure combination for whatever creative effect is desired, but they must be focused by guess, since no rangefinder is built-in—which is why they're as compact as they are.

110 POCKET CAMERAS/SUBMINIATURES

Sophisticated as some of these are, many serious photographers tend to regard them as most useful as a

"pocket" notebook"—a camera they can take along when it is not practical or possible to carry their regular equipment, such as on business trips. Well-made and capable of amazing sharpness in some cases, the best results from the tiny 110 negative are obtained when you process and print the film yourself, since commercial photofinishers are notorious for the low-quality work they do.

There are several reasons why the dedicated photographer does not really accept the 110 camera seriously. One is the very limited types of film presently available—one black-and-white emulsion, three color slide films and a small handful of color print emulsions. Another is the virtual impossibility of fitting most 110 cameras with filters and close-up lenses for special effects without constructing awkward home-made adapters.

A third drawback is the programmed exposure common to all but a handful of expensive 110 cameras (and shared by the 35mm rangefinder compacts), which prevents user control over shutter and aperture settings. And the increased size of many necessary to incorporate the features deemed desirable by their manufacturers has brought the more precision 110 cameras into direct conflict with the compact 35mm rangefinder cameras—why suffer with a 13x17mm negative when you can work with a camera approximately the same size that provides a standard 24x36mm negative format and gives you a choice of any 35mm emulsion rather than the limited choice of 110 films? The answer, of course, rests with your anticipated need for and use of the camera, but it has become more and more difficult for the

1. The compact rangefinder 35mm reached its ultimate in design with the Leica CL, manufactured in Japan for Leitz by Minolta.
2. The latest medium format SLR design, Rollei's SLX is highly sophisticated, largely dependent upon electronics for its operation and very expensive—listing for over $2400.
3-4. Less expensive but less versatile, the Olympus 35 DC and Minolta Hi-Matic G are representative of the rangefinder 35mm cameras available today.

beginner to make a choice he feels is correct.

Subminiature cameras like the Minox and Yashica Atoron with their 8x11mm negative formats and dependence upon film choices offered by their manufacturers have never been popular with large numbers of photographers. However, they continue to appeal to a cult of individualistic users, many of whom prize them more for the status involved rather than their well-known capability for quality results when used conscientiously. Since accessories for subminiature cameras are limited in number and offered only by the cam-

era manufacturer, investing in the "system" to accommodate various requirements can result in a large cost which can seldom be recouped either by trading them in or selling them to other private parties.

35MM CAMERAS

As discussed in the first chapter, these are available in three types: the compact 35mms, with and without rangefinders; the rangefinder 35mms; and the omnipotent 35mm SLR, undoubtedly the most popular type of camera used by today's amateurs. After exposing you to a variety of the fascinating special-purpose cameras available, the remainder of this chapter will be devoted to the features common to the 35mm SLR and how to use those features.

SPECIAL-PURPOSE CAMERAS

Several special-purpose/limited-use cameras have been placed on the market during the last few years, a few of which are of interest to serious amateurs. While all are quite expensive, they are also capable of delivering superb results. They are of use primarily to the professional and to those amateurs who are sufficiently interested in learning how to use them to create pictures generally unobtainable in other ways. For this reason, I'll discuss them in a bit more depth.
PANON WIDELUX/HORIZONT PANO-RAMA—Perhaps the most useful under a large variety of conditions are the 35mm panoramic cameras. The only new one currently available is the Japanese-made Panon Widelux, initially introduced in 1959 and now available in its latest version, the F7. In the early 1970s, however, the Russian-manufactured Horizont Panorama was briefly in vogue in this country, partially due to a highly favorable exchange rate, coupled with a brief fascination with Russian/Chinese photo equipment, and was imported both under its own nameplate and as the Kalimar Wide-X. As they are still current on the used market at prices that make them generally a good buy, the Horizont/Wide-X cameras also deserve our attention.

Imported by the Harrison Camera Corporation, 249 Post Avenue, Westbury, New York 11590, the Widelux F7 uses a curved film plane and a 26mm f/2.8 lens mounted in a cylinder that rotates from left to right when the shutter is released. As the lens travels its arc across the film plane, the narrow vertical slit of an all-metal focal-plane shutter also moves across the film at

3

4

the same speed of travel to produce a uniform exposure over the extreme wide-field (130-degree) negative. Because of this wide coverage, the resulting negative is 24x59mm instead of the traditional 24x36mm format of the standard 35mm camera. The elongated picture frame thus reduces the number of exposures obtainable from a 20- or 36-exposure roll of film to 11 or 21, respectively. The Widelux shutter can be adjusted to settings of 1/15, 1/125 and 1/250 second, and its lens stopped down to f/11. Focus is fixed and everything in view is sharp beyond seven feet at f/2.8, or sharp beyond three feet at f/11.

The Widelux F7 is equipped with an integral optical viewfinder, which comes very close to matching the camera's field of coverage while providing a sharp, brilliant image. A spirit level is built into the camera's top plate to help assure that the camera is level. Its knob-type film advance is a bit old-fashioned, but it works smoothly and easily, and the rapid-wind feature to which we've all become accustomed really isn't necessary here. The exposure counter resets automatically when the back is opened, and all this stark simplicity is contained within a die-cast aluminum alloy body weighing 30 ounces and exuding a quality and fin-ish (complete with gold lettering) comparable to the very finest 35mm cameras—and why not? At this writing, its list price is $675, including a plush leather case and strap.

A series of six Widelux filters is also available from Harrison and comes in a separate case comparable in quality to that of the camera's case, and fitted with loops for the shoulder strap. These currently sell for $54 and can be used with all late-model Widelux cameras that have the small attaching stud located over the camera lens inside the cylindrical housing. The filter travels with the lens during its panoramic sweep, and other than taping a filter gel over the front of the cylinder, provides the only means of filtering Widelux pictures.

Despite its more distinctive appearance, the Horizont Panorama operates on the same principles and has many similar features which combine to produce essentially the same result on a 24x58mm frame of film, but its 28mm f/2.8 lens covers slightly less in its horizontal field of view, or about 110 degrees. The lens is also fixed-focus and stops down to f/16. The shutter

operates at four speeds—1/30, 1/60, 1/125 and 1/250 second.

The Horizont's exposure counter, shutter speed and aperture controls are all combined within a three-section circular dial on the camera's top plate, and are somewhat more difficult to operate efficiently than the Widelux controls. The optical viewfinder detaches from the camera to allow film rewind and contains a spirit level that's visible both in the finder and from its top. A detachable hollow handle grip that holds two filters is included in its $450 retail price, as are a carrying case and cable release. This grip is really useful, both in storing the filters and in helping the user to hold the camera properly.

Using one of these panoramic cameras to take vertical pictures can be a mind-shattering experience when you first examine the proof sheet. You have to be very careful not to get your feet in the picture, and even when the camera is held so that its lens is perpendicular to the subject, elongation will take place vertically. This is caused by the change in angle from lens to subject as the lens cylinder rotates upward. Tall buildings seem to bend, twist and give the appearance that they are falling over backward. Avoiding this effect when using the camera vertically takes a good deal of practice.

3

1. **The most compact 35mm of its kind, the Rollei 35S features scale focusing and match-needle metering coupled to its f/2.8 Sonnar lens and Compur-type shutter. The lens barrel collapses for portability, making it about the same size as many 110 pocket cameras.**
2. **Kodak's Tele-Instamatic 708 features an electronic shutter, automatic exposure control and a normal lens which converts to a telephoto at the flick of a switch.**
3-5. **Top-of-the-line 35mm SLR cameras such as the Nikon F2A (with motor drive attached), Minolta XK (with interchangeable finders) and Leica R3 are "system" cameras, producing professional results under widely varying conditions with the vast number of specialized accessories available.**

4

5

but for those interested in special effects, it can just as easily be made to work for you instead of against you.

Projecting color slides and enlarging black-and-white or color negatives present other problems. Special slide mounts are available from Harrison which will fit either Widelux or Horizont slides, but you'll need a 2¼x2¼ slide projector to screen them. Printing panoramic negatives requires an enlarger that will handle at least 2¼, but preferably 4x5 negatives. You'll have to adapt the negative carrier with a black paper mask and use an enlarging lens whose focal length adequately covers the negative's diagonal.

HOLOGON ULTRAWIDE—Imported to this country for a number of years on an on-again, off-again basis, and last manufactured in 1973, the Hologon Ultrawide is essentially a 35mm camera built around the famed 15mm Zeiss-Ikon three-element f/8 Hologon lens, which is also available separately in a Leica M mount. With its 110-degree angular field and focus capability to 20

inches, the Hologon was one of the first ultrawide-angle lenses to appear, but the camera's last list price of $798 helps to explain why it never really found a popular reception awaiting it. Other than the lens and a built-in viewfinder matching the lens's field of view, the sturdy, well-made camera mainly features a synchronized focal-plane shutter with speeds from one to 1/500 second and a single-stroke lever film wind. Unlike the 35mm panoramic cameras, the Ultrawide's effects can be achieved with a more highly corrected lens attached to your own camera body these days, and without

spending much more money, if you shop carefully.

HASSELBLAD SUPER WIDE C—To solve the problem of extreme wide-angle usage for the professional, the Hasselblad Super Wide C was designed with a highly corrected eight-element 38mm f/4.5 Zeiss Biogon lens permanently mounted to the camera body. Fitted with a Synchro Compur MX leaf shutter with a full range of speeds from one to 1/500 second and flash synchronization, the Biogon has a 90-degree angular field of view—comparable to that of a 21mm rectilinear wide-angle in the 35mm format. As it

1

focuses to 12 inches, the rear element of the lens comes within an inch of the film. Although a Hasselblad in appearance, the camera is focused is by scale and viewing is done with a separate tubular reflecting viewfinder mounted on top of the camera body beside the shutter release. For critical work, a focusing screen adapter permits through-the-lens focusing.

The Super Wide C offers the Hasselblad system user one large advantage—it accepts the same interchangeable film magazine as other Hasselblad models, along with many of the other system accessories. While lens design has progressed to the state where owners of some 6x6 SLR cameras can now use fisheye lenses, the Super Wide C has won a place for itself and continues to prosper in essentially the same design configuration as introduced over two decades ago.

BROOKS VERIWIDE 100—Once manufactured in Germany, the current model of this camera is international in nature. Made in Japan under license from Singer-Graflex (U.S.), it's fitted with a 47mm Schneider Super Angulon f/5.6 lens mounted in a Compur MXV shutter (Germany) with speeds from one to 1/500 second. Basically, the camera was designed around the Super Angulon lens, whose 100-degree angular coverage produces a 2¼x3¼ rectilinear image on 120/220 fill film. Its lens mount and focal plane are a single unit machined for a perfectly perpendicular

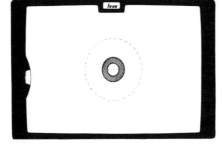

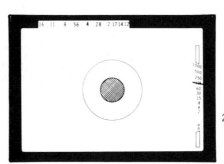

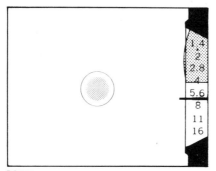

FIGURE A

relationship between the optical axis and film path. Designed in accordance with the Graflex X1 system, the Veriwide lens/spacer/focusing mount as-

2

sembly fits any Graflex X1 back accessory, including the wide-angle, Polaroid and Graflok backs.

One of the most highly corrected press/view wide-angle optics available, the six-element Super Angulon lens can be used at its maximum f/5.6 aperture without vignetting or loss of edge sharpness. While a full-focusing scale from 2½ feet to infinity permits accurate focusing on the principal subject, the tremendous depth of field of the lens will deliver a sharpness range from about eight feet to infinity at maximum aperture, and from about 2½ feet to infinity when stopped down to f/32.

The Compur shutter is synchronized for flash bulbs or electronic flash (use flat reflectors or tandem guns angled

3

1. Taken in an L.A. museum, this African veldt scene demonstrates both the scope of the Panon's wide-field capability and its ability to be hand-held for sharp exposures during a 1/15-second exposure.
2. The Brooks VeriWide 100, shown with Polaroid and standard backs.
3. The Panon Widelux F7 and the Russian-manufactured Horizont are representative of panoramic cameras. The Widelux is still in production, but the Horizont is found only on the used market.

slightly away from each other) and has a self-timer built in. The Veriwide's parallax-corrected eye-level optical viewfinder shows 92 percent of the picture area at infinity (88 percent on close-ups) and can be interchanged with a wire frame finder when photographing sports or other moving objects. Three bubble spirit levels are lo-

cated on the camera front to assist in critical camera placement and alignment when it's necessary that all lines within the picture retain their proper relationship.

CAMBO WIDE—Introduced at Photokina in 1976, the Cambo Wide is a new design manufactured in Holland and distributed in this country by Burleigh Brooks Optics, 44 Burlews Court, Hackensack, New Jersey 07601. Presently available as the Model 470 with a 47mm Schneider Super Angulon f/5.6 lens, or the Model 650 with the 65mm Super Angulon f/5.6 lens, a Model 1000 with the 100mm Schneider Symmar-S f/5.6 optic will also be marketed. Except for the focal length of the lens, all three versions are essentially

the same in design and operation.

While the Cambo Wide appears similar to other such cameras, there's one very important difference—it offers built-in lens movements. The front panel of the Model 470 has a 12mm lateral movement to either side (24mm total) and the Model 650 permits a 15mm movement (30mm total). In addition to these lateral movements, the front panel of both models can be turned 90 degrees; by doing so, the movements can be used in a vertical, as well as horizontal direction.

The camera body features a universal 4x5/9x12cm spring back fitted with a removable ground glass and built-in Fresnel screen. This allows the use of 4x5 or 9x12cm double sheet film holders, separate roll film holders which accommodate 120, 220 or 70mm rolls, the Polaroid 545 holder for use with 4x5 Polaroid sheet film, and the Polaroid 405 holder for Polaroid pack films, providing the user with the widest possible choice of emulsions.

Viewing is done either with the ground glass back, or with the top-mounted optical finder, with a detachable spirit level to assist in positioning the camera when used on a tripod. A hand grip at the left side of the body serves as a convenient means of hand-holding the Cambo Wide, while providing a means of releasing the shutter via a cable release. Like the Brooks Veriwide, the camera has been designed around what is probably the finest wide-angle optics for large-format users. The lateral front panel movement adds a measure of view camera versatility to a hand-held camera, and the universal back assures that virtually any large-format film can be used, resulting in negatives from 2¼ square up to 4x5 in size.

SINAR-HANDY—Compatible with the Sinar-p view camera system, this hand-held 4x5 wide-angle camera was also designed around the Super Angulon lenses, which are furnished in special helical focusing mounts and available in focal lengths from 47mm to 90mm. A tubular viewfinder and two-way spirit level take care of those functions, while an optional pistol grip with a cable release gives this odd-looking four-pound camera added versatility beyond its ability to interchange 4x5 and roll film backs.

WIDE-ANGLE VIEW CAMERAS—While a special wide-angle bellows is offered as an accessory by many view camera manufacturers, Calumet Photographic Inc., 1590 Touhy Avenue, Elk Grove

Village, Illinois 60007 produces a special short bellows Model CC-402 designed expressly for use with short focal lenses. The soft bellows design includes extra pleats to permit full swings and maximum flexing without restriction. By recessing the entire front of the camera, bellows compression is prevented, large lenses like the 90mm Super Angulon f/5.6 can be used, and the need for the recessed lensboard required when using standard view cameras (with or without the accessory wide-angle bellows) is eliminated. Its special side rails allow infinity focusing of any wide-angle lens, and the short monorail design results in a highly compact camera of its type.

LINHOF TECHNORAMA 6X17cm—Those interested in panoramic pictures without the curvature of the horizon usually associated with such wide-angle formats will find this camera the answer to their dreams. Taking four pictures on a roll of 120 film (or eight on 220), the Technorama brings 5x7 quality to a compact, hand-held camera. Its permanently mounted 90mm Schneider Super Angulon f/5.6 lens provides a 90-degree angular field of view with exceptional corner-to-corner sharpness; only those three-dimensional objects close to the camera and at the very edge of the frame will show exaggerated perspective.

A precision optical viewfinder frames the picture area and the reflected spirit level visible in the finder helps to prevent converging lines in hand-held pictures. A host of other features make the Technorama a versatile camera—Compur shutter (one to 1/500 second), cable release and tripod sockets, soft-pressure body release, two accessory shoes, automatic film-advance lock, exposure counter, and depth-of-field indicator—but the most fascinating is the flash synchronization.

Fitted with both hot shoe and PC connector, the Technorama will handle flash-illuminated panoramas in an interesting manner. Mount two "computer" flash units on a special bracket 30 degrees from the optical axis and you not only get even illumination over the entire field, but "in-depth" computer-controlled flash. If the photocell of one unit should react to a nearby object on its side of the camera, the other flash will ensure that the background still receives sufficient illumination. If you're interested, this one is the Rolls Royce of special-purpose cameras, listing at $2800 from HP Marketing, 98 Commerce Road, Cedar Grove, New Jersey 07009.

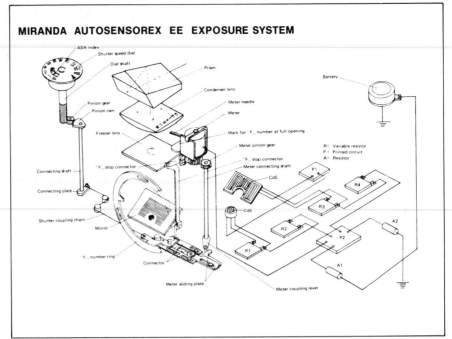

MIRANDA AUTOSENSOREX EE EXPOSURE SYSTEM

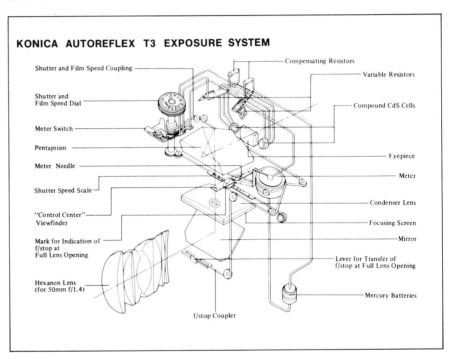

KONICA AUTOREFLEX T3 EXPOSURE SYSTEM

BUT DO YOU NEED ONE?—Probably not. The sole exception to this would possibly be a Widelux or Horizont. Although these panoramic cameras have definite purposes and limitations inherent in their design, they can often be put to good use by the creative amateur, with the results serving as an exercise in "seeing" while you're learning to use the camera to its best advantage. Because of the sweeping lens design and curved film plane, the panoramic principle is the only practical way of achieving a wider-than-normal field of view with a realistic image treatment which contains only negligible distortion.

For this reason, the panoramic camera has certain definite applications in specific fields, such as forestry, land surveys, legal, architectural, news and sports photography. This by itself can be sufficient justification if you're looking for an opportunity to indulge yourself by buying one, and once you have it, the creative applications of the camera are there for you to discover: perspective distortion, subject compression or elongation, simulated subject motion, etc.

BACK TO THE 35MM SLR

Now let's return to the 35mm SLR camera and examine why it is so very popular with both amateur and professional photographers alike, and how to use its features.

1. The Konica Autoreflex TC, a compact 35mm SLR and the latest offering from the company which introduced shutter-preferred exposure automation in 1966.

2. The Contax RTS—a resurrection of a fine old Zeiss name by Yashica and considered to be one of the finest handling 35mm SLR cameras.

The exposure control system used by most 35mm SLR cameras is either semiautomatic, also referred to as match-needle, or fully automatic. Older 35mm SLR cameras may be found without a built-in metering system, and these must be set by guess or with the help of a hand-held meter.

THE MATCH-NEEDLE SYSTEM

With the lens cap removed from the camera lens, look through the viewfinder eyepiece. At the side or along the bottom of the focusing screen, you'll see a meter needle and a fixed index notch—the exact location and configuration differ from one camera model to another (Figure A). Depending upon the camera in question, you may also see one or more of the following:

1—A plus (+) and minus (-) sign on the index notch to indicate needle alignment for one f-stop over- and one f-stop underexposure.

2—An indication of the shutter speed that is in use.

3—An indication of the aperture that is in use.

4—A light-emitting diode (LED) display in the form of arrows or an O.K.

5—A needle which moves from a small S (spot) to a small A (averaging) to indicate which metering mode you're using in those cameras equipped with more than one mode.

Regardless of the number or configuration of the display devices that are found in the viewfinder, the camera will be adjusted for a correct exposure as determined by the metering system when its needle is centered in the index notch. To do so, rotate either the aperture ring on the lens, or the shutter-speed dial on the camera body.

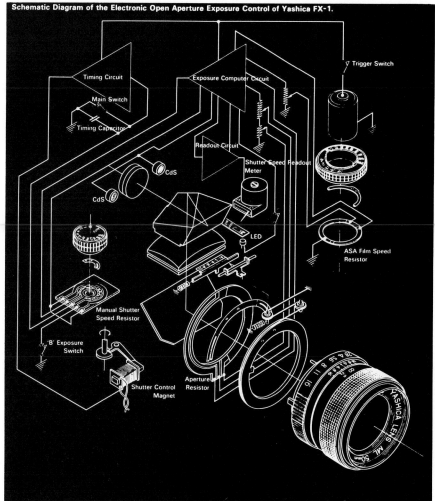

Schematic Diagram of the Electronic Open Aperture Exposure Control of Yashica FX-1.

As you adjust one or the other, the meter needle will move up or down according to the film speed for which the meter has been programmed (this is done when fresh film is loaded), the lighting conditions and your choice of lens/shutter adjustment.

For correct exposure, the needle must come to rest in the center of the notch; the plus and minus marks let you know when you're over- or underexposing by one f-stop. Some 35mm SLR cameras use a LED readout system calibrated in ½-stop incre-

Type A, L

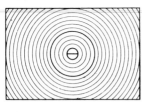

Type G

Type B

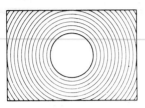

Type H

Type C

Type J

Type D

Type K

Type E

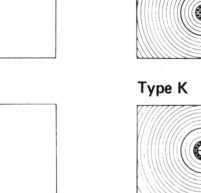

Type M

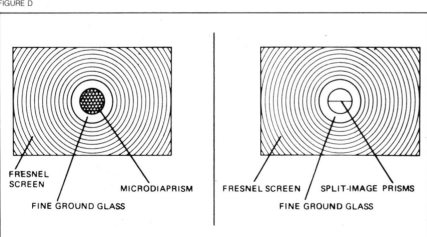

FRESNEL SCREEN

MICRODIAPRISM

FINE GROUND GLASS

FRESNEL SCREEN   SPLIT-IMAGE PRISMS

FINE GROUND GLASS

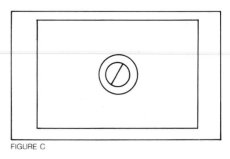

ments, permitting accurate over- or underexposure by ½ stop, one stop or 1½ stops. If you wish to deliberately over- or underexpose, align the meter needle to intersect the proper mark. With LED displays in the form of arrows, you generally rotate the aperture ring or shutter-speed dial in the direction of the arrow until the LED goes out; one such camera even signals you for a correct exposure with a bright red greeting, reading ''O.K.''

AUTOMATIC EXPOSURE CONTROL—SHUTTER-PRIORITY SYSTEM

The shutter-priority system of exposure automation is operated primarily by mechanical linkage and the trapped-needle concept which was first developed by Kodak in the late 1930s and used in its prewar Kodak Super Six-20 folding camera. To understand how it functions, as well as learn about its disadvantages or advantages, let's briefly explore a simplified model.

Regardless of manufacturer and design, each application of the shutter-priority system operates when light is received by the camera's photocell. With most such cameras, this means turning on a switch of one kind or another to activate the meter. The light striking the CdS cell(s) causes a current flow within the meter coil and it rotates, carrying with it a needle attached to the coil. The final position of the coil and needle depends upon the intensity of the light that reaches the photocell.

The needle moves over an anvil, or fixed metal bar, which is placed beneath, but very close to, the needle and covers the entire arc of swing. A movable trapping blade is located above the needle/anvil and is spring-loaded. This is operated by pressure on the shutter release and when triggered, gently pinches the needle between the blade and anvil, holding it securely in position.

As the shutter release is further depressed, a sawtoothed or step blade slides along the anvil until it reaches the trapped needle. This blade activates linkage as it moves, positioning a

1

2

3

1. Aperture-priority cameras use a manual exposure bias for user control over the metering system according to subject/background requirements.

2. The Fujica ST901 viewfinder uses a flashing digital LED display to inform the user of the approximate shutter speed selected by the camera's meter.

3-5. Depth-of-field preview levers are found either on the lens barrel or the body near the lens. As the aperture is always fully open for focusing, viewing and metering, this feature allows the user to manually stop the lens down to check field sharpness at any previously selected aperture.

stopping device to block movement of the lens's automatic (spring-loaded) diaphragm ring as it closes down. The closing action of the diaphragm happens when final pressure on the shutter button swings the mirror out of the way and releases the spring-loaded diaphragm ring. The diaphragm then closes to the position predetermined by the stopping device, and the shutter opens at that point.

In essence, the system converts light into electrical energy, which is then further transformed into both rotary and linear mechanical energy through the operation of a series of needles, linkages and gearing. Spring action has to be precise, and the shutter-release return spring must be sufficiently strong to override all linkage systems and restore them to their initial positions if the user decides not to take the picture at any time before releasing the mirror, which is the point of no return.

You receive a visual indication of the needle-trapping as it happens by turning on the meter, looking through the viewfinder, and slightly depressing the shutter release. As you move the cam-

4

5

era in the direction of differing light intensities, the meter readout needle in the viewfinder also moves. But there is a position in the shutter release travel where the needle locks (is trapped) and will no longer move despite changes in light intensity—this indicates that the needle has been trapped by the trapping blade and anvil.

The shutter-priority system has benefitted from considerable experience in design and application, and is reasonably accurate and responsive. But as you might gather from the discussion of its operation, shutter-release travel must be lengthy and pressure must be somewhat heavier than that required to activate the shutter on the average camera, because it must set each mechanical subsystem in operation. What we do with this exposure system is to provide the meter with a specified increment of time that we wish the shutter to remain open, and in return it delivers an infinitely variable aperture between the limits of the largest and smallest openings made available by the manufacturer, once the system has determined exactly what is required by light conditions.

But let's suppose that the light level is too low or too great for a correct exposure. What happens? The readout needle in the viewfinder will deflect above or below the marked aperture scale into a warning zone. This tells you to select another shutter speed, change the film speed rating you've keyed into the camera's meter or attach a neutral density filter—alternatives you must select and implement yourself, according to the situation at hand. Should the meter battery fail, all is not lost, as you can use shutter-priority cameras manually by selecting your own aperture until a new battery can be installed—the shutter is mechanically operated.

But the shutter-priority system has its own disadvantages. Each lens used with such a camera must incorporate a coupling device to function with the manufacturer's design; thus, a lens used with a Konica Autoreflex will not work on a Miranda Auto Sensorex EE body. Lenses, extension tubes, extenders, etc., will not work automatically with camera bodies other than the one for which they were designed. Since all manufacturers do not provide the same flexibility in terms of the number and types of lenses available for their body design, this can be a limiting factor in your choice of camera.

Although the diaphragm stopping device controls the aperture selection

with only a limited amount of movement, mechanical wear leading to a loss of adjustment can throw off the aperture by one stop or more, without the meter or you ever realizing it. But the shortcoming most discussed is the point at which the shutter-priority camera is locked into a selected exposure. Once the needle is trapped, the aperture selected by the meter can be changed only by freeing the needle and remetering. This means that pressure on the shutter release must be removed, the linkage configuration returned to its original position, and the process started all over again.

What does this process mean in practical terms for most of us? Well, if you trap the needle and complete the exposure, it means very little. What you must remember with this type of exposure automation is to not trap the needle and then wait several seconds be-

1-2. Self-timer operation differs slightly according to design. After pulling the small lever all the way toward the camera base, the timer is activated by either depressing the camera's shutter release button (1) or the tiny switch under the timer lever which is exposed when it is set (2).
3. The mirror lock-up feature is operated by a small lever very often found in this position.
4-5. To disengage the film transport, the rewind button is depressed and the rewind crank turned in the direction of the arrow. If making a multiple exposure, you simply depress and hold the rewind button while working the film advance lever rather gently.

fore completing the shutter release travel. Should you trap the needle and not wish to continue with the exposure at that moment, release the pressure on the shutter button until you're ready to expose, and then do so with a smooth motion, trapping the needle once more.

3

AUTOMATIC EXPOSURE CONTROL—APERTURE-PRIORITY SYSTEM

Basically, the aperture-priority system works like this—after keying the film speed into the meter to determine its sensitivity level, the lens aperture is selected and set by the user. When the meter is turned on, information about the preselected aperture is sent to the primary electronic center through a variable resistor attached to the aperture stop-down ring. This information is joined by data about the film speed, which is transmitted by a multifunction resistor. At the same time, the meter cells begin measuring subject light intensity and sending this data to the electronic center, where it's stored in a capacitor that acts like a memory bank.

When the shutter is activated by pressing the release in completely, the lens stops down to the preselected aperture as the mirror flips out of the way and the first shutter curtain begins its travel. The metering cells are temporarily disconnected from the control circuit, turning over their function to the memory bank. Battery power is diverted to an electromagnet, which restrains the second curtain, and to a timing capacitor. When the capacitor and electromagnet charges become equal, the control center de-energizes the latter, which then releases the second curtain to complete the exposure.

What we really have here is a mechanically operated, electronically governed shutter, not an ''electronic'' shutter as some advertisements might lead you to believe. By energizing the electromagnet, the shutter is trapped open until battery and capacitor resistance are equal—the so-called trigger level—at which time the electromagnet is de-energized to close the shutter. The length of time required by the timing capacitor to reach the trigger level depends upon the resistance value used in shutter speed selection. In elementary applications, this could be simply a variable resistor, but it usually

4

5

takes the form of a complicated network of resistors for film speed, aperture control, and for light level response functions.

While it's possible to provide the user with a visual readout in the viewfinder as to the shutter speed chosen by simply attaching a needle to a moving coil meter, not all aperture-priority systems are designed to do so. The trend seems to be in the direction of LED readouts of some sort; these require far less space and are also less fragile than a moving coil, but also require more battery power to operate. And should battery voltage level drop below a predetermined point, the meter stops functioning and you must resort to manual operation until the battery

can be replaced. With some designs, you're limited to a single speed under such conditions, and the newest ones lack even that; with a dead battery, the camera is useless.

Aperture-priority cameras use a manual override system. In the early designs, this was a limited range of shutter speeds at which the focal-plane shutter would operate mechanically on a step basis, permitting camera use manually or in a match-needle mode. The newest designs use an exposure compensation subsystem that programs the main system to provide over/underexposure by as much as two stops for use under special lighting conditions.

Proponents of the aperture-priority

system maintain that exposure is more precise with this system than with a shutter-priority camera, as the memory bank stores exposure data right to the moment of exposure when the mirror begins to rise. They also maintain that shutter-speed increments can be more minutely divided and controlled by an electronically governed shutter than can the differences between apertures operating via a trapped needle system. In the vast majority of photographic situations, these arguments are academic. However, one very solid fact about the aperture-priority camera remains a hard reality: You can obtain exposure automation with any lens that fits the camera, because no special lens mount is required as in the shutter-priority models.

Although these so-called "electronic" cameras are less subject to temperature and humidity factors, there remains to be answered the all-important question of gradual changes in the components that make up the electronic system. Over a long period of time, there may be alterations in the capability of the memory bank and timing capacitor, or resistors may experience a value change. In either case, incorrect data would operate the system without the user or the control center being aware of what happened, resulting in incorrect exposures. These questions are yet to be answered and can be determined only over a time span of a few years, but you can rest assured that if they do appear, manufacturers will correct any such problems as rapidly as they are discovered.

INSIDE THE VIEWFINDER

When you look through the viewfinder eyepiece of an SLR, you'll see the image that will appear on the film, right side up and unreversed on the focusing screen. Superimposed along the side(s) of the screen, you'll also find one or more of the data display devices previously mentioned, and in the center, a means of sharply focusing the image in the form of a circular focusing aid.

This center circle contains a fine-focusing collar, which in turn contains either a circular microprism or a circle split by a horizontal line (Figure B). If you point the inside circle at the object on which you wish to focus and then rotate the lens barrel, the image covered by the microprism will appear shattered or fractured when out of focus, snapping into definite sharpness when the object is brought into focus.

With those screens containing the

center split circle, or split-image rangefinder, vertical lines in any object at which it is pointed will appear in different planes if out of focus. Rotating the lens barrel until the two sections of the line are aligned will bring the object into focus. Recent variations in split-image design include setting the split on the diagonal (Figure C), and the use of a microprism circle set within another microprism circle. This functions in effect as a split-image device which permits you to focus on any line—horizontal, vertical or diagonal.

Regardless of the type of focusing aid used in the center, the rest of the screen is generally a matte Fresnel which can be used to check the sharpness of the area around the object on which you have focused. While most SLR cameras are fitted with noninterchangeable focusing screens, the so-called "system" cameras for which a large variety of accessories are provided will usually have a removable screen, with the manufacturer offering a number of different types for specialized purposes. A few of the 19 screens provided by Nikon are in Figure D.

THE SELF-TIMER

An important and useful feature found on most 35mm SLR cameras, this can be used when you wish to include yourself in the picture, if you're taking close-ups where one or both of your hands must appear in the scene, or for other such special applications. Simply set the camera on a tripod and prepare its controls for the exposure, then swing the self-timer lever into action and you're ready to go.

With most cameras, the total delay in shutter action provided by the self-timer is 8-10 seconds; you can pull the lever all the way down for the maximum delay, or only partially if you

1. To load a 35mm camera easily, hold as shown in the left hand.
2. To prevent stray light from entering the viewfinder and biasing the meter cells' reading whenever the camera issued at other than eye level, a blind is often built into the eyepiece of 35mm SLRs.
3. Insert a film cartridge and withdraw sufficient film to engage it with the take-up spool securely.
4. Hold the film aligned on the sprocket teeth with your right thumb while revolving the take-up spool with your left thumb to take up slack.
5. Alternately work the film advance lever and trip the shutter until both sets of sprocket holes engage both sets of teeth. Then close and lock the back and use the rewind crank to take up excess slack in the cartridge. Now when you advance the film, the crank should move unless something is wrong with your loading.

think that only 3-4 seconds delay will suffice. One of two methods is generally used to activate the timer mechanism—you either depress the shutter button in the usual manner, or there will be a small release button located at the top of the timer lever mechanism on the camera face to activate it. Once you've set the shutter action in motion via the self-timer, you step in front of the camera and position yourself; when the delay period is up, the camera will operate normally to take the picture. Since the self-timer is a clockwork mechanism operated by gears and springs, you should never force it. If you decide not to take the picture after setting the self-timer, refer to your camera's instruction booklet, as there are various methods used to override the mechanism.

Actually, the self-timer feature is far more useful to assure vibration-free exposures whenever you're using a long focal length or telephoto lens—few of us spend much time taking pictures of ourselves or our hands. But suppose that you have an 800mm lens mounted on your camera body. Any camera shake is going to be magnified 16X on the negative, causing a considerable degradation of the image. To prevent this, use the self-timer.

Focus and frame your subject, adjust the exposure and set the self-timer for its full delay. When you're ready to take the picture, trip the camera's release button (or the self-timer's release button) and the instant-return mirror will move up and out of the optical path. The camera now has several seconds in which to recover from any vibration that might be caused by the lens, the action of the mirror moving upward, or from the pressure exerted to trip the shutter. By the time that the shutter actually fires, all such vibration will have dissipated. Despite the fact that most SLR mirror actions are very well dampened against vibration, use of this technique will provide assurance that your negative will retain all of the clarity your camera lens is capable of delivering.

THE MIRROR LOCK-UP

Many 35mm SLR cameras feature a mirror lock-up mechanism. This feature may be required for the use of certain lenses, or when using a motor drive. Mirror lock-up devices vary in shape, position and location, but all are usually found on the side of or near the camera escutcheon. To operate a mirror lock-up device, you generally move the control lever up or down from a centered position. With some cameras, you push upward on the lever to lock-up the mirror and down to return it to normal operation; with others you push downward to lock the mirror and up to restore it.

The mirror lock-up device becomes especially handy when shooting with a tripod-mounted telephoto lens. Locking up the mirror *before* activating the self-timer is double insurance that you'll get no vibration from mirror action. If your camera is so equipped, take advantage of the feature and use the mirror lock-up whenever possible.

MULTIPLE-EXPOSURE PROVISION

Not too many years ago, photogra-

3

4

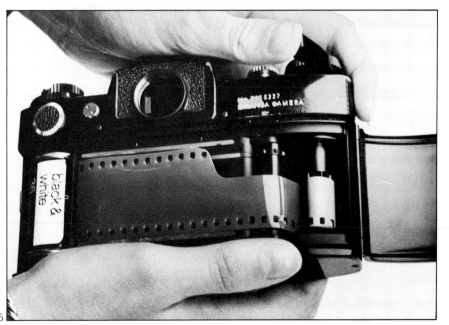

5

1

phers made double exposures (taking two pictures on the same frame of film by not advancing it after the first one) so easily and often so accidentally that all camera manufacturers built a double-exposure prevention mechanism into the film transport/shutter cocking operation. But in recent years, double and even multiple exposures have come into vogue as a creative means of expressing oneself.

Many recent SLRs will have a multiple-exposure device built into the camera. After turning the proper lever in the required direction, you simply depress the rewind button and stroke the film-advance lever to cock the shutter. This procedure can be repeated as often as desired and each succeeding image will register perfectly on the previously exposed one. As the multiple-exposure device disengages the film transport sockets, you should not forget to return it to its original position when you're finished with the function, or you'll end up with unwanted multiple exposures.

If your camera is equipped with this provision, you should refer to the instruction booklet for precise information on the procedure to be used. Some models require that you hold in the rewind button while cocking the shutter, but others do not; some exposure counters will keep track of the frames that have been advanced, while others count the number of exposures.

Readers who wish to make multiple exposures with an SLR not having this specific capability can do so, but should not expect precise registration of the various images with the method I'm about to describe. Start by taking up the slack in the film cartridge by turning the rewind knob and holding it while you make your first exposure. Still holding the rewind knob to make certain that it doesn't move, depress and hold in the rewind button while cocking the shutter with the film-advance lever. Make your next exposure and repeat for as many further exposures as you wish to make, releasing the rewind knob and button only prior to your final exposure.

Replace the lens cap, advance the film and release the shutter. This is known as shooting a ''safety'' frame and is required because when you throw the film-advance lever after making that final exposure, the film *will not* advance a full frame. It takes a portion of the advance lever's throw to re-engage the film transport and so the film will actually move only about ½ frame or less. This ''safety'' frame will prevent spoiling a portion of your multiple exposure.

EYEPIECE BLIND

Light entering the viewfinder eyepiece when the camera is used on a tripod or otherwise used without the photographer's eye placed tightly

1-2. The camera's meter is indexed for the film speed rating by lifting the shutter speed dial and revolving until the proper speed shows in the window (1) or by setting a separate film speed dial, usually located around the base of rewind lever.

against it will affect the metering system's sensor cells, overinflating the reading and leading to underexposure. To prevent this, cameras likely to be affected by such a problem contain some form of blind in the viewfinder which can close it off to stray light, freeing the user from peering through the finder while making lengthy electronically timed exposures and possibly jarring the camera by accidentally bumping up against it.

FILM LOADING

This should not present problems if you make a conscious effort to develop the correct technique at the very beginning. The following procedure is the way in which I load my cameras, and should work very well for you, although you may find slight modifications of your own that will make the method more convenient for you.

1—Holding the camera in your left hand with the lens facing downward and the camera back facing toward you, unlock and open the back, supporting it with your index and forefinger to prevent the weight of the back from springing the hinges. On some cameras, the back may come off com-

2

processor (unless you continue winding beyond 36 exposures). One of the latest wrinkles in camera design is a small window near the film-advance lever which indicates film movement or the lack of it.

7—When you reach the final picture on the film, you may find that the film-advance lever will not turn sufficiently to wind the film and cock the shutter. When you reach this point, it's time to rewind the film back into the cartridge. If you force the film advance in an attempt to "sneak" one more picture, you run the risk of pulling the film loose from the spool in the cartridge and the camera must then be unloaded in the darkroom.

To rewind, activate the rewind release (usually a small button on the camera bottom), lift the little crank from the rewind knob and turn it at a uniform pace in the direction indicated by the arrow. You'll feel a slight tension until the film disengages from the take-up spool, at which point the crank will revolve freely.

You'll find a few exceptions to this procedure with other 35mm non-SLR cameras; a handful load from right to left, and older screw-thread Leicas (and some of their imitators) load from the bottom of the camera. In such cases, the cartridge leader is attached to the camera's removable take-up spool and the two are inserted in their respective chambers from the bottom of the camera at the same time before the baseplate is replaced.

SET THE FILM SPEED

Once the film is properly loaded and you are certain that it is being properly transported through the camera, the metering system must be programmed with the speed of the film. To determine the proper setting, check the instruction sheet that accompanies each cartridge of film. This number will be given as an ASA, DIN or EI rating, and for our purposes, we can consider the ASA and EI numbers to be interchangeable. DIN is a European film-speed rating and each DIN number has an equivalent in the ASA system.

Locate the film-speed dial on your camera and chances are good that it will be marked in ASA numbers on one side, and DIN numbers on the other. Use the ASA side unless the film specifies only a DIN rating. On most 35mm SLR cameras, the meter is programmed by lifting up on the outer rim of the film-speed dial and turning it in the appropriate direction to align the index mark with the numerical speed of

pletely. If so, remove it and place it nearby where no harm will come to it.

2—Pull the rewind knob out from the camera as far as it will go. This will withdraw the split shaft attached to the knob and provide room in the film chamber for the cartridge.

3—Drop the cartridge into the film chamber so that the leader extends across the camera body, then push the rewind knob back in place with a revolving motion so that the split shaft will engage the slot in the cartridge spool. This will hold the cartridge in place. With cameras whose backs come off completely, you should slide your left thumb over the cartridge to keep it from sliding off the split shaft while you complete the loading.

4—Pull about three inches of the film from the cartridge with your right hand and insert the end of the leader into the take-up spool. Spool configurations differ considerably from camera to camera, but the spool will usually contain two or more slits for the insertion of the leader.

If the take-up spool slits do not show, the spool can be revolved with your right thumb until they do. Some spools use a slit with a sprocket tooth—the film is inserted into the slit and one of its perforations engaged with the tooth to prevent it from pulling

loose or disengaging.

5—The lower edge of the leader should now align with the bottom flange of the take-up spool. Make certain that the film is properly aligned and that the sprocket teeth engage the film perforations, then wind the film-advance lever while you watch the film move across the film plane and wind onto the take-up spool. Should the film slip off the spool, or not properly engage the sprocket teeth, make the necessary corrections and then close the camera back.

6—Release the shutter and *gently* turn the rewind knob in the direction opposite to that of the film's movement until it stops. This removes any slack in the cartridge by placing a slight tension on the film, and serves to indicate whether or not you've loaded the film properly.

As you wind and release the shutter two more times to move unfogged film into position for your first exposure, watch the rewind knob. If it does not turn each time you wind the film, the leader is not connected to the take-up spool and the film is not being properly advanced. Ignoring this step can prove costly, as you'll never know for certain that the film didn't go through the camera until your transparent negative or opaque slide film returns from the

1. To hold a 35mm SLR properly, cradle it in your left hand as shown and draw in your arms close to your body.
2. Stand erect, with your feet spread apart and one foot slightly forward to lower your center of gravity.
3. When a steady support is required, brace yourself as shown against a nearby wall, tree or other solid object.

the film. As you lower the ring back in place, make sure that it is completely seated or the meter may not function correctly. Some cameras use a click-stopped dial located beneath the rewind knob instead of a separate dial. This is rotated to align the proper speed with the appropriate index mark. If you haven't used the camera recently, activate the battery-check device to make certain that your power supply is up to par, then turn on the meter and you're ready to go.

CAMERA HOLDING SIMPLIFIED

Everyone who has ever used a camera before has developed his/her own method of holding it while taking a picture, but not every method used will minimize camera movement sufficiently at the time of exposure—and camera movement is a major cause of unsharp pictures. For exposures of 1/30 second or slower, it's strongly recommended that you either use a tripod, or brace your camera against some solid, steady object.

Although 1/30 second may sound quite brief to some readers, it's really a far longer time than most of us can hold a 2-4-pound instrument steady without some movement on our part. Remember that you're working with a small negative to make large prints, and unless the camera is held steady as a rock when shutter speeds of 1/30 second or slower are used, you're virtually guaranteed to pick up some slight image blurring. While you may think that you're holding the camera steady, there's almost always some slight body movement, such as that caused by breathing, which will contribute to a lack of sharpness in your negatives.

If you have not already developed a method of holding a camera, or if you're not particularly satisfied with the results your method provides, let me suggest that you give mine a try. Wrap the fingers of your right hand around the camera body so that the index finger rests comfortably on the shutter release, and the thumb fits between the body and film-advance lever. Cradle the camera in your left hand for additional support, with the left thumb and index finger around the focusing ring on the lens barrel. Pull your left arm in toward the center of the body, with the elbow resting against your chest. Draw the right arm in about three inches from your left arm and let it hang free—if you draw the arms too close together, you'll stiffen up and begin to shake from muscle tension.

Those who use their right eye for viewing should be able to operate the camera without removing it from their forehead. Since I use my left eye, I find that rocking the camera forward a couple of inches as I throw the film-advance lever lets me avoid gouging my nose and eye along the way. This is strictly a wrist action and as the camera is rocked backward after film advance is completed, it falls right back into position nicely, with but a moment's viewing lost. That's the penalty one pays for being left-eyed!

Once you've mastered the knack of holding your camera and releasing the

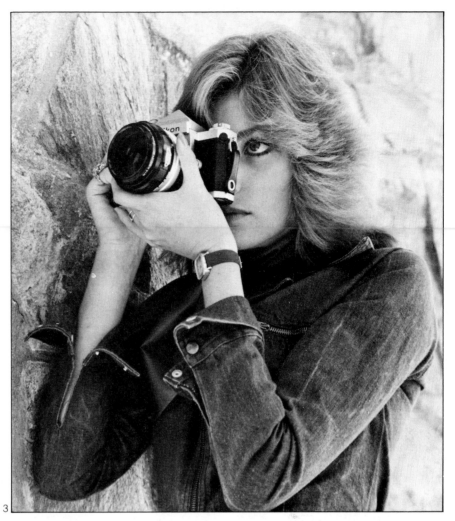

shutter properly, take a look at how you stand when taking pictures. Many people tend to stand flat-footed, that is, with their feet side-by-side. This may seem perfectly natural and comfortable at first, but try standing that way for awhile and see how quickly you begin to weave back and forth. Now, try spreading your legs slightly—about 12-14 inches apart should do it nicely—and with one foot slightly forward. This shifts your center of gravity to a lower point, turning you into a more stable base that is better able to resist a blowing wind and/or vibration.

If you find it necessary to brace your camera while shooting, and a tripod is not available, lean against a tree, wall, doorway or other rigid object. This will help to keep you relaxed and yet provides that extra measure of support that's especially important when taking pictures under low light levels, or whenever you're tired or during times of physical or mental stress. You may even find that resting the camera on a fence post, wall or park bench will provide a better camera angle. What you use to brace yourself is not terribly important—almost any solid object will do the job as long as it allows you to

rest the camera long enough to make the exposure without movement.

KNOW YOUR CAMERA

Just because you've spent (or are about to spend) a healthy sum on your camera doesn't mean that you should let it intimidate you with its array of dials, numbers, arrows and lights. Now you have an idea what they mean and how they're used. Your camera will function most efficiently for you if you're thoroughly familiar with its controls, how they operate and when to use them. While I've given you a quick rundown on the basic features and their relationship to one another, this chapter is by no means a satisfactory substitute for a complete run-through of the instruction manual that accompanies your camera; not only is the repetition unnecessary, but we have many other topics to cover in these pages. The great majority of camera instruction manuals are quite complete in their coverage, at least as far as using the individual features of your camera is concerned, and it's strongly advised that you carry the manual with you until you become fully proficient in the use of your camera. □

6

Basic Accessories & Their Use

Fast and easy to operate, the 35mm SLR is also extremely versatile in the number and type of accessories that can be used to extend its capabilities for virtually any type of photography. Cameras for which a large number of varying accessories are offered, such as the Nikon F2, Canon F-1 and Olympus OM-1/OM-2, are often referred to as ''system'' cameras—their basic body is regarded as the central point of a ''system of photography.'' By changing viewfinders, focusing screens, lenses and/or the addition of different accessories, the basic camera can be made suitable for almost any specialized use—photomicrography, astronomical work, sports or other action photography, slide duplication, etc.

Filters, interchangeable lenses and electronic flash are primary accessories that extend the range of your camera. As such, they're important enough to merit their own individual chapters. But there are other equally valuable accessories of which every photographer should be aware, some basic to taking good pictures and others important to protecting your equipment and the investment you've made. I'll cover those in this chapter and show you how to use them to best advantage.

AUTO WINDERS

Amateurs have long envied the professional photographer with his motor drive. There's something about the ability to shoot pictures at a rate of 3-5 per second that intrigues the average person. But motor drives are not only large and bulky attachments, they're also extremely expensive, often costing more than the camera and lens to which they're fitted. Some manufactur-

ers cannot adapt their basic body to a motorized operation, so they provide separate camera bodies with the function built in—an even greater expense to those committed to a particular camera because of their investment in lenses and other accessories. Beyond these limitations, motor drives also possess other disadvantages—they eat up batteries and film with an astounding amount of speed.

The normal motor drive operating at a speed between 3-5 frames per second will devour a 36-exposure cartridge of film in 7-12 seconds. Some motor drives actually use more than one motor; the Canon MF/MD drives use individual motors for shutter release and for film advance/shutter cocking, with a micro-relay switching automatically to tell which motor when to function. In a drive operated by a single motor, depressing the drive

1. Several manufacturers offer an entire system of accessories for use with their cameras—this is the Olympus OM-1/OM-2 system. In addition to system accessories, independent manufacturers offer a variety of other useful and usually less expensive items.
2. The motorized amateur camera was last seen in the form of Kodak's Motormatic 35—a spring-driven model of the late fifties.
3. The Topcon Super DM appeared in 1972 and introduced the motor winder concept. Although the first of the current crop of motorized 35mm SLRs at an affordable price, the Super DM lives on.

unit's shutter button turns on the motor that opens the first shutter curtain. A tiny micro-switch breaks the circuit and shuts off the motor for the duration of the shutter opening. When the second shutter curtain closes, the electrical circuit reopens to allow the motor to advance the film and cock the shutter.

While the motor drive provides rapid

3

2

fire power, many nonprofessional users found them less than desirable when used under constantly changing lighting conditions. There's simply no way you can match-needle exposure on the button under such circumstances at a 3-5 fps rate, especially if you're trying to follow-focus a moving object at the same time. While a motor drive can also be used to make single exposures without manually advancing the film, the unit loses its appeal when used in this manner, as the size and weight become overly important factors for nonsequence photography.

But with the age of electronic exposure automation, this objection to rapid-fire photography has been overcome and a new breed of motor drive, called the *automatic winder* has appeared in conjunction with the compact electronic SLRs. These junior motor drive units are not designed as much for rapid-sequence photography as for automatic film winding. Since film wind and shutter release are both done with the right hand, most users find it necessary to remove the camera from their eye momentarily between shots to accomplish this. Such a break in the operational use of the camera defeats one of the primary advantages of the electronic SLR—its ability to constantly monitor the subject and adjust exposure accordingly.

The auto winder concept is not exactly new; Topcon first utilized it with its Super DM camera in 1972. Although a well-thought-out approach and most functional, the Topcon winder was ahead of its time and instead of selling cameras by the bushel, it simply pointed the way for others to follow. Currently, auto winders are offered for use with the Canon AE-1/AT-1, Contax RTS, Nikkormat ELW, Nikon EL2 and FM, Olympus OM-1/OM-2, Pentax ME/MX, Topcon Super DM, Voightlander VSL 3 and Yashica FR. There are others on the way from manufacturers not mentioned but they will no doubt be available by the time this appears.

1

2

1. An auto winder gives you the capability of repeated exposures without removing your eye from the camera to wind the film. This feature has its advantages in action photography, or whenever you're shooting people pictures. To create this ghostly effect, Ron Berkenblitt held the rewind button of his camera depressed while taking four exposures of the same cyclist.

2-3. The new Nikon EL2 and the Nikon FM auto winders represent different approaches to the concept. The EL2 uses the same AW-1 winder provided with the recently discontinued Nikkormat ELW, while the MD-11 unit for the Nikon FM is more of a hybrid motor drive.

4. The AW-1 winder controls are centrally located and consist simply of an on/off switch and pilot lamp.

5. Removing the battery compartment cap from the AW-1 winder requires the use of a coin; using a fingernail will result either in poor contact or a broken nail.

HOW THEY DIFFER—Because of the variations in operation and capability of the auto winders provided for use with different cameras, those interested in the concept will do well to take this accessory under consideration before making a firm decision which camera to buy. For example, of those mentioned, only the Canon, Pentax and Contax winders are capable of continuous shooting—press down and hold the shutter button for sequence bursts up to two fps. The other winders mentioned require that you release the shutter button between exposures, slowing their rate of use and decreasing their convenience factor.

Attachment considerations are also of concern, unless you plan to install the winder unit permanently. All current winders connect to the camera bottom in different ways. The Contax RTS winder, which also fits the Yashica FR, uses a folding key for a direct connection without having to remove a bottom cover plate. The Olympus winder for the OM-1/OM-2 is fitted with a milled knob for attachment, but a cover plate must be removed from the bottom of the camera with a coin, and no place is provided to store it. If lost, a new cover should be obtained, because using the camera without it will allow dust, dirt and other contamination to enter.

The Canon power winder attaches in a similar fashion, but contains a slot to store the dime-sized cover. The Nikkormat ELW and Topcon Super DM winders attach directly to the respective camera bottoms without removing a cover, but don't put that coin away because you'll need it to fasten the winder securely in place. Which brings up an important point—if any of these winders are not securely fastened, they will not operate properly due to poor electrical connections.

Other factors are the differences in shape, size and weight. As you'd expect, each winder is the same length and width as the bottom of the camera model for which it's designed, and most are within a few millimeters either way of 1½ inches in height. When fitted to the camera, some have a tendency to unbalance the whole affair and the camera/lens/winder combination will pitch over forward when placed on a flat surface. Others are designed to rest upright without tipping the whole affair over because of a built-in hand grip which gives the camera/winder an L-shaped base to rest upon. The Nikkormat ELW and Contax RTS winders weigh approximately 15 ounces when loaded with six AA batteries; the other winders weigh somewhat less primarily because they use only four AA cells.

Battery life also varies, depending on the type of cell used and the mechanical design of the auto winder/camera film transport system. Some winders require a bit more juice than others every time they wind the film. How often you use the winder, as well as the intervals between pictures, will also

3

4

5

affect battery life in addition to the other considerations common to battery-operated devices, such as temperature, humidity, etc. But all should deliver between 140 to 170 36-exposure cartridges of film (5000-6000 exposures) when fresh alkaline energizers are used, reducing battery cost per film cartridge to a minimum far below that of most electronic flash units. When used for cold weather photography, consider regular manganese batteries instead of alkaline energizers. Manganese batteries are much more efficient in low temperatures, despite the fact that fresh ones will wind only 8-10 cartridges through the camera.

What happens when you reach the end of a cartridge of film? Some winders use an automatic shutoff device, others use a slipping clutch and most have a red signal or pilot lamp on the rear of the winder which indicates operation, and will remain lighted if the winder is unable to complete a cycle. Unlike the full-fledged motor drive that has its own frame counter built-in and will shut off after the 20- or 36-exposures for which it is set are taken, the auto winder uses the camera's exposure counter and can thus be caught in mid-frame at the end of a cartridge.

To solve this problem with any camera/winder combination, you simply turn off the winder and rewind the film into the cartridge with the camera's film rewind crank. Once this is done, you turn on the winder to complete the film transport/shutter cocking cycle, shut it off again and trip the shutter. This prepares the camera for unloading and reloading with a fresh cartridge. Obviously, it is not as handy as the motor drive that will actually rewind the film for you under power, but

1. The Canon AT-1 with power winder—identical to the AE-1 but match-needle exposure instead of fully automatic. One winder fits both cameras.
2. While many winders accept batteries in a loose configuration, the Canon uses a compartmentalized approach which clips into place to form a part of the winder.
3. The Pentax MX winder features a built-in hand grip and uses a Canon-type attachment screw. Like the Canon unit, it achieves its low weight by the use of plastic.
4. With its unique enclosed attachment screw, attaching and removing the power winder from the Canon AE-1/AT-1 is a simple one-hand operation.
5. The Canon power winder contains a cut-out slot to store the dime-sized cover plate that must be removed from the camera baseplate for attachment.

it is no less convenient than the camera is ordinarily.

DO YOU NEED AN AUTO WINDER?—Obviously, no—you don't *really* need one, but there's no doubt that it is a considerable convenience in several ways. It's probably the greatest boon for those who view with their left eye. If you're one of these unfortunate souls, you know the problem of trying to advance film quickly without losing continuity of shooting and composition by removing the camera from your eye—you're continually poking your

nose or jabbing your eye with that right thumb. The auto winder removes that problem once and for all, and if you can live with the increased size, bulk and weight of your SLR with the winder attached, you'll probably never be without it.

Its next greatest value comes in shooting pictures of people, where you often find the best expressions coming immediately after your subject hears the shutter click. With an auto winder, you can surprise them with a second shot right after the first and capture fleeting changes of expression while retaining composition.

Those interested in nature, wildlife or other such specialized areas of photography will find an auto winder invaluable, as some are equipped with provisions for connecting an intervalometer and/or a radio-controlled or electric shutter release. These can be used in conjunction with bulk film magazines which replace the camera back for remote control, time-lapse or self-actuating photography of subjects like animals, where the camera can be operated from a distance, your subject operates it by triggering the shutter by its presence, or you set the camera up and leave it to take pictures at periodic intervals while you do something else.

Because of their increased level of operational noise—click, whirr, click, whirr—you'll find times when it's inadvisable to use an auto winder (such as during a wedding ceremony), despite

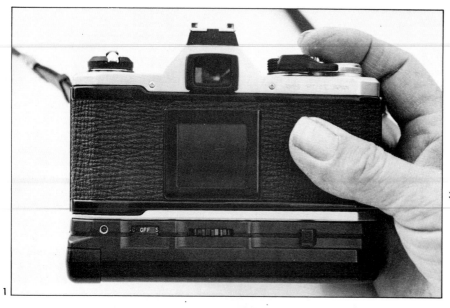

1. All controls are located on the back of the Pentax MX winder, with a switch position for single frame or continuous shooting. While both MX and ME cameras use a winder, they are not interchangeable.

2. The Olympus unit has no provision for winder attachment cover storage once it's removed from the camera baseplate, and is thus easily lost. Carry a spare or two in your gadget bag, as using the camera this way will invite dust, dirt and other contamination to enter the camera body.

3. Buy a solid, sturdy tripod with large operating knobs and a camera platform larger than your camera. Controls should operate with fluid precision and feature fast, sure locking and unlocking.

4. When using telephoto lenses over 200mm in focal length, the use of a tripod is a virtual necessity if you expect sharp pictures.

propriate for your desires, and as we know, this situation can easily be repeated several times in the next few years as winder technology moves into its second and third generation.

CAMERA SUPPORTS

There are many times when hand-holding your camera will be out of the question if you expect to get the best possible results from it: using long, heavy telephoto lenses; photographing sunsets and other relatively immobile or static subjects under low light conditions; working with perspective control optics to maintain the linearity of horizontal and vertical lines; and countless other applications.

Few photographers that I know really enjoy the prospects of working with a camera support—they're bulky, heavy and cumbersome to use in many cases, or so the folklore goes. Such supports are available in as many forms as human ingenuity can devise, but all do essentially the same thing: they provide a solid, steady support for taking pictures at shutter speeds of 1/30 second or slower.

While many photographers *can* hand-hold their camera at 1/60 second or faster without difficulty, it wouldn't be a bad idea to test yourself. Shoot a half-cartridge of film with a static object as your subject and use a

the temptation to do so. For the most part, using an auto winder is an addictive process; those who never bother to investigate one will probably never miss it, but once you do acquire (or use) one, you'll quickly come not only to appreciate it, but also to depend upon the convenience it provides. However, you shouldn't count on getting better pictures just because you have a winder—like any other accessory, how it is used is of more consequence than simply having it.

IN PERSPECTIVE—Earlier, I mentioned considering your camera purchase in terms of the winder available and its features. Just to prevent undue importance from being attached to my suggestion, the best approach is first to analyze the total requirements that you anticipate placing on a camera "system," and then narrow your possible selection to a couple of camera choices without letting the winder enter

the picture. At this time, you should then consider what each winder has to offer. For those with specialized needs, such as a provision for remote control operation, the winder might well make a difference and thus prove to be helpful in narrowing your choice to a single camera model or system—after all, no matter how fascinating, it's still only an accessory and should not dictate your choice completely.

Those who already own one of the models that will accept an auto winder will be limited to the features of the one manufactured to fit it. It's highly unlikely that you can justify trading in your equipment and starting over with a different camera brand just because the winder may not have all the features offered by a competitor. Remember, this is still a relatively new field and it is moving rapidly at this point—trade today, and tomorrow you may find a new design that's even more ap-

4

variety of shutter speeds, then finish off the cartridge with the camera firmly mounted to a secure tripod. When the film is processed, examine the results with a high-powered magnifier and determine what your lower shutter speed limit appears to be, then regard slower speeds as camera support situations. But before you do that, let's examine the various practical forms of camera supports (many are highly impractical) and how to select one.

TRIPODS—While a tripod isn't the only form of camera support that can be used to do the job, it is the *best*, if properly chosen and correctly used. Gunstocks, monopods, shoulder pods and grip pods all have their place in photography, but a tripod is by far the best possible insurance against camera movement. Yet you must be careful when it comes to determining your most important criteria for selection.

Most amateurs consider cost, size and weight to be most important—in that order. And although unfortunate, it's also true that most tripods are sold by these three factors. Buying the least expensive, smallest and lightest tripod is self-defeating, but if you were to stand in camera shops for a week as I have, you'd be amazed at just how many of the customers assume that if the three-legged monsters are small

enough and light enough to be carried easily, then they should be inexpensive. They feel that they shouldn't pay more than they absolutely have to for something that they'll probably use very little anyway.

Strangely enough, customers are willing to spend up to $1000 or more for a camera outfit without even blinking an eye, but how they begrudge the price of an appropriate tripod! For some reason, most try to keep their capital outlay for one below $30, if at all possible. Those readers who own such a tripod most likely have one that is not suited for their real needs.

If money were of no object, buying the steadiest, sturdiest tripod would pose no problem. But just as the smallest, lightest and most compact is not always the one best suited for your needs, neither is the sturdiest, steadiest tripod. Certainly, you wouldn't carry a 100-pound wooden tripod on your back as did the old-time photographers trekking through the wilderness, nor would you outfit yourself with a mule to carry the tripod and your equipment. So a certain amount of compromise is required when it comes to the selection of a tripod. The trick is to find the unit that involves the least amount of compromise while doing an adequate and efficient job.

Portability *is* a prime requisite of any tripod, but it's also the first feature that you should be willing to compromise. Those nine-sectioned legs which extend to form a 60-inch tripod. may be dandy for carrying, but they are so insubstantial once they're extended that they often invite shake from the nearest passing breeze. Ideally, the extended tripod should be absolutely rigid, with no tendency to waver or buckle when the weight of a camera and lens is applied to its top. Whether of U-channel or tubular construction, a two-section tripod is the best, a three-section one is perhaps a better all-around compromise and a four-section unit is usable only if you absolutely need that added 5-6 inches of height to meet the next requirement. Should you decide upon a three- or four-section unit, consider the center-pole leg braces which have certain advantages.

Those geared-center-column arrangements are also useful for making quick vertical adjustments, but the tripod should be sufficiently tall when the legs are fully extended to be used without having to crank up the column under most circumstances. Balancing a camera and heavy lens atop that solitary pole extended another 6-9 inches or more above the tripod only defeats the purpose of having chosen three solid legs to begin with.

Although just as important as selecting a tripod of sufficient height and sturdy design, the choice of pan head is equally overlooked by many enthusiasts. Since most inexpensive tripods come equipped with an inexpensive head, the amateur buys one and gets the other without bothering to consider that the two units are separate entities even though they are used together. If you have one of the old-fashioned ball/socket heads, get rid of it—they're not only outmoded but most are strained to their capacity when a moderately heavy camera and lens are fitted to the camera platform.

The camera platform of a good, solid pan head should be sufficient in size to hold the largest camera you can reasonably expect to use with it. It should revolve (pan) smoothly, tilt easily and lock securely in whatever position you decide on. While some heads use a single lever for both functions, those equipped with separate controls seem easier for many to use efficiently. The platform slotting should be sufficient to provide for balanced mounting of the camera body. Its tripod-attaching screw should be adequate in length to seat completely in the camera's tripod socket, and the wedging screw used to lock the attaching screw should be large enough to operate easily and attach the camera securely.

Quick-release features are popular on some pan heads these days, and a variety of such adapters have been marketed by accessory manufacturers. These usually work by attaching one portion of the release mechanism to the pan head and the other to the camera's tripod socket. Slip the two pieces together and flip a switch, turn a locking nut or slide a clamping device into place and the camera is supposedly secured to the tripod; reverse the procedure and you can separate them instantly, or so the sales pitch tells us.

Do you need the quick-release feature? Probably not—most that I've seen that are truly reliable require almost the same, if not more time and effort to operate than you'd spend releasing the wedging screw and spinning the attaching screw from the tripod—and the occasions when you need to attach or release your camera from a tripod very rapidly are few and far between. I'm certain that several manufacturers of such devices will take me to task for such an attitude, but I'd recommend that you forego the use of a quick-release device, especially when using long focal length lenses. For the most part, they simply introduce another weak link in what is already a tenuous chain, and the ones I've seen that are really solid and firm in use have not proven very handy for me to operate.

As there are literally dozens and dozens of tripods available these days, with more arriving on the market every month, a thorough examination of the various models can really cloud the issue if you're not firmly committed to the basic essentials. Don't let the addition of novelties such as quick-release mechanisms, spirit levels, and pan head markings for panoramic photography sway you from your real purpose—locating a solid, sturdy and functional tripod that you will not quickly outgrow as your interest in photography expands. Don't be afraid to consider *all* potential uses for your tripod when shopping around. Some permit leg adjustment to use the tripod almost at ground level, others allow the pan head to be removed and mounted to the bottom of the center column for low angle, close-up or copy work. But whenever you do consider such a special feature, make certain that it does not contribute to instability when used.

TRIPOD CARRY STRAPS—Lack of

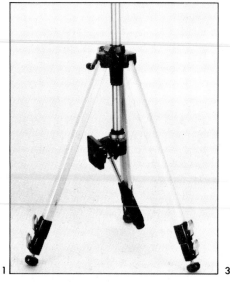

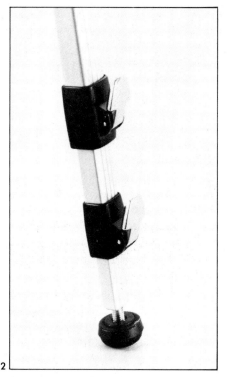

1. The reversible center column offered by the Prinz tripod shown (and other similar designs) is useful for copy work and close-up photography.
2. Whether channel or tubular in design, tripod legs should be easily adjusted and lock securely once the proper height is selected.
3. The center column of this Prinz tripod is geared, making precise adjustment far easier than those that are only tubular.
4. A locking cable release is necessary for time exposures with today's cameras. Set the shutter on B, depress the plunger and turn the locking screw to hold the plunger in and the shutter open. When the exposure is over, release the screw and the plunger will return, which will close the shutter.
5. Tripod-totes or carry straps such as these offered by Ambico are one useful way of carrying a tripod without interfering with your normal routine.

portability is probably the biggest complaint about working with a tripod. To make things a bit easier, you might consider purchasing a carry strap arrangement. These are especially designed for use with tripods and let you sling one over your shoulder much as you would do with a rifle. While some designs can prove a little awkward to install and remove quickly, others are clip-on, clip-off and work rather well.

Readers who search hard enough can even find a tripod quiver; this soft-vinyl carrying arrangement is similar to the quiver design used by Indians to carry arrows in days past, and is slung over the shoulder in a similar manner. There are also other types of tripod carry cases available, some with shoulder straps and others with handles. These may have either a top closure or

remain open like golf club bags.

Regardless of which arrangement you find most appealing, a carry strap, case or quiver will take the tripod out of your hands, freeing them for climbing, carrying other equipment, etc. If you plan on hiking or traveling more than short distances with your tripod and other equipment, some carrying arrangement should be considered to make the tripod more portable and keep it out of your way.

CABLE RELEASES/AIR RELEASES— While these devices more appropriately deserve a section all their own, the use of a cable release is highly recommended with the use of a tripod. Why go to all the trouble to provide a firm support for your camera if you're going to jar or wiggle it at the last second by pushing down on the shutter button with your finger?

Cable releases are nothing more than a flexible metal rod or plunger housed in a cloth, metal or vinyl tube that screw into or over the shutter release button to permit tripping the

4

shutter from a distance without touching the camera. These are available in various lengths to 36 inches, and will have either a straight or tapered screw-in thread, or a special fitting for Leica/Nikon models.

When buying one, fit it to your camera in the store and make certain that it works properly—don't take the salesman's word that a given cable release will work perfectly with your camera. Depending upon the design, it's possible that the end of the flexible metal rod may not protrude sufficiently when the release end is fully depressed to operate your shutter linkage properly.

Cable release design has changed very little in the past century, but you might consider one with a finger grip or support and a locking screw. The grip makes holding the end of the release easier and once the release has tripped the shutter, the locking screw can be tightened. This holds the cable pressure on the shutter linkage for lengthy time exposures without requiring that you stand beside the camera and hold the end of the release depressed. Because cable releases are small and often regarded as insignificant, it's a good idea to buy several. They're easily lost or misplaced by some of us, but even worse, they're the type of accessory you can never seem to find when you want them.

There are also a variety of air release devices that function in a manner similar to a cable release, but instead 5 of depressing a metal plunger to trip the shutter, you squeeze a rubber ball and air pressure operates a pneumatic trip pin. While cable releases are limited in length to about 36 inches, air releases come in lengths up to 20 feet, and if necessary, can be activated by foot pressure. The cost-conscious or gadget-happy photographer will be interested in those dual-purpose air releases which can be converted for use as a blower brush for use in camera cleaning.

HAND-HELD SUPPORTS—These are generally divided into three major categories: monopods, chestpods and shoulder braces, which includes gunstock designs. When compared to a tripod, most are lighter in weight and considerably more portable, but each type offers its own advantages and disadvantages. Those who are nature fans or enjoy hiking with their camera will find a monopod useful, as it can double as a walking stick. Monopods are single extendable tripod legs that screw into the camera's tripod socket and can be adjusted to a suitable height while offering some support for hand-held photography.

Manufacturers offer a considerable variety of monopods, most of which work quite well in providing support. But if you're trying to follow action where the subject not only moves across your field of view, but also at varying distances from the camera, you'll soon discover one of the major limitations of the monopod—it's one-third of a tripod.

Chestpods attach to the camera, transferring some of its weight from the arms to the body via a neckstrap and bracing arm that rests against your chest or waist. Ideal for use in close quarters and those times when you want to lug only a minimum of equipment with you, many chestpods can be easily fitted into your pocket for carrying. These are primarily useful for helping to steady long telephoto lenses.

Shoulder braces and gunstocks offer the most support but do so by sacrificing some of the portability and convenience of the monopod or chestpod. Virtually all are equipped with a sling for over-the-shoulder carrying; a few are even designed to fit into an optional sheath-type carrying case. As the camera/lens combination can be attached to a brace or gunstock for carrying, these are instantly ready for action whenever you are. Most are adjustable to the physical build of the user as well as to the equipment and some are even multiple-function, con-

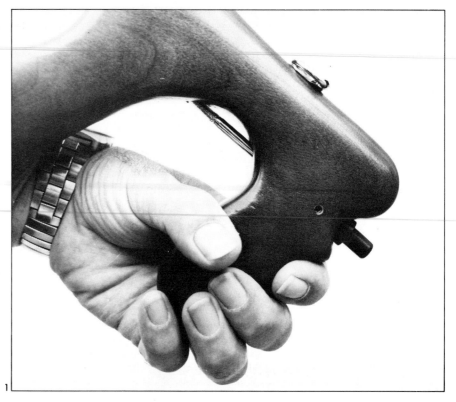

1. The cap-covered plunger of this Dasco gunstock saves much wear and tear on your trigger finger.

2. This zigzag slotting of a gunstock's support platform looks like a good idea, but try to mount the camera and you'll discover just how difficult it makes precise placement.

3. Camera supports come in all sizes and shapes. This Swagman offered by Porter's Camera Store, Box 628, Cedar Rapids, Iowa is especially useful in that it can be used as either a chest pod or bipod.

4. Spiratone's Dual-Range Telegrip uses an octagonal rather than the usual round tubing and will support a 750mm mirror lens without difficulty.

5. One-third of a tripod, the monopod is a single extendable tripod leg which can be adjusted for height. When collapsed, it makes an ideal walking stick and can also be used to drive off those unwelcome admirers.

verting to a chestpod or even a bipod for added versatility. You might consider the use of a shoulder brace or gunstock for action subjects, while a tripod would be better suited for static or immobile ones.

Unfortunately, not all such supports are created equal, and with the variety of available designs, making the wrong choice can aggravate, rather than solve your problems in hand-holding a camera. The first and most important consideration is that of *weight*. There's definitely a limit to the amount of weight an individual can comfortably hold at eye-level for any extended period of time, and this limit varies considerably from one person to another. Those interested in telephotography

should consider the current trend in long lens design toward more compact and lighter lenses before fitting their equipment to an overly heavy or bulky support.

A second, and related consideration is that of *balance*. The support used should offset as much as possible any awkward balance created by fitting a long lens to a camera body. Once attached to your equipment, the support should lend itself to normal and easy handling. Should a telephoto lens extend too far beyond the end of the support in use, you'll find it necessary to really dig the end of the brace into your shoulder or chest when using it, and this can prove tiring.

Once you've brought the support to

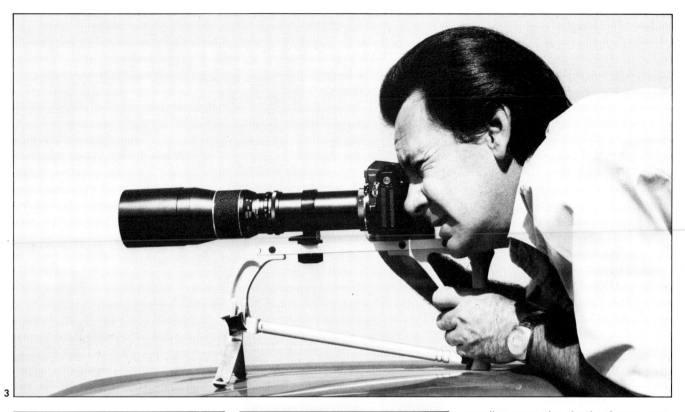

3

4

5

a shooting position, it should be fairly *comfortable* and *not interfere with accessibility* to the focus ring, zoom ring or other camera/lens controls. With braces and gunstocks, pay particular attention to how comfortably the shoulder end fits in with the contour of your body.

Consider the *degree of adjustment* which the support provides. Some of us have shorter or longer arms than the average person, and for maximum comfort, the amount of adjustment should be sufficient to place the camera at a proper distance for easy viewing when the support is brought up to its correct position for use. If you have to bend forward or backward to see through the viewfinder, it will affect comfort as well as the degree of stability offered by the support. Adjustment controls provided should be easy to grasp and operate, but should also lock securely in place.

Don't overlook the amount of difficulty encountered when fastening your camera and/or lens to the support

platform. Some platforms are far too close to the support rail; this is especially true with braces and gunstocks. This can be a deciding factor for those with large fingers, because mounting the equipment to the platform will require considerable fumbling with the tripod fitting screw. The size and shape of the platform should also be considered in relation to the location of your camera's tripod socket. If the tripod socket is located at one end of the camera's baseplate, and the support platform is very narrow or insufficiently slotted, you may find it impossible to mount the camera in a comfortable viewing position. Some tripod fitting screws extend higher above their support platforms than others, and de-

pending upon the depth of your camera or lens's tripod socket, may require the use of a washer or two if you wish to tighten the equipment securely and keep it from sliding around.

Shoulder braces use a cable release to trip the camera's shutter; these are usually mounted beneath the main support rail, secured to or through the front grip and activated by the index finger. How smoothly the release will operate depends upon its length and the degree of bend in the cable once it's attached to the camera. Generally speaking, the longer the cable release and the more gentle the bend, the less pressure required to trip the shutter. While all releases will operate smoothly enough when not connected to a camera, the actual amount of pressure required and the smoothness of release can only be determined with the camera mounted and the release connected. You should pay particular attention to this problem and to the release end that is operated by your finger. Those fitted with a button over the standard release shaft will be more convenient to operate, especially if the amount of pressure required is high.

While more portable than most tripods, many shoulder braces and gunstocks will not fit easily into a standard gadget bag. For this reason, you should decide in advance how you plan to carry one with you. You'll find some delightful supports are equipped with the cheapest of carrying straps and their method of connection can be

1

2

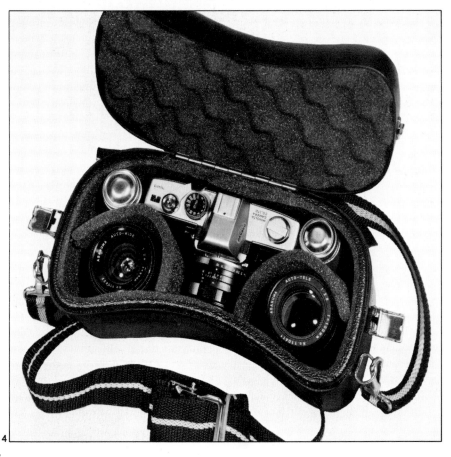

3

quite flimsy. You'll also find that some supports just do not hang right when placed over the shoulder, and it's not uncommon to find sharp metal edges that are likely to dig into your body and cause discomfort while carrying.

You should also be concerned with the *durability* of the support—how well will it stand up under use? If you plan only occasional use for it, virtually any of the available supports will perform quite adequately. But if you expect to make considerable use of a hand-held support you will find that durability is a very important consideration. Choose a design that is well enough constructed to stand up under repeated use without developing a wobble in the main support rail, eventual wear in the adjustment controls, or breaking the carrying strap. Don't overlook the comfort factor, since you'll be giving the support more than just an occasional workout and if it isn't comfortable to use, you'll gradually find yourself neglecting to take it along—a self-defeating solution to hand-holding the camera steady under adverse conditions.

GRIP PODS—These hand units are designed to function as a tabletop tripod,

4

camera handgrip and/or bracing device. One that's properly designed and well constructed can be a very useful addition to your support equipment, as it can be tucked in a gadget bag, handbag or carried in a coat or pants pocket without difficulty. Virtually all designs utilize a locking ball/socket arrangement at one end to attach and position the camera, and three fold-out legs at the other to form a stable base. Both are vital points of concern when selecting a grip pod from the many available, and as with the cable release, you should try one with your camera before settling upon a given make or brand.

The ball/socket arrangement should operate freely and smoothly until the locking screw is tightened securely. If there's still play in the head components, pass up that brand and try another. You'll be attaching at least two pounds and probably more, and if the ball/socket contains any play under these circumstances, the unit will be useless to you.

Check the legs for both construction design and the manner in which they are stored. Legs should be metal rath-

1. The ISE grip pod makes a handy handle. Grip pod designs vary widely, as does their construction, so shop carefully.
2. By extending the ISE grip pod legs and tilting the ball joint to the proper angle, it can be turned into a miniature shoulder pod that's amazingly effective with 105mm and shorter lenses when slow shutter speeds and a wide open aperture is a necessity.
3. When shopping for a carrying case, know roughly what you expect of it and what you want to pay before entering the store, then examine each design of interest with care, considering the factors discussed in the text.
4-6. How useful the case will prove in actual use is of prime importance. Traditional gadget bag designs (5) may be difficult to get into easily and quickly; preformed cases like the Vivitar Enduro (6) and Kustom Traveler (4) have their top hinged at the outside and are far more useful.

er than ABS plastic, and should be retractable for storage *within* the grip instead of simply folding into the side of the unit, popping out when a button is released.

Some of these units are also extendable, but I'd recommend that you approach such designs with caution. Since the basic requirement for a grip pod is stability, every compromise made to a single-section unit only serves to weaken the premise for its use. Also, beware of those extremely compact grip pods which have appeared recently—they're designed for use primarily with 110 cameras, and while the blister package will also mention use with 35mm cameras, don't be taken in by their cuteness and small size. For 110 cameras, and possibly a compact 35mm about the size of a Rollei 35/35S, they'll do the job well, but trying to use one with a 35mm SLR is really out of the question, regardless of what the manufacturer/importer says about it.

CAMERA CASES

For longer than I care to remember, camera manufacturers have pawned off ever-ready or ER cases on unsuspecting amateurs by including them in the price of the camera—buy both or none. Unfortunately, the ER case is probably the greatest misnomer with which the photographic hobbyist must suffer. To use one of the darned things, you must unsnap and fold the top section over the camera, where it hangs uselessly until you wish to put the camera down momentarily, when the top section must either be reclosed, unsnapped and removed, or it will poke the lens dead center.

To make matters worse, the camera must be removed from the ever-ready case to change film, and then replaced. If you wish to use a tripod or a flash bracket, the camera must also

come out of its case. While it is true that the attaching screw of such cases is threaded to fit on a tripod head or to accept a flash bracket, tightening that screw securely enough to accept either tripod head or flash bracket can physically damage the camera's tripod socket. If the screw isn't tightened *completely,* the camera moves on the tripod and the flash bracket swivels around the camera. In short, the ever-ready case simply isn't ever-ready for anyone other than a casual snapshot artist (who seldom uses a case anyway)—it's really a nuisance to the serious photographer, and you'll rarely see a professional use one. So how to protect your camera?

Sooner or later, most of us acquire a ''gadget bag'' of some sort. For many, this acquisition is one born not so much from need as from a feeling that it's the best way to approach the problem of carrying and storing equipment. Those souls unlucky enough to get stuck with an ER case generally use it (more or less) until they acquire a sufficient number of filters, accessory lenses, etc., at which time they look for a bigger case and/or a more suitable means of carrying everything around with them.

Unfortunately, most case purchases are not made with a predetermined plan, or even with a rough analysis of need, but from impulse or at best, a desperate feeling that something has to be done to keep the photographic paraphernalia we tend to accumulate ''all

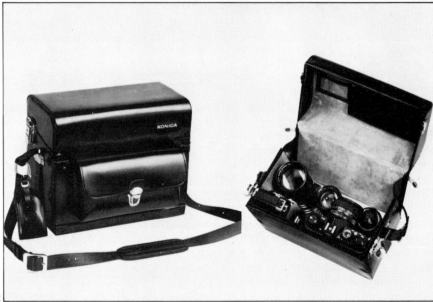

1. If you expect to give a camera case a rugged workout, consider the foam-lined aluminum type—I've found them most suitable, although I will admit that it's neat to have an assistant to lug them around.
2-5. Leather case designs vary widely in style and function—three types of the many available are shown here. The Konica SLR Pro Case is offered Konica camera owners (it will accept other SLRs too) to hold two bodies and four lenses which bayonet to fixtures in the case bottom. Exterior compartments hold miscellaneous items (2). The Prinz Cycler can be used as a shoulder bag or attached like a backpack for cycle/sports fans (3). The Prinz Soft-Leather foam-fitted case looks like luggage (4-5) but opens to hold a variety of equipment in a four-inch foam block that can be cut in whatever manner is most appropriate for your equipment.

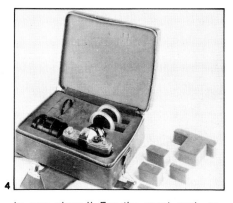

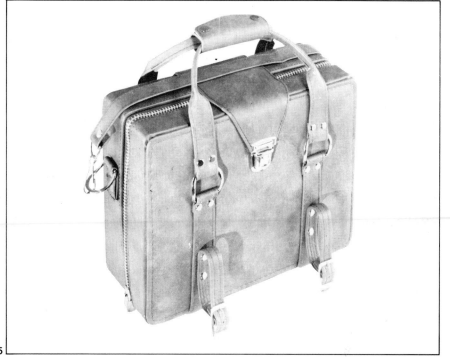

in one place." For the most part, organization and function become apparent to us only when total frustration sets in. This usually occurs after rummaging around the bottom of a too-small gadget bag for the 50th time, searching for a particular accessory that seems determined to remain hidden while the picture opportunity disappears. When you no longer need or want that particular piece of equipment, it comes out of hiding.

To efficiently use a camera, lenses, filters, lens shades and the rest of what you have, everything must be accessible and in its own logical place—one that's easy to remember and convenient to get at. Thus, a camera case of some sort is really a necessity, if for no other reason than to provide a means of equipment organization that will make the act of taking pictures more efficient and less frustrating.

Few camera equipment cases are designed and sold as a means of organizing photo equipment in a functional, logical manner. The primary purpose of most is simply that of holding your gear in a way that's convenient to transport from Point A to Point B. This can involve carrying by hand, tossing it in the trunk of a car, or checking it into the luggage compartment of some commercial means of transportation—airplane, bus or train.

In fact, the newest trend in design is to make the case look like luggage—ostensibly to fool the potential thief into believing that all you've got is a bag full of dirty clothes, rather than a thousand bucks' worth of highly negotiable hardware. It's a good ploy, but it seldom works. Most luggage is nondescript, ordinary looking—few camera cases can qualify in that respect, partially because they are used far less than ordinary luggage, and when they are, we tend to be overprotective of their appearance. Few people spend $50-$100 for a camera case and then deliberately scuff, mar, bang and crunch it to look like just another piece of luggage.

TYPES OF CASES—While the number and variety of protective cases is sufficiently great to confuse almost everyone as to which is best suited to their purposes, it is possible to make some sense from the situation by categorizing basic types as follows:

1—Traditional Gadget Bags: These are most often manufactured of leather or an imitation such as Durahide, and utilize a shoulder strap only for carrying. A zippered top closure or metal snap latch offers security, while one or more outside pockets generally have some type of buckle/strap closure arrangement. Elastic straps are often provided inside the top section for holding filters and other such small accessories. Generally speaking, these provide between 250 and 500 cubic inches of space, but equipment usually winds up being stored in a vertical fashion—and what you need always seems to be *under* everything else.

2—Pro Bags: Also manufactured of leather or an imitation, the pro bag opens by folding the top back; some use a zippered front opening for ready access to the inside. An inside shelf, semirigid dividers, an elastic pocket and/or tripod straps are offered with some models. Pro bags are provided with fold-over and snap-together straps which form a handle, or can be carried over the shoulder by means of a separate carrying strap included. This design usually offers 600 to 800 cubic inches of carrying space.

3—Rigid Contour Cases: Designed for a close, comfortable fit against the body (something lacking when carrying the traditional gadget or pro bag), these are usually made of high-impact Styrene or ABS plastic, have an adjustable waist belt in addition to the shoulder strap to prevent the case from bouncing against the body, and appeal to the active among us: hikers, cyclists, etc. The top or lid uses two or more metal snap clasps for closure and opens away from the body for easy access to camera and accessories. They are invariably compartmentalized and may even be foam-lined. Storage space is somewhat limited in comparison to other case designs, containing sufficient room to hold a camera body, three lenses and a couple film cartridges or other small accessories that can be tucked away in odd corners.

4—Soft Shoulder Bags: Offered in a wide variety of materials and designs, and variously described as shoulder, cycler, stowaway, hiker or traveler bags, these are usually zipper closure types with one or more side pockets and may even have a small snap-closure pouch or pocket at each end in addition. Some are semicompartmentalized inside with soft dividers and may offer as much as 1800 cubic inches of storage space, or as little as 550 cubic inches, although 1200 cubic inches seems to be average. All are carried over the shoulder and if loaded with expensive lenses, etc., offer little real protection against shock and other physical damage. Those who don't mind carrying their extra socks and hankies in this manner can provide additional protection at no cost.

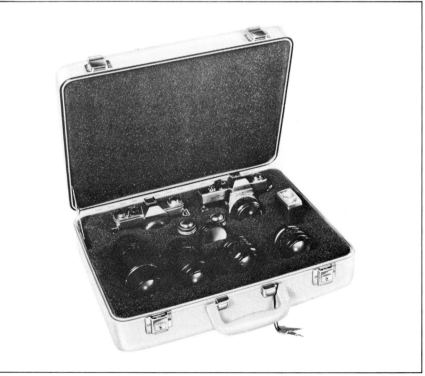

5—Compartment Cases: In addition to the designs discussed thus far, it's possible to obtain plush-lined cases in various sizes and shapes which have semirigid movable partitions, allowing their arrangement to suit particular requirements based upon the type and mix of equipment to be carried—one camera and four extra lenses, two cameras and two extra lenses, etc. You'll find these in leather, ABS plastic and other materials; many look like giant attaché cases or luggage and can be carried by hand or with the accessory shoulder strap provided.

6—Foam-Lined Luggage Cases: Made popular by the original Zero-Halliburton design, these may be manufactured of prestressed, heat-treated aluminum, of heavy gauge, heli-arc welded aluminum, aluminum sheets over a wooden frame, or ABS plastic—it all depends upon how much you wish to pay. With most such designs, the case lid opening interlocks with a neoprene seal to keep dust and mois-

ture out. Double-acting fasteners are generally used, and fitted with either a key-type lock or a separate three-digit, tumbler type combination lock.

The foam lining may be either a solid sheet which must be cut by the user to fit each piece of equipment that is housed in the case, or it may be pre-cut in one-inch segments that are removed as required to produce a cutout of the desired size and shape. Some users are satisfied with the die-cut type, but others prefer the greater flexibility of cutting the foam to suit their own particular needs. While this type of case may contain between 600 and 2000 cubic inches of space, much of it is consumed by the foam and thus cannot be used as a valid basis for comparison with other designs.

Incidentally, should you own a foam-lined case and find that the cutout configuration no longer meets your requirements, you should be aware that this medium-firm foam can be purchased in sheet sizes adequate to replace your old one. There's no need to sell or trade the case if you should change from one camera type or style to another.

SELECTING A CASE—Because few of us enter photography with a complete array of equipment to which there will be no further additions, the selection of a case is not a simple matter to be taken lightly. Today's purchase can easily become tomorrow's burden if it is no longer large enough to hold everything we wish to carry. For this reason, some advance planning should go into choosing the size and style of case that's right for the job. You should consider a variety of questions before settling upon a particular case or style of case:

1—Does it give you access to all of the contents without disturbing other items in the case?

2—Can it be placed on a flat surface safely if necessary?

3—Does it have provisions to prevent marring the surface on which it is placed?

4—Once it is set down, can it be moved easily without having to latch/lock everything up to avoid spilling the contents?

5—If there's nowhere to put the case, can it be opened easily, quickly and safely when it is slung over your shoulder?

To help you determine the practicality of a given case design, a variety of factors dealing with specific considerations such as those listed below should be taken into account.

3

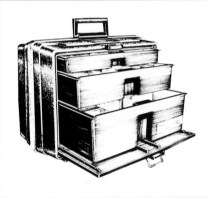

4

1-2. Polyester foam-lined aluminum cases are available in various price ranges, from the costly Halliburton (1) to the inexpensive Prinz Fieldmaster (2). The former features such exotica as a tumbler combination lock, heavy-duty hinges and strong handle mounts. How much use you plan to give such a case determines how much you spend. For most amateur use, the Prinz is most suitable, lacking only the prestige of the Halliburton name.
3. Especially handy if you're more of a camera swapper rather than a picture-taker, the Fiberbilt Adapt-A-Case features adjustable padded partitions, is available in ABS plastic or wood-grain fiber body construction and carries like an attaché case.
4. The Hoos Manufacturing Company offers a variety of innovative designs suitable for amateur and pro alike; this model 240 offers separate drawers to keep equipment at your fingertips.

1—Equipment Organization: Provision for separation of individual pieces of equipment? Facility to interchange equipment carried? Immediate and easy access to each item? Replaceability of partitioning?

2—Weight/Size: Efficient space utilization, with little difference between total bulk and useful capacity? Light weight for carrying? Shaped for ease in packing with other luggage; not awkward to hand-carry?

3—Equipment Protection: Exterior sufficiently rigid to resist deforming blows? Interior separations sufficient to hold equipment securely while preventing contact between items? Lining absorbs sharp shocks and excessive vibration? Provides adequate protection against inclement weather, excessive wind, etc?

4—Finish/Fittings: Handles, straps, hinges and locks are solid, work easily and will stand wear from frequent usage? Finish is durable, resists scuffs and does not transmit heat to the inside of the case? Access provided by the latch/lock system is quick and simple? Latches, fastenings and locks provide insurance against an accidental opening?

5—Security: Locks are strong, properly installed in the case and are difficult to pick, jimmy or pry open? Appearance will not attract attention from thieves? Provision is made or can be made for use of a personal identification tag or card?

6—Utility in Use: Can be placed on ground or other flat surface to work from without damage to case or equipment contained within? Access can be locked open; case top does not automatically close by itself? Can be moved from one position to another without possibility of spilling the contents? Access to the contents is permitted while the case is being carried over your shoulder?

7—Comfort in Use/Carrying: The handle or carrying strap will not cause

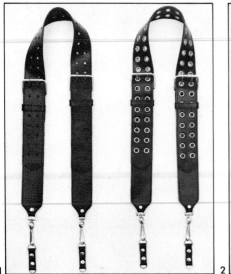

fatigue? Locks and fasteners have large, smooth gripping surfaces? There are no sharp corners or edges that might cause injury or discomfort while carrying or handling?

Obviously, not all of these factors will apply to each and every case design that you might consider, but they do give you a good idea of the type of thinking which should go into any such purchase before you actually part with the cash. It's not possible to establish that one design is superior to the others; a camera case is a very personal choice to meet a very personal need. But I've seen far too many amateurs get caught in the trap of buying and selling equipment cases in a desperate attempt to find the "right" one, and with the prices being asked these days, it's foolish to waste money in this way when it could be better spent on accessories that will make your hobby more enjoyable. Unfortunately, carrying cases are much like filing systems in that they all work well to an extent, and when you move beyond that point, the one you have becomes more of a liability than an asset. The idea is to minimize the need to change by thinking ahead.

SHOULDER STRAPS

There will be many times when you do not need to carry all of your equipment; simply having the camera and perhaps an extra lens and cartridge of film is sufficient. One reason many users suffer as long as they do with an ever-ready case is the handy shoulder strap it provides for carrying the camera without difficulty. But when you finally tire of lugging the nonutilitarian case around with you, the selection of a good, sturdy and useful shoulder strap becomes a primary consideration.

Most straps are provided by the camera manufacturer as a courtesy rather than as an accessory. A ¼- or ⅜-inch wide strap of plastic which connects to the camera body eyelets with a hook and eye arrangement is virtually useless. Not only does it cut into your neck or shoulder after awhile, it's also highly inadequate to support the amount of weight and stress you'll place on it. I can imagine nothing more horrifying to a photographer than to have the strap break as he leans over the edge of a railing at the top of the Eiffel tower, only to watch his gear plunge to the ground below—I once lost mine from atop a bridge in that same manner.

Having established a need for a sturdy strap that will do what it should without wearing a hole in your neck or shoulder, or contributing to camera damage, the question becomes one of selecting a suitable type from the dozens of styles and designs currently available. There's a good deal of controversy surrounding the most efficient means of connecting a strap to the archaic eyelet provided for the purpose

on most cameras. Obviously, no strap will thread through the eyelet, so there must be some intermediary between it and the strap.

One answer is the split-ring or variation thereof; these are available in circles, half-circles, ovals and differing triangular shapes, as well as in varying sizes. Split-rings can be hooked securely to the eyelet and provide a sufficiently wide area in which the strap may be connected. Strap connections depend upon the strap involved. Some simply thread through the split-ring and back into a locking arrangement on the strap, while others use quick release snaps on steel swivels which connect to metal eyelets in a short strap connector which attaches to the split-ring. The type you choose will depend upon your personal preference.

The split-ring has been criticized in the past as contributing to scuffing and scratching of the camera's top plate. This is usually caused by incorrectly selecting the size and style of split-ring. Use of the short connector strap design mentioned above generally pre-

4

5

1. Wide-band Camera Caddy straps by Ambico are typical of the many straps and manufacturer's brands on the market. I prefer the wide strap as a shoulder-saving device, and the rivet-lined cutout model doubles nicely as brass knuckles in those tight spots.

2. Narrow straps such as this one furnished with the camera are attached with a split-ring, but are not all that great if you carry the camera for long periods.

3. Ambico and other independent strap manufacturers provide a split-ring attached to a length of strap which attaches in turn to the strap proper by means of a snap hook-eye. This design prevents rubbing against the camera which wears off the finish off quickly.

4. Here are some of the many split-ring designs available. The leather buffer piece is used with certain strap designs to prevent strap wear on the finish.

5-6. Some straps such as Ambico's Tote-All Camera Caddy use an elastic piece sewn inside and divided by stitching to hold three film cans for an all-day shooting session (6). Ambico's Camera Clutch is an extra strap fastened to the tripod socket to hold the camera out of the way when not in use (5).

vents this problem; if not, small leather pads are also sold which attach over the eyelet and behind the split-ring to absorb any rubbing that might otherwise damage the surface.

When it comes to strap width and material, the sky's the limit. You'll find them ranging from the conventional narrow widths up to 1¾ inches, and made of denim, corduroy, web, leather or leatherette materials—in solid colors, plaids or tapestry patterns. A proper width is important and choosing it should be of primary concern once you've selected the attachment design most suitable. As to material, pattern and color, your selection will be determined by your personality.

PROTECTIVE (X-RAY) FILM CONTAINERS

By now, everyone is familiar with the antihijacking surveillance methods used at every airport of consequence here and abroad. Basically, such methods

6

rely upon subjecting every passenger and all luggage to an x-ray examination that will detect firearms, etc. which could be used to hijack an airliner. What many readers do not realize is that not only is the x-ray dosage dangerous to humans, but it can be deadly to any photographic film or transistor-operated device such as a pocket radio or calculator. While airport authorities are inclined to shrug off this dan-

ger as nonexistent and may even post signs assuring travelers that the surveillance device will do no damage whatsoever, this is not necessarily what happens.

Much controversy has surrounded this problem for photographers, some of whom have unfortunately relented to the assurances of authorities, only to end up with completely fogged film rather than the pictures they assumed they were bringing back. In other cases, no problems have been encountered. The crux of the matter seems to revolve around the type of screening machine used and the level of radiation that is emitted.

In an effort to solve the problem of those photographers who travel by air, Sima Products Corporation made available its Film Shield bag consisting of a layer of lead foil laminated between two sheets of tough polyester. The reusable container holds up to 15 cartridges of 35mm film and will withstand the abuse imposed by traveling, packing and repacking.

However, since the Film Shield bag was introduced, surveillance technology has taken another giant leap with the appearance of machines that subject luggage to a massive dose of radiation, some 10,000 times more than that of previous units. Fortunately, as of this time none of these high dose units are used in airports within the continental United States, but international travelers will find themselves confronted by one of two types of x-

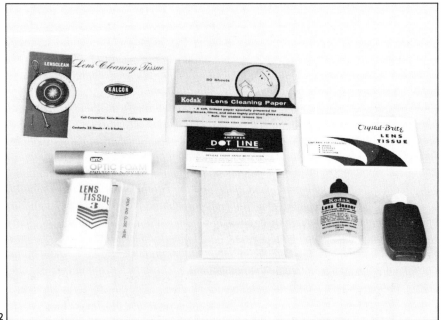

ray devices—the low dose and the high dose. Both are dangerous to all types of film, but while the Film Shield bag *is* effective protection against the low dose radiation, it cannot withstand a blast from the new units.

While your best bet is to ask for hand-inspection and refuse to subject your film to x-ray radiation, regardless of the attitude of surveillance personnel, the use of a container such as the Film Shield is insurance whenever you travel by air and carry film, whether exposed or unexposed.

CAMERA CARE ACCESSORIES

One of the leading causes of camera malfunction is neglect by its user—a situation easily remedied by preventive maintenance called camera care. Since the use of inappropriate cleaning materials and techniques can actually do more harm than continued neglect, you should be aware of the many different types of materials and accessories available, as well as basic hints on the correct ways they should be used.

CAMERA CARE KITS—Such kits are basic to maintaining your camera and

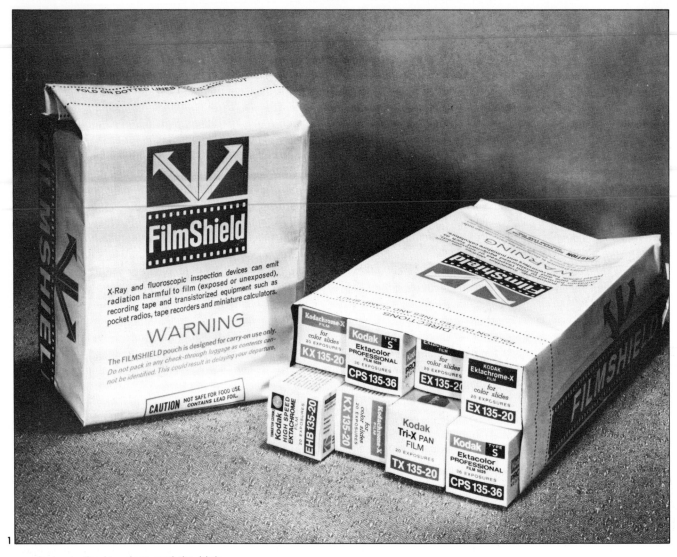

lens, and contain a small squeeze-bulb blower brush, a bottle of lens cleaning fluid, a supply of lens tissue and an antistatic cloth or chamois. While all of these items can be bought separately, the price of a kit is far more attractive

as an initial investment. If you shop around for one, you'll soon discover that regardless of the brand or house name, the only difference is price, with the exception of one or two kits that are on the market.

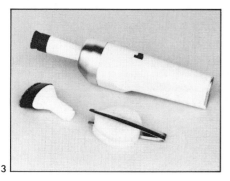

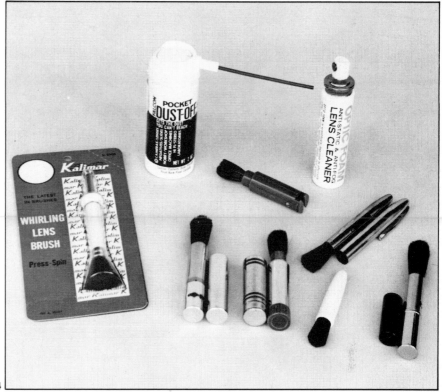

1. The Sima Film Shield protects exposed/unexposed film from low-level X-rays during airport security checks, and is reusable.

2. A small sampling of the various lens cleaning materials available; lens manufacturers generally recommend only the use of plain tissue, but fluid is often necessary to remove smudges and fingerprints from optical surfaces.

3. The battery-operated Super Auto Cleaner offered by Prinz is a miniature vacuum cleaner; instead of simply moving dust and dirt from one side of the lens to the other, it sucks the contamination into a replaceable filter.

4. Brushes and compressed gas are both useful in keeping your camera clean.

A handful of Japanese companies apparently manufacture all the others for sale under almost any name you care to have put on the package. In this case, buy by price alone and you'll get the same value for $1.95 that you'll get for $4.25. The other kits mentioned generally have a pack of double-ended cotton swabs included in addition to the four basic items, but the lens tissues furnished are impregnated with silicon, which would cause most lens manufacturers to cringe at their use—we'll see why in a minute.

BLOWER BRUSHES—A combination of the old-fashioned camel's hair brush and a syringe, you brush the lens surface with one of these and a gentle squeezing motion creates a surge of air to blow away dust and debris an ordinary brush might only move from one side to the other—contact with glass creates static electricity that tends to hold any debris on the surface. Although available in a great variety of sizes, styles and brand names, these too are manufactured in Japan by U.N., regardless of the brand name by which they are sold in this country.

Some are equipped with an attached snap-on plastic cap that protects the bristles while others come with a small accessory hose, the use of which allows you to direct air pressure into nooks and crannies far too small for the brush itself to reach. As with cleaning kits, price depends upon the brand name, and the least expensive

brush is essentially the same as the most expensive—just expect to pay more if you choose one equipped with a variation on the basic blower theme.

LIPSTICK LENS BRUSHES—These are identical in function and use to that of a ladies' lipstick tube, thus their name. Pull off the cap, rotate the base and the brush appears, ready for a quick touch-up to lens or filter. Because you can drop one in a pocket or purse without fear that the brush will get dirty or smeared with contaminants, this design proves useful in the field. Variations in approach take the form of a swing-out brush, a pencil/pen design, and the like.

Although available in a wide quality and price range, the one you buy should have one end of its bristles cemented to eliminate shedding or loss of hair; in a blower brush, they're usually molded in a plastic tube or handle to which the squeeze bulb is attached. Despite this, you can expect either brush to gradually lose its share of bristles through normal wear.

OTHER BRUSHES—You'll also find photographic cleaning brushes in a variety of other sizes and shapes. The most common usually resembles an ordinary household paint brush, with bristles varying from 1-3 inches in width, and is better suited for cleaning negatives. For cleaning lenses, the Staticmaster is perhaps the most useful, as it has a polonium strip attached beneath a safety grid under the bristles

to eliminate static electricity.

LENS CLEANING TISSUE—These are nonabrasive and absorbent, lint-free and chemically pure paper products used for removing smudges, fingerprints and dust from optical surfaces, and are usually packaged in booklets of 25 4x6-inch sheets, although their exact size depends upon the supplier. Larger tissues packaged by some companies are billed as suitable for such diverse uses as cleaning lenses and mopping up the darkroom—O.K. for the mop-up, but I'd keep them away from my lenses.

While Kodak manufactures its own tissue, the majority of other brand names are made by the same enterprising Japanese who provide the packages of tissues found in the camera care kits. Incidentally, facial tissues *are not* adequate substitutes, nor are chemically treated eyeglass-cleaning papers; the first will leave buckets of lint and can physically mar and damage the optical surface, while the latter will leave a chemical deposit (usually silicon) that can harm the coating.

LENS CLEANING FLUID—There is considerable disagreement about the liquid cleaning of a lens. In most cases, you'll find that lens manufacturers suggest using only lens tissue, but will make a recommendation about liquid cleaners to the extent they feel they have to. Most simply say to use a quality cleaner sparingly. The obvious question is, just what constitutes a

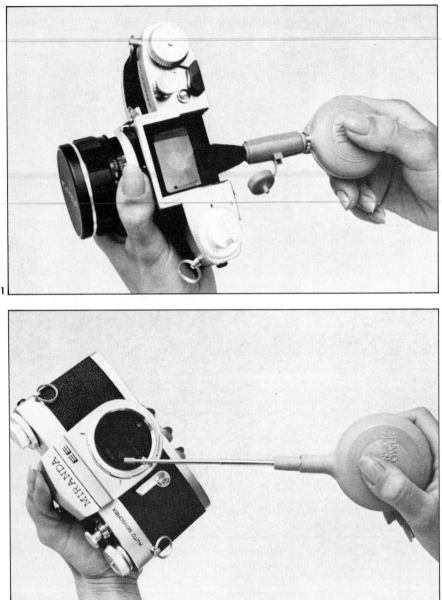

propellant in long stringy threads whenever the can is tilted in use. Since this stuff sticks to any surface, it can make a genuine mess of shutter curtains, lens's surfaces, etc. You should be extra careful whenever you use compressed gas, regardless of the brand, as it has been known to blow dust and dirt *into* the lens or shutter mechanism, where the contamination lodges and creates problems.

ANTISTATIC CLOTHS—Advertised as the ideal way to "wipe away" static electricity, these are available under a variety of brand names and promise to absorb smears, grease and oils, leaving your lenses "crystal clear" while providing resistance to misting and dust accumulation from static electricity—and all for a couple of dollars. Most measure about 9x11 inches in size and are invariably impregnated with a chemical substance, usually silicon. While *you* may find them handy to keep camera bodies and lens barrels clean, *I'd* hesitate to use one on my lenses. Despite the fact that they are designated as lint-free, fuzz eventually comes off every one I've ever tried after it's been used a few times. Should static electricity really prove to be a problem, the following device should solve the problem nicely.

VACUUM CLEANERS—How about a battery-powered device that uses the principle of suction for dust and dirt removal from optics and the inside of camera bodies? This is essentially a miniature vacuum cleaner, complete with internal filter to trap dust and debris—no more brushing it back and forth across a surface trying to get rid of it. The Prinz Super Auto Cleaner comes with two detachable brushes— one flat and the other round. You can use one for cleaning the interior of your camera, and reserve the other for lenses and filters.

WHAT YOU REALLY NEED—Unless you're a collector of photographic gadgets, all you really need to keep your equipment clean is one of the camera care kits and a couple of extra brushes. Why extra brushes? Well, the use of one should be reserved strictly for cleaning lenses, mirrored surfaces and your viewfinder focusing screens. Should you use the same brush on lenses that you clean the viewfinder eyepiece and other body components with, you'll invariably pick up some lubricant or the natural oils from your skin, which will then smear on the lens surface while you're trying to remove dust and dirt.

quality cleaner? Since most commercial lens cleaners are proprietary in nature, you won't get much of an answer from either lens or cleaner manufacturers. Analysis by a chemist generally turns up lots of water, some detergent and a bit of perfume. A trace of ammonia is also detectable in some, and in most others, you'll find some alkali.

In other words, lens cleaner is glass cleaner, which in turn is mostly water, although the water is undoubtedly distilled or filtered before manufacture. While I hesitate to equate lens cleaning fluids with Windex, there probably isn't a great deal of difference other than strength. This does not mean that you should clean your lenses with plain water and detergent, even though some sources will advise that any oily smudges can be removed by gently rubbing with a cloth dampened in a solution of oil-free liquid detergent and warm clear water, followed by a rinse

with a cloth dampened only with distilled water.

AEROSOL SPRAYS—Compressed gas in cans has made great inroads in the cleaning materials market since it was first introduced a few years ago—one or two quick squirts and dust and dirt go flying. Unfortunately, they often land right back where they came from if the aerosol spray is not properly used. When these first appeared, many used a liquid propellant and when the overzealous user vigorously shook the can before spraying, turned it upside down or tilted the can while in use (who bothers to read instructions?), the propellant was expelled, invariably depositing a residue and occasionally flashfreezing the surface of a lens, which can result in serious damage.

Solid propellants are now generally used, and you can operate these in any position, but some brands still have the nasty habit of spitting out the

3

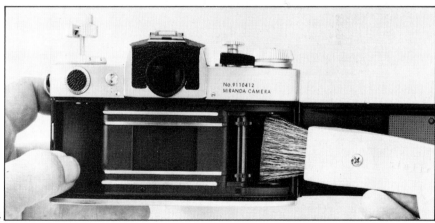

4

1-2,4. Brushes are offered in many sizes and styles, almost all of which are manufactured by the same company in Japan regardless of brand name by which they're sold here. The hinged cap design is handy in keeping the bristles clean after they're retracted into the nozzle (1), the extension tube which replaces the bristle for reaching tight spots with air may appeal to you (2), while the Staticmaster uses a polonium strip to neutralize static electricity (4).
3. Camera manufacturers will recommend that you breathe lightly on the lens and wipe off the moisture with a clean tissue, but lens tissue folded to form a pad and moistened with lens cleaner is the preferred method.

If you contaminate your favorite lens brush in this manner, don't throw it away; it can be cleaned by simply dipping the bristle ends in a small quantity of lukewarm water that contains just a dab of mild soap. Rinse thoroughly in clean lukewarm water to remove any residue, straighten the bristles while wet by using a dry comb, then air dry and comb once more before using the brush. Even if you don't contaminate the brush with camera lubricant or skin oils, it's a good idea to occasionally clean the bristles anyway; flicking them against the edge of a tabletop removes accumulated dust and debris.

CLEANING CAMERA BODIES

Put that impregnated antistatic cloth or chamois to work on the exterior of your camera. A medium stiff brush should be used to prevent dirt build-up in those hard-to-reach places as well as a cotton-tipped swab moistened with a little lens cleaner. Compressed gas also works very well here, but once inside the camera, be careful!

Never touch the mirror of a single-lens reflex with your finger, and don't rub it with lens tissue or cloth. This is a front-surface mirror and its coating is easily damaged. Manufacturers differ in

their opinion of whether to use a lens brush or compressed gas. If you clean your camera quite frequently, the brush should do an adequate job—if not, try the can of gas.

Use a blower brush, vacuum cleaner or compressed gas to clean the camera's interior, but avoid the focal-plane shutter regardless of what you use. The guide rails and pressure plate will gradually accumulate a residue of film emulsion which should be removed before it builds up and hardens sufficiently to scratch your film. Wad up a sheet of lens tissue and moisten it with lens cleaning fluid, then gently wipe the

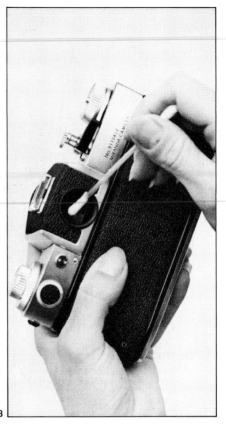

rails to remove such residue.

If your camera is equipped with an interchangeable focusing screen, you can clean the top of the screen with a brush, lens tissue and/or lens cleaning fluid, but never use tissue or fluid on the bottom of the screen, as this may destroy its surface. Compressed gas can also be used (on either top or bottom), but if your screen is not interchangeable, you'll find the vacuum device best for cleaning the bottom surface of the screen, as well as the mirror and mirror chamber, as it eliminates the problem of blowing or brushing dirt from one place to another without really removing it.

While the bottom of an interchangeable viewfinder prism is cleaned best with a soft brush or compressed gas,

the eyepiece is a slightly different problem. This tends to collect natural oils from your skin in addition to the normal amount of dust and dirt that floats around in the air. The combination quite often leads to smearing, and cleaning the eyepiece is most easily done with a cotton-tipped swab moistened with lens fluid. Wet the eyepiece with that end and dry it with the other, then brush or blow off any lint that still remains.

Many photographers completely overlook the battery chamber when cleaning their camera bodies. While this is not required very often, you should make it a practice to clean the contacts whenever you replace a battery. A periodic check for corrosion should be made every few months,

especially if you use the camera infrequently at times.

Several manufacturers offer a spray tube of solvent designed to clean battery contacts, and if you have a cartridge-loading 110 or 126 camera, go ahead and use it. But if you have a better camera, I suggest that you remove the battery and clean both sides of it (touching only the edges), as well as the contacts with a *pencil* eraser (not an *ink* eraser). Be certain to vacuum or blow out any residue in the battery chamber and wipe both sides of the battery clean with a soft lintless cloth before replacing it.

Chrome camera bodies have a tendency to pick up and retain surface dirt because of the natural skin oils deposited while handling and using the camera. This should be removed with a light application of lens fluid and a piece of lens tissue, using long continuous wiping motions, but don't scrub. If the dirt build-up is considerable, rubbing alcohol will usually remove it nicely—apply with a tightly wadded cotton ball. Either method will help restore the original luster and keep your camera shining. If you have a black-finish body, stick to the lens fluid, as rubbing alcohol has a tendency to leave a mist on some types of black finishes.

CLEANING YOUR LENSES

Wipe the lens barrel with a soft lintless cloth or one of the impregnated antistatic cloths. Use a clean lens

4

1. **Silicon-treated cloths keep the exterior bright and shiny but keep them away from optical surfaces. If your chrome is grimy looking, use gum eraser to restore a nice appearance.**
2. **The Prinz Super Auto Cleaner sucks dust and dirt from crevices that other brushes cannot reach. Use one brush for camera cleaning and reserve the use of the other for optical surfaces.**
3. **Cotton-tipped swabs moistened with lens cleaning fluid are ideal for cleaning viewfinder eyepieces. Any lint which remains can be blown off when finished.**
4. **To clean camera film guides, fold a sheet of lens tissue to form a small pad and moisten with lens cleaning fluid. Dampen deposits on the film guides until they remove easily—do not scrape off.**
5. **All batteries tend to give off a salt which will cause poor contact and corrosion. Periodic cleaning of such deposits with a pencil eraser will extend battery life and reliability.**

brush to remove dust and dirt from the glass surface, inverting the lens as you brush to allow the particles to fall off rather than simply move around. Compressed gas or one of the vacuum cleaners will also do the job when used properly. This is all there is to routine lens cleaning, as long as you do not rub or scrub. Problems develop when you get smudges or fingerprints on the front element's surface.

To remove such contamination, fold a piece of lens tissue into a small pad, moisten one corner slightly with lens

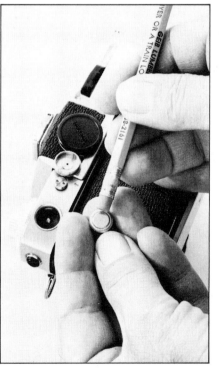

5

cleaner and using the pad with an index finger, touch the dampened portion to the center of the lens surface, wiping in a spiral motion toward the outer edge. Whatever you do, don't pour a few drops of cleaner on the lens and then rub or wipe it dry. The fluid can seep between the front element and its retaining ring, ending up

as a wet spot or streak between the elements. Should you get water droplets or a splash of chemical on the front element, use distilled water and apply it sparingly to dissolve the resulting spots in the same way you'd use lens cleaner.

I've mentioned distilled water quite often in connection with cleaning optics. In case you're wondering what's wrong with plain old H_2O, remember that in most parts of the country, you'll find quantities of minerals, however minute in size, in the water. If not removed by distillation of the water, these can act as fine grains of sand when pressure is applied to the fluid within which they reside. The end result can be scratching—not so much of the glass itself as of the coating applied to the glass to reduce flare and reflections.

OTHER ACCESSORIES

While there are literally hundreds of accessories, each of which hold interest for some photographers, I've restricted this chapter to the most useful and necessary of the lot. You'll find discussions of filters, lens cases/caps, flash brackets, and many others in appropriate chapters as we progress, so if I seem to have overlooked something of specific interest to you, don't despair, it's probably there. □

7

All About Lenses

There are two ways by which we can change the size of the image that a camera will reproduce on film: We can change the distance between the camera and our subject, or we can change the lens used to take the picture. While both will increase or decrease the size of the subject's image on the film, the relationship of the subject to its environment differs, depending upon whether we change the camera-subject distance, or use a different lens, as we'll see shortly.

For various reasons, it is not possible to deal with many subjects using the basic or "normal" lens that is fitted to the camera by the manufacturer—our subject may already be too far away, or too close to us, a different perspective may be desirable, etc. For those who have not yet bought their first accessory lens, a whole wide and wonderful world awaits you with the acquisition of an alternative lens.

For those of us with limited budgets, the choice of which lens to buy boils down to making an intelligent decision that will provide the most value (use) for the money involved, and as such, requires a good deal more investigation and understanding on our part than simply relying upon the judgment of a friendly camera salesman to tell us what we need. The world of interchangeable lenses can add new dimensions to your hobby, but if not approached with a dash of wisdom, it can also frustrate you completely. Far too many interchangeable lenses sold every year quickly find a more-or-less permanent spot in a dark closet or in the back of a seldom-opened drawer, just because their owners made one or more elementary mistakes when it came time to buy them.

But a little knowledge and a bit of foresight can make interchangeable lenses the most valuable and useful accessory you can purchase for your camera. You'll find what you need to know in order to make an intelligent decision about buying and using lenses in the following pages. With this basic information, it's then up to your imagination to put them to work for you.

LENS CHARACTERISTICS

Before we discuss the many kinds and types of lenses available, there are three characteristics common to all photographic optics with which we should be acquainted: focal length, lens speed and angle of view. While these have been touched upon briefly in other chapters, let's refresh our memory and add the other salient information necessary to understand these characteristics.

FOCAL LENGTH—The focal length of a lens is the factor which determines the size of the image reproduced on the film by the camera. It also determines the picture angle that covers the area of the subject, the brightness of the image at the film plane, the depth of field, etc. Light rays entering the lens run parallel along its optical axis, converging behind it on a "focal point" or "film plane." This distance between the optical center of the lens and the film plane is called the focal length.

The manufacturer of your camera equipped it with a lens he considers to be of standard or "normal" focal length for the negative format. Regardless of the type or size camera—rangefinder, SLR, folding or box, 110, 35mm or 120—normal focal length is approximately equal to the diagonal of the negative area it must cover. Although lenses considered as being normal for 35mm cameras range between 45 and 58mm, you'll find some 35mm compacts whose lenses do not interchange fitted with focal lengths as short as 38mm. These shorter focal lengths give a semiwide-angle or slightly larger picture image and are used for that reason. The 6x6cm SLR and TLR cameras using 120 roll film are usually equipped with a lens between 75 and 85mm.

Such lenses produce pictures whose perspective closely matches that seen by the human eye. Lenses with a shorter than normal focal length are called wide-angle. These bend the light rays entering them at a more acute angle and so produce a wider angle of view. If the focal length is greater than normal, we call the lens a long focus or telephoto; these bend light rays at a less acute angle and produce a narrow angle of view.

LENS SPEED—The "speed" of any lens is calculated by dividing its focal length by the diameter of its maximum aperture. As a general rule, the longer the focal length, the "slower" the lens. As the maximum aperture is designated by an f-number, so is the "speed" of the lens; if the maximum aperture is f/2.8, the lens is referred to as being an "f/2.8."

With any given focal length, the larger the aperture, the more light it passes, but the greater the difficulty in controlling optical aberrations caused by the bending of the light rays entering the lens. The large apertures of fast lenses require the use of larger elements, which in turn must bend the corner light rays at even sharper angles, and so increase these inherent defects. The faster the lens, the greater the design problems to be overcome, and the more costly it is to manufacture.

An adjustable diaphragm controls the brilliance of the image and depth of field in most lenses. Some, like mirror lenses, do not use a diaphragm as such, but have instead a single or fixed aperture whose value is calculated by comparing the effective ring area of the mirror to the disk-shaped aperture of a corresponding ordinary lens.

As we've seen, f-stop numbers or apertures are marked so that each consecutive marking denotes a halving of the next larger aperture, and doubling of the next smaller aperture. Since shutter speeds are designed according to the same principle, there are various combinations of apertures and shutter speeds that result in the same amount of light reaching the film.

ANGLE OF VIEW—This is the angle at the image side of the lens, as calculated on a diagonal of the negative, which the lens sees. The term is often used interchangeably with "field of view," which refers to the horizontal and vertical angles which the lens sees. Manufacturers have standardized on the use of angle of view as a descriptive factor, rather than field of view, although the latter is far more useful. Thus, a 50mm lens used on a 35mm camera with a 24x36mm negative format is said to have an angle of view of 46 degrees (computed on the diagonal) and a field of view of 27 degrees vertically and 40 degrees horizontally. Angle of view and horizontal field of view for the most common focal lengths are illustrated in Figure A.

The 16mm full-frame fisheye and a polarizing filter combine to add drama on the ground during a Mojave air race. (Ron Berkenblitt.)

LENS COATING

We tend to assume that light rays passing from the air through a lens will be transmitted virtually intact to the camera's film plane, but this is not so. Air and glass have different refractive indices, and when light passes from one medium to another with a differing refractive index, part of it is reflected and lost, and another part is absorbed by the glass. The reflected portion becomes flare and causes image degradation. Today's zoom lenses would not exist had not some means of reducing this light loss been found.

As early as 1817, optical designers realized that the chemical composition of optical glass tends to change with age, with the result that older lenses would transmit more light than new ones. Although this increased light transmission was desirable, it was not possible to duplicate the effect of nature until 1904, when an English scientist took out a patent covering the treatment of lenses with acid to create an effect similar to that of aging, but with far less time involved.

By 1935, the Carl Zeiss laboratories developed the technique of applying an antireflective coating to lens surfaces, but a single coating is effective only with certain wavelengths. By 1943, the Germans had developed a method of double-coating lenses, but the problems of production awaited more sophisticated developments in vacuum technology, and it wasn't until the early '60s that an American firm established the basis for multicoated optics.

Zoom lenses create a lot of flare by the very nature of their design, a factor that reduces light transmission to a minimum. Optical designers calculate the amount of reflectance or light loss at four percent for each uncoated glass surface. Thus, a six-element, five-group normal lens would have 10 uncoated surfaces (five times two), but the average zoom lens with its 14-element, 11-group design contains 22 uncoated surfaces (11x2). The application of a conventional single-layer coating as used on virtually all post-World War II lenses reduces the reflectance loss to about one percent, while today's multicoated technique cuts light loss to between 0.2 and 0.3 percent.

The purpose of multicoatings, of course, is to reduce the light reflectance of each different wavelength. To do so, the coating is colored, complementary to the wavelength color at which reflectance is minimal. The purple, red and blue coatings are meant to control reflectance in the green,

blue and yellow wavelengths, and account for the fact that many different hues can be seen when the front element of a multicoated lens is viewed by reflected light.

When Asahi introduced the concept of multicoating its lenses for the Pentax cameras a few years back, every manufacturer jumped on the multicoating bandwagon to prevent being lost in the competitive shuffle, but it has since been determined that multicoating does not really help *every* lens design, and manufacturers have reverted to the use of multicoating as an integral part of their optical design rather than a final step add-on in production. Multicoating has proven quite effective in reducing flare; so much so that some photographers avoid multicoated lenses like the plague because they prefer to work with flare as a creative tool.

MECHANICAL FEATURES

When you go shopping for your first accessory lens, you should be aware

that all lenses are *not* created equal. By this, I am not referring to their optical quality—we'll get to that in a moment—I mean how they are operated. You'll find manual, preset and various types of automatic lenses, some of which are more automatic than others. To make an intelligent decision, you should be armed with certain information and prepared to face the salesman, who will size up your pocketbook in many cases, and proceed according to what he thinks you will spend.

MANUAL-DIAPHRAGM LENSES—Once the only type available, manual diaphragms are no longer used except in special optics for which automation is either too expensive or too difficult to build into the lens barrel and mount. Lenses with a manual diaphragm have a single aperture ring which may or may not be click-stopped at each aperture setting. To use, you simply set the aperture according to your meter's recommendation, focus/compose and

then take the picture. The two biggest disadvantages of manual diaphragms lie in their speed of operation (slow) and for SLR users, the dimming of the viewfinder image that takes place as the lens is stopped down to its shooting aperture. Many users have a tendency to open the aperture to its maximum for focusing and composing their subject, but forget to close it back to its required f-stop before taking their picture, and thus spoil it by overexposing the film.

PRESET DIAPHRAGM LENSES—
Manual-diaphragm lenses were superceded by those using a preset diaphragm, for the most part. This type uses two rings, one which acts as a selector ring and can be set at any given f-stop on the aperture scale for the actual exposure. To use, you simply set the selector ring at the chosen aperture and then rotate the second ring to open the aperture to its maximum for viewing/focusing/composing.

1-4. The world of interchangeable lenses lets you vary image size and apparent perspective from a single camera position. These four scenes of a Ventura County (California) marina by Hank Harris show the different effects obtained with a 28mm (1), 50mm (2), 135mm (3) and 300mm (4) lens used on a 35mm SLR.

When you're ready to take the picture, you rotate the second ring in the opposite direction as far as it will go; this closes the aperture down, but only to the f-stop you "preset" with the selector ring. The big advantage to SLR users with this limited diaphragm automation rested in the fact that you no longer had to remove your eye from the viewfinder in order to correctly adjust the aperture before taking your picture.

The fact that lens barrel/mount automation is minimal helps to account for the difference in price when the identical optical formula is compared to that in an automatic mount. The primary disadvantage to today's camera users rests in the fact that built-in camera

metering and preset lenses are not compatible in many cases. Yet in some instances, you'll have to accept a preset diaphragm—many of the very long telephoto lenses are furnished only in a preset or manually operated diaphragm mount because of cost and/or the complexity of building automation via mechanical linkage into lens barrels of their size.

Preset lenses are available in fixed mounts (they fit only a particular make of camera) or in the T-2 system, which permits you to use one lens on a variety of different camera bodies by means of an adapter. If you own two different camera bodies and would like to use the same lens on both, buy it in a T-mount instead of a fixed mount, and buy a T-adapter for each body. That's all there is to it.

AUTOMATIC-DIAPHRAGM LENSES—
These are the ones preferred by most users today, as they take advantage of the camera body's automation and permit fully automatic diaphragm operation, along with cross-coupling to the built-in metering system. Camera manufacturers provide all lenses possible for their cameras in automatic fixed mounts; independent lens manufacturers offer their product either in fixed mounts for use with a particular camera body, or in the T-4 system, which fits a single lens to virtually any camera body by means of an adapter.

The difference between the T-2 and T-4 systems is primarily that of automation. The T-4 adapter transfers the automatic diaphragm operation and meter coupling from one body to another, while the T-2 adapter simply lets you connect the lens properly to different camera bodies without automation. With the advent of the open-aperture metering system—you no longer have to stop the lens down to its shooting aperture to meter correctly—Vivitar developed its TX adapter system, which provides for open-aperture metering if the camera body is so designed; the T-4 system does not provide this facility. There are also a few specialized lens systems that can be fitted to various camera bodies, but only by using their manufacturers' own interchangeable adapters, which are quite different from the T-2, T-4 and TX adapters. You should check this before buying such lenses.

Cameras using the aperture-priority system of exposure automation can use virtually any automatic-diaphragm lens that is available in a fixed mount, or with a T-4/TX adapter to fit the body. If you lose any convenience, it's usually that of open-aperture metering. But lenses designed for use with shutter-priority exposure systems require additional mechanical complexity in their construction, and you're pretty much restricted to the lenses offered by the camera manufacturer if you wish to use the camera's automation to its fullest.

RANGEFINDER CAMERAS—Lenses available for rangefinder cameras with lens interchangeability are somewhat limited because of the focusing problems inherent in the design of such cameras. Their viewfinders can incorporate only a few field frames (usually 35, 50, 90 and 135mm) and although shorter focal length lenses may be used in certain circumstances, all will require the use of a supplemental viewfinder. As for telephoto lenses, very few whose focal length exceeds 135mm can be used, as they are unable to couple with the camera's rangefinder, and focusing by scale is not sufficiently accurate for sharp pictures, as the longer focal length lenses have a limited depth of field.

Certain rangefinder 35mm cameras, such as the Leica, can be fitted with a reflex housing, which converts the camera to an SLR for all practical purposes. Manufacturers even supply short-mount lenses for use with such attachments to keep the combined overall length manageable. Leica owners today are pretty much restricted to using Leitz lenses, and even those are not fully interchangeable between the different Leica models. The sole exception to this is the older screw-thread-mount Leica cameras—lenses made by its various imitatiors can generally be used quite satisfactorily.

NONINTERCHANGEABLE LENS CAMERAS—Accessory optics may be made available for such cameras, either by the camera manufacturer or by independent lens houses. These generally take two forms—a slip-on or screw-in converter or auxiliary lens, or a front element which can be removed and replaced by another specially computed element to increase or decrease the effective focal length of the prime lens to which it is attached.

Converter lenses are usually limited in the degree of focal length change they can produce. Their power is expressed not in terms of effective focal length or millimeters, but rather by magnification ratio, such as 0.8X or 1.4X. They do not affect the speed of the prime lens to which they are attached. By their very nature, converter lenses tend to degrade the image qual-

ANGLE OF VIEW/HORIZONTAL FIELD OF VIEW					
Diagonal Angle of View	Horizontal Field of View		Focal Length in MM		
		35mm Format	6x6cm Format	6x7cm Format	4x5" Format
110°	100°	15	23	29	50
107°	97°	16	25	31	53
104°	93°	17	26	33	57
100°	90°	18	28	35	60
97°	87°	19	29	37	64
94°	84°	20	31	38	67
90°	81°	21	32	40	70
83°	74°	24	37	46	80
82°	72°	25	38	48	84
75°	65°	28	43	54	92
64°	54°	35	54	68	118
50°	44°	45	70	86	150
46°	40°	50	76	96	167
43°	36°	55	84	105	183
29°	24°	85	130	163	284
27°	22°	90	137	172	300
24°	20°	100	153	192	333
23°	19°	105	160	201	350
18°	15°	135	206	260	450
14°	12°	180	275	335	600
12°	10°	200	306	384	666
10°	8°	250	382	480	834
8°	7°	300	458	575	1000
6°2′	5°8′	400	610	775	1333
5°	4°6′	500	763	960	1667
4°1′	3°25′	600	915	1150	2000
3°7′	2°34′	800	1222	1533	2267
2°5′	2°4′	1000	1525	1920	3333

FIGURE A

1

3

ity somewhat, yet most users feel that they're better than nothing. If the converter lens is offered by the camera manufacturer, the camera's viewfinder will usually contain field-of-view markings for accurate framing; those supplied by independent lens manufacturers for use with a variety of cameras will come with an accessory viewfinder containing the field-of-view markings which is slipped into the camera's accessory or "hot shoe" mount.

Cameras using the convertible element design are limited to whatever focal lengths the manufacturer offers—

4

5

1-2. While a single coating (1) reduces a portion of the flare created when the camera lens is pointed in the direction of a point light source, or when photographing a backlighted subject, multicoating (2) nearly eliminates it, as shown in these comparison pictures which are provided by Honeywell Photographic.

3. The preset diaphragm utilizes dual aperture rings. The shooting aperture is set with the front ring (A) and the back ring (B) is used to open the aperture for focusing. Just before releasing the shutter, the back ring is turned as far as it will go in the opposite direction, closing the lens to the preselected f-stop.

4. Adding a Visoflex III to the Leica M5 allows the use of a 280mm Telyt f/4.8 telephoto and provides through-the-lens viewing and focusing by changing the rangefinder camera into an SLR.

5. Accessory lenses for use with rangefinder cameras are limited in number and focal length, and must often be used with add-on viewfinders.

usually between 35 and 135mm. Independent lens manufacturers do not offer convertible elements for such cameras, as they must be computed for a given optical formula, and the market for such is far too limited to interest the independent manufacturer. As the front elements which provide this variation in focal length are especially computed for the optical formula of the remainder of the lens, these are a good deal sharper but usually result in a change in maximum aperture; thus a 50mm f/1.9 lens may become a

135mm f/4 when the front element is changed.

WIDE-ANGLE VS. TELEPHOTO

Now it's time to take a look at some of the reasons for changing the lens on your camera, as well as some of the options you have. We'll start by considering both sides of the "normal" focal length first, then take a look at some of the more specialized optics available.

WIDE-ANGLE LENSES—The wide-angle lens has its strong and weak points. It will focus close to a subject, provides a considerable increase in depth of

field and permits you to record large subjects from a position close to the camera. But it also has the ability to produce an unpleasant distortion of perspective when you come too close to your subject, and when used in photographing distant scenics and landscapes, it can reduce the feeling of proportion to that of a single plane.

The imaginative user realizes that the wide-angle possesses considerable value as a creative tool. He uses its tendency to increase the apparent distance between near and far objects to produce a dramatic feeling of depth, which can often border on the three-

dimensional. He also takes advantage of its greater depth of field to produce sharpness from foreground to background that appears to defy perspective. And when shooting fast-breaking action and subjects in motion, he can prefocus a wide-angle lens for an approximate subject-to-camera distance and depend upon its depth of field to be sure that the resulting picture will be sharp, avoiding the need for constant and time-consuming refocusing in this manner.

For those who can't decide *which* wide-angle to buy first, there's an old adage that says that you should get one of approximately ½ the focal length of your normal lens, as this will provide a noticeable wide-angle effect. For most 35mm camera owners, this means either a 24 or 28mm wide-angle, yet many photographers prefer a 35mm lens instead of the standard 50-58mm as their normal optic. For those who like to play safe, the 35mm

is a good choice, but because its effect is limited (other than in widening your field of view), it has a tendency to bore many casual users. Focal lengths below 28mm begin to fall into the specialty category and most would advise you to consider them more practical as a second or third wide-angle purchase. Personally, I would advise that you go immediately to a 20-21mm, as the wide-angle effect is definitely present in that focal-length range, and if you're sincere in your determination to put the lens to good use, you'll find all kinds of situations in which it will prove ideal for you.

Wide-angle lenses are usually divided into the following major classifications, according to focal length: moderate wide-angles (28-35mm), rectilinear super wides (13-24mm), nonrectilinear or semi-fisheye super wides (15-17mm) and full-frame fisheyes. The following capsule descriptions can be of help to you in determining which will be most

useful in your photography.

1—Moderate Wide-Angle Lenses. By far, these are considered to be the most useful for the beginner, especially in the 35mm focal length. You'll get a somewhat larger area in your picture, but not really enough to require much cropping in the enlarger to get an effective picture. Such "overframing" sometimes takes place when a photographer does not compose with care while using a 28mm lens. While the natural tendency of most people is to use a 35mm lens from the same camera position as they would a 50mm, you should move closer to your subject when using a moderate wide-angle. This is not only good for your photographic vision (you'll begin to see things slightly different than in the past), but it allows you to make use of whatever degree of wide-angle "effect" your optic can produce.

Because the amount and degree of optical correction required with a

1. **Full-frame fisheye lenses invite flare and can be used effectively for creative photography. (Ron Berkenblitt.)**
2. **The full-frame fisheye will also get you in and out of tight places where few other wide-angle lenses can go, as in this model house shot by Ron Berkenblitt.**
3. **David Neibel found the 24mm perfect for capturing the isolation surrounding the ghost town of Calico, California. Sidelighting enhances detail to provide relief and depth in an otherwise flat scenic.**

35mm lens design is far less than with shorter focal lengths, optical distortion and vignetting are held to a minimum and the angle of view (see Figure A) is sufficient for a good deal of architectural and similar work. Its considerable depth of field is almost equal to that of the 28mm and the large maximum apertures available in the 35mm focal length make it a good lens for all-around use.

The 28mm optic delivers that little bit extra in terms of diagonal angle and gives a significant wide-angle effect.

For this reason, the 35mm is a good choice for general photography, with the 28mm touching the upper border of the more exotic wide-angles.

2—Rectilinear Super Wide-Angle Lenses. Until about a decade ago, wide-angle lenses below 25mm were filled with increasing amounts of optical distortion as you moved down the focal-length scale. And just two decades ago, focal lengths less than 28mm were almost nonexistent, but lens designers have made a considerable amount of progress in the recent past, and super-wide designs of good quality now abound, with more arriving on the market every year.

Rectilinear super wide-angles are corrected optically to reproduce a straight line as a straight line, and while such correction is very good, the shorter focal lengths do distort or exaggerate perspective whenever you come too close to your subject, or tilt the camera up or down at an extreme

angle. To use one successfully demands a keen sense of judgment and good taste on the part of the photographer if he wishes interesting and dramatic pictures. These focal lengths are often used by photographers specializing in advertising, fashion and product illustration to emphasize and exaggerate certain things.

3—Semi-Fisheye Super Wide-Angle Lenses. These are not optically corrected in the same manner as the rectilinear wide-angles, even though their focal length may be equal on paper. Despite any proximity in focal length between the two types of lenses, no comparison of rectilinear/semi-fisheye optics can be made on the basis of focal length—the angle of view of a semi-fisheye is far greater than that of a rectilinear super-wide of the same focal length. When the semi-fisheye meets up with a straight line, it curves it, and the effect increases as you move from center to edge of the pic-

1

ture area, resulting in barrel distortion—lines which bulge outward. Semi-fisheye lenses are great fun, as their high degree of curvilinear distortion provides a fascinating image-bending quality, but unless you work at it, it's easy to become disenchanted with the effect rather quickly.

4—Full-Frame Fisheye Lenses. These contain a large amount of barrel distortion; so much, in fact, that they reproduce their 180-220-degree field of view as a circular image on the film. Circular fisheyes, as they are also known, provide enormous depth of field, extending from infinity to within inches of the camera. Because of their expense and limited use, the amateur who has no specific need for this type of lens will be well-advised to forego it in favor of the circular fisheye converter lens, which costs only a fraction of what a true fisheye optic costs, but provides essentially the same effect with only a slight image softening near the edges.

The fisheye converter can be used with virtually any lens that accepts a 67mm or smaller filter, regardless of the negative format size, as it attaches to the prime lens by means of an adapter ring that screws in, like a filter. Provided you have the correct adapter, the converter lens can be used with almost any prime lens whose focal length ranges between 30mm and 200mm. For those who already own two or three different lenses for their camera, the fisheye converter can be used with all and will produce a different effect with each—the fisheye effect tends to diminish in intensity as the focal length increases.

In addition to the slight compromise in quality which the converter extracts, its other limitation of concern comes in the effective aperture of the conversion—this ranges from f/3.5 to f/90 and depends upon the focal length of the prime lens with which it is used, not its speed. When the convert-

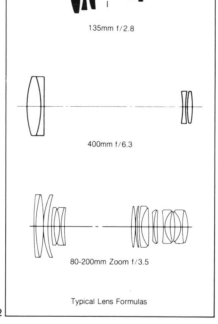

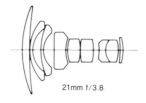

18mm f/4

21mm f/3.8

135mm f/2.8

400mm f/6.3

80-200mm Zoom f/3.5

Typical Lens Formulas

2

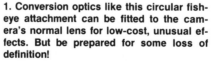

1. Conversion optics like this circular fisheye attachment can be fitted to the camera's normal lens for low-cost, unusual effects. But be prepared for some loss of definition!
2. These varied optical formulas are commonly used within their stated focal length categories, and show the complexity of modern lens design.
3-4. Two uses of the 35mm moderate wide-angle are shown by Jeff Blackwell. The wider field and greater depth of the 35mm makes it ideal or portraying people in their environment (4), while a slightly different angle of Los Angeles' new Bonaventure Hotel demonstrates its creative potential (3).

3

er lens is attached, the prime lens must be opened to its maximum aperture and focused on infinity. At the rear of the converter, there's a milled ring marked from 30 to 200 and this should be set to correspond with the focal length of the prime lens. To the front of this ring, there's a cutout containing the f-stop range (this changes according to the focal length setting) and a second milled ring with an index dot for setting the aperture according to the required exposure. Thus, the longer the focal length of the prime lens, the slower the speed of the combination. With a normal 50mm lens, the effective aperture will be f/5.6.

The converter lens multiplies the focal length of the lens with which it's used by a 0.15X ratio; thus a 30mm lens is turned into a 4.5mm wide-angle, a 50mm becomes a 7.5mm, and your 135mm equals a 20mm wide-angle. Considering this and the universality of attachment to most prime lenses, the fisheye converter becomes

a far more ideal investment for the serious amateur who wishes to partake of the flavor offered by the circular fisheye concept.

TELEPHOTO LENSES—Most beginners seem more attracted to telephotography. As long focal length lenses are available to 2000mm, selecting one that will be most useful can be a difficult problem, especially when your budget limits you to one or two lenses. Depth of field narrows rapidly as the focal length increases, making accurate focusing necessary. Apparent perspective is compressed and hand-holding the camera is increasingly difficult with the longer (and heavier) telephoto lenses.

Although it's the very long lenses that seem to fascinate the amateur the most, the practical focal length tends to be one of the moderate telephotos—85 to 135mm. These make an ideal choice for portrait work, as you can shoot a head-and-shoulders shot without having to move in so close to your subject that perspective distortion of features becomes a problem. The 135mm lens is also a good choice for isolating action during athletic activities and sporting events, and will allow close-ups of objects without introducing an excessive convergence of parallel lines.

From 200mm up, telephotos rapidly fall into the specialty category and are increasingly difficult to hand-hold. Under most circumstances, they should be used with a tripod, or camera shake will degrade image quality considerably. These are pick-and-choose telephotos; their angle of view is quite narrow and they won't work with every subject.

For those serious about photography, the telephoto is an important creative tool which has more value than simply bringing faraway objects up close, or overcoming the inaccessibility of the subject. At any given camera-to-subject distance, different focal length lenses give different perspectives to your picture, and the shallow depth of field inherent in telephoto lenses not only makes them quite easy to focus with accuracy, it also lets you throw distracting backgrounds or foregrounds out of focus to concentrate attention on the subject or to create a sharpness contrast between different areas of the picture.

Some of the medium-length telephotos are sufficiently compact and lightweight for hand-held shooting at 1/125 second or faster, but you will be well advised to use a tripod whenever

4

possible with longer lenses if you wish sharp, crisp results. A rule-of-thumb you can follow regarding the slowest shutter speed usable with a telephoto states that you should use the nearest reciprocal of the focal length of the lens—1/500 second with a 400/500mm telephoto, 1/250 second with a 200mm, etc.

To determine which focal length will be most useful to you, it's helpful to split the available range into the following classifications: moderate telephoto (85-135mm), medium telephoto (150-250mm), action telephoto (300-600mm) and the super long telephoto (750-2000mm). Each group has its own particular advantages and disadvantages, but as a general rule, the longer the focal length, the less use you'll find for it unless your photographic interest centers around specific areas like nature, wildlife, sports, or similar things.

1—Moderate Telephoto Lenses. Close-focusing capability and fast lens speed characterize this group. These are ideal for candid portraits because of their minimal distortion of features, keep you far enough from a subject to put him at ease while filling the negative area completely from 15 to 18 feet, and possess just enough shorten-

ing of the range of sharpness at any given aperture to permit the isolation of a subject from both foreground and background. Their flattened perspective is valuable for fashion work, product shots and still-life subjects. Traditionally, the 135mm seems to be the most popular choice for those who are new to telephotography.

2—Medium Telephoto Lenses. Generally more moderate in speed, these telephotos have a noticeable ability to compress perspective, and their magnification ratio (3X-5X) makes them handy for much outdoor work. You can manipulate both the subject's plane of sharpness and its perspective while bringing it close to the camera. For the most part, they should be tripod-mounted under most conditions, but there are a few which are small and light enough for hand-holding under many conditions, and more of the compact design are certain to appear.

3—Action Telephoto Lenses. Reaching this focal length, we've left the realm of telephotos that are useful substitutes for your normal lens to enter the world of the "occasional use" telephoto. These are great for sports photography, hazardous or physically dangerous subjects, dramatic landscapes, highly inaccessible subjects such as

stalking wild animals, etc.—they'll put you right in the middle of where the action is, while providing that sense of intimacy and immediacy possible in no other way. Fairly slow in speed, they usually require the use of some kind of camera support if you expect to get sharp pictures. Probably the most useful focal length in this category is the 400mm; at least, that seems to be the one preferred by most amateurs, who usually settle on the 135mm and a 400mm if they're restricted to two telephoto lenses.

4—Super Long Telephoto Lenses. Slow in speed, generally manual in operation and highly specialized in use, these are the lenses which produce pictures that really scream telephotography. Focusing is very critical, depth of field extremely narrow and their size/weight makes hand-holding out of the question. Special-purpose optics at best, these will deliver those larger-than-life sunsets you see so often, as well as many of the other highly effective telephoto treatments that

4

1-2. The appeal of the long telephoto is shown here. If you look long and hard enough at (1), you'll find (2). All it takes to pull the car out of the distance is a 600mm lens.

3. Equipped with a 400mm, you can bring an air race right into your own backyard, as this full-frame print by Ron Berkenblitt demonstrates. It's so neat that you'd almost think it was tabletop photography.

4. The compression effect of long lenses is shown in this apparently heavy traffic jam on the Hollywood Freeway. Be prepared for lowered contrast because of atmospheric haze when reaching out this far with a telephoto.

fascinate beginning photographers. While the results are impressive, so is the price tag required to get into the super long telephoto game and for many of us, they occupy a prominent place in our wish book.

ZOOM LENSES

Almost as desirable as the long telephoto lenses to many amateurs, zoom lenses represent an optical achievement unthinkable only a few decades ago. Essentially, any zoom lens will provide a variety of focal lengths, permitting the photographer to stand in one position and adjust the size of his subject's image to suit his requirements. In this respect, they are highly useful in teaching the fundamentals of composition, as you can see the precise effect of several focal lengths at one time, and frame the subject exactly as you wish.

When zoom lenses first appeared some years ago, they were large, bulky, heavy and slow in speed, as well as quite limited in the focal length

range provided, and as for quality, they left something to be desired when compared to single focal length prime lenses. But with the advent of computer optical design, multicoating techniques, new types of optical glass and several other factors that have recently come into play in the optical industry, today's zoom lenses no longer carry the stigmas of their predecessors.

With a continuously variable focal length through a given range, a single lens can provide wide-angle-to-normal-to-telephoto capability by simply sliding the zoom collar back and forth, or turning the zoom ring from one side of the lens to the other, depending upon the design. Once focused sharply at any given focal length, the zoom lens will remain sharply focused at every other focal length chosen; certain lenses similar in operation and effect to a zoom must be refocused at each focal length used, but these are not true zoom lenses—they're variable-focus optics instead.

By itself, the zoom lens is still larger

and heavier than a single focal length prime lens, but when you compare it to the several such lenses which it will replace, you see why many beginners can't wait to get their hands on one. The zoom also lends itself well to certain special effects, such as the implosion/explosion technique, or making multiple exposures, each of which is taken with the lens set at a different focal length. While most zoom lenses are not as fast as their single focal length counterparts, optical design is making considerable progress in breaking this barrier, and except for the long telephoto zooms which cover a considerable focal length range, we can look forward to faster zooms with each new generation to appear.

While zoom lenses have a good deal of potential for the creative photographer, their most beneficial aspect for the beginner lies in their ability to teach the fine points of composition and framing, as they permit instant and subtle changes in the image you record on film with none of the perspective problems inherent in changing your camera-to-subject distance. At each point in the zoom range, you can study the relationship of your subject to the background, the out-of-focus background effect, the impact of the subject within the total negative area, and its effect relative to any secondary

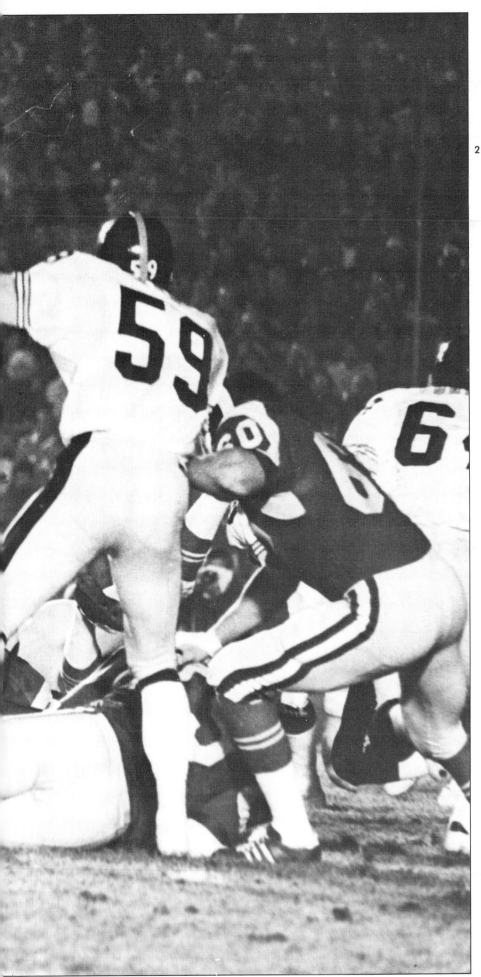

1-2. A favorite of sports photographers, the 200mm is the longest telephoto which you can safely hand-hold for action shots. Glenn Cooper (1) moved into the middle of an L.A. Rams vs. Pittsburgh Steelers game as Rod Phillips goes up and over with the ball, while Jeff Blackwell tightly framed the sidecar racers (2).

subject that might be included. Those who shoot color slides will find the zoom lens most useful in providing a quick and easy way of cropping in the camera to provide exactly the composition desired.

MIRROR OPTICS

More correctly known as catadioptric lenses, these utilize the optical principles of reflecting astronomical telescopes to good advantage. In the conventional or refracting telephoto design, the light entering the front element of the lens travels a straight path through the optical system to reach the film; in the catadioptric design, it doubles back and forth through a system of optically precise front-surface mirrors and lenses—thus its nickname, the mirror lens. This folding of the optical path leads to remarkable reductions in both size and weight when compared to other lenses of similar focal length, and makes it possible to hand-hold a mirror lens at high shutter speeds.

While each manufacturer uses his own particular design of mirrors and lenses in his catadioptric lenses, Vivitar has recently brought a very real innovation to the design of mirror optics with its Solid Catadioptric or "Solid-Cat" lenses. Unlike other mirror optics, the Solid-Cat is constructed by assembling two pieces of identical optical material together. Using a number of such spherically shaped lens elements cemented together to form what amounts to a single element, the solid glass construction results in an incredibly compact (3 5/16-inch long) three-pound lens, which lacks many of the disadvantages that are often common to mirror lenses.

And what are the disadvantages? They're tricky to manufacture because the arrangement of the mirrored surfaces must be very precise. And once this precision is obtained, the lens can-

1-5. The zoom lens as a compositional tool is demonstrated here, as well as the degree of reach possible with a 75-260mm. The sequence was photographed at 55, 105, 135, 200 and 260mm settings.

optic whose optimum focus is generally set at a 1:10 ratio for use in close-up photography. Its lens barrel permits a continuous and unbroken focusing range from infinity down to 8-10 inches or even less, depending upon the manufacturer. This near-incredible focusing range is made possible by lengthening the helical focusing mechanism to permit a greater separation between the film plane and the optical center of the lens. The barrel of a macro lens thus performs the same function as a bellows or extension tube with a nonmacro lens, but it does so in a direct and uninterrupted motion. This lengthening of the macro lens focusing barrel is often so great that the outer element of the lens ends up deeply recessed in the barrel, making the use of a lens shade quite unnecessary. Macro-corrected lenses are also available in what is known as a "short mount," that is, the lens itself does not have the capability of focusing, but must be used on a bellows instead.

The majority of macro lenses currently available focus sufficiently close to provide a 1:2 reproduction ratio, which means that the subject image on the film will be one-half its real-life size. To achieve a 1:1 ratio (or life-size image), an accessory intermediate tube is provided and when installed between the camera body and macro lens barrel, provides the necessary extension to increase the image size.

Depending upon the manufacturer, macro lenses may or may not use an automatic diaphragm. Some have auto-

not withstand shock, as impact tends to cause a misalignment of the mirror components. The hollow center of the light cone usually results in a fall-off of illumination from the center to the edge of the picture area. The size and intensity of this "hot spot" depends upon both the design and the quality of construction. Mirror lenses have no diaphragm; light transmission is regulated by filters built into the rear of the lens, or by varying the shutter speed. Because of its reflecting design and the differing types of mirrored surfaces used to transmit the light, most mirror lenses will transmit up to a full f-stop less light to the film plane than their rated speed. If this sounds discouraging, consider the advantages.

Mirror optics and especially the Vivitar Solid-Cat are far smaller and lighter in weight than their counterparts in the refracting telephoto design. They can be focused much closer to the camera,

lack the secondary color aberrations found in conventional telephoto designs and will turn out-of-focus highlights into ring-shaped donuts for spectacular special effects. The narrow depth of field can be maintained for creative use by manipulating exposure control with neutral density filters, which reduce the light passing through the lens just as additional smaller diaphragm stops would.

Catadioptric lenses are available in differing focal lengths from 150mm up to 2000mm, with a price structure ranging from slightly over $150 to several thousand. As you might expect, the better mirror optics are those which cost the most, but you haven't enjoyed telephotography until you've had an opportunity to experience the freedom offered by a catadioptric lens.

MACRO LENSES

The macro lens is a highly corrected

5

mation when installed directly on the camera body, but lose the capability when the intermediate tube is used; others provide automation regardless, and a few use a preset diaphragm. Macro lenses with full automation are often used as all-around "normal" optics by some photographer, and the newest zoom lens designs on the market are often billed as having "macro-focusing" capability. This is really better described as a close-focusing ability, as very few zooms of this breed really permit you to approach the subject at a distance close enough to provide a 1:4 ratio, to say nothing of the 1:2 ratio common to single focal length macro lenses.

Until recently, macro lenses were made 'available in 50-60mm focal lengths, but lenses with the same capabilities are now offered in focal lengths between 90mm and 105mm. These moderate telephoto macro lenses have definite advantages, especially when you're working very close to subjects where linear distortion might be noticeable—the longer focal length produces a more realistic perspective where lines are involved, and they can be used at a greater distance from the subject while providing the same image size. This is useful in

some circumstances where the camera and lens are so close to the object being photographed as to interfere with its correct lighting.

Why a macro lens instead of using the less-expensive bellows or extension tubes? One factor important to many is the convenience. Everything is in one package—no more fumbling in the gadget bag to find all the pieces, so to speak. Using a macro lens also eliminates the trial-and-error involved in adding, subtracting or changing extension tubes to achieve accurate framing and/or precise focus on the subject. With a macro lens, you simply move the camera/lens relative to the subject until the gross image size is reached, then fine-focus with the helical mount. Many macro lenses have a reproduction ratio scale engraved on their lens mount, making the task even easier. You just extend the lens barrel to the desired reproduction ratio and then find the camera-subject distance through the viewfinder.

PERSPECTIVE-CONTROL LENSES

Whenever the camera is tilted upward or downward sufficiently to disturb the parallel relationship between the camera's film plane and that of the subject, vertical lines converge toward

the center of the negative. This most often happens when we try to squeeze an entire building into the frame from too close a vantage point. The result is a building which appears to be leaning over backward, or tilting inward. This distortion of apparent perspective is visually disturbing to the eye, which rejects it as being unreal. While the effect on the eye is caused in part by the fact that we generally view prints from an improper distance and from an angle other than that used to take the picture, the fact remains that for some photographic work like architecture, such a distortion is unacceptable and must be avoided.

The problem does not exist with press/view cameras, as their many movements (tilt/swing, rising or falling front, etc.) allow the photographer to make the necessary corrections to restore the parallel relationship while including the entire structure. But other camera types do not have the same capability as a view camera, and thus the problem. For 35mm cameras (and some large-format SLR cameras), manufacturers make perspective control or PC lenses available.

Basic to all such optics is a shifting action of the lens itself, comparable in effect to the rising/falling front move-

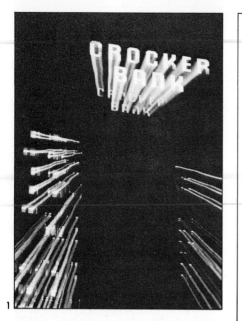

1

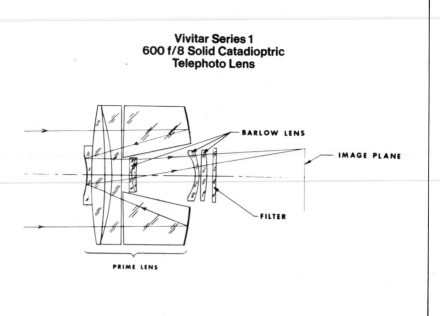

**Vivitar Series 1
600 f/8 Solid Catadioptric
Telephoto Lens**

BARLOW LENS

IMAGE PLANE

FILTER

PRIME LENS

2

ment of a view camera. Such lenses are designed with a greater than normal covering power so that they may be shifted a given distance (usually between 8mm and 11mm) in any direction, yet produce an image on the film without fall-off of illumination at the corners.

The latest developments in this optical field include a tilting movement perpendicular to the basic shift movement. This lets you manipulate depth of field at the same time you're correcting the converging vertical lines. Presently, this feature is available only in the Canon TS. Minolta has combined a feature called variable field curvature (VFC) with the basic shifting action of its Shift CA Rokkor lens. The air space between the front and rear groups of elements in a lens produces a flat focusing field which is determined according to the optical formula of the lens. By manipulating the size of the air space, the field curvature can be adjusted from convex through flat to concave, effectively altering the points of sharpness within a subject.

Because the PC lens must be free to move in any direction within its barrel, most designs utilize a manual or preset diaphragm to avoid the difficulties of designing a mechanical linkage that would work properly and withstand the stress of such movements. Minolta, at least, rejected this concept and has managed to solve the problem to provide an automatic diaphragm in its Shift CA Rokkor.

Perspective control lenses are moderate wide-angles, either 35mm or 28mm in focal length. Using them means working with a tripod if you expect to put the shift to effective use. But despite this handicap, if you chose

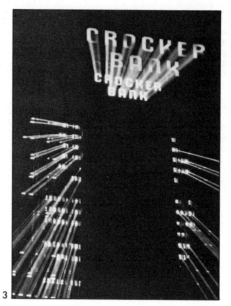

3

to view it as such, there are numerous uses for such a lens in addition to its primary purpose of controlling vertical line convergence. It can be used to shoot around corners, so to speak. By using the shift in a lateral or horizontal manner, it is possible to shift an undesirable object out of the picture area as if it wasn't even there. This application is especially useful when copying documents or photographs and you need to control unwanted reflections—you can shift them off the subject.

The perspective control lens can also be used to create panoramics; by shooting one shot with the lens shifted all the way to one side and another one with the lens shifted all the way to the opposite side, the two prints can be trimmed where they overlap in the middle and spliced together to form a single picture whose field of view is

**1,3. Creative uses of a zoom includes zooming from the shortest to longest focal length (1), and from the longest to shortest (3). It's also possible to stop the zoom ring at various points along the zoom (during a long exposure) to create a third effect similar to stop motion.
2. This diagram of the Vivitar Series 1 600mm Solid Cat shows why it's possible to keep the lens's size to a mere six inches while providing a razor-sharp catadioptric lens.
4-5. While the Vivitar Solid Cat is perhaps the most hand-holdable of mirror optics because of its small size and weight (5), mounting it to a tripod (4) is still highly recommended whenever possible. The beauty of this lens in addition to its excellent quality is that you don't get worn out lugging it around.**

considerably greater than that of the normal negative format. In addition to the control over depth of field possible with the Canon TS and Minolta Shift CA Rokkor lenses, the creative potential of perspective control lenses has hardly been scratched and your own ingenuity is the major limiting factor in making such a lens work for you. And just for the record, a PC lens functions exactly like any other wide-angle of comparable focal length; if you have one, it will take the place of a 28mm or 35mm wide-angle for routine work, as long as you can get by without the automatic diaphragm on those PC lenses that do not use it.

TELEPHOTO CONVERTER LENSES

An extension which fits between the camera body and its lens to increase the focal length, the telephoto converter or extender is an inexpensive optical device containing a negative or Barlow lens. Offered in two fixed powers or magnification ratios—2X and 3X—a

4

5

continuously variable or zoom model is also available which spans the same ratios. You may find some camera shops which still have 1.5X converters in stock; these were quite popular in the early days of the converter's design but are no longer optically adequate by current converter standards, and should be left to grace the dealer's shelf without disturbing the dust. All currently available converters contain the necessary mechanical con-

necting linkage to retain the automatic diaphragm feature of camera and lens when the converter is installed between the two.

A tele-converter will double (2X) or triple (3X) the effective focal length of any lens to which it is attached. Fit a 2X converter to a standard 50mm lens and you have the equivalent of a 100mm lens; use a 3X converter instead and the effective focal length becomes 150mm. And even though a

coverter is being used, your lens will still focus down to its minimum setting. Thus, it's not hard to see the potential of a pair of relatively inexpensive converters and two or three prime lenses in forming an extensive focal length capability. But are they all that good?

To answer this, we must look at some of the disadvantages involved in using a converter. As it doubles or triples the effective focal length of the prime lens without changing the size of the entrance pupil (width of the aperture), it also affects the effective aperture of the prime lens by the same ratio. Thus, a 2X converter used with a 50mm f/2 lens produces an effective focal length of 100mm, but with an effective aperture of f/4—a two-stop reduction. The 3X converter used with the same lens produces a 150mm lens with an effective aperture of f/5.6.

Most prime lenses in the 50mm focal length require that you close their aperture down about two stops for optimum definition—this means that you'll get the sharpest results at f/4. Add a converter and take into account the 2-3 stop reduction in the maximum effective aperture and the result is a viewfinder image that's considerably dimmer than before, which makes it far

more difficult to focus and compose with accuracy under some lighting conditions.

What makes optimum performance of the prime lens so important? Because the converter in effect magnifies or "spreads out" the center part of the image formed by the prime lens to cover the full negative format. Using a converter with a prime lens of good optical quality will deliver a fairly good image; with a fair or mediocre prime lens, the image will be poor. No converter can possibly improve the performance of the prime lens by itself—the best it can do is to retain most of the image quality of the prime lens.

This is further compounded by the fact that while the converter magnifies the center of the image formed by the prime lens, it also magnifies any optical aberrations present, as well as adding any aberration of its own to the final image. Modern lenses are usually well-corrected for aberrations, but regardless of how well-corrected they are, there's always a residual trace of one or more, and as converter magnifica-

tion increases, the resulting optical performance of the combination decreases quite rapidly.

When a converter is introduced into the optical system, its combination with the prime lens provides a depth of field equal to that of a prime lens of the equivalent focal length. Thus, a 250mm f/5.6 lens becomes a 500mm f/11 with a depth of field which is equal to that provided by a 500mm lens stopped down to f/11. This means that your 250mm and 2X converter will produce the same degree of space compression with the accompanying shallow depth of field that a 500mm prime lens would. For this reason, the use of a converter is subject to the same requirement for accurate focusing as that of the longer prime lens.

To return to our question of how good the converter is, all of them regardless of brand name will thus show some loss in image sharpness, as well as lowered contrast. Sharpness and contrast will both be better in the center of the image than at its edges, with image sharpness increasing slightly as

you close the aperture of the prime lens. To give you a means of comparison, you can expect to lose 25 to 50 percent of the prime lens's sharpness at the center, and perhaps 60 to 80 percent at the edges.

Exhaustive tests have turned up a few interesting facts about the use of converters that may be of help to you. Almost without exception, they seem to work best with prime lenses between 50mm and 105mm when used at close distances, and with prime lenses 400mm and greater when used at long range. They are not useful with most zoom lenses, as they tend to upset the fine optical balance of a zoom, and this combination should be avoided. When used with a 50-105mm prime lens, a converter works well for some portrait work, as the resulting picture will be slightly on the soft side, as if you had used a diffuser. When used with the longer focal lengths, the converter deals only with a small number of the light rays gathered at a narrow angle and so its best optical area—the center—is in control. This produces fairly good pictorial results, but the edges of the negative will be noticeably soft. When dealing with subjects which do not require high definition or contrast, such as the familiar red ball of the sun setting behind a landscape, a converter is more than adequate for the job.

MONOCULARS

In addition to the optics provided specifically for cameras and photography, there are other optical systems to

3

4

5

which photographers often attach their cameras—telescopes, microscopes, binoculars, etc. These are beyond our scope in this chapter, but the monocular is becoming fashionable once again, and as they are now offered in zoom models at a most reasonable price, they deserve at least a brief explanation for the reader, who may be sufficiently intrigued by them.

A monocular is half a binocular and makes a relatively lightweight auxiliary lens of considerable power which can be attached to the camera's prime lens by means of a screw-in adapter ring. These have been around for many years and the only thing new about the new ones is their zoom capability.

Much of what I've already mentioned about converters applies to the monocular. It lessens image sharpness to some degree, especially at the higher magnifications, but there is also a certain amount of vignetting (extreme light fall-off) at the corners of the negative. This is inevitable with the monocular/ prime lens combination and you should experiment to find the aperture setting which produces the least amount of vignetting when using a monocular.

The primary advantage of this optical accessory is its low cost—for those on a very limited budget who are willing to forgive its few eccentricities, the monocular concept represents a good, low-cost way to get into telephotography. Like any other high-powered magnifying instrument, a monocular is subject to all the other quirks of telephotography, so you should plan on using a tripod, cable release, mirror lock-up if

your camera has it and working on a clear day with a film rated at ASA 400.

WHICH LENS SHOULD YOU BUY?

Now that you're familiar with the broad spectrum of interchangeable lenses and accessory optics, and how they work, it's time to look at some of the factors involved in determining which type, focal length and brand of lens you should buy. In the past, the typical amateur photographer's selection pattern included a 135mm telephoto, a 35mm or 28mm wide-angle and a 400mm telephoto, in that order. But the popularity of the zoom lens and increased sophistication on the part of the buyer have changed the sequence to an extent; some form of zoom is generally the first lens bought today. So what should you buy?

The answer to that question will de-

pend upon a variety of factors, some of which involve how much you can afford to spend, what type of photography you're most interested in, how much automation you want and need, what's available to fit your camera, etc. And beyond these very real factors, a more subtle one can be expected to further complicate your decision. A revolution in camera design discussed earlier is also upon us as this goes to press, with smaller, more compact and lighter 35mm SLR cameras appearing on the scene. This design trend means that the entire range of optics available is also in the process of being reduced in scale and weight to accommodate the new compact bodies.

Primarily, the question of interchangeable lenses should be approached from the standpoint of your camera. If you do not have one, which

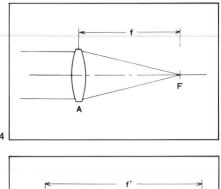

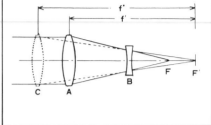

1

2

3

one will you buy? If you already have one of the older and larger 35mm SLR models, will you keep it or trade it in for a new compact model? The question of which camera is really more important than it appears on the surface. For example, all of the previous Nikon optics in the traditional Nikon F mount will fit the new Nikon cameras, but if you wish to retain the open-aperture metering capability, the lenses must be modified by Nikon or they will only function in a stop-down mode. Thus, if you buy a compact Nikon FM body with the idea of using the older optics, you should be aware that modifications will be required, a factor which has a significant bearing on the lenses you buy and use.

Once you're firmly committed to a particular camera body or camera system, you can refer back to our discussion of the advantages/disadvantages of the various types of interchangeable lenses available for help in selecting the appropriate type and focal length in view of your photographic needs and interests. Having settled upon a given focal length choice, the next step is to decide whether you will buy the lens provided by the manufacturer of your camera, one offered by a reputable independent lens manufacturer, or the off-brand bargain lens which is once more appearing on dealers' shelves with increasing frequency. If the lens you want or need is a specialized optic, such as a perspective-control or macro lens, you will probably be restricted to what your camera's manufacturer offers; if not, the field is wide open for you.

Optical quality should be your first concern, and here the camera manufacturer's lenses usually score highest,

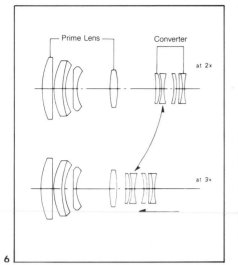

6

1. 50mm lens at infinity—no converter.
2. 50mm lens at infinity—2X converter.
3. 50mm lens at infinity—3X converter.
4. When light rays enter a convex lens (A), they form an image at F; the focal length is distance between A and F, or f.
5. Add a concave element to the convex lens and it will change the point at which the rays form an image from F to F'. The focal length of the lens is now the distance between C and F', or f''. By combining the concave and convex elements, we have increased the focal length to equal that of the convex lens alone at C; a net shortening of the lens while increasing the focal length.
6. By altering the distance between prime lens and converter, the magnification ratio can be changed. (Courtesy Komura Lens Manufacturing Ltd.)
7. 400mm lens at infinity—no converter.
8. 400mm lens at infinity—2X converter.
9. 400mm lens at infinity—3X converter.

but name-brand independent lenses may not be very far behind. For the majority of users who will never make enlargements greater than 11x14 or project their color slides beyond the 30x40 limit of their home screens, the differences in optical quality between the two sources is really academic. A more important consideration becomes the mechanical construction of the lens barrel, mount and diaphragm.

The economies in production are what make possible the lower prices of independent lenses, along with the fact that offering a single optical formula in a wide variety of mounts increases the potential market far beyond that enjoyed by the camera manufacturer, whose market is limited to those who use his product. To effect these economies, manufacturing tolerances may be greater. A helicoid focusing mount may be made of aluminum and use thick grease to provide smooth focusing action instead of the more expensive but precise brass mount with its fine and close-fitting threads. Diaphragm action may be less consistent and internal

7

8

9

baffling to minimize flare may not be as efficient.

These and other such considerations become very important if the lens is to receive more than just an occasional workout. You'll seldom find professionals using other than the lenses made specifically for their camera by its manufacturer, and for a very good reason. Automatic diaphragm operation must function within a given tolerance range, as it can affect exposure adversely should the diaphragm be even fractionally late in closing down once the shutter button is depressed. Independent lenses may very well be designed to sufficiently close tolerances initially, but under the wear and tear of continued and repeated operation, the less durable materials used in construction may result in an inordinate amount of wear which affects diaphragm operation much sooner than with those lenses whose quality control and manufacturing techniques are stricter.

The diaphragm will continue to function properly but its action will be a trifle late; the chances are good that you wouldn't even pick up on what's happened until the wear factor became so excessive as to be apparent. As you can imagine, few amateurs will put any lens through such a rugged pace, but the pro cannot afford to take such chances.

Should you even bother to consider the off-brand bargain lens? Your friendly camera salesman will most likely assure you that the white box lens is made by the same company who makes lenses sold under more reliable and better-known names, but that since the white box company does not advertise it can afford to pass the savings along to you in the form of lower prices. Sounds reasonable enough, and in some cases, it might even be true, but why take the chance?

To begin with, your friendly camera store that sells you the lens will not honor the warranty should you discover something to be wrong with the optic or its operation, but advise you instead to return the lens directly to the importer when any problems develop. Depending upon the importer, you might receive satisfaction, but there's also the chance that you might be out the price of the lens while incurring a good deal of frustration in the process of trying to resolve the matter.

The name-brand optics may cost more initially, but most such firms have either their own repair facilities or a network of authorized service centers across the country where repairs and adjustments can be made without a lot of hassle. I once bought a very expensive wide-angle for a large-format SLR and within a week after taking delivery of the new lens, the automatic diaphragm operation failed completely and I was stuck with a new wide-angle whose diaphragm had frozen half open. A quick trip to the authorized service center saw the lens restored to working order in a matter of hours, and at no charge to me. This is something to consider when weighing the pros and cons—price is not always the only factor to consider.

And when you think about the price of the off-brand lens against that of a used one of comparable focal length and speed bearing the camera manu-

facturer's name, you may find little or no price advantage, which brings me to the next point of interest—are used lenses worthy of your consideration as a means of conserving your money while obtaining top quality?

Unlike automobiles and other such material possessions, most camera lenses are not traded in because they're worn out or have been mistreated and do not function properly. Talk to any knowledgeable camera salesman with a few years' experience and he'll confirm that most lenses come his way because their previous owner (1) felt it wasn't fast enough, (2) didn't like the pictures it took—common with semi-fisheyes, (3) did not use it enough to justify keeping it or (4) was hung up on the status attached to another brand or a more recent optical design and traded his entire outfit for a comparable one of the more prestigious name or later design.

It's true that well-worn lenses do appear on the used market, but they're fairly easy to spot. Most used lenses are in pristine condition because they've been used very little and do present an attractive alternative for those on a limited budget. But there are a couple of considerations which you should keep in mind when shopping for one.

Some manufacturers change optical formulas fairly often, almost as if they are developing a lens piecemeal and using the consumer as a means of financing further development. Thus, if you read of a lens that's supposed to be a "super" optic and then look for a used one, you may well end up with a lens that appears the same externally, but is quite different optically. You cannot rely upon the salesman to know the difference, thus you should be able to research the history of lenses which you have a definite interest in obtaining secondhand. This requires a little work on your part, and perhaps a letter or two to the company to identify the lens by its serial number. Most secondhand shoppers find this part of the fun.

The other important factor to consider is obtaining a written agreement from the dealer that should the lens prove to be defective mechanically or optically within a specified timespan, it can be returned for credit. Most camera stores take a lens in trade without actually trying it out. For the most part, they put it on a suitable camera body and click the shutter several times while looking through the viewfinder. In essence, what they're really checking is the operation of their own camera

2

1. Lens shades either screw on or are built into the lens barrel and extended for use. Make sure the shade you use was designed for the particular focal length lens used.

2. Telescopes can be attached to your camera with special adapters. This 400mm is shown in use with a Shires camera support. (Photo courtesy of Shires Products.)

3. The Ritz Zoom Fotocular is a seven-inch monocular which gives you the capability of a 400-1000mm zoom lens when attached to the camera's normal optic. Fast film and a tripod are necessary.

body, but this "test" is usually sufficient as far as they're concerned.

ARE NEW LENS DESIGNS REALLY BETTER?

Some photographic innovations hold definite advantages while others are not really as great as the advertising copywriters would have you believe. When you read that Lens A is far superior to Lens B, take the claim with a grain of salt, at least until you can investigate the matter for yourself. Optical sharpness, for example, has not just reached a state of near-perfection; many prewar lenses will deliver just as sharp an image on today's films as will the most recent ones. In fact, camera movement while taking the picture, inaccurate focusing on the part of the photographer, and the use of a poor grade or inaccurately focused enlarger lens are culprits far more commonly

3

1. Lens cases come in a variety of sizes and styles. These Prinz cases are typical of the reinforced and cushioned type of "hard" case, with fitted lid, snap lock and carry strap.
2. Lens caps are a necessity for protecting front and rear elements when carrying the lens alone. Most slip on or snap in place—accessory caps will often screw into place.
3. A variation of the soft pouch case design, this Sima case uses air-filled pockets in the case wall for protection. Blow the case up and carry the lens, collapse it for easy storage when the lens is in use.
4. Soft pouch cases with fleece lining and drawstring closure represent another design, available to fit wide-angle (shown) or telephoto lenses.

encountered in unsharp pictures than are unsharp camera optics.

Certainly, there are definite advantages to certain new innovations. The use of aspheric elements (unknown a decade or two ago) provides one example. There are two ways in which spherical flare, a primary optical cause of image softness, can be managed— by using a slower maximum aperture (or stopping the aperture down), or by designing aspheric elements into the formula to maintain lens speed without sacrificing image quality at large apertures. While the latter seems preferable to many of us, there is a price to be paid in terms of size, weight and price. Aspheric elements are far more expensive to manufacture, and do not lend themselves to the present trend toward more compact, lightweight lenses.

Should you be concerned about such problems and the solutions used to bring them under control? The answer rests with you and the types of photographs for which you primarily intend to use the lens. Many such advantages turn out to be disadvantages to the creative-minded photographer; multicoating of optics was heralded as a tremendous advantage in reducing flare which some photographers like to use in a creative manner to enhance the pictorial qualities of their subjects. So before you succumb to the siren call of ''newest is bestest,'' think through the advantages and disadvantages carefully. If you're in the market for a used lens and you *know* that a previous formula had certain defects you would like to avoid, it may be necessary for you to buy the lens new in

order to get the more recent formula that does not possess the defects. But if the newest formula offers only marginal correction of such problems, it's questionable whether the newest one is worth the extra money to you.

LENS CARE AND PROTECTION

As interchangeable lenses can represent a considerable investment, often far in excess of what the camera body cost, certain precautions should be taken in their use, storage and carrying. For cleaning procedures and materials, refer to the discussion in the chapter on accessories.

LENS CAPS, LENS SHADES AND FILTERS—Most interchangeable lenses come equipped with both front and rear lens caps, which represent your first line of defense in protecting them. Whenever the lens is not attached to the camera body and in use, the caps should be securely in place. They not

3

4

lens cases are useful is an ambivalent one. Where extreme telephoto lenses are concerned, there's no question—you simply can't tuck an 800mm optic into the ordinary gadget bag. Those who use a foam-lined or compartmentalized carrying case should have very little need for separate lens cases. With other types of carrying arrangements, the individual lens case will protect your optics from scratching/scuffing by other accessories, but its use certainly slows down the speed with which you can interchange lenses.

Some manufacturers include a rigid carrying case in the price of their lenses, others offer the case separately and a few make no provision whatsoever for cases. In the wake of this "we don't much care" attitude on the part of lens manufacturers, a thriving business has grown up by firms dealing in such cases as accessories. These are available in several forms:

1—Rigid, preformed cases often lined with dust-catching velveteen. These use a snap-fastener lid and have provision for a shoulder strap which can also be used as a hand strap. This is the type generally provided by camera and lens manufacturers; when offered by independents, they're usually available in five different sizes and provided with removable foam sleeves to allow each size case to hold a range of lens sizes. The well-dressed photographer can also buy 35mm film cartridge cases of similar design/material using a zipper closure and attaching to the camera neckstrap.

2—Flexible lens pouches of soft leather or vinyl with a drawstring closure and ID tag attached. Also offered in general sizes to fit a wide variety of optics, these are most useful for tossing in the gadget bag or your luggage, as they do not lend themselves well to carrying over the shoulder or attached to a belt.

3—Inflatable lens pouches similar in type and design to the flexible pouches but inflated by mouth to the correct size and degree of firmness. They're touted as the answer to "what do I do with the case;" when not in use, you let the air out, fold it up and tuck it in your pocket.

Those who buy long focal length lenses will be wise to invest in some form of case if one is not included with the lens, but whether or not you use them for smaller optics will depend upon your personal preference and the type of carrying arrangement you've settled upon for the rest of the equipment you have. □

only keep the optical surface free of dust, dirt, smudges and scratches, they close off exposed avenues of entry to the internal mechanism and thus prevent dirt and other contamination from taking its toll. It's a good idea to have a spare or two on hand in case you lose or misplace one or more of them, which is much easier to do than you might imagine.

To protect a lens while it's in use on the camera body, many photographers turn to a skylight or haze filter and/or a lens shade. The lens shade (also called a lens hood) is useful, as it can serve a dual purpose in shading the front element from stray and unwanted light striking it (resulting in flare), while protecting against the possibility of damage from bumping the camera into other objects which could scratch or otherwise damage the front element. If a lens shade is used, it should be one specifically designed for the focal length lens or vignetting may take place at larger apertures. Most normal and moderate wide-angle or telephoto lenses are furnished with the correct lens shade. These may be separate screw-in shades, or built-in retractable units which are pulled forward for use and then pushed back into the lens barrel when not in use.

As for the filter, I personally do not recommend the use of one for the fol-lowing reasons: (1) it adds two more air-to-glass surfaces to the optical formula, which may cause some degree of image degradation and (2) people tend to have less regard for a filter than for the front element of the lens, and are thus prone to cleaning it by scrubbing, which can cause scratches and possible image degradation as a result. Despite this, you may feel more comfortable with a skylight filter protecting the front element of your lens. Special-purpose lenses such as fisheye optics cannot be fitted with either a lens shade or skylight filter, and will thus require extra care on your part, as their front element tends to protrude beyond the front of the barrel.

LENS CASES—Like the ever-ready camera case, the question of whether

Color Gallery

Hal Stoelzle

Hal Stoelzle

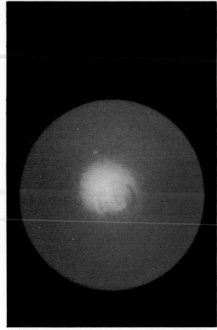

Kalton C. Lahue

David Niebel

Hank Harris

David Niebel

Ken Moore

Hank Harris

Ken Moore

Hank Harris

Kalton C. Lahue

Rick Oyama

Kalton C. Lahue

Gary Schuster

Don Snow

Michael Parrish

Ken Moore

Kalton C. Lahue

Kalton C. Lahue

Hal Stoelzle

Kalton C. Lahue

Ron Zuehlke

Hank Harris

Kalton C. Lahue   **Kalton C. Lahue**

Michael Parrish

Ken Moore

Jim Cornfield

Don Snow

Michael Parrish

John Chlumsky

David Niebel

Ken Moore

8

Filters & Lens Attachments

As we've seen, photographic film reacts to light in a somewhat different manner than do our eyes. As a result, it's often necessary to use a filter over the lens if you wish to recreate the scene as closely as possible to the way you saw it. By filtering out undesirable wavelengths or portions of the spectrum, you can alter the way in which the film records the image to intensify or subdue certain parts of the subject for emphasis.

A considerable variety of filters is available—some for use primarily with black-and-white film, others for use with color film, and a number that work equally well with both. In addition, it's possible to use certain filters designed for black-and-white photography with color film, if special effects are desired. Our discussion begins with the contrast filters for black-and-white photography, also referred to as correction or detail filters.

CONTRAST FILTERS

Over the years, volumes have been written explaining how and why filters work as they do. Actually, it's quite unnecessary to delve deeply into the theory of light and contrast filters to use them effectively—more often than not, this proves a source of great confusion and frustration, which serves only to interfere with their proper use. To make effective use of contrast filters, it's only necessary to understand and remember the following:

White light is composed of red, green and blue wavelengths, but as green and red combined will form yellow, white light can also be made by using blue and yellow wavelengths. When two colors combine to make white light in this manner, we call them complementary colors. Figure A shows

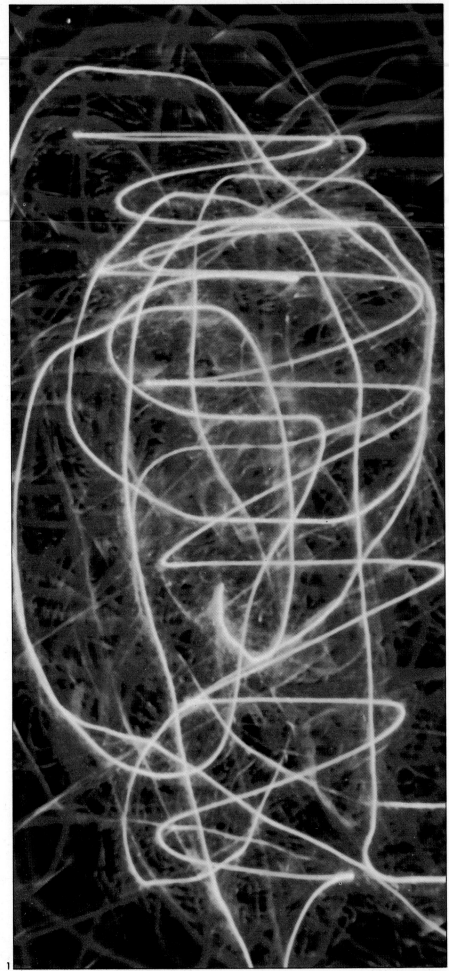

2

1. This shot was taken with a Polaroid 195 camera. A 45-second exposure was used at f/8 with a laser color burst filter taped onto the lens to catch this colorful sparkler. The sparkler was placed on a light stand to assure steadiness.

2. The careful selection and use of filters will add impact and intensify emotion in black-and-white photography. Gerald Strzykalski used a K-2 (yellow) filter for this striking sunset.

the relationship of primary colors (red, green and blue) and their complements (magenta, cyan and yellow). Thus, to lighten the color of an object, use a filter of the same color; to darken it, use one of the complementary color.

A colored filter will transmit only its own color, absorbing all other colors to some degree. As contrast filters are often made in varying degrees of density, a lighter one absorbs less of the light rays than a darker one of the same color. Colors farthest in wavelength from the filter's color are absorbed first and to the greatest degree; the darker the filter, the greater the degree of absorption. Thus, an orange filter will absorb more blue light than a yellow one, and a red filter will absorb more than an orange. Because of this, objects reflecting blue light rays will be increasingly darkened on the print as you move from the use of a yellow to orange to red filter. To see how this works, let's look at one of the most

common uses to which contrast filters are put.

As normal black-and-white film is overly sensitive to blue light, blue skies will be overexposed and reproduce as white on your final print. This hides any clouds in the sky (which are also white) and transforms what was a gorgeous view into a dull, flat-looking scenic on your print. But if you can find some way to reduce the amount of blue light rays that strike the film, the blue sky area on your negative will receive less exposure, reproducing darker on the print. At the same time, this allows the white clouds to register as white and so a degree of contrast is established between the white clouds and blue sky, just as it appeared in the original scene.

A yellow filter can be used to achieve this effect, as it will reduce the amount of blue light striking the film from the sky area, producing a near-normal cloud effect without changing the balance between other colors. An orange filter accentuates this contrast between cloud and blue sky, and a red one will make it even more pronounced. But as the latter two filters absorb increasing amounts of the blue wavelengths, greens also darken.

This effect can be put to use in other ways. Suppose that you want to photograph your green Christmas tree

covered with predominantly red ornaments. Without a filter, the green tree and red ornaments will appear about the same shade of gray on the print. But as a red filter absorbs blue *and* some green, the tree will not expose the negative as much and so appears darker on the print. As the red filter transmits the red of the ornaments, they will expose the negative considerably and thus appear light on the print.

The red filter doesn't really lighten the red ornaments; it darkens the green tree, which makes the red ornaments appear to be lighter. But as any contrast filter absorbs some of the light rays that would otherwise strike the film, it's necessary to increase overall exposure in order to compensate for the light rays that have been absorbed. This increase of exposure means that the light rays which are the same color as the filter through which they pass will also be increased proportionately, thus causing overexposure of that portion of the subject. In the case of your red filter and green tree, the increased red light rays will record darker on the negative and lighter on the print than normal. This means that although the red filter doesn't actually lighten the red ornaments in your picture, the increase in exposure it requires will. Which serves to bring us to a pair of equally fascinating theories—filter fac-

tor and no-factor—each of which has its own school of followers and should be considered whenever you use a contrast filter.

THEORY NO. 1—FILTER FACTORS

It's commonly accepted that the use of a contrast filter requires additional exposure to compensate for the reduction in light striking the film. By absorbing colors other than its own, such a filter allows less overall light to reach the film, resulting in underexposure. This filter factor is simply a number designated by the filter manufacturer to tell you how much the exposure should be increased whenever a particular filter is used. This factor is included on an instruction sheet accompanying the filter, and is usually also engraved on the filter ring along with the type/color and size (Red 52ø 8X). It may also be referred to as an Exposure Magnification or EM value.

A factor of two (2X) means that the exposure must be doubled, while a factor of four (4X) requires four times as much exposure. To simplify such calculations refer to Figure B. While this increase in exposure is generally stated in terms of f-stops, it can also be made by changing the shutter speed to a slower one. To do so, multiply the shutter speed which would ordinarily be used by the filter factor and the result is the new shutter speed for use *with* the filter. Thus, a 2X factor applied to a 1/250 second shutter speed results in a new one of 1/125 second. Figure C provides a handy reference at a glance for common filter factor/shutter speed combinations.

SLR camera manufacturers will tell you that by simply placing the filter to be used on the lens, the camera's through-the-lens metering system will make the necessary adjustments in exposure without further effort on your part, but this is not necessarily true. Like film, metering cells have their own light sensitivity range/pattern, and the two are not necessarily the same across the light spectrum. Depending upon the type of cell used, its placement and how it reads, different in-camera meters will give different exposure corrections, and not necessarily the right one; when deep contrast filters such as orange and red are used, most meters cannot completely compensate for the poor sensitivity of nor-

Yellow, orange and red filters absorb progressively more blue light, with an increasing effect on blue skies. Hank Harris found the red filter appropriate in accentuating the cloud formations over Grand Lake, Colorado.

Normal Aperture	Filter Factor							
	1.5X	2X	2.5X	3X	4X	5X	8X	16X
F/2	F/1.6	F/1.4	—	—	—	—	—	—
F/2.8	F/2.2	F/2	F/1.8	F/1.6	F/1.4	—	—	—
F/3.5	F/2.8	F/2.3	F/2.2	F/2	F/1.8	F/1.6	F/1.4	—
F/4	F/3.2	F/2.8	F/2.5	F/2.2	F/2	F/1.6	F/1.4	—
F/5.6	F/4.5	F/4	F/3.5	F/3.2	F/2.8	F/2.2	F/2	F/1.4
F/8	F/6.3	F/5.6	F/5.2	F/4.5	F/4	F/3.2	F/2.8	F/2
F/11	F/9	F/8	F/7	F/6.3	F/5.6	F/4.5	F/4	F/2.8
F/16	F/12.5	F/11	F/10	F/9	F/8	F/6.3	F/5.6	F/4
F/22	F/18	F/16	F/14	F/12.5	F/11	F/9	F/8	F/5.6
F/32	F/25	F/22	F/20	F/18	F/16	F/12.5	F/11	F/8

FIGURE B

mal black-and-white film to red. In general, a minimum increase of ½ f-stop with an orange filter, and 1½ f-stops with a red filter will be required in addition to the correction made by the camera's meter.

Perhaps the fastest, most effective way to compensate with an SLR camera or any light meter is to divide the factor into the normal ASA-EI speed of the film in use: $64 \div 2 = 32$, $125 \div 4 = 32$, $400 \div 8 = 50$, etc. Set the camera's meter at this new ASA-EI rating (or the one closest to it) while using the filter—but don't forget to reset the meter to the normal ASA-EI when you remove the filter.

Regardless of which method you choose to compensate for the filter factor—f-stop, shutter speed or film speed—it's preferable to give *less* rather than too much exposure if you have any doubts. More exposure than indicated by the filter factor will *lessen* the effect of a contrast filter, but underexposure will help to *increase* its effect. In fact, the wide exposure latitude of most black-and-white films today will take care of a 2X factor without any other compensation—all of which leads us to our second theory.

THEORY NO. 2—NO-FACTOR

A small school of thought embraces this theory for black-and-white photography, often attributed to W. Hartley Harrison, of Harrison and Harrison (filter manufacturer). In a nutshell, the No-Factor Theory tells you to expose for the darkest major object in the scene which is substantially the same color as the filter you're using, and let the filter absorb the other colors. To use our red filter with its 8X factor as an example, increasing the exposure eight times will overexpose any reddish objects in your picture by almost eight times, as the red filter transmits almost all of the red light. This will result in the loss of a lot of detail in the red objects in your final print. Let's see why this occurs.

	COLOR RELATIONSHIPS		
	This Color Filter:	Will Absorb (darken) This Color:	And Will Transmit (lighten)* This Color:
Primary	Red	Cyan (Blue & Green)	Red
	Blue	Yellow (Red & Green)	Blue
	Green	Magenta (Red & Blue)	Green
Complementary	Magenta	Green	Magenta (Red & Blue)
	Cyan	Red	Cyan (Blue & Green)
	Yellow	Blue	Yellow (Red & Green)

*The colors in this column will be lightened if the filter factor is applied to the exposure.

FIGURE A

Suppose you're photographing a large red building in a grassy field, backed by a blue sky containing a few fleecy white clouds. What happens when you shoot through your red filter and increase the exposure by three stops (8X)? The filter transmits nearly all of the red of the building, rendering it far too dense or "blocked-up" on the negative. When it is printed, the building will appear washed-out and lacking detail. But at the same time, the increase in exposure will effectively cancel out the blue and green absorption effect of the filter. As it absorbs most of the blue and green, the sky and grass should be rendered lighter than normal on the negative, but the three-stop exposure increase will cause them to appear about normal. Thus you really haven't darkened the sky; you simply destroyed the detail in your main subject, the building. You can print the negative to compensate for this by increasing the exposure in the enlarger, but you'll still experience lost detail and increased graininess from the overexposure in the camera.

According to the No-Factor Theory, you should expose for the main subject—in this case, the building. Take a spot reflected-light reading from the building with your light meter/camera meter and expose according to

that. This will expose the building correctly, leaving it full of detail while the red filter absorbs much of the blue in the sky to darken it and provide the desired contrast between the sky and the clouds. The key to which filter to use is the factor—if your filter needs a factor, you've selected the wrong one. Suppose the building was green; use a green filter and expose for the building and the sky will still be darkened. If you use a red filter in this case, the green of the building will be absorbed and the building will go black. Use a yellow filter with a yellow building, etc.

The No-Factor Theory applies only when you're using a filter which is the same color as a major subject in your viewfinder. If there is no major subject the same basic color as the filter you're using, you might be using the wrong filter, depending upon what you want to do with it. As with everything else in photography, selecting the right filter (and exposure for it) for the desired effect requires some thought on your part (as well as experimentation) if you want to get the most from it.

WHEN TO USE A CONTRAST FILTER

As we've seen, filters can be used in black-and-white photography to match the film's sensitivity to that of our eyes,

SHUTTER SPEED COMPENSATION FOR FILTER FACTORS				
Normal Speed	Filter Factor 2X	4X	8X	16X
1/1000	1/500	1/250	1/125	1/60
1/500	1/250	1/125	1/60	1/30
1/250	1/125	1/60	1/30	1/15
1/125	1/60	1/30	1/15	1/8
1/60	1/30	1/15	1/8	1/4
1/30	1/15	1/8	1/4	1/2
1/15	1/8	1/4	1/2	1
1/8	1/4	1/2	1	2
1/4	1/2	1	2	4
1/2	1	2	4	8
1	2	4	8	16

FIGURE C

or to alter the tonal relationship among objects which possess similar qualities of reproduction in black-and-white.

To add more zest to landscapes, substitute the use of a yellow-green filter for a straight yellow one. Although this will darken the sky in the same way as the yellow filter, it has the added advantage of lightening grass and foliage to produce more texture and detail—a big help during mid-summer months when foliage has a tendency to reproduce as a very dark gray on normal panchromatic film. It's also helpful for outdoor portraits when your subject has a suntan, as the green aspect of the filter will produce a healthy look in the red-brown tan while the yellow lightens blonde hair.

As artificial light contains far less blue and more red wavelengths, a pale blue filter will add life to skin tones. It's also useful outdoors under certain conditions. When shadows are lighted by a blue sky, the pale blue filter will increase shadow details while retaining whatever atmospheric haze is present. When using contrast filters, however, you should bear in mind that they will affect the film only when there is color present for them to work on—you can't darken an overcast gray sky or lessen the effects of white mist or fog with a contrast filter, as there is no color for it to absorb and thus darken.

There are also many other uses to which contrast filters may be put—a stain on a document or picture to be copied can be removed with the use of a filter of the same color as the stain. Detail and texture can be separated in subjects that are otherwise nearly uniform in tone and color, such as sand, wood grain, brickwork, etc., if a filter similar in color to that of the subject is used. Figure D will help you to decide which particular filter is most useful with a given subject, but experimentation should be the rule rather than the exception—at least until you feel you

understand exactly what a given filter will do under a variety of circumstances and situations.

Should you embrace the Filter Factor Theory or the No-Factor Theory? Again, experimentation is the answer. Try both and compare the results—it won't take you long to decide which one is the most pleasing. You may even decide that the subject and the effect desired will determine whether you honor the factor or disregard it. The choice is yours.

HAZE FILTERS

Not to be confused with fog or mist, true atmospheric haze is caused primarily by the scattering of blue and ultraviolet wavelengths by dust particles and water vapor present in the atmosphere. As normal film is overly sensitive to these wavelengths, the effect of haze appears in exaggerated proportion in your picture, causing a loss of detail in distant objects. Since haze scatters some green, but very little red and virtually no infrared wavelengths, its effect can be minimized by the use of a contrast filter. A light yellow, deep yellow, orange or red filter will progressively "cut" haze to render distant details with greater clarity, but they also alter the tonal relationships of other colors in the scene. Red filters penetrate haze more effectively than the human eye, while a blue filter exaggerates haze.

The so-called "haze" filter sold for use in black-and-white photography is really an ultraviolet or UV filter. As it is formulated only to retard ultraviolet rays from reaching the film, it *does not* penetrate haze. Since it absorbs only ultraviolet wavelengths (which are invisible to the eye), it is an automatic filter—if ultraviolet rays are present, it absorbs them; if not, it does nothing. For this reason, it can be used over the lens for all photography and since it absorbs no visible light, it has no

filter factor. Some photographers use a haze filter all the time to protect their lenses from dust, dirt and damage. This filter has more appropriate uses in color photography, as we'll see, but it can also be helpful for black-and-white aerial work when the use of even a light yellow filter might darken a very deep blue sky more than you desire.

You should realize that some UV filters on the market are simply plain glass. This absorbs ultraviolet (you can't get a sunburn through glass), but only the shorter wavelengths, to which photographic film is not sensitive anyway. To determine whether or not you're buying a real UV filter or one of plain glass, check its coloration—the true UV filter will have a very slight yellowish tint, while the one of plain glass is colorless.

INFRARED FILTERS

As the maximum penetration of atmospheric haze is obtained by infrared rays, a special film emulsion sensitive to the near-infrared range of the spectrum, as well as possessing the same basic blue (but not green) sensitivity of a normal film emulsion, is used in certain situations. With no filter over the lens, such a film produces results similar in nature to those of a normal panchromatic emulsion, except for its lack of sensitivity to green objects.

Place a red filter, designated as A or No. 25 over the lens and much of the blue and violet wavelengths are absorbed, allowing primarily infrared rays or radiation to reach the film. While many different densities of red filters will work, this particular one is probably the best compromise for most landscape/scenic work, as it allows use of the maximum ASA-EI with black-and-white infrared film. The orange G or No. 15 will deliver quite similar results should the appropriate red filter not be available.

The use of a No. 87, No. 87C, No. 88A, No. 88C or No. 89B filter permits *only* infrared radiation to reach the film. Although visually opaque, these filters will render maximum detail in distant scenics. The selection of a given red filter for infrared photography depends upon the precise effect desired and the emulsion used. As infrared rays are not emitted from a given subject in proportion to visible light, it is not possible to determine a correct exposure with a light meter, and any ASA-EI rating is nothing more than an appropriate guide or starting point for test exposures. But as the amount of infrared radiation seems to remain more or less constant throughout the day, as well as from day to day throughout the year, a test series of bracketed exposures with a particular subject should allow you to ''guesstimate'' the exposure for future pictures of similar subject types with a fair amount of accuracy.

A good starting point with an A or No. 25 filter on a sunny day would be 1/30 second at f/11, dropping this to 1/8 second at f/8 when the sky is overcast, although somewhat less exposure will be required for distant scenes. If you use a No. 87 or No. 88A filter, try 1/30 at f/8 in good weather and 1/8 at f/5.6 under overcast or dull conditions. With the No. 87C, start at 1/30 at f/4.5 and open to 1/8 at f/2.8 for overcast weather. For the best definition, the smallest aperture consistent with lighting conditions should be used.

By fitting your flash unit with a No. 87, 87C or 88A filter, it's possible to take photographs in the dark without the flash being seen. Rate the film at ASA-EI 20 and reduce the flash guide number by one half. In the heyday of flash bulb photography, specially coated bulbs (designated 5R or 25R) were available. These can still be obtained on special order (as of this writing), but it's worth noting that manufacturers have now started offering electronic flash units specifically designed for use with infrared film without a filter over the lens.

CONVERSION FILTERS FOR COLOR FILM

Color films are *balanced* for a particular mixture of the red, green and blue wavelengths which compose white light. Daylight films have a color sensitivity balanced to respond most accurately to average daylight—that mixture of skylight and sunlight found in middle latitudes at noon on a bright summer day. Any other light mixture will result in a deviation from the color norm of the film. This explains why daylight color films show a bluish cast when exposed under dull lighting conditions, and a reddish cast if exposed at early morning or late afternoon.

Indoor or tungsten films are balanced more on the reddish side to respond to the increased red content of artificial light, as measured by a color temperature scale designated in degrees Kelvin or °K. In the past, indoor color films have been designated as either Type A or Type B, depending upon the color temperature for which they are balanced—for photofloods at

1

3400°K. (Type A) or studio lights at 3200°K. (Type B). Some color films, primarily the negative or color print emulsions, make no such differentiation between daylight and indoor balance, as correction is made during the printing process.

You may have noticed on occasion how the prevailing illumination affects the color of familiar objects, but the human brain has an ability color film does not possess—it can adapt to different kinds of lighting as seen by our eyes, and so we visually accept things as appearing ''normal.'' With its assigned color temperature of between 5500 and 6500°K. (depending upon who does the rating), daylight is bluer in content than tungsten light, which has a color temperature of 3200°K., yet both appear white to the eye. If a piece of white paper which looks white outdoors in daylight is taken indoors, it still looks white under tungsten light, despite the difference in color temperatures. But color film cannot adapt to various light sources unless the color temperature of the light source used to illuminate the scene is converted to

1-7. We all know what filters do to skies, but how do they affect skin tones? This is an equally important consideration when you want to change the sky tone in outdoor portraits. In this sequence, Julie Swanson's hair is honey blonde and her complexion light. She wears a blue denim top and bright red scarf. All prints were made to a uniform exposure/development formula. No filter is used in (1). In (2) a light yellow filter is used. In (3) and (4), we see the effects of a light green and an orange filter, respectively. A red filter is used in (5), while a polarizing filter is used in (6). The final photo in this series (7) shows the effects of a blue filter.

that of the light source for which the film was designed to be used. Conversion filters convert daylight color temperatures to tungsten color temperature, and vice-versa.

Conversion filters are of two types: those which ''warm'' the light and those which ''cool'' it down. The amber ''warming'' filters absorb enough blue from daylight to convert it to the color temperatures of various tungsten light sources, while the bluish ''cooling'' filters absorb sufficient yellow to convert tungsten light to daylight color temperature. Other amber conversion

2

4

7

3

5

6

filters are used to bring the color temperature of zirconium-filled or aluminum-filled flash bulbs up to the color temperature of daylight for use with daylight color films. Figure E will be helpful in selecting the proper conversion filter for the film and light source in use.

LIGHT-BALANCING FILTERS

These are designed to make smaller changes in the quality of light reaching the film. Such changes will eliminate undesirable bluish or reddish casts, as when using 3200°K. lights with Type A film, or 3400°K. lights with Type B. In a technical sense, a light-balancing filter does its job by slightly adjusting the relative amounts of the primary colors which it transmits from the light source to the film. As with the conversion filters, there are two types of light-balancing filters: the 82 series (bluish) which cools, and the 81 series (yellowish) which warms.

Light-balancing filters will make the minor adjustments shown in Figure F. In a more pragmatic sense, they will absorb some of the orange found in pictures taken in early morning or late afternoon with daylight film (No. 82A), absorb some of the bluish cast caused by cloudy weather or when some electronic flash units are used with daylight film (No. 81A), and balance clear flash

bulbs when they are used with Type A (3400°K.) film.

To determine exactly which light-balancing filter is required to provide a "normal" color rendition, you'll need a color temperature meter. These are expensive and vary in their capabilities according to price—the more costly ones will measure all of the primary colors, which permits their use with all kinds of light sources, while less costly ones measure the relative amount of red/blue only and can thus be used only with tungsten illumination. Unless you're a stickler for color consistency (or a professional making his living from color work), you'll be just as well off shooting 2-4 different shots with different light-balancing filters and choosing the slide you like best. When used in combination, light-balancing filters

will produce stronger effects, but the results are quite difficult to predict with accuracy unless you use the mired system discussed below.

DECAMIRED FILTERS

While conversion and light-balancing filters permit you to make the most commonly needed changes in color temperature of the light striking the film, the mired system allows you to make any color temperature change you desire. In this system, each color temperature is given its own number, called a mired (short for *micro-reciprocal degrees*) value, which is found by dividing the color temperature into a million. By this formula, 3200°K. tungsten light has a mired value of 312 (1,000,000 divided by 3200) and daylight (as defined by Kodak) has a mired value of 182 (1,000,000 divided by 5500).

To obtain numbers that are easier to work with, mired values are rounded off and expressed as decamireds, or tens of mireds, so that tungsten light's mired value of 312 becomes a decamired value of 31, and daylight's mired value of 182 becomes a decamired value of 18. Decamired (DM) filters come in warming (red) and cooling (blue) series, and have decamired value designations of 1½, 3, 6 and 12. A No. 3 decamired filter causes a color temperature shift of three decamireds, or 30 mireds. A No. 3 and a No. 12 decamired filter combined will cause a shift of 15 decamireds, or 150 mireds.

Suppose that your film is balanced for daylight—this means a mired value of 182 (decamired 18). Should you want to use the film with 3200°K. tungsten illumination (decamired 31), you'll need a filter or combination of filters to result in a decamired shift of 13, or 130 mireds. A No. 1 and a No. 12 decamired filter will cause a color shift of 130 mireds. As you're using a film balanced for bluish daylight with a light source containing primarily yellow and

LIGHT BALANCING FILTERS

When Film Is Balanced For:	And You Wish To Expose It By:	Use This Filter Or Its Equivalent:	And Increase Exposure By:
3200°K. Light	3400°K. Light	81A	⅓ Stop
3400°K. Light	3200°K. Light	82A	⅓ Stop

This Filter:	Balances This Light For 3200°K. Film:	Balances This Light For 3400°K. Film:	And Requires An Exposure Increase Of:*
81	3300°K.	3510°K.	⅓ Stop
81A	3400°K.	3630°K.	⅓ Stop
81B	3500°K.	3740°K.	⅓ Stop
81C	3600°K.	3850°K.	⅓ Stop
81D	3700°K.	3970°K.	⅔ Stop
81EF	3800°K.	4140°K.	⅔ Stop
82	3100°K.	3290°K.	⅓ Stop
82A	3000°K.	3180°K.	⅓ Stop
82B	2900°K.	3060°K.	⅔ Stop
82C	2800°K.	2950°K.	⅔ Stop
82 + 82C	2720°K.	2870°K.	1 Stop
82A + 82C	2650°K.	2780°K.	1 Stop
82B + 82C	2570°K.	2700°K.	1⅓ Stop
82C + 82C	2490°K.	2610°K.	1⅓ Stop

*Approximate values—check by practical test for critical work. If used in combination, add the exposure increase for each filter together and open aperture by the total figure.

FIGURE F

red, you'll need bluish cooling filtration to match the tungsten light to the film, thus you'd use decamired filters B-1 and B-12.

The convenient thing about the mired system is its consistency. Unlike conversion and light-balancing filters, which provide different degrees of correction at different color temperatures, a decamired filter will *always* cause a color shift equal to its own value, regardless of the color temperature involved. As we've seen, decamired filters can be combined to obtain a desired value, but only filters of the same color can be combined—blue and red cannot be mixed.

In this same respect, it's not advisable to mix daylight with photofloods (3400°K.) or studio lighting (3200°K.) when working with color film, as there's no adequate correction possible with either daylight or tungsten-balanced films. The very best for which you could hope would be a compromise in which everything is slightly wrong. And as films balanced for 3400°K. are extremely blue-sensitive, it requires only a slight amount of daylight to result in that unwanted blue cast. If light sources *must* be mixed, they should be of comparable quality—daylight and electronic flash, daylight and blue flash bulbs, etc.

Decamired filters require a slight exposure increase; if used in combination, the increase necessary for each filter is added together and the aperture adjusted according to the total of the filters used. The casual user will find the simple charts that accompany decamired filter sets to be most useful,

RECOMMENDED FILTER USES, BLACK-AND-WHITE FILM

Filter	Factor*	Use
Light Yellow	2X	Slightly darkens sky to bring out clouds; absorbs some UV for haze penetration; improves contrast between subject and sky. Lightens yellows, darkens blues.
Yellow/Green	2X	Similar in effect to light yellow, but also lightens foliage somewhat; works well for outdoor portraits and beach pictures, but does not lighten suntanned skin tones.
Dark Yellow	3X	Similar to dark yellow, but more pronounced in effect. Emphasizes foreground subjects and increases shadow contrast in winter snow scenes; works well when photographing light-colored woods.
Green	2X	Lightens greens to help contrast in pictures containing much foliage, trees, flowers, etc.; emphasizes detail and improves cloud effect; will darken suntanned skin tones but beware of freckles. Lightens greens, darkens orange and reds.
Orange	4X	Produces a strong cloud effect, increasing contrast in outdoor scenics while absorbing UV and eliminating haze. This makes it good for distant landscapes, scenics and aerial work. Subdues lips and facial blemishes such as freckles; useful for better rendition of brick and stone surface textures, as well as photographing dark-colored woods. Lightens reds, orange and yellows, darkens blues and greens.
Red	8X	Cuts haze, produces strong contrast leading to exaggerated cloud effects; with slight underexposure, produces simulated night effects. Works well for architectural photos when building is light in color as it sets it off against a very dark sky. Try this for sunsets in black-and-white, and for copying blueprints and other such documents. Lightens reds and yellows, darkens greens.

° May vary according to density of filter and manufacturer.

FIGURE D

CONVERSION FILTERS

When Film Is Balanced For:	And You Wish To Expose It By:	Use This Filter Or It's Equivalent:	Or Your Pictures Will Look Too:
Daylight	3200°K. Light	80 A (4X)	Orange
Daylight	3400°K. Light	80 B (4X)	Orange
Daylight	Aluminum Foil Flashbulbs	80 C (2X)	Orange
Daylight	Zirconium Foil Flashbulbs	80 D (1X)	Orange
3200°K. Light	Daylight	85 B (1.5X)	Blue
3400°K. Light	Daylight	85 (1.5X)	Blue

FIGURE E

1-2. Infrared film and a red filter are used for dramatic emphasis. Shirley I. Fisher shot (1) with panchromatic film and no filter, then switched to infrared film with a red filter for (2).

as they tell you which filter(s) to use and when to use them—it's not as difficult as it might seem. Bear in mind that if you use the mired system, you will not need the conversion or light-balancing filters, as decamired filters do the same job but with even greater precision.

COLOR COMPENSATING FILTERS

Color Compensating or CC filters come in various densities of six different colors: red, blue, green, magenta, cyan and yellow. As these are the primary colors, a CC filter will control one color while leaving the others unaltered. The various densities permit close control of the amount of a given color to be absorbed. A CC20Y (CC for color compensating and Y for yellow) filter has a density of .20 to blue light (it absorbs about 37 percent of the blue light—see Figure G) and allows red and green light to pass. A CC50R (red) filter has a density of .50 to blue and green light (it absorbs about 68 percent of the two) while al-

lowing virtually all of the red light to pass through.

CC filters are used to make small changes to compensate for deficiencies in the color quality of light sources, deficiencies in film due to manufacturing tolerances, and for reciprocity failure in films. Since CC filters come in all the primary colors, almost any color correction can be made with them, and they're used when color rendition is critical. As color negative or print films have some color latitude,

they can be corrected with CC filters when they are printed, but for critical work with color transparency films, you'll have to shoot a test.

Color films are manufactured under strict controls, yet two rolls of the same brand of film may vary slightly in color balance. One roll of a given chrome film may require a CC10Y filter to produce "normal" color, while another roll of the same film from another emulsion batch may require no filter. Variations within allowable manufacturing tolerances, although usually held to within a CC10 filter of a "standard," are one good reason for shooting a test whenever color rendition is critical.

Whenever you use extremely long exposure times (as when shooting in very dim light) or very short exposure times (as when using electronic flash), you may encounter reciprocity failure in the film, which is a shift in color balance and a loss of speed caused by longer or shorter exposures than those for which the film was designed. For the majority of color films, the "safe" range of exposure times is between 1/30 to 1/1000 second. At longer or shorter exposures, you may have to use a CC filter to compensate for the color shift caused by reciprocity failure. Some manufacturers provide exposure and filter compensation data for very long or short exposures with their film instruction sheets; others don't, so you'll just have to shoot a test, look at it, and then decide what correction, if any, is required.

Although normally used to make color corrections, CC filters can also be used to make color creations. They can intensify colors, create moods and do all kinds of wild, interesting things for your pictures. To find out exactly what you can do with them, experiment. This will not only provide you with some unusual effects, it'll give you a better knowledge base of filter use.

In a similar vein, the contrast filters used for black-and-white photography can also be used with color films to produce interesting effects. These filters will give an overall tint to the picture; the deeper the filter density, the deeper the tint. Used selectively, a contrast filter can add drama, punch, mood or emphasis to a particular scene. Don't be afraid to use filters for purposes other than those for which they were designed—this is part of the fun of photography.

FLUORESCENT LIGHT FILTERS (FLD-FLB)

Fluorescent lighting does not produce a uniform or standard distribution of red, blue and green wavelengths. For this reason, it presents rather difficult problems, and results in undesirable color casts when used as the major illumination source for photography. While a tungsten lamp puts out a little blue, more green, even more yellow and much red (as we move from the shorter light wavelengths to the longer) in a smoothly increasing pattern, a fluorescent light may put out hardly

CC FILTER DENSITY/TRANSMITTANCE		
Density	Transmission (%)	Absorption (%)
.05	90	10
.10	80	20
.20	63	37
.30	50	50
.40	40	60
.50	30	70
.60	25	75
.70	20	80
.80	16	84
.90	12.5	87.5
1.00	10	90
2.00	1	99

FIGURE G

UNPOLARIZED LIGHT RAY

FIGURE H

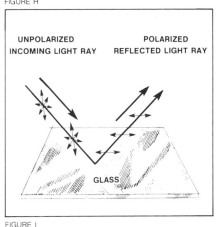

UNPOLARIZED INCOMING LIGHT RAY

POLARIZED REFLECTED LIGHT RAY

GLASS

FIGURE I

1. Ron Berkenblitt combined a 17mm full-frame fisheye lens with Plus-X film and a polarizing filter for this spectacular air race scene in the Mojave Desert.

any blue, some green, much orange and no red, or any combination you care to name. Fluorescent lights also vary in color quality from lamp to lamp, from brand to brand, with age and all other kinds of factors—there seems to be no two alike. Thus the filtration necessary for proper colors in a picture varies just as widely—from film to film, lamp to lamp, brand to brand, etc. There are so many variables that we just don't have room here to list the correct filtration for *every* possible combination.

Until a few years ago, color correction when working with fluorescent

lighting was obtained with CC filters only. While this method is still recommended if precise results are desired, there are also two fluorescent light filters which will remove most of the bluish-green cast from flesh tones photographed under fluorescent lighting. The FLD is used with daylight films and can cope adequately with a mixture of daylight and fluorescent lighting; the FLB is for use with tungsten emulsions and will handle a mixture of tungsten and fluorescent lighting with acceptable results. Either filter generally requires an increase in exposure equal to one f-stop, and as fluorescent lighting varies during AC cycles, it's highly desirable to keep the shutter speed used to 1/60 second or below if you wish to obtain uniformity in the quality of both color and illumination.

INFRARED COLOR AND FILTERS

Unlike normal color films, an infrared color emulsion does not try to deliver an accurate color rendering of a scene—it's designed to differentiate between objects which reflect infrared wavelengths and those that don't. Originally created for scientific use, this type of color emulsion has found popularity with both amateur and professional photographers because of the strange and even surrealistic properties with which it becomes embued when used with certain filters.

Exposed without a filter, infrared color film shows a strong propensity toward blue, but by photographing your subject through a yellow, green, orange or red contrast filter (those normally used for black-and-white photography), an entire range of effects both strange and unusual can be created. For example, a green filter turns foliage orange/red and shifts other colors toward magenta. A red filter produces similar orange foliage, but adds green skies with yellow clouds. Add a polarizing filter (to be discussed shortly) to the contrast filter and you can deepen all of the tones in the picture.

Like black-and-white infrared film, there is no established ASA-EI rating for infrared color film, but an EI of 50 is usually suggested as a starting point for bracketing a series of exposures when using a yellow, orange or red filter, and an EI of 20 for use with a green filter.

SKYLIGHT/HAZE/ULTRAVIOLET FILTERS

For most amateur photographers, a Skylight or Haze filter is the first purchase, and usually made at the suggestion of the salesman, who rec-

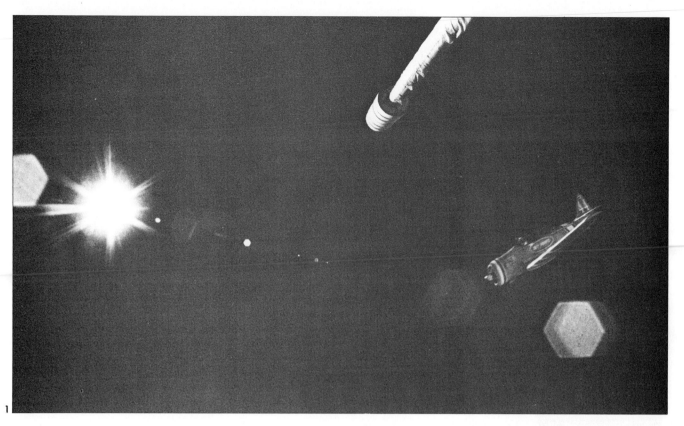
1

ommends its use to protect the camera lens from damage or contamination. All of these filters are used with color film to penetrate haze and reduce the bluish cast caused by ultraviolet wavelengths—especially prevalent in landscapes, pictures taken at the beach, or in shade or an overcast.

A compromise between a haze filter and the weakest of the decamired filters, the pinkish-colored skylight (often designated as No. 1A) hold back ultraviolet while adding a slight degree of warmth to your picture. Regarded by many as a good all-around choice for a basic filter in color work, the skylight works best with American and Japanese color emulsions. When European color films are used, the haze or UV filter often proves to be a better choice, as it does not produce the muddy flesh tones characteristic of the 1A when used with such emulsions.

Haze and UV filters are generally available in two or three strengths; which filter and which strength you use will depend mainly upon your personal taste in color rendition, as well as the film you're using. I would suggest that if you're a newcomer to photography, you resist buying any of these filters until you've shot a few rolls of color film and have had an opportunity to evaluate your results—you may very well find that the slight warming tendency of the skylight filter does not suit your personal tastes in color. If so, your money can be better spent in

some of the other areas we've discussed or have yet to consider.

NEUTRAL DENSITY FILTERS

Useful with both color and black-and-white films, a neutral density or ND filter is gray in appearance and absorbs all colors equally. This reduces the intensity of light reaching your film without affecting either the tone or color balance of your subject. While ND filters have no other function, they do possess the ability to absorb ultraviolet wavelengths, which makes the use of a UV or haze filter unnecessary whenever a neutral density filter is used over the lens.

You'll find this particular type of filter one of your most useful creative tools. For example, suppose that your camera is loaded with ASA 400 film and you're working outdoors on a bright sunny day. The proper exposure is 1/1000 second at f/16, but you wish to use a larger aperture to throw an unsightly background out of focus. The ND filter is your answer. A 2X ND filter lets you open up one f-stop; a 4X ND requires two stops; use the two together and you can open up three stops (2X x 4X = 8X). With one of each in your gadget bag, you can now select an aperture of f/16, f/11, f/8 or f/5.6, depending upon the effect you desire to have.

ND filters have many other uses. They permit the use of large apertures in portraiture when selective focusing

is desirable, correct flash exposures when the flash is very powerful or very close to the subject, and the use of slow shutter speeds to permit special effects such as the "explosion" technique with a zoom lens.

A special ND filter called a graduate-clear-to-neutral filter is also available. This is half clear and half neutral density and is used on scenes where the brightness range is beyond the latitude capability of the film. If you're trying to record a scene where the foreground is on the dark side and the background includes a bright, partly cloudy sky, there might be as much as five f-stops' difference between the foreground and the sky. This special ND filter will reduce that difference to something the film's latitude can handle by reducing the brightness of the sky without affecting the foreground. Like standard neutral density filters, this one is available in several strengths.

Incidentally, if you find it desirable to use a contrast filter with black-and-white film to bring out clouds, etc., it can be used in conjunction with the neutral density filter. Thus, if a three f-stop reduction is required, you can use a 4X ND filter and a 2X yellow filter, achieving the same exposure reduction as you would with a 2X and 4X ND filter combination.

POLARIZING FILTERS

Light rays normally vibrate in all di-

rections at right angles to their path of travel (Figure H). But when they pass through certain substances (such as water or glass) or are reflected from nonmetallic surfaces, much of the multidirectional vibrations are absorbed and the rays which pass through or are reflected now vibrate only in a single direction—and as such, are said to be "polarized" (Figure I). Such polarized light tends to create a glare or strong reflection. Light radiating from a clear blue sky at right angles to the sun is also polarized.

Neutral gray in color, a polarizing filter acts like a pair of Venetian blinds placed at right angles to each other. When the two blinds are aligned in the same direction, polarized light will be passed through the open slits. But turn one blind at right angles to the other and the polarized light will be prevented from passing. Nonpolarized light will pass through regardless of how the blinds are arranged, but by turning the two blinds relative to each other, you can govern the amount of polarized light which passes.

Polarizing filters for SLR cameras are two-piece units—the outer frame which screws into the lens and the inner frame containing the filter, which revolves within the outer frame. Those for non-SLR cameras are simply a disk which fits into an adapter ring for placement over the camera lens. SLR polarizers are fitted to the lens and rotated while looking through the viewfinder until the desired effect is achieved; to use the disk type, it must be held in your hand and rotated until the effect is correct, then mounted over the camera lens in the same position or alignment. In either case, if you cannot achieve the effect wanted, change your camera position slightly in relation to your subject and try again. Maximum glare/reflection reduction occurs when you're working at a 30-to-40-degree angle to the surface.

Polarizing filters are most versatile and can be used for both color and black-and-white work. This is the only filter which will produce a deep blue sky in a color shot without changing the other colors in the picture; in black-and-white work, it will darken the sky without altering other tonal values. Its glare reduction quality increases color saturation, penetrates light haze, and is especially useful in controlling glare and reflections when copying.

There's probably more misinformation about exposure compensation than any other phase of the polarizing filter's use, but there's no valid reason

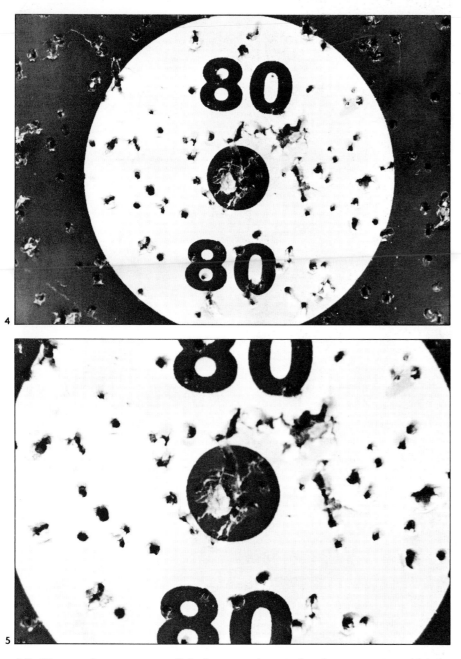

4

5

1-5. Close-up lenses are a satisfactory substitute for a macro lens, if you have only occasional use for moving in close to a subject. This sequence shows the magnification and sharpness possible. This is the closest focusing distance of 50mm lens—18 inches (1). A +1 close-up lens allows you to move in this close (2), a +2 close-up lens gets you this close (3) and a +3 close-up moves you in even closer (4). Here is what all three combined looks like (5).

for the confusion. The polarizing filter is a neutral density filter and has a built-in filter factor, which remains constant regardless of the position of the filter. As you rotate it, the sky will grow darker in your viewfinder, but this does not mean that you need more exposure to compensate.

There are a few exceptions to the rule, but they're due to the nature of the subject, not the filter. If you take a

meter reading from a scene which is full of reflections, then remove the reflections, the scene will appear darker than expected. You can eliminate this mental exposure juggling by using an incident-light meter, or taking a reflected-light reading from an 18-percent-reflectance gray cared.

If you're using an SLR with a built-in metering system, take a reading with the filter off the camera, then put it over the lens and apply the filter factor. In theory, the camera's meter will supposedly compensate for the effect of the polarizing filter, but some cameras will give erroneous readings, especially those which use half or split mirrors to direct light to the CdS cell.

Because many photographers think of the polarizing filter in terms of its ability to darken the sky without changing other colors, they tend to overlook

its usefulness with black-and-white film. But combine a polarizer and a red filter and you'll get dramatic black skies and a night effect. The yellow filter also produces a dramatic sky, but not as pronounced as the red filter; combine a polarizer with a deep green filter and you can approximate infrared results. Whenever you combine the use of a polarizer with another filter, always attach the polarizer to the lens first, then add the other filter.

SPECIAL-EFFECT FILTERS AND ATTACHMENTS

There is a wide variety of colorless filters and other lens attachments available which magnify, diffuse, distort, decrease and otherwise modify the image received at the film plane to create special effects with color or black-and-white film. While some of these "trick" filters and attachments have been greatly overused and abused in the past, all are enjoyable to work with, and can offer you considerable challenge at a time when you might feel that your photographic vision is becoming stilted. Before embarking on our Cook's Tour through the world of these devices, I should mention that although the following discussion is current as of this writing, manufacturers continue to bring new effect filters and attachments on the market.

CLOSE-UP LENSES

Also known as plus-diopters or portrait lenses, these optically change the effective focal length of your lens, allowing you to focus on objects closer to the camera than would otherwise be possible. Supplementary close-up lenses are available in strengths from +1 to +10, with some manufacturers offering fractional diopters (+¼, +½, +¾), and others offering units which zoom from +1 to +10 to cover the entire diopter range with a single attachment. The greater the diopter number, the closer you can focus to the subject. Such lenses can also be used in combination with each other, with the resulting power calculated by adding the individual powers (+1 and +3 = +4). When close-up lenses are used this way, the strongest one should be placed on the lens first.

While no exposure increase is necessary, it's a good idea to stop your camera lens down to about f/11 and use as fast a shutter speed as possible to reduce the possibility of vibration or camera movement. Depth of field diminishes rapidly at these close distances and sharp focus is essential. There is a minor loss of image sharpness when

close-up lenses are used, but you should be able to make an 8x10 print with almost no noticeable loss of sharpness from a 35mm negative taken with a +3 diopter. Close-up lenses can also be used with moderate to medium telephoto lenses to increase image size at the closest focusing distance of the lens.

SPLIT-FIELD LENSES

Available in fractional and full diopter strengths, these are half plus-diopter and half clear. Split-field lenses allow you to focus on an object very close to the camera through the diopter half and at the same time, retain the sharpness of distant objects through the clear half. Properly positioned, the dividing line between the two parts blends in and will not be noticed in the picture. A variation on this theme is the so-called two-field lens, which contains a half of a close-up lens and half of an optical filter, making it ideal for panfocus photography and half section blurring.

SPOT FILTERS

A wide variety of these are available. The Center Focus type is a close-up lens with a circular hole in its center. When the image in the hole is sharply focused, the convex lens portion surrounding the hole is out of focus, creating a blurring effect around the image. The Sand Screen or Center Image filter permits sharp focusing on the center of the picture with the edges whitening out in a semi-vignette. These are often available with a soft screen insert to diffuse the area which the Sand Screen whitens.

SOFT FOCUS/DIFFUSER

These are also available in a wide variety of types and effects, ranging from concentric circles inscribed on optical glass to irregular stippled or mottled surfaces producing minute light refractions. While all are intended to soften image lines, they vary in the type and amount of diffusion produced according to the pattern design and strength. Many photographers prefer to make their own by smearing petroleum jelly on a skylight filter.

The camera lens should be sharply focused on the subject before fitting the diffuser in place, but the aperture to be used is best selected afterwards, using the depth-of-field preview control as a guide. Small apertures minimize the effect and large apertures produce maximum diffusion. They can also be used on an enlarger to diffuse fine detail and blend highlight and shadow areas. While particularly useful in portraiture, diffusion filters can often be of benefit in landscapes, providing the lighting and camera angle are well chosen and planned.

LOW-CONTRAST FILTERS

Designed for those occasions when you do not want the brilliant, deeply

1-5. Shown is a normal lens at f/16 (1), a normal lens at f/3.5 (2), a center spot filter at f/16 (3), a center spot filter at f/3.5 (4), and a soft spot filter at f/11 (5).

saturated colors and well-defined color areas characteristic of today's color films, low-contrast filters desaturate and mute colors to produce dreamlike effects in which color areas blend and diffuse. Available in various strengths, these could set color photography back 50 years if you're not careful in selecting appropriate subjects.

FOG FILTERS

Another variation used to create an illusion of misty atmosphere and haze without reducing definition and subject sharpness, fog filters are manufactured from very finely ground glass. Offered in varying degrees of strength, they make the image appear as though in a natural veil of fog or mist. While real fog obscures in depth, with closer subjects more easily visible than those in the distance, the fog filter cannot duplicate this effect and so has a uniform appearance on both foreground *and* background. For this reason, it's best

trum effect. The grid pattern is available in 1mm, 2mm, 3mm and 4mm sizes. The finer the grid or mesh pattern, the smaller but more pronounced the effect will be; the coarser the grid, the more subtle and less intense the effect becomes, as fewer cross flares/stars are produced.

They're also found with interlocking triangular figure crosslines which produce a six- or eight-point cross flare/star effect, as well as being combined in the variable cross screen, which simply contains two ordinary cross screens, one of which rotates in the mount as does a polarizing filter to permit adjustment of the grids at varying angles. These tend to produce a long, wide and multicolored cross flare. Other varieties are constantly appearing, making the purchase of just the right one a problem of fitting each to the lens and examining the effect it creates.

The proper choice of cross screen is further complicated by the variations in effect names which manufacturers and distributors insist on giving to their own line in an effort to glamourize the effect and differentiate theirs from that of the competition—Snow Cross, Sunny Cross, Starburst, Crystal Cross, etc. They justify this in part by categorizing such filters as producing a four-, six-, or eight-point star effect (depending upon the grid pattern—see Figure J) instead of by the size of the grid.

The cross-screen effect seems to work best when used at apertures ranging between f/4 and f/8, as smaller apertures have a tendency to minimize or even lose the effect, while larger lens openings may produce out-of-focus cross flares. Incidentally, the finer grid patterns produce a slight measure of diffusion which softens the entire image. The aperture range at which a given cross screen works best is subject to experimentation, as the effect depends upon the size and pattern of the grid, as well as the focal length of the lens to which it's attached. Should you find that a 67mm cross screen produces exactly the effect desired when used with the 85mm

to avoid compositions containing a graduated foreground which leads into the background or the effect will not seem natural. Stick to portraits, foreground objects only or landscapes with no foreground when using one.

Although valuable in black-and-white work, fog filters are particularly effective with color subjects. As mentioned, those which contain a limited amount of perspective will give the best and most natural-appearing results, and a slight degree of overexposure, ranging from ⅓ f-stop for the weakest strength to a full stop for the strongest is suggested with them.

DUAL-IMAGE FILTER

Somewhat of a misnomer, this is not actually a filter, but more of an inexpensive matte device in that it contains an opaque semicircle in a rotating holder frame to permit positioning of

the black half for trick photography, particularly multiple exposures. The opaque portion prevents exposure of that portion of the film, and so it's possible to photograph the same object in two or more positions and/or locations. Like the split-field lens, the dividing line of the dual image filter must be positioned with care to blend it into the picture area so that the eye will be unable to discern how the effect was actually achieved.

CROSS SCREEN/STAR FILTERS

These special-effect attachment lenses contain minute cross line grooves engraved in an interlocking pattern at right angles to each other. When these lines intersect a point light source, they split its rays into a cross flare or star to create a bright specular highlight. With color film, the cross flare/star is refracted, causing a spec-

normal lens on your 6x6 SLR, don't expect that it will deliver the same effect if stepped down to fit a 50-55mm normal lens on a 35mm SLR.

On occasion, you'll find that the number of highlights in the picture will cause visual confusion when a cross screen is used (as with a busy city skyline at night). In such cases, you need a coarser grid pattern to limit the number of cross flares in the picture. Many photographers find them most effective when only a few flares are created, as in catching a reflection in the eyes of a model to create a star effect in her eye—a cliché of glamour photography some years back. But regardless of how you envision using a cross screen, experimentation is the best advice, and as you may have already realized, no single cross screen (whatever its name) will give you all the variations in effect in which you'll be interested. What this means is that you'll probably find yourself buying several different makes and grid patterns to cover the many different occasions on which you'll want to apply the technique.

When using a cross screen, remember that rotating the filter will change the orientation of the cross flare/star points, and that you should view the scene using the depth-of-field preview lever (or at the shooting aperture with SLR cameras which do not have this feature) in order to determine the precise effect on the film—this may have a bearing on your choice of aperture. Also remember that the nearer you are to a bright highlight or point light source, the larger and more intense the effect; if you're not particularly captivated by one effect, move the

camera position or change your angle slightly, as this will reorient the entire pattern effect.

PRISM ATTACHMENTS

Like cross screens, prism attachments are known by a wide variety of names—multi-vision, miracle image, mirage effect, trick photography, trick prism, multiple mirage lenses, etc. Regardless of the brand or trade name, these are available in a standard set of prism patterns (see Figure K) and each

1-2. Shown here are the effects of a soft spot filter at f/16 with sand screen insert (1) and a soft spot filter at f/3.5 with sand screen insert (2).
3-4. Diffusion filters produce different effects, depending upon who manufactures them and the means used to achieve the diffusion. The rippled surface diffusion filter was used for (3); David Neibel's use of a diffusion filter with an etched surface (4) turns up a more pronounced effect, similar to that of an out-of-focus lens. You can make your own diffusion filter to order with petroleum jelly and a haze filter, or use nylon stocking material stretched over the lens.

pattern produces a different effect. At this writing, the most recent innovation in prism attachment design is a compound multiple-image prism called Vari-Pair© by Spiratone and Variable Mirage by Prinz.

Essentially the same, they consist of a pair of identical double-faceted prisms in a rotating mount, which allows you to orient the prism as desired. When the prism axes are parallel, two identical side-by-side images of an object will be recorded; when the prism axes are set at right angles to each other, four identical images will result. In-between settings of the prism are possible to produce a variety of other patterns.

Offered in a double ring mount which screws into your camera lens, most prism attachments have a small handle on the front ring to let you

4

looking for, and so you should not be afraid to experiment.

The colored prisms previously mentioned are available in two types: a continuous and blending color spectrum which is incorporated in the glass, and a multi-faceted prism with a different color or hue applied to each facet. Both produce spectacular results, are quite expensive and may find only limited use in your photography.

Simple, plain backgrounds are usually preferable, as they emphasize the primary object of interest while holding background clutter to a minimum. Silhouettes against the sky, or night shots help isolate the image mix and usually produce interesting results. Try to select the prism attachment configuration best suited to the subject and don't get carried away with the technique—it's useful, but can easily be overworked. By the way, shoot the subject both with and without a prism attachment— who knows, you might prefer the non-effect picture after all!

POP FILTERS

Offered under a variety of trade names such as Kalt Pop, Spiratone Vibracolor, Prinz Exoticolor, etc., these are intense single-color filters used in the same way as normal black-and-white contrast filters to produce an overall cast on color film. They differ primarily in the result—while black-and-white filters will give a yellow, orange, green or red cast, the "pop" filters deliver a strong and unusual shade of purple, pink or aquamarine not obtainable on color film with other filters.

When you find a subject suitable for use with "palpitating pink" or "mystic marine," the result can be eye-blowing, but that's also the major limitation of a "pop" filter. It's not always easy to match a suitable subject with the filter, and if the two are not compatible, the result is usually a visual "blah." Filter factors differ with color and manufacturer, but all require an increase in exposure when used.

DIFFRACTION GRATINGS

Often called rainbow filters, diffraction gratings create spectrum effects on color film and have proliferated in the last few years, with almost every major manufacturer/distributor of filters offering their own variation on the theme. Originally, gratings were optically flat glass plates which contained very precisely engraved lines to diffract light rays from point light sources into a spectrum effect. But these are very costly to make, so using the engraved glass plate as a master, plastic repro-

change the position and pattern of the images created on the film, or to rotate the entire attachment during slow exposures without unscrewing it from the camera lens by accident. Should you become hooked on the prism effect, you can expect to part with a good amount of money, as these attachments are no longer inexpensive; in fact, the multicolored prisms list as high as $60 each in popular screw-in filter sizes, one reason why most dealers will obtain them only on special order by request.

Regardless of the pattern, the center segment of the prism will deliver the sharpest image, with diffraction softening the other segment images to some degree. This also varies with the choice of aperture. At large apertures, the center image will be slightly diffused, with a considerable loss of image contrast and color saturation af-

fecting the other images. But stop the lens down to f/16 and all the images will be distinct, bright and almost as sharp as the center one. As with the cross screen filter, you should rely upon the depth-of-field preview lever and check the effect at each usable aperture to get precisely what you want. After working with prism attachments for awhile, you'll become accustomed to visualizing the potential subject with one in mind, and select the most effective f-stop by second nature.

Prism attachments are most effective when used with the camera's standard lens. A moderate wide-angle lens tends to clump the images in the center of the picture area while causing corner vignetting; moderate telephotos will cause a divergence of the images to the side of the frame, often cutting part of each image off. Yet each of these effects may be exactly what you're

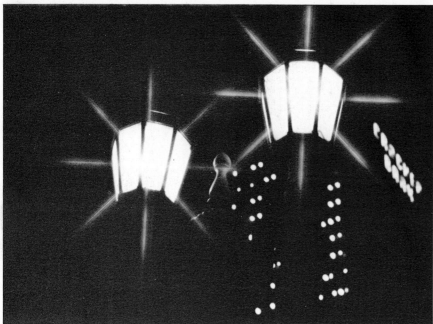

1-2. Cross-screens produce their maximum effects at around f/5.6 (1); stopping the lens down to f/16 reduces the effect, as in (2).
3-4. The same cross-screen filter was used for both pictures. What accounts for the difference in effect? The filter was rotated slightly during the exposure for (4).
5. This was taken with a fog filter at f/3.5.

ductions were made in much the same manner that record companies "press" thousands of discs from a single master. The latest technique of creating the gratings involves holography and has brought the cost down within reach of the average photographer, although they're still not inexpensive, by any means.

As with other special effect filters, several varieties are available and they can presently be catagorized in four major groups, each of which produces a different effect:

Linear produces repetitive patterns along a straight line.

Radial emanates the pattern from the point-light source much like the spokes of a wheel.

Circular surrounds the light source with ever-increasing rings of color.

Nebula emanates a multistreak burst pattern from the light to form a circle.

Actually, these descriptions are only very rough approximations of the various possible effects and as the state of the art advances, more and different types are certain to appear. Some diffraction gratings work most effectively with the lens wide open, while others require that you stop down considerably for the full effect. In this respect, they're much like cross screens or prism attachments. Experimentation is paramount, and that's one of the major reasons they're so very popular these days—the effects have not yet been completely exhausted and you can still "do your own thing" without feeling that everyone else has done it before you. Also, like the previously discussed filters and attachments, you'll probably

end up with two, three or even four different diffraction gratings before you're satisfied.

For those who wish to fit a large diameter lens mount at a more reasonable cost, or who use filter gels as a matter of course, diffraction gratings are also available in the form of sheets and long rolls from Edmund Scientific Company (100 Edscorp Building, Barrington, New Jersey 08007) and the Hollo Corporation (17785-D Skypark Circle, Irvine, California 92707). I've found a 4x5-inch sheet to be the most efficient way of outfitting both circular and full-frame fisheye lenses for some really mind-blowing effects.

Simply place the camera on a tripod so that you can use both hands, set and release the self-timer and use the 8-10-second interval to position the diffraction grating sheet in front of the lens in a U shape where it remains for the exposure. This material also works beautifully with special-effect cameras such as the Panon Widelux, as you need cut only a small piece from one end and fasten it to the moving lens cylinder with cellophane tape to hold it in place for the entire exposure over a 140-degree field of view! I've also taped small pieces over the lens of a 110 pocket camera to achieve some rather interesting effects on the tiny 13x17mm slides.

While most manufacturers recom-

5

mend a slight exposure increase when using their diffraction grating filters, I'd suggest that you experiment with exposures as well as with subjects and effects. You'll find a slight degree of under-exposure highly desirable for maximum color saturation when working against a light background; when used for night shots, you'll probably want to stay with the basic exposure recommended without the filter, as this will help intensify the color saturation against the dark of night.

CHROMATIC, DICHROIC AND COLOR IMAGE FILTERS

When French fashion photographer Jean Coquin was hired to photograph Pierre Cardin's autumn fashions a few years ago, he found it necessary to devise some means of hurrying fall along, as it was still summer. Recalling a prewar graduated Rollei filter, Coquin made his own graduated filters of various colors and hues to permit the introduction of the desired colors wherever he required them. The idea was so successful that it was made commercially available during 1975 under the tradename Cromofilter.

While Cromofilters are not yet available in this country (at this writing), a variety of Japanese imitations and variations have made their appearance (more are to come), and along with the diffraction grating, they are the hottest filter concept presently on the market. The Cromofilter and its imitations are tinted a particular color over one-half

of the filter area, with the remaining half graduated to neutral. Manufactured in threaded rotating mounts, the tinted half can be positioned where desired, preventing color overlap between two different areas of the picture, such as following a slanted horizon line. A second filter of a different color can also be threaded into the first, producing a two-color effect. When used in this way, a narrow neutral strip separates the two tinted areas. As with most special-effect devices, the careful choice of a chromatic filter can strengthen the mood of a scene, but

used indiscriminately, the results will be meaningless.

Izumar Chromostar filters, distributed in this country by Spiratone under its Colorflow trademark, are colored polarizing filters available in two types. In the single-color version, the color density varies from dense to an almost transparent hue as the filter is rotated in its frame. Four different colors are available. The bicolor version also changes color in this manner as the filter rotates, but continued rotation in this case carries through a change to a second color. For example, rotating

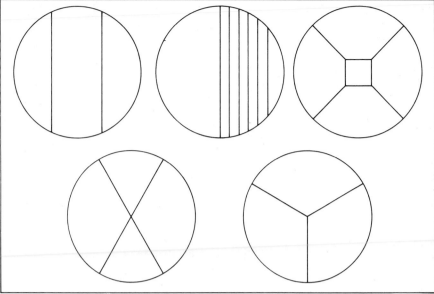

FIGURE K

1-2. The six-section concentric mirage lens has a variety of uses, but camera-to-subject distance is important in properly spacing the images. When you're too far away (2), they tend to blend; when too close (1), you may lose various parts of the image.

the red-blue bicolor filter changes the color from dark to light red, through magenta and then light to dark blue.

Another variation on the multicolor theme is found in the straight bicolor and tricolor color image filters offered by Prinz, Hoya and others. With these, the filter surface is divided into two or three sections, each having a sandwich containing a different color base. As the color combinations are permanent, the subject at hand will dictate whether the filter can be used successfully and with taste, or if the result simply becomes another novelty.

The degree of their effect differs, depending upon the focal length of the lens to which they're attached and the aperture used. With wide-angle lenses, the color border between segments is definite and pronounced, but as you increase the focal length into the telephoto range, the colors blend into each other gradually, with no definite border noticeable. The larger the aperture used, the more diffused and delicate the color gradation; as the aperture is stopped down, the colors become more intense. These two- and three-color filters have a 2X to 4X filter factor, depending upon the color combinations. When used with color print film, this fact should be mentioned to the color lab doing the printing, otherwise the printer will often attempt to correct the effect with CC filters, the end result of which is a uniformly ''dirty'' color rendition.

The chromatic filters and dichroic

polarizers are far more versatile than the multiple-color image filters, and they remain your best investment for serious use. The two- and three-color filters can be positioned as desired on the lens, but finding a subject where the multiple fixed color combination is both appropriate and useful is much like trying to find a suitable use for the pop filters, and proves to be a far more serious limitation to those who wish creative results.

STEPPING RINGS

For those who wish to use a given filter size with several lenses which require slightly different sizes, such as 49mm and 52mm, 49mm and 55mm, or 55mm and 58mm, a series of thin metal coupling rings containing female threads on one side and male threads on the other are available. These are referred to as step-up or step-down rings, depending upon the particular combination of threads and direction of use. To attach a 58mm filter to a 52mm lens mount, you need a 52-58mm step-up ring; if the lens takes a 58mm thread and you want to use a 52mm filter, you'll need a 58-52mm step-down ring.

These handy accessories can hold down your total investment in filters/ lens attachments should your lenses require various filter sizes, but they should be used judiciously. Although rings are available which will adapt filters over a 3-5 step range, and even more if the rings are used in combination, it's never a good idea to use a filter more than one step smaller or three steps larger than that required. A filter that's too small will cause vignetting; one that's too large can cause flare while protruding from the lens mount, inviting damage.

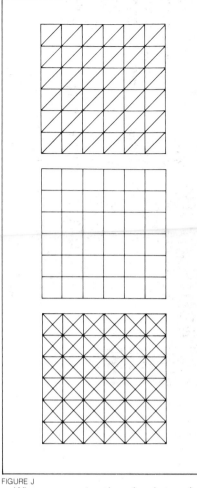

FIGURE J

Whenever a stepping ring is used, it should be screwed into the lens mount part way, the filter then installed and both tightened until barely snug. Overtightening can result in binding of the threads and an inability to free the stepping ring from the filter and/or the lens mount. If stepping rings are used very frequently, you might consider the purchase of a filter wrench. Made of plastic, this simple but handy device fits around the outside of the filter, ring or attachment and provides sufficient leverage to separate the two when binding does take place. *Never* tap the filter or lens mount in an attempt to free threads that bind, as it can cause permanent damage to the lens and/or attachment.

PURCHASE, HANDLING AND STORAGE

While we might presume that common sense would rule in these areas, past experience has proven such presumptions to be incorrect and so a few words on the subject are in order before we close out this discussion. Filters and lens attachments will generally last a lifetime unless damaged, and for this reason, it's more economical to buy *good* ones. Here's why.

Whenever you place another piece

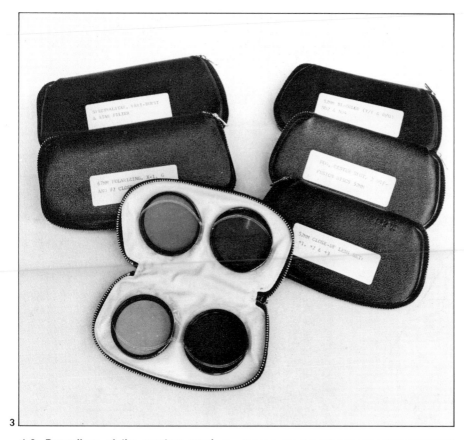

3

1-2. Regardless of the aperture used, a mirage lens will soften all but the prime image. But as the aperture is stopped down, image clarity increases from center to edge.

3-4. There are more ways to carry filters than you can count, but few of which are really convenient. Even the stack-cap method (center top, 4) allows the entry of dust between the filters. My personal favorite are the Prinz filter cases shown in (3). These hold four filters under transparent plastic. Label the outside of the zipper case and you have the handy equivalent of a tobacco pouch, with ready access to any filter.

4

of glass in front of that expensive optic on your camera, you're introducing a potentially disruptive element to the carefully calculated formula of your lens. To paraphrase an old saying, if the manufacturer of your lens had wanted a filter there, he would have provided it. As a potentially disruptive element, the filter you use had better be as perfectly plano-convex and free from distortion as possible, its color mass uniform, and it must be free of all other optical imperfections—or your pictures will suffer. Remember, an expensive lens formula, no matter how carefully calculated, is only as good as its weakest element—in this case, the filter you use. That's why camera manufacturers often offer their own filters manufactured to their specifications, and charge accordingly.

Now, I'm not suggesting that you must buy Zebra filter because you own

a Zebra camera, but I am holding the Zebra quality level up to you as a level to be attained in your own filter purchases. There are plenty of good filters and lens attachments offered by independent manufacturers, but there are also dogs in the same showcase. So know your manufacturer—an obscure off-brand name may be a bargain over the counter but it could be a disaster on your lens.

Color permanence is important. Most filters sold to amateurs today are laminated, that is, two pieces of optical glass with a gelatin filter between and treated with heat and pressure to form a single unit. Some even skip the gelatin and provide the color by adding dye to the cement which holds the two glass pieces together. The "dyed-in-the-mass" optical glass filter is on its way to becoming little more than a memory these days. But despite the method of manufacture and what some filter companies will tell you, *all* dyes are subject to change from exposure

to temperature extremes and light, and the more exacting control and quality that goes into the manufacture of a filter, the better the end product.

Once you've acquired more than one filter/lens attachment, their care and protection becomes a problem. Most filters and attachments are supplied in screw-together containers of hard plastic; a few come in soft or padded vinyl pouches. Regardless of how they're packed, the most important thing is to keep them protected adequately from the possibility of scratching or chipping when not in use.

The "stack cap" concept of storage and carrying has proven relatively popular in recent years. This simply involves screwing all of your filters together to form a single unit and protecting the stack at both ends with a screw-in and screw-on cap. While certainly desirable from a storage standpoint, the stack cap method does have disadvantages which can outweigh its portability, especially after you've accumulated a fair number of filters and attachments.

For reasons no one quite fathoms, dust still manages to work its way between the stacked filters, settling on their surfaces and often making a thorough cleaning necessary before use, particularly if the filter stack is frequently carried in a gadget bag. There's also the problem of screwing the stack together too tightly and not being able to separate it to use the filter you've selected, as well as the distinct possibility of damaging several expensive filters by accidentally dropping the stack while removing or replacing a filter.

Despite the space problems posed in carrying a variety of filters with you, the best answer still remains the use of the case supplied with the filter. Write the type, filter factor and size (if you use more than one size) on the outside of the plastic case with a permanent-ink marker for easy reference without removing the filter from its case. Protect stepping rings in a similar manner, carrying them in their box instead of loose in your gadget bag, as the fine-pitch threads are extremely susceptible to damage.

The world of filters and special-effect lens attachments can add immeasurable enjoyment to the hobby of photography, but these accessories should not be acquired in a haphazard fashion. Think about what you can do with a particular one and how much use you'll give it before adding another item to your gadget bag—then *use it!* □

Composition

Sooner or later, anyone who writes about photography must lock horns with the subject of composition and with rare exception, it's a losing battle. No matter how he approaches the topic, the self-proclaimed expert will critique his treatment to death, often using contradictory statements that have been repeated so often they're now clichés. Unfortunately, clichés play a large role in our daily lives and so we have a tendency to accept them as gospel, especially if they've been repeated many times by our "experts."

To cite an example, we've all heard the popular saying, "Rules are made to be broken." This happens to be one that our "experts" are fond of applying to photography in support of their contention that the "best" pictures break all the established rules of composition that collective experience has formulated over the years. Yet what they fail to recognize is that before you can *break* the rules, you must first *know*, *understand* and be able to *apply* them, and that's our purpose in this chapter. Composition is regarded by many as perhaps the dullest topic in photography, but I don't think you'll find this treatment one that will put you to sleep—after all, composition is highly personal, and there's no reason why we can't have a little fun with it.

We all take bad pictures from time to time, but whether your pictures are good or bad from a creative standpoint, the most important thing is that you make a conscious effort to improve your ability to create with a camera—in other words, to learn from your mistakes. Without some understanding of the subject's elements and how they can best be arranged, your pictures will seldom rise above the category of snapshots, even if you possess the best, most expensive camera and equipment available. You may even have sufficient expertise to create

1. Hank Harris found a natural "Rule of Thirds" in this still life. Despite the subject's linear aspect, the eye enters on a diagonal, with only momentary distraction in the center before moving on.
2. Composition is personal; how you arrange your subject matter will depend upon how you "see" the world around you. Michael Parrish used several of the traditional rules of composition in capturing this aspect of Toledo while in Spain. Can you spot them?

technically excellent pictures, but unless you have a firm grasp on the principles of composition and how to make them work for *you,* you'll never bridge the gap between expensive snapshots and interesting photographs.

Even the purist or the documentarian who uses his camera to capture reality precisely must work with photographic composition if he is to rationally present his subject matter. So, if you've excused your poor pictures on the grounds that you've simply recorded what you found in front of your camera (the camera never lies), you really have no excuse at all, and even less reason for taking pictures.

CONTROLLING COMPOSITION

I've always regarded the essence of

composition as the structuring of a highly personal view of the world and how to best present it within the confines of a two-dimensional format. In this respect, what turns on one person may well make another cringe. The idea that composition is a rigid, unbending set of rules is as erroneous as those who believe that compositional rules are outmoded and "everything goes." There are classic concepts of composition and when used as a general working guide, they provide a point of departure for the photographer who seeks to improve his work by providing a basic understanding of and feeling for what he's working with. Upon reaching this point of visual literacy, you are then able to present your point of view by controlling the composition of your pictures in such a way as to strengthen what you are trying to say with them.

However, don't fool yourself into believing that once you've mastered the basics, you have finished learning and can now take prize-winning pictures one after another simply by rote manipulation of the rules. No matter how high up you climb on the ladder,

1

eyes and we see it in full color, in three dimensions with great depth, and with a field of view approaching 160°—or about the same as a full-frame fisheye lens. The camera sees in terms of the type of film with which you loaded it, in two dimensions with a very limited degree of depth, and with a fixed field of view determined by the photographer's choice of lenses. But the most important difference is the interaction of the eye with the human brain. When you look up at a building, the parallel lines *do not* converge in the image you see as they do when seen by the camera lens. They do not converge because the human brain makes an accommodation in the mental image which the camera is incapable of accomplishing.

When you look at someone or something from an unusual angle, or from a very close distance, the distortion recorded by the camera lens on the film is transformed by the brain so that our eye does not see it in real life. While the camera depends upon the far more sophisticated vision of the human eye in selecting and treating the subject with which it will deal, it has none of the magical qualities of accommodation and transformation with which the eye is endowed by the brain. And so, that breathtaking sunset captured by the camera lens falls flat upon your memory when you see the finished picture for the first time a week or so after taking it, just as the multicolored field of flowers waving gently in the breeze turned into just another flat and sterile mass of grays forming a world you do not recognize.

Once you learn to manipulate those elements that go into creating the moment in time you wish to preserve, there are "tricks" which can be played upon the human eye and memory. And it's the understanding of this manipulation of elements that constitutes what I call the psychology of composition.

PSYCHOLOGY OF COMPOSITION

A picture will have either a fast or slow discharge quality, depending upon the subject and the way in which it's treated photographically. In the case of the former, its content and message are grasped by the viewer immediately. For this reason, the degree of visual and emotional impact that the picture possesses will depend upon the impression(s) it transmits to the viewer in that single moment. While it's true that such a picture will require more time on the part of the viewer to absorb its lesser details, their importance

there's always another rung above you. So, our first task is to discover the factors that govern good composition and learn how to effectively apply the resulting guidelines. Once you've accomplished this, you can begin to manipulate the basics in such a way as to further the impact of your particular point of view. Rather than being a rigid framework, or no framework at all, composition should be regarded as a flexible tool for improving your photos.

THE CAMERA AS AN EYE

How many times do you look at your finished pictures with less than satisfaction because they fail to transmit what you considered the essence of the subject as you saw it when you snapped the shutter? A thing of beauty may be a joy forever—or at least until you see your picture of it—but there are definitely ways in which you can

1. The massive strength of this San Francisco bridge is captured in Jeff Blackwell's vertical composition. Check your own bridge pictures—how many of them are horizontal?
2-3. Here's reality, as seen by Rick Oyama's eye (2) and his camera lens (3). Both were taken with a 17mm wide-angle, yet note the lengthening of vertical lines and the excessive perspective distortion in (3), resulting from a too-close camera placement.

avoid this sort of visual letdown and carry the original excitement right through to the print on display or the slide on the screen. To understand how, we must review the comparison of the human eye and the camera lens for a moment. This fundamental comparison has a far greater implication than the simple mechanical aspect so often used as a basic concept in explaining how a camera works.

Most of us see the world with two

2

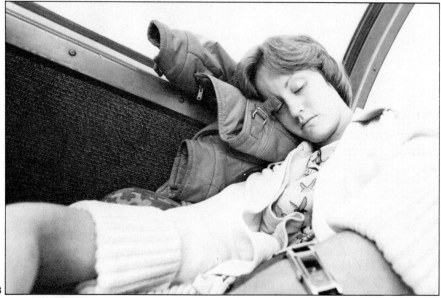

3

is usually only relative to the thrust of the principal object(s) in the photo.

Given the same single glance, a slow discharge picture may appear to possess little, if any, power. Like other abstractions, it must be perceived as a matter of space, time, color or object relationship—factors which all contribute heavily to any meaning that the viewer receives or deciphers as being present. The physical content of a slow discharge picture may be no greater than an isolation of form, shape, tone or texture, but such photos will usually have a far deeper emotional meaning, and one that has a tendency to build with visual study.

ACCEPTING REALITY SELECTIVELY

To some, photography is nothing more than the recording and reproducing of reality; to others, it involves a complex rearrangement of reality. Both positions represent the extremes of composition and as such, are rejected by most serious photographers. But it is possible, and at times certainly desirable to alter the appearance of certain aspects of reality in order to gain a specific effect.

The use of a filter will improve upon the tonal renditions within the subject, while contrast can be controlled by increasing or decreasing the development process. In the same way, it's possible to alter the size/distance relationship between objects in the picture to achieve a specific effect. In all such cases, we must compensate for the eye's ability to transform and accommodate, and to do so successfully, it's necessary to know exactly the effect sought and how to obtain it correctly without depending upon our eye to guide us.

There are also situations in which reality fools the eye, as in the case of optical illusions. Many may recall the old optical puzzle encountered as a child in which a light area of a given size when banded by a darker one appears larger to the eye than a dark area surrounded by a lighter one, even though both are exactly the same size, as shown in Figure A. For the same reason, the gray tone of the circles in each of the five boxes in Figure B is

identical, but to the eye, the circle in box E seems much lighter than the others.

But there are also times when this kind of illusion reverses itself, as in the case of haze and fog and their relationship to distant objects. On a clear day, foothills or mountains appear to be much closer than when seen on a hazy day, despite the fact that the haze or fog makes them lighter. To understand why this is so, we must consider the relativity of detail.

RELATIVITY OF DETAIL

The presence or lack of detail produces an interesting subconscious effect on what we see and what we don't see. When looking at a picture or even a scene in real life, the human eye tends to travel immediately to the lighter areas, where it can recognize and absorb whatever detail is present. If a sufficient amount of detail exists in such light areas, the eye ignores the lesser amount found in the darker areas, reserving it until last, if at all. But what happens should the detail in lighter areas burn out or not even be present? The eye simply searches out whatever detail it can find and then judges distance accordingly. The amount of detail present in foothills when seen on a clear day makes them appear to be much closer to us than on a hazy or foggy day, when the eye must search for its clues elsewhere.

By now, you should recognize that there's a good deal of psychology involved in composition and its correct application. At the same time, you've discovered what is responsible for the majority of pictures that fail to communicate their message to a viewer. Despite all our good intentions, our

1-2. Abstractions such as (1) are slow discharge pictures, requiring that the eye study the image for its full impact. Yet Hal Stoelzle's message in (2) is immediate, accentuated by the perspective compression of his 180mm lens.

eyes can and often do play tricks on us when we try to transfer the reality of life to a photographic print or slide via the camera. To be successful in all cases, you must see beyond that which your eye sees and know when and how to introduce controls that will reinforce or override, as the particular situation may require.

COMPOSITION IN THE CAMERA

The recognition of and differentiation between good and poor composition should begin even before you raise the camera to your eye. You should train yourself to select the appropriate treatment for any picture opportunity by mentally considering the alternatives and the equipment required to obtain the desired effect. If this sounds difficult, let me assure you that it really isn't once you've had an opportunity to analyze the various basic rules involved. With only a bit of practice, you'll find that the principles involved in good composition will become second-nature in your thinking. Once this happens, you'll sort out potential picture possibilities and select the most promising one almost automatically.

It's certainly possible to improve a photograph considerably in the darkroom, but it's also foolish to think that you can just snap away all day with your camera and then correct every error that you made in the evening while working with an enlarger. Off-the-cuff shots may well turn out to have good composition, especially after

you've reached the point where you make automatic decisions correctly, but the majority of good pictures are created in the camera with a conscious effort on the photographer's part. Darkroom composition under an enlarger is really an adjunct to, and not a replacement for judicious camera use, and should be reserved only to improve an otherwise good picture.

KEEP IT SIMPLE

If you asked me for a single rule of composition on which you could base your photographic efforts, the most useful one I could pass along would be, "Keep it simple." Many photographers, from rank beginner to the tech-

nically accomplished amateur, automatically make the mistake of crowding everything they possibly can into a single picture. The end result is a massive jungle of conflicting visual cues that cause the eye to wander without direction, often giving up before it finds whatever you were trying to say. For this reason, "move closer to your subject" is probably the best advice one can give to the beginner, but somehow there seems to be a psychological block which prevents many from following such a simple direction. It's almost as if they are afraid of not getting *enough* into the picture.

Those who shoot family pictures are especially guilty in this respect. The re-

sult is an exercise in eye-squinting to determine if the subject really was Aunt Mary—there's an equally good possibility under such circumstances that you're actually looking at Uncle Fred. The simple act of moving closer to the subject corrects a number of other compositional problems that usually afflict such pictures: poor framing, incorrect camera placement, distracting backgrounds, etc.

Simplicity is not always easy to achieve, so here are a few tips on how to approach it, which will be amplified shortly. Don't forget that the eye moves almost constantly, and the camera lens is static. The eye shows us a composite of a scene—the camera

does not. The eye picks out significant detail from what it sees, the camera does so only if it's properly used. Pictures taken from eye level often have nothing extraordinary about them—try a high or low angle. Focus selectively to control the foreground or background in such a way as to draw the eye directly to your subject without wasted motion. Use lighting to emphasize form and texture; use filters for contrast. Fill the frame for impact. Arrange your composition in such a way that its appeal is self-evident and the viewer is not forced to search for it.

If you can remember simplicity as your major goal whenever you take a picture, you've made a giant step for-

1

2

1-3. Many photographers use a red filter to bring out the sky; Ralph Merzlak wanted to emphasize Cristo's latest "sculpture" by darkening the ground for contrast on an overcast day (3). Controlled development can achieve the opposite—a reduction of contrast in which light and dark tones blend together, as in this pseudo-storm shot (1). David Neibel depended entirely upon tones in (2).

3

ward in the direction of better photographic composition.

BALANCE

As we've already seen, photographic composition has to be considered with the human eye in mind. From early childhood, our eyes are taught certain behavior, the most important of which is a left-to-right movement within a field of view whose shape is fluid or unlimited. Reducing reality to two dimensions in a photograph and then asking the eye to interpret it is bad enough, but at the same time, we've imposed a geometric frame of necessity in these negative dimensions.

With a 35mm camera, the horizontal is 1½ times that of the vertical, while with other cameras, the horizontal and vertical are often of equal dimensions. This format structure must be taken into consideration, both in terms of arranging the subject elements and in viewing the finished prints—and whether it is 5x7, 8x8 or 11x14, it's artificial. Even the so-called "ideal" negative

format that permits enlargement to standard paper sizes without losing any of the image is restrictive in this sense. Balance is thus a prime consideration, and balance in any photograph is interdependent with the negative format.

As the eye has been preconditioned to move naturally from left to right, so it is reasonable to begin compositional arrangements of the elements from the bottom left corner to lead the eye into the picture and direct it to the main area of interest. Should action of any kind, whether static or active, be involved, it should also be directed from left to right if at all possible, and on a diagonal line into the center of the picture area.

Balance can also be applied in terms of the picture's tonal scale. Think of the tones in terms of weights and you should be able to balance the picture on an axis close to its center. For example, if all the light tones are placed on one side and the dark ones on the other side, you end up with a lopsided picture, with the visual weight of the dark tones dragging the light ones down. This is easily illustrated by a typical scenic shot with the horizon line placed directly through the center; the bottom half is a nearly uniform landscape containing a variety of darker tones, while the top half is a nearly white sky.

Since most of us will immediately reject such a picture as being visually flat, we reach for a filter that will dark-

en the light sky tones and lighten the darker ones in the landscape. In doing so, we're applying the concept of balance by shifting the tonal scale to interrelate the tones. When working in color, this concept is applied by making certain that the primary subject the strongest color in the scene, wi

all others subordinate to but harmonizing with it. In black-and-white work, this principle can be applied by placing the lighter tones closer to the center, with the darker ones positioned toward the edge. In essence, you're framing with tones, a topic that we'll touch upon in greater depth somewhat later.

FUNDAMENTALS OF COMPOSITION

To achieve simplicity and balance, there are a number of simple and basic concepts which the beginner can follow to assure that his pictures will have at least a semblance of compositional strength. As he works with these tools, he finds that they are often inter-

dependent, and ignoring or breaking one has an effect on the others. Let's first consider the primary subject.

USE A STRONG CENTER OF INTEREST—Sounds simple, right? It is, but you must be careful how you interpret it, since the center of interest may form only a portion of your subject matter, and placing it directly in the center of your negative format will create a static illusion that causes the eye to lose interest immediately. Although you want and need a strong center of interest, you don't want it in the center of your picture area. So where should you put it?

Follow the *Rule of Thirds* in positioning the center of interest in your picture. This can be applied by mentally dividing the picture area as you see it into thirds, both horizontally and vertically. This will create a grid pattern of nine equal blocks and four intersections—and it's at one of the four intersections where your center of interest should be placed. Which intersection will depend upon the other elements in your total composition. Although you should avoid the use of more than one center of interest, a secondary subject will present no real problem as long as its placement does not detract the eye's attention from the primary center of interest.

Should a secondary subject be included, photographic balance will come into play. Both the center of interest and the secondary subject should be located in the format according to the Rule of Thirds, and an attempt should be made to create a feeling of depth by positioning the two at varying distances from each other and from the camera. Whenever the secondary subject falls in the same plane as that of the primary center of interest, it's likely to detract from the strength inherent in the latter, resulting in a weakening of the total effect.

CAMERA PLACEMENT AND ANGLE—It's always humbling to watch a group of tourists taking pictures. They climb off the sightseeing bus, shoot a few quick snaps and buy a souvenir before scrambling back aboard, only to repeat the whole procedure at the next stop. If you remember that those are the same pictures that will bore their unfortunate neighbors for countless winter evenings filled with dull slide shows, you'll suddenly count your knowledge of composition (however slight) as one of your greatest photographic blessings.

Whenever you find a subject that's worthy of your camera, don't just step up to it, shoot a snap and then run to the next one. Walk around and look it over from various angles; consider their virtues and vices before selecting the best two or three angles from which to take your pictures. With a bit of practice, you'll soon be able to choose a camera placement and angle

that complements the subject.

When the background is cluttered, try shooting from a low angle to use the sky as a backdrop. Or you might try a higher angle and shoot down, especially if the weather is overcast and bleak, since overcast skies add little to most pictures. Regardless of the angle you decide on, consider what its effect will be on your subject before you release the shutter. If you're fairly close to a person and use a low angle, you may accentuate the neck, chin or nose. This can result in a proportional distortion of perspective and an unappealing, even unflattering picture. The same holds true with the subject's nose and forehead when you're shooting from a high angle and are too close. In such cases, it's best to step back from the subject until the perspective regains its normal look.

Be careful *where* you place the camera. Beginners have a tendency to look through the viewfinder and then back away from their subject. While the viewfinder is primarily thought of as a means of positioning the subject in the picture area, it is also a tool which can be used to eliminate everything around the subject that does not add to the picture. Forget about cropping the negative in the darkroom and concentrate on cropping before you shoot. You'll end up with a far better picture as a

1-2. The inherent ability to change size/ distance relationships by lens focal length can be seen in Shirley I. Fisher's use of the 50mm and 250mm lenses on a Hassleblad for these scenics.
3. Reality fools the eye in this optical illusion. Both blocks and both squares are identical in size—or are they?
4. Another optical illusion—while the gray tone in all five circles is identical, most people would insist that E is lighter.

result. Of course, it's possible that you'll find that judicious cropping under the enlarger will improve it even more, but think of the problems this would present if you had not taken the trouble to eliminate those unnecessary and distracting elements before snapping the shutter.

Because the Rule of Thirds is closely interrelated with both camera placement and angle, you should visualize the grid created by its application whenever you explore various possibilities. It's possible that an otherwise perfect camera placement or angle simply will not work properly because the lighting on the center of interest is not right. If this is the case, you should change the lighting if possible, choose an alternative camera placement or angle, or just wait until the lighting is more appropriate.

LINES AND SHAPES—Lines and shapes of some sort are found in every picture situation, and how you make

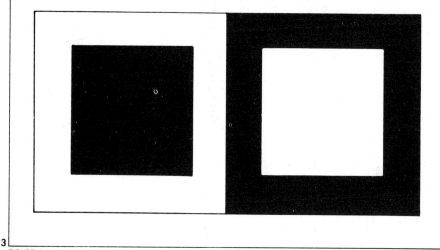

2

3
FIGURE A

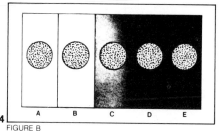

4
FIGURE B

est. Vertical lines can often be used as a balancing factor to hold the eye's attention on the center of interest by blocking any easy exit from the picture. But whatever you do with them, analyze their effect first and consider alternatives before immortalizing them on film and calling it a day.

Diagonal lines possess a dramatic and emotional appeal, and can be used to lead the eye into, through and even out of the picture with ease. Such lines can also foster the illusion of depth, as in the case of railroad tracks, wherein the perspective created by the converging lines suggests a dimensional quality, especially when photographed at a low camera angle. The lines used may be real ones, or they may be imaginary lines created by the placement of the subject matter, such as a group of skiers winding their way down a slope. Although there's no real line involved in such a winter scene, the S-shaped curve inherent in the skiers and their path creates the same effect as if the line were actually there. By placing your subject matter along an imaginary line, you can create virtually any line effect you want.

As a general rule, lines should lead into the picture area from left to right (following the direction in which the eye normally moves) and are most effective when they are strong enough to direct the attention of the eye along their path. Almost anything can act as a leading line—a road, stream, even a shadow or other tonal contrast—it's simply a matter of selecting the correct angle of interpretation to have it lead into the picture and to the subject as desired.

The conventions of composition tell us that there are three basic shapes that can and should be used wherever possible in arranging the main elements within a picture: the triangle, the circle and the ''L.'' The triangle and especially the circle are supposed to convey a feeling of unity and a sense of symmetry when properly used.

If your subject happens to settle into a basic triangular shape with its base line resting on the lower third of the picture area—that's neat. But don't knock yourself out trying to get just the

use of them will determine to a large degree how successful you are in mastering the techniques of composition. Let's look at lines first, starting with the simplest one of all, and the one that seems to give most amateurs their most difficult problem—the horizon line. Many of us almost automatically use it to cut the picture in equal halves—the least effective way of treating it—and the picture invariably ends up being a visual dud.

Instead, look at the horizon line in terms of the effect you wish to achieve. If it's spaciousness you want in a scene, run the horizon line below the center, leaving ample room for those fluffy white clouds to stand out against an expanse of blue sky. But if depth and closeness are your goals, the horizon line belongs in the upper third of the picture area.

The same approach holds true for vertical lines—try not to divide the picture area into halves but use them to cut the picture unevenly. Lines may also be used to produce a pattern effect wherein the horizontal and vertical lines create their own subdivisions and lose their identity as individual lines, or they may be used to create a natural frame for the primary center of inter-

camera placement, lens selection, etc. that will deliver this effect. All too often, the means becomes the end in applying compositional rules, and you can get mired down in the mechanics. You'll find that both the triangle and circular shapes work best in landscapes and still life pictures.

The most useful of the three is the "L" shape. This can be placed in any position—right side up, upside down, reversed—and is commonly used as a framing device, which we'll touch on a bit later. The use of horizontal and vertical lines within the picture to form an "L" will add a visual strength to your work that's difficult to obtain in any other way.

FOREGROUND AND BACKGROUND CONTROL—Photographing a subject as you find it in real life differs considerably from the studio shot, where compositional elements can be manipulated at will. While the real world demands that you work within the specific confines which it places on you, it also provides room for sufficient creative control in most cases, but you have to be alert and take advantage of it. Every potential picture contains both a foreground and a background, and unless you exercise the necessary control over each one, they can easily upset the balance in your finished picture. Your model may be the most beautiful girl in the world, but if your rendition of her beauty happens to include a tree branch or telephone pole that appears to grow from her head, the entire mood is ruined and so is your picture.

Backgrounds seem to pose the most problems for many amateurs. Those living in highly congested urban areas often find background control to be perplexing, because there are few wide open spaces where one can "lug" his subject to take the picture, and many subjects can't be "lugged" at all, but must be treated within the confines of their environment. Since you must live with the background whether or not it's actually connected to the content of your picture, the secret lies in knowing how to make it work for, instead of against you.

The first concern is simply that of being aware that your background *does exist.* Far too many photographers are so eager to take the picture in a hurry and move on that they pay

Haze and fog change the relationship of distant objects, adding depth that really doesn't exist in the picture. To put this fact to work as Ralph Merzlak did, you must understand the relativity of detail.

no attention to the background until it's too late to change it. Suppose you're working in an available-light situation—an ugly lamp to one side of your subject may not bother your eye when looking through the viewfinder, and if it does, you mentally decide to crop it out in the darkroom. But the lamp's effect will be considerably out of proportion to its value in the final picture; even if you crop it out, you must somehow compensate for the effect its light will have on the area near its location. This may mean burning in that area, or even further cropping.

If the background is cluttered and filled with distractions, try to clean it up by changing camera placement or angle; moving the subject (if possible) is another alternative, as is selective focus or the use of another focal length lens. Watch out for strong horizontal or vertical lines, such as those of a brick wall or shingled house—in cases like these, it's better to substitute foliage or the sky for your background.

Consider the case of two models, one with dark hair and one with light. A sky background will work far better with the dark-haired girl, since it frames and contrasts with her hair, which would blend into a foliage background. But when the model is a blonde, foliage provides a better backdrop as it will show her off to better advantage than the light sky. There are occasions when a blend is more appropriate than contrast but you'll seldom go wrong balancing light against dark and vice versa as a general rule.

When everything else fails, you can try selective focus. Open the aperture to a large f-stop and use the depth-of-field preview lever while you focus carefully to throw the area immediately

1-2. Composition in the camera—should it be vertical or horizontal? Many would automatically choose the vertical, but a good case can be made for the horizontal—take your pick.
3. Keep it simple. Jeff Blackwell applied this tenet of composition and found it can be deceiving. The longer you look at this street scene from his viewpoint, the more complex it becomes visually. Here's a hint to start your search—note how everything tends to fall into block designs?
4. Simplicity often involves symmetry, where one half of the picture is nearly a mirror image of the other. (Hank Harris.)

behind your subject as far out of focus as possible. If you work with other than a single-lens reflex or view camera, you'll have to guess at the effect and it's a good idea in such cases to bracket your focus over at least three points because you'll get a different degree of background control with each, and you can select the most effective one from the proof sheet.

Foregrounds present a different 3

4

problem—they are too often ignored and left empty. What you do to and with a foreground depends to a great extent on where you decide to place the horizon line and primary center of interest. If either the horizon line or the center of interest is positioned in the lower third of the picture area, there may be very little you can or should do, but this is more often than not the exception, especially when you're dealing with outdoor scenes and most especially landscapes.

One method of control that can work quite well is to place a secondary subject in the foreground, or compose your picture to include one. This will add a feeling of spaciousness, as well as a degree of depth to an otherwise flat scene. But whatever foreground objects you use must be compatible with or at least complementary to the center of interest, or they can easily distract the eye completely. When compatible or complementary, secondary objects also tend to draw some of the emphasis that would otherwise be directed to the background. Thus, the use of a foreground object often becomes a matter of personal taste and not an inviolable rule—the key here is not so much whether or not they are used, but rather *how* they are used.

Static foreground objects should relate to the rest of the picture; if you include people who happen to be in the camera's field of view, they should be looking into the scene rather than at the camera. Proper framing helps to direct the eye to the center of interest and in some cases, can even act as a leading line. Many of us recall quite vividly a scene used in countless Hollywood ''B'' westerns—the magnificent Indian chief standing erect and silhou-

1

2

3

1. Properly used, the horizon line can produce an adequate foreground and background without overemphasizing either.

2,5. Two examples of the circle as a compositional tool. David Neibel went all the way in his interpretation of an old hay rake, while Ron Berkenblitt broke up the circular staircase with a vertical, combining light and dark tones to further emphasize his subject.

3. Using diagonal lines to lead the eye into this train derailment, Hal Stoelzle added depth to his picture. Many would photograph such a scene head-on, ending up with a mass of horizontal lines and little eye appeal.

4. Use the "Rule of Thirds" as a guide in positioning the center of interest. While X marks the spot(s), don't place your subject directly in the center of the negative.

etted against the setting sun at the left of the screen, his arm outstretched into the picture area as he points out the unsuspecting wagon train below to his followers crouched at the bottom of the frame. While this technique was used so often that it became a movie cliché, there's no doubting its effectiveness as the eye travels into the picture and right down his arm to the center of interest. It's not only most effective, but also highly dramatic.

One precaution to observe: When you include people as foreground objects for effect, watch their clothing, especially in a black-and-white picture. Depending on the film and any filter combination you use, the figures may inadvertently blend into the background or even into other elements in the foreground. In most circumstances, the foreground and background bear a definite interrelationship with each other and should be treated in this way,

not as separate and distinct entities. By making them work in unison, you can further emphasize and even strengthen the center of interest.

FRAMING TECHNIQUES—Occasionally you'll find that you can greatly improve a picture simply by adding an object in the foreground to be used as a frame that will concentrate the eye's attention on your primary subject. To do so effectively, it may be necessary to change your camera position slightly or even use a wider-angle lens.

Those scenic landscapes which contain no foreground objects to provide a sense of scale will often appear visually flat. But if you can manage to arrange several objects around the edge of the picture darker in tone than the primary subject, you can create a visual "frame" that will concentrate the eye's attention where you want it, while providing the needed sense of depth. In addition to partially filling the

empty space with a contrasting object, it acts to block the eye's quick exit and may even serve the same useful function as does our Indian friend's arm in directing the eye to the center of interest of the picture.

Other objects that you would ordinarily avoid, such as columns, arches, window frames, etc., can often be put to good use in creating framing effects that will heighten the appeal of your pictures. Using a frame can prove a valuable technique in controlling dis-

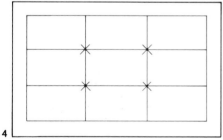

4

5

cipline in your composition, so long as it remains visually subordinate to the center of interest. Under most circumstances, both the frame and the center of interest should be in sharp focus, but on occasions you'll find that deliberately throwing the frame out of focus will help rather than hinder the eye. You'll also come across subjects on occasion that demand the use of a frame, even though there is nothing in the immediate area to serve the purpose, but don't let that stop you from applying your knowledge of composition. Take the picture just the same and later we'll discuss how to improve such pictures in the darkroom.

When using the framing technique for an effect, try underexposing the foreground object slightly to produce

good black tones in the picture. To do this, take a meter reading from the shadow areas of the frame and close the aperture down two stops (or increase the shutter speed accordingly); if you wish to lose the shadow detail in the frame itself to produce a semisilhouette effect, close the aperture down another ½ stop.

TONAL CONTROL AND LIGHTING—
Anytime you work with black-and-white

film, whatever you photograph will be reproduced on the film in varying shades of gray. For the most effective results, you must understand this gray scale transference and how tones can be manipulated to achieve a pleasing effect in a black-and-white print. What this tells us is simply that there is more than one way in which a subject can be treated. If you do not understand tonal control, you will often be disap-

1

2

3

1- 2. John Guarante combined near-horizontal lines and diagonal tones in an effective way (1), while Hal Stoelzle turned an oil field into a mass of verticals compressed by his 180mm lens (2).
3. Here we see another use of lines to lead the viewer's eye where the photographer intends. The early morning fog pushes the background back to emphasize the work crew. (Jeff Blackwell.)

pointed in your pictures and fall back on the old excuse that the subject really wasn't photogenic after all. Such cop-outs are quite unnecessary, as tonal values can be manipulated to a large extent by your choice of film, filter and processing technique. These areas are treated in greater depth in their own chapters; for our purposes here, it's sufficient to make you aware of their existence and value as manipulative tools.

My purpose in this chapter is to help you relate your ability to manipulate tonal values to their effect in composition. As I mentioned earlier, the eye will seek out lighter areas and tones first, in preference to the darker ones. Keep this in mind when composing your picture and try to treat your center of interest so that it either contains or is surrounded by the lighter tones. When possible, you should include a wide range of tonal values from white to black, but don't overlook the inherent possibilities in using only a part of the tonal scale for high or low key, high contrast or other unusual effects.

It's quite possible that a given picture area will contain several unconnected light areas. Remembering the effect of balance, it's a good idea to avoid placing one directly at the edge of the picture area whenever possible, as it will lead the eye's attention away from the center of interest by drawing undue attention to itself. When all else fails, close off the eye's avenue of escape by substituting a frame for the unwanted light tones. Once you know what tonal values are and how they will reproduce in the final picture, you can distribute them within the framework of other compositional rules—to create an effective picture, you must distribute them as skillfully as possible. So at this point, it's a good idea to briefly review light and how it can be used to alter tonal values.

Controlling the intensity and direction of light will allow you to create texture, dimension, emotional impact and even alter the appearance of shapes, figures or patterns to suit your requirements. While the professional and the serious amateur may find it more appropriate to return to a particular scene at a different time of day in order to capture precisely what he has in mind, many of us are unfortunately regimented into a schedule that demands we either take the picture now or lose it forever. Under these circumstances, it may be sufficient to change the placement or

angle of the camera, because the treatment of other compositional elements in a picture depends to a large degree upon the lighting.

In dealing with most outdoor photographic situations, lighting can be classified in one of three major catagories: frontal, back-, or sidelighting. Many find front lighting the easiest with which to work, but it does lead to a flat appearance and a lack of contrast in the subject. Filters can be used to change tonal values (add contrast) in a front-lighted situation, but control here is somewhat limited, as filters work only on complementary colors—while you can separate blonde hair from a blue sky with the help of a yellow or polarizing filter that darkens the sky, no filter will separate a green dress from green foliage.

Sidelighting is trickier, in that filters are not as useful under this lighting condition. Although sidelighting causes deep shadows which may achieve the desired contrast in some pictures (especially scenics), when people are involved, the shadows can cause a gross distortion of their features. One side of the face will usually be over-lighted, while the other is un-derlighted, often to a degree where balance is not obtainable by natural means. Under such circumstances, you should look for a source of natural fill light—a reflective surface such as walls, sand, or water will usually help considerably. If none of these is handy, the use of a reflector or fill flash is indicated.

Backlighting is the most difficult for many to work with; our eyes compensate to a considerable degree while the exposure meter and camera cannot. When shadows constitute the greatest portion of your picture area, an increase in exposure greater than that

3

1. **Balance—some hate it, others love it. Hal Stoelzle was fascinated with this supermarket magazine rack in San Bernardino, California, and his subject obligingly took up a symmetrical position.**

2,4. Hal Stoelzle used a modified "L" shape to provide a frame for his interpretation of solitude (2); David Neibel threw foreground flowers out of focus to frame his pretty model (4).

3. You can break the rules and come up with an effective picture—if you know and understand them to begin with. First prize winner in the Fuji, "Picture America" contest, Anna Lee Cutrone bent the rules backward to come up with this delightful picture of her children at play.

5. Whether tonal, line or form, symmetry can be dull if not handled with care. Hal Stoelzle broke up the inherent static nature of this subject by waiting for just the right moment.

4

5

recommended by the meter is necessary to keep the shadow detail from going black. At the same time, *too* much additional exposure will cause a loss of detail in the highlight areas. Balancing the two—shadow and highlight detail—makes backlighting difficult for many amateurs to use, although the accentuation of compositional elements creates an opportunity for some very striking pictures.

To work well with a subject lighted from behind, you must be thoroughly conversant with lighting, film, exposure and development, as the proper interaction of all is necessary to achieve the desired results. You can't use a high-speed film, normal exposure, standard developer and normal processing times if you expect to maximize the necessary shadow detail in a backlighted shot.

BE COLOR CONSCIOUS—When you replace the black-and-white film in your camera with color, you shouldn't overlook most of the aspects of com-

position which we've already covered, as they still apply, but with some modifications. You now have to replace the tonal scale in your thinking with a consideration of how the colors in the scene will interact with each other. While there's a difference between what the human eye sees and the ren-

dition of various color films, it's not as difficult for most to learn the use of a color wheel as it is to acquire a mental "feel" for translating the world of color into a gray scale.

Many of the same psychological factors come into play. The eye accommodates itself to the scene and in so

FIGURE C

doing, reduces our ability to see color exactly. Color film reproduces what it is programmed to ''see'' through the camera's lens so its rendition of a particular color may differ considerably from our mental comprehension of it. For example, suppose that a girl wearing a white wedding dress poses for an informal portrait in the garden. She's standing beside heavy foliage on a green lawn. Everything looks O.K. to the eye in this case, but to the film, everything is seen as green, including the girl and her dress, to a degree. What the film sees that we do not is the green reflecting from the darker foliage and lawn area into the highlight areas of her dress and skin.

Those of you who have taken color pictures in snow country on a bright day without any filtration were probably amazed to discover a bluish cast in the shadows of certain pictures, something not remembered in the original scene, as you did not ''see'' it that way. While it's possible to attribute such results to a bluish shift caused by processing, or a tendency of a particular color emulsion to overemphasize blue, the photographer who's color-conscious knows that his eyes played a trick on him. The shadow areas in the snow were filled with light reflected from the bright blue sky (and consequently contained blue), but our eyes saw them differently.

Composition for a color picture requires a conscious distribution of colors. While light tones draw the eye first in a black-and-white picture, it's the warm colors (red through yellow) that attract initial attention in a color shot. Cold colors are the blue-greens. With this firmly fixed in your mind, you can achieve the same light-dark relation-

1. This is just another subject for the tourist's camera and treated as such here. But there's a picture within the picture—check the contents of the circle.

2. Here's your other picture—a detail shot culled from the unsightly mess the previous photo. The camera was dropped to achieve a plain background and a red filter was used with Ilford FP4 film.

3. This picturesque church was photographed with a 28mm lens in order to get it all in the frame. As both sides of the church lean inward toward the center, our eye tells us that this is unreal.

4-5. Switch to a telephoto lens instead of the wide-angle and concentrate on the unusual details rather than the whole building. Such pictures are far more effective than the distortion of photo 3 this page.

ship of black-and-white photography by treating the warm/cold aspect of color photography in the same way.

Colors opposite each other on a color wheel are called complementary and produce a contrasting effect when used together; those colors on each side of a given color on the wheel are known as adjacent colors and contribute a harmonizing effect. Using complementary and adjacent colors wisely and in good taste will improve your color composition; disregarding colors and their psychological content may produce a striking picture in a few cases, but generally the effect is less pleasing than you might think.

Leaf through any book containing color pictures by accomplished photographers and you'll discover that the most effective ones contain few colors which are generally grouped in large areas. As color photography has its own requirements in terms of lighting and exposure, you should refer to the appropriate chapters in this book for definitive information on how to best work with it. For our purposes here,

it's sufficient that you equate the warm/cold relationship with the light/dark of black-and-white photography and function with that knowledge in composing your color pictures.

BE SELECTIVE—Do you know Joe? When he became interested in taking pictures, he went the route and bought the very best camera, with the fastest lens and all the accessories. In a manner of speaking, there's hardly any photo situation that Joe is not equipped to handle, at least from the equipment angle. But his expensive camera and accessories gather dust in the closet because no matter where he goes or what he does, Joe can't seem to find anything interesting enough to train his lens on.

Today's cameras represent a considerable investment and as such, deserve to be used to the fullest. While you don't really need the world's finest camera to take the world's best pictures, many people believe that the mere act of buying the latest camera with all the up-to-the-minute features will automatically give them better pictures. I'm willing to concede that owning a top-flight camera may give a per-

3
FIGURE D

4
FIGURE E

son the *incentive* to take better pictures, but if he/she doesn't get satisfactory results with last year's SuperDooperFlex K, swapping it in for this year's SuperDooperFlex L isn't going to improve the pictures taken with it.

As a photographer, your subject matter is the world and it's all around you—your job is to discover and interpret it with a camera. The first premise you should accept is simple enough—if you can learn to see picture opportunities, you can take a good photograph of almost anything. But waiting for the unusual or unique to take place right

5
FIGURE F

before your lens is a guaranteed method of assuring that your camera will soon wind up beside my friend Joe's in that dusty closet—you'll quickly get tired of carrying it around for "nothing." Visualization is the key to *seeing* potential pictures, and while we are regarded as a "visually oriented" society these days, this may not be as true as the mass media and our educators would have us believe.

The best way to start training your eye to *see* picture material is to load the camera with film and set out to *see* what you can *see*. Look at Figure C as an example. By itself, there's nothing particularly striking, exciting, unusual or even interesting in what the camera captured, and you might well ask with justification, "Why bother to take the picture at all?"

Well, for many, this constitutes what we call a "record" shot; they saw something different from their way of life and so recorded it exactly as it was. But the beauty of the unusual design that initially caught their eye was not transferred to the print, where the eye has ample opportunity to study the ugliness that surrounds it. Yet in every record picture taken, there's invariably a detail or two shot that *can* become striking, exciting and interesting, if only you train your eye to *see* it.

Look at the extreme right side of the record picture and then go to the next illustration, where the camera was moved in close and its angle lowered to take advantage of the sky for a backdrop. Here's your picture; one of several possible detail shots that could be taken of subject material contained within the original record shot. The mood evoked by such detail pictures is considerably stronger than that of the original record shot, and also far more fascinating.

Look at it another way. Figure D is the result of much composition care to avoid the unsightly street lamps, bus and traffic signs and other assorted trappings of modern society. To capture the entire building, it was necessary to use a 28mm wide angle lens; the result is a mass of converging lines seen by the camera but not by the eye. The end result is hardly flattering to the subject matter or to the memory. It's far better to concentrate on selected portions of the church using a telephoto lens, as in Figure E, to emphasize that which caught the eye's attention in the first place, or as in Figure F, whose mood seems to sum up everything that the building represents.

There's *always* something to photo-

FIGURE G

FIGURE H

graph, but too many people spend their time looking for that "big" picture and then try to put it all on film at once. Be selective and your pictures will be far more interesting and powerful than if you try for the big picture every time out, and your camera will stay out of that dusty closet, providing you with the enjoyment you expected when you first bought it.

THE BUILDING-BLOCK TECHNIQUE— One of the most effective ways in which you can work to improve your sense of composition is to use the "building-block" technique. To see how it works, let's consider a typical situation faced by those who want to move out of the "snapshooter" category. We've given our model a bicycle and our first picture (Figure G) is the type of snapshot many take—nothing

exciting about it in the least. So let's move the camera in closer for the second go at it, but that pole growing out of her head (Figure H) is just one of the many problems left to overcome. As the direction of the lighting is opposite to our pose, let's change her position and our camera angle (Figure I) as we move in even closer—this serves to eliminate several of the problems.

But she still appears static in her pose and does not project any hint of her personality. So we'll change the pose again (Figure J) and move in even closer. Things are beginning to shape up now, but that background is in focus and still very cluttered. Despite a better compositional use of triangular lines (arms versus back), the effect remains awkward. To eliminate these problems, we'll have to come in still closer. The bicycle handlebars are sufficient now to serve as our prop, and with a joke or two, we'll get the more relaxed, natural pose shown in the last picture. This time, Julie's good-natured humor and personality begin to project themselves, and we finally have a picture, not a snapshot.(Figure K).

By studying this series, you'll see that applying several of the fundamental rules of composition one at a time will build a picture that goes far beyond the initial attempt—the point at which most people stop. You can do the same, if you stop and think before releasing the shutter.

COMPOSITION IN THE DARKROOM

Now that we've explored the fundamentals of composition with the camera, let's take a look at the ways in which your pictures can be improved after the fact. For openers, the most efficient way to treat each roll of film is to make a proof sheet of all the negatives before printing any individual ones. This contact sheet will allow you to study what you have and decide upon the methods of printing you want to use before committing a particular negative to the time-consuming and often expensive business of enlarging.

A magnifier should be used to view the proof sheet and let you check both the sharpness and composition of the negative. Keep a sharpened China marker (grease pencil) handy to try different cropping effects such as reducing the picture area horizontally or vertically if an improvement seems likely to result. If you don't like the first try at marking off a new composition, wipe the marks from the proof sheet with a paper tissue and try again. Before moving into actual techniques, we should consider the picture format.

PRINT SIZE VS. NEGATIVE—Picture format means the actual dimension of the finished print, not the original size of the negative, although it's the negative size that causes a portion of our concern. For reasons of tradition more than anything else, we are primarily concerned with standardized sizes of finished prints: 4x5, 5x7, 8x10, 11x14, etc. Yet most of the standard negative formats available to us will not proportionately enlarge to fit one of the accepted standard print formats. And herein lies the problem—if you have composed the subject matter to fit neatly into the negative format, you're going to have to compromise when it comes to printing. There are two choices: cut into the composition sufficiently to fit the standard print size you

FIGURE I

FIGURE J

FIGURE K

1

desire, or enlarge the entire negative as close as possible to the desired print size, accepting as a result a nonstandard print that will fit neither commercial frame or photo folder.

To clarify the problem, let's take the 35mm camera's 24x36mm negative as an example. Enlarging it to 8x10 means that you can only use 24x30mm of the negative area, which represents a waste of about one-sixth of the original area available. If you enlarge the entire negative, you'll end up with a print 8x12 inches in size. In the same way, a 2¼x2¼-inch negative enlarges proportionately to 9x9 inches, yet if you fit the square format on a sheet of 8x10 paper, you'll end up with an 8x8 print. Making an 8x10 from this negative means wasting nearly ½ inch at the top and bottom, or at each side.

For those who do their own darkroom work, the answer is to leave a fractional space at each side of the negative when you compose with the camera; in other words, compose carefully in the camera, but not right up to the frame edge. On the other hand, there's nothing in the rules that says you must stick to the accepted standard print sizes; after all, magazine edi-

tors feel free to adjust print sizes and shapes as they see fit, no matter how much time the photographer spends in creating the exact composition he feels is most appropriate to the subject.

SUBJECT SIZE—Many negatives will permit more than one cropping. By this, I mean that after you've completed your initial attempt at improving the treatment of your subject, you may find it possible to raise the enlarger head, refocus the image and crop even more. As an example, a full-length picture of a young lady might become a head-to-knee shot after cropping, but if you increase the subject size to fit the same print dimensions, you may well end up with a head-to-bust shot as the most pleasing of all.

CROP FOR STRENGTH—Regardless of how carefully you've composed your subject before snapping the shutter, there are few occasions when you'll print the entire negative area and let it go at that; yet it's good mental discipline to attempt such perfect composition in the camera. Learning to *see* under the enlarger using the adjustable frame of the easel as a tool is a skill you should master if you do your own

1. Hal Stoelzle was on the scene as 2000 motorcyclists roared across the California desert near San Bernardino in an environmentalist's nightmare. Photographed with a 28mm lens, the picture was severely cropped at the top and bottom to remove excess empty space which detracted from the power of the two-wheeled legions on the move.
2-3. Pictures are made in the camera, but sometimes saved in the darkroom. By tight cropping, Hank Harris removed the many distracting elements to come up with a touching portrait of his subject.

darkroom work. Even if you don't, you should be able to specify the cropping desired to those who print for you.

Once you've settled upon the size of the subject image (by moving the enlarger head up or down) and the shape of your print (by adjusting the easel margins), your next step is to position the subject within the image area. This is accomplished by moving the easel around until your subject is positioned in that part of the image area which seems to best suit it. You'll find that quite a large number of variations are possible with most subjects, and it might be a good idea to actually make several prints with the subject positioned in different portions of the image

area and settle on the most effective one later.

TONE CONTROL—The selection of the paper grade, surface and tonal rendition can be used to influence the compositional effect. You would not print a portrait of a bewhiskered sea captain on a silk finish paper, nor would a rough or coarse finish be appropriate for a young lady's portrait. Since the appearance of the resin-coated enlarging papers, manufacturers have been trying to reduce the variety of paper surfaces and finishes they offer, and you will gradually find it more and more difficult to acquire paper surfaces that can be used to emphasize the nature of the subject. Uniformity seems to be the goal these days, but as long as the choice is available, avail yourself of the opportunity it offers.

The choice of a cold-tone paper to portray a vivid sunset would destroy its effect, whereas the use of a rich sepia tone instead would enhance it. Tonal control can be complete, as in overexposure of a backlighted subject for a silhouette effect, or local by virtue of dodging and burning-in techniques, which will be covered more fully in the appropriate chapter.

THE END—OR THE BEGINNING—In the preceding pages, I've attempted to introduce you to the mysteries of good composition in a practical manner. But no photographer should walk with a crutch for long. Guides such as these are useful to avoid awkward stumbling around the ins and outs of composition, but a feeling for tasteful and effective subject arrangements should be cultivated, so don't limit yourself to the narrow confines established here. Now that you know what it's all about, break out of the pattern today, then go out and make a unique photograph. □

10

Using Artificial Light

More books and articles have been written about artificial lighting and lighting techniques than any other subject in photography. Unfortunately, the majority of these do not really clarify the topic for the novice, but serve only to further confuse him. While it's true that some photographers just seem to have an inborn knack in visualizing the effects of various lighting schemes, handling their lights and lighting setups with ease and finesse, most of us find it a struggle which we attempt, usually without much success, and soon give up. The end result is a return to on-camera electronic flash and a bad taste in our mouths when someone mentions the word "lighting."

Strangely enough, artificial light is not that difficult to work with—it only seems that way. Somehow or somewhere, we've fallen victim to the mistaken notion that only the very accomplished can meet the challenge. For those who have never worked with artificial lighting beyond the use of on-camera electronic flash, this chapter will help you avoid the problems many amateurs encounter with it; readers who have already tried and given up will find a step-by-step method to success in the following pages. My intention is not to make you a past master in the art of lighting, but simply to provide a proven formula for success that will serve as a solid foundation for further experimentation on your part. To do so, it's necessary to adopt the proper mental attitude and reduce lighting to its basics.

YOUR MENTAL ATTITUDE

Mental attitude is more important than you might think—if you've tried working with artificial lighting and given

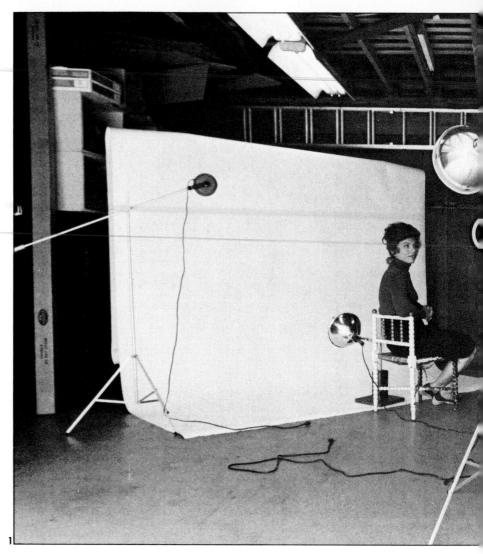

1. A home studio in the author's garage—setup time is 15 minutes. Lighting equipment and background stand can be acquired for less than $150.

up in disgust, you know what I mean. To be successful, you must realize that there is *no proven formula* in lighting a particular subject—the variations possible are infinite, and depend upon you and what you want to accomplish. There are, however, basic or elementary lighting setups with which you should be familiar, as these provide the foundation upon which you'll build.

Concentrate upon your subject rather than the "rules of lighting." While I will provide you with basic lighting diagrams later on, these are not meant to be followed religiously, but are included only as a guide to give you an idea of the approximate location of each light used to take the pictures that illustrate the different effects possible. Each subject with which you work is different, and what works well with one is not guaranteed to work with others. Thus you should light each subject individually, according to the type of ef-

fect you want to achieve, and how well the subject lends itself to that type of lighting and effect.

Remember that what you see is what you'll get. The difficulty here is that while we all see, not all of us really "see." If this sounds slightly confusing, you probably suffer from the problem I'm about to describe. Many of us will take great pains to set up a particular composition, moving things here and there to arrange everything perfectly, yet never notice until the final print is made that the lighting was all wrong, or that there's something in the background or foreground of the picture which visually detracts from our subject. We paid great attention to what we saw, but we didn't *see* everything that we should have. Carelessness perhaps, but more likely the result of an eye that's not fully trained to completely visualize the end result. This requires experience as well as an awareness of the problem, and occasionally plagues even the most accomplished photographer.

Don't forget that in most cases, there's very little difference in principle

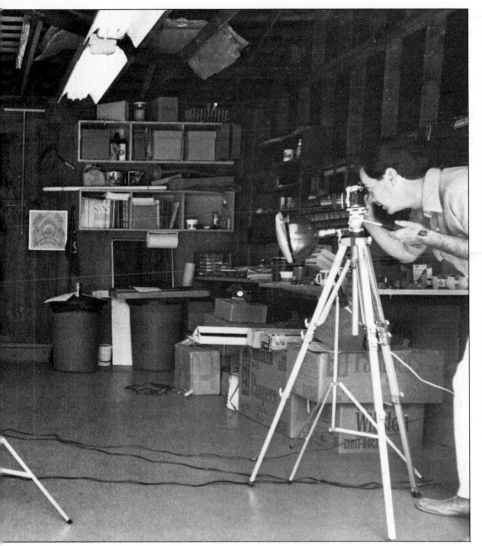

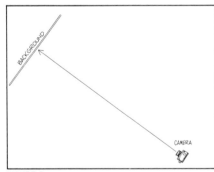

FIGURE A

ginning and end of your shooting session—a small price to pay for professional results.

Your primary problem will be that of providing a suitable background for whatever or whomever you wish to photograph. While there are various ways of solving this problem, including background roller shades which fit into standard window fixtures, most are too restrictive in nature when used without some adaptation. The easiest answer is to build a free-standing background support unit. You can do this with wood if you have the tools and the talent, but considering the amount of time and materials involved, you'll be ahead of the game by acquiring one of the inexpensive metal support units such as that offered by Prinz.

Each leg of this support rests on a three-legged base, the unit requires no nuts, bolts or washers to assemble, it provides a sufficiently sturdy holder for seamless background paper, drapes, display screens, etc. and can be easily adjusted for the height and width desired. With this and a roll of background paper, you're in business. Should you wish to photograph still-life subjects, tabletops, etc., the addition of a standard foldaway card table which can be placed in front of the support unit and background will suffice. If you wish, the background paper can be unrolled to form a background and then draped across the table to form a single, unbroken blend between photographic surface and background.

With this problem out of the way, you can now turn your attention to the basic lighting equipment necessary. You should have four lights: three of the aluminum reflector variety and the fourth a small spotlight which will accommodate a 500-watt bulb. Older slide projectors were often equipped with tripod sockets specifically to serve this purpose, and can usually be located in thrift shops or second-hand stores for a few dollars. The aluminum reflectors should be at least 10 inches in diameter and of parabolic design; the deeper reflectors of the bullet type will not be satisfactory for your needs.

Each reflector and the spot should be attached to an adjustable light stand with fold-up or permanent tripod legs. Four simple stands are adequate, but if your budget can provide for it, the type of leg that uses rubber tire casters with toe brakes can be a great help in expediting the exact placement of lights. These are also available in folding or permanent leg designs. When extended to its full height, the

between natural lighting outdoors and artificial lighting indoors. In one case, you manipulate your subject or camera position to take advantage of lighting which you cannot change; in the other, you manipulate the lighting to suit the subject and camera position. Generally speaking, the best artificial lighting scheme approximates the same results you'd obtain outdoors with natural illumination. The exception to this is those occasions when you find it appropriate to use artificial lighting to create unusual, dramatic or mysterious effects not usually found in nature. Great care is required in such cases if

the end result is to be visually appealing. One example is light primarily directed from below the subject; another is cross lighting, which results in prominent shadows that criss-cross—neither lighting effect is found in nature, but both can produce highly effective pictures if properly used.

THE HOME STUDIO

One dandy excuse for avoiding the use of artificial lighting is that you really have no place where it can be used—you can't afford to rent a studio, there's no camera club in your vicinity so equipped, and there's no suitable place around the house where you can really dig in and go about your business without creating havoc and inconvenience and moving furniture all over the place. But for slightly more than the cost of your lights, I'm going to show you how to put together a compact, portable studio arrangement that can be used in your garage with little more difficulty than backing the car out into the driveway. Setting up and tearing down the entire studio shouldn't require more than 15 minutes at the be-

light stand should be about seven feet tall. Taller stands may be desirable in some cases, but before you invest in what amounts to a more expensive unit, make certain that you have sufficient height available in the garage for their use.

Complete the basic lighting arrangement with the use of No. 1 photoflood bulbs. Many amateurs make the mistake of buying the largest, brightest bulbs they can find. The light output of such bulbs is great for small apertures and depth of field, but when used too close to your subject (another common mistake), their harsh brightness can play havoc with it. The No. 1 photoflood bulb will provide sufficient light in most cases, and draws comparatively little current, which reduces the danger of overloading an electrical circuit when you light up. Yet their life is fairly short (3-4 hours), so don't keep them on when it's not necessary. You'll also want a sufficient number of heavy-duty extension cords long enough to con-

1-3. A single light can be very versatile, if used properly. Hank Harris demonstrates three uses of the candle shown in (2), with all three pictures taken by its illumination. Exposures on ASA 400 film were in the ½ second at f/5.6 range.

nect the lights to each other, or individually to an AC outlet. With these components in hand, you have the basic necessities, but what about a few handy accessories that can increase the versatility of your lighting setups?

Probably the most useful accessory is a heat-resistant clip-on diffusion screen to fit the aluminum reflectors. This will provide a considerable amount of control over both the intensity and quality of light in which you bathe your subject. Another useful add-on is a two-section boom arm fitted with a tripod locking device to be used on one light stand—the reflector is then attached to one end of the boom. For this use, a bullet reflector 6-9 inches in diameter will be more useful than the wide parabolic type. The boom will

give you the ability to provide overhead illumination for highlighting a model's hair, or otherwise adding a touch of distinction to your subject.

You might also consider a pair of barndoors for one or two of your lights. These are useful when the light is used near to or opposite from the camera lens, as they permit shading the lens from the light rays. They also allow you to direct your illumination a bit more specifically to the subject when desired. Those who work primarily in color might consider the acquisition of gel holders and a set of gels to fit over the aluminum reflectors in a manner similar to the diffusion screens. These are highly desirable whenever you wish to direct a number of colored lights on your subject for effect.

The final accessory of value would be an umbrella for bounce-light photography. Umbrellas can also be used effectively in electronic flash photography, are available in either square or hexagon shapes and come in various fabrics and colors. A neutral white designed for soft shadows and diffused shoot-through lighting effects will probably prove most versatile for the beginner. The silver is a standard, all-purpose material suited for main, fill-in and outdoor use, while a super-silver adds extra accent with more contrast and less light loss. Gold, black and silver blue are also available for special purposes, none of which we're ready to attempt at this time.

A sturdy tripod will be necessary to hold the camera, and an incident-light meter is useful in determining correct exposures. You can use a hand-held reflected-light meter, or the built-in camera meter, but only if you understand the metering system you have

and how to use it properly. For most beginners, a used incident-light meter will make it far easier to determine correct exposure. Those who don't own a hand-held meter will find this a good time and opportunity to acquire a back-up to their camera's meter. Should you use a hand-held reflected-light meter, I recommend that you also work with the neutral gray (18-percent reflectance) card to avoid some of the problems which we discussed in the chapter on exposure.

The lens with which you work will depend to some extent upon what focal lengths (if any) you have other than the camera's normal lens. If absolutely necessary, you can use the normal lens by placing the camera far enough from the subject to prevent distortion and then cropping the excess negative area in the darkroom. For most subjects, whether you're shooting portraits or tabletops, a moderate telephoto is best. Which one depends upon two factors—what you have available and the amount of working distance your garage studio provides. To get more distance in a two-car garage, you can work on the diagonal instead of the linear dimension, as shown in Figure A. While a 135mm is ideal for most portraiture, you'll find an 85mm or 100/105mm to be equally useful when you must work at closer camera-subject distances.

For black-and-white photography, you'll want a slow- to medium-speed panchromatic film that has a fine grain structure and moderate contrast level. If you intend to photograph people, the greater tonal gradations of such emulsions can be put to good use. Avoid the high-speed color emulsions, whether you're shooting slides or negatives from which you'll make prints. Color films in the ASA 25-100 range will provide sufficient speed while assuring you the sharpest image possible.

LIGHTING—A BASIC APPROACH

One reason amateurs become quickly befuddled by artificial lighting is the way in which they approach its use. After settling upon a suitable lighting diagram which they hope will achieve a specific effect (it apparently did for the guy who drew it), they position all the lights according to the diagram, throw a switch and bam—instant sunlight in all directions. Unable to tell which light is doing what, they begin to fiddle with each in turn, readjusting its position until the total effect becomes overwhelming, and usually much worse than when the lights first came on.

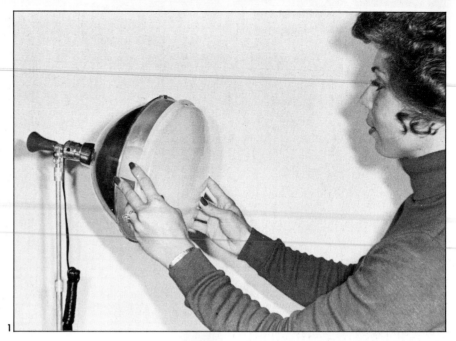

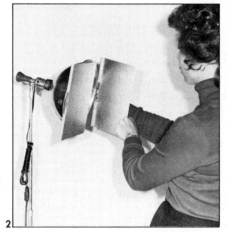

As with composition, the key to success in working with artificial lighting is simplicity—never use more lights than absolutely necessary to create the desired effect. Like the old adage about too many cooks spoiling the soup, the use of too many lamps and too much light can destroy the effect of any lighting you might attempt. The correct way to approach lighting of any subject is through a build-up technique, similar to that discussed in improving composition.

To do this properly, work from darkness to light in order to evaluate the effect of each light on the subject. Reduce the overall illumination of your "studio" to a level adequate for work, but not sufficiently bright to cause difficulty in judging the contribution of each light to the total effect. When building up your lighting one step at a time, make sure that you're satisfied with the placement and effect of each before adding another. This is best done by placing the light with any that have been previously positioned turned

1-2. Home lighting equipment will accept barn doors (2) or diffusion screens (1). Both are inexpensive and a great help in controlling the light. While the author used Prinz lighting equipment, these accessories will fit all similar arrangements. 3. Portraiture is probably the most common use for artificial lighting, but there are many other uses too. Photo by Jim Cornfield.

off. Now evaluate the effect of the light by itself, then turn on any other lights you've already positioned while you switch the one in question on/off several times to study how it relates to the overall effect.

Begin by placing a main light aimed at the subject from a point about 20 degrees above the camera-subject axis and at one side of the camera about 45 degrees away. When photographing a person, make certain that the nose shadow does not extend to the lip. Then add your second or fill light at a similar point above the camera lens, but close to it on the opposite side of the camera. This will illuminate details lacking in the shadows cast by the main light and should be weaker in intensity, either by use of a smaller lamp or by placement at a somewhat greater distance from the subject than the main light. The fill light must not add its own shadows within or across those cast from the main light—too little fill is always better than too much.

Now add your third light (a spot) from behind to make the subject stand out from the background. Your subject should be positioned far enough from the background to avoid casting a prominent or otherwise objectionable shadow. To reduce the possibility of any such undesirable effect, a fourth light can be directed at the back-

3

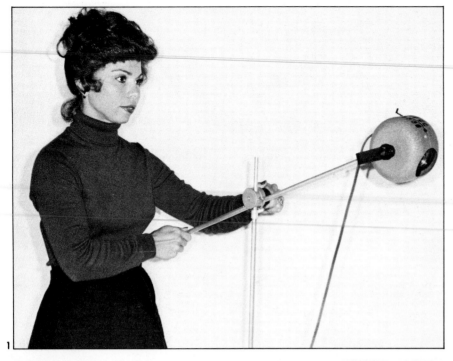

THE FOUR-LIGHT TECHNIQUE

Why four lights—why not one, two or three instead? Each of these combinations certainly possess an infinite capacity for variations, as the following examples will demonstrate. But our four-lamp technique, which will be described in greater detail below, produces a uniform or standard illumination that can be used with virtually any subject you might care to photograph. The possible variations in the use of a main, fill, accent and background lighting arrangement are unlimited, and by manipulating the four lamps according to subject distance, intensity, quality and direction of illumination, and contrast, practically any degree of sophistication you desire in lighting can be achieved easily. Before we move into the actual use of these lights, their placements and the effects you can expect, let's take a quick but closer look at what each one does.

THE MAIN LIGHT—The most important of the lights you will use, this one determines the mood of your picture by means of the light and dark areas it creates. When used for portraits, it serves to establish the general structure of the subject and creates a modeling effect on the face. With a subject positioned approximately six feet from the background, the main light should be placed between eight and 10 feet from the subject.

THE FILL LIGHT—An important complement to the main light, this is primarily used to balance the level of illumination, offsetting some of the harshness created by the main light, especially in the shadow areas. In doing so, it establishes the lighting ratio. When both main light and fill light are positioned at the same distance from the subject, the lighting ratio is said to be 2:1— those subject areas illuminated by both main and fill lights receive two units of light, while the shadow areas created by the main light receive illumination from only the fill light, or one unit. A lighting ratio of 2:1 is considered suitable for most average pictures and is a good one for the novice to work toward. One experience is gained in working with artificial lighting, he can then attempt other ratios for harder or softer effects, as the subject might demand. Placing the fill light above but close to the lens prevents it from casting secondary shadows visible to the camera, and eliminates one very common mistake made by most beginners, and some experienced photographers.

ground to light either a portion or all of it. The end result is shown in Figures B and C.

Regardless of how many lights are used, the goal for which you should strive is a picture that appears to be lighted by *one* source of illumination, rather than many sources. The farther you place a light from your subject, the weaker its illumination falling on the subject will be, but the more sharply defined the shadow edges will be. When working with subjects other than people, the lighting effect should be built up one light at a time but in a manner which will carefully pick up each surface and its texture. Lighting a

small object with a light placed low to glance across its surface will produce the desired texture. When photographing still lifes such as food, try placing the main light at the back of the subject and using one or two weaker lights at the front to lighten up the shadows.

The preceding example of building a lighting effect is not intended to make you a master of the use and control of artificial illumination, but rather to demonstrate a step-by-step approach to working with lights, observing the effect of each as you position and adjust it. Now we're ready to look at some of the potential in our home studio.

FIGURE B

1. This tiny spotlight by Prinz is one of the few of its kind remaining on the market. Use on the end of an adjustable boom, it's a great help in highlighting hair and other overhead uses.

2. If your lighting stand will not adjust low enough for use as a background light, you can use a clamp-on reflector unit and a piece of broomstick as shown. Ingenuity is the answer.

ACCENT LIGHT—Usually a spotlight, this is used to add highlights to hair and/or edge-light the contour of a cheek. As it functions from a position behind the subject, careful placement is required. The accent light must not cast unwanted secondary shadows, nor can its light be allowed to strike the lens and create flare. If an assistant is available to move the light according to your direction, considerable time and wasted motion between cam-

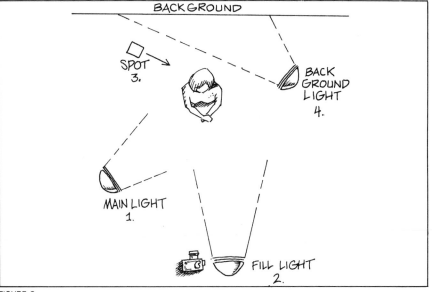

FIGURE C

FIGURE D

era and light for adjustment purposes can be saved. If not, the photographer can fall back on a law of optics which states that the angle of reflectance is equal to the angle of incidence of the light. Here's how to put it to work:

Place the accent light directly in front of the camera lens and in line with its axis. With only the accent light turned on, walk slowly around the subject until you can pick out a position from which the highlights are most appropriate, then move your light to that exact place. Determine its proper height, check through the viewfinder just to be sure and take the picture.

BACKGROUND LIGHT—This can be either a flood or spot and can be used in one of two different ways:

1—For general background illumination, both subject and background must receive equal amounts of light. The background light is positioned in this case with the help of a neutral gray card and a reflected-light meter.

2—To separate subject and background where one is dark and the other light in color. It can be placed to result in an intermediate background tone or at one side to give an uneven effect. Placed directly behind the subject and facing the background, it will

create a light spot which gradually fades into darkness.

You can control how bright the background will be, or how much the light will fall off from edge to center in various ways—bulb wattage, lamp-to-background distance, angle of placement, the use of barndoors, etc. Like the accent light, proper use of the background light requires experimentation to find the effect most appropriate for a particular subject and specific interpretation of the subject.

These are the basic elements of the four-light technique of lighting, and you'll find those complex lighting ar-

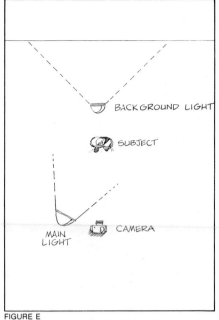

FIGURE E

rangements used in large photo studios are really nothing more than varied applications of these same principles, using several lights of each kind rather than just one. In such cases, integration of the lights might appear to be overwhelming, but it's all done in the same way as we're going to do it now. While you're free to select your own subject matter, I enjoy photographing the opposite sex, and so acquired the services of an attractive nonprofessional model to demonstrate some of the things which can be done by using the four-light technique and relying on the basics.

LIGHTING ARRANGEMENT NO. 1

With your subject situated several feet from a light background, the main light is positioned to the side of the camera and directed at her. The background light should then be placed behind her and directed on the background. Using an incident light meter, take readings from both the subject's face and from the background, adjusting the placement of the lights until the two meter readings are equivalent. This will produce a background tone which approximates that of the subject's face. Notice that the lighting on her face is rather even but somewhat flat. (See Figures D and E.)

FIGURE F

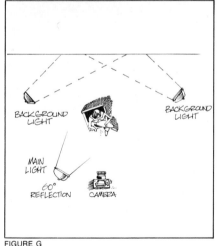

FIGURE G

LIGHTING ARRANGEMENT NO. 2

Should it be desirable to have the background tone somewhat lighter than the subject's face, leave the main light where it was in Arrangement No. 1, but use a background light on each side of the subject, positioned outside the area seen by the camera. This will result in a lighter background and provide separation from the model's face,

but does not change the basic lighting of her features, which remains rather even and somewhat flat. (See Figures F and G.)

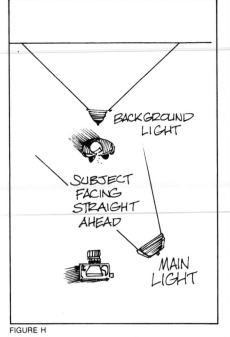

BACKGROUND
LIGHT

SUBJECT
FACING
STRAIGHT
AHEAD

MAIN
LIGHT

FIGURE H

FIGURE I

LIGHTING ARRANGEMENT NO. 3

Position the main light at the right side of the camera and direct it at the subject. Use a single background light placed behind her and slowly move the main light's position until you have thrown one-half of the subject's face into shadow. Use the incident-light meter to adjust the placement of the main light until the exposure reading from the half of her face that is illuminated is twice that of the background.

In places where you're cramped for space, the main light may end up too close to her face for comfort. If so, increase the distance between her and the background. As this will reduce the intensity of the background light's effect, you can now move the main light farther away from her face, retain the required reading and make her far happier and cooperative. (See Figures H and I.)

FIGURE J

LIGHTING ARRANGEMENT NO. 4

A distinct variation can be achieved with the lighting pattern developed in Arrangement No. 3 by simply having the subject turn 45 degrees from the camera so that illumination from the main light will now strike both sides of her face. Although the shadows created are both deep and harsh, notice the considerable increase of depth in her face over that of Arrangement No. 1 and No. 2. (See Figures J and K.)

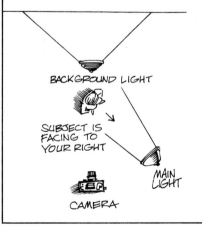

FIGURE K

FIGURE L

LIGHTING ARRANGEMENT NO. 5

Even greater depth can be created just by lightening the background. To do this, leave the main light in place, keep the subject's position unchanged and replace the single background lamp behind her with one located on each side and positioned out of view of the camera. (See Figures L and M.)

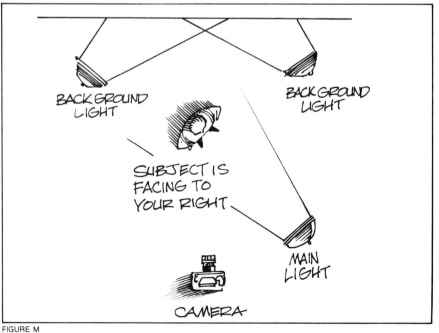

BACKGROUND LIGHT

BACKGROUND LIGHT

SUBJECT IS FACING TO YOUR RIGHT

MAIN LIGHT

CAMERA

FIGURE M

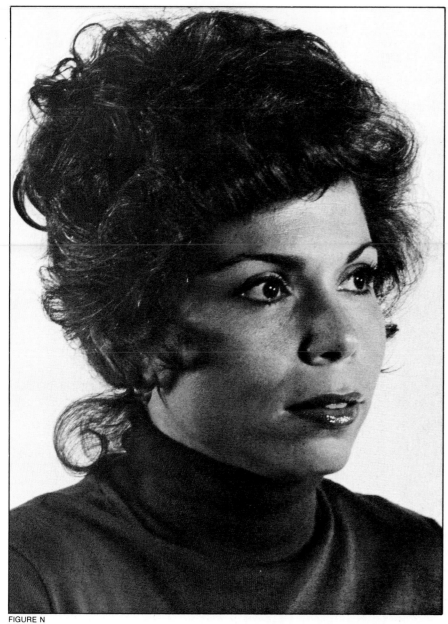

FIGURE N

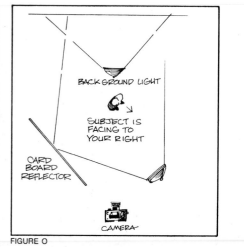

FIGURE O

LIGHTING ARRANGEMENT NO. 6

Replace the two background lights used in Arrangement No. 5 with the single background lamp used in Arrangement No. 4. Open up the shadows in the subject's face by positioning a sheet of white cardboard on a light stand quite close to her and on the side opposite the main light. This will reflect light spill from the main light into the shadow areas to permit details to register. Notice how the face begins to take on a more natural form. This is the basic principle of the fill light, which will be used next. (See Figures N and O.)

FIGURE P

FIGURE R

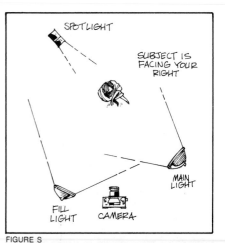

FIGURE S

LIGHTING ARRANGEMENT NO. 8

Remove the background lamp, but do not change the position of the main or fill lights. Position your spotlight behind the subject and on the same side as the fill light. Use the incident-light meter to adjust the spotlight's position until the exposure reading from the area illuminated by the spot is just a bit greater than that taken from the area illuminated by the main light. Why didn't the background go black in this case without the use of a background light? Because a sufficient amount of light from the main and fill lamps affected it. (See Figures R and S.)

LIGHTING ARRANGEMENT NO. 7

Remove the reflector, leave the rest of the lighting unchanged and place a fill lamp close to the camera on the side opposite from the main light. Use the incident-light meter to adjust the distance of the fill lamp from the subject until the exposure reading obtained from the shadow side of her face is one-half that of the reading taken from the highlight side. Now we're making real progress, as a far more natural shape and tonal relationship is beginning to appear, along with delineation of her features. (See Figures P and Q.)

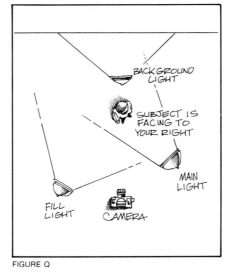

FIGURE Q

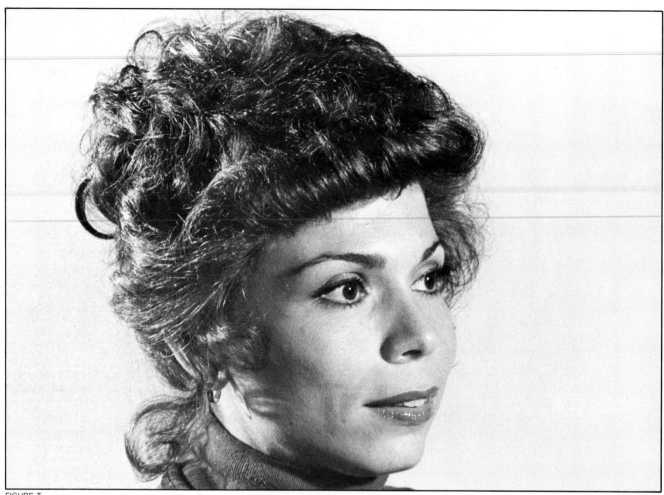

FIGURE T

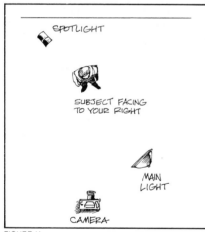

FIGURE U

LIGHTING ARRANGEMENT NO. 9

Now remove the fill light from Arrangement No. 8, leaving the placement of the subject, spotlight and main light unchanged. The background will now go dark because only the main light affects it. The shadows will also go dark again, but there are still highlights in the hair in a semibacklight situation. (See Figures T and U.)

LIGHTING ARRANGEMENT NO. 10

Move the main light to the opposite side of the camera and have the subject turn to face it. Position another light behind the subject on the opposite side and leave the spotlight unchanged. It may be necessary to readjust its placement slightly, depending upon the subject's position. (See Figures V and W.)

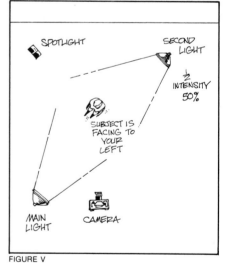

FIGURE V

FIGURE W

FIGURE X

LIGHTING ARRANGEMENT NO. 11

To achieve this effect, simply remove the spotlight from Arrangement No. 10 (See Figures V and Y). Compare the results and determine which you prefer, Figure W or Figure X.

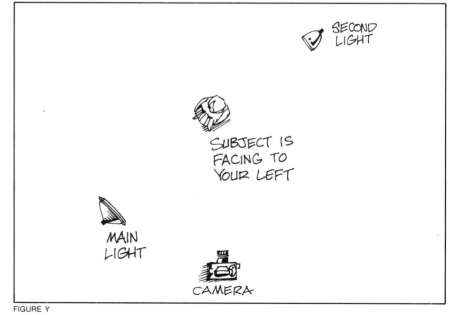

SECOND LIGHT

SUBJECT IS FACING TO YOUR LEFT

MAIN LIGHT

CAMERA

FIGURE Y

LIGHTING ARRANGEMENT NO. 12

Now position your subject about 18-24 inches from the background and have her face to your right to achieve a profile as seen at the camera position. Locate the spotlight on your right side and point it at the subject's face without allowing it to spill light over onto the background. Position the main light to the left of the camera and adjust it until her profile casts a shadow on the background immediately to the right of her face, as seen from the camera. (See Figures Z and AA.)

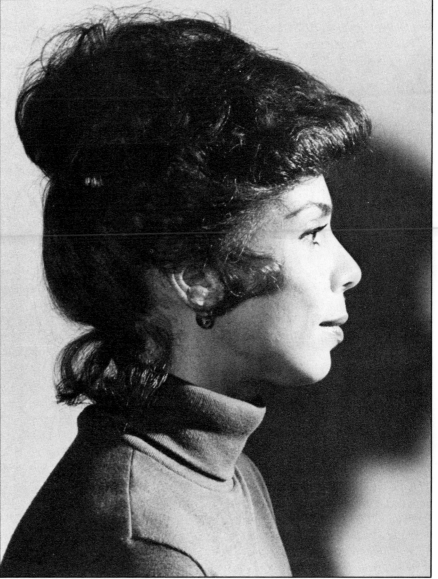

FIGURE Z

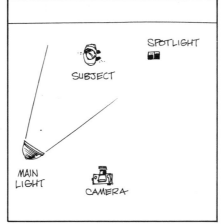

FIGURE AA

FIGURE CC

FIGURE DD

LIGHTING ARRANGEMENT NO. 14

Rearrange the light and umbrella positions as shown in Figure DD. This will provide soft, diffused illumination bathing the subject from a single light source. As in Arrangement No. 13, study the effect and try to determine how useful the addition of a second umbrella and light would be on the other side of the camera.

FIGURE EE

LIGHTING ARRANGEMENT NO. 13

Arrange an umbrella to the left of the camera and light it as shown in Figure BB. This will bounce the illumination from the umbrella to the subject. Study the effect—would the use of a second light/umbrella combination on the other side of the camera improve the picture? (See Figure CC.)

FIGURE BB

SPOTLIGHT

SUBJECT
FACING
FORWARD

CAMERA

FIGURE FF

LIGHTING ARRANGEMENT NO. 15

Move the subject back to a position approximately six feet from the background and place the spotlight directly behind her head on axis with the camera lens. No other illumination is used. This produces the dramatic rim effect of backlighting. The partial delineation of her head and shoulders outline, surrounded by the black emptiness, produces a surrealistic rendition. Hardly flattering, but dramatic. (See Figures FF and GG.)

EVERY SUBJECT IS DIFFERENT

If you've followed along with the 15 lighting arrangements covered above, you can see some of the versatility inherent in the four-light system, as well as the potential of the umbrella. You should have also realized at this point that it's not always necessary to use *all* four lights in the same arrangement. Try some or all of these suggested light placements for yourself and you'll see that my initial contention is indeed correct—lighting is basically simple in itself, it's the photographer who complicates it unnecessarily. Just remember that my diagrams are only *approximations* of where your lights should be placed.

And why only approximations? Because each and every subject you photograph will appear different once it's under the lights. If we're talking about portraits, for example, stop and think of the wide variations in hair styles, facial shapes and placement of features that you'd get if you were to stop four different people at random on the street. Yet with the four-light system, there's a means of lighting each one for whatever effect you desire, simply by raising, lowering or moving your light placement slightly. Don't forget that you'll get on the film just what you see under the lights—the trick comes in "seeing" what the light really does. If you build up your lighting arrangement one lamp at a time and evaluate its effect and relationship to others already placed, you'll turn out pictures you can't help being extremely proud of. □

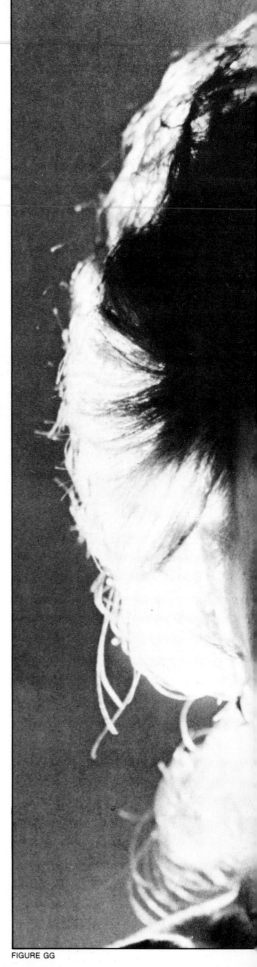

FIGURE GG

11
Electronic Flash

Whether it's used in the professional's studio or at home by the serious amateur, continuous artificial lighting works fine—just as long as you have an AC outlet, plenty of extension cords and a relatively immobile subject. But suppose you want to work outdoors after dark, or without lugging around a truckload of reflectors, light stands and other accessories? The earliest photographers had no option but to put their camera away when the sun faded in the western sky until the invention of a magnesium dust called flash powder made it possible to take pictures under such conditions.

But flash powder had its failings—it was erratic, dangerous to use and hard to control for a proper exposure with the "open shutter—ignite powder—close shutter" technique. The arrival of the flash bulb in 1929 gave rise to the "bottled explosion" concept. The early ones were inconsistent but safe and easy to use. They produced light through a very rapid burning of one or more combustible metals by passing an electrical current through a thin filament to ignite an explosive paste which in turn scattered through a quantity of magnesium or zirconium wire which burned in the rich oxygen trapped within the bulb.

Concurrent with the development of the flashbulb, Dr. Harold Edgerton of M.I.T. was also working to develop the basic circuitry necessary to convert electrical energy into a brief burst of light. For the historically oriented, Will-

It's not electronic, but it is flash—flash powder, that is. Until the mid-30's, this was commonly used for indoor pictures by pros and serious amateurs. In spite of its danger and other shortcomings like smoke and fumes, or temporary blindness if you looked directly at the magnesium flash when it ignited, flash powder gave very even illumination. (Eastman Kodak Company.)

1

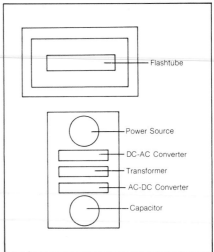

FIGURE A

iam Henry Fox Talbot made the first "electronic flash" photo in 1851 when he photographed a rapidly whirling newspaper page with the light from a brief electrical spark. But the state of the art advanced slowly from Fox Talbot's cumbersome hand-cranked generator, Leyden jars and open-air spark gap until Dr. Edgerton succeeded in 1932. Dr. Edgerton worked with the Heiland Research Corporation to refine his circuitry concepts and manufacture usable electronic flash or EF units, yet electronic flash did not become practical until after World War II, and then only for the professional. Early units were large, used extremely high voltages and were hardly what we consider as portable in nature.

But the flash bulb is no longer dominant—EF technology has progressed considerably in the past three decades, making astounding gains in circuitry and packaging in just the past five years. It's now possible to buy an electronic flash unit no larger than a pack of cigarettes which has the capability of unleashing more light than the average flash bulb used 25 years ago, and repeating this light output as often as desired with only a few seconds rest between each flash. The breakthroughs have come so rapidly in recent years that those who have not kept pace with the developments can find the choice of the "right" electronic flash unit for their needs as confusing as selecting the "right" camera. So let's begin our consideration of electronic flash with a look at its advantages and how it works.

WHY ELECTRONIC FLASH?

It's convenient. You don't have to carry a carton of flash bulbs around, and then find some place to dispose of

each one as you use it. There's no possibility of running out of bulbs or getting burned trying to remove a used one from the flash gun.

It's less expensive. Today's flashbulb systems such as the G.E. FlipFlash can cost you as much as $2.79 for eight pictures—take 80 shots and you've spent more than the cost of an EF unit with a comparable light output.

It's reliable. Flash bulbs have always been subject to corrosion and thus erratic in operation—just when you wanted it most, the darned thing wouldn't go off. In the early days, it was standard procedure to scrape the contact point free of any corrosion and then wipe saliva on it for insurance that contact would be adequate. Both Magicubes and FlipFlash were developed to eliminate the reliance on an electrical current from the camera to fire the bulb. But EF units use highly sophisticated electronic circuitry which does not have to contend with the corrosion problems of bulb-type flash.

It's uniform. Unlike flash bulbs, which often fumed, fussed and sputted for as much as a full second, one flash is immediate and exactly like another in intensity and duration, as long as

1. Early EF units were large and bulky. The Heiland Strobonar I (center) appeared in 1949, the first portable to operate from either AC or a wet-cell battery pack. This was followed in 1951 by the Strobonar II (right) built for the government with a rechargeable wet-cell pack, and in 1953 by the Strobonar V (left) using a high-voltage cell for 3-5 second recycle. (Courtesy Honeywell, Inc.)

2. Today's amateur line is a far cry in size and features from those early Strobonars. This is a sampling of the popular Hanimex EF line, and ranges from the peanut-power X130 to the highly sophisticated BX550 with thyristor circuitry and bounce flash capability.

3. On Strobonar's 25th birthday in 1974, Robert L. Pennock of Honeywell demonstrated how the press photographer did it before EF. The 1949 Strobonar I design was replaced by the Futuramic (center) in 1958; today's Strobonars range from the shoe-mounted model at right to its companion handle mount or the "potato masher" design.

the unit's capacitor is given sufficient time to charge fully.

It's fast. With bulbs, the shutter opens *after* the flash goes off, and closes *before* it ends. Depending upon your shutter speed or subject movement, it's entirely possible to end up with a well-exposed blur. Not so with electronic flash. The flash duration ranges from 1/1000 to 1/30,000 second—fast enough to stop *any* motion, whether of camera or subject.

It synchronizes. Because of the brief duration, synchronization with most cameras is far more efficient than with bulbs. When used with a leaf shutter, EF can be synchronized at any shutter speed, but because of the nature of the focal-plane shutter's operation, it can be used only to speeds of 1/60-1/125 second, depending upon the particular shutter.

It's comparable to daylight. While the clear flash bulb is all but gone today, bulbs give off a reddish light unless coated with a blue corrective dye,

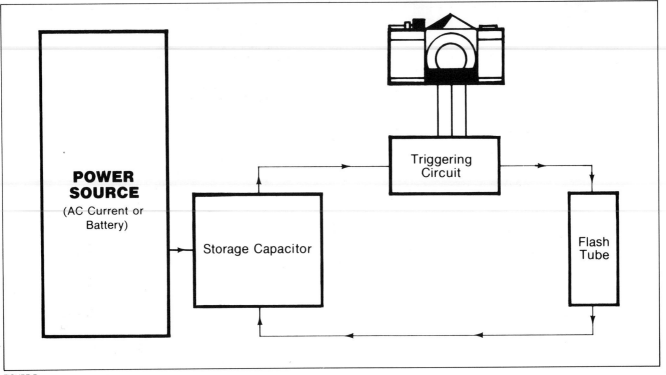

FIGURE B

which reduces the intensity of illumination somewhat. But the light from an EF unit falls within the color-temperature range of daylight-balanced color films, and will deliver excellent color rendition with none of the problems associated with the use of bulbs.

With all these advantages, electronic flash seems to be the answer to a photographer's prayer—and for the casual user, it is. But electronic flash does possess at least two drawbacks for the serious amateur.

1—When and how will the light strike the subject? Except for the large, expensive studio units with incandescent lamps built-in for modeling purposes, it's impossible to answer this question with any assurance when EF is used. Experience helps as a guide, but you can never be absolutely certain of its exact effect, except when you are using a ringlight.

2—What exposure do you use? It's not possible to measure electronic flash with an ordinary hand light meter, or even the one built into your camera. For studio work, a special flash meter can be obtained, but at a considerable expense. Under other than studio conditions, exposure is determined as with bulbs by using a guide number (GN). Divide the GN by the flash-to-subject distance and the result is the aperture to be used. The GN will differ according to the EF unit in question, as well as its manufacturer, who may be overly optimistic about how powerful his product really is. As we'll see later on, it's

best to determine your own guide number for a particular EF unit.

HOW ELECTRONIC FLASH WORKS

Regardless of their circuitry design (which will be discussed at length later), all EF units have one thing in common—they produce light. To do this, each must have two major components: a flashtube filled with inert gas, and a power supply system (see Figure A).

The sealed flashtube is filled with xenon, whose molecules are ionized when charged with high-voltage electricity. The molecules become electrically conductive in this state and give off light between the tube's electrodes for as long as the electricity is applied. By controlling the application of electricity to the xenon-filled tube, the flash duration can be as brief as 1/30,000.

Electronic flash units can be powered by either DC (battery) or AC (household) current; some units accommodate the use of both. DC-powered units may use either high- or low-voltage batteries. The high-voltage units are compact, use simple circuitry and can recharge their capacitors quickly to reduce down time between flashes. But high-voltage batteries are large, heavy, expensive, deteriorate rapidly whether in use or not, and cannot be recharged. Such EF units are usually found in studios, or used by news photographers.

Low-voltage units utilize ordinary battery cells or the rechargeable nickel-cadmium (nicad) type. While

their power source is smaller and lighter, the recharge or recycle period between flashes is longer and the electric circuitry more complicated. Portable amateur EF units are generally of the low-voltage type, but pack a surprising amount of light (Figure B).

When the EF unit is switched "on," direct current from the low-voltage battery is converted to alternating current and stepped up by a transformer to the higher voltage required for a brilliant light flash—no step-up in voltage is necessary with high-voltage battery units. While this voltage step-up takes place, you'll hear a high-pitched "whine" which is characteristic.

As the AC current is transformed to a higher voltage, it's converted back to DC and sent to the capacitor, which serves as a storage unit in the power supply system until the electrical circuit is closed (Figure C). When this happens, the current surges out of the capacitor to the flashtube, where it jumps the electrodes to create the flash of light (Figure D).

This process of charging (or recharging) the capacitor is called recycling, and varies in the length of time required according to the size of the capacitor, circuitry efficiency and state of the power supply. Recycling time is shortest when the battery is new, and gradually grows longer as the battery wears out, through either use or age. Very cold temperatures also affect recycling times adversely, according to the type of battery in use.

The energy-storing capacitor tends

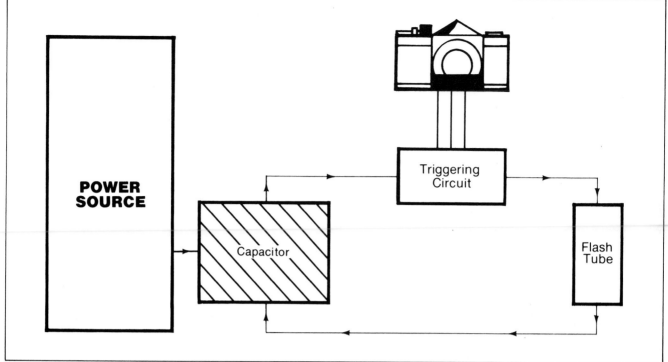

FIGURE C

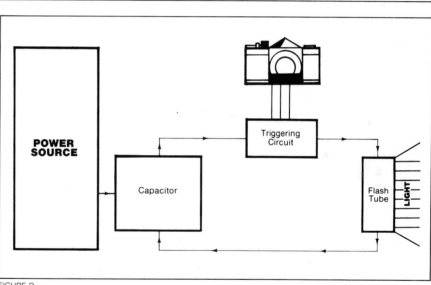

FIGURE D

to deform when not used frequently. After a few weeks of inactivity, it may require considerable battery power to reform the capacitor to hold the energy. If the EF unit can be used with AC current, it's a good idea to plug it in for a few minutes every month or so to prevent the capacitor from deforming. If the capacitor has deformed, AC current will reform it quickly, without the massive drain on the unit's battery.

A small neon bulb called a "ready light" is connected to the capacitor. When the capacitor reaches a predetermined state of charge (usually 70-85 percent), this light comes on to inform the user that the unit is ready to flash

again with a predictable amount of light. Some manufacturers have a tendency to set the threshold of the ready light low so that potential purchasers of their product will be impressed by its "quick" recycle time.

Triggering the flash as soon as the ready light comes on will result in consistent underexposure with such units, as the capacitor is not *fully* charged. Unless the unit's instruction booklet specifically states that the ready light indicates a 100-percent charge, it's a good idea to wait 5-20 seconds *after* the ready light glows before releasing the next flash.

Repeated constant use of the power supply system builds up heat rapidly while recycling takes place. To prevent damage to the unit, some circuits may contain a heat-sensitive switch which

will turn the system off and allow it to cool once a certain level of heat is reached under such usage.

Electronic flash circuitry contains two gaps or open points—the flashtube and the triggering switch. Remember that under normal circumstances, xenon isn't conductive to electricity. But by coating the flashtube with a thin transparent coating of an electrically conductive substance, some of the initial energy from the capacitor is encouraged to flow across the tube when the triggering switch is closed. This is sufficient to alter the normal state of the xenon and make the inert gas an electrical conductor. The rest of the capacitor's charge follows, and is discharged between the electrodes at each end of the flashtube. A built-in reflector behind the tube disperses the

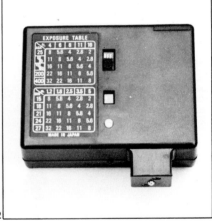

FIGURE F

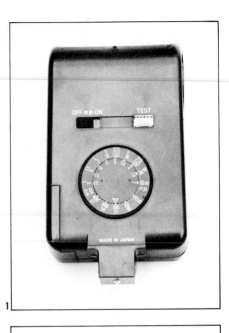

1

2

flash in an orderly manner.

Installed between the flashtube and capacitor, the triggering switch closes to allow current flow when the camera's shutter button or the EF unit's "open flash" button is depressed. To function on command from the camera, the EF unit must be connected to a set of flash contacts or switch in the camera's shutter. This connection can be made remotely by a PC cord which attaches to the camera, or directly by means of an electrically wired accessory clip on the camera body called a "hot shoe" (Figure E). The PC cord is a convenience when the flash is not mounted directly to the camera, or when the camera has no hot shoe.

Regardless of the light source—bulb or electronic flash—its triggering must be synchronized to the shutter's action to assure that the flash goes of while the shutter is open. This exposes the negative uniformly to the maximum amount of light available. But flash bulbs and electronic flash have widely differing operational characteristics. Bulbs require a certain length of time after igniting (usually measured in milliseconds) before reaching peak intensity. This means that the bulb must be ignited and the shutter's action *delayed* slightly so that when it opens, the flash will be at or near maximum intensity. This type of synchronization is referred to as "M" sync.

Electronic flash has no such delay—command and it's there. As a leaf-type shutter opens fully at all speeds, the EF can be triggered *after* shutter action

starts and because of its very brief duration, can be used with all shutter speeds. With a focal-plane shutter, the situation is somewhat different. The EF fires as the first shutter curtain reaches the far side of the negative and before the second curtain starts its travel. At speeds faster than 1/60 second with horizontal or 1/125 second with vertical focal-plane shutters, the second curtain starts its travel before the first one reaches its destination. Thus, EF can only be used at these or slower shutter speeds, or part of the negative will not be exposed by its brief flash. Electronic flash synchronization is designated as "X" sync. If your camera has an M-X switch, it must be correctly positioned for proper synchronization; some switches use a bulb outline and lightning bolt instead of the letters M-X.

OPERATIONAL CHARACTERISTICS

Just as electronic flash units all function in a similar manner to produce light, they have certain characteristics in common.

LIGHT OUTPUT—This is an area of considerable confusion, as manufacturers tend to use various methods of expressing the amount of light their particular units will produce—watt-seconds (Joules), guide numbers based on an ASA 25 film, effective candlepower seconds (ECPS), beam candlepower seconds (BCPS), etc. Each is incompatible with the others, as figures from one system cannot be translated meaningfully into another, and none is really accurate.

The quantity of light delivered by any EF unit is determined by (1) the watt-second rating of the power supply, (2) the flashtube, (3) the reflector design and (4) the circuitry. The first factor, watt-seconds, refers to the amount of raw power available, but due to differences in the other three factors, it's entirely possible for two different EF designs with the same watt-second rating to deliver different amounts of light to a given subject.

The more energy the power supply stores, the brighter the light. The larger or more efficient the flashtube, the brighter the light. The size, shape and surface of the reflector affect the light output; generally speaking, a large reflector delivers more light than a small one. A bowl-shaped reflector delivers more light than a shallow one, and a polished surface delivers more light than a matte surface. The average reflector will increase light output of a flashtube by 10 times—approximately three f-stops—by directing the light in a forward direction.

Flashing through a Fresnel screen concentrates the light even more, mak-

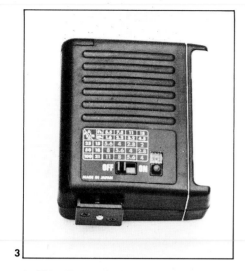

3

4

1. This Hanimex EF calculator is representative of those found on many EF units and used to determine correct exposure with the guide number system.
2-3. Less expensive EF units, like these Hanimex models, use a color-coded printed table instead of a calculator dial for direct reading.
4. Standard equipment of the Topcon Super DM, this 50mm RE GN Topcor M f/1.4 lens features automatic flash settings by means of a focus-linked GN scale. Set the scale to correspond with your EF's output and the lens aperture will open/close as you focus, eliminating the need to calculate the correct f-stop. Focus-linked flash is provided on most adjustable 110 pocket cameras.

ing it more intense but decreasing the area of coverage—useful with telephoto lenses. Flashing through a diffusion screen disperses the light over a greater area, but reduces its intensity—useful with wide-angle lenses.

COLOR TEMPERATURE—Electronic flash units normally produce light with a color temperature range between 5500°K. and 7000°K. This variation in color temperature is dependent upon the manufacturer, but for the most part, EF can be used with any color film emulsion balanced for daylight illumination, and it can also be mixed with sunlight for fill-flash and other effects. Some manufacturers apply a slight gold or amber tint to the flashtube in an effort to slightly ''warm'' the color temperature of the light produced and give color pictures a much more pleasing appearance.

COVERAGE ANGLE—Light emitted from the flashtube falls off proportionately in intensity as you move right or left of center. The permissible amount of such fall-off is 50 percent at each side and is measured by the coverage angle. At either limit of the coverage angle, the light will be exactly one-half of what it is head-on. This means that a subject at the limits of the coverage

angle on either side of center will receive one f-stop less exposure than a similar subject directly in front of the unit. But merely having all subjects of interest within the unit's coverage angle does not guarantee proper exposure—consider the subject at the limit of the coverage angle but which is on the same plane as a subject directly in front of the flash (Figure F). The coverage angle of most EF units is adequate for use with a 50mm lens on a 35mm camera; some units have an angle sufficient for use with a 35mm wideangle lens, while others provide accessory lenses to do the job.

FLASH DURATION—As we've seen, the duration of electronic flash is very brief, which makes it ideal for stopping action and minimizing the effect of camera movement. It also makes things far easier on human subjects (especially small children), as the very short flash is not nearly as blinding as that from a longer-lasting flash bulb.

Flash duration is controlled by many things, among them voltage (the lower the voltage in the circuit, the longer the duration), watt-second rating (the greater the watt-second rating or energy stored in the capacitor, the longer the duration), number of lampheads on one power supply (a second lamphead on the circuit will cut the duration in

half), the arc-length of the flashtube (the longer the tube, the longer the duration), and the internal width of the flashtube (the wider the tube, the longer the duration).

You can't do much to change the flash duration of most units, although some are equipped with half- and quarter-power settings, which will decrease the duration. If the flash duration is 1/10,000 second on quarter power in a variable-power unit, it will be 1/5000 second on half power and 1/2500 second on full power. The newer automatic flash units have durations which vary from 1/500 to 1/50,000 second, depending upon flash-to-subject distance. When used on manual instead of automatic, such units will operate at the longest duration possible.

While short flash durations have their advantages, they also pose problems at times. If the flash duration is too short, the bottom layer of a three-layer color film will be underexposed, causing reciprocity failure or a shift to blue in the picture. While this bluish cast can be corrected when prints are made from color negatives, a yellow or amber ''warming'' filter such as a No. 81B may be necessary for critical work with color slide films.

In situations where existing light is

1

2

very strong, it may register on the negative when EF is used at slower shutter speeds. This will cause a "ghost" image in action shots, so a shutter speed that's sufficiently fast to keep the existing light from exposing the negative should be chosen. But this effect can also be an advantage. By using a slow shutter speed with electronic flash to give dim existing light an opportunity to register on the negative, you can record things that would otherwise be washed out by the flash at higher shutter speeds, such as lights on a Christmas tree. In fact, you can use the shutter speed to control the lighting ratio between the existing light and the flash—the slower the shutter speed, the greater the effect of the existing light on the picture. You'll need to experiment with the technique before it can be applied with certainty in every situation, but the control it offers is worth the time and effort.

POWER SOURCES—Operating an EF on AC current is the least expensive and provides the quickest recycling time, with no worry about battery strength. In the past, many manufacturers included this capability in even the lowest-priced units, but as AC usage is not terribly popular with most amateurs, who find the AC cord a nuisance that's forever in the way and/or pulling out of the socket as they move around, it's now included mainly in the higher priced, sophisticated units.

Replaceable batteries—usually penlight (AA) cells—are the most popular power source. The common carbon-zinc types are very inexpensive to buy, but recycle slowly and expire quickly in a high-drain application such as EF—40 shots more or less usually drain them dry. The alkaline type are more expensive, but they cost less per flash produced, last far longer and recycle the unit much quicker.

Nicad batteries, which can be recharged hundreds of times, are also popular. For those who use flash very

often, the nicad will quickly pay back its much higher initial price and over its lifetime, will deliver the most economical power. But nicad batteries are not as ideal for those who use flash only occasionally. They tend to die suddenly and if repeatedly used to only a portion of their capacity, are difficult to bring back and hold a full charge—a characteristic known as the "memory effect." If you use nicads and can't understand why they don't seem to deliver as many shots per charge as they should, chalk it up to this phenomenon. Let them run down completely and then recharge fully—this should restore their capability completely. In fact, it's a good idea to do this every few months anyway to keep the cell healthy.

EXPOSURE DETERMINATION

Most amateur EF units will be equipped with either an exposure calculator dial (similar in appearance to that of a light meter) or a table on which the calculations have already been done for you. Their use is the easiest method of calculating the correct exposure. With a calculator dial, simply set its pointer at the ASA speed of the film in use and then read the appropriate f-stop opposite the flash-to-subject distance on the dial. If a table is used, you generally locate the film

speed and read across until you intersect the proper flash-to-subject distance to determine the aperture.

Some manufacturers provide what they call GN lenses. These contain a guide number scale coupled to the aperture ring; set the GN of your flash and the lens will automatically set the correct aperture as you focus on the subject, eliminating the frustrations of having to stop and calculate the correct f-stop for each different picture. But for the fastidious, or those working in color who require or demand as accurate an exposure as possible, it will be necessary to become involved in determining the exact guide number for your particular EF unit.

A guide number is simply the product of a distance and an aperture that gives proper exposure with a given film and flash unit. To use the guide number, just divide the distance from the flashtube to the subject into the guide number, and the result will be the proper f-stop to use. For example, if the guide number for your film and unit is 45, and your flash unit is 10 feet from the subject, the proper f-stop will be f/4.5 (45 divided by 10 equals 4.5). If your flash is 20 feet from the subject, the proper f-stop is 2.3, or midway between f/2 and f/2.8 on your lens. If you recall the inverse square law, you'll remember that it says,

3

4

5

1-5. This series of five photographs provided by Vivitar demonstrates the results of a guide number test. We would select (2) as the best exposure, but some might prefer (3). To obtain the results in (2), a guide number of 130 would be used; for (3), the guide number becomes 180—see why you should establish your own personal guide number?

of exposures at ½-stop intervals (f/5.6, 6.3, 8, 9.5, 11, etc.) and write the f-stop used on a card to be included in the picture area somewhere to help you remember which exposure was made at which f-stop. Give the EF time to recycle completely between shots (at least one minute) and have the film processed normally. When it returns, look at each slide carefully and select the one which you feel is best exposed. Multiply the f-stop in that picture by 10 (the distance you used to shoot the slides) and you'll have an accurate guide number for that particular EF unit. This does not mean that you can buy another of the same make and model and expect that it too will perform exactly the same—there may be as much as ½ f-stop difference between two such units. If you buy a second one, make the same test.

Suppose that f/5.6 provided the best exposure. This gives you a guide number of 56 for that unit when used with the same film. Let's assume that you used an ASA 25 emulsion—your guide

"double the distance, quarter the light." It just happens that f/2.3 lets four times as much light strike the film as f/4.5.

Dividing the guide number by flash-to-subject distance is exactly what the exposure calculator on the EF unit does, but manufacturer-provided guide numbers are often inflated somewhat and thus not entirely dependable for critical work. The best procedure is to determine your own guide number in the following manner. Place a subject exactly 10 feet from your flash unit, measuring the distance carefully. Use slide film in your camera, as it has relatively little exposure latitude and is not corrected in printing. Make a series

number for ASA 25 is 56, right? But now you wish to use the EF unit with an ASA 100 film—what's the guide number going to be? You can always repeat the test with ASA 100 film, but there is a mathematical way to calculate the new guide number that is just as accurate, and far faster.

Your guide number with ASA 25 film is 56, or f/5.6 at 10 feet. As ASA 100 film is four times (two f-stops) faster than ASA 25 film, f/11 should be the correct f-stop when used at 10 feet with ASA 100 film, thus the guide number should be f/11 times 10 feet, or 110. Now that you have the new guide number for your flash and ASA 100 film, you can determine the correct exposure at any flash-to-subject distance by simply dividing that number into the guide number to find the proper aperture. Those who find such math confusing can refer to Figure G to translate an ASA 25 guide number into one which can be used with ASA 100 or ASA 400 film.

Now suppose that you want to use a film with a nonprogressive film speed, such as ASA 64 or ASA 320. This can get slightly complicated when you try to work out the difference in speed in your head. So now you'll have to refer to this formula:

$$\text{New Guide Number} = \text{Old Guide Number} \times \sqrt{\frac{\text{New ASA}}{\text{Old ASA}}}$$

To use the formula, first divide the ASA speed of the film you've been using into the ASA speed of the film you plan to use. Next, find the square root of that answer and then multiply the square root by the guide number of the film you've been using. The result will be the guide number for the new film.

Now that you've gone to all this trouble to determine a guide number that is accurate for your particular EF unit, let me caution you again that a guide number is just that—a guide. They're calculated for "average" subjects, whatever that may represent. When you're taking a picture in a small

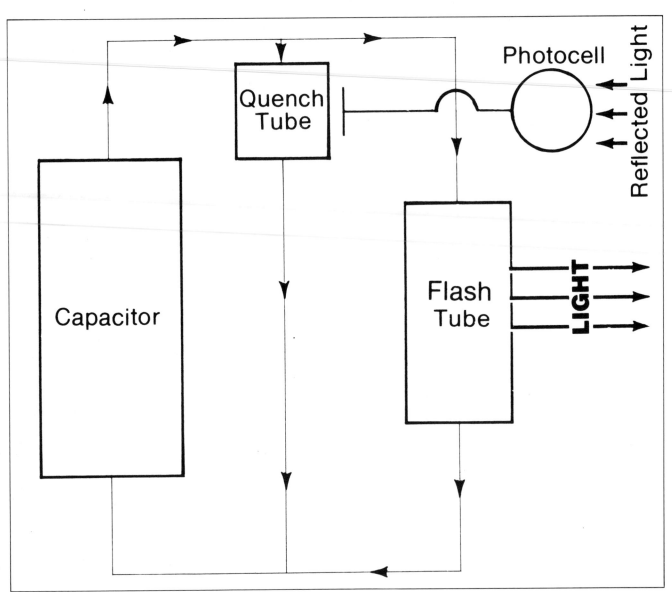

Photocell

Reflected Light

Quench Tube

Capacitor

Flash Tube

LIGHT

FIGURE I

room with white walls, they will reflect back a good deal of the light from your flash and the result will be an over-exposed picture if your choice of exposure was based entirely on the use of the guide number. In such a case, you should close the aperture down one or two f-stops—a better idea is to bracket a series of three exposures whenever possible.

The same situation in reverse applies to large rooms with dark walls, or shooting outdoors at night. Very little if any light will be reflected and so your picture will be underexposed when exposure is based on flash-to-subject distance alone. In a case like this, it's a good idea to open the aperture an f-stop or two to compensate for the lack of reflection and get a properly exposed picture. Here too, the best approach is to bracket when possible.

If you're really exacting, you should shoot a test roll of film whenever you change anything—film type, flash unit, lens, environmental conditions, etc. For

black-and-white photography, such precision isn't really necessary because of the film's far greater latitude. In most cases with black-and-white film, you can use the calculator on the EF unit and you'll get satisfactory results. Exposure with electronic flash is as simple or complex as your requirements—no more, no less.

MANUAL VS. AUTOMATIC FLASH UNITS

To this point, I've discussed electronic flash in terms of units where the user determines the exposure, based on his own experience and the unit's guide number. As such EF units have a constant flash duration, the exposure is controlled manually by changing the f-stops on your lens, based on flash-to-subject distance. We call these manual EF units. But manual units are not very handy when you're working with fast-moving subjects such as children at play, or shooting sports activities.

As automatic EF units expose the

film properly throughout a preestablished distance range, they save you the time and trouble of determining and setting the f-stop for each picture you take, which can be a very useful feature when things start to move quickly. Such EF units use a constant f-stop (some provide a choice of two or more f-stops that can be used) and vary the flash duration to control the exposure.

When the flash is triggered, its light is directed to the subject and reflected back into a light-sensitive cell or "sensor" mounted on the front of the EF unit. This sensor is connected into the circuitry and sends electrical signals to a solid-state analog computer (Figure H). When a predetermined amount of light sufficient for a proper exposure has been reflected from the subject, the computer shuts off the light and the remaining energy is switched into a quench or dump tube, where it can dissipate without affecting the picture (Figure I). Thus, while a manual unit might produce a flash duration of 1/1000 second, the automatic unit may quench the flash after a 1/5,000 second exposure, and the remaining energy from the capacitor is discarded by the shunt circuit.

The more sophisticated automatic EF units are equipped with a sensor which provides a choice of aperture settings. These let you preprogram the flash system to take into account your requirements for depth of field or to provide a margin of error in focusing. A choice of settings also allows you to use various speed films, or lenses whose maximum aperture might not correspond to the one specified for use with a single-aperture automatic unit. Thus, the greater the number of sensor settings available, the greater the opportunity for creative alternatives with automatic electronic flash.

ENERGY-SAVING CIRCUITRY DESIGNS—The quench tube described above solved the problem of what to do with energy in excess of that required for a correct exposure with automatic EF units—it handled the surge of electricity without giving off any illumination. But quenching the flash in this manner wastes considerable battery power, especially when working at a fairly close range where the full power of the flash is not required. The partial power switch was incorporated as a means of conserving battery power under such circumstances and thus producing more exposures from a set of batteries.

As of this writing, the most recent advance in energy saving uses a thyristor circuit or high-speed switch (Figure J). Instead of dumping the excess energy into a quench tube where it can dissipate, the thyristor circuit simply shuts off the EF unit when sufficient light has reached the subject for a correct exposure. As the unused part of the capacitor's charge does not leave the capacitor, less power is required to recharge it. This results in two distinct advantages—when maximum light output is not required, less time is lost in recycling and as less energy is needed, the batteries will last even longer.

To conserve battery power between shots, most photographers turn the unit off. But while you're waiting for a particular event to occur, the capacitor may have discharged. Once the ready light goes off, you have no way of knowing just how much juice the capacitor contains. If things suddenly break and you shoot without turning the unit back on, you may get only a

EQUIVALENT GUIDE NUMBERS*		
ASA 25 *(feet)*	ASA 100 *(feet)*	ASA 400 *(feet)*
16	33	65
20	39	79
23	46	92
26	52	105
30	59	118
33	66	131
36	72	144
39	79	157
43	85	171
46	92	184
49	98	197
53	105	210
56	112	223
59	118	236
62	125	249
66	131	262
69	138	276
72	144	288
75	151	302
79	157	315
82	164	328
85	171	341
89	177	354
92	184	367
95	190	380
*Rounded off to nearest whole number.		

FIGURE G

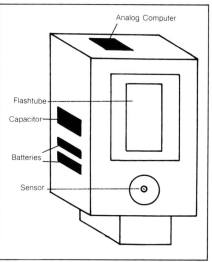

FIGURE H

partial flash, but if you stop to turn it on, you'll miss the action while waiting for the capacitor to recharge fully. The recent incorporation of a special "monitor" circuit in some EF units solves this problem; it conserves battery power by switching the power supply system on and off as necessary to maintain the capacitor at full charge. As this keeps the flash constantly ready for use without excessive battery drain, it also considerably reduces the power drain on the batteries between flashes.

A SYSTEMS APPROACH TO ELECTRONIC FLASH

For many years, manufacturers and photographers alike treated electronic flash as simply another source of "bottled light." Manufacturers added hot shoes to their cameras and EF units

were clipped in place and used on-camera. This results in flat lighting with unnatural shadows, and what is best described as the "red-eye" syndrome—when flash and camera lens are next to each other, the light from the flash penetrates the pupils of a subject's eyes, bounces around through the red blood vessels in the retinas and reflects back to the film carrying a pink or reddish coloration.

Those interested only in snapshots paid little attention to the problems of on-camera EF; more serious amateurs found them obnoxious and sought new ways to be more creative with their use of electronic flash. The best solution to these problems is, of course, to get the EF away from the camera, and to do this, whole new industries arose with a variety of ingenious and not-so-ingenious flash bracket designs.

But EF manufacturers finally got the message and just as the systems approach to camera design resulted in a host of multicomponent accessories, application of the same design philosophy has resulted in a considerable extension of the photographer's control over his use of electronic flash. Just as Honeywell pioneered the automatic EF, Vivitar has led the way in applying the systems approach to electronic flash, pointing the way for other manufacturers to follow. For this reason, the components of the Vivitar 283 flash system are described below as typical of the accessories this design concept includes. Other companies are in the process of building their own systems approach to electronic flash, which may or may not include each and every accessory described.

THE VIVITAR "LIGHT MACHINE"—This highly sophisticated, extremely versatile and portable EF system is built around a basic electronic flash unit, the Vivitar 283. Using the 283 flash and its innovative accessories, the photographer has a wide control over the intensity, direction, color and coverage angle of his lighting, and can now create effects limited primarily by his own imagination rather than the equipment.

The basic flash unit is an automatic thyristor design fitted with a click-stopped flash head. This tilts up to 90 degrees for bouncing light from ceilings or walls at varying angles. A bounce compensator circuit automatically increases the light output to compensate for light dispersion whenever the unit is set for 45-degree, 60-degree or 75-degree bounce positions. A removable remote sensor permits the use of any one of four apertures (f/1.4,

f/2, f/4 and f/5.6), and connects either to the flash unit or to a standard camera accessory shoe to compute the correct exposure for either direct or vertical bounce flash.

A removable battery holder utilizing four AA alkaline batteries provides the basic power supply option, and a spare holder preloaded with fresh batteries can be snapped in place in seconds should those in the EF fail. The 283 can also be operated on standard 120-volt household current, by a rechargeable nicad battery pack or with a 510-volt battery for heavy-duty or sequential flash operation.

A snap-on lens/filter adapter permits the use of a filter kit and the variable-angle lens kit. The filter kit includes a 4X neutral density, Type B conversion, ultraviolet, and red, blue and yellow filters for use in light control, correction or in creating special effects. The variable-angle kit includes dispersion lenses matched to the field of view of

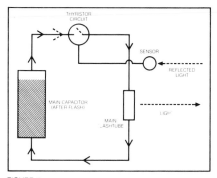

FIGURE J

1. This is the Sunpak 411 Flash System.
2. The Vivitar 283 "Light Machine" Flash System is shown here.
3-5. The versatility of the Vivitar 283 flash system is shown here by the use of bounce flash (3), Lens/Filter Adapter use (5) and Soft Light/Bounce Diffuser Kit (4).

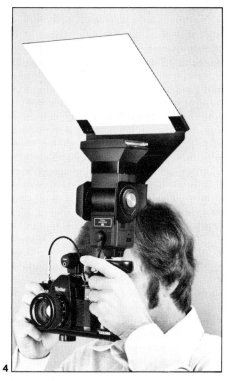

a 21mm and a 28mm wide-angle lens, and concentration lenses for use with telephoto optics. As the adapter accepts one or both types of inserts at the same time, filters and angle lenses can be combined in whatever manner the photographer finds appropriate.

The soft light/bounce diffuser is a portable "ceiling" in effect. This accessory accepts a standard 90-percent white reflectance card (usually the opposite side of an 18-percent gray card used in determining exposure) and snaps onto the 283 flash to produce soft light with consistent quality regardless of the surroundings.

A variety of integrated camera grips/flash brackets/camera platforms and connecting cords, along with a pouch carrying case round out the 283 system. Other manufacturers such as Sunpak and Honeywell offer their own competing systems based upon different design configurations, and by the time this appears in print, there will undoubtedly be others.

In addition to illustrating the considerable amount of versatility which the systems approach to flash unit design provides, the foregoing discussion serves to point out the fact that choosing the "right" electronic flash is becoming an increasingly difficult task.

HOW TO PICK YOUR ELECTRONIC FLASH

Actually, there is no "right" EF unit for every purpose, although the system units such as the Vivitar 283, Sunpak 411, etc. probably come as close as humanly possible at the present time. At last count, I numbered seven EF units among my souvenirs, and all have a very definite use in my photography. Hopefully, you won't become this deeply involved in electronic flash photography, but there's no doubt

about it, selecting an EF unit from the abundance presently on the market can prove to be a major headache—and if you make a mistake, forget about trade-in value; it hardly exists with electronic flash units despite the fact that some cost as much as a fairly good camera. So how do you make sense of the row after row of EF units you'll find at a well-stocked dealer? Read on.

Don't get carried away with comparisons of features offered by various EF units until you've first decided exactly

what you want it to do. You know the types of pictures you'll be taking with EF, and you should be able to arrive at an approximate guide-number range necessary to handle your requirements. It's not a good idea to buy extra power when you have no real need for it, but many do so on the assumption that it's nice to have the capability there just in case. I would answer this by reminding you that power and portability are directly interrelated—the more powerful the EF unit, the larger, heavier and bulkier it tends to be. If you only occasionally use flash, investing in a thyristor circuit unit is not really economical, as you will have no great need for the energy-saving feature. Other considerations should center around the necessity (not the desire) for fast or slow recycling, fully automatic computerized output, the use of various types of power supplies, manual control, etc. Once you've thought through your requirements and have a general idea in your mind of the specifications you require, it's time to embark on the hunt.

First determine which units match up with your specifications and fit each one to your camera to see how it feels, how it affects handling and balance, whether it interferes with film replacement or your use of the operating controls, how easily it can be connected/disconnected for on/off camera use, etc. In short—evaluate each one of interest as best you can in terms of user convenience.

Now take an unbiased look at the quality of each unit still under consid-

eration. Is it well-made and sturdy? Are the controls centrally located and do they function easily? Is the calculator or exposure table well thought out and easy to use and understand? The most likely point of failure will be the PC cord, as it contains very fine wire and with the inevitable twists and turns, bends and kinks which occur, these fine strands are bound to give way. Obviously, a detachable PC cord is ideal, but make certain that replacements can be easily obtained should you lose yours. If the PC cord is permanently attached, try to determine what's involved in replacing it, which brings us to a consideration of repairs.

As the majority of electronic flash units are manufactured abroad these days, EF repair service is about on a par with that previously discussed for lenses. If you buy a recognized brand, the importer/distributor should have a well-established service network, but many lesser-known and private brands will require return of a defective unit (which happens more often than they would like to admit, and which the dealer will not replace) directly to the importer, who may or may not honor the warranty—if he's still in business.

At first glance, this may seem a lot of work and a lengthy procedure to go through just to buy a flash unit. But with today's price structure, the pur-

1. For realism and a natural-looking picture, remove the flash from the camera and place it outside the window.
2. Direct flash results in the same effect produced by direct sunlight, with distracting shadows and a flat, lifeless appearing subject.
3. You can bounce light from any white ceiling or wall to duplicate the diffused light of a room, but don't bounce from colored surfaces when shooting in color, as reflected light contains color cast.
4. Hiding the flash beside the fire, but out of the camera's view, gives the illusion that your subject is illuminated by the fire and not the flash.
5. Bounce light from a large white reflector can be used to duplicate the diffused light of an overcast day.

chase of an EF unit for many amateurs takes on the proportion of a major investment, especially if you want one to do more than blow out an occasional burst of light for a family snapshot or two. For that purpose, almost any small, inexpensive unit should suffice. Once you've decided which units will do what you require, are convenient and well-built, then it's time to talk about price.

If you go into the store and start with the price factor, or ask the salesman for his recommendation, you're very likely to get exactly what you asked for—a bargain. Unfortunately, it probably won't be what you need, but one which the dealer got a special price on

4

from the distributor, one that's been discontinued (which happens very frequently in the fast-moving world of EF and is a good reason to stick with a brand name) or one from a slow-moving line which the dealer would like to unload. So do it right and you'll end up all right.

USING ELECTRONIC FLASH

Now that you have an electronic flash, let's see what you can do with it. EF can be used in a wide variety of ways—on-camera or off, as the sole source of illumination or to balance existing light by filling in shadow areas. It may be used to simulate sunlight, or bounced off a reflective surface to appear as natural light. In short, electronic flash can be used in virtually every way you would ordinarily use sunlight or artificial lighting. Like so many other aspects of photography, your imagination is the only limiting factor, as the equipment is available to do almost anything you wish.

ON-CAMERA FLASH—This is the simplest and easiest way in which EF can be used, although not the most creative. While it does not always provide the most appropriate or desirable lighting, the sheer convenience of having the light source attached to your camera cannot be discounted. It's especially handy when shooting sporting

5

events and other fast-moving subjects where you must also move quickly, without having to worry about where the flash is and if it's positioned correctly. With a manual unit, exposure calculations can be made quickly and transferred to the camera; with an automatic unit, no such calculations are necessary—just keep your eye on the ready light and shoot.

OFF-CAMERA FLASH—This possesses the greatest potential for creative use of flash. Off-camera use can be as complex as a studio lighting arrangement, or as simple as holding the flash off to one side and slightly above the camera. The benefits of such a change in flash position will be immediately apparent in the natural appearance and better modeling of the subject, with far fewer harsh shadows, and no washed-out foreground. Exposure calculations are no more difficult with the flash off-camera, as long as you remember to calculate on the flash-to-subject distance rather than camera-to-subject.

For dramatic proof of the difference between the two techniques, try a simple comparison test as follows. Place a subject 10 feet from your camera, shooting one shot with the flash attached. Then disconnect and elevate the unit a foot or so above the camera, shooting another picture. Now move the flash at one-foot intervals in a 90-degree arc around your subject, shooting a picture at each point as you go. The resulting proof sheet will be more convincing than you might believe from this description.

BOUNCE FLASH—Reams have been written about this flash technique and variations on the theme abound. For those readers limited to a single flash unit, bounce flash can be the answer to the vexing problem of what to do

with the flash unit once it's off the camera. With bounce flash, there's no real need to remove the flash—you simply point the flash head toward a ceiling or wall. Many current units offer this capability in the form of a tilting flash head; for those whose units do not have this feature, the use of a simple flash bracket or a bounce flash shoe will accomplish the same thing.

When bounce flash is used, the more expensive automatic EF units will provide automatic exposure compensation by means of a tilt head with sensor pointing at the subject, or a removable sensor which can be properly positioned according to the circumstances; using automatic units whose head and sensor are fixed (or manual units) will require that you calculate the correct exposure. Tables are often provided which purport to take into account the flash-to-ceiling distance as well as the ceiling-to-subject distance, and additional factors such as variations in wall/ceiling colors and surface textures, but these are overly complex and most often prove useless in your particular situation. Here's a simple way to reach a correct exposure for black-and-white photography using

1-2. These photos show the difference (1) without flash and (2) with flash.
3-4. Beautifully exposed background (4), but did you really want a silhouette? If not, use flash to fill in the dark areas and expose those important details correctly.

bounce flash in any normal room.

Find the correct aperture for direct flash at 10 feet with your EF calculator and then set the lens at an aperture two stops larger—if direct flash requires a setting of f/16, the bounce flash aperture should be f/8. Using this setting, you can vary the camera-to-subject distance from 6-12 feet and your exposure will still be correct, as the flash-to-ceiling-to-subject distance is not normally affected by horizontal changes between the EF and the subject in rooms 10-15 feet long with 8-12-foot ceilings.

Working with color film requires more accuracy, as its latitude is not sufficient to accommodate an error ± one f-stop as is the case with black-and-white film. Where possible with color, you can apply the two-stop method if you can also bracket your exposures ½ stop in either direction.

Another problem can arise when you're using an automatic EF with a

can hold the camera with your right hand and the flash with your left, you can bounce the light without too much difficulty. The left hand can also be used for focusing when necessary, if the EF design isn't too bulky. You should use the camera with a neckstrap that's drawn up short—this allows the camera to hang down where you can wind the film by pressing the camera to your body as you throw the film advance lever. The neckstrap is also good insurance against the possibility of losing your grip on the camera and dropping it.

One last caution with this technique when shooting in color—beware of color casts caused by bouncing light from colored surfaces. Your eye will not notice the tint reflected from a nearby red wall to the face of your subject, but the film will pick it up with absolute fidelity. Take care to bounce your light from a surface as white or neutral as possible and keep your subject a sufficient distance from colored surfaces that might be close enough to pick up the bounce and reflect their color to the subject. If necessary, you can bounce the light from a large sheet of white poster board or paper—I've even heard of press photographers bouncing the flash from their own shirt front when shooting a head-and-shoulder portrait in an auditorium.

choice of aperture settings—which one should you use? Each aperture setting on the sensor has a maximum range of effectiveness at which the flash will function for a proper exposure. With direct flash, the choice is easy to make, as you can accurately determine the flash-to-subject distance. But the flash-to-ceiling-to-subject distance of bounce flash can vary considerably, depending upon the size of the room, the height of the ceiling and the angle

at which the flash head is tilted. To be on the safe side with bounce flash, use the largest aperture possible with a low-power unit (GN of 40 or less) and the next-to-the-largest aperture with a more powerful one. A few of the highly sophisticated EF units contain a test button—when fired, this will determine if you're bouncing sufficient light for a proper exposure.

You do not need elaborate or complex setups to use bounce flash; if you

1

WINDOW FLASH—Let's suppose you wish to photograph a person indoors. If you've done this before, you know that on-camera flash will produce a deep shadow which seems to join your subject to the wall behind, yet if you separate them too much, the entire background will drop off quickly into murky darkness. Either way, the result is less than perfect. Here's how you can avoid both ends of the problem and come up with that perfect picture.

Place your subject *in front* of a window. Take a meter reading for the outdoor scene, just as though you were going to photograph it through the window, and then set your exposure according to the reading. Now select your camera-to-subject distance and then determine the proper aperture for a flash exposure. If it's the same as that required for the outdoor exposure, you're O.K. If not, the flash-to-subject

distance must be adjusted until it is.

This is usually done by reducing the intensity of the flash with a Neutral Density Filter or clean white handkerchief over the flash head. For example, if the outdoor exposure required is 1/60 at f/8 and the flash exposure 1/60 at f/11, a 2X neutral density filter over the flash or a single thickness of handkerchief will cut the light sufficiently. The same thing can be achieved by moving the flash unit back to the appropriate position by means of an extension flash cord. As a third option, move both camera and flash back until the flash-to-subject distance requires an exposure of f/8 and then change to a zoom or a longer focal length lens to compose the shot as you desire it.

Once you've balanced the required exposure by one of these methods, simply go ahead and shoot. There'll be

no shadow on the glass, and the picture will look perfectly normal as the illumination from outdoors and that from your flash are in balance. As firing the flash directly at the glass will result in a reflection, you should either angle the EF unit slightly, or open the window if doing so will not interfere with your composition. When possible, select a window where the outside view will not visually detract from your subject—large masses of foliage or other nondescript backgrounds are most ideal, as you're not able to use selective focus with this technique to throw the background completely out of focus.

USING FLASH OUTDOORS—Let's step out into the sunlight for a moment and explore one of the most useful and easiest applications of electronic flash, yet one which seems to thoroughly confuse many beginning photogra-

2

3

1. Expose for existing light and place your EF at a distance sufficient to slightly underexpose the shadow areas.

2. "Duplex look" is one of many variations of the doubletake portraiture possible. The EF was fired with its test button from one position for the first pose and moved to a second position for the second pose. (Jim Cornfield.)

3. Under overcast conditions, turn the flash into your main light and use existing illumination as fill—see the text for advice on this trick.

phers. Often called "synchro-sunlight," the use of flash to fill in deep shadows created by bright sunlight will inevitably produce a better picture, especially when shooting close-ups or medium close-ups of people outdoors.

Your subject will generally find it necessary to squint (or wear dark glasses) when you work outdoors with bright sunlight coming over *your* shoulder, and the result is not usually very flattering. If the subject complains (and who wouldn't?), you can make the grand gesture and switch places, but now the sun is in *your* eyes, and the subject is backlighted. Now you've got a real situation on your hands—if you expose for the face, the background will be hopelessly overexposed. But expose for the background and the face will go dark. What to do? Use fill-flash!

Many amateurs tend to make the use of fill-flash more difficult than it really is, when the truth of the matter is that it's simpler to use than conventional indoor flash. It all works on the guide number system plus the fact that the guide number system goes to pieces when applied outdoors. If this sounds confusing to you, I'll clarify it as soon as we've explored a hypothetical situation. Your camera is loaded with ASA 100 film. Focusing on the subject tells you that you're five feet from him/her. As the subject is sidelighted, you want to lighten the shadow side of the face in order to pick up some detail.

Check your EF unit and determine the guide number for ASA 100 film— we'll assume it to be 80 in this particular example. Now divide the distance (five feet) into the guide number (80) and you arrive at the proper aperture, f/16 (80 divided by five equals 16). Set

1

2

the lens at f/16 and take a meter reading in the usual manner. With leaf-type shutters, you can simply pick the shutter speed which correlates with f/16 on the meter dial and shoot away to your heart's content. Those using a camera with a focal-plane shutter will probably have to vary the flash-to-subject distance in order to balance the flash exposure with that required for the sunlight. The same techniques can be used here as with window flash—a neutral density filter or white handkerchief over the flash, moving the flash position away from the camera, or changing the focal length of the lens which is used.

From this discussion, you might assume that both the sunlight and the flash fill-in had been equally balanced, and that the resulting picture will be flatly lighted and thus uninteresting. But this is not the case in reality, as the guide number system goes to pieces when used outdoors. Indoors, where you calibrate your flash unit in terms of guide numbers, you had sev-

eral highly reflective surfaces (walls, ceilings, small rooms, etc.), all of which added up to a specific guide number. But there are no reflective surfaces outdoors to augment the light from your flash. As a result, the effective light output is reduced to one-half, or even one-quarter its indoor rating.

This reduced efficiency outdoors allows the flash to act merely as a fill-in light and thus open up shadows. That's really all the mystery there is to using a flash fill outdoors. You simply pretend to balance your flash unit's output to the available sunlight in terms of lens apertures and then make your exposure. The final effect will be one where the sunlight has made the basic exposure, with the flash serving to fill in deep shadows. Once you've mastered this technique, and it doesn't take very long, you'll use it often, as the resulting pictures are far better than without the lift that your flash will provide.

When the weather is dull, try turning this outdoor fill flash technique around to simulate sunlight. To do this, you must make the flash provide your main lighting and use daylight as your fill source. Here's how: Determine your proper daylight exposure and then

close the aperture down one extra stop. If the required exposure is 1/60 at f/5.6, use f/8. Now divide your EF guide number by the aperture in use to establish the correct flash-to-subject distance (56 divided by 5.6 equals 10). Position your flash at that distance from the subject and it will now act as the main light—the reduction in exposure from natural lighting will change its function to that of a fill light source.
OPEN FLASH—For really creative results from electronic flash, try this technique. It's really very simple—you just set the camera shutter on B or T (use of a locking cable release is recommended with the B setting) and fire the flash by hand using the open flash or test button. If done with the room lights on, the film will record an image from both the ambient light and the flash. This will record a sharp and a blurred image at the same time, providing a feeling of motion.

Another application is called "painting" with light, where you fire the EF several times from different positions in a large dark interior or outdoors at night to light the subject. A less complex application of painting with light is the dual portrait or "doubletake," which shows two aspects of a subject

1-2. Two variations of the action montage possible with open flash in which posed shots simulate motion. Subject placement with each successive flash should be rehearsed. (Jim Cornfield.)

1

2

3

4

in the same picture. With this procedure, the subject changes position between flashes. For example, the first flash might show a frontal pose with the subject facing the camera, while the second pose is a dramatic profile. The desired end result must be preconceived and worked out in the camera viewfinder so that the two images will be positioned properly and not overlap.

A slighly more difficult application of the doubletake, the "perspective doubletake" records two images of the subject, but the images differ in size, giving a feeling of depth to the picture. This approach requires that the subject be rehearsed in the two poses desired, and is easiest to accomplish without a hitch if set up with the room lights on and a chair placed at each position for the subject. If the flash-to-subject distances are unequal, you'll have to work with two different apertures, as well as two different focus settings. Once the subject is acquainted with what is required of him/her, turn the room lights off and flash for the first pose. While the unit recycles and you refocus the camera, have the subject move slowly to the second position and arrange his/her pose. Then flash the second position, close the shutter and bring up the room lights.

How to determine the proper focus settings on the lens in the dark? Place

a small piece of adhesive tape on the focusing index mark of the lens, and a second small piece on the correct distance setting on the footage scale. To refocus, simply align the two pieces of tape using your index fingernail as a straightedge. If you're working in color, try using a different color gel over the flash head for each flash—and don't forget to compensate in your exposure for the gels.

You can also use open flash to create an action montage by having your model go through a predetermined movement against a dark background very slowly while you make repeated flash exposures. The result is a multiple-image picture which contains a dramatic illusion of movement. Some of the highly sophisticated EF units now available are fitted with a switch

1. **In this shot the main light provides the primary lighting.**
2. **Here the fill light softens shadows created by the main light.**
3. **Adding a second fill illuminates the background. This does away with distracting shadows and makes your subject stand out more emphatically.**
4. **A backlight emphasizes hair texture.**
5-6. **Two of the available meters for determining EF exposure, the comparatively inexpensive Wein WP500B (6) was one of the first and has earned a well-deserved reputation for accuracy. The Minolta Flash Meter II (5) shown with its various accessories provides an instant digital readout of the aperture.**
Unless otherwise credited, all creative flash pictures and corresponding artwork reprinted by courtesy of Vivitar.

for multiple flash on a single exposure to give a stroboscopic effect. If your unit has this feature, you can use it to make multiple-image pictures of normal subject movement.

MULTIPLE FLASH—Lighting arrangements for using electronic flash in studio-type setups are identical to those discussed for continuous lighting in the previous chapter. EF units placed in the same positions as continuous lamps will produce the same basic effects. The primary differences come in how the various units used are activated, and how the exposure is calculated.

There are various methods of connecting a multiple EF setup; which one

5

6

you use will depend to some extent upon the EF units. Some have a PC socket built in so that the unit can be connected to others by means of a long flash extension cord. Those which use a PC cord can be connected to a single cord which plugs into the camera's PC socket—this is done by leading flash extension cords from each unit to a multiflash flash tip connector which feeds all lines to a single one leading to the camera. Units which will function only in a hot shoe can be fitted with a hot shoe adapter. These terminate in a short PC cord and can then be plugged into the wiring setup. Like continuous lighting, the primary disadvantage to all these solutions is the spider web of connecting wires which results.

A far more convenient method is the use of remote flash triggers. These are sold as accessories to convert your EF units into "slaves," or units which fire

upon a command from your "master" unit. Priced about the same as an inexpensive EF unit, a remote flash trigger contains a switching circuit that is sensitive to light. To use, you simply connect the triggering device to the PC cord and turn the EF unit on. When the flash designated as the master unit fires, the triggering device picks up the light signal and closes the circuit of the remote units, firing them instantly. In addition to doing away with connecting cords completely, the remote triggering devices are much less of a problem to carry, store and use than are extensions cords.

Offered by various manufacturers, they vary considerably in configuration and features. Some have no provisions for mounting, while others use a suction cup base or bottom-mounted foot fitted with a tripod thread. The degree of sensitivity is adjustable on some and depending upon the manufacturer, the sensitivity angle will vary between 45 and 180 degrees. While the narrower sensitivity angle limits to some extent where the flash can be placed relative to the master unit, using one with the wider angle does increase the risk of another light source accidentally triggering the slave.

Regardless of how a multiple EF setup is arranged, your exposure is calculated only on the main light, unless you have several lights directed at the same highlight area of a subject. Under these circumstances, you should stop the lens down somewhat, but ex-

actly how much will depend entirely upon the number of lights in use, their output and distance from the subject.

For those desiring on-the-button flash exposures every time with multiple EF setups, an electronic flash meter can be used. These range from the comparatively inexpensive direct-reading Wein Flashmeter to the new multipurpose but expensive digital units such as the Minolta Flash Meter II. The pioneer in this field of exposure determination, the Wein WP500B is also a breeze to use. Simply place it at the subject's position facing the camera, set its exposure index dial to match the speed of your film and turn the unit on. Fire a test flash and read the correct f-stop from the scale. Set the camera's lens to this aperture and you're in business.

Although it may appear complex to the beginner, electronic flash is by far the most versatile artificial light source available to the photographer. With today's automatic units, anyone can use it successfully by learning no more than how to attach the EF unit to his camera and turn it on—yet the creative potential remains to be explored as you become more serious about your picture-taking. The more you come to know and understand about lighting, the more you'll appreciate the many convenient and creative aspects of electronic flash, and the better your pictures will be. And who knows—you might even end up with seven EF units—just like me! □

12

Working With Available Light

Sometimes called existing light, available-light photography involves working with whatever illumination is present, without the use of flash or other forms of supplemental lighting. As such, available-light photography is generally characterized by lower levels of illumination than are encountered in more normal photographic situations, and many amateurs often think of it in terms of push-processing and the proverbial black cat photographed in a coal bin at midnight.

While this is a part of available-light photography, it is by no means the only definition. Whenever you think of taking pictures indoors by whatever light is present in the scene, or when you work outdoors at twilight or after dark, you're thinking in terms of available-light photography, much of which can be accomplished without resorting to extraordinary processing techniques. This chapter is designed to give your creative juices a shot in that direction.

WHY AVAILABLE LIGHT?

Realism is one answer; freedom and mobility are others. Available-light pictures have a realistic look that even the best pro finds difficult to duplicate with his skillful use of artificial lighting. By taking advantage of natural illumination, you can create a mood—a sense of atmosphere—that would otherwise be impossible to attain. And there are times and places when the use of flash is simply inappropriate—during stage shows, wedding ceremonies, candid photography, etc. Those disturbed by the decay of urban areas find that street scenes at night project

an entirely different visual experience—one that's often colorful, exciting and clean by comparison with the same area pictured during the day.

You don't have to burden yourself with all kinds of accessory lighting equipment—just a camera, light meter and on occasion, perhaps a lightweight camera support. This means far less to carry and think about, leaving you free to concentrate upon the subject itself and how it can be best treated. People will pay less attention to you (everyone *knows* that you can't take pictures at night without a flash) and you'll be able to take pictures that better reveal your subject's personality.

CAMERAS AND FILM

Virtually any 35mm camera available today can be used for pictures by existing light—an f/2 or faster lens and a high-speed film will give you far more capability than you might imagine. Quite often, you'll be able to hand-hold the camera using a 1/30 second exposure, but a lightweight tripod for time exposures can prove invaluable on occasion. If you're a bit shaky at 1/30 second, pick up a grip pod and use it to form a compact shoulder pod just to be on the safe side; a cable release will also come in handy, as well as a small flashlight for checking camera settings in the dark.

While cameras with rangefinder focusing are generally preferred for their brighter viewfinder image and greater ease in focusing under low light level conditions, an SLR shouldn't pose too many problems in use, as you'll generally be working with the lens wide open. This makes focusing far easier, especially if you have a split-image focusing screen.

The built-in camera metering system can be either a blessing or a bust, depending upon how familiar you are with its eccentricities, and how effectively you use it. I prefer to leave the camera's meter off and use a hand-held reflected-light meter with a 10-degree angle of view—this approximates the area seen by the 85mm telephoto I generally use as my normal lens for available-light work. Sticklers for absolutely correct exposure may prefer a 1-3-degree spot meter, but these are not as handy to stuff in your pocket, and consume valuable time in use—I'd rather bracket three quick shots and be sure I carry away the

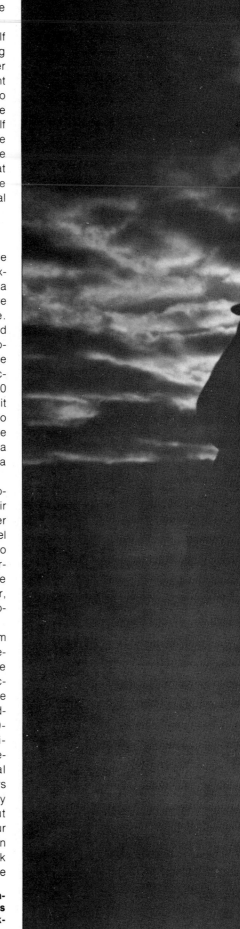

Available light lends itself to dramatic interpretations. Gil Gonzalez captured this lonely figure against the windswept background of an approaching snowstorm.

picture than to spend the equivalent time (or longer) metering a subject, especially in changing light conditions. But whether you use your camera's metering system or a hand-held meter is really immaterial—it's *how* you use it that counts.

There are plenty of different film emulsions available which are suitable for available-light photography. For black-and-white work, there's Kodak Tri-X and Ilford HP5, both normally rated at ASA 400 and easily used at EI 800 by taking advantage of the film's latitude, or EI 1600 (two stops less exposure than normal) by extending development 50 percent. Just be certain that the contrast level of your subject is fairly low when exposing at EI 1600, as much shadow detail will be lost with high-contrast subjects. There's also Kodak 2475/2485 films with a nominal EI of 1000, as long as the inherent graininess does not prove objectionable. These can also be push-processed, but whether the quality will exceed that of Tri-X or HP5 pushed to the same EI level is debatable.

For color photography, you can choose between the new Fuji and Kodak color print emulsions rated at ASA 400, and both can be used at EI 800 although you should expect that the color rendition will suffer accordingly. Those who prefer color slides can work with Kodak High Speed Ektachrome Daylight (ASA 160) as long as it remains available, picking up an extra 2½ stops by exposing at ASA 400 and using a Kodak Special Processing Envelope ESP-1, available at photo dealers. With this mailer, Kodak labs will push-process the film to 2½ times its normal speed. The same mailer can be used for special processing of any of the professional Ektachromes, doubling the effective speed of each.

GAF presently offers the fastest color slide film available—GAF 500—with an ASA of 500. This can be exposed at a speed of 1000 and will be push-processed by the GAF Processing Laboratory, P.O. Box 910, Binghamton, New York 13902—just include an extra $1.00 in the regular GAF processing mailer and mark the film cartridge as having been exposed at "ASA 1000." Depending upon the lighting conditions, you may also find GAF 200 (ASA 200) or Fujichrome R-100 (ASA 100) to be adequate in speed for such work as rainy-day photography, or shooting stained glass windows, etc.

Using daylight color films will result in a warmer than normal color rendition under artificial illumination, but it's

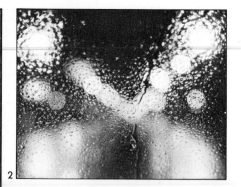

1. Calculating exposure for night shots like this one by David Neibel should not be left to an automatic exposure camera; the photographer needs to insert his own judgment, which may even include overriding the camera's exposure recommendation at times.
2. Rain drops on the windshield turn this interpretation of on-coming traffic into an abstraction. Available light pictures of this kind shot in color are especially striking. (Ron Berkenblitt.)
3. The L.A. Rams lead the Tampa Bay Bucs 10 to 8 as Pat Toomay and his teammates watch the action on the field. Glenn Cooper pushed Tri-X two stops to EI 1600 for this shot.

definitely preferable when working with fluorescent lighting or a mixture of daylight and tungsten illumination. For the most part, it all boils down to a matter of personal taste, but I'd suggest that you match your film to the lighting conditions and avoid using filtration wherever possible, as you'll lose about an f-stop and sometimes more when a filter is used. This can prove to be self-defeating unless you have a tripod and a static subject, and in some cases might even push you over the brink into problems with reciprocity failure. The sole exception would be fluorescent lighting. Here an FLD or CC30M filter should be used with daylight film, and an FLB or CC50R with tungsten illumination—especially if there are people in the picture.

WHAT TO PHOTOGRAPH?

Adverse lighting conditions offer all kinds of subjects for your camera.

Look around your home and you'll see dozens—parties, holiday activities (including the Christmas tree), your children, family members enjoying group activities—the list is long. But as these subjects and activities are always present, let's move outside the home to take a look at some of the things that may tempt you on vacation or other once-in-a-lifetime experiences.

SHOOTING IN THE RAIN

Most amateurs put their cameras away when it rains, and why not? Who wants to get wet deliberately—and who wants to risk his expensive camera in the rain? But rainy weather has its own charm and appeal, just as a sunny day with blue skies, an overcast day with its diffused lighting, or the aftermath of a snowstorm—and you take pictures under those conditions, right? So why not rainy days? Should it happen to rain while you're on vacation, don't let it interfere with your picture-taking—you may never have another opportunity to return, so make the best of it!

Of course, I'm not suggesting that you stand on a street corner and snap away during a torrential downpour; there are some occasions when the weather is just *too* inclement. But even on days with heavy rainfall, there are times when it lets up considerably, and with a fast film, wide aperture and a shutter speed of 1/60 second, you should come up with some first-class pictures that are different. Try to stay with a 1/60 second shutter speed where possible, because the normal tendency is to work more quickly in wet weather and camera shake at slower speeds becomes more difficult to avoid. If you're shooting black-and-white film, don't worry too much about underexposing by one stop or so—the resulting low-key effect will often accentuate the atmosphere and can even improve the picture. Make prints on both normal and hard grades of paper and select the effect you like best.

To work most efficiently in wet weather, you should wear a waterproof jacket or coat with pockets that are

3

sufficiently large to hold your camera if possible, and whatever accessories you think necessary, such as extra film, lenses or a meter. Wear a cap; a wide-brimmed hat only acts as a trough to collect water which will be deposited on your camera whenever you move your head. One good way to protect your camera is to use clear plastic bags. Two or three judiciously used with rubber bands to hold them in place and a bit of careful tearing or cutting here and there of the bag and you can make most cameras safe from the rain. Another dandy waterproofing method is to use that cling-wrap material manufactured to cover food in the refrigerator. This is clear enough to be stretched across the lens and photographed through in many instances, thus you can wrap the entire camera in it for rainy weather work. If the lens is exposed to the elements, use a lens shade and carry a package of lens tissue to remove any drops of rain that may blow onto the front element.

As for subjects, look for the unusual which emphasizes the bad weather—

people scurrying across the street with umbrellas, the fellow with no raincoat or hat who's drenched while waiting for a bus or taxi, pavement and buildings glistening with rain, reflections and catchlights from puddles. Interesting subjects are all around you. Some types of subject matter should be avoided—landscapes lack sufficient contrast in such weather and tend to fall into a uniform mass of dull tones. But seascapes can be inspiring, especially if you can capture wild surf, windblown trees and dark clouds. If you've never tried rainy-weather photography, now's the time to let your imagination run wild.

PHOTOGRAPHY AFTER DARK

If you don't use your camera after dark, you're missing out on some of the best picture opportunities you'll ever come across. Night photography adds a change of pace to your normal photo routine and should be considered an indispensible part of vacation/travel photography, as vacation spots (like your own home town) take on a

completely different mood after dark.

Street scenes, city skylines, floodlighted structures, neon signs, brightly lighted marketplaces, fairs and parades—all are fair game for the knowledgeable available-light photographer. Night scenes taken during or just after a rain or snowstorm offer interesting reflections and other effects, adding a touch of visual interest to what would otherwise be dark, empty areas in your picture. Cross-screen and star filters will also produce a different effect, especially when used with colored point-source lights.

Whenever possible, try to avoid large areas of total darkness in color pictures—these tend to reproduce as a sickish green/black or brown with the faster emulsions, especially when you're exposing scenes which include small areas of bright lighting. For this reason, some subjects are best photographed just before dark when the fading twilight will provide a slight tone in sky areas. If this is not possible, try to fill in otherwise blank areas with reflections or other tones.

Fountains and floodlighted buildings may appear mundane during daylight hours, but once the sun goes down and the lights come on, they are ideal subjects, as modern architecture often makes after-dark lighting an integral part of its design. Some subjects will stand by themselves, but others may benefit from including a person silhouetted in the foreground. Use a tree branch or other such object to frame your subject for a different effect.

Multiple exposures of neon signs can give a Las Vegas-type effect to virtually any city after dark. You can create unusual montages in this manner, scattering the images at random across the frame, or carefully placing each one. A zoom lens is useful here, as it will permit variations in the size of the signs while keeping your camera placement in safe areas away from traffic or careless pedestrians.

There's usually sufficient illumination in theatrical or shopping districts to permit using your camera without a tripod. Don't overlook window displays, as they often offer unusual subjects. If you shoot a window display straight-on, place your lens against the glass to avoid reflections, or shoot from an angle if necessary.

Now and then you may be working with a tripod and a lengthy exposure while people and traffic are still on the street. If someone should decide to walk across your field of view, don't get upset, as he won't even be recorded on the film, but the light from auto head lamps and taillights will leave streaks. This is fine when you're looking for a ghostly effect, but unless such streaks are definitely desired, simply cover the lens with your hand while traffic passes by and increase your exposure accordingly.

Amusement parks and fairs usually offer superb opportunities for imaginative pictures. For example, you can photograph the lighted Ferris wheel while it's stationary for one effect, use a slow shutter speed while it's moving for another, or apply the explosion effect with a zoom lens to draw the colors out in a pinwheel-like pattern. Detail shots of individual attractions, the midway or lighted structures can be taken with the camera hand-held, as the illumination around these areas is generally quite bright.

Firework displays are best recorded with the camera on a tripod and the shutter left open to catch several bursts on a single frame. If you want the individual lines in the burst bright and thick, use a wide aperture; closing

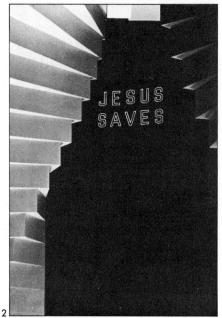

1. After-dark scenes of the city do not necessarily require the use of a tripod, fast lenses or push processing. Many like this are lighted sufficiently to work at 1/30 at f/2.8 with ASA 400 film.
2. By day, this would have no impact at all, since the black area hides a series of ugly apartment buildings. But shot after dark, the essence of the subject changes completely.
3. Another type of city scene which gains impact from the use of existing illumination. Flash would totally destroy the impact in this scene.

it down will cause them to record darker and thinner. Placing the camera where you can include other objects such as buildings or statues in the foreground will add a feeling of depth and relative size to such pictures. If you're caught without a tripod, don't give up—you can shoot with the camera hand-held using the widest aperture and a 1/30 second shutter speed for many firework displays.

Lightning bolts are photographed in a similar manner, but the camera must be tripod-mounted with the shutter open as you have no idea when or where a bolt will appear in the sky. For this reason, the use of a normal or wide-angle lens will increase the odds that you'll catch the bolt in your field of view. Try to pick a spot where there are no bright lights in the immediate vicinity, but do your picking with care, as lightning has been known to destroy

tripod, camera and photographer. As you might imagine, photographing lightning bolts from a position in the middle of an open field or standing beneath a tree can be dangerous, so look for a location which offers protection as well as a good vantage point.

If you have interchangeable lenses for your camera, use them—don't restrict yourself to the camera's normal lens. I've already mentioned the use of a zoom for special effects; a moderate telephoto will fill the frame more effectively when you're shooting fireworks displays, and a wide-angle is quite appropriate when photographing city sights at night. As very fast wide-angles can be obtained in 24-35mm focal lengths, here's an opportunity to combine the apparent perspective distortion of the lens with the effects of night photography. As most of your pictures will be taken from street level, the wide-angle is probably the most convenient of all lenses when shooting city scenes at night. You'll often find that the space in which you're free to move about will be restricted by traffic, pedestrians and buildings; thus the ability to work closer to your subject and still obtain the same image size as you'd get with the 50mm optic will be appreciated.

3

Telephotos are great by day—you can fold distant planes together, compress objects into close proximity and make a street of moderate traffic look like the traffic jam of all time. But lens speeds beyond 135mm are quite restrictive, particularly when the aperture must be stopped down to provide adequate depth of field for the subject. This brings the shutter speed out of the hand-held realm and into a tripod situation, limiting the usefulness of such a lens severely. Telephotos up through 135mm can be obtained with a speed of f/2.8 or faster, and these will prove useful to some extent for night photography. I prefer my f/1.8 85mm over most other focal lengths for hand-held photography.

Using a moderate telephoto when shooting city scenes does have one redeeming advantage. There's nearly always some convenient place to brace your camera—a lamp post, fire hydrant, railing, wall, etc. The grip pod can often take the place of a regular tripod in such photography, as you can angle the camera on the ball/socket head and press the grip pod firmly against a nearby solid object for support.

INDOOR PHOTOGRAPHY BY AVAILABLE LIGHT

Indoor entertainment and sporting events such as the circus, an ice show, boxing match, basketball game, etc. all provide a variety of available-light opportunities. Flash simply won't carry the necessary distance to photograph such spectaculars, but you'll always see a raft of bulbs go off from the stands during a performance, invariably by the box-camera crowd. We know how their pictures come out, so the question here is how to get the best results by available light.

The first step toward good pictures is to select your seats with your camera in mind when buying your tickets. If you're familiar with the facility where the performance will take place, so much the better, as you'll be able to determine which lenses will be most useful. It's also a good idea to find out the type of lighting used—entertainment events are generally lighted by carbon arcs or tungsten lamps, while sporting activities will use fluorescent or tungsten indoors, and mercury-vapor illumination for baseball/football games outdoors. This will help you to decide on either daylight or tungsten color film.

As such events contain a good deal of motion and activity, you'll want to work with one or more of three possible techniques: (1) use the highest possible shutter speed, (2) look for the peak of action when participant movement is momentarily slowed, and (3) watch the direction of motion relative

1. If motion is appropriate to the subject, don't be afraid to use a slow shutter speed when working with available light. Glenn Cooper deliberately chose a slow speed to emphasize the action during a night football game.
2. Even the lowly 110 pocket camera can be used for available-light photography. This store mannequin was photographed through the glass window with a Ricohmatic 110X using an exposure of 1/30 at f/2.8 on Kodak Verichrome Pan film (ASA 125 film.)
3. Assignment—capture the Nikon School in action for Petersen's Nikon System book. Working solely with the overhead illumination shown, Kodak Recording Film 2475, and a 21mm f/3.8 wide-angle lens wide open, author of this book hand-held at ⅛ second.

to your camera position. Action is easiest to freeze with a moderate shutter speed when it's moving toward or away from you, and most difficult to capture at such speeds when it moves across your field of view. In this case, you can choose between panning with the direction of movement for a sharp subject against a blurred background (which emphasizes motion), or shooting as the subject appears in your viewfinder and accepting whatever blurring you get as indicative of motion. Camera-to-subject distance should also be taken into consideration; the farther away your subject, the slower the speed with which you can capture the action.

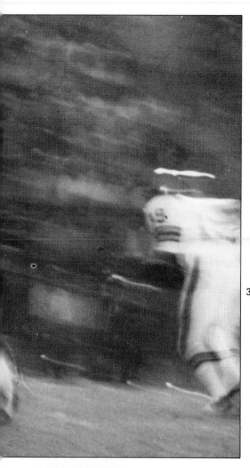

Gorgeous settings for color pictures often characterize stage shows and musicals. Because of the uniformity in lighting, they permit the use of a basic exposure for much of the performance. When the lighting changes, use this rule of thumb—open up one stop for dim lighting and two stops for very dim lighting. A fast film and wide aperture will often allow a 1/60 or 1/125 second shutter speed—fast enough to stop most motion while preventing camera

shake. A tungsten emulsion will give the best color rendition under stage lighting.

Before walking into the show with your camera, make certain that picture-taking is not prohibited by the management. The larger houses and better-known shows often frown severely on amateurs in the audience taking pictures, considering them as distractions even without the use of flash (which, incidentally, is a definite no-no). In such cases, it's often possible to arrange to take pictures during a dress rehearsal. This can prove to be an even better opportunity, as your camera location will not be restricted to the same degree as during a regular performance—you can move around the theatre and work from the best vantage points without distracting an audience.

Museums and art galleries also offer a variety of subjects for your camera, although you should investigate the policy of a particular institution before lugging in your gear to shoot. A few have total restrictions against taking pictures, while others only prohibit the use of tripods and flash units. Because of the nature of many of the exhibits and the manner in which they are displayed, available light proves more suitable anyway. Such displays are skillfully lighted for effect (often behind glass), which flash would destroy, so take advantage of the artistic effect the museum personnel have achieved and shoot with a fast film and wide aperture setting.

Some of the most interesting subjects are dioramas—exhibits which have a painted background to place the subject in its proper environment. These are often quite elaborate, with a great deal of care taken to make them

as realistic as possible. You can make even more realistic pictures of such dioramas by throwing the painted background slightly out of focus with a wide aperture. The largest dioramas will not have a glass front, but there will be a railing beyond which you are not allowed. A wide-angle lens used with the camera resting on the railing will permit tack-sharp negatives and slides by preventing camera movement.

Try to pick a day when attendance is low—weekends are usually not very good for photographing displays—and work quietly and unobtrusively, carrying only an extra lens, grip pod and cable release if possible. While the choice of lens will depend a great deal on the particular institution and how it has arranged the displays, I've found a 24mm wide-angle and 85mm telephoto to be most useful in addition to the camera's normal lens; both are fast enough to do the job and hand-holding the camera proves no problem.

As churches contain some of the world's most significant architecture, both ancient and modern, they often provide interesting subject matter by themselves, in addition to the family events which you might wish to record such as baptisms and weddings. For the amateur photographer, the use of flash is not only inappropriate, it's futile in most cases when you are trying to document the church interior unless you have several extension or slave units—the vast interior of most churches simply soaks up the light from a single unit with no appreciable benefit beyond a few feet.

If you can work from a balcony, you'll not only have an ideal vantage point, but the railing can be utilized as a camera support as well. You'll want to use a moderate to medium telephoto

from this position, as well as a moderate wide-angle. These two focal length extremes will allow you to capture both an overall view of the interior and close-ups of detail like the intricate sculptures, carvings and designs found in such structures.

Stained-glass windows make another fascinating subject and some of the finest in the world are found in cathedrals, especially those in Europe. Depending upon the intensity of the illumination shining through the glass, the use of a tripod may be required and if so, it's a good idea to ask for permission to set it up and record the windows. Abroad, you should expect to pay a fee for such permission, as a charge is often made by the church authorities.

An averaging meter reading works best for determining correct exposure because of the extreme contrast of a stained-glass window. Meter to expose for the richer colors when they are predominant, as the clear whites will

bleach out anyway. Once you've determined the "correct" exposure, it's a good idea to bracket two ½-stops on either side, or at least one full stop. Generally speaking, all your slides will be suitable for projection or viewing, but the slight difference in exposures will produce variations in the intensity of the colors, and you may prefer the effect of one taken with slightly more or less than the "correct" exposure.

Because a stained-glass window requires very little depth of field, you can work with the lens wide open—just be sure to focus carefully. The use of a lens shade is a good idea whenever there is bright cross-lighting entering from another nearby window. Try to fill the frame as much as possible with the window and if you're working with a tripod, use a cable release just to be on the safe side.

Hobby and trade shows abound these days, and if you're a connoisseur of cameras, guns, cars, flowers, etc., you may want to photograph

some of the displays. Some collectors collect photographs of unusual items related to their hobby, and such exhibits are generally rich with subject material. For example, if custom cars are one of your interests, photographing what others have done to their vehicles can provide you with a file of ideas for future projects.

This type of attraction is usually well-lighted from above, with individual exhibits and displays often containing their own lighting arrangements to spotlight that which the owner feels will be of interest. While the overall illumination is likely to be fluorescent or mercury-vapor, individual lighting arrangements will probably use tungsten lamps. For black-and-white photography, this simply means low-contrast lighting, but if you're shooting in color, choose your film according to the type of light which will predominate in the majority of your pictures.

You can meter this type of subject quite easily and as with stage shows,

4

5

one basic exposure will often handle most of the general views you'll take. Be sure to check your exposure whenever you take detail shots, and carrying a low-powered EF unit to punch light into deep shadows, such as those under the hood of a car, will often prove useful. There are usually no restrictions on the use of flash at such shows unless it's a pet show where live animals are on display.

DETERMINING EXPOSURE

While it's not too difficult to train yourself to look at a normally lighted scene and calculate the necessary exposure accordingly, available light is tricky to ''guesstimate'' with accuracy because the human eye adapts so easily to changes in illumination. Even a highly sensitive light meter can be fooled by available light; thus the use of a meter is not an automatic guarantee that you'll end up with the correct exposure.

First of all, let's define ''correct exposure'' in terms of available-light photography. As in all other types of picture-taking, the correct exposure is really the best exposure for the subject at hand and your desired interpretation of it. In available-light work, the idea is to reproduce your subject so that it appears as realistic as possible in your finished picture. While writing this, I received a box of slides from the lab which contained a bracketed series of exposures of a street scene taken during the waning moments of twilight before darkness settled over the city. Yet several of the slides appeared to be taken in near-daylight with the street lights on—an interesting effect, but one that is hardly realistic. Pictures taken under such conditions should appear as dark as the subject did to you when you took the picture.

The point to hang onto here is simply that although we often worry about underexposure when dealing with available-light photography, overexposure can also be a problem with poorly lighted scenes. This is especially true of color slides, as there is no correction you can make once the slides are processed. While they may certainly be acceptable as visual images, the slides will not contain true reproductions of your subject. With black-and-white shots, the problem is more one of washed-out highlights and blocked shadow areas, but some compensation can be made during enlarging to bring the subject's reproduction closer to where it belongs. So if you can't ''eyeball'' such subjects accurately, and you can't place absolute faith in what your meter tells you, how can you determine the best exposure?

METERING IN AVAILABLE LIGHT SITUATIONS

Whether built into the camera or hand-held, your exposure meter is the best guide you have, but you can't just point it at the subject and shoot away. You must first know and understand the eccentricities which plague all types of metering systems—see the chapter on exposure. Once you're thoroughly familiar with how to best use the device you have, as well as understanding its limitations and how to overcome them, you must be able to

evaluate the evenness of illumination with which you're working.

When the illumination is fairly even, as in an office, factory or department store, a normal reading with your reflected meter will generally be sufficient. An incident meter will have to be considered in terms of the subject's level of reflectance—cut exposures by ½ stop for light subjects and increase by one stop for dark ones.

You'll probably encounter uneven lighting conditions more often in available-light work—it's dramatic but requires a good deal more forethought on your part in interpreting what the meter tells you about the light. A reflected-light meter is generally more useful than the incident type, but must be used with care, as large areas of light or dark will influence its reading heavily. When the smaller areas in the scene are most important, a straight reading will give you an incorrect exposure. My preferred meter for such work has a 10-degree angle of view, which covers the field of an 85mm telephoto, but makes it a narrow-angle meter when working with focal lengths

below that—the shorter the focal length of the lens, the more of a spot meter it becomes.

With uneven lighting and large patches of light or dark in the scene, you should meter those areas of most importance to you and average the exposure readings when there's sufficient difference in brightness to warrant it. Should one important area call for an exposure of 1/30 at f/4 and another for 1/30 at f/2, set your aperture at f/2.8 for the best exposure.

METER TYPES

A moment ago, I mentioned the reflected-light meter as being more useful than an incident type for determining exposure under available-light conditions. This is, of course, a personal opinion and depends upon the type of available-light work most frequently done. The problem with the incident-light meter is that it must be subjected to the same illumination which falls on your subject and thus it's not always possible to meter neon signs (which emit rather than reflect light), concerts or stage shows where

1. Glenn Cooper caught this dramatic shot of Rob Scribner on Kodak Tri-X pushed to ASA 1600.
2. A tripod is a necessity here, as well as careful exposure determination. A hand-held CdS meter is recommended for such work. If it doesn't have a restricted angle of view, take your readings of both highlight and shadow areas from a close point of view and average them for the best exposure compromise.
3. This black-and-white reproduction of one of the color slides referred to in the text was taken at night, but the combination of fast film, a slow shutter speed at wide-open aperture, and push processing gives it the appearance of near-daylight. To be effective, such pictures should appear as dark as the subject did to your eye when you shot it.

a spotlight is frequently used, and other like situations.

The reflected-light meter has its own disadvantages. Under some circumstances, it may be necessary to take readings from a point close to your subject, and it's here that I find my 10-degree angle meter most useful. While it's not as accurate as the 1-3-degree spot meters available, it's an acceptable compromise in terms of size, weight and functional use, requir-

2

3

ing far less time to pick up an approximate brightness range ratio.

Thus far, I've considered meters primarily in terms of the hand-held variety. While I personally feel them to be more versatile than any built-in metering system, there's no reason why you can't use the one in your camera to obtain acceptable exposures, as long as you apply the same principles of use discussed above. The primary difference becomes one of automation—if you utilize your camera's meter as suggested, you'll find yourself working in a match-needle mode rather than applying full automation to permit point-and-shoot photography.

METER SENSITIVITY

The more sensitive your meter is to low light levels, the more efficiently it can determine your best exposure.

CdS, silicon-blue and GAP meters all work reasonably well in dimly lighted situations, subject to their own particular eccentricities in terms of color sensitivity, memory effect, etc. Inexpensive meters, regardless of type of cell used, tend to lack sensitivity to low light levels, or if they possess it to some degree, may not be reliable—a fault which can often be traced to a meter scale that is too compressed to allow easy reading of the low end.

If your meter falls into this category, you don't have to trade it for a more expensive/sensitive one to work successfully with available light. Divide the speed of your film by a factor of five and then set your meter to the resulting figure instead of the higher film speed rating. Now take your meter reading from a clean white handkerchief or the white side of an 18-per-

cent gray card illuminated by the same light which strikes your subject and you'll arrive at the proper exposure.

A good way to insure that you'll come away with a usable negative or slide is to bracket available-light shots whenever possible, especially those readers who are not accustomed to working with such low light levels. Take a series of three shots, one at a stop over and one at a stop under the aperture on which you've settled as being appropriate for the subject. Keep a record of the exposure given various subjects, check it against your negatives or slides after processing and make a mental note of how successful you were in arriving at a ''correct'' exposure for the scene.

AND FINALLY . . . .

Use a tripod whenever possible and take advantage of the T or B setting on your shutter for extended exposures. Remember the reciprocity failure effect when shooting color with exposures longer than one second and open the aperture ½ stop for those exposures between one and 10 seconds, or one stop for those which exceed 10 seconds. Avoid the use of filters which require an exposure increase whenever you can, and take advantage of push-processing when necessary. Look for unusual subjects, treat them with imagination and you'll find uses for your camera long after you're accustomed to putting it away because ''it's too dark to take good pictures.'' □

13

Instant Camera Photography

I can think of no single advance in photo technology over the past half-century whose impact compares with that of Dr. Edwin H. Land's "picture-in-a-minute" process introduced in the autumn of 1948. Continuing developments in the processes and equipment have taken us from those deckle-edged sepia-tone prints of the first Model 95 Land camera through high-speed black-and-white prints in 15 seconds, and full color in 60 seconds. While "60-second" photography has exposed millions to the fascination of photography in that time, it has also proven invaluable in scientific and industrial applications.

But Land and his associates didn't stop there—his fondest dream was a camera that would produce a completely finished picture, with no need to time the development process, no negative to peel away from the positive print, and nothing to discard and litter the landscape. Called the Polaroid SX-70 Land camera, it was a dream realized almost 24 years to the date he had first introduced his process to the public in a Boston department store. Although the SX-70 process was greeted with far less awe than a less-sophisticated generation had bestowed on the original Model 95 almost a quarter-century earlier, instant photography took a tremendous leap forward.

Eastman Kodak, who was then coating the Polacolor film emulsion under contract to Polaroid, had also long savored the idea of instant photography, and when Polaroid began to manufacture its own SX-70 film, Kodak decided to enter the arena with its own instant products. Soothsayers immediately foretold the demise of Polaroid, as Kodak's overwhelming resources and

long-established capabilities were well known as decisive factors in molding the photographic market in whatever direction it wished—their cartridge-loading still cameras and sound-on-film movie cameras had long proven that.

And so three years after the SX-70 Land camera appeared, Kodak's instant cameras and film were ready for market and were introduced in the spring of 1976. Contrary to what the "experts" had predicted, Polaroid did not fall by the wayside; if anything, the company and the market it serves are healthier for the competition. For the first time in the history of instant photography, the public has a choice between types of cameras and films—a choice which has actually expanded the instant photographic segment of the market. Photokina '76 was the scene of a demonstration by Agfa of its forthcoming instant process, and several Japanese firms including Fuji are working on their own. For the present, however, let's examine the Pola-

roid and Kodak processes to see how they work, how they differ and which will best serve the needs of those interested in instant photography.

THE SX-70 PROCESS

The original SX-70 camera of 1972 was a stunning technical achievement—ultraminiaturization had compressed hundreds of electronic components into three tiny "brain" centers neatly packaged within a 24-ounce, 1x4x7-inch, leather-covered, injection-molded plastic body, along with a 12,000-rpm motor which propelled hard, dry and durable picture "packets" outside the camera within 1.2 seconds after exposure where they developed completely by themselves.

The SX-70 film was another astounding achievement, involving a complete restatement of the basic Polaroid dye/developer concept that used new emulsions, interlayers and coating technology, and which combined with the multilayer positive sheet to form an

1. The Polaroid Pronto! RF faces the Kodak EK6 Instant camera for the moment of truth. Which system you choose will depend primarily upon the user convenience factors and color rendition of the two different films.

2. Polaroid's SX-70 Model 3 camera is the latest derivation of the original SX-70 design. This inexpensive model retains most of the sophisticated electronics but features a bright viewfinder system and manual focusing.

integral structure of 17 microscopic layers. As the film packet was driven automatically from the camera between two tiny steel rollers, the reagent pod ruptured to spread its contents uniformly between the bonded negative and positive sheets.

Opacifying dyes within the reagent produced a chemical curtain to shield the negative's still-sensitive layers from exposure to external light. Migrating dyes from the negative then pushed through the reagent within seconds to begin forming the color picture on the inner surface of the transparent posi-

tive sheet and as this process intensified, left the fully developed color image against a highly reflective layer of white pigment.

Because the final picture rested above this chemical background, it appeared to have a remarkable luminous quality, as if it were illuminated from behind, a characteristic that lent a three-dimensional feeling to the subject. As there was nothing to peel apart, throw away or even time (development was completely controlled by the process), the pictures could be tucked in your pocket to continue the development process while you took other shots.

Stunning technical achievement that it was, the SX-70 camera and film had their share of minor "bugs" that remained to be worked out when they made their debut, but this is something encounted by every new advance—

Kodak has had its own share of difficulties with new color emulsions in recent years, difficulties that were resolved fully only after the products were in actual field use. The original SX-70 Land camera had an optical system design in which the image tended to float in the viewfinder, thus the user was really focusing on an aerial image rather than one on a conventional ground glass. Those without 20/20 vision often encountered difficulty in focusing the camera properly. To correct this, Polaroid immediately installed a split-image rangefinder—after aiming the center of the viewfinder at a vertical line in the subject, the focusing wheel was rotated until the two halves of the line were brought together to form a single line once more, and the camera was then in focus.

Unlike other automatic exposure cameras, which use a battery (eu-

THE POLAROID SX-70 LAND CAMERA

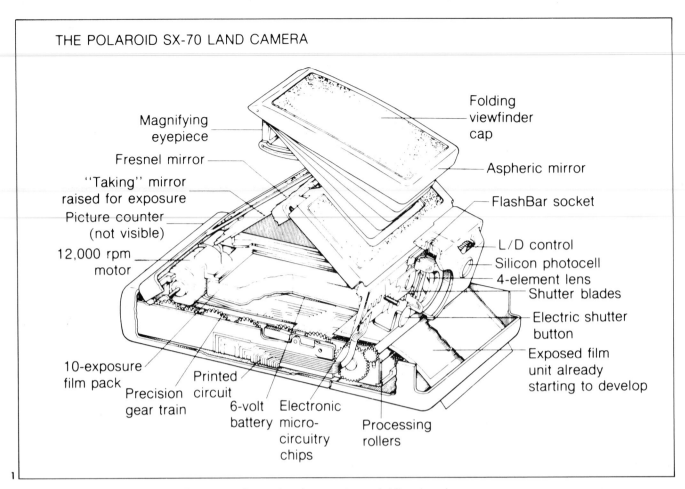

Labels (clockwise from left):
- Magnifying eyepiece
- Fresnel mirror
- "Taking" mirror raised for exposure
- Picture counter (not visible)
- 12,000 rpm motor
- Folding viewfinder cap
- Aspheric mirror
- FlashBar socket
- L/D control
- Silicon photocell
- 4-element lens
- Shutter blades
- Electric shutter button
- Exposed film unit already starting to develop
- 10-exposure film pack
- Precision gear train
- Printed circuit
- 6-volt battery
- Electronic micro-circuitry chips
- Processing rollers

1

phemistically referred to as an "energy cell" by battery manufacturers), the SX-70 contained no power source of its own. A new type of battery had been designed in conjunction with Ray-O-Vac and was incorporated in the base of each film pack, supposedly assuring a constant and fresh power source for the camera's motor, electronic circuitry and flash system. Unfortunately, the battery's storage and shelf life was somewhat less than the reputed six months, and many users bought fresh film packs only to find that the camera would not work. Since there was no other provision made in the SX-70 for alternate power sources, the camera simply would not function if the film pack's battery voltage was insufficient. Resolving this problem required considerable time and certain new approaches to battery design/packaging, but should no longer be encountered with film packs that have not reached their expiration date. Despite these and other minor aggravations, SX-70 development continued, with a less-expensive Model 2 in 1974 and an inexpensive Model 3 using a reverse Galilean-type viewfinder and scale focusing system in 1975.

THE POLAROID PRONTO!

The following year saw the first Pronto!, a low-cost, nonfolding Land camera using SX-70 film packs. Focused by rotating the lens bezel to align the marked subject distance with an index mark, the Pronto! used a three-blade scanning aperture shutter system with speeds from one to 1/125 second, and a 116mm f/9.4 three-element plastic lens with apertures to f/22. Shutter design was similar to the two-blade sliding aperture SX-70 shutter, but was recomputed especially for the Pronto! with a third blade added to ensure a complete light shield over the film, a function served in the SX-70 models by the mirror transport.

Once the camera was focused, exposure was automatically controlled for both daylight and flash pictures by a center-weighted silicon diode photocell coupled to three integrated circuits. The Pronto! also offered automatic fill-flash capability in which the electronic circuitry triggered the flash after a delay computed by the electronics to permit a reading of the existing light level.

The Flash Bar uses M-delay type bulbs and so the light output builds up to full intensity and then drops off in a bell-shaped curve, which requires several milliseconds. The Pronto! metering system is smart enough to select whatever portion of the light output it needs to complement the existing illumination,

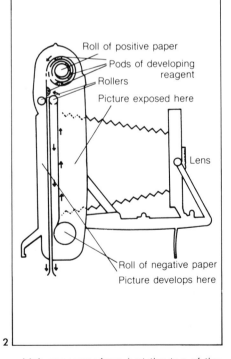

Labels:
- Roll of positive paper
- Pods of developing reagent
- Rollers
- Picture exposed here
- Lens
- Roll of negative paper
- Picture develops here

2

which may vary from just the toe of the flash output to its entire curve.

An interlock circuit prevented the camera from operating whenever the forward-facing side of a Flash Bar was expended, thus signalling the user to either reverse or replace it without the loss of a picture. Like the original SX-70, the first Pronto! used a slip-on

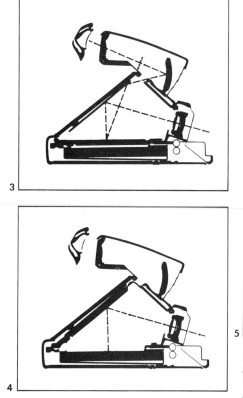

3

4

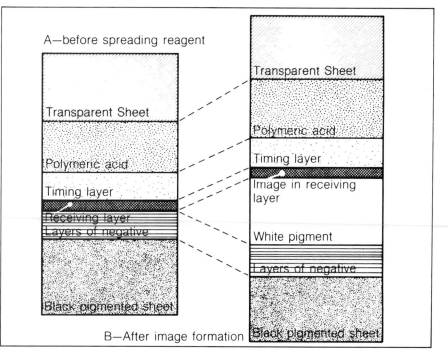

A—before spreading reagent

Transparent Sheet

Polymeric acid

Timing layer

Receiving layer

Layers of negative

Black pigmented sheet

Transparent Sheet

Polymeric acid

Timing layer

Image in receiving layer

White pigment

Layers of negative

Black pigmented sheet

B—After image formation

5

1-2. These schematic diagrams explain the basic features of the original Model 95 Land camera with its roll film (2) and the SX-70 with its self-developing picture packet (1). Like everything else, the tools of instant photography have become as complex as the age in which we live.

3-4. In the SX-70 viewing system, light enters through the lens, strikes a permanent mirror and reflects down onto a special Fresnel mirror which bundles it into a beam and projects it out through a small exit hole in the camera. The light beam strikes an aspheric mirror just below its centerline and passes through the magnifying aspheric eyepiece to the user's eye. The scene is presented to the user right-side-up and correctly positioned left-to-right (3). When you touch the shutter button to take a picture, the Fresnel mirror rises up against the camera's back and brings a trapezoidal "taking" mirror into the light path. This reverses the image into the correct left-to-right orientation as it reflects it downward onto the now uncovered negative in the film pack. A small rubber flap attached to the pivoting carrier (which hold the Fresnel mirror and taking mirror) seals the exit hole at the camera's top to prevent a light leak during exposure.

5. Drawn approximately to scale, this schematic cross-section shows the SX-70 film packet before and after development. The white pigment in B is spread with the reagent and forms the highly reflecting surface that contributes to the brilliance of the final image.

adapter unit so that the camera could be mounted to a tripod.

THE LATEST FROM POLAROID

Toward the end of 1976, the SX-70 Alpha 1 appeared. An improved version of the original model, the Alpha 1 incorporated the automatic fill-flash and used-flash bar features of the Pronto!, as well as a low-voltage detection system to determine if the film pack's battery was sufficiently strong for operation, and other little circuitry touches here and there designed to increase the camera's versatility. A built-in tripod socket did away with the awkward tripod adapter. At the present time, four SX-70 models are currently in production—the Alpha 1, Alpha 2, Model 2 and Model 3.

Responding to the challenge by Kodak, Polaroid expanded the Pronto! line in 1977 to include the Pronto! B, Pronto! Extra and Pronto! RF. The Pronto! B and Extra models differ primarily in trim and accessories included in the base price—the Extra comes with a self-timer and tripod adapter, which are available separately for the Pronto! B. The Pronto! RF incorporates a superimposed-image rangefinder in the viewfinder—turn the lens bezel until the two images coincide and the lens is in focus—with the self-timer and tripod adapter included with the camera. All lens/shutter/exposure system specifications of the original Pronto! have been carried over to the second-generation models.

Polaroid has also continued to improve its SX-70 color film. The most recent version contains an antihalation coating to reduce internal reflections while in the camera, and an increased latitude in processing temperature. The antihalation coating produces an image that appears to be considerably sharper than previous SX-70 pictures, and the modification in processing latitude now permits its use at temperatures between 45°F. and 95°F. Processing is also quicker, with better color rendition overall, greater color saturation and more natural flesh tones.

THE KODAK INSTANT PROCESS

As you might expect, the Kodak approach to instant photography is not compatible with the Polaroid SX-70 process; its cameras are considerably different in size, shape and styling, and will accept only the Kodak Instant Print film cartridge (designated PR-10). Three Kodak instant cameras are available—the EK4 and EK6 models introduced in 1976, and the new Kodak Handle—with a folding EK8 (made in West Germany by Kodak A.G.) to be offered later. Except for their method of film transport, the EK4 and EK6 are identical.

THE EK4/EK6 INSTANT CAMERAS

These two models share an electronic shutter with speeds from 1/20 to 1/300 second, and a 137mm f/11 coated triplet lens. The exposure system is controlled by a tiny integrated circuit containing a silicon photosensor that determines the correct exposure for both daylight and flash pictures. The plastic lens can be focused from 2½ feet to infinity using one of three focusing methods—by a focus scale marked in feet/meters, by zone focus symbols, and/or the use of a "zooming circle" device incorporated within the viewfinder. This distance finder can be used between four and 25 feet by aiming it around an adult head seen in the viewfinder. A three-element projected frame viewfinder is fitted with a rub-

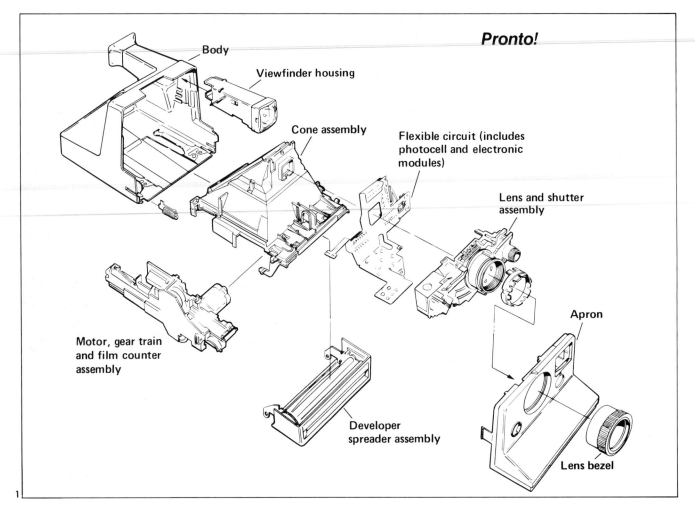

Pronto!

Body

Viewfinder housing

Cone assembly

Flexible circuit (includes photocell and electronic modules)

Lens and shutter assembly

Motor, gear train and film counter assembly

Developer spreader assembly

Apron

Lens bezel

1

ber eyecup to help the photographer in proper eye positioning.

Designed to accommodate FlipFlash, the two cameras operate at f/11 with automatic focus-linked exposure between four and 10 feet. A red low-light level signal appears in the viewfinder whenever an exposure of 1/20 at f/11 is insufficient, while a Lighten/Darken control provides a manual exposure override of ± one f-stop. A mechanical exposure counter is built into the camera close to the viewfinder eyepiece for convenience. When there's no film in the camera, the counter remains blank; if the pack is empty or when the safety cover is in place, symbols on the counter indicate so.

While the EK4 uses a manual film transport requiring about four revolutions of the folding hand crank to expel the exposed picture from the camera's bottom, the EK6 has a motor-driven film transport. This ejects the print from the camera about three seconds after pressure on the shutter button has been released. Both cameras incorporate a battery test button to determine the condition of the power source that operates the electronic exposure system—and powers the EK6 motor. Unlike the Polaroid SX-70 system, Ko-

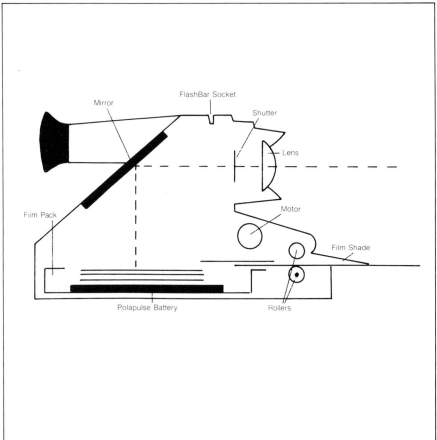

Mirror

FlashBar Socket

Shutter

Lens

Film Pack

Motor

Film Shade

Polapulse Battery

Rollers

2

3

1. The interrelationship of the components which make up the Pronto! are shown in this exploded drawing.
2. Compare this Pronto! schematic with that of the SX-70 and you'll understand the price differential.
3. The original Pronto! Land Camera contains a precision-molded three-element plastic lens in a rugged ABS plastic body, along with a sophisticated electronic exposure control system.
4. Easy to hold, the Pronto! is the lightest, most rugged camera ever manufactured by Polaroid.

4

dak chose to house its batteries (also a new design) in the camera body.

Both cameras are loaded by rotating open a hinged film door on the bottom and inserting a Kodak Instant Print film pack. The pack can be loaded in only one way, and so matched colored loading lines are used on both film pack and camera to help in properly orienting it. An extractor lever assists in removing empty film packs.

As with the Polaroid SX-70 process, obtaining the image seen in the viewfinder and turning it into a picture requires a tightly controlled sequence of interdependent events. The image must be correctly focused, and its exposure properly measured and controlled. The film must be expelled as the camera readies for a new exposure. Doing all of this requires an effective means of focusing the camera, controlling exposure and ejecting the self-developing picture from the camera.

Kodak chose a type of distance-finding device to help the user focus. As light comes into the distance finder through the camera front, it illuminates an opaque square of plastic which has a transparent circle in it. The image of that circle is then superimposed in the center of the viewfinder image by means of a system composed of an aspheric lens, mirror, positive lens and beam splitter.

As the camera lens moves during focusing on the subject, the mechanically coupled circle's image changes in size, but retains a correct relation to a nine-inch circle. By focusing the circle closely around the head of an adult subject (which is calculated to average nine inches), the lens is thus focused on the subject. Since the f/11 aperture provides relatively great depth of field, highly critical focusing isn't really necessary. When no people are in the picture, you focus either by setting the distance with the focus slide or by the zone symbols.

The electronic exposure control package contains an integrated circuit chip with a silicon photosensor to read the light reflected from the subject. If the light is insufficient for a good picture, the exposure center turns on a red signal in the viewfinder to indicate the need for flash. Inserting a FlipFlash cancels the low-light signal. During flash exposures, the same silicon cell reads the light reflected from the subject to help control the exposure.

By measuring the light reflected from the scene, the integrated circuit controls the lens opening and shutter duration. Shutter blades and diaphragm are controlled by a single electromagnet, functions which require two electromagnets in most other electronic shutters. The IC chip also responds to the Lighten/Darken control, extending control of exposure to those situations where the user feels the need of manual corrections.

When you press the shutter release, the exposure control must first decide whether the aperture should be f/11 or f/16. With bright scenes, it selects f/16 and as the shutter release is depressed, the shutter opens to expose the film at the required shutter speed. But if the camera decides upon f/11, the shutter will operate at a point between 1/20 and 1/80 second.

THE KODAK HANDLE

A year after Kodak entered the instant camera business, the Handle appeared. Obviously designed for the "point-and-shoot" photographer who hasn't yet jumped into instant pictures, this third and lowest-priced Kodak instant camera features an integral handle (thus the name) which makes it more inviting to carry along on vacations and trips than the other EK instant models.

The Handle is equipped with a two-element 100mm f/12.7 coated plastic lens which functions at f/18 under daylight conditions, switching to its maximum aperture only when a Flip-Flash is used. Focusing is not necessary, as the lens is factory-focused for sharp pictures from four feet to infinity. A silicon-cell exposure system similar to that used in the EK4/EK6 models adjusts the shutter speed within a 1/15-1/300-second range, and varies the shutter speed for flash pictures to provide a 4-8-foot range.

While the Kodak Handle is rectangular in shape and is used in a horizontal position, it's far from compact compared with the vertical EK4/EK6 models. As the Handle uses a straight-through light path instead of the internal mirrors and reflected light path of the EK models, the shorter focal length was almost a necessity to keep the size of the camera within reasonable proportions.

Other features of the Handle are comparable to the EK series—a projected frame viewfinder with low-light signal, a fold-out crank to dispense the print from the camera's top and activate the self-processing cycle, mechanical exposure counter, ± one f-stop L/D control, LED battery check, flash interlock to prevent FlipFlash firing when the film pack cover is in place or camera/film pack is empty.

THE KODAK EK8

Designed and manufactured by Kodak A.G. in West Germany, this variation uses the same lens, shutter and exposure control system as the EK4/EK6, and differs primarily in its folding book-like body, rangefinder focusing from 3½ feet to infinity, and use of standard AA batteries instead of the Eveready size J or #539.

KODAK INSTANT PRINT FILM

Kodak's film is complex, containing some 19 layers within each picture packet. As the packet passes between the rollers that break the activator pod, an opaque black layer of carbon forms a so-called "darkroom" to permit processing to take place without interference from ambient light. This utilizes a positive/reversal process in which only unexposed silver halides are developed—the SX-70 process uses a negative/positive film with a white pigment formed to block out ambient light during development; this white layer also serves to hide the negative after development.

While the Polaroid SX-70 process produces dyes within the emulsion by using "color-coupler chemicals" to mix with development by-products in each of the three color layers, Kodak uses a new chemistry that releases preformed dyes as a result of development. These dyes migrate to an image-receiving layer in the picture packet to form the color image. The five top layers of the packet compose the image-receiving section, and it's here that the dyes eventually end up after passing through the opaque black layer and an opaque white layer of reflective titanium dioxide, which provides all of the

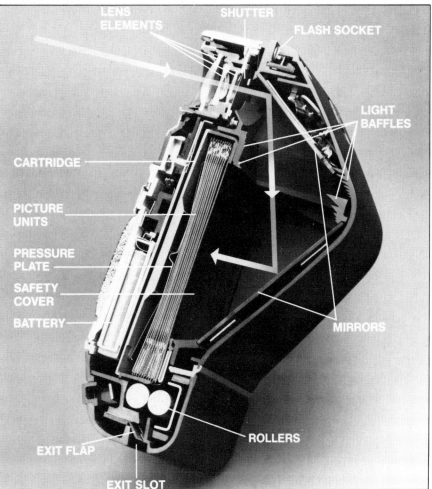

1. Kodak's instant cameras are designed for use with flip-flash for indoor pictures.

2. Kodak's initial entries in the world of instant photography, the EK4 and EK6 are identical except for the method of film transport. The EK4 uses a hand crank, while the EK6 is motorized.

3. The latest generation of Pronto! includes something for everyone. Left to right—the Pronto! B is basic, the Pronto! Extra has a self-timer adapter, and the Pronto! RF incorporates a coupled rangefinder for ease in focusing.

4. The Pronto! Extra comes complete with a self-timer and tripod adapter to put you in the picture. The tabletop tripod shown is an optional extra and can be used as a hand grip.

5. Slice an EK4/EK6 in half and you'll see how the light reaches the film. Each film cartridge contains its own pressure plate to keep the picture units aligned in the focal plane.

whites within the picture, as well as the white border of the finished print.

HOW THEY COMPARE

The first comparison one generally makes between the Polaroid and Kodak instant picture systems concerns the radical difference in appearance and styling. The unusual design of the EK4/EK6, with their ungainly pyramid-like hump in the back, is necessitated by the pair of internal mirrors that reflect the image from the lens to the film, and herein lies one of the primary differences between the two instant-picture approaches—the Polaroid SX-70 and Pronto! cameras expose their film through the front of the picture packet, while Kodak exposes through the back.

To compare the Kodak instant cameras with other than Polaroid's Pronto! models is unfair, as the SX-70 cameras are far more sophisticated, more versatile and considerably more expensive. The EK4/EK6 cameras are some 11 ounces heavier than Pronto!, which is also a more compact design; one is used in a vertical mode while the other is horizontal in operation. Despite what both companies profess in their advertising, neither the EK instant cameras nor the Pronto! are really take-it-wherever-you-go cameras. Privately, both companies recognize the inherent limitations of lugging an inexpensive instant camera and sufficient film packs on a trip of any kind, and in a rare unguarded moment, the people in Rochester have even characterized their new cameras as being "socially oriented indoor cameras for taking people pictures"—a description that can be loosely translated to a phrase which makes Polaroid executives cringe at at its mere mention—they're a party camera. Of course, this doesn't have to be true—there are many noted professionals who work very creatively with instant photography. But for most of us, the initial attraction to instant photography comes about for one reason—it's great for parties!

Regardless of the use to which you might put it, the camera itself is really of less importance than the results—especially when those available are as close in features as the Kodak models and Pronto! True, there are differences in focusing methods, exposure range, flash systems, etc., but when you compare the two designs, the advantages and disadvantages of each pretty much balance out. Neither one is exactly a dream to hold and use, but you can become accustomed to either quite quickly, although I doubt that anyone will ever fall in love with the present instant cameras to the same extent they once embraced their old Box Brownie.

Since it's the results that we're really interested in, let's look at how the SX-70 process stacks up against that offered by Kodak. Remember that both manufacturers are constantly working to improve their film products, and so the evaluations which follow are based on the emulsions available at this writing. Probably the most striking difference and the one generally noted first is that of size and surface. Polaroid produces a 3½x4½-inch print containing a 3⅛-inch square image covered by a smooth, glossy surface of clear plastic; EK prints are 3 13/16x4 inches overall, with a 2⅝x3 9/16-inch image area covered with a fine satin pebble-grained plastic surface which Kodak calls Satinluxe©.

Kodak prints tend to be on the cool or bluish side, especially noticeable when the film is used in the shade or on overcast days. They possess a longer gradation scale, offering subtle differences in color rendition and fidelity, but have less overall contrast. Skin tones often go bluish-green on hazy days or in weak sunlight, although other colors remain highly realistic.

· While Kodak prints go to the cool side, SX-70-type prints invariably head

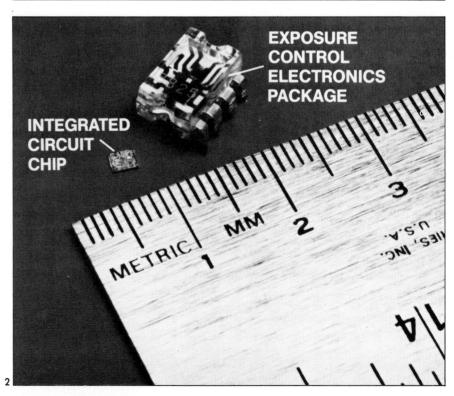

ZOOMING CIRCLE DISTANCE FINDER

CLOSE-UP SETTING

COLLECTOR

FOCUS

VIEWFINDER IMAGE AXIS

NEGATIVE LENS

MIRROR LENS

BEAM SPLITTER

EYE LENS

FOCUS SLIDE

GROUP SETTING

ZOOMING CIRCLE RETICLE

ASPHERIC LENS

ZOOMING CIRCLE IMAGE AXIS

MIRROR

POSITIVE LENS

VIEWFINDER RETICLE

1

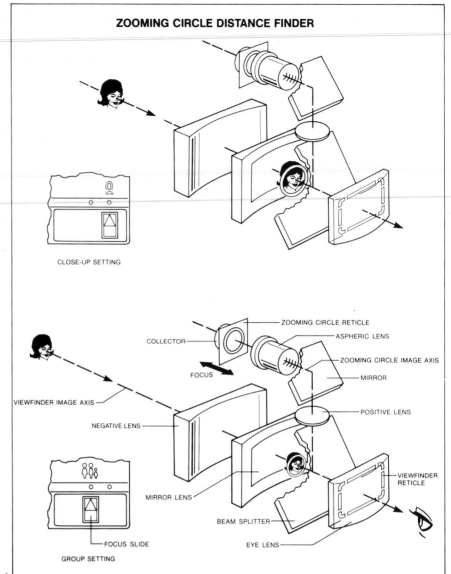

EXPOSURE CONTROL ELECTRONICS PACKAGE

INTEGRATED CIRCUIT CHIP

METRIC   MM   1   2   3

U.S.A.

2

3

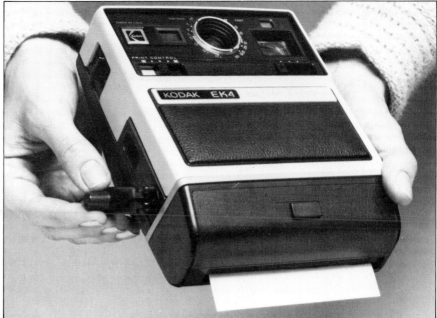

4

1. Operation of the Kodak EK4/EK6 zooming circle as a focusing assist device is explained by this schematic.

2. The EK4/EK6 exposure control system is operated by an IC chip which monitors exposure functions, computes battery condition when the battery check button is depressed, and turns on the low-light signal when flash is necessary.

3. To insert a Kodak film pack, rotate the door at the bottom open, line up the colored lines on the pack with those in the camera and push in place. An extractor lever facilitates pack removal.

4. After taking a picture with the EK4, turn the crank approximately four full revolutions and the print will be ejected from the camera's bottom.

5. The EK4/EK6 film transport mechanisms do the same job, but one uses a hand crank, the other a motor. In each, a gear-driven single-revolution clutch and cam advances a transport slide whose claw delivers an exposed print to the nip between the rollers. The roller pair then drives the print through the exit slot in the bottom of the counter.

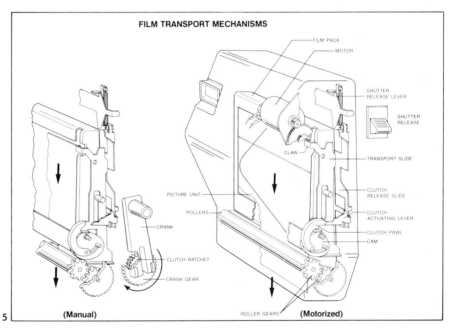

FILM TRANSPORT MECHANISMS

FILM PACK
MOTOR
SHUTTER RELEASE LEVER
SHUTTER RELEASE
TRANSPORT SLIDE
CLUTCH RELEASE SLIDE
CLUTCH ACTUATING LEVER
CLUTCH PAWL
CAM
PICTURE UNIT
ROLLERS
CRANK
CLUTCH RATCHET
CRANK GEAR
CLAW
ROLLER GEARS
(Manual)   **(Motorized)**

5

in the direction of greater warmth. For this reason, they seem to possess more life—partially because of their greater saturation and higher level of contrast. This warmth tends to extend right into the whites, throwing them slightly off-white in color. The glossy surface of Polaroid SX-70 prints combines with the higher inherent contrast to give the appearance of greater sharpness of detail, but Kodak prints benefit from their cleaner color differentiation, and the matte finish does not call attention to fingerprints and smudges as prominently.

Which film reproduces colors most accurately? Neither—both deviate from what the experts call "normal and accurate" color reproduction, but they do so in opposite directions. This places the choice of one type of print material over the other squarely on the potential user, where it really belongs. Which-

ever way you like your color, one will probably give it to you.

And how about their ability to compensate for incorrect exposure? Both films possess a very limited latitude—with low scene contrast, ½ f-stop in either direction is about the maximum leeway; even less tolerance is shown in high-contrast situations. The more exposure given either film stock, the more its appearance of sharpness seems to suffer. In a nutshell, you've got to be very close to "right on the button" if you expect really acceptable photographs.

Flash photography is yet another story; neither the Pronto! nor the Kodak flash systems are really adequate, as both deliver uneven coverage from their respective Flash Bar/FlipFlash configurations. Whether all in a row or

stacked one on top of another, those tiny bulbs just can't provide even illumination across the picture area. You may be far more satisfied in this respect with one of the electronic flash units now being provided by accessory manufacturers.

Nor are their automatic exposure systems as discriminating as they should be when the cameras are used for indoor flash close-ups of people. Flesh tones tend to wash out but the surrounding tones will come up satisfactorily. Overriding the system by ½ or even a full f-stop (one-two clicks of the Lighten/Darken control on either camera) will usually deliver a far better print than the normal setting when you're working at a distance of about 4-7 feet.

The temperature in which the film is

1. **The Handle is the newest Kodak instant camera. Its integral handle is convenient for carrying and provides a steady grip for picture-taking.**
2. **Like the EK4, the Kodak Handle uses a fold-out crank to advance the film, but the picture emerges from a slot in the top of the camera.**
3. **A "point-and-shoot" model, the Handle requires no setting—its lens is factory-focused and the silicon cell exposure system computes the shutter speed for the single aperture (f/18) lens.**
4. **The Handle exposure control package.**
5. **The Handle exposure path and lens.**
6. **The Handle transport mechanism.**

used is another important consideration. Both Kodak and SX-70 type prints will differ in results, depending upon the ambient temperature, with Kodak prints exhibiting the greater amount of color shift within the suggested 60-90°F. range. At the upper end of the range, the cool shift becomes very pronounced, while at lower temperatures, the shift goes over slightly to the warm side, accompanied by some loss of saturation.

Polaroid suggests 45-90°F. for its film, and color shifting within that range is less, although some loss of saturation coupled with an increase in contrast can be expected. You'll get optimum results with either film when used at temperatures between 68 and 75°F. The temperature range within which these materials will work satisfactorily is one area that both companies are working feverishly to improve—Polaroid made a considerable gain with its recently upgraded SX-70 stock—and one in which you can expect to see significant changes in the coming months, especially for Kodak who's clearly at a disadvantage here.

INSTANT-PICTURE TIPS

As the finished picture is deposited in your hand 1.2-1.5 seconds after it's taken, it is not difficult to assume that your camera will deliver a good instant picture every time you trip the shutter release. Unfortunately, that's a delusion fostered by the very immediacy of the process. *Good* instant pictures actually require *more* work on the part of the photographer.

All the standard rules of photographic technique, composition and lighting apply to instant pictures. If you expect the picture to be sharp, focus must be

as accurate as possible, with the camera held steady to prevent movement. Since darkroom cropping is out of the question, you must fill the frame with your subject. Lenses are not interchangeable, so your camera angle and placement must be selected with care. Lighting must be carefully evaluated, as the film's latitude is very narrow and the self-development process allows you absolutely no control as did the peel-apart process.

USING THE L/D CONTROL—Taking that second picture because the first one didn't come out just right is probably the most common problem with instant photography. It's also one of the most expensive, as each picture can cost you between 70 cents and $1, depending upon whether or not you use flash. But this problem can be minimized, if you approach instant photography realistically. For example, the L/D control on your Pronto! or EK4/

EK6 is your most useful tool in obtaining good pictures on the first snap, but to use it properly you must understand what it does and when to use it.

To manually bias exposure in instant photography, a lever or knob is moved on the camera. This slides a graduated neutral density wedge in front of the photosensor (see ND filters in the chapter on filters). This changes the programming of the exposure system, permitting a ±1 f-stop control with the Kodak cameras, and a ±1½ f-stop adjustment with the Pronto! While instant-camera manuals state that use of the L/D control is not necessary under *most* conditions, you should accept that statement with a grain of salt.

As we've already seen, satisfactory results with flash generally require a one- or two-click bias (each click represents ½ f-stop) toward the Darken position with either system. For the best results outdoors with the least expenditure of film, you should learn to evaluate *each* subject/scene before you release the shutter. The automatic metering systems used by both Polaroid and Kodak are subject to the same optimism which afflicts the built-in meters of most 35mm SLR cameras.

Since the metering systems *average* the various intensities of reflected il-

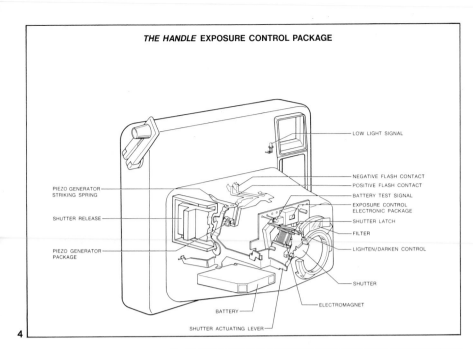

THE *HANDLE* EXPOSURE CONTROL PACKAGE

LOW LIGHT SIGNAL

NEGATIVE FLASH CONTACT
POSITIVE FLASH CONTACT
BATTERY TEST SIGNAL
EXPOSURE CONTROL
ELECTRONIC PACKAGE
SHUTTER LATCH
FILTER
LIGHTEN/DARKEN CONTROL

SHUTTER

ELECTROMAGNET

PIEZO GENERATOR
STRIKING SPRING

SHUTTER RELEASE

PIEZO GENERATOR
PACKAGE

BATTERY

SHUTTER ACTUATING LEVER

4

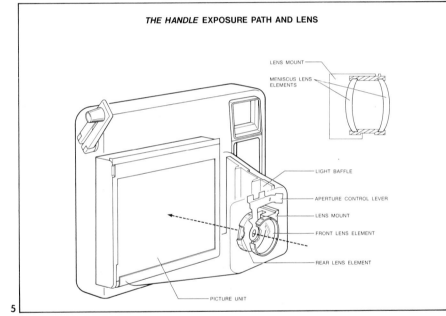

THE *HANDLE* EXPOSURE PATH AND LENS

LENS MOUNT
MENISCUS LENS
ELEMENTS

LIGHT BAFFLE

APERTURE CONTROL LEVER
LENS MOUNT
FRONT LENS ELEMENT

REAR LENS ELEMENT

PICTURE UNIT

5

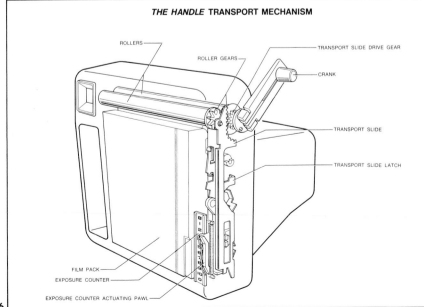

THE *HANDLE* TRANSPORT MECHANISM

ROLLERS

ROLLER GEARS

TRANSPORT SLIDE DRIVE GEAR

CRANK

TRANSPORT SLIDE

TRANSPORT SLIDE LATCH

FILM PACK
EXPOSURE COUNTER
EXPOSURE COUNTER ACTUATING PAWL

6

lumination within a scene, a subject with a very bright or very dark background will result in a picture containing a correctly exposed background, while the subject will be either over- or underexposed. If you learn to spot such situations and make the necessary corrections with the L/D control *before* taking the picture, you'll be far more pleased with the results.

Study your subject through the viewfinder and evaluate it in terms of relative brightness, lighting and contrast levels. If your subject is a person you're photographing at the beach, in snow country or near a large, light-colored object such as a wall, you should provide more exposure for the tones of primary interest by moving the L/D control toward Lighten. Light-colored (highly reflective) subjects placed against a dark background will require less exposure, and so the L/D control should be shifted toward Darken.

One other note of interest for EK4/EK6 users: When the red low-light signal comes on in the viewfinder, it indicates that the camera's exposure system is already operating at its maximum—1/20 at f/11. Moving the L/D control all the way to Lighten *will not* affect the picture in any way, since the manual override can only bias exposure within the normal operating range of the camera's exposure capability.

USING FLASH—In addition to the exposure bias required for best results with the Flash Bar/FlipFlash systems, there are a couple of other hints which should be kept in mind. These flash systems distribute light in a somewhat uneven manner across the camera's field of view to a useful distance of approximately 10 feet. Use of the L/D control will not affect flash pictures taken more than 10 feet from the subject. As the flash exposure is mechanically linked to the focusing mechanism, proper exposure (as well as a sharp picture) is very dependent upon correct focus of the lens on your subject. Depth of field just won't do the trick.

When there's more than one person in your picture area, try to either arrange them so that all are approximately the same distance from the flash, or choose a camera position that places them within the same plane. Grouping of your subjects in this way will result in each one receiving about the same amount of exposure. If you have three people in the picture and they are arranged at varying distances from the camera, the facial features of the one in the foreground will wash out from too much light, while the one farthest from the camera will appear very swarthy from too little light—not particularly flattering if it happens to be a girl. Granted, you may end up with "Murderers' Row" or a lineup, but at least they'll all appear normal because of the more evenly distributed lighting and more uniform exposure.

In addition to subject arrangement with flash pictures, exercise care in choosing a background. Whatever you select should be plain and simple, of approximately the same reflective quality as that of your subject(s) and about six feet behind. If closer, the shadow cast by the head from the flash has a tendency to join the head to the background. When the background is too far away, it drops off into blackness, visually pulling medium- and dark-colored hair with it. The result is a face which peers at you from blackness.

HANDLING INSTANT PRINTS—Every user of the "peel-apart" Polaroid films has encountered a wide variety of problems after exposure—stains, streaks and strange patterns which appear as the result of pulling the tabs too quickly, too slowly, or at an incorrect angle; incorrectly separating the negative from the positive; improper handling of the film pack during camera loading, or of the film packet during development. But these and similar problems are all part of the past with the self-developing Polaroid SX-70/Kodak PR-10 print films. Just be certain to turn the hand crank on the EK4/Handle cameras with a smooth, continuous motion or uneven development can occur.

Film packs should still be handled only by their edges; pressure on the center of its protective cover can fog the edges of one or more film packets. Opening the camera after the protective cover has been ejected from the film pack will also fog the top picture. There should be no need to open Pronto!, but if the EK6 ejects its print very slowly, or stops in the middle of the process, the batteries will have to be replaced, and this means opening the camera. Should battery replacement in the middle of a film pack be necessary, open the film door in subdued light. This will prevent fogging any print packets left in the pack other than the top one.

Should you decide to let a print develop inside your coat or shirt pocket when taking pictures in cold weather, do so with care. Print packets should be handled gently between ejection from the camera and full development. If you bend, flex, fold or otherwise

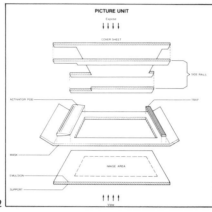

1. The Kodak EK8, a top-of-the-line folding model manufactured in West Germany by Kodak A.G., uses the same lens/shutter combination as the EK4/EK6 and is to be available in the United States soon.

2. Each picture unit is a seven-piece sandwich containing two supports, sensitized emulsion and chemicals. When the pod is burst by the camera rollers, it spreads a smooth black coating of alkaline activator across the inner surface of the integral imaging receiver. Side rails aid in determining the thickness of the spread, and the trap opposite the pod collects the excess, if any. The activator containing a black opacifying agent and the other opaque layers in the integral imaging receiver form a darkroom for processing. The dyes liberated by the development process pass through the opaque layers above it and form colors in the picture.

change their natural flat configuration during this time, you may cause irregularities in processing at various places within the picture packet. This is fine when you're trying for artistic or creative effects, but for normal prints the results may be disastrous.

Incidentally, it may be tempting to cut an SX-70 or Kodak instant print apart to see "what makes it tick." This is unwise, as each packet is a sealed unit containing a caustic fluid which will stain fabrics, carpeting, etc., and actually cause an alkali burn on contact with human skin. Should fluid escape for any reason, thoroughly wash

the affected areas that it contacts with plenty of water; in case of contact with your eyes, flush with water and seek medical attention immediately.

Whenever you take more than one picture at a time, be careful of where you place the prints to develop. I've seen many Pronto! users run back and forth across a room shooting pictures one after the other and letting them drop all over the floor. When the film pack was empty, they would retrace their steps to pick up the developing prints. If you do this, you run the risk of one or more pictures being stepped on, either by yourself or by others in the room—who expects to find developing pictures on the floor?

As each picture packet has to be pulled from the Kodak models by hand to complete the ejection process, you're more likely to look for a place to set it down while shooting multiple pictures with one. Don't leave them in direct sunlight or on a hot or very cold surface, since the considerable difference in temperature will adversely affect the development process, and you may find what would otherwise have been good pictures are now either too light or too dark.

FILM STORAGE—Like all other photographic film and sensitized materials, both SX-70 and Kodak PR-10 films can be damaged by extreme heat and humidity. The high temperatures involved will cause a color shift and age the undeveloped image-forming materials prematurely, reducing the quality of the pictures yet to be taken quite severely. For this reason, you should not store your camera and/or film in places like the rear window deck of a car, or in its glove compartment or trunk—all common places to find amateur cameras. Should you do this by mistake, let both the camera and film return to normal temperature before attempting to take pictures.

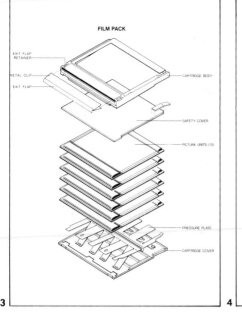

FILM PACK

EXIT FLAP RETAINER
METAL CLIP
EXIT FLAP
CARTRIDGE BODY
SAFETY COVER
PICTURE UNITS (10)
PRESSURE PLATE
CARTRIDGE COVER

3

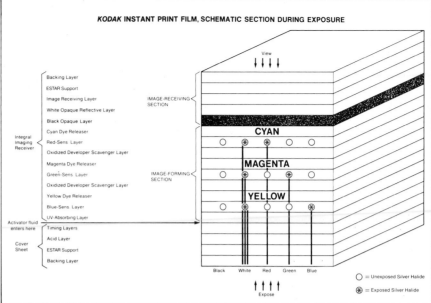

***KODAK* INSTANT PRINT FILM, SCHEMATIC SECTION DURING EXPOSURE**

View

Backing Layer
ESTAR Support
Image Receiving Layer
White Opaque Reflective Layer
Black Opaque Layer
Cyan Dye Releaser
Red-Sens. Layer
Oxidized Developer Scavenger Layer
Magenta Dye Releaser
Green-Sens. Layer
Oxidized Developer Scavenger Layer
Yellow Dye Releaser
Blue-Sens. Layer
UV-Absorbing Layer
Timing Layers
Acid Layer
ESTAR Support
Backing Layer

Integral Imaging Receiver

Activator fluid enters here

Cover Sheet

IMAGE-RECEIVING SECTION

CYAN

MAGENTA

YELLOW

IMAGE-FORMING SECTION

Black   White   Red   Green   Blue

Expose

○ = Unexposed Silver Halide
✳ = Exposed Silver Halide

4

3. The film pack seals 10 completed picture units in a lighttight package. After the pack is loaded into the camera, its safety cover will be ejected from the camera, as will each picture unit after exposure. The pressure plate keeps the picture unit flat on the focal plane before and during the exposure.

4. After light from the subject strikes the film, exposure takes place in the red, blue and green sensitive layers of silver halide emulsion. White light is made up of all three colors, as we have already seen, and so exposes in all three layers. Where no light strikes the film, no exposure will be able to occur.

5. In reversal emulsions, the exposed silver halide grains do not develop, it's the unexposed grains that do. Thus, red light exposed the emulsion in the red sensitive layer. As a result, these grains did not develop, thus preventing the cyan dye from being released. But where no exposure took place, development did. Thus, the blue and green sensitive layers were developed, liberating yellow and magenta dyes. These released dyes then migrate through the black opaque layer and the white opaque layer, and combine in the image receiving layer to form red. Corresponding activity takes place in the other emulsion layers. White and black are reproduced in the same manner.

Keep film in its protective box until you're ready to use it. If you break into the foil wrapper but decide against using the film at that time, store it in a refrigerator. Remove at least two hours before intended use to let the film reach room temperature. Should you stock up on film in anticipation of a particular event, it should be stored in the refrigerator until a few hours before you use it.

Don't store a loaded camera in a hot or humid place, and if you use a dark-colored compartment case for carrying, don't leave it in the sun, as dark cases retain heat and can affect the film in-

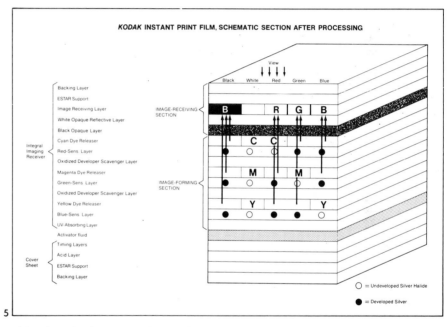

KODAK INSTANT PRINT FILM, SCHEMATIC SECTION AFTER PROCESSING

View
Black   White   Red   Green   Blue

Backing Layer
ESTAR Support
Image Receiving Layer
White Opaque Reflective Layer
Black Opaque Layer
Cyan Dye Releaser
Red-Sens. Layer
Oxidized Developer Scavenger Layer
Magenta Dye Releaser
Green-Sens. Layer
Oxidized Developer Scavenger Layer
Yellow Dye Releaser
Blue-Sens. Layer
UV-Absorbing Layer
Activator fluid
Timing Layers
Acid Layer
ESTAR Support
Backing Layer

Integral Imaging Receiver

Cover Sheet

IMAGE-RECEIVING SECTION

B   R G B

C C

M   M

Y   Y

IMAGE-FORMING SECTION

○ = Undeveloped Silver Halide
● = Developed Silver

5

side. An aluminum or other light-colored case is recommended for transporting quantities of film in hot sunny weather, for use at the beach, etc.

When you purchase instant-camera film, you'll notice that the end of the box carries the legend "Use before" with a date stamped beneath it. Because the development chemicals contained within each picture packet can deteriorate with age and varying storage conditions, it's sold with an expiration date somewhat shorter than conventional photographic materials. Always check this date when buying new boxes of film. If you shop at some of the smaller photo stores, there's a possibility that their stock may have exceeded demand, although both SX-70 and PR-10 films move rather quickly wherever they are sold.

If you've bought several boxes and

do not use them all before the expiration date has passed, don't worry—provided that you've stored them properly, there's a reasonable safety period built into that stamped date. Should you run into one of those rare occasions when a store is selling outdated instant-camera film, it's just as well to pass up the bargain. You have no idea of the conditions under which the film has been stored and you're likely to get a big surprise when you start taking pictures with it. Stick with fresh film and as a general rule, buy only what you intend to use in the immediate future. Stocking up on instant-camera film is not really a good idea, and as it's sold in all kinds of outlets, there shouldn't be any difficulty in obtaining a fresh pack when you need one.

CAMERA CARE—Both Pronto! and the Kodak instant cameras are hardy beasts, and although designed to survive the anticipated rough handling generally accorded a family camera, they should be stored and carried in a case such as those offered by their manufacturer or one of the independent accessory manufacturers. Not only will the use of a case protect the camera from those devastating blows and accidental drops that occasionally afflict even the most sure-fingered user, they also help to keep the camera clean—a factor which is of prime importance in obtaining sharp, clear instant pictures free from defects.

The world in which we live is full of dust and dirt, much of which travels in the air around us and seems to be attracted to camera lenses above all else. If allowed to accumulate to a sufficient point, this can actually form a cloudy mist on the front surface of the lens, which will gradually lead to pictures with a slighly foggy or misty appearance. Thus, instant camera lenses and viewfinders should be treated to the same care as other cameras.

In addition, those mirrors inside your instant camera seem to be attractive places for dust to hold conventions. Unless they are kept clean, specks of dust will gradually accumulate, showing up eventually in the form of small dark, shadowy spots in the same place on print after print.

Except for the Kodak Handle, the instant camera design doesn't lend itself to cleaning of the interior as easily as do other types in which the camera back is removable, but a rubber syringe or a can of compressed gas will do an adequate job providing you don't allow the contamination to really build up. To clean, you should hold the camera with the film chamber facing down so that as the moving air from the syringe or aerosol can dislodges the dust, it will float downward and out of the chamber. Whatever you do, never try to clean the mirror(s) with a brush, cloth or other cleaning material—remember that the mirror is a part of the instant camera's optical system; one decent smudge on this and your pictures will suffer.

On occasion, you may find that one of the reagent/activator pods of a film packet will prematurely break. This is most likely to happen when the film's temperature is very high and the camera is used after exposure to high temperatures for some time. When this happens, the chemical will harden into small deposits on the surfaces of the camera's rollers and leave a repeating pattern of spots on consecutive prints.

1

2

3

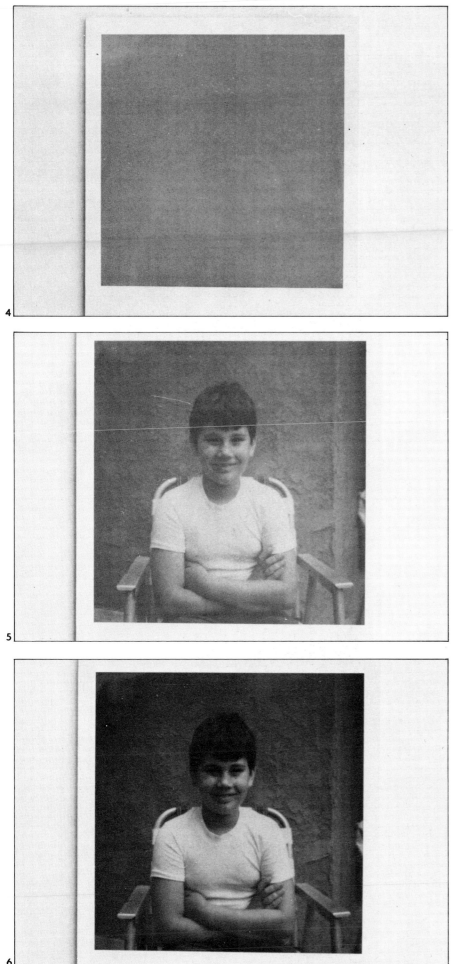

Should this happen, moisten a cotton-tipped swab or a piece of soft, lint-free cloth with water and wipe the contaminated area of the rollers until the deposits come free from their surfaces. Rotate the rollers to place the residue where it can be easily removed. As this is highly caustic and can cause problems identical to those described in cautioning you not to cut the film packet, you should take care that the residue does not fall on the floor—be certain to dispose of the swab/cloth in a closed trash container out of the reach of any children who might happen along.

Those who use the Kodak models will do well to remove the batteries from the camera body and clean the contacts in the camera whenever it's stored for an extended period of time, or when its use is not anticipated for several weeks. Although the six-volt size J batteries are rated with a life expectancy of one year (calculated as a minimum of 20 film packs), batteries often do strange things and should they corrode inside the camera, the resulting mess could render it useless.

INSTANT SPECIAL EFFECTS—Suppose you're of an artistic or creative nature and wish to use the instant-picture process as a means of self-expression rather than just the documentary snapshots most users take. While the cameras available are not the most versatile ones in the world, there are many avenues open to the truly ingenious among you willing and able to risk a pack of film now and then to see exactly what can be done when an unusual idea crosses your mind.

Some imaginative souls have already broken new artistic boundaries by ejecting an exposed film packet from the camera and using the edge of a coin, a stylus or other semi-blunt device to etch, sketch or otherwise mess up the inside of the packet to achieve impressionistic results. But most of us will be more interested in the less subjective and more controlled effects obtainable with devices made for use with conventional cameras. With the help of colored filters, multi-image lenses, a corrugated or otherwise distorted piece of plastic, etc., it's possible to enhance a mood, examine the many facets of reflections and distortions, or to simply

1. Three stages of print development are shown in this series of Kodak Instant Print (left) and Polaroid SX-70 Film (right) pictures. From top to bottom—just after appearing from the camera, three minutes into development and full development.

1

2

devise an image that differs from the reality around us.

Colored filters normally used to alter contrast in conventional black-and-white photography can be used to produce drama, add illusion and simulate fantasy in instant pictures. As these require exposure compensation, the filter material should cover both lens and meter cell. For this reason, the gelatin filter squares obtainable at camera stores work best. You can build a filter holder that will fit over the lens and meter cell, tape the gel in place with masking tape, or simply hold it in front of the lens/meter cell. Just take care to handle the filter gel only by its edges, and keep it free from scratches, smudges and other contamination.

Multi-image lenses can also be used to produce prism-like effects. For best results, the camera should be placed on a tripod so that you can take adequate pains to center the multi-image attachment over the camera lens. You should also avoid covering or casting a shadow on the meter cell while working with them.

Various other filters and lens attachments designed for conventional photography can also be used with your instant camera. You might also try photographing subjects through transparent/translucent materials which will diffuse or distort the image for a different effect. For example, those translucent shower curtains with their impregnated patterns will produce a number of unusual and interesting effects when used in front of a backlighted subject. Or try holding a fisheye converter lens in front of the instant camera lens for a really different outlook on the world in front of you!

WHAT TO DO WITH THE PICTURES?—To fully appreciate your in-

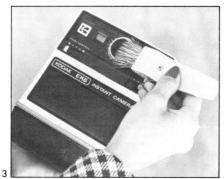

4

3

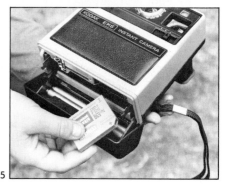

5

stant pictures, they should be organized and easily available for viewing—tossing them in the back of a drawer is not conducive to long life or enjoyment of them. You'll find that writing on the borders of an instant print for identification purposes does not work out very well, as the surface lamination prevents ink from adhering. Write or type any desired information on self-

1. An accessory case is a good idea if you plan to travel with either the Pronto! or an EK4/EK6 camera. This is the Prinz case for the Kodak Instant Cameras.

2. The Prinz Polalite electronic flash fits either SX-70 or Pronto! models, offers a high/low light range and provides an even better pattern of light distribution than do Flashbars.

3-4. While a soft brush will keep the lens and exterior of your instant camera clean (3), removing dust and dirt from the film compartment is best done with an aerosol can of compressed gas (4). Be sure to use clean brushes.

5. If Kodak Instant Cameras are to be stored for any length of time, be sure to remove the batteries. This caution does not apply to Polaroid models, as their power supply is contained within each film pack.

6-7. Accessory electronic flash units for the Kodak models vary greatly in size and shape, as shown by this ITT Magic-flash (6) and the Braun BK-100 (7).

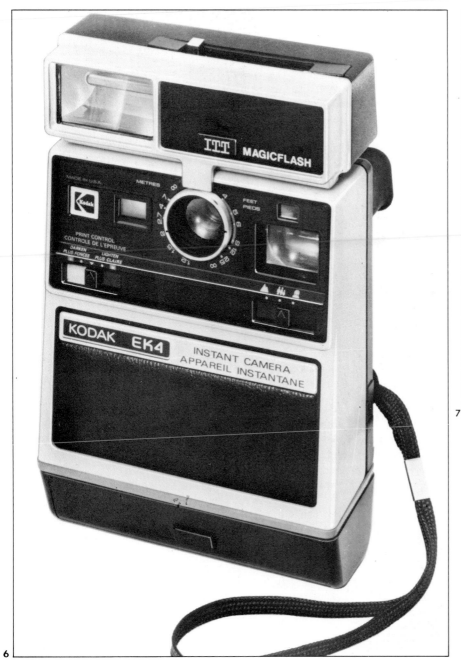

6

7

adhesive labels and apply these to the oversized margin of either SX-70 or Kodak prints.

Should you store your pictures in an album, it should be one which specifies use with instant pictures; both Kodak and Polaroid offer such. Recently processed prints that are not able to breathe and thus dry adequately (a process which may require several weeks) tend to darken somewhat. Don't try to mount instant prints in an album using rubber cement, household glue or the dozens of other such alternatives, as the impurities in these types of adhesives can cause a chemical reaction that may ruin your picture. For those interested in dry mounting with heat, this is a surefire method of destroying an instant print.

However you choose to store or dis-

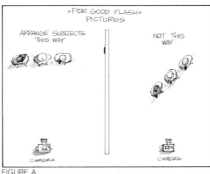

FIGURE A

play them, remember that long periods of exposure to sunlight or fluorescent lighting will result in a gradual deterioration of the image, so stick to a cool, dry place for the original and have a copy print or enlargement made of those you wish to keep out for friends and family to enjoy. Again, both Kodak and Polaroid offer this service for their

product, and as long as the original print is sharp and well-exposed, the copy prints and enlargements will be of good quality. Kodak even offers a reproduction service which turns an instant print into a slide for those who enjoy projection.

AND THE FUTURE?

Instant photography has made considerable strides in the past few years, and with the anticipated competition from Japanese and German instant print materials which should be appearing, perhaps sooner than you might expect, both Kodak and Polaroid will continue their concentrated efforts to keep ahead of their soon-to-be competitors. In the meantime, you can expect that a greater choice of instant cameras will also be made available in the foreseeable future, primarily because Kodak has extended an offer to other manufacturers that will permit them to license the necessary patents to produce their own versions of instant cameras designed to utilize the Kodak PR-10 film pack. From where I stand, the greater the competition, the more the consumer can expect to benefit. While Polaroid has done a commendable job of promoting ''picture-in-a-minute'' and ''instant'' photography over the past three decades, it finally appears that the baby is about to burst out of its swaddling clothes and walk upright—we can only be the richer photographically for it. □

15
You & Your Darkroom

If you're one of those hobbyists who lets your photo dealer or the corner drugstore process your pictures, you're missing out on much of the real fun of photography. You're also missing out on the many learning experiences that developing your own film and making your own enlargements can offer. It's one thing to invest a good deal of your time, money and effort in your hobby, acquiring just the right equipment to make it possible to compose, light and photograph your subjects as you wish, but quite another to hand over the exposed film to a lab service and let them finish the job.

Certainly, it's true that there are some photo techniques we just can't do ourselves—such as processing Kodachrome film—but if you're going to do just half the job, why go to all the trouble in the first place? It's equally true that few of us can afford the services of a custom lab every time we want a routine picture printed. And even if we could, it's still quite difficult to describe the precise effect desired from a given negative, even if you could stand right beside the printer and look over his shoulder—which you can't. You might as well expect it—the more serious your interest in photography becomes, the more you'll come to recognize the truth inherent in the old saying, "If you want it done right, do it yourself." And to do it yourself, you need a darkroom.

WHAT'S IN IT FOR YOU?

How will you benefit from a darkroom and darkroom work? There are several immediate benefits that you'll enjoy, as well as some which won't become apparent until you've become involved in doing your own developing and enlarging. Assuming that you'll start off with black-and-white darkroom work, let's look at a few.

1—Quality is perhaps the most obvious—the quality of the negatives and prints you'll bring out of your own darkroom. Even the novice can surpass the results provided by a commercial laboratory. Automatic machinery is great for mass production, and that's what constitutes the American photofinishing industry—get the film in, soup it and get it out. Volume is money; stopping the line long enough to dust a negative interrupts that flow and consequently, it isn't done. That comes under the heading of "custom" printing—and for that, you pay extra!

The majority of photofinishers in this country are geared to the snapshot artists—those camera users who consider themselves great if they come up with a recognizable image, much less one that's good. You'd be surprised at how many beginners never progress beyond that point in photography. So if you place your films in with theirs for processing and printing, you'll get the same average or below average results which are returned to them, and you'll pay the same cut-rate price they do. But are the results really worth it?

Not really, and here's why. As the economics of photofinishing preclude the use of "hand" labor in most cases, computerized printers are used to move the negatives as quickly as possible. This means that like the photoelectric exposure meter, which tends to reduce everything it sees to an 18-percent gray tone, the printing machine averages every negative it handles in such a way as to work with under- and overexposed as well as properly exposed negatives. Neither the machine nor its operator (if it even has one) understands the effect for which you're striving in your work, and so the production line goes its merry way, while you get back prints which in no way resemble what you set out to achieve when you took the picture.

2—Regardless of how carefully you have composed and exposed with the camera, many of your pictures can be materially improved by a bit of experimentation under the enlarger—selective cropping, varying image sizes, dodging, burning-in, a change in paper contrast, etc. You can be as creative as you like with your camera, but in the final analysis, it's the creativity in the darkroom that really makes the picture, as we'll see in an upcoming chapter, and to apply this creative touch, you need to do your own darkroom work.

3—The speed of the process accounts for much of the popularity of

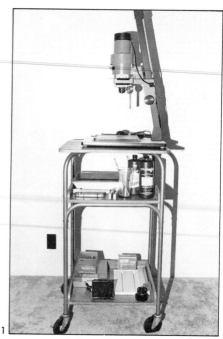

1. **A projection cart can serve as a mobile arrangement for those who must work in temporary quarters. All the essentials can be wheeled from the closet to the kitchen, or wherever you work.**
2. **A permanent darkroom arrangement lets you keep everything set up where it's handy. There's a place for everything here, and everything is kept in its place. There's nothing worse or more inconvenient than a messy darkroom.**
3. **Since this darkroom is long and narrow by design, the wet and dry areas are on the same side, but well separated by the manner in which the sink arrangements are designed and constructed.**

instant photography—people just don't like to wait a week or 10 days to see the results of their picture taking. The delay in finding out how your pictures came out while you wait for the lab to return your work has other disadvantages—you may have fouled up somewhere along the line but by the time you learn your mistakes, it may not be possible to reshoot the subject. Or the lab may lose or ruin your film—it does happen, you know. But even if everything comes out O.K., some of the thrill is gone by the time you get your prints back—there's a genuine thrill in shooting your pictures during the day and looking at the finished prints before retiring that evening for a well-earned rest. Although not always possible with color, it's well within the realm of feasibility for those who work with black-and-white.

4—Doing your own darkroom work will naturally cost you a larger than ordinary investment to acquire the necessary equipment and materials, but if you're one of those photographers who is accustomed to paying photofinishers on a more-or-less regular basis, you'll

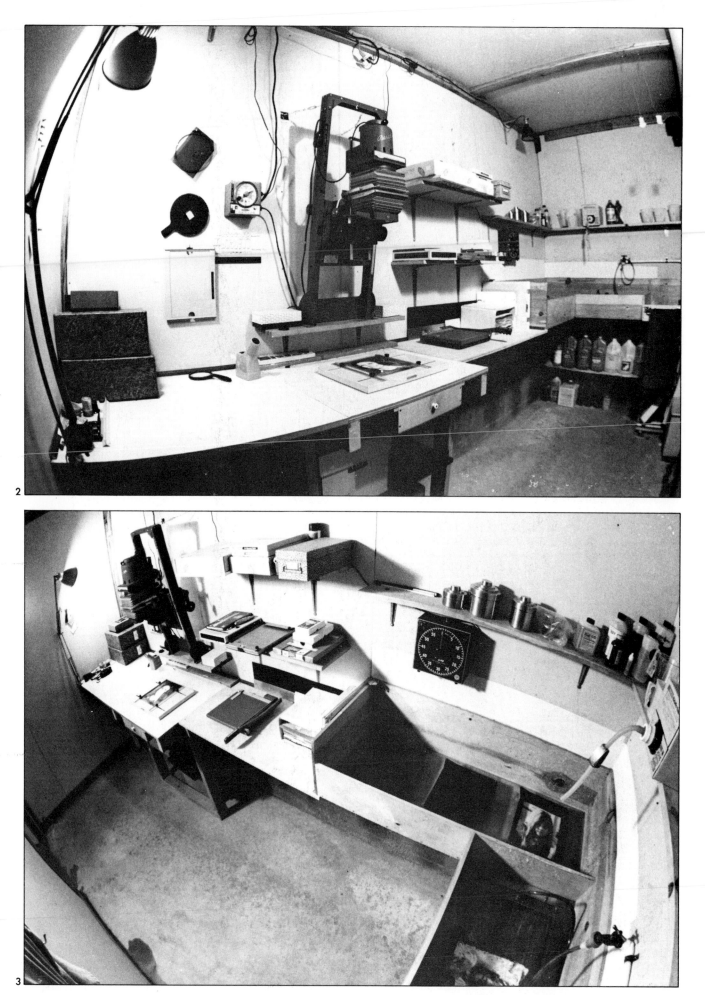

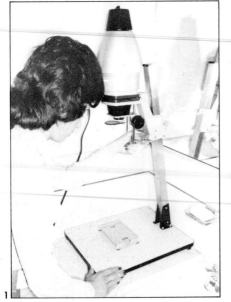

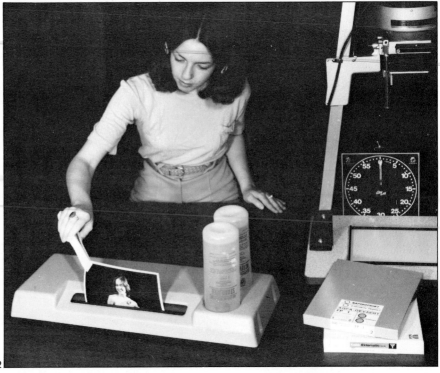

realize a considerable savings over the long run. This can either be regarded as a bonus from your hobby or invested in better equipment and more supplies to help you take and make better pictures at lower cost.

5—Most important, you'll see almost immediately what you've done wrong, or hopefully, what you've done right. It's one thing to look at a negative and try to envision the finished print, it's another to actually translate that negative into that print. Many times in the past, I've sneaked a look at negatives I've shot and then gone to bed feeling secure that I had the job well under control—only to learn the next day in the darkroom that I had really blown it. My lighting wasn't quite correct, my exposure was really too little or too much for the interpretation I desired, my composition wasn't as great as I had thought when I snapped the picture; I could go on, but you've got the idea, I'm sure.

6—The darkroom is where you put it all together, the place where you apply all you've learned about photography to turn out a finished print that demonstrates the sum of your knowledge and the skills you've acquired in your hobby, as well as discovering those skills you need to acquire. It's also the place where you quickly learn what you did wrong behind the camera (as I've already mentioned), and whether or not you can apply other techniques to salvage your mistakes and turn them into usable pictures after all. It's where you refine your thinking about composition, lighting and exposure, where you can build on past experiences to formulate new approaches and techniques, where you'll distill the essence of the hobby you enjoy.

TEMPORARY OR PERMANENT?

What kind of darkroom do you need? Any kind: whatever your life style, living standard and pocketbook can afford. Sure, we'd all enjoy a lavish permanent layout, complete with air conditioning and filtered running water along with those other niceties of life many call home, but it isn't really necessary. If you have sufficient unused space which can be devoted to a permanent darkroom setup, that's fine. but those who are renters, apartment dwellers, mobile-home owners, or just plain cramped for space can still have a darkroom. It'll just have to be more carefully planned around the temporary use of space normally used for other living purposes—a closet, bathroom, bedroom, the kitchen after everyone else has turned in, etc. Where there's a will, there's a way—I know of one chap in England who finally acquired running water piped into his house and immediately thereafter, he redecorated and comverted the old outdoor bathroom into a permanent darkroom. Hopefully, you won't have to go to such extremes to provide adequate darkroom facilities for yourself.

If you happen to live in the right geographical area, it may be possible to acquire the use of a suitable darkroom simply by joining a camera club or a local photographic center sponsored by your adult education or parks and recreation department. Rental darkrooms are also available in larger urban areas, as are darkroom schools, where you can learn the fundamentals.

1. Smaller enlargers like this Bogen 6x6 take up a minimum of space, and can be used in the kitchen or bath, as long as you have space for the developing trays.
2. You can eliminate the necessity for trays, running water and messy solutions with a stabilization processor like this Portertown Global Goose unit.
3. Mounting the enlarger to the wall has several advantages. It gets the enlarger up and out of the way, permits vibration-free operation, and for extra large blow-ups, the bench space beneath it can be removed.
4. Bench space should be designed at a comfortable height so that you don't have to stoop or stretch to work.
5. A deep sink arrangement for trays prevents splashing and spilling of solutions, helping to keep cleanup to a minimum. Note the work flow pattern as it progresses around the toe of the "L"-shaped design, with chemicals stored underneath the sinks.

Depending upon your exact circumstances, it may be more practical to pay the modest fees required and take advantage of such facilities for as long as you need.

PROBLEMS YOU'LL ENCOUNTER

Makeshift or temporary darkrooms can be as simple or as complex as you wish, space permitting. The space you select must be large enough in size to hold at least a minimum of equipment safely—enlarger, trays, timer, safelight, etc.—while permitting free access to it. You should be able to control temperature and air circulation for personal comfort as well as maintaining a satisfactory temperature range of your chemicals.

But there are several problems that

3

4

5

must be solved when using such spaces. The primary one comes in satisfactorily darkening the area. A darkroom must be just that —*dark*. If stray light leaks from under or around doors, through windows and curtains, etc., you'll encounter all kinds of problems with film and paper fogging. Opaque blinds can be purchased and used with makeshift light traps along the edges. On a less expensive but less convenient note, you can also tape sheets of corrugated cardboard or poster board over windows and then stuff towels, rugs or blankets along the bottom of loosely fitting doors which would otherwise leak light.

Absolute darkness is necessary only for short periods of time while loading exposed film onto a developing reel, unexposed film into a bulk-film loader or sheet-film holders, etc. But during that brief time, the room you use must be *totally* dark, or you're going to wind up with some form of fogging. On vari-

ous occasions, I've been forced to use small closets that were not perfectly lighttight to transfer film from my camera to the developing tank reel. While this *can* be done successfully if you work quickly enough (the room appears dark to your eyes, but it really isn't perfectly dark), this is usually the time when something goes wrong—the reel refuses to accept the film for no apparent reason, or the film cartridge slips out of your hand and drops to the floor, where you can't find it until your eyes become accustomed to the darkness and you spot it lying at your feet—but then it's too late.

Rather than take such chances, spend a few minutes to run the following test before you commit your film to such hazards. Simply place a sheet of white paper against some dark background in the closet or room you wish to use and then turn off the room lights and wait about five minutes—count to 400 slowly under your breath. If you can't see the paper where you placed it at the end of that time, the room will suffice for your purposes. But if you can see it, however faintly, you'd better seal up some cracks before using the room.

If this is not possible, for whatever reasons, the use of a film changing bag is another alternative. This is a sack or bag made of opaque cloth with a zipper closure at one end and two elastic-band sleeves at the other. To use, you open the zipper and place your developing tank and film inside, then zip it up. Inserting your hands through the sleeves, you are able to open the film cartridge or break the seal on the spool and insert the film

onto the developing reel without fear of light leaks. After placing the reel in the tank and replacing its top, you can withdraw your hands and remove the tank from the zippered end. Changing bags must be kept clean and free from dust and dirt inside.

Photographic enlarging paper is far less sensitive to light than film, thus negatives can usually be enlarged in rooms which will not meet the requirements for handling films. To check on whether or not such stray light will interfere with enlarging, perform the following test. Turn off your safelight and place a sheet of the paper you're using on your working area with the emulsion side facing upward. Scatter several coins across the paper surface and leave them there for approximately five minutes. Then remove the coins and without turning up the safelight, slip the paper into the developer. Leave it there for two minutes to simulate full development, then fix the sheet and bring up the white light for inspection of the results.

If the paper is pure white, with no trace of the coins showing, the amount of stray light which might be entering your working area is of little or no concern, as long as you do not leave a box of paper open during your entire session in the darkroom. But should the paper appear to be slightly gray and thus show where the coins were placed, even if their location is ever so faint, you'll have to do something about the amount of stray light before you can use the area to make enlargements. Analyze what can be done, do it and then repeat the test a second or even a third time if necessary before considering the problem solved.

Another problem is that of cleanliness. If you expect to obtain good results in the darkroom, you must practice cleanliness and view your work area as a source of contamination which must be kept under control. Whether you're using a temporary or permanent darkroom arrangement, you should wash and dry the counter space before setting to work with your equipment. Make sure that the equipment itself is clean and free of dust. If you've wiped your developing tank with a cloth which leaves lint all over, and you don't remove it before loading another film for development, you have no one but yourself to blame for all those wiggly little lines that are certain to appear on your negatives.

Equipment cleanup is equally important. If you pour chemical solutions in and out of the developing tank's top and do not clean it after every use, you can expect a gradual buildup of hypo that will affect developer and photo solutions, which are incredibly sensitive to contamination by one another, resulting in a reduction of efficiency and chemical staining. An ample supply of clean, dry, lint-free towel material—paper or cloth—should be kept handy for wiping up spills and keeping your hands free from chemicals, etc.

Many of the problems of cleanliness can be solved by organization. If you lock onto a pattern of operation, there's less of a possibility that you'll accidentally knock something over, or pour the wrong chemical into the wrong tray. Chemical containers should be clearly marked and kept out of your way but where they can be easily reached if necessary—and not on the floor where you can tip them over as you move around. The better your darkroom organization, the more efficient your work will flow, the higher quality it will be, and the more you'll enjoy working in the darkroom.

MAKING THE MOST OF THE TEMPORARY DARKROOM

While you can keep all of your equipment stored in boxes and lug them all out whenever you want to set up for work, there are more efficient ways to handle the temporary darkroom which must be set up and then torn down each time it's used. One such is a projection cart; this is an ideal means of storing all of your equipment when it's not in use. The large casters make it easy to move the loaded cart from room to room, and

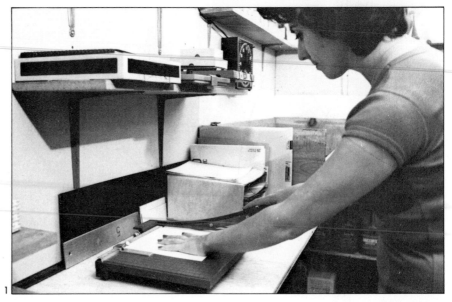

the toe locks on the casters will hold it firmly in place.

Those who are handy with tools can build a suitable cart without difficulty; those who are not can purchase one used from an audio-visual dealer. They come in a variety of heights and sizes, so look them over carefully before you buy and make certain that the one you get will hold everything you have. You can keep the cart with your equipment intact and store it in a closet or handy corner, rolling it out whenever you want to work. A large plastic cover will prevent dust and dirt from accumulating on the enlarger, as long as the cover is tied or taped securely around the enlarger's support girder. Such carts can also be built or bought with enclosed drawers which will let you store everything including chemicals and paper in its own specific place.

Depending upon how much equipment you have and the size of the enlarger you use, one of the inexpensive

1. A clean area is necessary for cutting paper and trimming prints. Keep a wastebasket handy and clean up the paper scraps as you make them.
2. For travelers or those without a permanent darkroom, a film loading bag like this one from Star-D allows you to transfer film from your camera to the developing tank without having to darken a closet. Just be sure to keep the bag clean inside and free from dust.
3. Another answer to the permanent darkroom facility is a rental darkroom, or a school like Kirk's Darkroom, shown here. The latest in equipment is generally available, along with various other equipment that you might not be able to afford in a home darkroom.
4. Stainless steel sinks are excellent, if you can afford them. A sheet of corrugated plastic makes print agitation in large trays much easier without worry of spilling solutions.

TV carts designed for holding a portable television set can make a good low-cost option. Discount department stores sell these with caster wheels in the $15-20 price range according to

3

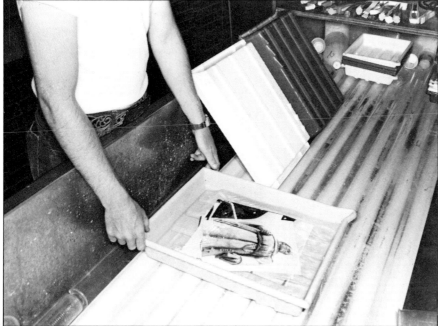

4

Those who have sufficient unused space which can be devoted to a permanent darkroom facility will do well to consider such. A minimum of 5x8 feet in floor space is generally adequate, but the more space you have, the more you can do with it. The temporary darkroom is adequate, but if you use it frequently enough, you'll soon get tired of setting up and tearing it down. This tends to discourage even the most ardent fan from working in his darkroom if he only has a few prints to make—it's too much trouble to get everything ready and then have to clean up afterwards. This means that the temptation is great to let things slide until your printing accumulates to the point where you suddenly discover that you now have more prints to make than you can handle in one evening.

DESIGNING THE PERMANENT DARKROOM

The location of the space you use isn't too important—it can be in the attic, cellar, garage or a spare room—just as long as it's sufficient in size, has electricity and running water (or is close to a source of both) and can be temperature-controlled easily. Converting any area into a darkroom requires considerable thought on your part, as it should be designed for efficiency and comfort. Exactly what you do with the space and how you arrange things

size. Check the store's demonstrator which is already assembled and make certain that the design is inherently sturdy—as these are intended to support a 35-50-pound television set, there should be no real question about the ability to hold your equipment, as long as there's no wobble in the legs when all the attaching bolts are tightened securely in place.

The type and size cart necessary will depend upon your own specific needs

and requirements, but should you settle on an audio-visual model, try to avoid the heavier carts constructed of metal. While these are dandy for durability, they also exceed what you'll need in terms of strength and thus extract a considerable penalty in the amount of effort required to move them over carpeted floors and wooden thresholds with ease. If possible, it's a good idea to stick to the lighter designs of metal tubing and particle board.

will depend a great deal upon how much room you have available, its configuration and the extent to which you become involved in darkroom work. While I'll pass along a few hints here, you'll find a good deal of practical help in two Kodak publications: Darkroom Design for Amateur Photographers (AK-3, 10 cents) and Darkroom Design (K-13, $2). These are available either from your local photo dealer or directly from Eastman Kodak Company, Department 454, 343 State Street, Rochester, New York 14650.

The darkroom should be divided into two major areas—a wet and a dry side. The wet side should contain counter and sink facilities, your developing trays, chemicals, print washer and a plastic wastebasket or some other trash container suitable for holding bad wet prints that you will not fix and wash. The sink should be large enough to hold at least an 11x14 tray, with hot and cold running water—preferably from separate faucets if possible. While a sheet of pegboard over the sink area can be used for storing developing tanks, reels, thermometer, etc., shelving is even more desirable if available. You'll want a room light fixture on the ceiling or wall, as well as one which will illuminate the hypo tray for print inspection, with a safelight and timer placed by the developing tray.

The dry side will contain your enlarger, timer, safelight and white-light fixture, and storage space for paper, chemicals and enlarging accessories such as easels, extra enlarger lenses and bulbs, dodging/burning-in tools, etc. Sufficient counter space about three feet high should be available for working; cover it with linoleum or vinyl material for easy cleanup.

Contrary to what you might think, the walls should be pastel or white, not black in color. Dark walls are unnecessary when the darkroom is blacked out for working with film or other sensitized materials in the dark, and when you're enlarging, light walls will reflect the safelight's output for more even illumination. Film and paper storage should be in lighttight drawers, or other containers such as a paper safe. Storing sensitized materials in the boxes in which they come is not a good idea if the boxes are to be exposed to white light for long periods of time. Boxes tend to warp and allow light to seep in to fog the contents. As high heat and humidity will affect sensitized materials adversely, keep your paper and film away from sources of heat or hot water pipes.

1

2

A portion of the dry side counter space near your paper storage area should be devoted to a paper trimmer so that enlarging paper can be cut into useful sizes or test strips when necessary. Since you'll do a considerable amount of standing, there should be rubber pads or discarded pieces of carpeting placed on the floor in front of the enlarging and tray areas to help ease the wear and tear on your legs and feet. If you plan to cover the entire floor area, use a material that will not stain if chemicals are splashed on it. A plain wood or concrete floor painted light gray is most practical. The paint will reflect safelight illumination, making it easier to locate negatives or other items accidentally dropped, protect the surface beneath it from chemical stains, and make clean-up a breeze.

You should have sufficient electrical outlets available to avoid having to hang several plugs in one socket. If necessary, you might tack one of the electrical socket strips sold for home workshop use along the wall over the counter. This will provide separate plug-in facilities for each electrical device used (safelight, enlarger, timer, etc.) and prevent cords from becoming tangled and in your way. Keep the outlet strip well above the counter top so that any spilled liquids will not be able to get to the sockets.

Some form of ventilation will be necessary. You can either install an exhaust fan in an outside wall to replace stale with fresh air, or use a strategically placed fan to do the job. A small electrical heater will be useful where central heating is not available to your darkroom area, but this should be used only on the dry side of the darkroom.

Remember, darkroom efficiency and comfort are the ultimate goals of any design or configuration, whether permanent or temporary. You should not fall into the trap of equating luxury with efficiency. Having lots of elaborate or expensive equipment does not necessarily mean that your darkroom will function any better than one that is sparsely outfitted with inexpensive or economy equipment. What you're really interested in is reducing the amount of time and effort spent under a safelight and having a drum print dryer isn't going to help you if it's placed at the wrong end or opposite side of the working area.

This is precisely why I emphasize that you should think through the design of your own darkroom space carefully before you commit it to wood, plaster and fixtures. Take several sheets of graph paper and sketch out different equipment locations to scale. Then analyze each in terms of how accessible the various pieces of equipment will be when you need to use them. Work with an L-shaped design, a square-U configuration and separate areas with no connecting counter

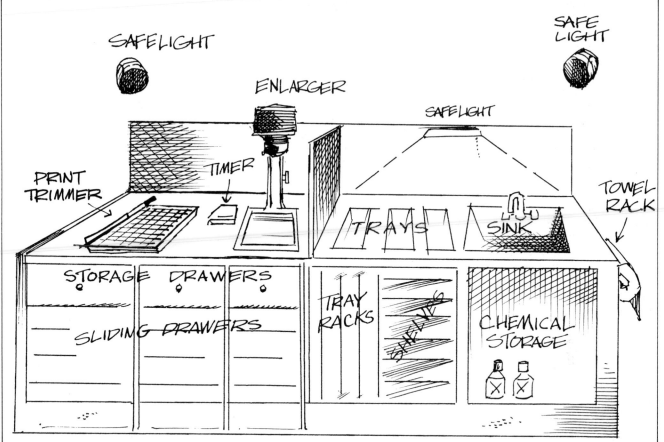

³
FIGURE A

1. This is the best type of print washer available. Again, it's the type of equipment you'll find in a rental or school darkroom, since such units are far too expensive for most home darkrooms.

2. Ample working space is the prime necessity in any darkroom. Your sink should be large enough to perform tasks such as ferrotyping prints, in addition to simply holding the trays.

3. Before you construct a thing, you should draw up various floor plans for your permanent darkroom, giving consideration to the amount and size of the working space available, and how it can be used most efficiently.

space to see which one seems most useful. If any of your friends have their own darkroom, spend some time in it and try the design on for size, evaluating how you could make it more functional; if it works, don't be afraid to adapt the design to your darkroom.

You'll find that the time spent thinking about your darkroom and its facilities will pay off handsomely once you consolidate your ideas into a firm plan of action. By not having to modify a hastily planned darkroom as you discover its shortcomings, you'll also save a fair amount of money in both construction costs and equipment bought. As you work in your darkroom, you will find a number of modifications helpful in personalizing it.

For example, you may want to make

provisions for jotting down ideas that come to mind, or for keeping track of exposure data and other information as you strive to achieve the best possible result from a particular negative. Perhaps you'll find the lighting controls to be less satisfactory than you first thought, and so modify them to permit foot control, or that the addition of more shelf space or partitioning of the space you have will make it more useful to you.

There are innumerable ways to take a basic darkroom plan and make it respond more efficiently to your own working methods, but these are touches here and there which you'll come across as time goes by, and no matter how hard you try to anticipate such while designing your darkroom, you'll never really catch them all until you put the operation into actual use.

DESIGN HINTS

While the Kodak publications mentioned earlier will provide you with definitive information in terms of construction, here are a few ideas to keep in mind while you're planning your facility on paper.

1—Locate your darkroom in a corner if possible. This way, you'll only have to build and frame two walls.

2—Design your darkroom in multiples of four to utilize wallboard panels with

a minimum of cutting and trimming.

3—Don't forget to provide entry/exit space—a door—in your design. A double length of opaque curtain material which drapes onto the floor is actually more suitable than a wooden door if your entry/exit is into a hall or otherwise relatively dark area.

4—Work your design around existing facilities. If running water and electricity must be piped/wired in, consider the placement of your sink and room light fixtures to require as little plumbing/electrical work as possible.

5—Don't design counter space too deep—18 to 24 inches is the most useful for the average person. If your counters are deeper, you'll find space going unused, as it's not convenient to stretch while you're working.

DARKROOM EQUIPMENT

The type of darkroom facility you have—temporary or permanent—will have some bearing upon the particular equipment with which you furnish it. Those who must work with a temporary darkroom should try to look ahead to the day when they will have a permanent one, and buy equipment with that in mind. To help you make wise decisions, we'll look at the various types available in the following chapter and determine exactly what you'll need to start working. □

16
Darkroom Equipment

The darkroom equipment you buy should be regarded as a long-term investment. It's something you'll use for years to come and as such, you should consider each and every item you purchase individually, and on its own merit. Buy the best that you can afford after carefully weighing the advantages of the different types available. While their price is tempting, stay away from those inexpensive darkroom sets which include "everything" you need. While they're ideal for a youngster who's just acquired an interest in photography, they're nothing you will want for your purposes.

It doesn't pay to skimp on what you invest in darkroom equipment. Consider a photographic thermometer, for example. You'll depend on what it tells you to determine chemical temperature and development time. If your thermometer is off by a few degrees, every roll of film you develop and every print you make will be affected. To assure yourself of the best possible results, you should have the best you can possibly afford.

Those who are about to furnish their first darkroom will find the following list of equipment for film development useful. I'll cover each item in turn and then we'll discuss what you need for printing and enlarging your negatives.

FILM PROCESSING EQUIPMENT

1—Developing Tank
2—Safelight
3—Photographic Thermometer
4—Timer
5—Film Washer and Film Dryer
6—Measuring Device/Funnel/Stirrer
7—Chemical Storage Bottles
8—Film Cartridge Opener/Scissors
9—Film Clips
10—Squeegees/Sponges/Towels

ROLL FILM DEVELOPING TANKS

Probably the most important pur-chase you'll make, film developing tanks are available in a variety of styles and types, which are designed to hold single or multiple developing reels. Once loaded, the roll film developing tank allows you to perform all other operations under normal room illumina-tion, and protects the film from scratches, fingerprints and other blem-ishes, providing that you've loaded it correctly. While each manufacturer claims his is the most versatile and convenient, you'll have to determine for yourself which style and type is most useful for your purposes.

Essentially, all roll film tanks, regard-less of manufacturer, operate on the same general principle. The exposed film is threaded onto a grooved or flanged reel of metal or plastic. The loaded reel is then placed in the cylin-drical tank and a lighttight cover is fit-ted over the tank and locked in place. Lightproof openings in the cover allow you to fill the tank with chemicals and drain them out when that particular step of the process is completed.

Agitation of the film during develop-ment is accomplished with some tanks by inserting a special rod provided with the tank into the center opening of its cover. This engages a shaft in the de-veloping reel and when the rod is turned, the reel turns with it. Other tanks are designed for agitation by in-version (turning the tank over), and to accomplish this a special cover is pro-vided that fits over the openings in the tank lid so that chemicals will not spill out when the tank is inverted.

As you look at the wide variety of developing tanks on the market, you should consider three aspects of tank development in general before settling upon a particular type.

FILM LOADING—This can be the most perplexing part of using a developing tank. Basically, there are three different ways in which exposed film can be loaded into the tank. The first, and least popular today are those tanks in which a separate plastic apron takes the place of a reel. These aprons come in specific sizes to fit a given film size and have crinkled edges to permit the chemical solutions to contact the film. After the film is inserted into the apron, it is placed in the tank and a weighted plate is placed on top of the apron.

Disadvantages of this type include keeping the apron free of chemical contamination, and difficulties in prop-

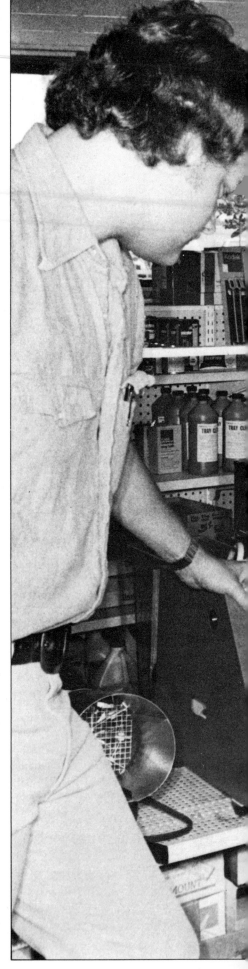

Like your camera, darkroom equipment is an investment. Compare features before you buy, and don't settle for less than quality equipment.

erly seating lengths of film in the apron. If the film is not seated correctly, the crinkled edges of the apron will leave a series of regularly spaced marks on one edge of the film. Tanks using aprons generally require 16 ounces of solution and will only develop one or two rolls at a time, depending upon the size of the film (1-120/620; 2-35mm).

Plastic tanks using self-loading plastic reels are quite popular these days. Such reels contain spiral grooves that prevent the film from touching itself as it is wound into a coil around the core of the reel. A small ball bearing built into the reel core provides the self-loading action. After inserting one end of the film into the reel entrance, one side of the reel can be twisted back and forth to produce a ratchet-like action that moves the film onto the reel without having to touch it by hand.

When it works properly, this self-loading feature is most convenient, but if the grooves are damp from a previous use, the film may hang up at that point and refuse to move further. There are two ways in which this source of frustration can be eliminated. Should the film hang up on the reel when partially loaded, immerse both reel and film in water and continue working the reel—with both the film and the reel grooves wet, the film can generally be loaded the rest of the way onto the reel without difficulty.

To prevent this from happening, follow this suggestion when you're finished with the tank: Immerse the reel in a film drying solution such as Kodak Photo-Flo, shake off the excess and let it air dry before putting the reel away. While this promotes complete drying of the plastic grooves, it also acts as a natural lubricant, making it possible to push an entire 36-exposure length of 35mm film onto the reel without even using the ratchet action.

Some reels of this type are adjustable, permitting you to develop any

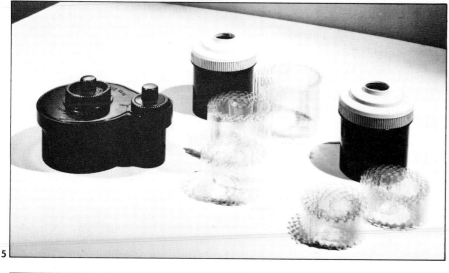

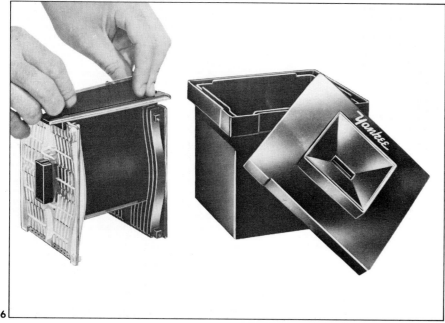

1. **Most manufacturers offer a complete line of developing tanks. The stainless steel Omega line features vinyl covers and caps, and offers both single and multiple reel tanks.**

2. **Film developing tanks come in several styles. One type is represented by the stainless steel tank/reel like the Honeywell Nikor, while the adjustable reel plastic tank is another.**

3. **The Kustom Universal tank combines the virtues of the adjustable plastic reel with the inversion agitation capability of the stainless steel type with its snug-fitting cover.**

4. **Another type of tank is the vinyl tank with stainless steel reel offered by Yankee Photo Products.**

5. **Kodak Kodacraft tanks use an apron of plastic with crinkled edges instead of a reel. The Kodak daylight-loading tank for 35mm film shown at left is no longer manufactured, but can still be found at swap meets and in used camera departments in photo stores.**

6. **The Yankee Agitank is an adjustable tank for developing cut film from 2¼x3¼ to 4x5. Loading the sheets of film in the rack is done in the dark with the help of a loading bar.**

size film from 110 to 620 by adjusting the spacing between the reel edges on the core, which is grooved at appropriate intervals according to film size. Other reels are nonadjustable and will thus accept only the size film for which they are made.

Plastic tanks with self-loading reels are available in single or multiple reel capacity, making it possible to develop several rolls of film at the same time in the same solution. The amount of solution required depends upon the size of the tank and the size/number of films being developed, but it can be as little as five ounces for 110 or nine ounces for 35mm film.

The third type, and a popular choice for years, are the spiral reels of stainless steel wire, which may be used in either stainless steel or plastic tanks. While they are simple in design, sturdy in construction and excellent for circulation of solutions, they are also easy to clean and dry for immediate reuse.

However, they are the most frustrating for many beginners to load properly because the film is attached to the wire core and then wound onto the reel from the inside out. To do so properly, the film must be held by the edges with one hand and slightly bowed or curved as the reel is turned in the other hand to feed the film in place on the wire spiral. If it does not feed properly, the film will touch the previous layer and prevent even development, resulting in several ruined negatives.

Various loading attachments and devices have been provided to make loading the stainless steel wire reels easier and more positive, but all have proven deficient in at least one aspect—they touch the entire surface of the film while it is loaded, and can cause scratching of the film back. Stainless steel tanks are also available in single or multiple reel capacities and because of their design, use the least amount of solution of any tank type.

AGITATION METHOD—While film agitation is necessary to move exhausted developer from the film's surface and replace it with fresh solution during the process of development (more on this in a later chapter), there are more old wives' tales than you can imagine about how it should be done, with each and every practitioner claiming that his method is the best. Agitation is certainly one of the most important steps in proper film development, but the method used is immaterial—just as long as agitation is consistent.

Basically, there are two ways of agitating film while it's developing. The inversion method requires that you turn the tank over in a 360-degree revolution, while the rotation method involves turning the reel back and forth. Which one you use will depend upon the design of the tank you buy. Most stainless steel tanks use a center-fill/drain opening and provide a sealing cap to permit inversion without spilling the solutions. Most plastic tanks with center-fill and edge-drain openings do not permit inversion agitation. Just to confuse the issue, the current trend in tank design is to provide for both types of agitation. If you have psychological hangups about one particular method, or if one seems more convenient to you than the other, look for a tank which provides that type of agitation.

FILM CAPACITY—Not too many years ago, most tanks held only a single reel. If you wanted to develop several films at one time, you resorted to such tricks as loading two films back-to-back (not

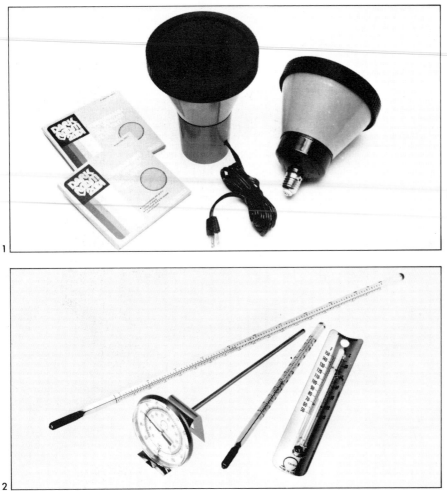

1, 3. Darkroom safelights are available in a variety of styles. These table/wall combination units with interchangeable filters by Arkay (3) are the most practical for permanent darkrooms, in the author's opinion. The globe-type such as the Kindermann (1), may be more useful to the temporary darkroom worker.

2. An accurate thermometer is a necessity, especially for color work. Omega is one manufacturer offering a complete line of tray, tank and dial thermometers.

4-5. These two timers by Omega represent an old and a new approach to darkroom timers. The audible Repeating Timer II (4) is an electromagnetic unit with audible and visual signals, and can be used for timing multiple prints. The Program Timer (5) lets you preprogram a sequence up to 30 minutes long, with intervals as short as 15 seconds. As each part of the sequence is completed, the timer automatically switches off the equipment to which it's connected. The sequence begins again when you press the bar.

6. Arkay's Time-Trol features a digital readout, and can be adjusted for the best viewing position from anyplace in the darkroom.

7. Accurate temperature measurement is useless if you cannot time the processing steps correctly. This Omega 60-second timer is an electrically operated, updated version of an old clockwork favorite with darkroom workers.

emulsion-to-emulsion) on the same reel, or you bought more than one tank. In the heyday of the Nikor stainless steel tank (before the expiration of patents allowed everyone to jump in with the same design), their popularity was greatly enhanced because they offered tall tanks that would hold 1-7 reels on a stainless steel lifting rod.

Today's tank systems, such as the Omega, Paterson or Prinz lines, offer sufficient variety to drive the layman crazy. You can buy tanks to hold single reels, double reels, or virtually any multiple you wish up to 14 35mm reels or eight 120/60 reels at a time. Sounds great, but there is a hitch. The multiple reel tank works fine as long as it's filled with solution, but trying to develop one or two reels in the tank and filling it with chemicals is wasteful, whereas reducing the amount of chemistry used so that it only covers the one or two reels you want will result in uneven development.

What this means is that those who develop both single and several rolls of film as the occasion warrants will find it necessary to own two or more tanks, along with the appropriate number of reels required to cover their needs. Fortunately, manufacturers make this easy for you, as tanks and reels are available separately. Thus you can tailor your purchases to your exact requirements without having to buy tanks with reels when you only need one and not the other.

SHEET FILM TANKS

These are used for processing sheet or cut film taken from film holders used with press and view cameras, and are generally constructed of plastic, hard rubber or stainless steel. Most have no covers—the sheets of film are inserted in individual metal hangers whose channel construction is perforated for efficient agitation and then hung in the tank. Since such tanks are not lightproof, they must be used in total darkness for all operations. Generally, a separate tank is used for each chemical, with the individual hangers removed from one, drained and then inserted in the next tank, rather than attempting to pour the solutions in and out. Obviously, this type of tank with its individual stainless steel hangers runs into a considerable investment (over $100 for three tanks and 12 hangers) and is thus not economical for the amateur photographer unless he uses only sheet film.

For the occasional sheet film user, Yankee Photo Products offer their 4x5 Agitank at a cost of less than 20 percent of the tanks and individual holders just discussed. This injection-molded plastic tank contains a removable film rack that adjusts to handle 12 sheets of film from 2¼x3¼ to 4x5. When each sheet of film to be developed is slipped into its own grooved channel, the rack is returned to the tank and the snap-on lid provided is set in place, permitting the remaining steps to be carried out in daylight.

SAFELIGHT

For many, buying a safelight for film development is a waste of money. Modern general-purpose emulsions are all panchromatic and as such, are best handled in total darkness. It is possible to use a dark green safelight, such as the Kodak Filter No. 3 when loading

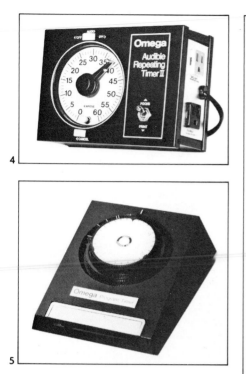

4

5

and developing panchromatic films, as long as the film is kept at the required minimum distance from the safelight, but the amount of light in which you have to work is so faint as to be virtually useless.

But those who work with certain specialty films, such as Kodak Kodalith, will find a dark red safelight (Kodak Filter No. 2) useful, since you can load the film under this illumination as well as visually check on its progress during development.

6

PHOTOGRAPHIC THERMOMETER

Necessary for checking and adjusting chemical temperatures, the photographic thermometer is mandatory for color work, since solution temperatures must be maintained to within ½ or 1°F. in nearly every processing system. Thus the thermometer you use should be accurate within ½°F. over the critical range of 68-100°F. to be useful in developing black-and-white and color.

Thermometers are provided in two types—the dial and the mercury-in-glass, or standard straight thermometer. The dial type is easiest to read but the standard type is generally more accurate. Some dial thermometers have a needle adjustment feature that can be used to calibrate the thermometer when necessary. The best idea is to have one of each type. Compare the dial against the straight, note any difference in readings and then use the dial for convenience, double-checking it with the other when you're unsure.

TIMER

For film development, this can be as

7

simple as a clock or a watch with a sweep-second hand. Those kitchen timers which allow you to preset a specified interval that ends with an audible alarm are useful only for timing the overall development period; the sweep-second hand is necessary to indicate agitation intervals and to time the duration of each agitation cycle.

Perhaps the best approach here is to stick with the watch or clock until you're ready to invest in an electric interval timer that is better suited for automatically timing exposure during enlarging. These usually feature both the sweep-second hand and an audible or visual indicator at the end of a preset interval, but are fairly expensive.

FILM WASHER AND DRYER

Many amateurs wash their film after fixing by simply removing the cover and placing the tank beneath a moderate stream of cool water for 30 minutes or so. Unfortunately, this is not the best way to remove fixer from the film. Hypo is heavier than water and tends to settle at the bottom of the developing tank because the water circulation pattern in this method is poor. Some tanks even come with a hose that connects to the faucet and is fed into the shaft of the reel, forcing water down into the tank and removing it by overflow at the top. This amounts to essentially the same thing as the previous method, but since the water

1. Paterson offers a filtered wash attachment for roll film tanks.
2. Arkay provides roll film wash units in varying sizes for washing one or more reels at a time.
3,5. Here are two styles of darkroom graduates: the Kustom 20 oz. graduate (3) and the Honeywell (5). Both are marked in ounces and milliliters
4. Funnels are inexpensive and help prevent spillage when solutions are transferred. The filtered insert in this Kustom funnel is useful in reducing contamination from unmixed chemical particles, etc.

stream is actually taken to the bottom of the tank by the hose, it can be slightly more efficient in some cases.

Unfortunately, commercial attempts have all but failed to convince amateurs that these methods are not really satisfactory for washing negatives. Occasionally, a new film washer design will come onto the market, but few sell in sufficient quantity to survive for long. What you really need is a container with a few small holes near its bottom to allow the hypo-laden water to flow out under the force of gravity. If properly washed negatives are of concern to you, this is the way to get them. As this method is far more efficient in actually disposing of the hypo removed from the film, the duration of the wash period can be cut by 40 percent.

When your wash is over, the film must be dried. For most, this means hanging it up to dry. How fast and how clean it dries will depend on where you hang it. The air in most homes (and many darkrooms) contains a good deal

of dust particles floating around and these seem to love damp film hung up to dry. In fact, it sometimes seems that every piece of loose dust and lint in a 10-block radius has decided to honor your film with its presence. Since this is especially true of dry air when the humidity is low, I'd suggest that you hang the film in a shower cabinet after running the shower sufficiently to produce moisture in the air. This tends to keep dust from floating around.

If this is not possible, or if you wish more consistency in your ability to dry film whenever or wherever you wish, a special portable film drying unit such as the Prinz Jet Rapid is ideal. This compact dust-free unit can be hung on the wall out of your way, as it only occupies a space 8x8 inches when not in use. To use, the collapsible plastic bag is lowered and up to three rolls of film are hung in it. When the unit is switched on, it blows thermostatically controlled, filtered warm air, which dries the film inside within 10-15 min-

utes. As the fiberglass filter is removable, it can be washed and reused. This permits you to keep the potential dust level to an absolute minimum at all times.

MEASURING DEVICE/FUNNEL/ STIRRING ROD

As many photographic solutions are created by dissolving powder in specified quantities of water, some accurate method of mixing your chemicals is necessary. This usually takes the form of a graduated measuring container or cylinder on which the measurement intervals (usually ounces) are clearly marked. Avoid the use of metal household measuring cups or containers because the chemicals will react with the metal, rendering the container unsuitable for use either in the kitchen or for mixing chemicals.

You'll need one large enough to handle the largest solution quantity you plan to mix. Those who buy and mix developer and hypo by the gallon will need a 64-ounce or 2000ml (milliliter) container; mixing by the ½-gallon will make a 32-ounce or 1000ml container necessary; and mixing by the quart, will necessitate a 16-ounce or 500ml cylinder. Smaller ones are also useful for measuring out only a few ounces of developer. These are available in plastic, glass or stainless steel.

To properly mix chemicals, you'll

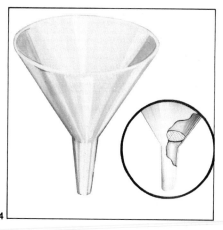

need something to stir the solutions. The use of household utensils such as a large kitchen spoon is *not* recommended. Not only is this an unsafe health practice, but the shape of a spoon is not adequate for crushing crystalized chemicals to make certain that all are properly dissolved in the water. Plastic or stainless steel stirring rods made especially for this purpose have a wide bottom for crunching up those bits that refuse to dissolve by themselves, and usually have some means of hanging them up attached to the opposite end. Get one long enough to work with the largest graduate or mixing cylinder you use.

Transferring the chemicals from graduate to storage container to developing tank and back to storage container can be a messy job, so I recommend using a funnel to keep spillage at a minimum. These are sold by the quantity they'll handle—eight, 16, 32 ounces, etc.—or by the designations small, medium and large. Some funnels even contain a stainless steel filter to remove contamination from solutions. A couple of these in different sizes are handy, as is the two-in-one arrangement in which a large and small funnel combine to form a single unit. You'll need both plain funnels and filter funnels, the latter for mixing chemicals and the other for transferring them.

CHEMICAL STORAGE BOTTLES

Used to store photographic solutions after they are mixed, polyethylene bottles will not break when dropped and

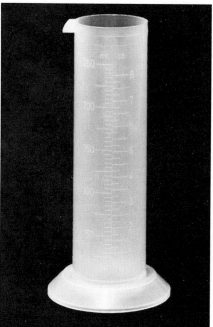

are thus more practical than glass. Most are brown or blue in color, as solutions stored in clear bottles may deteriorate if left exposed to daylight for long periods of time. The latest designs such as the Prinz DataJug® and Camrex/tainer incorporate white spaces on the bottle for writing pertinent data—contents, date mixed, dilution, time and temperature, directions for use, etc.—that can be reused if you change the contents.

Oxidation is the enemy of all photo chemicals—if stored for long periods of time, a half-empty container of developer can be rendered useless. In the

days before the use of plastic bottles became widespread, it was a common practice to add a sufficient quantity of marbles to the bottle to occupy the space left by the solution removed. It worked fine, but can you imagine pouring the last four ounces from a gallon jug filled with marbles?

When mixing up a relatively large quantity of a stock solution such as developer, from which only a small amount will be used at any one time, it's not a good practice to store the entire quantity in a single container. Store it in four or eight separate containers each filled to the top and use your solution from one at a time. You'll also find collapsible polyethylene bottles which can be compressed as the solution is used. In this way, the formation of an air space above the chemical level can be prevented.

FILM CARTRIDGE OPENER/SCISSORS

Opening a roll of film to remove the film from the paper backing requires nothing more than a fingernail to slit the gummed paper strip that keeps the roll intact. At one time, removing the spool from a 35mm cartridge posed no serious problem either. A simple sharp rap of the protruding spool end would pop off the retaining cap on the opposite end and provide immediate access to the film inside.

But Kodak and some other manufacturers changed over to a cartridge design with a crimped end a few years back, which immediately rendered that method of opening a 35mm cartridge obsolete. Kodak and others do sell special cartridge end remover devices, but you can work just as efficiently with a can opener of the type once used to puncture beer and soda cans. Just fit it over the cartridge end and apply pressure. Presto, the cap comes off. But either method—cartridge or beer can opener—makes the cartridge unsuitable for reloading.

Those who load their own film will either use a pop-type cartridge such as the Kodak Snap-Cap, which is opened with the sharp rap on the spool end, or a more durable design in which the cartridge cap actually screws into the cartridge proper. The latter has the longest life and is by far the least likely to leak light.

Film removal from the 110/126 cartridges is a bit different. To remove 110 film, insert a ballpoint pen or similarly shaped object through the little opening in the back of the cartridge and push out the paper backing where you can reach it. Pull gently on the paper until you feel the film appear, then continue pulling on both paper and film—they'll be drawn out together and when the film comes free of the cartridge (it's not attached), discard the cartridge with the paper backing and proceed to load the film.

The 126 cartridges are best unloaded by snapping them in half, then separating the two pieces of the film chamber with your thumbs as you'd pry open a clam shell. When these come open, the film, paper backing and spool can be withdrawn. Remove the film from the paper backing as you would with an ordinary roll film by slowly tearing the retaining tape free from the paper backing. If you tear it too fast, you'll create static electricity that may fog one or more frames.

Scissors are handy for removing tongued leaders from 35mm film, and if used to cut the film just beside the tape which attaches it to the cartridge spool, will prevent the possibility of fogging from static electricity. They're also necessary should you decide to remove several frames shot at the beginning of a cartridge for immediate development. Much of the remainder of the unexposed film can be salvaged by following this procedure:

1—Advance and release the shutter twice, then open the camera back and slipping one finger under the film, raise it away from the film channel sufficiently to use the scissors without damaging the camera's focal-plane shutter. Cut the film with the scissors, depress the rewind button and pull the film to be developed from the take-up spool. Trim the tongue and load onto the developing tank reel.

2—Now, remove the cartridge and trim a new tongue by feel. Insert the tongue in the take-up spool and advance the film once to make certain that it's securely attached to the spool, then draw the film over the film plane and drop the cartridge in position, en-

1-2. Honeywell offers a loading stand for standard stainless steel reels (1); Kindermann provides larger units for 35mm and 70mm film (2).
3. A film squeegee such as this one by Yankee is inexpensive and promotes film drying without water spotting.
4. A film drying cabinet such as those offered by Kindermann and Prinz is most useful. This diagram shows how most such driers operate.

gaging the rewind knob. Check to make sure that the film is relatively tight across the film channel, that both sets of sprocket teeth engage the holes along the edges of the film and then close the camera back. Advance the film one more frame and you're ready to shoot. If doing this in the dark unnerves you somewhat, you can always turn on the light after loading the film to be developed and recut your leader tongue to thread the camera under normal room illumination, but you'll lose an extra 2-3 frames this way. This may make it impractical to bother with it if you're working with the remainder of a 20-exposure cartridge.

FILM CLIPS

These are used in pairs to suspend each washed roll of film for drying; only one clip is required when drying sheet film. The top clip holds the film attached to the wire, clothesline or other surface while the bottom clip should be weighted to keep the drying film from curling. Some clips contain teeth which pierce the end of the film when

the jaws are squeezed together to assure that it will not gradually slip out of the clip and end up in a crumpled heap on the floor.

Usually made from either stainless steel or plastic, the choice of film clip design appears to be a highly personal one, especially because there are many types available, but all do the same thing to varying degrees of efficiency. Most have lips or hooks for hanging the film up, and a hole for storing unused clips on a nail or hook in the wall. The major problem with the plastic clips is a tendency to break in half after repeated use.

Clothespins can also be used in an emergency, but are not recommended for constant use as they have a tendency to let the film slip free, and have been known to break in two at just the wrong moment. Those who swear by clothespins instead of film clips usually use the wooden kind and drive small brads through each gripping surface, so that when the pins are closed, the brads will puncture the end of the film in two places and prevent it from slipping free.

SQUEEGEES, SPONGES, TOWELS

These are all required for darkroom cleanliness. Once the film is ready to hang up for drying, the use of a photographic squeegee will remove any loose particles of emulsion, water drops, solution scum, etc. from the film. The squeegee should be wet and

2

3

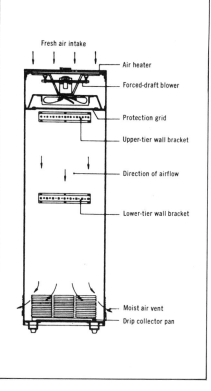

4

Fresh air intake

Air heater

Forced-draft blower

Protection grid

Upper-tier wall bracket

Direction of airflow

Lower-tier wall bracket

Moist air vent

Drip collector pan

squeezed as dry as possible several times before use—this will both soften the spongy surfaces and remove any lightly embedded particles or contamination that would otherwise scratch the film. When you're finished with the squeegee, it should be stored away from where dust, dirt and other contamination can collect on the sponge surfaces.

Some photographers prefer to use a chamois or even a clean piece of water-absorbent terry cloth to wipe the film semidry, but this is a tricky procedure for the beginner and can easily result in nonrepairable scratching of both film base and emulsion. You're way ahead of the game by using a squeegee with care, or allowing the film to drain by itself after treatment in a solution of wetting agent (like Kodak Photo-Flo), which promotes quick, even drying of the film without water spotting.

Individual sponges are useful for sopping up any spilled chemicals or water splashes. Towels are necessary to keep your hands dry. Whether developing film or making prints, you should remove any chemical solutions from your hands by washing them immediately. Although expensive, paper towels are ideal—at least those that do not produce lint. If you use cloth towels, be certain that they're washed be-

tween sessions in the darkroom, since contamination from one session can get on your hands in a later session if you use the same towel over and over without cleaning it.

MISCELLANEOUS ITEMS

You'll find a wastebasket useful in keeping the area around you clean. Cut-off film leader tongues, paper backings and spools, pieces of 35mm cartridges—these should all be disposed of before beginning work. The less clutter you have around you, the better. When enlarging, you'll want a trash container that will accept wet prints you do not wish to fix or wash, sheets of paper spoiled in other ways, etc. A medium-size plastic trash container lined with a small plastic trash bag is ideal, as it will prevent the accumulation of solutions which drain from unfinished prints from messing up the bottom of the container.

Should you have several rolls of film to develop at one time, and being able to identify them in the same sequence in which they were taken is important to you, you'll want some means of marking each one as it's loaded onto its reel. This can be done with a waterproof marking pen used on the very tip end of the film leader back after the tongue is cut off. You can establish your own identification system—letters, numbers, dots, etc. Those who do not trust the marking pen will find a single-hole paper punch perfect for the job. Used like a pair of scissors, this will

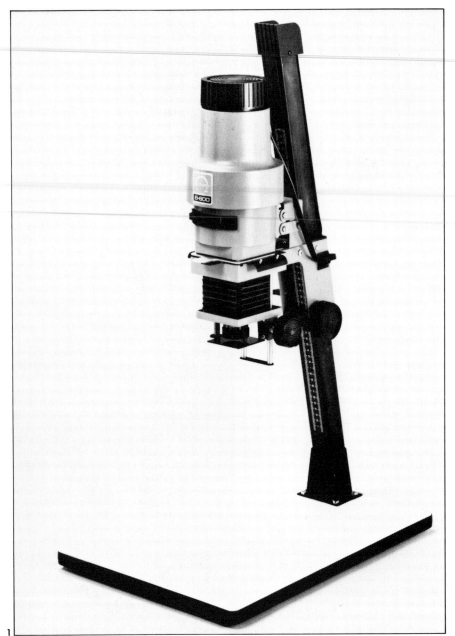

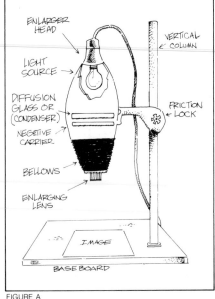

FIGURE A

1. Lowest priced of the Omega line, the B-600 accepts an optional dichroic color enlarger head.
2. The Prinz 6x6 condenser enlarger is available in a kit with four negative carriers and lens.
3. Omega's new C67 condenser enlarger features a double-walled, flanged-U cross-section for strength, rigidity, and vibration resistance. The front of the head slides up for easy condenser cleaning, and an optional color head extends its versatility.

ENLARGER

The most expensive darkroom item you'll buy, the enlarger should be chosen with great care. Unfortunately, too many amateurs do not regard it with sufficient import. Old ideas die hard, and one of these is that an inexpensive enlarger is satisfactory as long as you have a quality camera and lens. The truth of the matter is that many inexpensive enlargers will cause a considerable loss of quality in the final print, regardless of the camera used to take the pictures. To prevent this, you should consider your enlarger purchase with care.

For the most part, all enlargers function in basically the same way, sharing certain basic components that are shown in Figure A. The baseboard and support rail form an L-shaped support for the main unit or enlarger head. This enlarger head contains the essential parts of every enlarger—light source, diffusing glass or condensers, negative carrier, focusing tube or bellows and enlarging lens.

The light source provides illumination for exposure of the negative to the sensitized enlarging paper located in an easel or other holder on the baseboard beneath the lens. To distribute this illumination evenly over the negative, a diffusing glass or condenser

punch ¼-inch holes in the leader or you can clip the edge of the film to remove a specified number of tiny semicircular pieces.

As you work in your darkroom and develop more and more rolls of film, you'll undoubtedly run across other handy items for which a use will arise—I've specified only the major necessary items.

It's time now to move on to the equipment which you'll require in order to make prints or enlargements from your developed negatives. Here's what is necessary in addition to those items purchased for film development that can be used for enlarging purposes.

PRINTING EQUIPMENT

1—Enlarger
2—Enlarging Lens
3—Contact Printer / Proof Printer

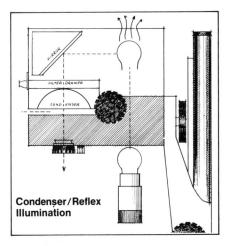

Condenser/Reflex Illumination

4—Safelight
5—Paper Easel
6—Trays / Print Tongs
7—Print Washer / Print Dryer
8—Paper Safe
9—Paper Trimmer

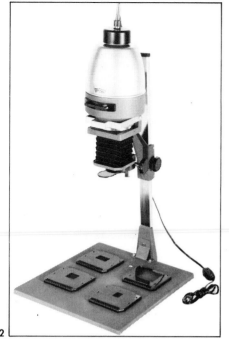

2

system is used. The negative carrier is a removable device that holds the negative flat and in proper alignment for the light to pass through on its way to the paper below. The overall size of the picture projected by the enlarging lens is controlled by moving the enlarger head up or down on the vertical support column by means of a friction lock device, while fine focusing of the image is achieved with the bellows. Some less-expensive enlarger designs use a spiral-threaded focusing tube instead of a true bellows.

These are the essential components of any photographic enlarger, and they perform the stated functions with varying degrees of efficiency. For example, to increase the overall picture size, the enlarger head is moved up or away from the baseboard. The simplest method of performing this is the friction lock mentioned; more sophisticated designs use a counterbalance device in conjunction with the friction lock to make enlarger head movement less of a task and more precise in operation. The even more sophisticated models will have a cam arrangement that automatically focuses the enlarger lens as the overall image size is adjusted—a considerable convenience, because it reduces the amount of trial-and-error adjustments that must be made to achieve an exact image size.

There are four primary factors involved in selecting an enlarger that's appropriate for your needs. These should be thought through with care before you settle on a particular make or model.

ENLARGER CONSTRUCTION—The

3

main requirement of any enlarger is that of rigidity—it must not move during an exposure. And rigidity is a function of the baseboard/vertical column design. The upright single tubular column is the least efficient design in this respect; incorrect design or a baseboard that's too small can cause the weight of the enlarger head to pull the column forward sufficiently to destroy the parallel alignment of negative and enlarging paper enough to cause a slight unsharpness in one part of the print. Such support systems are sensitive to virtually any vibration and may cause slightly blurred prints regardless of how

sharply you focus the lens. Amateurs tend to blame both problems on the quality of the enlarging optic used when the enlarger design itself is what's at fault.

Some manufacturers have attempted to overcome these inherent defects of the single tubular column design by changing the support column used to an I-beam and slanting it forward, resulting in what amounts to an inclined beam design. This requires the use of a larger baseboard, but does away with the possibility of flare and fog in the form of light reflected from the column striking the enlarging paper. Oth-

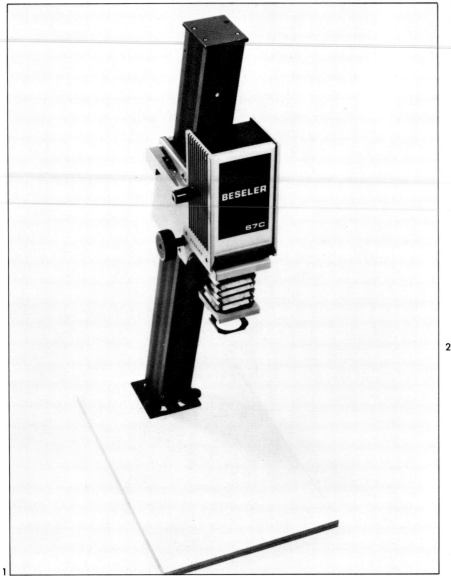

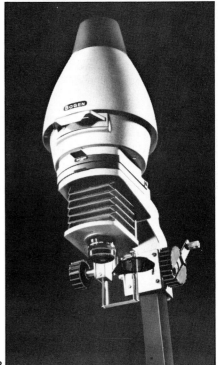

ers have gone to a braced girder construction in which struts and braces are used with the enlarger head mounted between two beams for maximum rigidity.

Don't jump to the conclusion that one design is far superior to another, as it remains for the enlarger manufacturer to translate the design upon which he settles into reality, and it's just as possible to produce a braced girder enlarger design with inherent tendencies toward vibration as it is to manufacture a single tubular column design without such tendencies. The major point of concern here should not be the particular design used, but how well that design has been translated into reality.

The small, lightweight enlargers generally utilize a single tubular column support, and many are designed to be disassembled for storage after use. These are especially prone to alignment difficulties because of the constant put-together/take-apart routine

1. Beseler uses an I-beam support girder on its 67C.
2. Beseler offers a wall mounting bracket which makes it easy to produce king-sized prints.
3. The Bogen 6x6 is an inexpensive but highly practical enlarger for the beginning darkroom worker.
4. The Honeywell Nikor 6x7 is another new system enlarger. Note the simplicity of design.

through which they must go. When considering an enlarger, take into account the support system design and try to determine to your satisfaction how well the manufacturer has achieved his goal in producing a vibration-free system.

NEGATIVE SIZE/DEGREE OF ENLARGEMENT—While enlargers are manufactured that will handle any negative size from the tiny 8x11mm Minox to 8x10 negatives, the most popular are built around the 35mm, 6x6cm and 4x5 negatives. Those who use only one negative format will have no difficulty in selecting the right enlarger

because of negative size, but if you use more than one format, you may be tempted to buy an enlarger that will handle them all.

While this is both a money-saving and space-saving idea, it does have its limitations, depending upon the variation in size between the formats used. Some formats are best handled by special enlargers designed expressly for their use—one example is the Minox. As a Minox camera has a curved film plane, the enlarger used should also have a curved plane in its negative carrier to assure maximum sharpness

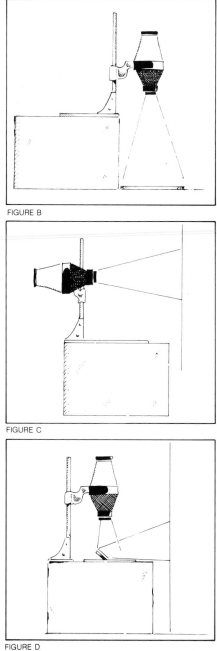

FIGURE B

FIGURE C

FIGURE D

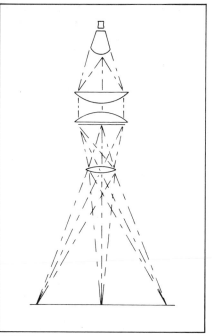

FIGURE E

from corner-to-corner. Many enlargers will accept a negative carrier holding the 8x11mm Minox negative, but only the enlarger offered by Minox provides the curved plane in its carrier to properly accommodate the negative.

Another problem encountered in such dual use of an enlarger is that of even illumination. As we'll see shortly, it's entirely possible to have a 6x6cm enlarger whose illumination pattern is fairly even except for a slight hot spot in the center—no great problem when a 6x6cm negative is used, but insert a 110 negative in the same enlarger and you may not be pleased with the results. Dual function enlargers should have an accessory condensing lens when such small negatives are used in order to properly redirect the illumination through the smaller negative.

If you work with two or more formats, make your first enlarger purchase one that will work with the largest of the formats and buy the negative carriers and enlarging lenses to allow use of the smaller ones. As soon as your finances permit it, you should acquire a smaller enlarger so that each format can be used in an enlarger designed for it.

Maximum enlargement size is determined by the focal length of the lens used and the height of the support column, or the distance it allows the enlarger head to be separated from the baseboard. The higher the enlarger head and/or the shorter the focal length of the lens, the larger the enlargement you can make. Some 35mm enlargers permit no larger than an 8x10 print to be made, while most 6x6cm enlargers fitted with the proper lens for the 35mm format will allow an 11x14 print.

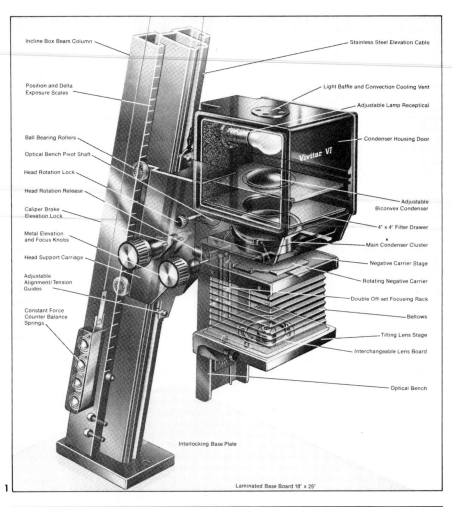

Incline Box Beam Column

Position and Delta
Exposure Scales

Ball Bearing Rollers

Optical Bench Pivot Shaft

Head Rotation Lock

Head Rotation Release

Caliper Brake
Elevation Lock

Metal Elevation
and Focus Knobs

Head Support Carriage

Adjustable
Alignment/Tension
Guides

Constant Force
Counter Balance
Springs

Stainless Steel Elevation Cable

Light Baffle and Convection Cooling Vent

Adjustable Lamp Receptical

Condenser Housing Door

Vivitar VI

Adjustable
Biconvex Condenser

4" x 4" Filter Drawer

Main Condenser Cluster

Negative Carrier Stage

Rotating Negative Carrier

Double Off-set Focusing Rack

Bellows

Tilting Lens Stage

Interchangeable Lens Board

Optical Bench

Interlocking Base Plate

Laminated Base Board 18" x 25"

1

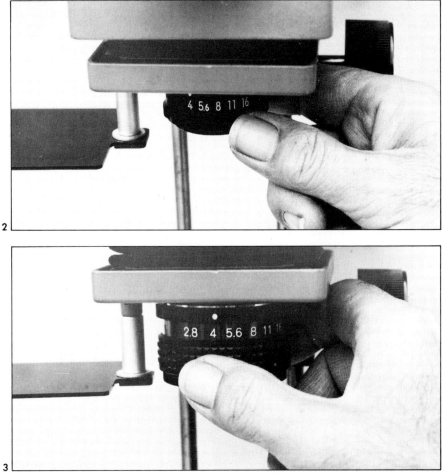

2

3

Enlargers which are more expensive and thus more sophisticated may have a head that can be rotated 180 degrees on a vertical axis. This lets you turn the baseboard toward the wall, clamp it in place to prevent the unit from falling over and then revolve the head to project your image on the floor (Figure B). Another method occasionally used by enlarger manufacturers is to provide a 90-degree head movement on a horizontal axis for projecting the image on a wall (Figure C). Specialty companies offer 45-degree mirror devices for fixed-head enlargers, which will also reflect the image onto a wall (Figure D). Whatever enlarger you buy should be able to produce the maximum size enlargements you'll require without resorting to the use of ultra-short focal length lenses or mirror devices. Some manufacturers offer their enlargers with a choice of column height—standard or extra long (XL)—to suit your needs.

ILLUMINATION—Every enlarger contains a light source to provide illumination to make the enlargement. In addition to the light source, either a condensing lens system or a diffusion device is used to spread out the rays from the point light source (enlarger bulb) so that the illumination reaching the enlarging paper will be evenly distributed. How well these designs do their job depends upon the manufacturer involved.

An enlarger may be designated as a diffusion type by simply painting the inside of the lamphouse white. This is not very effective but it is done on occasion. Placing a sheet of white opal glass between the enlarging lamp and the negative carrier is the usual manner in which a diffusion-type enlarger is manufactured. Diffusion-type enlargers are simple to design, inexpensive to manufacture and when opal glass is used as the diffuser, the resulting prints can be of high quality, provided that the light source is efficient to begin with, and that a good enlarging lens is used.

Such enlargers tend to produce less light than condenser types, as the opal glass absorbs a percentage of that produced by the bulb. Enlargements made with a diffusion-type enlarger will require a longer exposure time, especially when working with slightly dense negatives. Such negatives will also be somewhat more difficult to focus because of the reduced light output to the easel.

When condensers are used to spread the illumination evenly over the

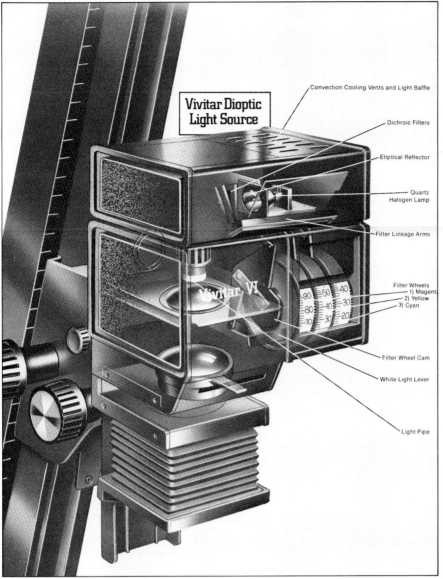

Vivitar Dioptic Light Source

Convection Cooling Vents and Light Baffle
Dichroic Filters
Eliptical Reflector
Quartz Halogen Lamp
Filter Linkage Arms
Filter Wheels
1) Magenta
2) Yellow
3) Cyan
Filter Wheel Cam
White Light Lever
Light Pipe

FIGURE F

1. The first really significant enlarger design in years, the Vivitar VI TM offers such features as a rotating negative carrier, tilting lens stage, and inclined box beam column. The big news about this unit is shown in Figure F.

2-3. When choosing an enlarger lens, look for convenience features as well as optical quality. The f-stop numbers should be large enough to stand out boldly under safelight illumination (2) and a large milled aperture ring for easy adjustment (3) is also desirable.

negative area, we refer to the enlarger as a condenser type. Condenser lenses concentrate the light rays from the enlarging bulb and must be designed with accuracy and ground with precision if they are to do their job properly. As a result, this type of enlarger is more expensive than the diffusion type (Figure E).

As the diffusion enlarger produces a softer light, resulting in lowered contrast than that from a condenser enlarger, it also tends to hide fine scratches and other blemishes on a

negative that the condenser type will accentuate. The more brilliant image of the condenser enlarger makes focusing easier and faster, especially with dense negatives. Which is best? Many prefer the crispness of the condenser enlarger for black-and-white work, but the diffusion enlarger when working with color negatives. Only you can determine which is best for you, since it depends on the type of prints you wish to make.

You can, however, determine how evenly the illumination is distributed in a given enlarger by means of a simple test. With the enlarger set up as if to make a print and focused on a negative, remove the negative and then turn on the enlarger to give the enlarging paper beneath it a brief flash of exposure. Develop the paper fully and inspect the results under a white light after it's fixed. The sheet should be a uniform gray—if there are any dark spots or other deviations from the uniform gray pattern desired, the illumina-

tion is not even. Incidentally, keep a spare enlarging bulb or two on hand and never attempt to substitute a household or other electric bulb should your only enlarging bulb burn out. The filament structure is different and you will not usually get acceptable results.

Enlarger design has remained relatively static in recent years, with the emphasis placed upon refinement of the existing system designs rather than new ones. But Vivitar has just introduced an enlarger line using what it calls a Dioptic Light Source that promises to touch off a design war in the enlarger industry. Basically, this innovation provides either condenser or diffusion operation at the user's option for both black-and-white or color.

The light from a quartz-halogen bulb with a prefocused dichroic elliptical reflector is transmitted to the enlarger's condenser system by means of a fiber optic system, which has given rise to the nickname "light pipe enlarger" (Figure F). This fiber optic transmits 2-3 times as much light to the enlarger baseboard as do other designs with similar bulb wattage, and does so at an unusually cool temperature, as its dielectric properties form an efficient insulator between lamp and negative. This means that negative temperature is unlikely to rise more than 3°C. above ambient temperature, reducing the problem of negative buckling to a minimum. When desired, an optical diffusion filter can be inserted in the lamphouse to alter the illumination from condenser to diffusion type, giving the user the ability of matching the light to the image requirements.

There's little doubt that the time is ripe for enlarger innovations, and should the Vivitar "light pipe" design meet with consumer acceptance as expected, you can look for a number of rapid changes in enlarger design, something that has not taken place in the enlarger industry since the fluorescent or cool light craze of the 1950s.

NEGATIVE CARRIERS—There are two types of negative carriers in use, each with its own operational advantages and disadvantages. Use of the glass type carrier is pretty much restricted to larger format enlargers today. While this has the advantage of holding a negative perfectly flat between the two sheets of glass, thus preventing buckling of the negative due to excessive heat from the enlarger bulb, the glass carrier has a tendency to produce concentric bands of colored light called Newton's rings, an effect caused by the lack of perfect contact between

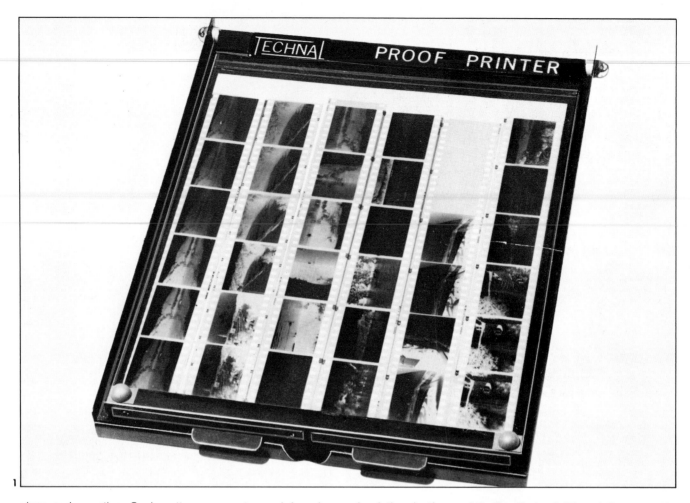

1

glass and negative. Such patterns are more than just a simple nuisance, as they will show up clearly in the print and cannot be removed. Some carriers are made using a special glass that prevents the formation of the Newton's ring effect, but these are expensive and are not available to fit the less expensive enlargers. The glass plates also have a tendency to attract and hold dust and lint, making it difficult to keep all four glass surfaces (and the two sides of the negative) clean.

For these reasons, the glassless carrier is far more common these days. Consisting simply of two metal frames hinged at the back with matching cutouts to fit a given negative size, glassless carriers offer no protection against heat generated by the enlarger lamp, and will thus permit the negative to buckle or ''pop'' during lengthy exposures—especially if the emulsion is ''green'' (contains moisture)—which results in unsharp prints.

To prevent this from happening, some photographers will place the negative in the enlarger and turn on the light for several minutes before placing the paper under the enlarger to make their print. This presumes that the ''warm-up'' period will give the negative a chance to pop if it's going

to, and focusing and printing is then carried out. While it's not a totally satisfactory answer, this does work on some occasions.

Well-designed optical systems of an efficient enlarger will hold negative buckling to a minimum and new approaches such as that taken by Vivitar with its ''light pipe'' design promise to reduce the occurrence of this darkroom nuisance even further. As for your choice, I'd suggest the use of a glassless carrier for negative sizes through 6x6cm, because dust and dirt can create more havoc than an occasional negative buckling, but go with the glass carrier when you enlarge 4x5 negatives, since flatness can pose distinct problems with negatives that are this large.

CHOOSING YOUR ENLARGER—While price is usually the determining factor in the purchase of an enlarger, a low budget should not prevent you from obtaining the very best you can get for your money. Should you find that a lack of funds limits your choice too much, let me suggest that you seriously consider a used enlarger in good condition from a reputable photo dealer. There isn't too much that can go wrong with an enlarger that cannot be determined on the spot. The primary

1-2. The Technal (1) and Paterson (2) represent two different approaches to proof printing. The Technal uses a negative clip along one edge of the cover glass to hold the negatives in place, while Paterson uses individual negative channels for each strip.
3. If you want contact prints from negatives up to 4x5, the Yankee printer will do the job.
4. Contact printing negatives to make a proof sheet is one easy way of identifying what's on each roll of negatives in your filing system.
5-6. Kustom offers two different types of paper safes: the multishelf design with sliding cover, and the single paper container design.

concern is that the negative carrier and baseboard alignment is parallel, and that the illumination is spread as uniformly as possible across the negative. Both can be checked out in a matter of minutes in the back of the store, as the proof of the pudding is in the image it projects.

You'll find it best to avoid the inexpensive or bargain enlargers, off-brand units, and those loaded with dubious features such as automatic focusing. This particular feature is a convenience, but nothing more—its presence or absence will not improve or reduce the quality of the final print, and as the *actual* focal length of an enlarging lens

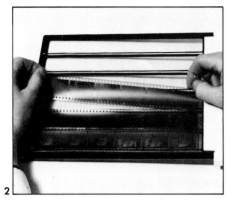

2

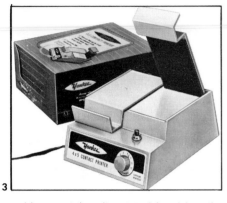

3

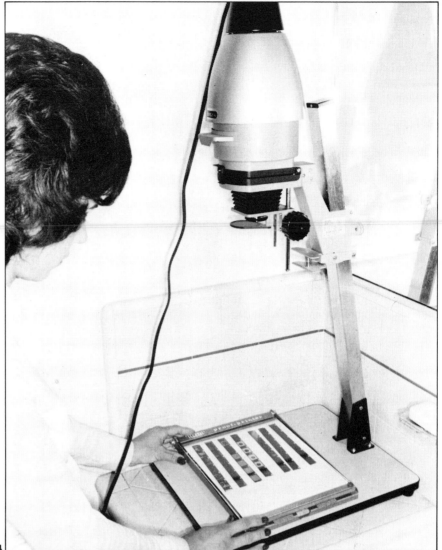

4

seldom matches its *stated* focal length, each cam used in the auto focusing system must be individually tailored to the lens in use, or it will not hold a sharp focus automatically throughout the entire range of magnification.

In general, you'll get the most for your money from those name-brand enlargers which you see nationally advertised. While cute little enlargers such as one manufactured in China are fine as curiosity items for the affluent darkroom worker, they are by no means capable of the results you should both expect and demand from your enlarger. To this point, I've mentioned nothing about the quality of enlarging lenses, and since the optics you use are also a highly critical point in producing good enlargements, they're discussed next.

ENLARGING LENSES

In the '30s, it was not uncommon to find manufacturers of inexpensive cameras offering attachments to turn their product into an enlarger, claiming that your "fine" negative should be enlarged through the same "fine" lens which originally took it. Leitz did it with the Leica and so it sounded logical to owners of Argus and other lesser 35mm cameras.

Perhaps some sincerely believed this, but I have no doubt that the use of the appropriate lens would probably not have improved the quality of the prints that were made in this manner. Yet the success with which the con-

5

6

cept was sold to the photographic public only reaffirmed Barnum's original dictum: There's one born every minute.

To do its job properly, a lens used for enlarging negatives must differ from that used to take pictures in two very important ways. It must be corrected to provide maximum image sharpness at very short distances, and it must also possess as flat a field as possible to deliver sharpness over the entire print area. This lets out lenses designed for picture-taking, since a flat field is of concern only in macro lens design. In

addition, a high degree of correction for chromatic aberration is necessary for visual focusing, and correction for spherical aberration is also required, as the lens is generally focused at its maximum aperture and then stopped down to make the exposure.

Like normal camera lenses, the focal length of the enlarging lens used should be roughly equivalent to the negative diagonal, but because of the short object distance (lens-to-paper), it's possible to use a shorter focal length lens to produce larger images, providing that it's appropriately corrected optically.

Most enlarging lenses are of triplet (three-element) or Tessar designs, but more complex formulas have become common to provide better correction for color work. Lens speed usually ranges between f/2.8 and f/8, but the faster optics are mainly useful in focusing with dense negatives. For best results, an enlarging lens should be stopped down one or two stops from its maximum aperture if you want the sharpest possible image and uniform light distribution. Unlike camera lenses, you can stop an enlarging lens down *too* much—many are subject to a diffraction phenomenon and to focus shift when used at their minimum aperture.

Optical quality should be the prime requirement when selecting an enlarging lens. While you can expect that the higher-priced optics will deliver better pictures than one of the $13.95 variety, this is not always true. There appear to be considerable differences among even the quality lenses. If you buy an enlarger equipped with a lens by its manufacturer, you're sort of stuck with it unless you can afford to replace it with a better one. Thus the quality of the lens should be a determining factor in your enlarger selection. But if the enlarger can be bought without a lens, then you should select a high-quality, name-brand enlarging lens of appropriate focal length that will fit your enlarger. As with the enlarger itself, you should not try to skimp on the lens—why take pictures with an expensive SLR and then enlarge them with a box camera lens?

While you're looking over the field, there are a couple of nonoptical conveniences that you should keep in mind. The aperture numbers should be sufficiently large and legible so they can be easily read under a safelight. They should also be click-stopped, since stopping an enlarging lens down precisely without click-stops can be difficult in the dark. As an option in place of click-stops, consider the preset feature found on some enlarging lenses. This operates just like the preset feature on camera lenses—set one ring at a specified f-stop and then use the other ring to open the aperture while focusing and close it to make the exposure.

CONTACT PRINTER/PROOF PRINTER

Once very popular home darkroom items, the contact printer has virtually disappeared from the scene. The near-dominance of the 110/35mm formats and the emphasis on big prints regardless of negative size have rendered it practically useless. The few remaining commercial units, such as that offered by Yankee Photo Products, are designed for contact printing 4x5-inch negatives.

When contact prints are desired, they can be made by simply placing a clean sheet of plate glass over the negative and a sheet of printing paper to create a sandwich of glass, negative and emulsion side of the paper, in that order. You can also use a printing frame available from most photo stores. Contact prints are best made on the slower contact printing papers since the speed of enlarging paper is often too great for satisfactory results.

Proof printers are very much in vogue today, and are useful in making proof sheets of your negatives for purposes of evaluation and filing. These are available in a variety of styles, but generally amount to a sheet of glass hinged to a foam-lined base. To use a proof printer, a sheet of paper is placed emulsion side up on the base, the negatives are arranged as desired on the paper and the glass top is closed to create a sandwich. Some proof printers have clips or other means of attaching the negative strips to the underside of the glass so that they won't overlap or curl when you close the printer. While you can make proofs using a sheet of plate glass as described for contact printing, the proof printer is far more efficient when more than an occasional proof sheet is required.

SAFELIGHT

The safelight you use for enlarging must provide sufficient illumination to allow you to work efficiently and without eye strain, and it must also be

3

1. This Bogen easel is typical of standard easel design. The two movable arms allow adjustment for prints up to 8x10.

2. Larger units such as this Saunders-Omega easel provide for adjustment of all four borders.

3. Saunders-Omega also offers easels for those who wish to make borderless prints. This type of easel does away with messy gums and sticky tapes used by older borderless easels to hold the paper flat against the easel.

4. The Speed-ez-el by A. J. Ganz is a one-size unit which provides a standard ¼-inch border, and is available in all standard paper sizes.

5. For multiple prints from one negative, Saunders-Omega offers this versatile printing easel.

"safe"—the light it transmits must not affect the sensitized papers with which you're working. Whether or not you have a safelight as described under the section on film developing equipment, you will need one with at least two filters for work with enlarging papers—a light amber (Kodak Filter OC) for black-and-white, and a dark amber (Kodak Filter #10) for color printing.

Safelights are available in a variety of styles and sizes, the least useful of which are those of the traditional acorn or cup design. You should visit a couple of photo stores and look over their safelight selection to find the size and style that will be most useful for your purposes. Some are designed to plug into wall sockets, others are suspended from extension cords, and a number are meant to be wall-mounted or placed on your work counter. You should consider the following points:

1—Does the safelight use interchangeable filters? Are they a standard size? Can they be easily changed without interrupting your routine?

2—Filters deteriorate with age. They also break on occasion. Are additional filters readily available at a fairly reasonable price?

3—Will the safelight provide sufficient illumination for your darkroom? Is the maximum wattage too great, and if so, can smaller wattage bulbs be used in an efficient manner?

4

5

4—Is the safelight bulb a standard one, or does it have a special size base or unusual filament, making it difficult to obtain a replacement bulb on short notice?

5—Can the bulb be changed safely and without interrupting your routine, or does the unit require a home tool kit to get into just to replace the bulb?

6—If you have a permanent darkroom arrangement, you will have need for more than one safelight. Is it possible to standardize on style so that filters and bulbs are interchangeable between units? This will save money and cut down on the number of filters and bulbs that must be stored as replacement units.

TESTING YOUR SAFELIGHT—It's not a bad idea to test a safelight's efficiency to determine if the filter is indeed suitable for the paper you generally use, if you have located it at an adequate distance from your work, or if the bulb is too powerful. Simply exposing a piece of enlarging paper to the safelight illumination for several minutes and then developing it will not really give you a satisfactory answer, since fog caused by a safelight does not always appear on the white border of a print, but just in that area exposed to a white light. Thus, your safelight may be degrading the quality of highlights in your prints without your realizing it.

To properly test your safelight, briefly expose a piece of enlarging paper without a negative in the enlarger—you'll want a medium gray tone when the paper is developed. Now place the exposed paper in your normal work area or beside the developer tray and quickly cover about one-quarter of it with a piece of cardboard. Expose this to safelight illumination for one minute, then move the cardboard to cover one-half of the paper, wait another minute and cover three-quarters of it, exposing this final section for two minutes. You now have a sheet of enlarging paper that contains four test strips, with

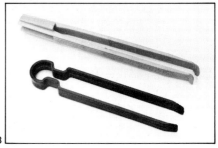

sections exposed for four, two, one and zero minutes.

Develop and fix the sheet of paper, then inspect it under a white light. If the first three-quarters of the paper appears essentially the same in tone and the last quarter is slightly darker, your safelight is O.K. Any difference in tone between the center two strips and the one that remained covered during the exposure to the safelight indicates that your safelight is too close to your paper, provides too much light, or is fitted with the wrong filter for the paper you're using.

PAPER EASEL

This device holds the enlarging paper flat, provides a means of creating a white border around the print if desired, and allows you to shift the position of the paper under the enlarger to print just a portion of a negative if desired. Easels come in two types—fixed and adjustable.

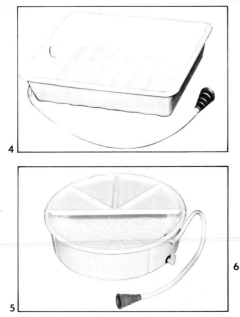

4

5

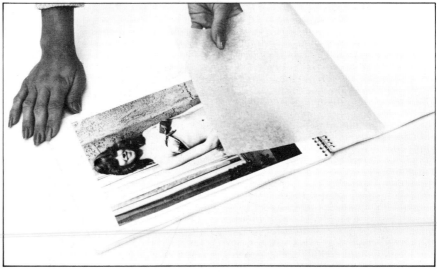

6

1. The Ambico Wave tray is the first significantly different tray design in years. The bottom of the tray is angled so that it can be rocked for easy agitation; solution is poured out through the capped spout on one end, and provisions are molded into the design to hold print tongs and a thermometer without their slipping into the solution. You have to try this one to appreciate it.

2. Standard print trays are offered in various sizes. Look for a ribbed or channeled bottom such as these Arkay trays use. This design makes it easy to slip a print tong under the paper.

3. Print tongs come in a variety of sizes, shapes and tips. The Yankee tong (top) has angled tips, while the Kustom design below it uses a coating on the tips to protect the soft emulsion of wet printing papers from damage.

4-5. Print washers are pretty standard in design for home darkroom use. Two styles by Kustom are shown here.

6. A blotter book is the least expensive, but also the slowest way of drying prints.

7-8. Inexpensive electric print dryers such as these two Arkay units are also fairly standard in design. Some use only one side for drying (7), while others use both sides (8). The latter are called flip-over dryers.

Similar to a picture frame without the glass, the fixed easel is used by simply sliding a piece of enlarging paper of the appropriate size into the channel guides. As some fixed easels accept only one paper size, you must buy a separate one for each paper size you'll use. Other fixed easel designs are divided into sections, with an 8x10 area on one side and three or four smaller standard areas on the back—more convenient from a storage standpoint. The fixed easel is quite handy when you're enlarging to a standard size and want a uniform white border on each photograph.

Adjustable easels are available in a

7

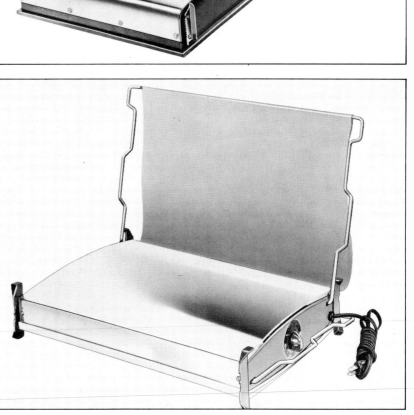

8

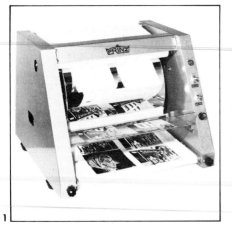

1

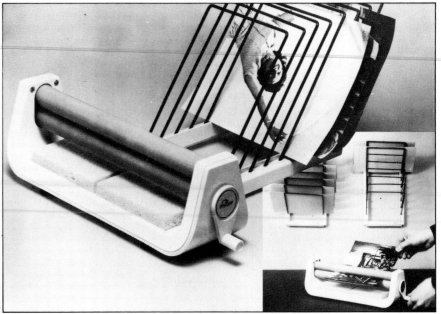

2

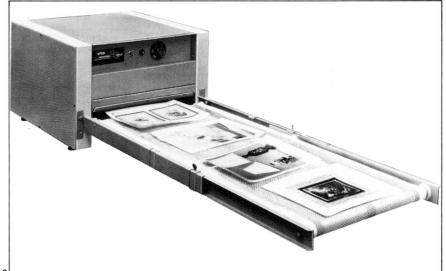

3

variety of maximum paper sizes and use adjustable masking blades that lock as desired. This lets you (1) vary print size/shape from a square to an extremely narrow rectangle, (2) crop to size on the easel in addition to cropping by changing the easel's placement, and (3) use paper of any size/shape between the minimum and maximum accepted by the easel. For the beginner, the 11x14 size is best.

For those who wish to make borderless prints, there are variations in easel design to do so quickly and easily. The adjustable borderless easel uses retaining bars to hold the paper both flat and in perfect register. Vacuum easels come equipped with a small hand vacuum pump and keep the paper in place and flat by means of tiny holes in the vacuum base. Other variations on the borderless theme include easels which use rubber pegs or some form of adhesive.

Want to make multiple prints on a single sheet of 8x10 paper? Multi-size easels are offered that use interchangeable click-stop masks. These are furnished with the easel and permit up to eight wallet-sized prints on each 8x10 sheet. This design allows you to make a test strip quickly, or do volume printing of a single negative in smaller than 8x10 sizes.

TRAYS/PRINT TONGS

Required for processing the enlargements after exposure, you'll need one tray for each solution used. While it's possible to get along with three trays—one each for developer, short-stop and hypo—the meticulous worker will use six—developer, short-stop, first hypo bath, second hypo bath, hypo eliminator and water. The latter serves as a container for prints that are ready to be washed.

Shallow trays work best for developer and short-stop solutions, as prints will be moved through these chemicals quickly. Deep trays are more useful for

hypo, hypo eliminator, and/or water baths, as prints will accumulate in these solutions. The trays should be one size larger than the largest print you generally make to permit easy insertion and removal of the paper without fumbling.

The once-popular hard rubber and porcelain-enameled trays have been replaced by stainless steel and high-impact plastic. While the stainless steel trays are nice if you can afford them, the plastic variety are just as suitable at a far lower price, and will not chip, peel or crack if of good quality. While white or yellow trays are best in terms of visibility, some manufacturers offer trays in red, white and blue for those who like color-coding as a way of remembering which is which. As trays have a tendency to stain, they should be thoroughly cleaned after each use with liquid detergent and hot water to prevent stains from accumulating.

Print tongs act as an extension of your fingers in handling wet prints, keeping your hands clean, dry and free from chemical contamination. For those whose skin is irritated by photo chemistry, the print tong is a virtual necessity. A wide variety of print tongs are available, many of which may well prove less then useful to you. Don't rush out and buy the first set you come across, as you'll probably end up not using them.

To do its job properly, a print tong should satisfy the following requirements. It must:

1—be manufactured of lasting material, impervious to photographic chemicals and staining;

2—be designed for easy, comfortable use without requiring a finger-tiring amount of pressure;

3—have a tip designed to permit easy sorting and selection of a particular sheet of paper from many in a tray

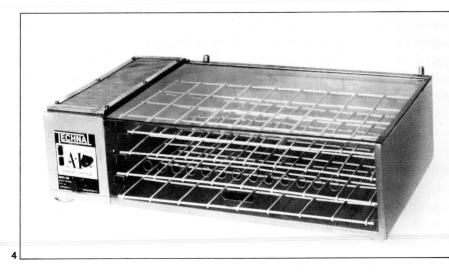

4

6

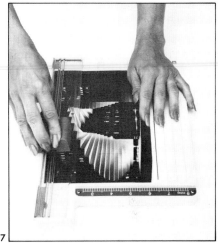

7

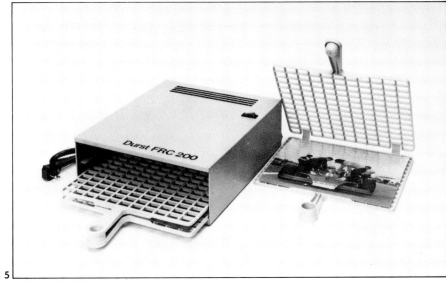

5

1. The Prinz Jet Roto Dryer is ideal if you dry enough prints to make the investment in a drum dryer worthwhile.
2. Falcon Safety Products offers its inexpensive RC Dryer which consists of two rollers to remove excess water and a rack in which the prints can dry.
3. Prinz also offers a motorized RC Dryer. The feeder belt shown is an option which eliminates the hand feeding of wet prints into the unit.
4-5. The Bogen Technal RC Dryer (4) offers still another approach to drying RC prints. Warm filtered air is directed through the racks, drying prints in minutes. A variation on this design is the Durst FRC 200 dryer (5). Prints are loaded on the plastic-coated grids and inserted into the front of the unit, where they are dried by warm recirculated air.
6-7. The newest designs in paper trimmers are represented by the Honeywell-Nikor Safety Trimmer (6) and the Paterson Trimmer (7).

without awkward fumbling or hesitation;

4—grasp and hold one or more wet sheets of photographic paper without slipping;

5—do this without scratching, marring or otherwise damaging the paper surface;

6—have a provision to rest on or against the tray when not in use, without dripping on the counter or slipping into the solution;

7—be color-coded for easy identification under the safelight to prevent chemical bath contamination by using the wrong print tong with the wrong solution.

You should be especially careful in print tong selection if you intend to work with the new color printing and resin-coated photo papers, as these have emulsions with a far greater sensitivity to scratching and tend to be more slippery in nature than standard photo papers. Print tongs that work well with the standard papers will not necessarily be efficient with color or resin-coated papers.

PRINT WASHER/PRINT DRYER

Washing prints is usually done in a manner as inefficient as washing negatives, but there are a larger number of inefficient commercial devices for print washing available. The most popular seems to be the tray siphon device, followed by deep trays that hook to a faucet by means of a flexible hose and

function in a similar manner to the tray siphon. They accept water at one end and eliminate it at the other. Too often, however, the water drain is not located at the bottom of the tray, so prints swirl around on the surface while the hypo permeates the water at the bottom of the tray and remains there.

The most efficient print washers are the stainless steel drums that are perforated and revolve in a deep container of constantly changing water, but these are both large and expensive. Because proper print washing can be difficult in the amateur darkroom, the use of a hypo-eliminator bath before washing is highly recommended.

Towels, blotters and ferrotype plates can be used to air dry the washed prints. You'll get a dull finish with the first two and a mirrorlike or glossy finish with the latter. All of them dry prints very slowly. More efficient than any of these is the electric print dryer, which comes in various sizes and designs. These produce dull finish prints by themselves, or glossy prints when used with ferrotype plates. The ideal way to dry large numbers of prints is with an electric drum dryer. Prints are fed into the dryer and around its drum on a moving belt, coming off completely dried in a matter of minutes. These are large units, costing $200 and up, and require a permanent place in your darkroom. The flip-over electric dryer is better suited to the temporary darkroom worker.

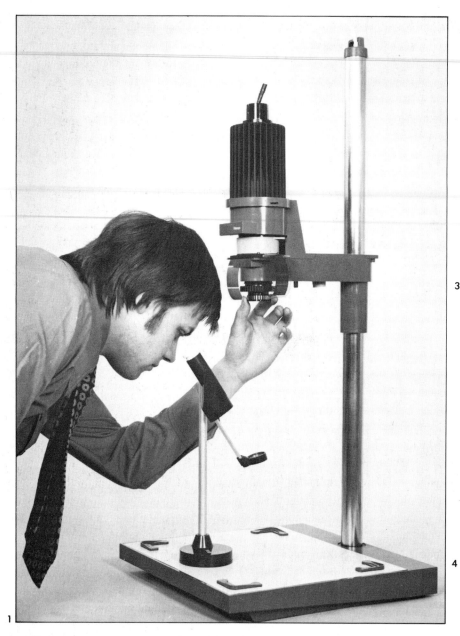

1

3

4

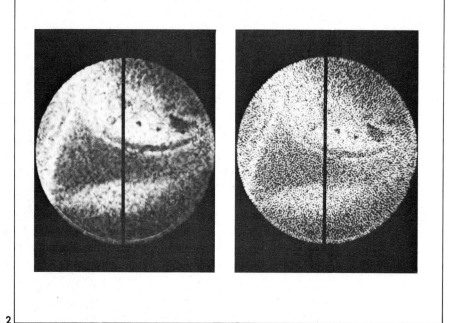

2

Resin-coated papers should not be dried on conventional electric dryers, as they cannot tolerate the heat. Convection dryers that take the form of modular plastic-coated wire racks are the least expensive, but you can buy electric units which dry resin-coated prints by warm forced air. Such dryers are usually used in conjunction with a squeegee or some other device to remove excess water from the print.

PAPER SAFE

As long as it's kept in a drawer or other relatively dark place, you can store sensitized paper right in the box in which it comes, but this makes it inconvenient to use. And should you work with more than one grade or type of paper at a time, there's always the possibility of mixing them up or forgetting to replace the top of the box securely before turning on the room light. Do this a few times and you'll have more than paid for a paper safe.

A more convenient and practical way to store photographic paper where it's available at the touch of your finger,

5

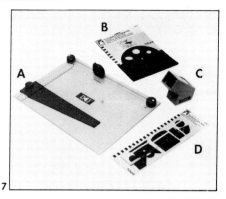

7

1. **Focusing aids which allow you to focus on the grain may be useful to some darkroom workers. The Paterson focuser is shown in use with Paterson enlarger.**

2. **This shows the difference between an out-of-focus grain pattern (left) and one that's sharply in focus (right). This is what you should see through your focusing aid.**

3-4. **Omega offers its Micromega critical focuser (3) and a lower-priced version (4). Both are based on the technique of focusing on the grain of an aerial image from the projected negative.**

5. **Some darkroom addicts prefer the use of a hand magnifying glass over the grain focusing device.**

6. **The Star-D dodging kit comes complete with a handle and various sizes and shapes of dodging attachments.**

7. **Durst offers a paper cutter (a), vignetter kit (b), focus finder (c), and a dodging kit (d)—all items of interest to serious darkroom workers.**

this lightproof container amounts to a small chest-type storage cabinet with roll top door and inside shelves for separating paper by type, grade and size. Paper safes are generally made of plastic these days, although Brumberger still offers its very durable metal unit with a door that closes automatically. As design features are very similar, you can shop by size and price without going wrong.

PAPER TRIMMER

While you can get along without a trimmer, it's a very useful addition to any permanent darkroom facility, especially if you make many prints smaller than 8x10. At one time, it was also a money-saving device, as cutting 4x5 or 5x7 sheets from larger sizes was far less expensive than buying the smaller sheets precut. But manufacturers caught on eventually and current paper price schedules reflect no savings. The primary usefulness of a paper trimmer

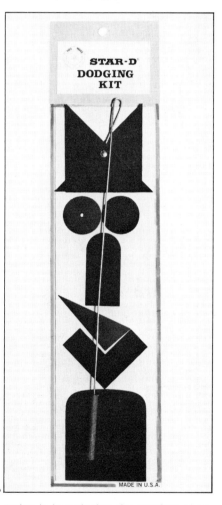

6

today is in reducing the number of paper sizes you must keep on hand. They are, however, quite handy if you do very much print mounting for display, and I'll say more about them in a later chapter.

MISCELLANEOUS ITEMS

In addition to the wastebasket and clean-up materials mentioned under film developing equipment, you'll find several miscellaneous items useful and

perhaps even indispensible for enlarging. The most important is some means of removing dust and lint from negatives before printing. This can take the form of a rubber syringe, blower brush or other such devices discussed at length in the chapter on camera care equipment. I prefer the use of a can of compressed gas to remove loose dust, and a Staticmaster brush for removing stubborn particles without scratching the negative.

Speaking of scratches, you'll find a small jar of petroleum jelly most useful. Applied lightly and uniformly to the back of a scratched negative, this possesses the same refractive index as the base of most films, and thus renders such scratches invisible in the final print. But don't try using it on the film's emulsion since the refractive index differs and it will not work.

Focusing aids come in a variety of types and if you have difficulty in achieving sharp print focus for reasons other than an unsharp negative or enlarging lens, such a device may prove useful, although some photographers I know simply use a powerful magnifying glass. The most efficient focusing aids let you focus on the negative's grain pattern.

Personally, I prefer the use of a Focus Spot. Although no longer available, this special high-contrast pattern on a negative strip was designed to assure corner-to-corner sharpness and is most handy for presetting focus when printing very dense negatives. Of course, if you're stuck without any focusing aid and can't seem to zero in on correct focus for a dense negative, you can always focus on the frame line between two negatives.

I'm positive that you'll come across other small but useful darkroom accessories that will make the hours you spend under a safelight more pleasant and profitable. We'll discuss a few of them when we reach the chapter on making enlargements. Now it's time to look at some of the chemistry and other materials for your darkroom. □

17

All About Developing Film

Whether black-and-white or color, negative or slide, selecting the right film and exposing it properly according to your subject's requirements only puts you a third of the way toward a high-quality image. Just as important is the choice of developer and how you use it to turn the latent image into as good a negative as possible. Many amateurs regard film development with somewhat less importance than it deserves, yet the proper choice and use of a developer or color chemistry is as important to the final print as the proper selection of film and exposure. For that reason, you should understand the process of film development and how it works—without such knowledge, you can hardly expect to make an intelligent decision about developers and the various options open at this point.

THE MYSTIQUE OF DEVELOPMENT

Let's focus on black-and-white film first. Changing a latent image on film into one that is both visible and permanent (called a negative) requires that the exposed film be developed and fixed. This process involves the use of four solutions: (1) a developer to make the image visible, (2) a stop bath to halt the developer's action, (3) a fixer to remove undeveloped silver and make the image permanent, and (4) a wash bath of ordinary water to remove all traces of the fixer.

Today's developers are a far cry from those used by photographers of the last century, yet their basic formulations have not really changed that much. You will find a great variation in the ingredients of various developing formulas, but all contain one or more chemicals which perform the following functions: (1) vehicle or solvent, (2) developing agent, (3) activator or accelerator, (4) preservative, and (5) restrainer. Using different chemicals to perform these functions, or varying their proportions, results in different developing formulas, each of which will produce its own individual results on a given film emulsion. Since it's the *result* that determines the particular developer you should use, let's briefly examine what each of the above does in order to give you a better understanding of why proper developer selection is so important to your negative.

VEHICLE/SOLVENT

Because the chemicals which compose any developer are dissolved in water, this becomes the vehicle which carries the ingredients to the silver bromide crystals in the emulsion where the developer does its work. At the same time, the vehicle causes the emulsion to swell in the same way a solvent would, thus its other name. This swelling action permits the chemicals to reach all of the crystals—without it, those crystals at the bottom of the emulsion would not react to the chemical action of the developer within the necessary timespan.

DEVELOPING AGENT

Hundreds of chemicals are available that will turn the latent image into black metallic particles, but few are able to differentiate between those crystals exposed by light and those not so exposed. Most current developers do not depend on a single developing agent, but combine the effects of two in an effort to retain the best features of both. For example, two of the most commonly used are metol and hydroquinone, both hydrocarbon derivatives from benzene which date from the 1890s.

A rapid worker, metol gives detail to shadow areas and used alone, makes a useful soft-working developer. But combined with the slower-acting hydroquinone, which provides a good tonal range and the necessary highlight density, the result is a negative containing a good tonal range, good highlight density and good shadow detail. Interestingly enough, when these two are combined, they produce a far better negative than either used by itself. It's not unfair to say that the hydroquinone produces the negative and that metol adds the quality.

A third commonly used developing agent is Phenidone. This is a proprietary agent discovered by Ilford and is found primarily in Ilford developers. Although not a benzene derivative, it has similar properties to those of metol and is far more efficient in activating hydroquinone, since about 1/10 as much will do the same job. When used with hydroquinone, it produces lower contrast and tends to give a higher fog level than metol, but it also produces less skin irritation for those sensitive to chemicals. Unlike metol, it is seldom used alone.

ACTIVATOR/ACCELERATOR

In order to trigger the action of the developing agents, the vehicle must

1. Unless you understand what photographic chemistry does and how it works, picking the right developer can pose a problem.
2. Producing salon quality prints such as this one by Shirley I. Fisher requires more than a casual acquaintance with processing chemistry and printing papers.

Kodak Packaged Developer	Developing Times (in Minutes)—Small Tank*				
	65 F	68 F	70 F	72 F	75 F
PANATOMIC-X Film					
D-76	6	5	4½	4¼	3¾
D-76 (1:1)	8	7	6½	6	5
MICRODOL-X	8	7	6½	6	5
MICRODOL-X (1:3)†	—	—	11	10	8½
VERICHROME Pan Film					
D-76	8	7	5½	5	4½
D-76 (1:1)	11	9	8	7	6
MICRODOL-X	10	9	8	7	6
MICRODOL-X (1:3)	15	14	13	12	11
PLUS-X Pan Film					
D-76	6½	5½	5	4½	3¾
D-76 (1:1)	8	7	6½	6	5
MIRCODOL-X	8	7	6½	6	5½
MICRODOL-X (1:3)	—	—	11	10	9½
TRI-X Pan Film					
D-76	9	8	7½	6½	5½
D-76 (1:1)	11	10	9½	9	8
MICRODOL-X	11	10	9½	9	8
MICRODOL-X (1:3)	—	—	15	14	13
DK-50 (1:1)	7	6	5½	5	4½

*Agitation at 30-second intervals throughout development. Primary recommendations are in bold type.
†For greatest sharpness (see developer instructions).

FIGURE A

contain an alkali, such as sodium carbonate. The greater the alkali content, the more rapidly the developing agents will work. For this reason, the alkali or activator is sometimes referred to as an accelerator.

PRESERVATIVE

At this point, we have a functioning developer, but one which will oxidize rapidly, as developing agents are highly susceptible to oxygen in both the vehicle and the air. Thus, our developer will quickly turn brown and lose its ability to work on the exposed silver. To prevent this, a preservative such as sodium sulphite or potassium metabisulphite is added to prevent interaction of oxygen with the developing agent(s). When formulating your own developing chemistry, the preservative must be added *before* the accelerator if you are to prevent oxidation from taking place.

RESTRAINER

As stated earlier, few of the potential developing agents can differentiate between those silver bromide crystals exposed to light and those unexposed, and even the ones that can discriminate in this respect do not do so perfectly. As development is a function of the emulsion, the time and temperature, agitation and the chemical make-up of the developer, we call it a ''rate'' process. Leave a piece of exposed film in a developer long enough (rate) and *all* of the silver bromide crystals will turn black.

As some unexposed crystals will begin to turn even during the normal developing time, the result is an overall gray density called base fog. Since this fog is undesirable, its build-up is prevented by the use of a restrainer, usually potassium bromide, which also happens to be a by-product of the process of development. Organic restrainers such as benzotriazole are used with Phenidone-base developers, as the quantity of potassium bromide necessary to prevent fog formation is sufficient to cause staining. Since organic restrainers are very potent, they often result in a loss of emulsion speed.

WHY SO MANY DEVELOPERS?

If that's all there is to it, why is the market crowded with so many different developers? Simple—just as there's no universal film emulsion suitable for all occasions, there is no single developer that will produce the many variations in negative or print characteristics that photographers demand on different occasions. No single chemical formulation can deliver a full tonal scale, high maximum density, low maximum density, short development times, maximum energy for forced development, etc. Thus while the many developers available all use certain basic chemicals to perform the necessary functions described above, each one is designed to develop negatives according to the special properties assigned to its use.

The advice is often passed on to pick one developer and stick with it through thick and thin, on the assumption that if you can predict what it will do, you'll have no difficulties. While this is sound advice for the rank beginner, nothing could be less useful to the photographer interested in obtaining the best negatives his expensive equipment can deliver. To help you further understand the necessity for discrimination in picking developers, let's move one step further and look at those factors which affect what you get with any developer.

FACTORS AFFECTING FILM DEVELOPMENT

As mentioned earlier, development is a rate process. Regardless of the formula used, its action is dependent upon several factors.

TIME/TEMPERATURE—Because the duration of the development process is interrelated to the temperature of the solution, the manufacturer of a particular developer will specify an optimum length of development at a given temperature. Variations in duration from that specified for a given temperature will affect both negative contrast and density. Warmer than specified temperatures will speed up the rate of development, increase density and contrast, and cause excessive negative granularity. Temperatures colder than specified will slow developer action to its minimum. The normal temperature for all development is 68°F.

Because it may not be possible to adjust the temperature of the developer to exactly the recommended temperature, developer (and film) manufacturers will usually make available a series of recommended times and temperatures, any one of which will produce results comparable to development at the recommended 68°F. temperature. These are known as time/temperature development charts (Figure A).

You should not attempt development

1. This time/temperature table is provided by Eastman Kodak for use with Kodak films and developers. Other film and photo chemistry manufacturers provide similar data for their products.

2-3. Uneven development can result from the lack of, or improper agitation (2). In some cases, it may be possible to hide such negative defects by using techniques such as diffusion (3) in printing.

at temperatures other than those recommended, as problems can arise. For example, hydroquinone is not very active at temperatures below 60°F. and will result in a lack of negative contrast; at temperatures above 80°F., the film emulsion can soften sufficiently to reticulate (wrinkle) or receive other damage. While some color processes depend on such high temperatures, you should be careful when handling the film to prevent unnecessary damage to the emulsion surface.

DILUTION/EXHAUSTION—The strength of the developer affects the process of development. Some developers are designed to be used full strength as mixed; others can be used either at full strength or diluted with water. When used in a diluted form, the duration of development must be increased as specified by the manufacturer.

Each time a developer solution is used, the level of its chemical activity decreases for two reasons—its developing agents are gradually used up and by-products accumulate (such as potassium bromide) that act as additional restrainers. To some extent, it's possible to compensate for this decreased activity by lengthening the duration of development. A more satisfactory method of compensation is called replenishment—the periodic addition of a small quantity of highly concentrated developer to the original solution.

AGITATION—Probably no aspect of film development is as misunderstood as agitation. Because of the chemical activity that takes place when developer contacts the film emulsion, it is necessary to periodically bring fresh developer to the film's surface. This is accomplished by moving the solution around in the tank at recommended intervals.

Improper agitation affects the rate of development, negative contrast and uniformity of development. If you do not agitate the film at all, you'll get uneven density across the negatives because of a phenomenon known as "bromide drag." As the developer working on highlight areas exhausts itself very rapidly, it releases a relatively large amount of potassium bromide (a restrainer). This is slightly heavier than the rest of the developer and so it sinks to the bottom of the tank, but in doing so, acts upon other areas of the film over which it passes. This additional and unneeded restraining action of the excess bromide causes stripes of unequal density for which there is no known remedy.

Excessive agitation speeds up development, increasing negative contrast and overall density. This results in increased granularity and a reduction in acutance or edge sharpness. And if constant agitation is carried out with the same repetitive motion, streaking may also occur. Figure B is a checklist of other common side effects that may result from improper agitation.

The situation is further confused for many amateurs because manufacturers of different developers recommend different methods of agitation. Kodak specifies five-second agitation in a circular motion every 30 seconds, while Ilford recommends 10-second agitation every minute. Does this mean that you should agitate your film one way in a Kodak developer, and in another when using Ilford? Not really—the answer lies in formulating a single method for yourself and being consistent in its use. You may settle upon five-second agitation every 30 seconds, or 10-seconds every minute; you may agitate in a circular motion or invert the tank. The secret to correct agitation is in not mixing methods or intervals—pick one and stick by it.

TYPES OF FILM DEVELOPERS

As mentioned earlier, there is no "universal" developer that will work its miracle precisely as desired under all circumstances—each formulation is designed to provide specific and measurable results. For this reason, developers can be classified in one of several general categories.

STANDARD/FINE-GRAIN DEVELOPERS—These are the basic film developers, which produce negatives with moderately fine grain, a good tonal range with sufficient highlight and shadow detail, and normal contrast. Such developers can be divided into two general subgroups—the metol/hydroquinone or MQ developers such as Kodak DK-50 and D-70, and the Phenidone/hydroquinone or PQ developers like Ilford Microphen.

EXTRA-FINE-GRAIN DEVELOPERS—Advances in film coating and emulsion techniques have made it possible to produce sharp negatives with fine grain using the standard developers, thus the extra-fine-grain solutions are somewhat less popular today. While they deliver a

1

better grain structure with lower contrast, these have a couple of important liabilities. Because they achieve the finer grain structure by dissolving the edges of the silver particles to reduce their size, extra fine grain developers tend to result in a loss of image sharpness. Those interested primarily in sharpness rather than grain will find this drawback of concern.

A second liability is the slight loss of emulsion speed. While you'll occasionally encounter an extra-fine-grain developer for which its manufacturer claims an *actual increase* in film speed, such claims should be taken with a grain of salt. Nowhere are there more disputed and conflicting opinions and claims than in the area of what an extra-fine-grain developer will or will not do. If you find this difficult to understand, bear in mind that photographic scientists do not completely understand the process of development. It's a situation much like trying to explain electricity—it's there and it works, but precisely why and how is still theoretically in dispute.

For example, grain was long believed to be the major culprit in creating an unsharp image, but this fault is now credited to a lack of acuity or apparent edge sharpness between contrasting areas. This change in theoretical base has given rise to a whole new group of developers, to be discussed next. Until

recently, it was popular to explain a more visible grain pattern as the result of silver particles in the emulsion "clumping" together as a result of the violent chemical effect of development, but this physical "clumping" has been abandoned recently for the newer concept of optical clumping—a visual effect caused by the depth of the silver that constitutes the image. Yet extra-fine-grain developers like Kodak Microdol-X and Ilford Perceptol have their own admirers who swear by the results and so these developers are not likely to pass from the scene as long as such controversy continues.

ACUTANCE DEVELOPERS—Primarily formulated abroad, these are "surface active" or "compensating" developers which work only on the surface of the emulsion, instead of developing an image throughout its entire depth. The theory states that the deeper development takes place within an emulsion, the more diffused the image becomes, with the diffusion causing a lack of image sharpness. Thus, if only the surface of the emulsion is developed, this diffusion is held to a minimum and apparent sharpness of the image is increased. Actually, it is not sharpness that is increased, but rather the loss of sharpness is minimized when compared with that provided by other developers (Figure C).

1. Alternating light and dark striations are another form of negative defect caused by improper agitation. In this case, there is no remedy or way in which the defect can be hidden.

2. Litho developers are used with high-contrast films like Kodalith, where a high degree of contrast is desired between the black and white areas, as in this tone line print by Shirley I. Fisher.

3. This diagram illustrates how a compensating developer differs in its manner of working. As light penetrates to the film base, it spreads out as shown in (A). With a standard developer, the developed image is thicker and has a "coarser" outline. A compensating developer acts only on the emulsion surface (B). This produces a sharper image, and one that is more clearly defined. (Courtesy, Beseler Photo Marketing)

Another reason for the apparent increase in image sharpness when using an acutance developer is the so-called "adjacency effect." This states that developer will move from an area where it has little work to do to an adjacent one where there is much work to do. Thus, developer moves from the edge of a shadow area to the edge of a highlight area. By this reasoning, the highlight edge is developed to a greater degree, and the restrainer released by this activity acts to further hold back development of the shadow edge, resulting in a net increase in apparent edge sharpness because of the visual contrast created by the slightly underdeveloped/slightly overdeveloped boundary between the two areas. The Ultra-Fin formulas manufactured by Tetenal in West Germany and marketed in this country by Beseler are representative of high-acutance developers.

HIGH-CONTRAST DEVELOPERS— These special developers are formulated to provide the highest possible contrast between light and dark areas, and are used mainly with high-contrast emulsions for copying of line drawings and graphic arts work. Also known as "litho" developers, they are generally caustic-hydroquinone in nature— hydroquinone used as the sole developing agent with a greatly increased concentration of accelerator, preservative and restrainer.

To prevent rapid deterioration of such formulas, some litho developers are mixed and stored as two separate solutions, to be combined just before use. The "A" solution contains all the chemistry except for the accelerator, which primarily constitutes the "B" solution. Kodak Kodalith and D-8 developers are typical of the very-high-contrast developers, while Kodak D-11 and D-19 provide a more moderate level of high contrast—each has different applications and uses.

MONOBATH DEVELOPERS—These combine the separate processes of development and fixation in a single solution, eliminating the necessity of precise timing and reducing the effects of temperature and agitation to a minimum. Monobath formulas appear and disappear with regularity, seldom lasting long enough on the market to gain much acceptance, as they're totally inflexible—there's no way to alter the development rate to accommodate difference in film types, exposure, subject contrast, etc.

These are the major types of developer commonly used today. It's fair to assume that among the great variety of commercially prepared developers available, you'll find one or more suitable to your needs. If not, there are literally volumes of formulas available by which you can create your own particular developer.

PREPARED DEVELOPERS—Manufacturers package developers in various sizes, according to the photographer's needs. Some are offered in liquid form, either for use full-strength or after dilution with water. Most also come in powdered form, to which the user adds a specified quantity of water to prepare a "stock" solution, which may either be used as is, or further diluted with

2

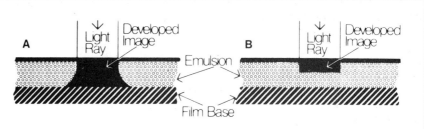

FIGURE C

water to make a "working" solution.

Liquid formulas are more expensive than the powdered ones, and small-quantity packaging costs more per ounce than large ones. Prepared chemicals have the advantages of uniformity and convenience and do away with the necessity of storing and compounding a wide variety of chemicals to produce a given formula.

USER-COMPOUNDED DEVELOPERS— Those who want or need special formulations not available in commercial packaging, or who wish to experiment with one or more of the exotic developer formulas, may wish to invest in darkroom scales and the necessary containers and measuring devices for storing and mixing bulk chemicals into personalized formulations. With these possible exceptions, compounding your own developers today offers no advantages, convenience or economy over buying prepared developers ready for immediate use.

MIXING POWDERED DEVELOPERS PROPERLY—There's more to film developing than simply mixing up the developer, pouring it into the tank, agitating the film as specified and then pouring it out when the recommended time interval is up—and it all begins with properly mixing your developer. Some will question what could be simpler than adding a premeasured quantity of powders to a specified quantity of water. For openers, the *kind* of water used is important Despite the fact that tap water is safe to drink, it may not be sufficiently *clean* to use as a developer vehicle unless filtered first. There may be sand, grit or chemical buildup from inside the water pipes—all minute particles swirling around in your graduate. In hard water areas, there will be quantities of mineral deposits in the water. Drop any or all of this stuff on a dry emulsion and you won't have a chance of getting a clean negative.

If you draw water through an aerated

attachment on your faucet or filter, you'll have all kinds of air bubbles that only time will break up. Should you continue mixing the developer at this point, you're actually mixing in a contaminant (air) which will begin oxidizing the developer even before it's used. The alternatives are two-fold—wait until the bubbles all disappear, or remove the air by boiling the water.

Many powdered developers are packaged in separate containers, with instructions to mix one package into the water *thoroughly* before adding the other. To assure that the powder will dissolve completely, the water must be at a specified temperature. If the first package is not thoroughly mixed before adding the second one, you can end up with small lumps of undissolved powder settled at the bottom of the container. These must be crushed up with the stirring rod and those too small to be crushed should be removed by straining. Otherwise, you'll pour contamination into the tank in the form of undissolved concentrate—highly active chemical lumps—which may dissolve during agitation, with varied and unpredictable results.

If a sufficient quantity of powder remains undissolved and settled at the bottom of the container, the developer may not be strong enough to fully develop the film within the alotted time, and you'll end up with underdeveloped negatives and no clue as to why. For this reason, it's always a good idea to shake the bottle of solution slightly before use, even if you use the utmost care in preparing your stock solution. Developer which is used time after time gradually acquires a number of byproducts of the process of development which are heavier than the other chemicals in the vehicle. This can upset the uniformity of results, especially if you should use some of the newer types of chemical containers, which use spigots or draw spouts to remove developer for use from the bottom of the container. Don't take chances—shake your bottle to keep everything in solution.

REPLENISH OR DISCARD?—Developers gradually lose their potency. This is caused by repeated use to process films and/or by oxidation from exposure to air, both in use and while stored. The oxidizing effect of air can be minimized by mixing a sufficient quantity of developer at one time to fill a specific container, and keeping it tightly sealed, and by using a container from which air can be removed. This

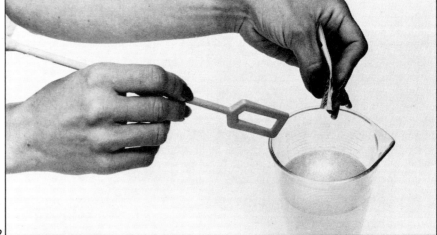

may be done by squeezing plastic bottles or by adding marbles or other small pellets to offset the air space in glass containers which are not full.

The gradual decline in strength caused by reuse can be offset by extending the duration of developer each time the solution is used, but a more accurate method of maintaining its potency is by periodic replenishment. The developer manufacturer will specify the exact replenishment method, interval and rate; the replenisher may be a special solution, as with Kodak Microdol-X, or simply a concentrate of the original solution. This method is preferred by the cost-conscious photographer, as it allows the maximum

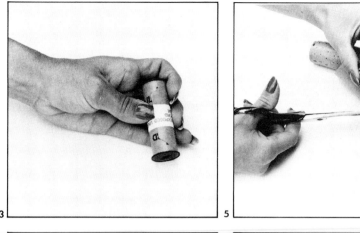

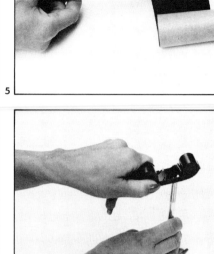

utilization of the developer.

If you use the replenishment method, you should make a notation of the date you mixed the developer and keep an accurate record of the number of films developed so that you can replenish the solution *before* it is exhausted, and discard it when appropriate. This will remove much of the uncertainty surrounding whether or not the solution is still good, or should be discarded.

THE STOP BATH

Once the development time is over, there must be some way of halting the process, or it will simply continue. Because developer is an alkaline solution, the most effective means is to treat the film to a slightly acidic solution or stop bath, as this will neutralize the alkalis in the developer. The most common stop bath used is a solution of acetic acid diluted in water.

When developer is poured out of the tank and replaced with stop bath, the film should be agitated thoroughly—agitation stops development immediately and evenly, preventing any possibility of streaking. Stop bath can be purchased already mixed, or you can buy acetic acid in bulk and mix your own. If you do so, be certain that the proportions are correct, because too strong a stop bath may affect the apparent granularity of a negative be-

1. A shower cabinet is one of the best home drying areas for those without a darkroom since it usually contains little dust. A squeegee should be used to remove excess water and prevent water spots from forming as the film dries.
2. Prepared chemicals are mixed by adding the contents of the package to a specified quantity of water. A stirring paddle is handy for breaking up any lumps and assuring that the powder is totally dissolved before use.
3-5. To prepare roll film for loading on a developing tank reel, work in total darkness and break the paper seal with your thumbnail (3). Unspool and separate the film from the paper backing as shown in (4) to avoid fingerprints. Cut the tape which holds the film to the paper backing (5). If scissors are not handy, the tape can be torn in two, but you should work slowly to prevent static electricity from fogging the film.
6. Film is removed from a 110 cartridge by poking a pencil through the cartridge opening. This pushes the film up where it can be grasped by the fingers and withdrawn from the cartridge. To unload a 126 cartridge, it must first be snapped in half.

cause of the immediate change from alkaline to acid on the film surface.

Glacial acetic acid is far stronger (99 percent) than the 28-percent solution used in stop baths, and must be mixed differently if used. To mix a stop bath from 28-percent acetic acid, add 1½ ounces to 32 ounces of water. If glacial acetic acid is used, it should be reduced to a 28-percent solution by

adding three parts of glacial acetic acid to eight parts of water, then this can be used as above—1½ ounces to 32 ounces of water. When mixing acetic acid with water, you should always pour the acid into the water—doing it the other way can result in spattering and possible burns on the skin, especially when reducing glacial acetic acid to a 28-percent solution.

You might want to use an indicator stop bath. These contain a dye that changes color as the stop bath nears exhaustion. Under an amber safelight, the indicator stop bath will appear clear when fresh, but turns dark as its acidic properties diminish.

Some photographers omit the stop bath, using a water rinse instead between development and fixing, but this is a very inefficient practice for several reasons. Water slows down the action of the developing agents, but does not stop it completely—it remains for the fixer to completely halt development. This puts an undue strain on the fixing solution, as the alkalinity of the developer contaminates the acidic properties of the fixer, prematurely weakening it.

There is also the possibility of image streaking due to development of the film continuing at uneven rates during the water rinse. Omitting the stop bath in favor of a water rinse may also cause heavily used fixer to react with the developing agents, precipitating the silver content of the fixer out on the film and resulting in a surface stain called dichroic fog. Prints which are not treated to a stop bath between developer and fixer are likely to stain while in the fixer.

Thus, the stop bath performs several important functions. It halts the process of development quickly and evenly, it prolongs the useful life of the fixer by acting as a chemical buffer between the alkaline developer and acid fixer, and it prevents the formation of dichroic fog, or negative staining.

FIXER/HYPO

Once the film has passed through the development and stop bath phases, it now carries a photographic image, but one that is not yet permanent, as the unexposed silver which remains in the emulsion is still light-sensitive, and will turn black when exposed to light unless removed. To do this, a fixing or hypo bath is used to remove the unwanted silver by making it soluble. This process is often called ''fixing'' or ''clearing'' the negative. Like developer, a fixing bath contains various ingredients which perform specific func-

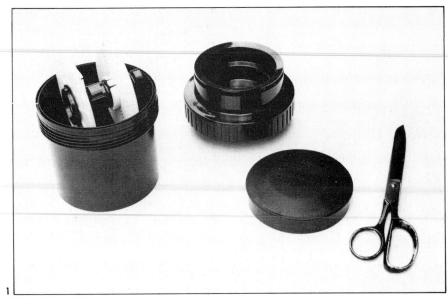

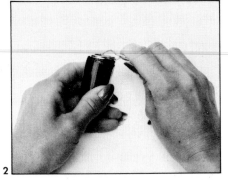

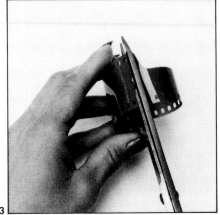

tions. Water is again used as the vehicle or solvent to carry the fixing action to the emulsion. To the water is added the following:

DISSOLVER—A thiosulfate is used to dissolve the unexposed and undeveloped silver. Standard fixing baths use sodium thiosulfate (also known as hypo, hence its name), while rapid fixers depend upon ammonium thiosulfate.

ACCELERATOR—While developing agents require an alkali in which to do their job, thiosulfates need an acid to promote their action. Acetic acid is generally used and potassium metabisulphite may be added to quickly neutralize any alkalinity carried over from the developer.

PRESERVATIVE—Like developer, fixer requires a preservative. This is used to retard the formation of sulfur and prevent the acid from decomposing the thiosulfate. The same sodium sulfite used in developers is added to fixers for this purpose.

BUFFER—Sludge is a by-product of the fixing process and if allowed to form unchecked, will quickly destroy the fixer's power. Boric acid is used in many fixers as a buffer to prevent sludge formation and increase the hardening power of the solution.

HARDENER—Because the soft, swollen gelatin is very prone to injury from handling at this stage, potassium alum is used to shrink the emulsion back to a compact, hard state. This minimizes the possibility of damage to the emulsion during the rest of the processing cycle, as well as once the emulsion is finally dry.

PROPER FIXING—Just as fixer is a rather complex chemical formulation,
its use is not as casual as many amateurs tend to think. While the manufacturer will state that a negative should be fixed only for a period twice as long as it takes to clear the film, excessive fixing will result in a deterioration of the image. When film or a print is left in the fixing bath too long, the exposed and developed silver that forms the image will begin to dissolve, causing a loss of fine shadow detail in negatives and highlight detail in prints. Negatives loaded with fixer also require a far longer wash time to remove the contamination. Insufficient fixing does not fully prepare the unexposed, undeveloped silver for removal from the emulsion and it will remain there regardless of the duration of washing. Such residual silver compounds will eventually decompose, forming the yellowish stain that's often found on many old negatives and prints.

Experienced darkroom workers will use a two-bath system of fixing for both negatives and prints. The first bath is used for a period of three to five minutes and then the film/print is transferred to the second bath where it remains for an equivalent length of time. When the first bath exhibits signs of near-exhaustion (you can check this with a commercial hypo test solution), it is thrown out and replaced by the second bath, with a new second bath mixed from fresh fixer.

HYPO ELIMINATOR AND WASHING

Once the film has been completely developed and fixed, it carries a permanent silver image, but the products of fixing must be removed as completely as possible to assure that the image remains stable and permanent. The careful darkroom worker will use a hypo eliminator bath before washing

1-2. To prepare for film loading, separate the developing tank as shown and place a pair of scissors to the right before turning off the room light (1). Now use a bottle opener to pry the end from crimped 35mm cartridges, such as Kodak uses (2). With noncrimped cartridges, a sharp rap of the cartridge spool on a hard surface will pop the end off.
3. Cut the leader tongue with scissors. You want a nice even cut, as jagged edges can scratch the film as it is spooled onto the developing reel.
4. Slide the end of the film into the reel's loading grooves and then work the film onto the reel by its edges.
5. Just before reaching the end of the film, use the scissors to cut the film from the spool.
6. Insert the loaded reel into the developing tank, replace the tank cover securely, and you can turn on the room lights.

the negative/print. This removes much of the fixer from the emulsion and thus shortens the length of the wash bath necessary.

The normal length of the wash bath depends upon the water temperature and its rate of flow. The cooler the water, or slower its rate of flow, the longer the time required to assure that as much fixer as possible is removed. Complete removal of fixer that has entered the paper base of prints is next to impossible, but the use of a hypo eliminator solution will assure that the remaining amount will not have an adverse chemical effect at a later point in time. This is very important to those who wish archival quality, where the image will last longer than its base.

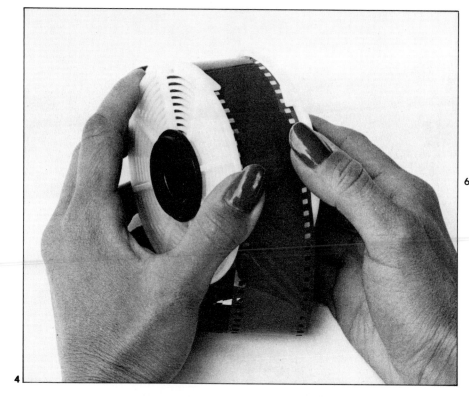

WETTING AGENTS AND DRYING

After the film has been washed, it must be dried in as dust-free an area as possible. Proper drying is as important as any other step in the development process. If water droplets are left on the surface of the film when drying starts, there is a differential shrinkage of the emulsion, resulting in small circular spots on the emulsion, and chemical waste deposits from the water may leave a whitish deposit on the back of the film.

One way to promote rapid, even drying is by removing the water droplets with a viscose sponge, chamois or film squeegee. Each will do the job, but must be used with considerable caution as their use involves a physical pressure on the surface of the film. A tiny speck of dirt from the wiper or an equally tiny granule from the wash water can cause scratches on your negatives that will be impossible to repair. Some photographers bypass the use of these devices, preferring instead to use their wet fingers as a squeegee. This has an equal disadvantage in that natural skin oils may be deposited on the surface of the film, leaving a smudge that's difficult to remove once the surface is dry.

The most efficient and effective way to promote rapid, even drying without risking physical damage to the film is the use of a wetting agent, such as Kodak Photo-Flo. A post-wash treatment in a wetting agent breaks down the surface tension of water, causing it

to run off freely instead of collecting in spots. Other solutions such as Yankee Instant Film Dryer operate on the same principle of evaporation once used by hurried press photographers who dunked their negatives in rubbing alcohol for a fast dry before printing—the chemical displaces the water in the emulsion and then evaporates very quickly, leaving the emulsion hard and dry in only a fraction of the time normally required for adequate drying.

COLOR FILM CHEMISTRY

To this point, I've discussed the chemistry of development in terms of black-and-white film only. Now let's take a quick look at what's involved in turning your color films into negatives or slides.

NEGATIVE COLOR FILM PROCESSING—Current negative or color print films primarily use C-41 chemistry, although GAF Color Print Film still utilizes the older C-22 process. All of the necessary chemicals are provided in kit form, either by the film manufacturer or by such independent companies as Unicolor and Beseler. While the chemicals and sequence in which they are

used are basically the same, the length of time in each solution may differ from one manufacturer's chemistry to another.

The color developer is used first, followed by a water rinse, the bleach, another rinse and fixation. Some combine the bleach and fixing steps into a single bleach/fix bath, which reduces the total processing time considerably. After a final wash, a stabilizer bath is used as a safeguard to ensure image permanence.

REVERSAL PROCESSING—Color slide film is more complicated to develop (GAF slide films require 14 wet steps) and takes approximately one hour to complete (except the new Kodak E-6 process). While GAF film has its own process and chemistry, all other transparency films available for home processing use the Kodak E-4 or E-6 process. The sole exception is Kodak Ektachrome Professional film, available in roll or sheet film sizes only. This is an E-3 process.

The basic difference between the E-3 and E-4/E-6 processes lies in the method of image reversal. The E-4/E-6 emulsions are reversed chemically for consistent results. With the E-3 process, reversal is accomplished by a physical reexposure of the film after the first developer, stop bath and rinse have been used. This is done by exposing the film for a given time to a specific light source at a recommended distance. Inconsistencies in these three factors and their application can lead to differences in the processed slides from one roll to another. Whether reexposure is chemical or physical in nature, the film is then treated to a second or color developer (the first developer produces a black-and-white image), bleach-fix, wash and stabilization prior to hanging the film up to dry.

While reversal is achieved by chemical fogging in the color developer, a reversal bath is used between the two developers in the E-6 process. The total wet processing time of E-6 films is 50 percent shorter than that of the E-3

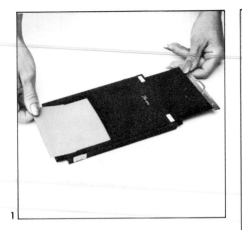

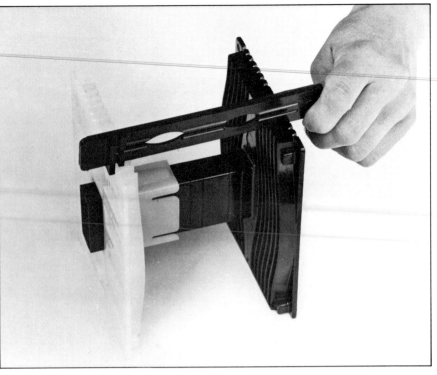

process. This was accomplished by designing the chemistry to function at a much higher temperature (100.4 ± 0.5°F.) than either the GAF (75 ± 0.5°F.) or E-4 (85 ± 0.5°F.) chemistry. Processing time was further reduced by the use of a hardened film emulsion to withstand the higher processing temperature, as this permits elimination of the prehardener/neutralizer steps of the E-4 process.

DEVELOPING YOUR OWN FILM

To develop your black-and-white film, you'll need the following equipment and chemicals:

1—A developing tank which accepts your film size.

2—A darkroom thermometer.

3—A graduate or other measuring container.

4—A timer, clock or watch with a sweep second hand.

5—A pair of film clips for each film.

6—Developer, stop bath, fixer, hypo eliminator and wetting bath solutions.

LOADING THE TANK—To load your tank most efficiently, remove the lid and reel, placing them beside the tank on the counter in front of you. If the reel is adjustable, make certain that it's set to the proper width to accept your film. Place a pair of scissors to the right of the tank lid, then turn out the room lights.

With roll film, break the paper seal and unroll the protective backing until you feel the end of the film. Handling it only by the edges, continue to unroll the film and backing paper, letting the paper curl into one roll and the film into another. When you reach the strip of adhesive holding the two together, carefully remove it and let the paper and spool fall to the floor. The adhesive strip can be pulled from the film, cut with the scissors or carefully torn in half between the film and paper, depending upon which method is easiest for you. If peeled or torn, do so very slowly to prevent static electricity that

can cause fog markings to appear on the last frame or two. Feed one end of the film into the entrance flanges of the reel and work it in place according to the design of your reel (see the chapter on darkroom equipment), touching only the edges.

The 110/126 cartridge films are loaded in the same manner once the film has been removed from the cartridge. In the case of 126, the cartridge

1. To unload a sheet film holder, withdraw the dark slide as shown and fold down the bottom. Grasp the sheet carefully by one corner and pull it carefully from the holder.

2. The Yankee cut film tank uses the loading bar design shown. As each sheet is loaded, the bar is moved until its teeth click into the next notch on the top of the "reel." This indicates that it is properly positioned to load the next sheet.

3. The sheet film is inserted into the loading bar as shown. It will enter the correct film channels in such a way as to prevent the insertion of two sheets in the same channel.

4. An accurate thermometer should be used to check the developer temperature before pouring the chemical into the tank. If necessary, readjust the temperature until it is correct. This Beseler dial-type color thermometer is ideal for both black-and-white and color processing, as it can be calibrated to within ½°F.

is broken open; with 110, the film and paper backing are withdrawn together without breaking the cartridge—unless the paper backing has been completely wound into the cartridge. Incidentally, 110 film is not attached to the paper backing, but 126 is.

If developing 35mm film, you'll need a can opener (one that punches triangular holes in pop cans) to remove the crimped end of Kodak cartridges; most other factory-loaded cartridges can be opened by sharply rapping the spool end against the counter top. Remove the spool of film and cut off the tongued leader with the scissors. Insert the end of the film into the reel entrance and feed the film from the spool onto the reel, again according to reel design. As you approach the end of

5

7

6

9

8

the film, slowly tear it from the adhesive strip attaching it to the spool, or cut it with the scissors just before the tape. If you cut it, cut close to the tape to avoid damaging the final frame on the film.

Sheet films are removed from their holders for developing by pulling the holder slides out a couple of inches. This allows the bottom edge of the holder to be folded out flat and provides access to the film inside. Grasping the film sheet by its end, slowly withdraw it from the holder grooves and insert in a film hanger of the appropriate size, or slip into the proper grooves in the cut-film rack if using a tank like the Yankee Agitank. You can develop one or two sheets with a standard reel tank if necessary, as long as the sheets do not overlap. Trying to develop more than a couple of sheets in this way will inevitably lead to problems with overlap, ruining portions of both sheets—use the proper developing device instead.

Once the film has been loaded correctly onto the reel, replace it in the tank, secure the cover or lid and turn on the room lights. At this point, I should mention that there are two ways in which you can proceed. One is to fill the tank with developer at the recommended solution temperature and set your timer *before* turning out the lights to load the film. When the loaded reel is inserted in the tank, the timer is started to begin timing the developing cycle according to the time/temperature chart for the film/develop-

5. Pour the solution into the tank and start timing the development process as soon as you're finished.
6. Tank designs like this Yankee Master provide an agitation rod.
7. If you prefer inversion agitation, simply replace the vinyl cover and the Yankee tank can be inverted without spilling solutions out of the cup.
8. Whether you agitate by inversion (shown), or with the agitation rod, time the procedure accurately. A sweep-second hand on your watch will do for those without a darkroom timer.
9. Wash the film thoroughly. The method shown is not ideal, but will suffice for those without a permanent darkroom.

er combination you're using. The tank lid is then replaced and the tank rapped sharply to prevent air bubbles from adhering to the film emulsion.

The second way is to insert the loaded reel in the empty tank, replace the cover/lid and then pour the developer into the tank through the appropriate opening in the top with the room lights on. The tank should then be rapped sharply to prevent air bubbles as you start timing the cycle.

PREBATH—Some photographers prefer to immerse the film thoroughly in a prebath of ordinary water at the proper temperature and agitate it thoroughly before replacing with the developer and starting the cycle timing. This softens the emulsion and accustoms it to the developer which will follow, while

preventing the formation of air bubbles. There's no hard and fast rule concerning the advisability of using a prebath—it's simply a matter of approaching the problems of air bubble formation from a different viewpoint.

THE DEVELOPMENT PROCESS—Throughout the development cycle, agitation should be uniform, slow and gentle—do not shake the tank vigorously. Whether you choose to agitate by inversion or by rotating the reel will depend upon your tank and your own personal preference—just be certain to agitate according to a preselected pattern/time sequence and you'll be O.K. When the timer signals the end of the development step, the solution is removed from the tank and replaced with the stop bath.

Once again, this can be accomplished under normal room illumination by pouring one solution out and the other in, or it can be done by turning off the lights and removing the lid, then pouring out the developer and replacing it with stop bath, replacing the cover before turning on the light again. The primary difference is one of time—to pour the solutions out and in through the proper tank openings can take as much as a full minute; to replace the solution in the dark can be done in a matter of seconds. One way is no more efficient than the other insofar as development is concerned.

Agitate and time the stop bath cycle, then replace the stop bath with the fixer, agitating it periodically. How long the film remains in the fixer will depend upon the strength and freshness of the bath, but it should not exceed twice the length of time required to change the film's milky appearance to one that is perfectly clear. As the tank lid can be removed safely once the film has been in the fixing bath for 60 seconds, this can be determined visually. I'd suggest constant agitation in the fixer for the first minute and then removal of

the film to inspect the degree of clearing that has taken place.

Once the fixing cycle is complete, drain the tank of the solution and immerse the reel in the hypo eliminator for the period recommended by the manufacturer of the brand you use. ·Then wash your film for at least 15 minutes (30 minutes if you do not use the hypo eliminator bath) under running water at the same temperature as the rest of the process—68°F., or as close as you can regulate the temperature of the flowing water to that point. Should running water be unavailable, changing the water every five minutes for a period of 15 minutes (30 minutes without hypo eliminator use) will usually be sufficient.

Remove the film from the tank and replace the plain water with a wetting bath solution. Agitate the film for 30 seconds in this and then remove the film from the reel and hang it up to dry with the film clips, making certain that they're securely fastened to the film ends. If you use a squeegee, sponge or chamois in place of a wetting bath, hang the film up and gently remove all water spots from both the emulsion and film back, taking particular pains to avoid touching the emulsion with your fingers during this step.

Once the film has dried, cut the strip into lengths which will fit your negative filing system and file the negatives accordingly. That's all there is to developing black-and-white films; color film processing is a bit more complicated.

DEVELOPING COLOR FILMS

Color film development uses similar

equipment and follows essentially the same "pour solution in—time—pour out and replace" sequence as does black-and-white development, but due to the greater number of chemical baths used in some processes, the relatively brief duration of some of the steps and the extreme accuracy required in temperature control, the procedure requires more care.

1. Film clips are made of metal or plastic. Many prefer the metal type like these Prinz clips with their twin teeth that hold the film securely, and the clip for hanging up the film.
2. The Prinz Jet Film Dryer is a compact unit which can be located wherever convenient, as shown. Forced warm air will dry your film dust free inside the vinyl bag in 10 minutes. When not in use, the bag can be collapsed for storage.
3. As soon as your negatives are dry, they should be cut up and inserted in whatever negative preservation system you use. These are standard glassine enevelopes.
4. A removable filter prevents the unit from sucking dust from the air into the drying unit. This filter can be cleaned as necessary.
5. When you're finished with the Prinz dryer, the cord is folded up and placed on top of the filter. Fold the vinyl bag for storage and place on top of the filter/cord to prevent dust from accumulating. All that remains is the metal housing mounted to the wall.

Temperature control is by far the most difficult and the most critical part of the process, and a thermometer accurate to ± ½°F. is an absolute necessity, as is some way of maintaining the solution temperature during the first developer. Other steps usually have a sufficient ± deviation to make temperature control less of a problem. Should the difference between the room and solution temperatures be too great, you'll need some way of maintaining constant temperature control during processing. This can be done in various ways, but the one most common and practical for the amateur is the use of a water jacket.

A water jacket is simply a container larger than the developing tank in which water of the correct temperature is poured and the tank inserted (the water must not cover the tank). If temperature control of the water jacket is maintained by adding hot/cold water as required, the temperature of the solution inside the tank will also be constant to that of the water jacket. As stainless steel is very sensitive to temperature changes and transmits them rapidly, many who develop color film prefer the use of a stainless steel tank over the plastic ones, as any adjustments made in the water jacket temperature will be transmitted far more quickly to the film inside.

Should the color chemistry used involve a reexposure of the film to light, the use of either a stainless steel reel or a plastic one with a translucent side is recommended if reexposure is to be done without removing the film from the reel. The latter method is, of course, the best way to assure proper reexposure of the entire film, but some find it very difficult to replace the film on the reel without damaging the soft emulsion.

Chemical contamination must also be avoided, especially if you plan on using the color chemistry more than one time. Bleach and color developers are not particularly fond of each other, and if not rinsed thoroughly from the film *and* reel, can cause color spotting to take place. This means that you should clean your equipment carefully after each use.

As the various color processes differ considerably, it's not practical here to follow each one step by step.

The instruction sheets furnished with each particular chemistry are quite comprehensive in the details of preparing and using the chemicals and should be followed as closely as possible if you wish the best results.

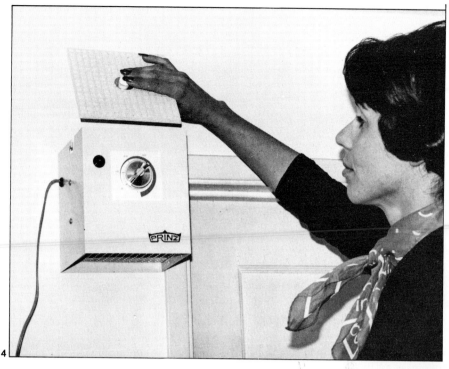

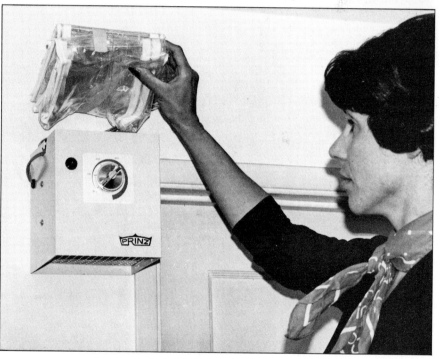

NEGATIVE AFTERTREATMENT

Years ago when there was no grade four paper on which thin negatives could be printed, or grade zero for dense negatives, the techniques of intensification/reduction as means of controlling negative contrast, density and image quality played a prominent role in many darkrooms. But with the wide range of paper grades and the variable-contrast papers available today, the importance of these once-essential darkroom tools has diminished, especially since it's now possible to obtain predetermined contrast characteristics (at least to some extent) by a careful selection of film/developer combination.

You can use a compensating developer with those fine-grain emulsions that are inherently contrasty, a standard developer with fast emulsions which have low contrast, etc. Manipulating the development time/temperature is another way of contrast control; in fact, the list of options is much longer than I have space to list. My point is simply that other and more convenient techniques have displaced intensification/reduction, although they do not always do the job as well, or even do the same job. So if you've never

GAF COLOR SLIDE CHEMISTRY AR-1

Processing Step	Time In Minutes	Temperature	Remarks
First Developer	12	75°F ± ½°F	Increase to 16 minutes for 1 stop push.
Shortstop/Hardener	3	75°F ± 3°F	Agitate vigorously for first minute.
Wash	6	70°F–75°F	Running water.
Second Exposure	2	—	Use photoflood at 3 feet; expose each end of reel for 1 minute; rinse every 30 seconds to prevent overheating of emulsion.
Color Developer	12	75°F ± ½°F	
Shortstop/Hardener	3	75°F ± 3°F	Agitate vigorously for first minute.
Wash	6	70°F–75°F	Running water.
Bleach	4	75°F ± 2°F	
Wash	3	70°F–75°F	Running water.
Fixer	4	75°F ± 3°F	
Wash	4	70°F–75°F	Running water.
Stabilizer	½	75°F ± 3°F	
Wash	½	70°F–75°F	Running water.
Final Rinse	½	75°F ± 3°F	

worked with these two techniques, now's a good time to learn.

INTENSIFICATION—When you want to build up printable density in under-developed negatives, intensification is one very useful way to do so; with underexposure, it's not as helpful. As intensifiers work by adding to the density of blackened silver areas (highlights), they must have something on which they can work. If there's *no* exposed silver in the *shadow* areas of a negative, you cannot expect to intensify what isn't there to begin with.

Many less-than-perfect negatives can often be handled by the choice of paper grade. But take as an example the classic case of underexposure and overdevelopment—the resulting negative is contrasty but thin. Using a soft paper grade reduces contrast in the highlights, but the shadows remain empty. Switching to a contrasty paper grade may help to separate existing shadow detail to the degree that it exists, but you'll lose all tone in the already contrasty highlights. Thus, neither paper choice will do the job adequately enough.

The use of an intensifier will help build highlight detail (density), but will have proportionately little effect on the shadows, and so it won't help with such a negative (underexposed and overdeveloped). Intensifier works best with a properly exposed but underdeveloped negative, one which has both highlight and shadow detail, but is thin and lacking in contrast. Intensifier will increase both shadow and highlight detail in this case, but will add most density to the highlights, thereby increasing the contrast back to normal.

There are several different forms of intensifiers available, but most must

KODAK E-4 PROCESS

PROCESSING STEP	TIME IN MINUTES	TEMPERATURE	REMARKS
Prehardener	3	85°F ± 1°	Total Darkness
Neutralizer	1	85°F ± 3°	Total Darkness
First Developer	7	85°F ± 0.5°	Total Darkness
First Stop Bath	2	85°F ± 3°	Total Darkness- Do Not Use 2nd Stop Bath
Wash	4	80°–90°F	Running Water
Color Developer	15	85°F ± 3°	
Second Color Bath	3	85°F ± 3°	
Wash	3	80°–90°F	Do Not use 1st Stop Bath
Bleach	5	80°–90°F	Running Water
Fixer	6	80°–90°F	
Wash	6	80°–90°F	
Stabilizer	1	80°–90°F	Running Water

KODAK C-41 PROCESS

Processing Step	Time In Minutes	Temperature	Remarks
Developer	3¼	100°F ± 0.5°	Total Darkness
Bleach	6½	100°F ± 5°	Total Darkness
Wash	3¼	100°F ± 5°	
Fixer	6½	75°F	Normal Room Illumination For Remaining Step
Wash	3¼	100°	
Stabilizer	1½	75°F	

be prepared by the user, as Kodak's Chromium Intensifier is virtually the one commercial formulation remaining on the market. In addition to this, there are copper and mercury intensifier formulas, as well as the so-called "proportional" intensifiers, like uranium.

As it is the most readily available, chromium intensifier is thus the most useful for many amateurs. Its formulation is done in two packets of dry chemicals—a bleach and a clearing bath—to be mixed with the specified amount of water. As these chemicals are extremely poisonous, they should

be mixed by *adding the powder to the water,* and kept away from children once mixed. Trays and other containers used with either solution should be washed thoroughly when you're finished to prevent the possibility of contamination of other chemicals.

The handy thing about using a chromium intensifier (other than its prepackaging) is that all steps involved can be carried out in subdued illumination. The negative to be intensified should be as free from hypo as possible, and must be soaked in water for 10 minutes to soften the dry emulsion.

BLACK-AND-WHITE NEGATIVE DEFECTS

DEFECT	CAUSE
Thin negative, detail, low contrast.	Underdevelopment; developer too cold, too diluted, exhausted.
Thin negative, no detail, low contrast.	Underexposed.
Thin negative, high contrast.	Underexposed and overdeveloped; underexposure of a contrasty subject.
Dense negative, low contrast.	Overexposure; light fog; developer too warm.
Dense negative, normal contrast.	Overexposure and overdevelopment.
Dense negative, excessive contrast.	Overdeveloped; developer too warm, too concentrated.
Texture pattern on emulsion. (Reticulation)	Extreme changes in temperature of solutions.
Negative spots.	Undissolved chemical particles resting on film during development.
Stains.	Exhausted developer; forced development; developer too warm.
Airbells.	Lack of agitation.
Mottled marks.	Lack of agitation.
Fingerprints.	If black, hands were contaminated with developer while loading film; if white, fingers were contaminated with hypo.
Overall fog.	Light struck film during loading or development, possibly from safelight.
Reversed image.	Partial reversal of the film by light striking it during development.
Film is blank.	Film was not exposed; developer was badly contaminated or incorrectly formulated/mixed.
Uneven development.	Lack of agitation.
Clear spots (pinholes).	Dust on film during exposure or development.
Translucent spots.	Grease on film during loading, can be caused by normal skin oils if film is incorrectly handled.
Black streaks along edges.	Fog caused by light leak in camera or film cartridge; roll film not wound tightly.
Wiggly lines, flashes of lightning, rows of dark dots.	Static electricity marks, film wound or rewound too quickly on cold, dry days.
Uniform colored stain.	Antihalation backing not removed.
Elliptical spots on emulsion.	Water drops not removed before drying.
Blistering of the emulsion.	Excessively acidic stop bath or fixing bath.
Scratches or abrasions.	Foreign matter in camera; film wound too tightly (cinched); dirt imbedded in sponge or squeegee.

FIGURE B

At that time, the negative is placed in the "A" or bleach bath (68°F.) for 3-5 minutes, or until the black image has turned yellow. A good rinse in plain water removes the excess bleach solution and then the negative is transferred to the "B" or clearing bath (68°F.) for about two minutes, or until the yellow stain of the bleach disappears and a nearly white image is what remains.

Another rinse bath follows, and then the bleached and cleared negative is redeveloped in a nonstaining developer until the white image has blackened completely—Kodak Versatol mixed 1:4 or Kodak Dektol mixed 1:3 are both good choices. Once redevelopment has been completed, the negative is then washed for 10-20 minutes in running water—no fixing is required—and then dried. If more intensification is necessary, the entire process can be repeated several times, or until the limit of intensification has been reached.

REDUCTION—A reducer has an effect opposite to that of an intensifier. It reduces the density of negatives that are too dense.

There are two basic kinds of reducers. The first is the standard Farmer's Reducer, which is available in handy packets from Kodak. This reducer removes equal amounts of density from all parts of the negative, and is therefore best used on overexposed but normally developed negatives, which are too dense all over, but of normal contrast.

The other kind of reducer is called a proportional reducer, because it takes most density away from the densest parts of the negative, and least density away from the thinnest parts of the negative. Proportional reducers are best used with overdeveloped (contrasty) negatives. You can make a proportional reducer by using Farmer's Reducer but using just 1/10 as much of the ferricyanide, or by adding six grams of ammonium persulfate to 250ml of water.

Reduction takes place rapidly once it begins, and the negative must be removed before it reaches the exact point of reduction desired. To halt further reduction, you'll need a solution of five percent sodium sulfate into which the negative is transferred, then wash for 20 minutes before drying. And don't forget one very important thing about reducers—whatever you remove

from the negative in this way cannot be replaced.

HANDY HINTS—Intensifying or reducing sheet film negatives presents no great problems, but if you're working with 35mm negatives, you'll find a pair of tweezers highly useful. If surrounding frames on the negative strip are valuable to you, the negative to be treated should be cut out of the strip, because the chemical action will affect all negatives on the strip, and it's difficult to treat the third one from the end without treating the others at the same instant.

When the process is finished, give your negative a 30-second treatment in a wetting bath. If you've cut out single frames, hanging them up to dry can pose problems, so shake the negative free of excess solution and stand it up on its edge—the frame will curl somewhat, making this position easy to use. After a few seconds, any remaining moisture will collect at the bottom sprocket hole area and can be removed by gently touching this area with a dry cotton-tipped swab. Trying to wipe such small negatives dry with a sponge or chamois is asking for trouble you don't need.

UNICHROME
(E-3 OR E-4)*

Processing Step	Time In Minutes	Temperature	Remarks
First developer	8	80°F±0.5°	
First stop bath	2	75°–80°F	Do not use wrong stop bath.
Rinse	3	75°–80°F	Running water
Reexposure	30 seconds on each side of reel		Use No. 2 photoflood 12-18 inches from film.
Color developer	8	80°F±1°	
Second stop bath	2	75°–80°F	Do not use wrong stop bath.
Rinse	3	75°–80°F	Running water
Bleach	5	75°–80°F	
Rinse	1	75°–80°F	Running water
Fixer	2	75°–80°F	
Rinse	6	75°–80°F	Running water
Stabilizer	1	75°–80°F	Do not squeegee.

*Can be used with GAF, Agfrachrome, E-3 or E-4 films—follow separate instructions furnished.

Remember, these solutions are poison and should be handled with care. It's a good idea to work in a well-ventilated area and practice the ultimate in cleanliness to prevent contamination at a later date.

PUSH-PROCESSING FILM

Sometimes it seems that photographers fall into one of two categories—those who seek maximum quality from whatever emulsion they use, and those whose quest in life is to extract every bit of speed and then some from their film, which usually carries a high ASA speed to begin with. The former are eternally in search of the ultimate fine-grain developer, while the latter just as earnestly seek a magical potion that will endow the film emulsion with qualities that its manufacturer was unable to provide.

Entrepreneurs among us prey commercially on both groups with outlandish formulas, fantastic additives and unusual procedures, and do very well practicing their own forms of black magic which emulsion chemists and physicists reject, yet the quest continues. Of the two, push-processing is of greatest interest today. The idea of photographing the proverbial black cat in a coalbin by the light of his eyes at midnight intrigues even the most practical of us, and sooner or later, we're tempted to give in and try it ourselves.

At the risk of offending those who swear by their own particular process, formula or technique, let me define push-processing as nothing more than an attempt to capitalize on the built-in latitude of a film's emulsion by "extending" or "forcing" development to obtain a printable negative in spite of

COLOR SLIDE PROCESSING PROBLEMS

Defect	Cause
Image too light	Overexposure; excessive first development
Image too dense	Underexposure; insufficient first development; exhausted first developer
Milky appearance	Insufficient fixing
Brown cast, mottle or streaks	Insufficient fixing
Random pink or purple spots on film	Bleach/fixer contamination
Residue/scum on film when dry	Hard water residue

underexposure in the camera. Some also define push-processing as an attempt to artificially increase the emulsion's sensitivity to light by means of a chemical additive, but let's take them one at a time.

Super-speed developers are available that claim an increase of speed in the neighborhood of 3-5 f-stops. A similar increase can be obtained by using most standard film developers. Why? Simply because both take advantage of the film's latitude to achieve an *apparent* increase in film speed rather than a *true* increase. How much advantage is taken and how well the result turns out will depend upon the given developer/film combination in question.

Some emulsion types react more favorably to push-processing than do others; some developer formulas are more amenable to extending development than others. The trick lies in finding the best combination. Regardless of the combination used, negatives which have been push-processed will exhibit more noticeable grain and more

contrast than those processed according to the manufacturer's recommendations. The higher you attempt to raise the effective film speed, the more shadow/highlight detail you lose, although it is often possible to obtain an acceptable picture by printing such negatives on a softer than normal grade of enlarging paper. The results depend entirely on the circumstances under which the exposure was made—the subject, how it was lighted, its brightness range, film speed, and other such external factors.

WHAT EXTENDED DEVELOPMENT DOES—By increasing development time up to 50 percent longer than that recommended by the film manufacturer, you can get negatives that will produce acceptable prints on a softer than normal paper grade when the amount of underexposure is held to no more than one f-stop. Underexposure amounting to more than one f-stop will result in negatives which contain progressively greater contrast, overall granularity and increased density in all areas except those shadows which are underexposed to begin with. Thus it is not possible to fully accommodate the lack of sufficient exposure by simply extending development. Here's why.

When the film manufacturer creates an emulsion, he follows uniform industry standards in determining its speed as represented by an ASA rating. These standards require that the ASA rating represent the *minimum* exposure necessary to produce a negative that will deliver an excellent picture with a full tonal range and normal contrast. So the speed or emulsion sensitivity to light as reflected in the ASA rating is both an inherent characteristic of the film, and one established at a minimum exposure threshold. Thus, providing less exposure than required by the ASA rating will not permit the shadow areas of most subjects to receive sufficient light to record the detail they contain. And if detail *is not recorded*, it *cannot be developed*.

Those who are conservative in their view toward the value of push-processing will concede that up to a one-third f-stop in effective film speed is possible by extending development. This results from shadow detail which is borderline; that is, it received sufficient exposure to appear slightly when subjected to extended development, but would not have shown up at all during normal processing.

Others more liberal in their appreciation of push-processing often tend to attribute their ability to satisfactorily photograph a low-contrast subject with less than a minimum exposure to a significant gain in film speed. While such negatives contain adequate density, you must remember that such subjects will have little or no shadow detail to be recorded in the first place. In other words, the brightness range of the subject is compressed, resulting in greater than normal film latitude. This allows exposure of the film at an exposure value considerably higher than its assigned ASA speed, yet with no appreciable reduction in the quality of the picture.

SUBJECT CONTRAST—Subject contrast and how it's lighted plays a large role in determining the minimum amount of exposure necessary to produce an acceptable picture—as does your own personal definition of the word acceptable. Normal exposure and processing use the film's latitude to handle contrast within acceptable limits to produce a negative of excellent quality.

Average-contrast subjects contain important highlights, mid-tones and

UNICOLOR K2			
Processing Step	Time In Minutes	Temperature	Remarks
Developer	3¼	100°F ± 1°	Time critical
Blix	6-7	100°F ± 5°	Not critical beyond minimum
Wash	3-4	100°F ± 5°	Not critical beyond minimum
Stabilizer	1-2	75°F	Not critical beyond minimum

UNICOLOR E-6			
Processing Step	Time In Minutes	Temperature	Remarks
First developer	6½	100°F	Agitate first 15 seconds, then 2 seconds every 15—include drain time.
Rinse	2-3	92°-102°F	Fill tank and drain 6 times—total of 6 rinses is more important than time.
Reversal bath	2	92°-102°F	Agitate first 10 seconds only.
Color developer	6	99°-101°F	See first developer.
Stop bath	1	92°-102°F	See first developer.
Rinse	2	92°-102°F	See first developer.
Bleach	3	92°-102°F	See first developer.
Fixer	2	92°-102°F	See first developer.
Rinse	2-3	92°-102°F	See first rinse.
Stabilizer	½	Ambient	Agitate 10-15 seconds only.

BESELER CN2 (C-41 PROCESS)			
Processing Step	Time In Minutes	Temperature	Remarks
CN2 Developer	16	75°F ± 1°F	Extend development by 2 minutes after every 2 rolls processed.
CN2 Bleach-Fix	9	75°F ± 1°	
Water Wash	4	75°F to 100°F	
CN2 Wetting Agent	½	68°F to 100°F	
OR			
CN2 Developer	8	85°F ± ½°F	Extend development by 1 minute after every 2 rolls processed.
Water Wash	4	75°F to 100°F	
CN2 Wetting Agent	½	68°F to 100°F	

shadow detail, or what we call a middle brightness range. Low-contrast subjects primarily contain a short brightness range, whether of highlights, middle tones or shadows—often the result of relatively flat lighting. High-contrast subjects possess bright highlights as well as deep shadows, resulting in an expanded brightness range, and one that is often beyond the capability of the film to record both of its ends satisfactorily.

Push-processing such high-contrast subjects as a performer working under a spotlight on an otherwise dark stage will result in extreme contrast with a loss of quality at both ends of the brightness range. Under such circumstances, it is often better to expose for the important area of the subject—highlight or shadow—and let the rest go its own way, as push-processing will deliver little more than a hard-to-print negative, the results of which will turn out to be an unacceptable print.

OTHER FACTORS TO CONSIDER— We've all occasionally met up with a

fellow photographer who claims fantastic results with push-processing techniques and has the prints to prove it. But one very common explanation for his success lies in the equipment he uses. For example, it is not uncommon for manufacturers to accept as much as a 20 percent ± deviation from marked shutter speeds as being within the acceptable range. Thus, it's possible to use two identical cameras set at 1/500 second and receive a 1/400-second exposure with one but a 1/600-second exposure with the other. The difference amounts to ½ f-stop.

Add to this error similar tolerance errors in lens diaphragm and light meter operation, and it's possible that one could shoot an ASA 400 film at ASA 1000 and come up with identically exposed negatives as those taken by another photographer who rated the same type film at its assigned ASA 400 speed. Taken by itself, the first instance is certainly impressive, but when it's compared to the second, it indicates little more than the need for equipment adjustment.

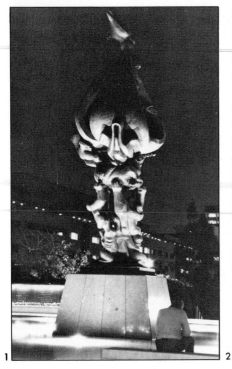

1

2

4

3

1-3. Taken on ASA 400 film, these three negatives received the same exposure, as calculated by a hand-held meter. After processing as indicated below, uniform prints were made on Kodak RC medium hard paper. Photo (1) received 50 percent overdevelopment in a standard developer, (2) was developed in a high energy developer, and (3) was developed in standard developer treated with Factor 8. Note the considerable difference in highlights, shadows and gradation between the three prints.

To get acceptable negatives when using my very expensive fully automatic 35mm SLR, I find it necessary to set the ASA index dial to one-quarter the value of the film's specified rating (ASA 125 film to ASA 32, ASA 400 to ASA 100, etc.). When a subject is metered with my hand-held meter set at the film's rated ASA, the meter indicates the same exposure as the camera's meter when set at one-quarter of the rated ASA. Thus, if the camera meter is set at the rated ASA, there's a full two-stop difference between the readings—and my negatives come out underexposed by that amount. Sending the camera back to the distributor to determine the problem brought me only reassurance that all systems are functioning within the factory-specified tolerances. While my particular problem lies in the wrong direction, if it were the reverse, I would be able to get good negatives with the camera's meter set at ASA 1600 instead of ASA 400, and with push-processing, I could shoot at two stops underexposure, or ASA 6400.

In addition to problems of this nature, there are other less obvious ways for the unwary to arrive at incorrect conclusions about increases in ASA ratings. Some habitually overdevelop their film unwittingly—their thermometer is inaccurate, they don't use one, or they haven't bothered to check the time/temperature table to discover that the manufacturer has changed his recommendations since they last read it.

Others can arrive at the same conclusion just as easily by using a standard developer but in a highly diluted form. This tends to produce a compensating effect that flattens gradation, so to increase contrast back to the desired level, they overdevelop. As this results in additional density, they mistake it for overexposure and thus increase the ASA rating to take care of the "overexposure problem."

The manner in which the exposure meter is used can also fool even experienced hands. If you habitaully keep your reading confined to the foreground or shadow areas (or use a bottom center-weighted metering system incorrectly), you'll give more exposure than necessary. Your neighbor may read both highlights and shadows and give the same subject less exposure than you did. Assuming exactly the same development for both negatives, you'll end up with one that's denser than his, despite the fact that you both used the same ASA index. Naturally, you'll assume the rating is too low and readjust it upward to achieve the desired "normal" exposure—when all you've really done is to compensate for an incorrect metering technique.

Please don't leave this section with the impression that I attribute all success in push-processing to a combination of incorrect techniques and defective equipment—I'm merely raising the point that we all too often accept what we are told without question. If the shutter dial says 1/500, we assume that the shutter operates at 1/500 second when set at that position—but does it really?

HOW BIG A PUSH?—How far can you push a given film with acceptable results? That depends upon the factors just discussed, such as subject contrast, lighting, technique and equipment accuracy, as well as film/developer combination. Fortunately, there's an easy way in which you can easily arrive at the most appropriate ASA rating

5

4. This proof sheet shows the results of the test described in the text to determine how far you can satisfactorily push a given film and developer combination. The bottom strip was exposed at ASA 400 and from left-to-right, the negatives received one stop overexposure, normal exposure as recommended by the meter, and four successive half-stop increments toward underexposure. By selecting a negative from the overdeveloped strip at the top (see text), which will give a print of equal quality, you can determine just how much you can safely push a given film and still get good results. As this technique takes into account any individual differences in equipment used, it results in an absolutely accurate recommendation.

5. The wedding of Michu and Juliana during the 1976 Ringling Brothers and Barnum and Bailey Circus took place under a huge spotlight. The resulting contrast level was excessive but by exposing for the spotlight illumination, an acceptable tonal range was provided for the center of interest. A hand-held meter used intelligently excels in situations such as this.

for use in determining the absolute minimum exposure required by a given film to obtain a printable negative of acceptable quality.

To do so, you'll need two rolls of black-and-white film, such as Kodak Tri-X or Ilford HP5. Both rolls should carry the same emulsion number, indicating that they are from the same batch of film and thus identical in characteristics. The emulsion number is a series of numbers/letters located on the film box panel with the expiration date. Now pick a subject similar in contrast to the type you would generally photograph with push-processing in mind—this step is important, as the subject must be truly representative or you're performing the test for nothing.

Set the exposure meter dial (built-in or hand-held) to the recommended ASA 400 rating and carefully determine the "correct" exposure, then photo-

graph the subject, bracketing your exposures in ½-stop increments from one full stop *more* than the meter indicates as necessary to four full stops *less,* for a total of 11 shots.

Repeat the photo sequence with the second roll of film, but this time, you should readjust the exposure meter for each shot as closely as possible to the following ASA indices, beginning with the one full stop "overexposure"—200, 280, 400, 560, 800, 1100, 1600, 2200, 3200, 4400, 6400. This final exposure at ASA 6400 is equivalent to the four full stop "underexposure" of the first roll. As you've shot both rolls in the same progressive sequence, comparison should be simple once developed.

Now process both rolls in the same developer—the first roll normally and the second roll with development extended by 50 percent. Examine each roll and pick both the negatives that appear to have the best potential for producing good prints, and those in which the lack of shadow detail starts to show up. A contact proof sheet will prove useful in helping you make the selection if you're not good at "reading" negatives alone. Make straight prints—no dodging or burning-in allowed here—of all negatives selected, taking care to select the appropriate grade of paper contrast.

The best print from the normally exposed/developed film should come from the negative made at the rated ASA film speed—400. If it doesn't, either your equipment is off or your metering technique is faulty. Using this print as a comparative base, examine those made from the pushed negatives and select the one that contains the maximum quality loss you can accept.

Once you've determined which picture in the sequence you've selected, you've arrived at the highest ASA setting you can use for underexposure and forced development.

WHAT ABOUT CHEMICAL ADDITIVES? —Some developers like Acufine and Ilford Microphen are especially formulated to create the maximum possible chemical reaction to the light-struck silver halides in the emulsion. These so-called "maximum energy" developers tend to alter the response of the emulsion in such a way as to build up more density than normal for a given amount of contrast. Put another way, they compress the upper and lower tonal scale, requiring extended development to reach a normal contrast level. This provides an adequate negative density with less exposure. By the definition of some, this distortion of the tonal range results in a usable film speed increase, accompanied by a noticeable increase in granularity. As such developers tend to blacken more silver grains than do normal developers, the result is a visual "clumping" effect, and so they are compounded in such a way as to prevent grain from growing excessively large. Unfortunately, there's a limit to their ability in holding grain size down.

From time to time, "miracle" chemical additives appear on the market, making claims that can stagger the unthinking photographer. Suppose I told you that I have a bottle which will increase the speed of your film by up to *eight* times! Now before you dig down into your pocket, stop and think a moment. An increase in film speed of this magnitude actually represents three f-stops, thus an ASA 400 rating becomes an apparent ASA 3200. What's so great about that? Photographers constantly expose ASA 400 emulsions at a 3200 rating and then push-process them.

O.K., now let's look closer at my "super" additive. To use it, I'll let you *double* the normal ASA rating of your film for purposes of exposure calculation. This means that you're actually underexposing by one f-stop. My processing recommendation is a 50-percent increase beyond the normal developing time. If you think about it, you'll realize that you're doing little more than push-processing, as described earlier.

You want more speed? Extend development 100 percent and I'll guarantee two f-stops. Add a little more of my miracle solution, triple the developing time and you can claim three f-stops. Now if you haven't caught on to me yet, I'll clue you in. My magic bottle

transforms your standard developing formula into one that approximates a maximum energy developer—nothing more. Certainly, I'll claim tighter grain structure and reduced contrast, and to some degree, I'll deliver on those promises. But so will a maximum energy developer. Actually, I'll give you nothing you can't get for less money somewhere else.

Despite all the claims made for and by various chemical additives, there are basically only two ways in which the sensitivity of silver particles in the emulsion can actually be increased—by exposure to mercury fumes or by a brief pre- or post-fogging of the film with a very dim light. Each will produce about a one-stop increase in speed, but the former is extremely dangerous to use and the latter very tricky. Both require extensive experimentation on

the photographer's part, and the end result is rarely worth the time and trouble. You'll be far ahead of the game if you ignore claims such as the ones I made, and stay with more orthodox methods of eking the maximum sensitivity possible from your film. Yet, being human, I'm sure you don't believe me—so step right this way!

PUSH-PROCESSING COLOR FILMS— Color negative and positive films can be successfully push-processed. Yet any time you deviate from the recommended exposure and processing with color materials, you should be prepared for a color shift to take place, along with an increase in contrast and more pronounced granularity. The degree to which such defects appear will depend upon your film and the amount of push you give it, as some emulsion types lend themsleves better to push-processing than others. This is also true of the chemistry.

The limit in pushing negative color films is usually two stops, as contrast and fog levels increase considerably and quickly above this point, resulting in a rapid deterioration of image quality. But the new ASA 400 color negative emulsions recently made available allow the use of an effective film speed of 1600—a notable breakthrough that now puts color users right behind those who work with black-and-white.

While the same theory which applies to black-and-white push-processing—you can't produce image detail where none exists on the film—applies equally to color negative emulsions, the same is not true of slide films. In fact, it's quite possible to pick up an effective increase in film speed when push-processing slide film. If you're wondering why, remember that color positive films are a *reversal* process.

The maximum possible density (or blackness) of a positive color film is always greater than the amount required by a correctly exposed slide. Because of this, the potential density of the emulsion is never fully used to record your subject—if it were, the slide would be much too dark, or underexposed. So if you deliberately underexpose a positive color film by one stop, the film *will record* shadow detail, even though the slide which results is too dark for normal viewing.

As shadow detail has been recorded, increasing the length of time in the first developer will lighten the exposed areas of the emulsion, which has the effect of *restoring* shadow detail. This amounts to full compensation for the underexposure and results in an effective increase in speed. But to the previous defects noted as a result of push-processing color films, we should also add an increasing reduction in the maximum density or blackness with color slide emulsions when they are push-processed.

Can you push your own color films? Yes and no. The Kodak C-41 chemistry does not lend itself well to push-processing, and the new E-6 emulsions are also a bit tricky to work with in this way. Where the manufacturer offers a pushing service, as in the case of certain Kodak and GAF emulsions, you're better off letting their labs do it for you, since your control over important variables is always less than that of a well-equipped lab designed and staffed for such. On the other hand, if you enjoy a challenge and are willing to accept the consequences, pushing your own

1-2. The results of the test shown on the proof sheet indicate that the author can depend upon reasonably good results when 50 percent overdevelopment is given to the film after exposure at double the ASA index (2). While not completely the equal with normal negative exposure and development (1), the pushed negative will deliver a fairly good print.
3. Nightclub and stage photography can be tricky. This was photographed under a blue spotlight, causing a considerable loss of quality in all but the brightest highlights.

color film may be right up (or down) your alley.

TWO-BATH DEVELOPMENT

A half-century ago, the serious photographer had no difficulty in exercising total control over the development of his negatives. Because he used sheet film, he could photograph three scenes with greatly varying contrast levels and treat each one accordingly in the darkroom. The roll-film user of today has no such control—he must treat all of the negatives on a roll alike during development. Those concerned with obtaining the finest negatives possible will keep a record of what they shoot and then develop the film to achieve maximum negative quality in the highest percentage of shots on the roll, trusting to exposure latitude and the gods to pull the rest through. But sometimes, that is not good enough.

Once very popular, the concept of two-bath development has been kicking around for many years now, but is

mainly used today by professionals who care enough to give their negatives the best development possible—many amateurs are totally unaware of the benefits offered by two-bath or water-bath development. Yet it offers the opportunity to exercise control over the tonal gradation of each negative on the roll—just as if you were processing each one individually. Like any other specialized photographic technique, there are several variations of the concept in use. To give you an idea of the range of possibilities inherent in two-bath development, let's look at three such possibilities.

THE STRAIGHT WATER-BATH PROCESS—Whenever you're faced with extremes of contrast such as those provided by the combination of very bright sunlight and predominantly deep shadows, you generally expose for the shadows to pick up the essential detail in them. This means that highlight areas will be grossly overexposed. The straight water-bath process offers a means of bringing the shadows and highlights into a manageable proportion by balancing out the extremes in exposure through development. Essentially, the trick is one of letting shadow detail develop while retarding the highlights from complete development.

To develop a film by this process, place it in the developer for a brief period until the image begins to appear. While you'll be unable to deter-

1

mine this state exactly, it usually requires between 20 to 40 seconds. At this point, remove the film from the developer and place it in a tank of plain water at the same temperature as the developer. Leave it there without agitation for two minutes, then return it to the developer for a period of time double that of the initial immersion.

Remove the film from the developer once more and return it to the water bath—this time for four minutes. A third trip to the developer for 20 seconds follows, with a final water bath treatment of 10 to 15 minutes. This should complete the process, providing even development of the negatives without the blocked highlights or lost shadow detail resulting from normal processing. The resulting negatives will be far superior to those obtained by under-

development (as a means of reducing the contrast level) and the prints made from them will be much better than trying to dodge or burn-in areas of normally developed negatives.

Naturally, you should experiment with this process before trying it on negatives that cannot be replaced. You might find it useful to use a desensitizer bath prior to development. This will permit you to develop the film by inspection using a dark green safelight and will give you an opportunity to establish your own pattern of alternating development with the water-bath treatment—the figures I've provided work for me, but as your method of determining exposure and the type of subject matter with which you work might differ considerably from mine, it's best to experiment until you arrive

1. Here's the result of intensifying the negative used to make the print in photo 3 on page 359. Since chemical intensification increases the density in proportion to the existing image density, the highlights have been intensified to a greater extent than the shadows. While this results in an overall contrast increase, the print *is* better.

2-4. Kodak Chromium Intensifier is a two-solution bath used with a nonstaining developer, such as Kodak Dektol diluted 1:3. The first bath is a yellow bleach (2) and is used until the black image on the film has bleached yellow. I use tweezers to prevent staining my fingers and damaging the film, as a film clip might do. After a water bath, the film is placed in the clearing solution. This removes the yellow stain and results in an almost white image on the negative (3). Another rinse is followed by redevelopment until the white image has darkened completely (4). Wash the film in running water for 10 minutes and dry.

2

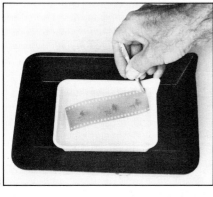

3

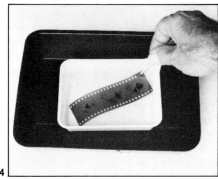

4

at the optimum for yourself.

If you're wondering why the water-bath process is recommended for contrasty negatives, the answer is simple. Shadow detail, which received less exposure than the highlights, absorbs the same amount of developer as the highlight areas. Under normal development, the overexposed highlight areas will develop much more quickly and with more vigor than the shadow areas. But when immersed in water, highlight development ceases while the slower and less vigorous shadow detail continues to develop. Returning the film to the developer "recharges" both areas of the negative and the process repeats itself until the entire negative has satisfactorily developed. At this point, the shadow detail has developed normally, while the overexposed highlights have

developed less than they otherwise would, thus balancing the great discrepancy in exposure.

THE SPLIT-DEVELOPER PROCESS—A variation of the two-bath procedure involves splitting the chemistry of the developer into two separate parts. The first solution will contain just a developing agent and preservative; the second bath, just an accelerator. To use this process, you'll have to mix your own developing chemistry, as it's not available in a prepared form commercially. Before giving you the formulas and mixing instructions, let's look at the benefits it offers.

When the film is placed in the first developer (actually the Kodak D-23 formula), it begins to develop very gently. While the highlights only reach a medium density, the shadows literally absorb developer. Transferring the film to the second bath containing the accelerator speeds up the action of the D-23, which rapidly exhausts itself in the highlights while the shadows continue to develop. The end result is a negative with a finely differentiated tonal scale from shadows that exhibit very good detail to clean and unblocked highlights.

Use the first bath at 68°F. for four minutes (including drain time), agitating constantly for the first 60 seconds. Then give the tank a single inversion every following 30 seconds. Without using a rinse in between, pour the second bath in after draining the first and agitate constantly for one minute, giving the tank a single inversion every 15 seconds thereafter for a total time of three minutes. Fix and wash the film as you usually do.

To mix the solutions, use the formulas below. Before adding the metol, drop a pinch of the sulfite in the water and dissolve completely by stirring.

Then stir in the metol until it too is completely dissolved, adding the remaining sulfite last while stirring the solution constantly. When everything has dissolved, add the cold water. The first solution is used full strength; the second solution as mixed according to the formula is a stock solution, and should be diluted one to 30 parts of water for use.

FIRST SOLUTION
(Kodak D-23 developer)

24 oz.	Water—not to exceed 125°F.
¼ oz.	Metol
3 oz.	Sodium Sulfite (anhyd)
	Water to make a solution total of 32 oz.

SECOND SOLUTION

15 oz.	Water—not to exceed 125°F.
265 grains	kodalk (Sodium Metaborate)
	Water to make a solution total of 20 oz.

COMMERCIAL TWO-BATH DEVELOPERS—There is a commercial variation of the split-developer process—Beseler UltraFin 1 + 1. This develops different areas of the negative more or less according to the exposure given those areas. Basically the developing agent, the first bath's chemical formula is such that *all* of the film absorbs it equally, but development does not begin until the second bath is introduced. When the second bath is added, the absorbed developer is then activated, becoming exhausted more rapidly in areas of greater density (highlights) than in areas of lesser density (shadows). This results in a continuing development of the shadow areas to bring them up to a greater than normal density (with more shadow detail) without a block-up of the highlights by overdevelopment. While the chemistry and its operation are different from the preceding formula, the end result is quite similar.

IN CLOSING . . . .

Film development is a fascinating process and can be as simple or complex as you wish to make it. While I've only touched on the basics in this chapter, there's a good deal more to the subject for those who are interested. Let me suggest that in addition to your regular photography, you do a bit of experimental work and try various developers to see what they will do. While this advice deviates from what you may read elsewhere, it's the one sure-fire way to learn the ins and outs of your hobby. □

18

All About Enlarging

Throughout the book, I've emphasized working toward obtaining the best possible negative. Now that you have it, it's foolish to compromise at this point. The quality of your final picture is very much dependent upon your choice of photographic printing paper, as well as how you expose and process it. The choice of printing paper and chemistry is just as important as selecting the correct film/developer combination. For that reason, let's begin our look at enlarging with a consideration of the materials to be used.

PHOTOGRAPHIC PAPER

Whether designed for enlarging or contact printing, photographic paper consists of a gelatin emulsion containing silver halide particles in suspension and coated on a paper base. The speed, contrast and image tone of the emulsion are determined by manipulating the chemical composition of the silver particles with additives. Black-and-white photo paper has several important characteristics: emulsion speed, color sensitivity, contrast grade, paper surface, paper base, and image tone/base tint.

EMULSION SPEED—Like films, photo papers possess different degrees of sensitivity to light (speed), as well as to different portions of the visible spectrum. This is necessary to provide manageable exposure times that are neither too brief to time with accuracy, nor too lengthy to cause negative damage from over-heating and buckling. Contact printing paper is slow in speed and cannot be used efficiently for enlarging purposes. While enlarging paper is much faster, it also varies considerably in speed from one type to another. The fastest papers are most useful for high-volume production

work, making large blowups from small negatives, or working with very dense negatives.

The speed of photographic papers is determined according to standards set by the industry, and are expressed as American Standard Paper Speeds, or ASAP ratings for tray development. Papers designed for mechanical or stabilization processing carry a designated speed called Effective Paper Speed (EPS) rather than an ASAP rating. Although comparable in one respect to

ASA ratings for film emulsions, there is no direct relationship between the two.

If you wish to use a paper brand, surface or contrast grade with which you are not familiar, the ASAP speed furnishes a comparative basis for exposure determination. By comparing the speed of the unfamiliar paper with that of your usual type, you can arrive at an exposure which will deliver approximately the same type of print on the new paper. To use the ASAP speed in this manner, multiply the rating of your

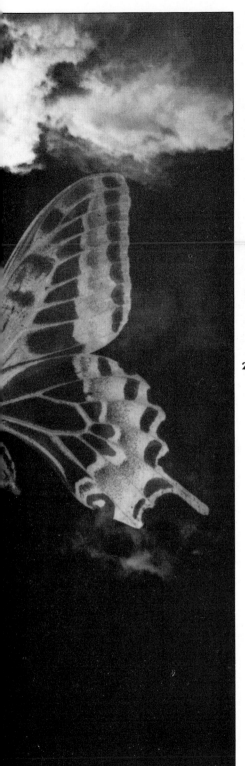

1. Colored paper stocks can add an extra dimension to your creative photography. Shirley I. Fisher originally printed this on a gold paper for effect.

2. How to select the right paper surface from a stock like this? Most dealers supply sample books which show each surface they stock. Browsing through the books will help you to make the right kind of choice.

known paper by the optimum exposure time and then divide that figure by the speed of the unfamiliar paper to determine its base exposure. Like ASA ratings of film speeds, ASAP speeds are meant for use primarily as a basic or starting point in determining proper exposure, and may require some adjustment to accommodate the efficiency (or lack of such) of your particular equipment.

COLOR SENSITIVITY—Silver halides alone are sensitive only to the blue,

violet and ultraviolet portions of the spectrum. To make them sensitive to other wavelengths, special sensitizing dyes are used. This is the principle behind variable-contrast papers, in which filters are used between the light source and enlarging paper to change its contrast by controlling the relative exposure provided to the blue- and green-sensitive emulsions coated on the paper.

Sensitizing dyes are also used with special papers like Kodak Panalure. This particular paper is used primarily to make black-and-white prints from integrally masked color negatives, and so its emulsion must be as sensitive as possible to the visible spectrum in order to achieve a proper tonal balance in transferring the negative's image to the paper.

CONTRAST GRADE—Photographic emulsions coated on printing paper have an inherent contrast more aptly referred to as gradation. This is the response of the paper's emulsion to the contrast or density range of the negative to be printed.

A normal gradation produces a print in which the degree of contrast is more or less equivalent to that of the nega-

tive. A soft gradation produces a print with lower contrast than that of the negative, and is thus used with negatives whose contrast level is excessive. The hard gradation delivers a higher contrast level than that contained in the negative, and is useful in adding contrast to prints from negatives which lack a sufficient amount.

Photographic printing papers are assigned contrast grade numbers/names. These serve to indicate the density range of negatives which can be printed on each paper grade with satisfaction. Generally speaking, grades 0 to 1 are soft gradation papers, 2 is normal, and 3 through 6 are increasingly hard in gradation. But while industry standards govern the ASAP speed of photo papers, no such standardization exists in the assignment of contrast grade designations. Thus, the No. 2 paper of one brand may not necessarily be comparable with the No. 2 paper offered by another manufacturer in terms of its gradation characteristics. The only way to become familiar with such differences is to actually work with the paper in question until you become fully acquainted with its eccentricities in gradation.

The type of enlarger used has a bearing on the paper grade chosen. While this also differs according to the efficiency of the enlarger's optical system, enlargers of the condenser type generally produce a print with greater gradation than those from diffusion-type enlargers, and the same negative printed with both types of enlargers may require two different paper grades to produce a satisfactory print.

PAPER SURFACE—Photographic papers are manufactured with various degrees of gloss—from the high gloss of a ferrotyped print to the virtual absence of gloss in a matte paper. A variety of textures are also provided, ranging from perfectly smooth through a silklike finish to rough or pebblelike textures. Surface textures have long been considered important in creating an effect that complements the subject matter of the print, and in providing a certain amount of reality to black-and-white prints. Such surfaces possess a unique quality in permitting the darkroom worker to achieve a range of subtle and not-so-subtle effects.

Unfortunately, the choice of textures has been considerably reduced in recent years, partially as a result of decreasing consumer demand for their use accompanied by a rise in demand for other papers, and partially as an industry means of reducing inventory

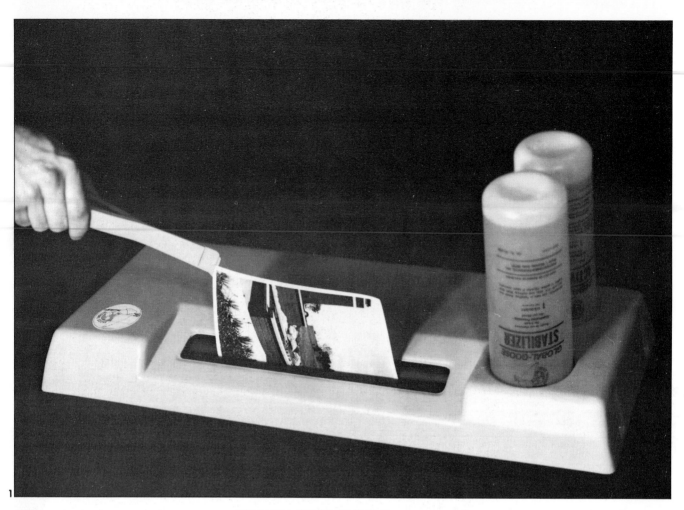

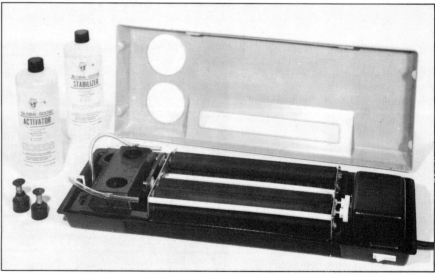

and production costs to devote more facilities toward the more popular ones.

Paper texture and sheen are not interdependent—textured papers can have a sheen, just as smooth surfaces can be matte. The paper you choose will depend to a large extent upon the use to which the print will be put. The best tonal reproduction, maximum sharpness and definition are achieved with the use of a smooth, glossy finish. Should it prove desirable to hide fine detail or small imperfections, a matte paper with a coarse texture can be used. As reflections are a common distraction to viewing prints, those to be placed on exhibition are best made on a matte or semi-matte surface—this tends to reduce reflections to a bare minimum.

The smaller the size of the print, the more desirable it is to use a smooth surface, as coarse surfaces reduce the apparent sharpness of small images. Silk-finish papers are the worst thing that ever happened to the amateur photofinishing industry for this very reason. Large prints designed to be viewed from a distance make more effective use of surface texture, and can better stand the coarser finishes.

PAPER BASE—All photographic print-ing papers use a paper base on which the light-sensitive emulsion has been applied, but the introduction of a water-resistant resin-coated base a few years ago considerably changed the complexion of the photographic paper business, as well as practices in the darkroom. By coating the standard paper base with resins, processing times can be reduced because the base does not absorb chemicals and water to the same extent as the "conventional" papers, now referred to as fiber-based. As a result, the resin-coated papers dry much more quickly, cutting total time from negative to finished print to only a fraction of that required with conventional papers.

Photographic printing paper comes in three weights or thicknesses—single, medium and double weight. This refers to the paper stock on which the light-sensitive emulsion is coated. Single-weight (SW) paper is suitable for most general work; medium-weight (MW) is the heavier designation for many of the

RC papers; double-weight (DW) is the heaviest and is generally used when the print will be exhibited or subjected to rough handling. With the increasing popularity of the resin-coated papers, some manufacturers have tended to reduce the thickness of their DW fiber-based or conventional papers slightly; thus many of today's double-weight papers are not as thick as they were a few years ago.

IMAGE TONE/BASE TINT—In addition to different surfaces and textures, photographic papers produce different tones according to the type of paper used. The silver image can vary from a deep blue-black through neutral and warm blacks to a brown. This color is called the image tone. While a particular paper type is manufactured to produce a specific tone, variations in developer type, development time/temperature and drying conditions can affect the silver image tone.

The paper stock used as a base has a color of its own—this is known as the base tint—and is designated as cream, warm or cold depending upon the amount of yellow or blue cast in the paper. To provide additional brightness in finished prints, some papers contain a fluorescent brightener.

Image tone and base tint have importance in paper selection primarily when artistic considerations are involved, as they can lend a degree of supporting strength to the statement you wish to make about your subject. The following suggestions are offered as typical guidelines for the beginner:

1—General usage, copy work, reproduction: These are pictures basically intended to convey information to the viewer, so use a white-base paper with a neutral black or warm black tone.

2—Portraits and character studies: This covers a wide field, but generally a warm brown tone complements skin tones and the base tint is selected according to the subject matter. For example, a cream base is ideal for head-and-shoulder portraits, while a white base is more appropriate for wedding portraits or where the subject is wearing mainly white clothing.

3—Pictorial, landscapes, scenics: Match the tone/tint to the subject matter for creative printing. As an example, use a cream base and warm tone for sunsets, a white base with cold black tone for seascapes, or a white base with neutral black tone for snow scenes, etc.

4—Commercial and industrial work: As these are basically informational rather than creative in nature, stay with

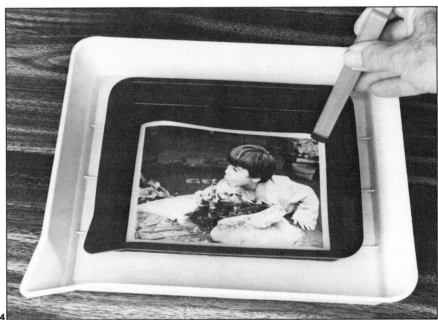

1. Want maximum production with a minimum of fuss? Try the stabilization process. The Portertown Global Goose unit shown will deliver a finished 8x10 print every 10 seconds. This eliminates the need for mixing chemicals, working with trays and lets you work without having running water nearby.
2. Stabilization processors are really simple units and will operate for years without giving problems. The paper passes through a series of motor-driven rollers which guide it through the activator solution and into the stabilizer. Liquid level valves attach to the solution bottle to control fluid feed into the solution trays beneath the roller assembly.

3. A stabilization processor must be kept clean. After use, remove both the roller assembly and the trays, then wash both in warm water to dissolve any chemical accumulations or build-up.
4. For ease in controlling solution temperature, try the tray-in-tray method. Cooler water in the larger tray will help to prevent the temperature of the solution in the smaller tray from rising above a normal working level.

a white base and neutral black tone where possible.

VARIABLE CONTRAST VS. GRADED PAPERS

As we've seen, the choice of gradation offered by a printing paper can accommodate the lack of or excessive contrast in the negative. There are two types of papers which make this accommodation, both offering different advantages to the user.

VARIABLE-CONTRAST PAPERS— Designed to permit contrast control during enlargement by the use of appropriate filters, this type of photographic paper has the advantage of limiting the inventory of paper you

must keep on hand since one box provides any contrast you might require during a printing session. The contrast range of most variable-contrast papers equals that of four contrast grades of graded paper and with the appropriate filter, can produce grades in-between those offered by the normal graded paper, or seven choices of contrast in half-grade steps.

Suitable filters are available in squares (mounted or unmounted) or sheets and are manufactured of acetate or gelatin. The acetate type is not recommended for use between the enlarger lens and easel, as it can degrade and distort the projected image. Because most enlargers sold in recent years have a color drawer for using color printing filters, this is a good place for your variable-contrast filters.

GRADED PAPERS—These are generally faster in speed, offered in contrast grades above/below the range possible with variable-contrast papers, and are more uniform in speed among grades. For example, each of the three lower contrast grades of Kodak Kodabrome RC paper have the same speed, with the two higher grades rated at one-half the speed of the three lower ones. This makes exposure calculation far easier when switching among several different grades during a printing session.

Graded papers have two major disadvantages. Your control over contrast changes with a given grade is limited

to your choice of developer and development time. As it's not practical to work with several different developers during a single printing session, this can become a handicap in some cases. The other disadvantage rests in the amount of paper you must keep on hand and store, some of which may well deteriorate from age before it's completely used up. If you're constantly working toward obtaining the best negative possible, you should have little use for grades of more than one step above/below normal, but just when you don't have it on hand, you suddenly find a need for it.

SPECIAL PAPERS

While these are fewer in number and type with each passing year, there are several special photographic papers of interest. Luminos paper is available in

1. The proof sheet is an ideal way to select those frames you wish to enlarge. File it with your negatives and you'll never be at a loss to find what you're looking for very quickly.

2. The Spiratone Printer-Proofer™ eliminates the difficulties of proofing 35mm negatives found with some proofer designs. Both ends of the negative strip are secured under individual tabs.

3. Sunlight proof sheets can be made with a proof printer and Kodak Studio Proof paper. These sepia-tone proofs allow you to verify exposure, composition, etc. without resorting to a darkroom. Use this to select the frames to be printed and then make a permanent proof sheet at the same time.

4. A proof sheet is a necessity when working with 110 and other such small negatives. You'll also need a magnifier (8X will do fine) to check the proof sheet, as the images are far too small to inspect without one.

a special linen cloth type, while both Luminos and Supreme offer colored paper stock in a variety of pastel and psychedelic/iridescent tones. While each of these offers interesting possibilities, they're primarily novelty papers. Of more interest to the serious darkroom worker, Kodak Panalure paper can be used for making black-and-white prints from color negatives.

Making a black-and-white print on ordinary blue-sensitive paper from a color negative results in an unsatisfactory tonal rendition. As normal papers "see" the color negative as though you were printing it through a blue filter, red objects turn out too dark and

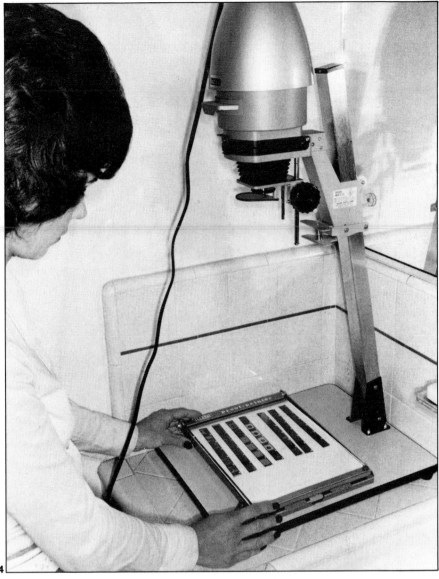

blue objects too light. This becomes most unpleasant when both red and blue objects in the negative are in close proximity, as this aspect tends to visually accentuate the incorrect rendition of tones.

Kodak Panalure is sensitive to all three primary colors and so reproduces everything in the color negative according to the appropriate gray tone, just as a panchromatic film emulsion would. In addition to this more normal rendition of the tonal scale when translating it from a color negative to a black-and-white print, it's possible to alter tonal balance during enlarging by fitting color compensating (CC) filters over the enlarger lens. If more dramatic changes are desired, try using the same contrast filters that you would use for black-and-white photography. Filter usage with Kodak Panalure follows traditional rules—a filter will lighten the tone of all objects similar in color, and darken those which are complementary in color. The chapter on filters will refresh your memory on filter usage if necessary.

Where production speed is of more importance than the permanence of the print, stabilization papers can be used. These require the use of a special processing machine and solutions instead of the usual tray and chemicals of the ordinary darkroom, but finished prints take only 15 seconds and are virtually dry upon emergence from the processing machining.

Stabilization papers contain developing agents within their emulsion and can be processed by simply applying an activator to their surface, which the processing machine does in a uniform and orderly manner for even develop-ment. A stabilizing agent then neutralizes the activator, converting the remaining silver into reasonably stable chemical compounds which remain in the paper instead of being washed out. For this reason, stabilization papers deteriorate relatively quickly once they're processed—even if kept in a dark place, they will generally show signs of deterioration within a few months—but by fixing and washing in the same way as ordinary papers, they can be made permanent if desired. Ordinary photo paper cannot be processed by stabilization, but stabilization paper can be processed with normal photo chemistry if the need arises.

PAPER STORAGE AND HANDLING

Like film, photographic paper can be damaged by improper storage and handling. When storage temperature is maintained between 40°F. and 50°F., with a relative humidity of between 40 to 60 percent, its physical and photographic characteristics remain relatively

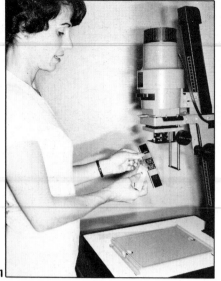

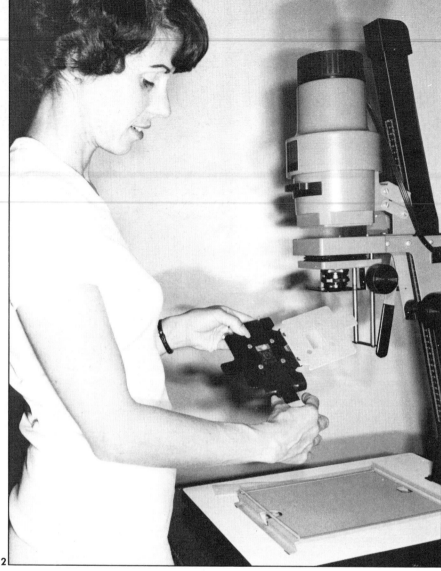

stable. But excessive variations in temperature and humidity will cause both the base and the emulsion to deteriorate rapidly. High temperatures and humidity can cause a fungus growth to form on the emulsion, while excessive dryness or a very low relative humidity will lead to brittleness of both the paper base and emulsion, resulting in excessive curling and a tendency toward cracking when used.

As photographic paper gradually deteriorates with age, it's marked with an expiration date, just like film. This date is an indicator provided by the manufacturer of how long his product will maintain its quality under proper storage conditions, and does not mean that paper whose expiration date has passed is no longer good. Outdated paper, like outdated film, can retain its quality beyond the stated date, as long as the recommended storage conditions have been met. The problem with buying outdated paper is mainly one of gambling upon what those storage conditions have been. It's a good idea to buy only fresh paper with an expiration date of at least one year beyond the date of purchase.

Although it's possible to work with the paper directly from the box, the unused portion should be kept wrapped in the black paper provided with it. This can prove a source of frustration while printing, especially if you're working with several different grades or surfaces of paper, meaning several different boxes. For 11x14 and smaller paper sizes, a more efficient way to store your paper is in a paper safe. These lighttight containers usually have 2-4 shelves inside, each of which will hold up to 200 sheets or so. Whenever you add a new supply of paper to an existing one, be sure to

put it underneath the older paper so that the older stock is used first.

Proper handling of photographic paper is of equal importance. Nothing is so frustrating as to watch a print over which you've labored long and hard to dodge and/or burn-in just right come up in the developer perfectly—and with a big fat thumb print right in the corner! As photographic emulsions are very sensitive to fingerprints, they should be handled only by the edges or the very tip of the corners, and with hands that are both dry and free from chemical contamination. Natural body oils and sweaty fingers will do just as much damage as chemicals.

Avoid unnecessary handling, as this can cause kinks or cracks in the dry surface that are not visible until the processed prints dry. Close the paper safe door or replace the box cover before turning on the white light. In fact, you should make it a practice to do this as soon as you've removed a sheet of paper, since leaving the box

1. Before inserting the negative in the carrier, dust it gently but thoroughly on both sides with a clean camel's hair brush such as the Staticmaster. This brush eliminates dust-attracting static electricity.

2. Carefully place the negative in the carrier. This step can lead to multiple negative scratches if not done correctly, or if the carrier itself is dirty.

3. Open the enlarger head with one hand, position the negative carrier and then close the head.

4. Check the image on the easel for dust spots and lint marks. Remove any you find by opening the enlarger head and using a can of aerosol gas as shown. A brief squirt will do the job.

5. Now adjust the height of the enlarger head until you have approximately the image size desired. Height adjustment controls vary in design, but the majority are located somewhere on the column.

6. The lens focusing control will be found on the bellows. With the lens wide open, adjust the focus until the image on the easel is sharp. If this changes the image size too much, you may have to readjust the height and then refocus.

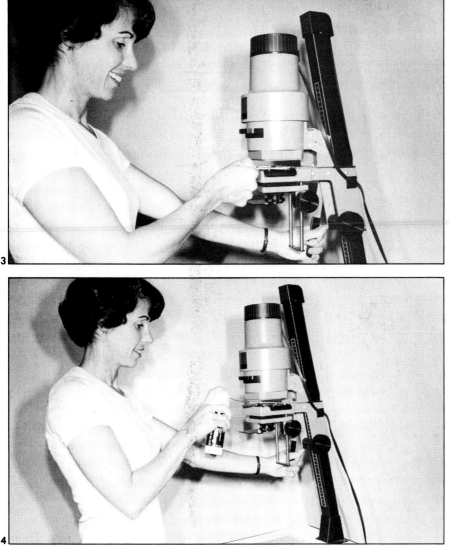

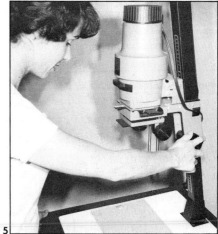

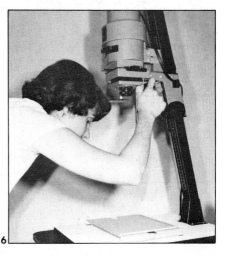

or paper safe open will expose the paper to safelight illumination as well as stray light from the enlarger while it's on—and that's just asking for trouble.

As safelight fog can also degrade the image on the paper while it's in the easel or developing, try to keep the paper in the shadow of your body and turn the safelight off or point it in another direction while you compose and focus the image. If possible, try to keep the safelight off while you're exposing the paper and during the first 30-60 seconds of development.

If you find it necessary to write on the back of an unprocessed sheet of paper, do so lightly with a soft pencil after placing the paper on a hard, smooth surface to prevent the writing from showing through on the face of the print. Special pens with fast-drying waterproof ink are available for writing on the back of resin-coated papers.

PROCESSING PHOTOGRAPHIC PAPERS

Processing black-and-white prints is a three-chemical procedure involving a developer, stop bath and fixing solution. Those interested in maximum print life will also use a hypo eliminator after the fixer to reduce the wash time and ensure the removal and elimination of virtually all the hypo from the paper.

PAPER DEVELOPERS—With rare exceptions, developers used with photographic papers differ from those used with film, although their chemical action on the paper's emulsion is very similar in nature. Paper developers are formulated to emphasize the image tone of a given type of paper, and are selected by experienced photographers on that basis. Some, like the very popular Kodak Dektol, are considered to be neutral and are thus useful regardless of the image tone of the paper. Unlike film developers, those used to develop prints cannot be replenished and should be discarded when you've finished printing or when the solution becomes exhausted.

Each package of photographic paper contains a data sheet. This data sheet contains the manufacturer's recom-

mendations for the correct time/temperature that will provide the optimum print quality, as well as a useful range of development times. While prints can be developed by inspection, you'll find it best to keep the time and temperature constant, varying the exposure as necessary until the print reaches its desired density within the specified time/temperature frame. To avoid the unnecessary waste of paper, exposure can be determined by use of a test strip or an enlarging exposure meter, which we'll discuss later.

It's important that the developer be maintained as closely as possible to the recommended 68°F. temperature, because significant variations in temperature mean corresponding changes in exposure—a waste of both time and material, since the resulting prints are far from the best possible. When necessary to maintain temperature control, you can place the developer tray in a larger one filled with water that's several degrees above or below that of the developer. If room temperature is normal, the developer will then remain at 68°F. or close to it. During summer months, when developer temperature tends to rise quickly, the liquid-filled plastic cubes used for cooling drinks

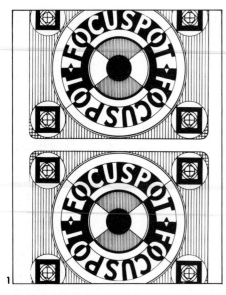

are very efficient in temperature control and can be used directly in the developer. As they will not melt and dilute the solution, such cubes provide a quick and easy way of holding developer temperatures at the correct level.

Paper developers are usually concentrates or stock solutions designed for dilution before use. A given quantity of developer has the capacity to process a certain number of prints before it becomes exhausted and must be replaced with a fresh solution. This capacity is subject to several conditions—the size of the prints being made, the length of time it stands in the tray (oxidation), the type of pictures being developed (dark ones reduce developer activity more quickly than light ones), and contamination by short-stop or fixer. A contaminated, over-worked or oxidized developer turns brown, indicating chemical exhaustion. If used beyond this point, the developer can stain the print surface or its base, ruining the print.

The developer tray used should be large enough to let you work with the prints easily. The usual recommendation is one size larger than the maximum size prints you intend to make. Don't skimp on the developer—use enough in the tray to cover the prints while they are developing. Prints should be agitated during development by rocking the tray gently, or uneven development is likely to result. Keep your fingers off the paper surface and use print tongs to remove the prints for inspection or to place them in the short-stop.

STOP BATH—Hold the print by one corner to drain excess developer when development is complete and then slide it into the short-stop. This bath halts development quickly and evenly,

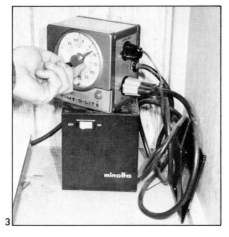

prevents the formation of scum on the print surface, and protects the fixer from contamination by the developer. Contamination will destroy the fixer's acidity and prevent the print emulsion from hardening satisfactorily.

As ordinary stop baths are colorless, there's no way to determine their efficiency, so the use of an indicator stop bath is recommended whenever you're making more than a handful of prints. These contain a yellow dye that turns bluish when the stop bath is exhausted or contaminated. A stop bath that's too strong will cause a mottle or water-soak condition in the paper base, as will lack of proper agitation when the print is initially immersed.

FIXING BATH—This is the same chemical as used for fixing films, but the same solution should not be used to fix films and prints interchangeably, as the differences in the silver compounds formed from the different emulsions will quickly reduce its ability to fix either film or print. This leads to premature exhaustion and insufficient fixing, which can result in a stain that's next to impossible to remove.

After draining the print of stop bath, it should be placed in the tray of fixer. This should be a deeper tray than that used for development, as prints will accumulate here for several minutes before they are transferred to the wash bath. As with film, the fixer makes the print's image permanent by turning the unexposed silver into soluble compounds which can be removed by washing.

Fixing a single print in fresh solution is a relatively quick process, as the fixer contacts all surfaces of the print evenly. But as prints accumulate and/or fixer reaction time slows down, they should be agitated and separated from each other to assure that the fixing action takes place uniformly. Prints left in the fixing bath longer than recommended will require an excessively long wash time to remove the silver compounds.

The life of the fixer is dependent upon the amount of silver compounds it contains. Once this silver concentration reaches a certain level, insoluble compounds begin to form which washing cannot remove from the paper. As with developer, fixer life is also dependent upon the size of the prints being fixed, print density (light ones leave more silver than dark ones), and contamination level. The two-bath fixing method described in the last chapter is especially useful in assuring proper print fixing.

HYPO ELIMINATOR—Prints treated with a hypo eliminator bath prior to washing will require only about one-third the usual wash time, and will contain far less chemicals when dried than will nontreated prints washed for the full duration specified. A hypo eliminator bath is neither required nor recommended for use with RC papers.

PRINT WASHING—When fixer or silver is left in a print after washing, they eventually form a silver sulfide which either stains the print or causes it to fade. For this reason, a proper wash is of equal importance to correct fixing.

Conventional papers have an absorbent base, which makes it virtually impossible to remove every trace of fixer and silver. For this reason, SW prints should be washed under running water for approximately 10 minutes, and DW paper for about 30 minutes, using some method of removing the fixer-laden water from the bottom of the washer. This may be a siphon device attached to a regular tray, or a standard print washer.

The length of the wash bath and the rate of water flow are both immaterial if the prints are allowed to cling to each other while washing, or lie in a pile on top of the water or at the bottom of the washer. Where prints larger than 5x7 are being washed, you should agitate them frequently to insure adequate washing. Placing too many prints in a washer at one time reduces the effectiveness of the bath and can lead to hypo staining.

When a batch of prints is already in the wash cycle and you have another group ready to wash, place the second group in a separate tray of water to await their turn in the wash bath. If you dump them in with prints already partially washed, the contamination from the fixer will affect the partially washed prints as well, and require that you start the wash cycle all over again.

Washing resin-coated papers requires a different technique, as the duration of the wash bath is far shorter. Prints should be continually agitated under a flow sufficient to change the water at least once in four minutes. RC prints should not be overwashed.

FUNDAMENTALS OF PRINTING

A print is basically the positive reproduction of your negative, and to obtain it, you must go through a variation of the same procedure as that necessary to produce a negative—exposure, development, fixing, washing and drying. But while the negative is unique and fixed both in size and in shape by the camera that made it, a print can be made in any size/shape/quantity that you desire.

During the process of printing, it's possible to manipulate exposure, contrast, content, perspective, etc. to improve upon the negative image for creative purposes. When these tools

1. **Excessively dense negatives are difficult to focus. Substitute a high-contrast negative like this to focus the enlarger, then replace the dense negative and make your exposure.**
2. **The test strip is the oldest and least expensive way of determining printing exposure. It can be made either horizontally or vertically, depending upon where the most important tones are located in the negative. In this case, skin tones are centered, thus a horizontal test strip was made. The superimposed figures show exposure times for comparison with another method of exposure determination shown in Photo 4.**
3. **Some timers connect to your enlarger and turn it off once the exposure is completed. This type is ideal for accurate exposures when you're making several identical prints of a single negative.**
4. **This test print of the same negative used for the test strip in Photo 2 shows the results with the Kodak Projection Print Scale. According to this, a 12-second exposure will produce the best skin tone rendition.**
5. **The Kodak Projection Print Scale is an inexpensive density wedge made on acetate and produces far more accurate results than the usual test strip, with far less effort.**

are used properly, they can often enhance the creative content and the visual effect of your picture. Before moving into the various tools and techniques, we should first consider the two possibilities of printing a negative—by contact and by enlarging.

CONTACT PRINTS—A contact print is one made directly from the negative by placing the printing paper in contact with the negative. This results in a print of the same size/shape as the negative. Because of the smaller negative sizes popular today, contact prints are not very useful; there really isn't much that you can do with a 1x1½-inch print from a 35mm negative when it comes

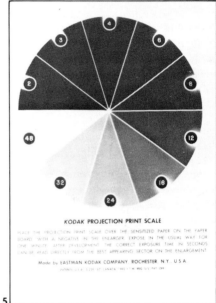

to exhibition or display.

But contact printing is useful in making a proof sheet. This is a "multiple" contact print of all the negatives from one roll of film or of one particular subject, printed together on a single sheet of paper. The proof sheet is an inexpensive way of negative comparison to decide which ones merit enlargement, a useful tool in deciding how the negative might be cropped (if at all), and what special techniques could be of value in producing the best enlargement. Proof sheets are also useful as a record of your work, allowing you to locate individual negatives with ease from your negative file.

Proof sheets are generally made on 8x10 paper. This will hold 20 or 36 35mm negatives cut into four or six strips, 12 2¼x2¼ negatives cut into three strips, or four 4x5 negatives. For ease in reading, all the negatives should be oriented in the same direction and in the order in which they were originally taken. To minimize the inevitable differences in density and contrast between four to 36 individual negatives on a single sheet of paper, it's a good idea to make your proof sheet on grade No. 2 paper. This makes it possible to calculate deviations from normal paper contrast and provides a point of reference which is helpful in choosing the appropriate paper grade to be used for enlargements of individual negatives.

Once the proof sheet has been processed and dried, it can be marked with a black grease pencil or China Marker to indicate cropping and printing instructions easily read under a darkroom safelight. Red pencil markings are not as useful, as they tend to disappear under the safelight. Gently wiping the proof sheet surface with a paper tissue will remove the pencil marks when you're ready to file the proof sheet; if marks are left on the paper for several weeks, they may prove stubborn to remove. In such cases, dampen the tissue with cigarette lighter fluid and the marks will rub off easily without a trace.

For "quick and dirty" proof sheets when you want to check negative quality or picture composition without setting up the darkroom for a single print, Kodak Studio Proof paper is very useful, as it requires no chemical processing. Studio Proof is a printing-out paper which produces a reddish-brown image when exposed to sunlight or an ultraviolet light source. Because the image will eventually turn completely dark just from exposure to normal room illumination, this paper is useful only for proofing. Should you desire permanence of the image for any reason, overexpose the paper to produce a very dark image and then place it in a tray of fixer. This bleaches the image somewhat while making it permanent, and with normal washing and drying, the image will last indefinitely.

Care should be taken when using Studio Proof to keep its temperature and humidity at the recommended levels, as it has a tendency to turn brownish and mottle. Buy it in the 25-sheet package and keep it in the refrigerator or such deterioration may take place quite rapidly.

Interpreting what you see on the proof sheet can be tricky, unless you take certain things into consideration. It's not unusual to enlarge a "perfect" negative only to find that the larger print is less than perfect. For example,

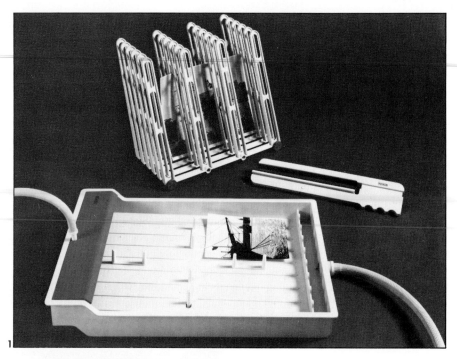

negative contrast and density will often look much better in the small print on the proof sheet than they actually are. Other negatives which may well make excellent prints can appear less appealing on the proof. You should thus regard the proof sheet as an *indicator* of potential interest rather than an *absolute measure*, and look for subject matter and treatment instead of technical quality.

HOW TO MAKE A PROOF SHEET—For best results, you should use a SW paper with a smooth surface and glossy sheen of the same contrast grade and speed as your usual enlarging paper. If proofing color negatives in black-and-white, use Kodak Panalure paper. At a minimum, you'll need a sheet of glass and a light source. Your enlarger will serve as a suitable light source by raising its head with the empty negative

carrier in place until the field of light produced is somewhat larger than your proof paper.

Place a sheet of paper under the enlarger with its emulsion side facing upward (with only the safelight on) and arrange the negatives to be proofed on it, with their emulsion side facing down. This positioning results in what we call emulsion-to-emulsion contact, and assures that the prints will be properly oriented left-to-right. To hold the negatives and paper in close contact for sharp registration, lay a piece of clean glass (8x10 minimum, 11x14 preferred) on top of the sandwich. Stop the enlarger lens down to f/8 and expose for 10 seconds.

Process the proof sheet just as you would an enlargement, and once it's in the fixer safely, turn on the white light and inspect the finished proof. If it's too dark overall, your 10-second exposure was too great; if too light, make another and increase the exposure accordingly. Many times, the black border around the negatives will be helpful in determining how appropriate your exposure/development was, especially if you decide to develop the proof by inspection rather than time/temperature. Anything less than a good, cold black indicates that either exposure or development was off.

A wide variety of proof printers is available at your photo dealer, and acquiring one has a number of virtues over the use of a sheet of glass as described above. Basically, such proof printers are two-piece units—a sheet of heavy clear glass hinged at one end to a metal or plastic base containing a

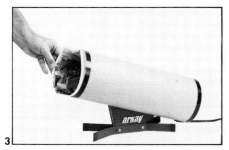

1. Paterson offers this unique print washer for RC paper. The adjustable pegs in the washer keep prints separated for rapid water flow and prevent the usual bunch-up of prints in the center of the washer. Also shown is an RC paper squeegee and drying rack.

2. For those who want super accuracy in determining printing exposures, CdS enlarging meters like this Paterson unit are available. To use, the meter is placed on the baseboard with the diffusing screen held under the lens. The meter dial is rotated until its neon lamp lights. The correct exposure can then be read directly from the dial.

3. The Arkay tubular 814 dryer handles RC paper quickly and is a very compact unit which can be easily stored.

4. The blotter book is the least expensive way to dry prints. RC prints dry rapidly, but conventional papers require a considerable drying period in the book.

5. To minimize print curl with the blotter system, use a blotter press. These consist of individual blotter sheets between two hardboard covers and are held together with adjustable straps.

sponge-rubber pad. The hinged plate may have clips or grooves to hold six six-frame 35mm negative strips, or three four-frame 120/620 strips in place. After positioning a sheet of paper on the sponge-rubber pad (emulsion facing upward) and loading the negatives into the hinged plate's clips/grooves (emulsion facing downward), the plate is closed to form a sandwich. Some proof printers have locking snaps or clips to provide uniform pressure on the negative/paper, while others depend upon the weight of the glass plate to produce sharp image registration.

The commercial proof printer just described is far easier to work with when your negatives have a tendency to curl instead of laying flat. The clips/grooves in the hinged plate hold them in position and prevent the curl from causing the negative strips to overlap one another or buckle as the plate is closed. It also makes life easier on the negatives since the possibility of getting fingerprints or scratches on them while making a proof is minimized.

ENLARGEMENTS—Now that you have a proof sheet and have decided which negatives to enlarge, let's walk through the process step-by-step. Having decided which negative to enlarge, and how great the degree of enlargement will be, you should study the proof sheet to determine if any printing control should be exercised to improve the quality of the finished picture. For our purposes here, let's assume that you're going to make a straight enlargement this time, and then we'll discuss the basic techniques of print control that are available to you.

PREPARATIONS FOR PRINTING—WHITE LIGHT ON—The greater the degree of enlargement, the more prominent any dust, dirt or lint on the negative will appear in the finished print. Use a camel's-hair brush to remove loose particles from both surfaces of the negative. I find the Staticmaster brush ideal for this, as its polonium strip neutralizes static electricity which often forms when a negative is brushed, especially on dry, cold days.

Position the negative to be enlarged in the negative carrier's cutout with its dull (emulsion) side facing down. To make the projected image appear right-side up on your easel, insert the negative with its bottom edge facing away from you. This means that vertical negatives will face to your right, unless your negative carrier has a provision to orient vertical shots from top to bottom.

Close the carrier gently to avoid stirring up dust, and just before inserting it into the enlarger, tilt the carrier under the light projected through the enlarger lens at a sharp angle and examine it carefully to make certain that you've removed every troublemaking particle. Slide the carrier into the enlarger just as carefully, checking the top surface as you go. An aerosol can of compressed gas comes in handy at this point, as you can insert the slender nozzle into the carrier slot in the enlarger and "pick off" individual dust/lint specks with a short burst. Once you're satisfied that you've got every spot of dust, close the enlarger head down on the carrier slowly and you're in business.

If you think that I've overemphasized the problem of negative cleaning before printing, just remember that every speck you remove before means one less spot to retouch on the finished print. And few things are more frustrating than to make a print using manipulative controls and have it come up just right in the developer, only to find that you've got one or more dust or lint marks in the wrong places which must be spotted out or otherwise hidden if the print is to be used. Thus the little extra effort you exert at this point can save you considerable trouble later.

PREPARATIONS FOR PRINTING—WHITE LIGHT OFF, SAFELIGHT ON—You must make two adjustments—one for print size and one for a sharp image. Turn on the enlarger lamp and

Once you've adjusted the print size and sharpness to satisfaction, you can set to work. Turn off the enlarger lamp, insert a sheet of paper in the easel and stop the lens down two or three f-stops from the maximum aperture, where most enlarging lenses give their best performance. Stopping down too far can actually cause a deterioration of image sharpness, will lengthen the duration of exposure sufficiently to introduce the possibility of negative buckle from overheating, and with some enlarger optics, can result in a focus shift. For a straight print, the ideal exposure is about 10 seconds and the aperture selected should provide this exposure time or one quite close to it.

Those relatively new to enlarging will find the next step to be the most difficult problem they'll face in the darkroom: How to determine the proper exposure time without wasting half a box of paper. Experienced workers will be able to ''guesstimate'' the exposure with a surprising degree of accuracy, but unless you fit into this category, the answer is to make a test strip.

While we've already seen the use of a test strip in checking safelight illumination for fog, let's go over the procedure briefly as it relates specifically to exposure determination in enlarging. Begin by placing a strip of enlarging paper about two inches wide on the easel face up, and cover approximately 5/6 of it with a piece of cardboard. Turn on the enlarger lamp for a total of 60 seconds, uncovering another 1/6 of the paper every 10 seconds. When the one-minute exposure is finished, turn off the enlarger. Process the test strip in the developer for two minutes, place in the stop bath for 5-10 seconds and then place it in the fixer. After a couple of minutes there, turn on the white light. Remove the test strip from the fixer, rinse it briefly under running water and inspect the results. One of the six exposures will produce a segment on the test strip that is representative of the result you want—and that's the exposure you'll give the print.

Those who wish to be more precise about exposure determination in enlarging will be interested in the use of a print scale or meter. An example of the former, the Kodak Projection Print Scale is a square of film that contains 10 pie-shaped wedges graduated in density from light to dark. This is placed on a square of enlarging paper and the enlarger is turned on for 60 seconds with the aperture set at f/8. After processing and fixing the test

position your easel under the lens. If the easel is adjustable, be sure that the margins are set to the desired width, then raise or lower the enlarger head until the image size is approximately the same as that of the print desired, as represented by the easel area. This will establish the gross size of the print.

With the aperture wide open, focus the lens until the image is sharp. This will establish the final print size. If too large or too small, readjust the enlarger head in the appropriate direction and refocus until the final print size matches the easel area. Those with good eyesight should not have any difficulty in focusing the image sharply— the trick is to pick certain areas of the subject such as catchlights in the eyes, letters on a sign or other similar objects where light contrasts with dark

to make the determination of precise focus easy.

If you have difficulty with focusing, you might find one of the enlarging magnifiers that focuses on the grain useful, although many workers simply rely on a high-powered magnifying glass. With negatives that are particularly dense, focus can be a problem regardless of how good your eyesight is. The use of a special high-contrast focusing negative in place of the negative you wish to print will allow you to set the focus precisely for that particular degree of magnification, or you can simply move the negative in the carrier and focus on its edge along the frame line separation. Incidentally, you can make your own focusing negative by simply taking a discarded one and scratching several fine lines across the emulsion with a needle.

1-4. When you do your own printing, you're the judge of how the subject will be interpreted. Variations in tonal control are possible by slight changes in exposure without using control techniques. Depending upon the desired effect, each of these could be considrered a good print when viewed by itself, but (2) is clearly the best when the four are all seen in a series.

square, the wedge that appears most natural or normal is selected. The number contained within that particular wedge is the proper exposure time in seconds.

There's also a wide variety of special printing meters, which determine the correct exposure by use of CdS cells with neon indicators, or test probes used to read specific areas of the print. Some meters provide an averaging reading, while others utilize a spot reading. All are expensive, complex to use *properly* and of little use to the average darkroom buff unless he's also a collector of equipment.

Having determined the appropriate exposure for the negative to be printed, you now place a full sheet of enlarging paper in the easel, turn on the enlarger lamp and time the exposure. Don't touch either the enlarger or the bench/counter on which it stands during the period of exposure, as even the slightest vibration can be enough to blur the print slightly. A foot switch is an ideal way to control exposure duration—stepping on the switch turns the enlarger on and removing foot pressure shuts it off again. For those exercising printing control during the exposure, this leaves both hands free for manipulation of the print as desired. There are various other methods, including the use of a sheet of card-

board held under the lens with the lamp on. You remove the cardboard, time the exposure and replace the cardboard beneath the lens to cut off the light reaching the easel while you turn off the lamp. Personally, I prefer to turn the line switch on/off to make an exposure.

After the enlarger is turned off, remove the paper from the easel and slide it into the tray of developer face up with one hand while rocking the tray slightly with the other to assure that the solution will cover the entire print surface as quickly as possible. I know old-timers in the darkroom who turn the paper over so that the emulsion faces down and then place it on top of the developer's surface, dunking the paper into the solution by tapping the center lightly with a print tong. You'll discover endless variations on each of these steps as you go along, but you'll eventually settle on an exact procedure that is most comfortable for you. From the developer, the print is removed, drained and immersed in the stop bath, passing along each of the steps described earlier—from developer to stop bath to fixer to hypo eliminator and then to the wash bath.

PRINT DRYING—How this final step is carried out will depend upon the type of paper used—conventional or resin-coated—and your own personal preferences. Air drying by placing the washed prints between blotters, blotter books or blotter rolls is the simplest and least expensive method—but it's also the most time-consuming and for SW papers, the least satisfactory. If you want a glossy finish, the prints must be squeegeed onto a ferrotype plate and allowed to air dry. Subjecting the ferrotype plate to heat from a radiator, hot air vent or other such source inevitably results in uneven drying and the prints end up with a warping effect called "oyster shell"—circular ring imprints which crack the print surface as it pops free from the plate.

A step up the ladder in time saved and money expended are the various flatbed and flip-over print dryers, which contain one or more hot-plate type heating elements housed within their metal case. The flatbed model has a single drying surface while the flip-over has two, much like joining two flatbed models together bottom-to-bottom. Most of these dryers are not suitable for glazing print surfaces without the use of a ferrotype plate, despite the claims made for them. Buying the dryer amounts to investing in a heatbox

1

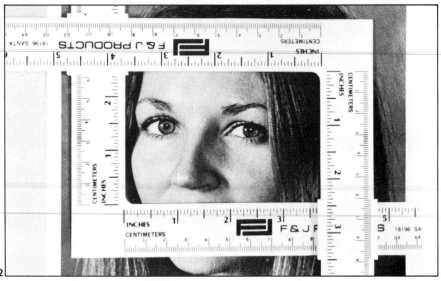

2

for ferrotype plates. Unfortunately, many produce heat that's unevenly distributed or difficult to control temperature-wise regardless of the thermostatic controls with which many are fitted—don't buy one without a thermostatic control!

Rotary drum dryers are the only really satisfactory electric dryers available. Squeegeed prints are simply placed on the continuous canvas belt—face up for glazing, face down for matte finishes—and retrieved from the print table when the drum has completed a full revolution. Disregard the drum dryers that you must turn by hand; if they're not motorized, they won't work any more efficiently than the flatbed or flip-over types. For the average amateur in his darkroom, the motorized electric drum dryer is a neat, convenient and professional way to go, but the number of prints he dries at one time will seldom justify having it.

Electric dryers are the source of more problems than they solve. Flatbed and flip-over units often turn out prints with wavy edges because of uneven drying. Their canvas aprons become quickly contaminated with hypo if prints are insufficiently washed, passing the contamination along to carefully washed prints that follow. Ferrotype plates tend to produce an erratic glaze, leaving blank spots at random on the print surface regardless of how carefully the prints were squeegeed and rolled in place. Scratches on the ferrotype plate surface transfer to the print and a dirty ferrotype plate, insufficient hardener in the fixer, exhusted fixer, and too little/too great a wash time are all reasons why the one print you desperately want simply will not come off the plate by itself, and when assisted by a friendly hand, ends up with cracks in the print surface.

If the foregoing sounds like I'm discouraged with the drying of conventional prints, then you'll begin to un-

3

derstand why resin-coated paper has proven so popular since it was first introduced. Resin-coated papers have the advantage of delivering a perfect glaze from every sheet of glossy paper, but cannot tolerate heat to any great extent. Thus simple convection racks are being used in increasing numbers to hold these prints while they air dry, usually a matter of 10-15 minutes. Other manufacturers have recently designed low-heat forced-air units to cut drying time somewhat.

PRINT CURL—Another source of considerable frustration to the amateur working with conventional papers, print curl seems to afflict all fiber-based papers to some degree, and is worse with SW papers than heavier stock. Several manufacturers sell print flattening solutions in concentrated form, which work like a wetting agent with film when diluted for use, but I've nev-

er been able to reduce print curl significantly with any of these. Fresh paper has less of a tendency to curl than older paper, and both temperature and humidity play a role in the degree of curl encountered.

Print curl can be minimized when using a flatbed or flip-over dryer by removing the prints before they are completely dried and placing them between blotter sheets under pressure. Should you slip up and dry them completely, put the prints face down on the dryer's canvas apron as soon as it has been filled with more wet prints. Moisture in the form of steam which leaves the apron will enter the dry prints and cause them to reverse-curl somewhat without cracking the emulsion. Deposit the prints between blotters, apply pressure and wait.

The lack of significant print curl remains another point in favor of resin-coated papers. While such papers generally possess a slight convex curl before processing, it disappears as soon as they hit the solution. Should you encounter problems with resin-coated paper curling when dry, it indicates that your wash time is excessive; reduce the duration of the wash to the period specified by the manufacturer and your problems with print curl will disappear.

PRINT CONTROL

In addition to the strictly technical aspects of making a good quality print from your negative, there are various creative considerations which can be exercised at your option to enhance the appeal and impact of a straight print. Each of us has an idea in our mind's eye of exactly how our final print should look, and these techniques of print control should be used toward achieving that end result.

4

5

6

1. **Despite your careful composition in the camera, many pictures can be improved by further cropping in the darkroom. Use a pair of L-shaped cards as shown to help determine how the print can best be improved by cropping.**

2. **Devices like the Crop-It are even handier than the homemade variety, since they interlock and move together to maintain proportions.**

3-6. **The advantages of cropping and other print manipulative devices are shown in this series. The basic picture (3) contains a distracting background and an out-of-focus object at the left of the frame. Both are removed and the composition strengthened by cropping as in (4). Changing to a vertical format (6) further strengthens the picture. For those who object on the basis that diagonals should lead the eye into the picture from the left, the negative can be flipped and printed (5) to provide that effect, as long as there is nothing in the picture to tell the viewer that it was printed backwards.**

TOTAL CONTROL—Techniques offering total control deal with overall considerations that affect the entire print: size, shape, cropping and contrast. The size of the print you make will depend upon the quality and condition of your negative, and the use to which the print will be put. To illustrate this concept with extremes, you wouldn't attempt to produce a satisfactory wall mural from an 8x11mm Minox negative, nor use an 8x10 negative to make a wallet-sized picture.

Tradition has established a number of size restraints centered around the 8x10 and 11x14 sizes. Photographic paper is manufactured in standard sizes, frames and other mounting devices are made to fit these sizes, and people *expect* to see their finished prints conform. But from a creative point of view, size should more properly be a by-product of the print's use, as long as the negative has the potential to deliver the size desired without

introducing technical considerations such as excessive granularity, lack of apparent sharpness, etc.

Shape is another creative aspect limited to negative proportions by manufacturers, who produce standardized paper shapes, generally rectangular in nature and approximately proportional to negative formats. Yet by simply changing the proportions of the print, it's often possible to emphasize a feeling of width or height in such a way as to increase the visual impact of your print. To this end, cropping much of the top and bottom from a rectangular negative to eliminate excessive foreground and background can result in a narrow picture which appears to have been photographed with a wide-angle rather than the normal lens.

If the standard 8x10 print you make doesn't seem to have the strength you think it's capable of, use it as a ''work'' print. Try masking it with paper

strips in various ways to determine exactly where its strength lies. In this manner, you can quickly find out if a different shape or proportion will really improve its visual impact. Should you settle upon a shape that works better, simply mark the print with a grease pencil as a guide for reprinting.

Although you should always work toward achieving the best possible composition when taking a picture, there are times when you'll see a more effective way of presenting your subject after the fact. By enlarging only a section of the negative, you may strengthen its impact or change its emphasis. Known as cropping, this technique is generally used to remove extraneous material from the foreground, background or sides of the picture area. In addition to strengthening the creative impact of your work, cropping can often be used as a means of salvaging a technically imperfect negative by eliminating such defects as light fog, uneven development lines, negative scratches and emulsion blemishes.

To determine whether or not composition can be improved in the darkroom by cropping, use a pair of L-shaped pieces of cardboard with a work print or proof. These will form a variable frame that can be moved around on the print and adjusted to mask-off undesirable portions of the picture area. Working with a variable frame in this way will generally show you several different proportions that are more effective than those of the standard paper format.

When using this technique, bear in

1

2

mind that shape will have a direct relationship with size in this case. If you select only a small portion of the negative to be enlarged, the size of the enlargement possible will be limited by the degree of grain and the sharpness of the negative—the larger you blow-up the small negative segment, the less sharp and grainy the resulting print will be. Sectional enlargements of this type can often substitute for the telephoto lens you didn't have when you took the picture.

While it's possible to achieve such cropping by simply adjusting the enlarger head until the desired segment of the negative fits the easel size as required, the stray light spilling around the easel from the remainder of the negative may be sufficiently strong to degrade your image quality. In cases where cropping is extreme, it's a good idea to make a mask from opaque paper roughly equivalent in size to the desired negative segment. This will reduce the possibility of light from the negative's edge striking the enlarger column and reflecting back onto your paper in the easel.

As we've seen, contrast can be manipulated through the choice of paper grade and variations in exposure/ development times. When a pictured printed on a normal paper grade (No. 2) contains muddy grays in place of clean blacks and whites, a harder gradation of paper (No. 3-6) will improve the contrast level. Similarly, if the picture exhibits a lack of detail in the blacks and whites when printed on the normal grade paper, try a softer grade

(No. 0-1). The same effects are achieved when working with variable-contrast papers through the choice of printing filters.

As the latitude of photographic papers is very limited, normal exposure/ development always produces the best print. But where the desired change in gradation is less than the full step between paper grades, or when you're out of the necessary grade, alterations in exposure/development can prove a useful substitute. A slight increase in exposure followed by shortening the development time slightly will produce a softer gradation—decreasing the exposure and increasing the development gives a harder gradation. How acceptable the results will be when you deviate from the norm in cases like this will depend upon how great the deviation is, and how the particular paper used reacts to it—not all papers will tolerate this practice with the same results.

A couple of precautions are in order whenever you practice contrast control by varying the exposure/development

cycle. The briefer the development time, the more the print should be agitated to prevent a mottle or streaks from appearing. When development is increased, it's best to do so with the safelight shielded or turned away from the developer tray, since longer than normal development times invite safelight fog to occur.

LOCAL CONTROL—Sometimes it's not desirable to alter the relationship of the entire print relative to what it already is—perhaps just one or two small areas are affected, requiring local rather than total control. There are three ways in which such local contrast control can be exercised: dodging (holding back light from a particular area to make it lighter), burning-in (giving additional exposure to certain areas to make them darker) and the technique of selective development.

The first two techniques are used to improve the basic appearance of your print without changing its overall effect, and are usually the first methods of creative print control with which most amateurs work. Both require more manual dexterity than equipment, although the use of a foot switch is highly recommended as a means of controlling the enlarger light, because it frees both hands for the necessary manipulative procedures.

DODGING—By holding light back from reaching certain areas of the print, you are exposing that area for a shorter length of time. To prevent light from exposing the print in such areas, experienced darkroom workers often use their hands by forming the necessary shapes (which may be unusual at times) with their fingers.

The less-experienced will generally work with odd sizes and shapes made from cardboard and attached to a handle of fine but stiff wire. Beginners are urged to either make their own dodging tools in this manner as the occasion for their need arises, or to buy the commercial dodgers sold for this use.

Whatever device you employ, it must be in constant motion during the entire exposure or the dodged area will show up in the print with an edge that's sharply defined from light to dark, and the handle will be revealed as a fuzzy streak. Whether fluttering, circular or concentric in nature, the type of motion used is not of great importance—just as long as it's used continuously.

Where should the dodging tool be held for best results—close to the paper or close to the lens? For the most part, it doesn't really matter—the positioning will depend upon the size of the shadow cast by the dodger, relative to the size of the area to be dodged. But in some cases, you'll find it virtually impossible to work close to the paper (especially with your hands) without leaving some kind of noticeable change in density at the edge of the dodged area, usually caused by light spill-over from the dodging tool onto those areas immediately adjacent to the one being dodged.

This problem can be avoided by employing what the scientific-minded among us would call the penumbra. A shadow cast by an object close to the easel is simply the difference between

2

3

full shadow or fully lighted. But by moving the dodging tool further from the paper (closer to the lens), a "gray-out" occurs between the fully lighted and full shadow areas, resulting in a partially shaded area known as the penumbra. This placement minimizes any density changes and combined with movement of the dodging tool, is sufficient to result in a smooth blend between dodged and untouched areas of the print.

BURNING-IN—By allowing more light to reach certain areas of the print, you are exposing those areas for a greater length of time. This technique is useful where shadow detail exists, but negative density or brightness range is such that it doesn't appear when the highlights are held to a normal printing exposure. Burning-in is the reverse of dodging, and as such, uses the opposite tools. Where you might work with a small circle as a dodging tool, the sheet from which the circle was cut would serve as an appropriate tool for burning-in a similarly shaped area. Again, experienced workers will use their hands for burning-in, because you can adjust the size of the opening through which light passes infinitely and immediately. Like dodging, whatever tool you use must be kept in constant motion to prevent a "halo" effect, and the burning-in device can be positioned wherever appropriate between easel and lens, as light spill-over is not a problem of concern here. Should it occur, it will only serve to shorten the duration of burning-in and help reduce your work.

You can create a highly useful tool for burning-in which will probably receive more work than any you could buy. Take an 8x10 card (the one accompanying your paper should work nicely) and trim off the corners as

4

5

1,3. The texture screen effect can be slight (3) or exaggerated (1). Negative defects can often be hidden by using the appropriate screen. If chosen properly, the corrective effect becomes a creative one at the same time. (Photo [1] Michael Parrish and [3] Hank Harris.)
2. The use of texture screens is a popular control technique. This example shows how one of the many Paterson screens will alter a basic print.
4-5. Control techniques can be used in creative as well as corrective ways. San Francisco's Trans-America Building stands beside an example of the city's older architecture (4). To demonstrate its stability during an earthquake, Ralph Merzlak dodged the building while moving the easel at five-second intervals.

shown in the accompanying illustration. Then use a sharp-bladed knife to cut a circle about the size of a quarter from the center. The trimmed corners will give you three different shapes which will come in handy when those light corners of your print require just a little touch-up to prevent their distracting effect from interfering with the subject.

The center hole serves a dual purpose. When using the card for working on edges or corners, hold it with your thumb in the hole for a firm grip and to prevent light from passing through; when working on small areas within the print, hold the card by its edge and adjust the placement between lens and easel until it's correct for the area being burned-in.

IT'S ALL A MATTER OF TECHNIQUE—Dodging and burning-in as means of controlling contrast in selected areas of the print are effective only if it is impossible to tell that you employed the techniques in making the print. Practice is very important, and for anything other than a simple touch-up of a single area, you should diagram such difficult negatives once you've recognized the problems and what must be done. Made on a separate card or right on the work print for filing, this diagram should show the rough boundaries of each area controlled, as well

plex print, only to find that while the majority of the print is satisfactory, one or two areas remain too light even after full development. But before you throw the print away and attempt to duplicate it by repeating the tedious process, you might consider selective development as a means of bringing up the light area(s) to match the rest of the print. If successful, this could save you from having to make another print. Selective development is accomplished by the use of hot water or concentrated developer on the affected area of the print.

The technique works on the principle that development can be accelerated or forced by increasing either the developer concentration or the temperature at which the chemical action of development takes place. To use it, you'll need a small container of concentrated developer and a few swabs. For relatively small areas, the cotton-tipped swab is suitable; for areas larger than a dime, you should make your own swabs by wrapping narrow strips of an old handkerchief around the ends of thin wooden dowels. These should be prepared in advance and on hand when needed.

After developing the print for the full period recommended, remove and rinse it briefly under running water. Put the print on a hard surface, such as an overturned tray, with its emulsion side up and, dipping the appropriate sized swab into the concentrated developer, touch it lightly to the area of the print requiring further development. Use a circular motion and don't rub the print surface—you're working for a chemical reaction, and the amount of pressure applied has nothing to do with that (at the worst, it will remove the emulsion). Taking care that the developer does not spread into adjacent areas not requiring treatment, repeat the process until you're satisfied with the degree of darkening achieved. At this point, place the print in the stop bath and continue processing as usual.

The use of hot water is an alternative method which lends itself best to the treatment of larger areas, such as skies that require only a slight degree of darkening. For efficient results with this method, you'll need either a sink or tray of metal which can be heated by means of hot water. Lifting the print from the developer by the two corners opposite the area to be treated, lower it onto the wet sink or tray surface, allowing only that portion requiring darkening to touch the hot surface.

Heat from that surface will penetrate

1. Diffusion is another control technique which can be used in both a creative and correct manner. The Pic-Trol is an adjustable diffusion device for enlargers, but it can also be adapted for use with a camera if you choose.
2-4. A straight print is not always the most flattering (3). It can be softened by printing through a piece of nylon mesh (2) or with the enlarger thrown slightly out of focus for a part of the exposure (4). (Ron Berkenblitt.)

the paper base and accelerate the action of the developer in and on the emulsion. Provided the amount of heat is sufficient, you'll notice the darkening effect beginning to occur almost immediately after contact is made with the hot metal. Don't overdo it, as the print must go back to the developer before you've reached the necessary stage of darkening, thus the process will continue. Like any other method of local control, selective development by concentrate or hot water requires sound judgment on your part, as well as practice, and you should not expect absolutely perfect results without it.

OTHER PRINT CONTROLS

A variety of other controls on print contrast can be exercised, but generally speaking their use involves a change in the basic nature of the print rather than simply a modification of it. The soft-focus effect of diffusion is one such control popular with darkroom buffs for both creative and corrective purposes.

DIFFUSION—A soft-focus effect can be produced in the camera by using some form of diffusing material over the lens (see the chapter about filters), but many prefer to add diffusion in the darkroom as desired, and for a very good reason. A sharp negative can be used to make a diffused print, but a diffused negative will never produce a

as the exposure used. If you should find it necessary to reprint the negative for any reason, you'll have a road map to help in duplicating the original treatment you used.

Study the contrast distribution of the work print carefully and figure out exactly what needs to be done to achieve the desired effect. As dodging and burning-in are different sides of the same coin, it should be relatively simple for you to determine which technique will prove most efficient for your needs—burning-in a small area will give an effect very similar to that obtained by dodging a much larger area, and the technique you use should be the one which presents the least amount of work. You should avoid mixing the use of both techniques in the same print whenever possible, since it can become overly complex and difficult to exercise precise control over the end result.

SELECTIVE DEVELOPMENT—There may be occasions when you've dodged or burned-in a relatively com-

4

sharp print. And should you decide that diffusion is not really appropriate to your subject matter after viewing the finished print, all is not lost if you added the soft-focus effect in the print.

True, there's a distinct difference between diffusion created in the camera and that manufactured in the darkroom, but only the knowing, critical eye can spot that difference. When diffusion is created in the camera, highlights will spread into the shadow areas; diffusion manufactured in the darkroom is just the opposite in that shadows spread into the highlights. From a visual standpoint, the former is more effective but as I said, only the critical eye can tell.

Diffusion has its own unique place in the creative process, but of primary concern to us at this point is how to use it in contrast control (total control) and in hiding negative scratches, abrasions and blemishes (total control used as local control). Depending upon the method of diffusion used, it will be necessary to print on a paper one or two grades *harder* than you would normally use.

Diffusion in the darkroom can be produced in numerous ways using various materials. One form is to throw the image out of focus slightly; a variation on this involves a two-part exposure with the enlarger in sharp focus for part of the exposure and slightly out-of-focus for the remainder. A variety of diffusion devices are sold for darkroom use, or you can fit a diffusion filter over the enlarger lens. Transparent acetate underneath the lens will produce one effect—crumpling the acetate and then smoothing it back out before use will give another. Darker

FOCUS HERE

1-2. When the camera is pointed upward with a standard lens, vertical lines converge (1). The easiest way to correct this effect is to shoot the picture with a perspective control lens, but if you don't own one, you can often correct the effect in the darkroom. A slight tilting of the easel can reduce the effect (2) to a point that is not visually disturbing.

3. Negative distortion can be controlled in the darkroom by tilting the easel as shown. The point of focus should be about one-third the distance from the high point of the easel, and the lens stopped down for uniform critical focus.

4. Blocking the easel at just the right angle when trying to control distortion can be a problem. The Saunders Company offers a special tilting base to hold the easel, solving the problem nicely.

5. Professionals usually create diffusion in the camera by smearing petroleum jelly over a filter. The effect varies according to the amount used. Ron Berkenblitt used this technique to give his subject a ghostly appearance.

shades of nylon mesh taken from a ladies' stocking can also be used, as can petroleum jelly smeared on a filter or sheet of glass placed between the lens and easel.

The latter technique holds considerable potential for variations in effect. A thin coat produces a mild diffusion while a thicker one gives a stronger effect. Coat the edges but leave the

center clear and you'll get an effect similar to that of the center-spot filter, etc. In addition to providing the desired diffusion, this technique also has the advantage of obscuring scratches, dust that's embedded in the emulsion, and other negative defects of that nature. While it's not recommended that you deliberately diffuse such negatives just to "save" them, it's nice to know that if a touch of diffusion would otherwise help that particular picture, it will also take care of the defects.

DISTORTION CORRECTION—Every work of art is a distortion of reality, but not every distortion of reality is a work of art. Distortion in photography is inevitable under certain circumstances, but it can be corrected to some extent in the darkroom. If you're fortunate enough to own an enlarger which permits tilting of both lens and negative carrier, you can correct a fairly high degree of distortion, but most amateur enlargers do not have this kind of control. So instead, you correct distortion to some degree by tilting the easel during enlarging.

Using a sheet of white paper in your easel, manipulate it until the desired correction is obtained. You'll need a variety of things of different thicknesses that can be used to support one or two ends of the easel, or you can buy special swivel socket devices which fit under the easel and tilt it at predetermined angles. Using this technique is fairly simple if you remember that converging lines are corrected by tilting the easel in the opposite direction. Thus to correct distortion at the top of the negative, you must elevate the bottom of the easel.

Focus the image with the enlarger lens wide open, concentrating on a point about one-third the distance from the highest point of the easel, as shown in the illustration. When you have achieved the maximum sharpness possible with the lens wide open, stop it down until all parts of the image are critically sharp; this usually means stopping down all the way. A hint when using this technique: Make fairly

5

change in the background or top portion of the print. Some dodging may be necessary to maintain a satisfactory balance.

Of equal importance with the tonal changes produced, you'll find that this method of distortion correction will necessarily involve a condensation of horizontals, and squeezing them together in this way will alter the appearance of the subject considerably, especially if the person viewing the picture is familiar with the subject. Yet done carefully, you can get acceptable results with this technique and when you consider that once the distortion is immortalized on film, there is no other satisfactory way of correcting it. But I can guarantee that after you've worked your way through the hassle of setting up the easel correctly and calculating the exposure and dodging necessary to produce an acceptable print, you'll think twice about pointing your camera upward without a PC lens on the front.

AIM FOR GOOD PRINT QUALITY

You should become your own best critic. There's an old saying to the effect that if something is worth doing, it's worth doing well, and that idea should be uppermost in your mind when working under the safelight. If you've put in the time, money and energy to reach the moment of decision, the end result should be the very best that your equipment and ability can produce.

Before we move on to a consideration of color printing, I'd like to leave you with a checklist for good print quality—one you can use to critique your own work.

1—Did I use the paper grade, type and surface most appropriate for my subject matter?

2—Is the print really sharp? If not, is the lack of sharpness intentional, and if so, does it contribute to the feeling imparted by the picture?

3—Are the specular highlights really white, and the diffuse highlights a light gray as well?

4—Are the dark shadow tones a rich black? Are the middle and light shadow tones dark, but not as dark as the black tones?

5—Is there adequate tonal separation in the mid-tone range?

6—Are negative imperfections completely invisible, with no signs of retouching or spotting apparent?

Good technical quality lies within the reach of every photographer, and there's no justification for sloppy work or poor print quality. □

large prints because the closer the easel is to the lens, the smaller the lens opening required for uniform sharp focus. So if you can't get critically sharp focus over the entire print by stopping the lens down, try making a print one size larger.

This technique does have several drawbacks, but if a perspective control lens was unavailable to take the picture, distortion control in the darkroom may be the only answer. Because of the inclined plane of the tilted easel, the light rays from the enlarger will reach the foreground of the print in about one half the time of those which constitute the background. This will result in a modification of the exposure necessary to produce a good print, and will also cause a major tonal

19

Color Printing

If you can make good black-and-white enlargements, there's no reason why you can't do your own color printing. The state of the art has advanced significantly in the past few years with the introduction of Cibachrome and continuing improvements in other color chemistry and printing papers. Further improvements designed to deliver even better results with far less time and effort on your part will continue to appear, and at a faster tempo than ever before. So there's little point in describing step-by-step procedures for the color printing systems presently available. Technological change and the simplifications in materials and chemistry forthcoming would soon render any such information useless to the reader.

What is of greater value is an understanding of the principles behind color printing—why the processes work—and the equipment necessary to put you in the mainstream of today's burgeoning interest in do-it-yourself color darkroom work. So let's begin our discussion of color printing by examining what you need to make your own color prints.

EQUIPMENT FOR COLOR PRINTING

Beyond the same general equipment necessary to make black-and-white prints, such as the enlarger, a timer, an easel and an accurate thermometer (± ½°F.), you'll need a set of color printing (CP) filters. If your enlarger is equipped with a filter drawer, it will accept acetate CP filters between the lamp and negative; if not, you'll need the more expensive, optically clear gelatin color compensating (CC) filters for placement between the lens and easel. Those who have the latest in color enlargers, or whose black-and-white enlarger is part of a "system" and accepts a color conversion head in place of the standard lamphouse, will use the

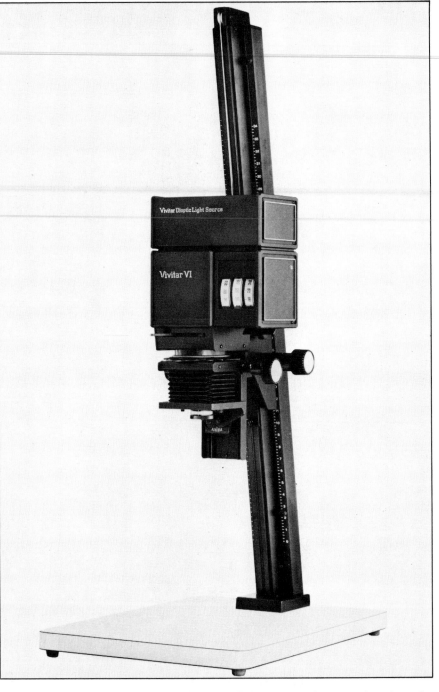

built-in dichoric filters. We'll get into a more comprehensive discussion of filters shortly.

You'll also need a subtractive calculator. This is a matrix-like device which will help you to determine both the exposure and filter combination (pack) necessary to make a correctly exposed and balanced print from your negatives. On a more advanced level, you might wish to invest in an electronic color analyzer once you've mastered the basics of color printing. This device stores information programmed into it on the basis of an average negative and the print made from it, and will then provide exposure/filtration data for other negatives by comparing them with the stored data.

Print processing can be done by tray, but as this means working in the dark, you'll probably buy a print processing drum anyway. These tubular plastic drums allow all processing steps to be carried out in normal room illumination once the exposed paper has been loaded in the dark and the end cap of the drum secured in place. Chemicals are poured in and out of the drum through lightproof baffles, just as with a film developing tank. The paper's soft emulsion is thus protected from scratching and is systematically processed with proper agitation, just as you process roll film in a tank.

Print processing drums usually provide a means of manually agitating the print by rolling the drum back and forth

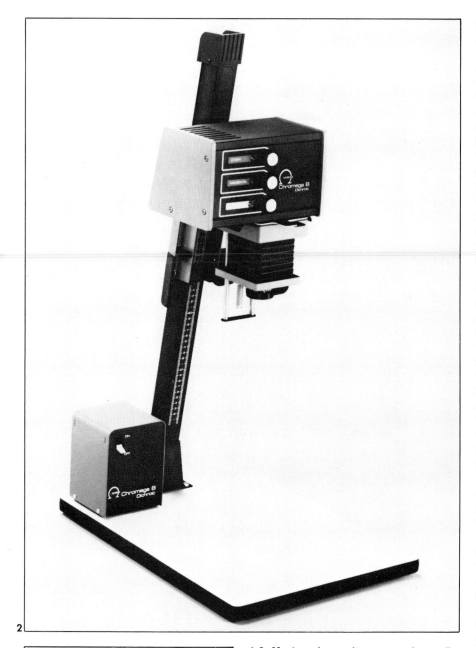

kept absolutely clean, or it will become a major source of contamination—and regardless of exposure/filtration choices, color chemistry just will not function properly when contaminated. You should use different beakers for each chemical, labeling them clearly to avoid future mix-ups; waterproof marking pens will do the job satisfactorily. You should also mark your chemical storage containers *and their caps* in the same way. The print processing drum must be washed thoroughly between prints to avoid possible chemical contamination. If it isn't kept clean, you'll end up with ruinous stains on every print you make.

Those who have worked with black-and-white materials have no doubt become accustomed to printing in a darkroom under a fairly bright safelight. There are yellow safelight filters for use with color printing materials (Kodak No. 13), but since they are very dim by comparison to the one used in black-and-white printing, and since you'll probably choose to work with a print drum for processing anyway, the safelight can be easily eliminated from consideration. Exposing the paper and loading it into the processing drum are the only steps performed under the safelight anyway, and they are just as quickly and easily done in the dark.

You'll also need color printing paper and chemistry, both of which are offered in a "kit" form, or can be purchased individually. There are several different color printing systems available today, all of which work equally well provided that you understand what you're doing and why. To set to rest any misconceptions you might have about color printing, let's begin by clarifying two terms which you'll run across frequently.

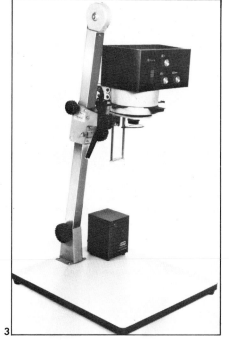

1-3. Most modern enlargers can be easily adapted for color printing. These three represent the wide range of price and features available to today's amateur. The Vivitar VI (1) is one of the latest designs and includes the new Dioptic Light Source. The Omega B-600 with Chromega B head (2) is a moderate priced design that is more traditional than the Vivitar VI, but also a recent addition to the Omega line. The Bogen 67 Dichro (3) is also moderately priced, and features a reflex light path using a dichroic reflector bulb.

on a level surface, but you might want to consider the use of a motorized agitator base. Its consistency of motion assures a uniformity of agitation, and you can put the free time offered by the motorized unit while it agitates the print for you to better use in selecting other negatives for printing, or just cleaning your work area.

Cleanliness is very important in color printing—there's no room for sloppiness here. Your thermometer must be

ADDITIVE VS. SUBTRACTIVE PRIMARIES

Additive primaries are those spectral wavelengths in white light to which color emulsions—paper or film—are sensitive: red, blue and green. When wavelengths of these three colors are mixed or added together, we see a different color as a result, and so does the film emulsion. The colors we see will depend upon which primaries are added together, and in what proportion this mixing takes place.

Subtractive primaries are those colors which are formed by the process of mixing equal amounts of any two of the additive primaries. Thus the subtractive color formed in this way is a

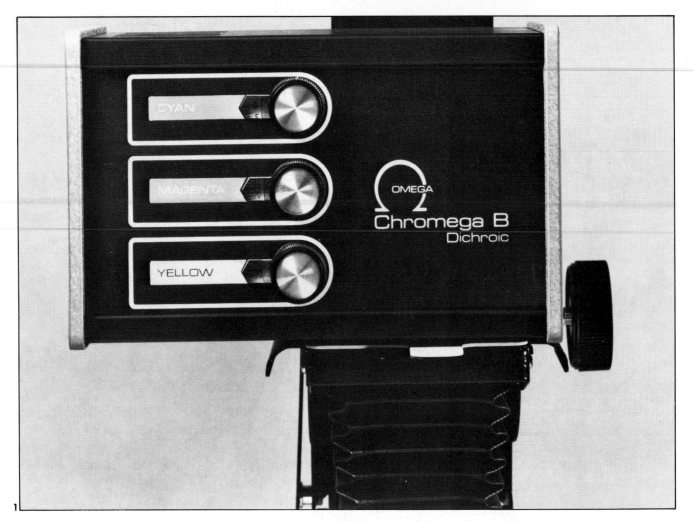

1

complementary one. Equal parts of blue and green will produce cyan, red and blue will produce magenta, and red and green combine to produce yellow. The dyes used in color emulsions are subtractive in nature.

While it is possible to make a color print by exposing a negative through three different filters (one at a time), there are several drawbacks to such a tricolor printing system for the casual amateur. As color balance and print density depend completely upon the exposures through the red, blue and green separation filters, an electronic color densitometer is a virtual necessity for good work, and these are expensive. While excellent prints can be made by the fastidious technician using the additive or tricolor printing process, today's color printing systems for amateur use are all based on the subtractive primaries.

HOW THEY WORK–Color films have separate layers of emulsion placed one on top of each other, and each of these layers is sensitive to only one color. When you take a picture with color negative film, each different color found in the subject is reproduced on the appropriate emulsion layer. Thus

the cyan layer records only red portions of the subject, the magenta layer only green and the yellow layer only blue. Colors other than the three additive primaries record proportionately on the proper layers. After processing, a color negative contains a reproduction of the subject formed by the combined images of the three layers—these images are complementary in color to the original colors of the subject.

This is possible because of chemicals called color couplers embedded in the emulsion, which react during development to form color dyes. The couplers in a given layer combine with developer to form that layer's complementary color, in proportion to the amount of exposure received from the additive primary color to which that particular layer is sensitive. Yellow and red couplers also function as a mask to automatically compensate for incorrect dye absorption during printing. Kodachrome film is the sole exception to this, as the couplers and dyes are both contained in the processing solutions.

COLOR PRINTING PAPERS

Color printing papers differ from color film in two major aspects—the base

1,3. Color printing filtration is provided in one of two ways. Most manufacturers offer color printing filters, as this Unicolor set (3). More expensive, but more convenient and precise is the dichoic color head (1). This contains permanent dichroic filters which provide continuously variable and repeatable color correction.
2,4. Comparative cross-sections of a typical negative color emulsion (2) and color printing paper (4).

and emulsion structure. As a print is designed to be viewed by reflected instead of transmitted light, the base material used is a highly reflective but opaque paper rather than the transparent acetate material of film. The emulsion layers of papers used for printing color negatives have a structural difference in that the order of sensitivity is reversed (Figure A) from that of color film and reversal papers used for printing color transparencies.

Papers used for printing color negatives are classified as either type A or type B. These differ in several respects. Type A is generally resin-coated, disperses its color couplers in the emulsion by means of tiny globules and can be evaluated for proper color balance only when dry. Type B paper uses a baryta coated base, prevents

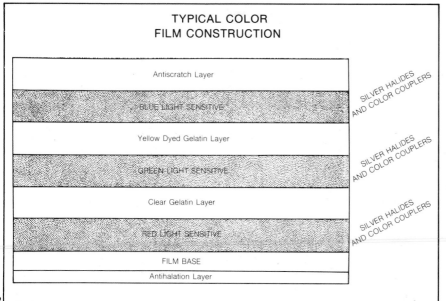

TYPICAL COLOR FILM CONSTRUCTION

Antiscratch Layer

BLUE LIGHT SENSITIVE — SILVER HALIDES AND COLOR COUPLERS

Yellow Dyed Gelatin Layer

GREEN LIGHT SENSITIVE — SILVER HALIDES AND COLOR COUPLERS

Clear Gelatin Layer

RED LIGHT SENSITIVE — SILVER HALIDES AND COLOR COUPLERS

FILM BASE

Antihalation Layer

2

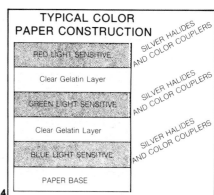

TYPICAL COLOR PAPER CONSTRUCTION

RED LIGHT SENSITIVE — SILVER HALIDES AND COLOR COUPLERS

Clear Gelatin Layer

GREEN LIGHT SENSITIVE — SILVER HALIDES AND COLOR COUPLERS

Clear Gelatin Layer

BLUE LIGHT SENSITIVE — SILVER HALIDES AND COLOR COUPLERS

PAPER BASE

4

FIGURE A

coupler wandering by attaching the molecules to larger organic groups, and can be evaluated for color balance while still wet. Like black-and-white resin-coated papers, Type A requires less wash time, dries rapidly and without curl. Type B paper does not have these qualities to the same extent, but is less expensive to use.

Unlike the processes in which the paper contains only silver and couplers, with color dyes formed during processing, Cibachrome is a reversal paper for printing color transparencies that utilizes a dye/bleach system. Cibachrome paper is manufactured with three layers of dye in it—cyan, magenta and yellow—and when processed, the excess dye is removed to form the color image.

Color printing paper is used in basically the same way as black-and-white paper. But there is one additional factor to be considered when printing color—filters are required to obtain the best color balance from each negative. Color papers are generally manufactured so that some combination of yellow and magenta filters will usually produce the necessary correction. In rare instances, you'll find cyan filtration to be necessary, but all three are never used at the same time, because the result of combining the three subtractive colors is a neutral density, or black. Since an understanding of filtration and how it is manipulated seems to be the major pitfall for beginners, let's see if we can clarify the problem at the outset.

USING COLOR FILTRATION

Color printing or CP filters absorb or reflect a portion of the undesired wavelengths of the visible spectrum. Three

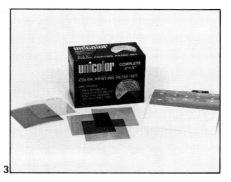

3

types are in general use today—acetate CP, gelatin CC and dichroic—and the manner in which they function and are used differs.

ACETATE CP FILTERS—These are thin acetate sheets that contain a certain color dye in a specific, measured density. Acetate filters are the least expensive, most convenient and therefore the most widely used at the present time. As acetate has a very poor optical quality, such filters should be placed between the light source and the negative, not between the lens and easel. Most modern enlargers have a drawer built into their head to accept printing filters.

When located in such a filter drawer, CP filters modify color temperature by absorbing a part of the enlarger lamp's output according to their color and density. Dye density values differ according to the manufacturer and system with which they are designed to be used, but are additive in nature. If a filtration change of .60 density in magenta is required, you can add a .40 and a .20 to get the necessary .60. A minimum set of filters for color printing regardless of the paper and chemistry used should include the following: one each in cyan, magenta and yellow in

densities of .05, .10, .20 and .40, for a total of 12. To these you should add an extra .40 magenta and .80 yellow filter, as well as a UV filter for absorbing whatever ultraviolet might be emitted by the enlarger lamp.

Should you decide to work with only one type of paper and chemistry, buying the filter set offered by its manufacturer will equip you for any contingencies you might encounter, whereas using the basic pack above might not. It's more expensive initially to buy the entire set filters—some of which you may never use—but at least you'll have the satisfaction of being able to cope with a difficult negative if necessary.

GELATIN CC FILTERS—These are used between the enlarger lens and easel with enlargers lacking the capability of working with acetate or dichroic filters, generally the older units. Because of their location, CC filters must be kept absolutely free of scratches, dust, dirt and other contamination. CC filters must also be kept parallel to each other and the entire pack must be perpendicular to the optical axis of the lens, or distortion may occur. To prevent loss of definition and flare, it's necessary that you hold the number of CC filters used to achieve the required filtration to an absolute minimum. For this reason their density range is far more comprehensive.

When working with CC filters, it will still be necessary to use a UV filter and some provision for incorporating it between the negative carrier and the enlarging lamp should be made. As these can also be obtained in glass, you might try placing it inside the enlarger right on top of the condenser if no other suitable place can be found. Both CC and CP filters should be inspected occasionally for fading and cleaned regularly to keep them free of all foreign matter. Because of the problem of fading, it's not a good idea to expose such filters to daylight, high temperatures or humidy for extended periods of time.

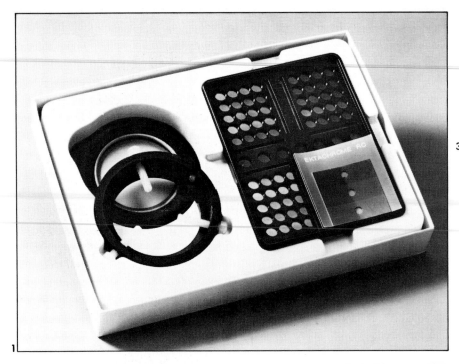

1

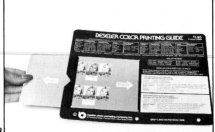

3

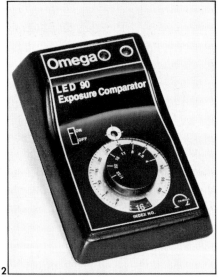

2

1-3. Exposure calculation and color filtration are the two factors in color printing which confuse most amateurs. Low-cost answers are offered in the form of print calculators. Omega offers a Reversal Print Calculator (1) and its LED 90 Exposure Comparator (2) for use when printing color transparencies. The Beseler Color Printing Guide (3) is a comparison device which uses a modification of the "ring around" approach.
4-7. Color analyzers represent electronic state-of-the-art for darkroom workers. The Beseler PM2M features a plug-in modular programming bank (4). Each module stores and recreates a separate program. Omega's SCA 100 is a one-piece analyzer with a silicon blue cell detector and is not much larger than a pocket calculator (5). The Soligor/Melico SM 20 takes advantage of the latest CMOS integrated circuits to minimize darkroom space required (6). The EPOI MM-7 allows analysis of very thin or dense negatives without changing the color balance setting (7).

DICHROIC FILTERS—These are microscopically thin films that have been deposited on a glass substrate by a vapor process and *reflect* the unwanted wavelengths from the visible spectrum. Unlike acetate CP or gelatin CC filters, which are used in a pack with density changes made by substitution or removal from the pack, only a single dichroic filter is necessary in each subtractive primary color. The degree of filtration with the dichroic type is controlled by positioning of the filter, and so they must be mechanically operated within the enlarger head by a dial on the outside, which is calibrated in fine increments to permit highly precise changes in filtration.

Because of their design, function and operation, dichroic filters are sold as a unit incorporated within a continuously variable enlarger "color" head, or a conversion head to replace the one you already have for use in black-and-white work. These special color heads contain a tungsten-halogen lamp and the necessary mechanical linkage, as well as light-mixing chambers. Light mixing is very important when using dichroic filtration, as the modified part of the spectrum which has been subjected to the dichroic filter(s) must be completely mixed with the unmodified white light that bypassed them.

On rare occasions, you might find that the maximum dichroic filter density provided by the enlarger will not be sufficient for printing a particular negative. If the enlarger head will accommodate acetate CP in addition to its integral dichroic filters (some will, oth-

ers won't), there's no reason why the two cannot be combined for use.

FILTRATION HINTS—How do you tell which color filter and which density to use? This isn't as difficult a procedure as it might seem at first. In color printing, it's only necessary to get one color correct and the others will look right. In most cases, you'll make the necessary color changes by adding or subtracting just magenta and yellow filters, either alone in combination as required. The important point is to learn to identify which colors you must correct and what the corrections must be.

There are several things you must remember about color printing filtration if you expect to work with it efficiently and without costly frustrations. The smaller the filter's density number (.05), the less the correction it provides; the greater the number (.40),

the more correction it gives. A moderate correction is in the neighborhood of .15-.20. The color balance of paper emulsions tends to vary from batch to batch, just as with color film emulsions; thus you may find a paper filter adjustment recommendation for an initial color bias packaged with a new box of paper. If the bias is stated as -.10Y, for example, you should start filtration calculations with a .10Y filter in place, as this amount and type of correction is required to bring the paper to a "normal" color balance.

Once you've determined the predominant color in a test print, your correction for that print is to *add* more of the same color filtration to the filter pack. This may sound strange—if the print already has excess magenta, for example, why add more of that same color? The answer is simple—because increasing the filtration of the excess color is the way in which you reduce its influence in the print. You can also subtract a complementary color filter from the pack, a more desirable practice when possible.

To obtain a pretty accurate idea of the exact filtration required on a second print, try viewing the first one through the actual printing filters. Position the filter over the print in such a way that light will not pass through the

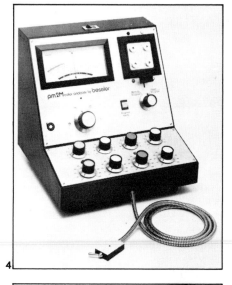

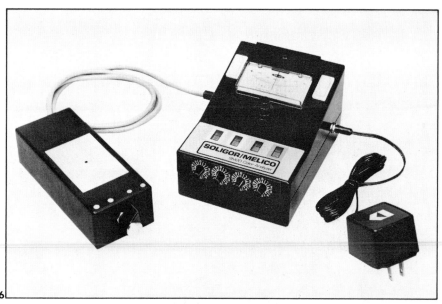

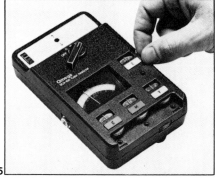

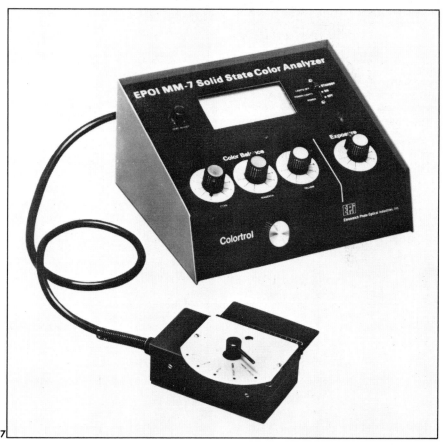

filter before reaching the print. This should also be at a distance sufficient from your eye that you can see only the print through the filter. Now scan the mid-tones through different filter densities until you find the one that offers the best correction, then remove half its strength from the filter pack, as the filter's effect on color printing paper is generally greater than it seems when you view through it. Should you find this technique useful, some manufacturers offer a color print viewing kit which may be used in place of the actual printing filters.

To put this into concrete terms, let's assume that a .10M filter makes the print appear correct—indicating that it has too much green at this point. If you remove .05M filtration from the pack, you'll be right on the mark. One point to remember when determining filtration—you're printing to suit your own tastes and if you find that a slight deviation from normal makes the print more effective, use it.

Remember that filters of the same color combine their densities when added to the pack—a .10Y, a .20Y and a .30Y equal a .60Y. But when two different filters are added together, as a .20M and a .20Y, their densities *do not* add up to a .40R, but remain a .20R instead. To keep yourself pointed

in the right direction and avoid any confusion which might otherwise arise, keep this fact in mind when correcting color imbalance.

Filter pack changes may also affect exposure times. If a given exposure produced a satisfactory print density, but with poor color balance, that same exposure may not produce an equally satisfactory print density once the filter pack is changed. This is due to two factors—a change in the degree of filtering action and the change (if any) in the number of filters through which the light must pass. Color printing systems

usually provide a table or scale of factors to be applied to a basic exposure according to the filter pack changes necessary.

Filter factors are not relevant when working with dichoric filters, as these completely block the wavelengths to which they are complementary, producing virtually no effect upon other wavelengths. Because the dichoric filter modifies the enlarger's light by partial movement into the light beam, as we've seen, there are no additional surfaces to consider when the degree of filtration is changed.

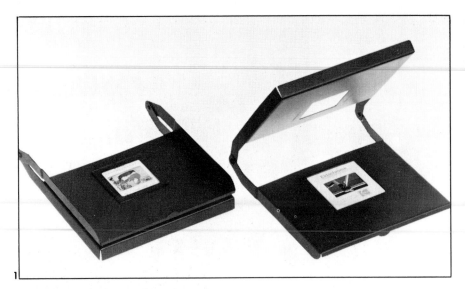

1. **Spiratone makes carriers which are specifically designed to hold 35mm color slides without removing the transparency from the mount when making color prints. These carriers are designed to fit all Spiratone enlargers.**
2. **An accurate timer and footswitch such as these from Omega are a must in your color darkroom.**
3. **The Prinz 8x10 color processing drum is a low-cost alternative to tray processing method.**

DETERMINING BASIC EXPOSURE AND FILTRATION

That first print is always the most difficult one to get by. As there are so many variables to be controlled in producing a properly exposed and correctly balanced color print, it's highly unlikely that you'll make a perfect print on your first try, even if you have a darkroom filled with the latest and most sophisticated analyzing equipment. Unless you use one of the calculating devices for determining exposure and filtration, the basic filter combination usually recommended as a starting point is a 50M + 50Y (.50 magenta and .50 yellow) for daylight-balanced films, but for emulsions like Kodacolor II, which are balanced for flash bulbs, a 30M + 30Y is a more suitable combination. As for exposure times, a test strip is the most practical determinant when you're "winging it."

Once you've made a first print, you can evaluate any changes necessary in exposure and color balance. For the latter, a "ring-around" is generally suggested for beginners on a budget. A "ring-around" is simply a series of test prints which vary in known quantities from a standard print which contains acceptable color balance, and these are offered by various manufacturers and are used by comparison. After finding a print on the ring-around which is a close match to your own

first print, you read the correct amount and color of filtration that should be added to your filter pack. The ring-around is most useful when your initial color balance is way off—for those prints closer to being correct, the previously mentioned method of viewing the first print through actual filters is

THE SUBTRACTIVE CALCULATOR

Virtually every color printing system includes a subtractive calculator. This is an inexpensive device that helps you determine the correct exposure/filtration necessary to make good color prints from your negatives with a minimum of fuss. In case the idea of using something like the Kodak Projection Print Scale used in black-and-white printing has already popped into your mind, let it pop right back out. The sensitivity of different emulsion layers varies with the level of illumination and exposure time, so exposure predictions made with such devices tend to be highly unreliable.

Subtractive calculators come in different sizes and shapes and thus function slightly differently from one manufacturer to another, but all perform the same function in basically the same manner, so the description which follows will provide a fundamental understanding of how they work—specifics are best left to the particular one you might own or buy. To use a subtractive calculator, place it on a sheet of color paper in your easel. With the negative to be printed in the enlarger, contact-print the calculator using the lens opening and exposure recommendation provided by the calculator manufacturer. There should be no filtration in the enlarger at this point other than the UV filter. The image from your negative will pass through a special diffuser sup-

plied with the calculator. This "scrambling" device is used to blend all of the negative tones so that the calculator can provide the average exposure and filter information for that image.

Once it's processed, the test print is evaluated according to the specific procedure that accompanies the particular calculator in use, and the proper filter pack/exposure time determined accordingly. After placing the appropriate filter pack in the enlarger's filter drawer, you're now ready to expose your first print according to the recommendations of the calculator. If your negative contains the right combination or "mix" of average tones, your print will be satisfactory from an exposure standpoint, and hopefully the color balance will be what you want.

Of course, subtractive calculators can be fooled by an unusual negative, just as built-in camera metering systems can be fooled by an unusual negative. This usually happens when your negative contains a predominance of one color or another, as in the case of a sunset. The best way of dealing with this type of problem is to recognize the potential printing difficulty at the time you take the picture. By exposing an extra frame at the same time and including a gray card in this otherwise identical negative, you'll have an "average" reference point which will not fool the calculator. When you come to print these negatives at a later date, make the calculator print from the frame that contains the gray card and then switch negatives, printing your original negative using the exposure/filtration data determined by the calculator from the second negative.

Subtractive calculators can be used with dichoric enlarger heads, but as the calculator is actually made up of tiny pieces of acetate filter material similar to that of CP filters, there's a distinct possibility that your dichoric head will not produce precisely the same color of light as acetate filters at equivalent settings because of the differences in filter materials. But at the worst, you'll only have to make additional filter corrections once you view the print made with the calculator-provided data and the dichoric filter head.

Where these two unlikes are to be used together, it's a good idea to make your initial calculator print with some filtration dialed into the lamphouse (50Y + 40M is a good starting point with Kodak Vericolor II). Doing so means that you'll reduce the amount of filtration to be called for by the calculator and in turn, reduce the per-

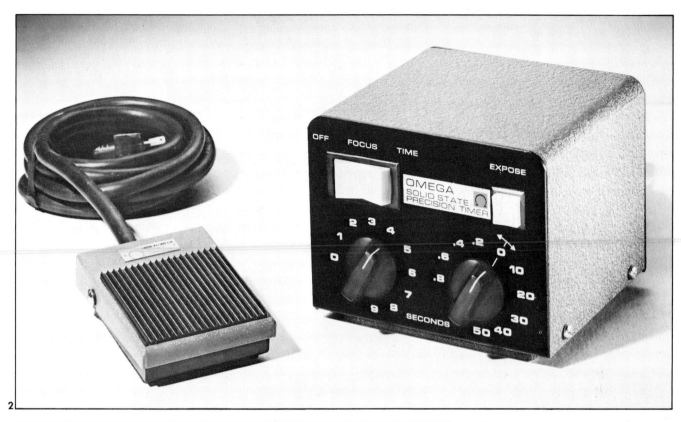

The integrated program involves the blending of *all* tones in a negative. This is usually accomplished by placing an integrating or diffusing filter in the enlarger's light path. The analyzer then records an average tone, produced by the blending of all the tones in your negative. As long as you work with "average" negatives, the integrating method is fast, simple and repeatable. But since this type of program depends upon the integration of all tones in the negative, it's sometimes possible to accidentally fool the analyzer by attempting to print a negative that's not average, such as one containing a predominance of a single color.

The spot-reading program is more precise in that the program you record relates to filtration and exposure data necessary to reproduce a single, specific and preselected tone from your negative. Since a spot reading is not fooled by surrounding areas and tones, this is considered by many as the most accurate way to work. While you can make a spot-reading program for any desired tone (flesh, a gray card, your red car, etc.), it's important that you match future negatives exactly with the same single tone programs you've already selected.

It's also important to remember that not even a color analyzer can tell you how a good print should look; visual judgments like that are far too subjective and reflect your own personal tastes. You can begin to rely on a col-

centage of error if there really is some discrepancy between calculator and dichoric head.

THE ELECTRONIC COLOR ANALYZER

This is an electronic device that eliminates the necessity of making a test print from each new negative. Once you've made a good print from a reference negative, the exposure and filtration information required to make that print is stored in the analyzer—this is known as "programming" the analyzer. Programming is a routine procedure which usually consists of nothing more than turning a few dials on the analyzer unit until a meter needle indicates the proper setting. The procedure is repeated for cyan, yellow

and magenta values, as well as for the enlarger lens setting.

Once it's correctly programmed, the analyzer will then *compare* all future negatives you want to print with the information stored in it about the reference negative. The result of this comparison will be the amount of filtration and/or exposure you must add or subtract in order to make a good print with any other negative. There are basically two types of programs used with a color analyzer—the integrated program and the spot-reading program. Both have certain strengths and weaknesses; the type with which you work will depend upon the specific analyzer used and the kinds of negatives you normally print.

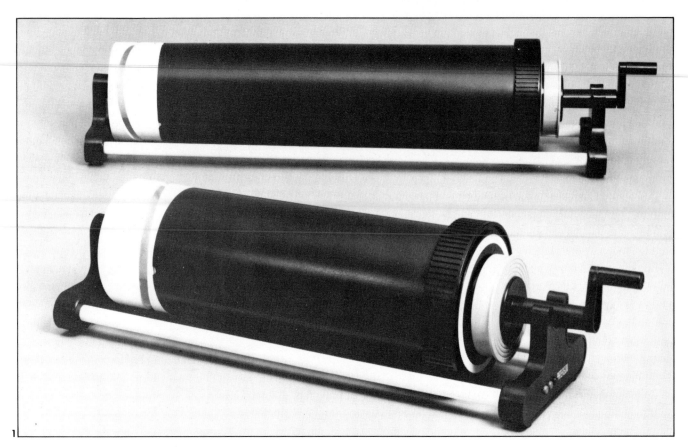

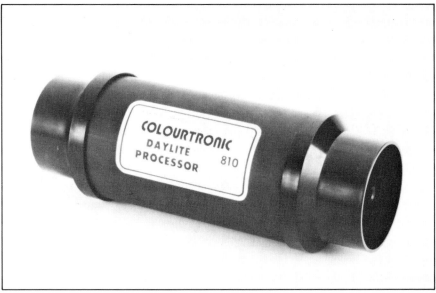

or analyzer only after you've made a good print that lives up to your expectations fully, whether by trial-and-error or by using a subtractive calculator.

MAKING AND USING COLOR PROOF SHEETS

There are three good reasons for making a color proof sheet—cropping, filing and editing. Since there's no really accurate way in which you can view a color negative and determine from it how it will look when a print is made, a color proof sheet can become an extremely valuable tool in your color printing. By providing side-by-side comparisons, a proof sheet lets you select the cropping that will prove most complementary to the image. It also gives you a means by which you can choose between two or more similar frames which may vary only slightly in hue or in depth of field. And as with black-and-white proofs, it can be filed along with the negatives for future reference once you've finished printing.

The proof sheet is the most economical and quickest way in which to make color prints from all the negatives on a single roll of film. The approximate exposure and filtration necessary to expose the proof can be obtained by applying any previous experience you might have had with color printing. If you've made color prints before, use the approximate filtration and exposure settings that you've found correct in

the past. For those who've never made a color print before, the use of a subtractive calculator is recommended to make a print from an average negative. Once this is done and you've made a satisfactory print, simply use the exposure and filtration data indicated by the calculator and transfer the negative used from the negative carrier back to the proof printer. Make a proof just as you would with black-and-white negatives, and you're on your way.

If all the negatives on the proof sheet look good, simply place the ones you wish to print in the negative carrier one at a time and make your enlarge-

ments without changing any of the settings. As the same light passed through this negative, it will make a good enlargement if it made a good contact proof. Should some of the frames on the proof sheet appear too dark or too light, you must make the necessary exposure adjustments to compensate for the discrepancies before they're printed. And should the exposures prove correct but the negatives show a difference in color balance from one frame to the next, use the technique mentioned earlier of viewing the proof through the printing filters. This will assist you in evaluating

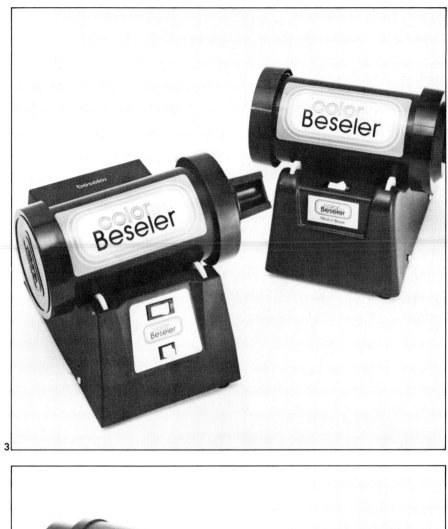

3

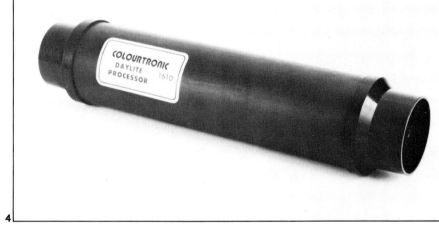

4

1. Paterson offers drums for 8x10 and 11x14 prints; a hand agitation cradle is also provided.
2,4. Colourtronic provides a variety of drums for processing prints from 4x5 to 30x40 inches.
3. Motorized bases for continuous or intermittent agitation are available from Beseler Photo Marketing.

the required filtration changes.

The deeper you get into color printing, the more likely it is that you'll encounter negatives that will challenge the traditional ways of determining exposure and filtration. Some may lack an average blend of tones while others will defy a spot-reading program on the analyzer. In these cases, the use of a color proof sheet offers a helpful alternative to the tedious and wasteful trial-and-error method. By printing those difficult negatives along with known reference values, you'll be able to make some useful side-by-side comparisons and evaluations concerning the required exposure and filtration corrections.

REVERSAL COLOR PRINTING NOTES

At one time, it was necessary to make an internegative from a color slide if you desired the best possible results, but modern reversal printing no longer requires this rather tedious procedure for good prints from the positive/positive process. There are basically two approaches to reversal color printing—chromogenic development (Kodak Ektachrome paper) and the dye/bleach (Cibachrome) process. Both resemble negative/positive printing but have one distinct advantage— you can compare the final print with the original slide to check whether or not your color rendition is correct. This is not possible where a color negative is involved.

The few differences between positive/positive and negative/positive printing are important. When a change is necessary in the filter pack to correct color balance, you *remove* filters of the same color you're trying to correct, or alternately, *add* filters which are complementary in color. Reversal color papers tend to increase contrast in the translation from slide to print, but this is necessary to produce a good color saturation. For this reason, slides of normal or slightly soft contrast will give better prints than those having a good deal of "punch" or an excessively long tonal range.

The data sheet furnished with the reversal paper used will suggest tentative exposure and filtration recommendations, which you should follow unless your slide differs considerably from average. When specified the UV-absorbing filter and a heat-absorbing glass should also be used. Test-strip exposures should be made in a geometric progression using a factor of two—10, 20, 40, 80, etc. Smaller factors are not useful in positive/positive printing, as color reversal paper requires relatively large exposure changes to effect relatively small density changes.

SPECIAL PRINTING TECHNIQUES

Just as with black-and-white printing, it's possible to achieve unusual effects with color materials that can change otherwise mundane pictures into something unique. There are numerous good books on the market which delve rather deeply into such processes and the procedural steps involved, something I do not have sufficient space to deal with properly. But to give you a few hints on the potential beyond multiple printing and creative color techniques, here are a few possibilities.

BLACK-AND-WHITE COLOR PRINTS— Try making color prints from your black-and-white negatives. With a properly chosen negative and appropriate filtration, the effect can be really dramatic. Remember that the color

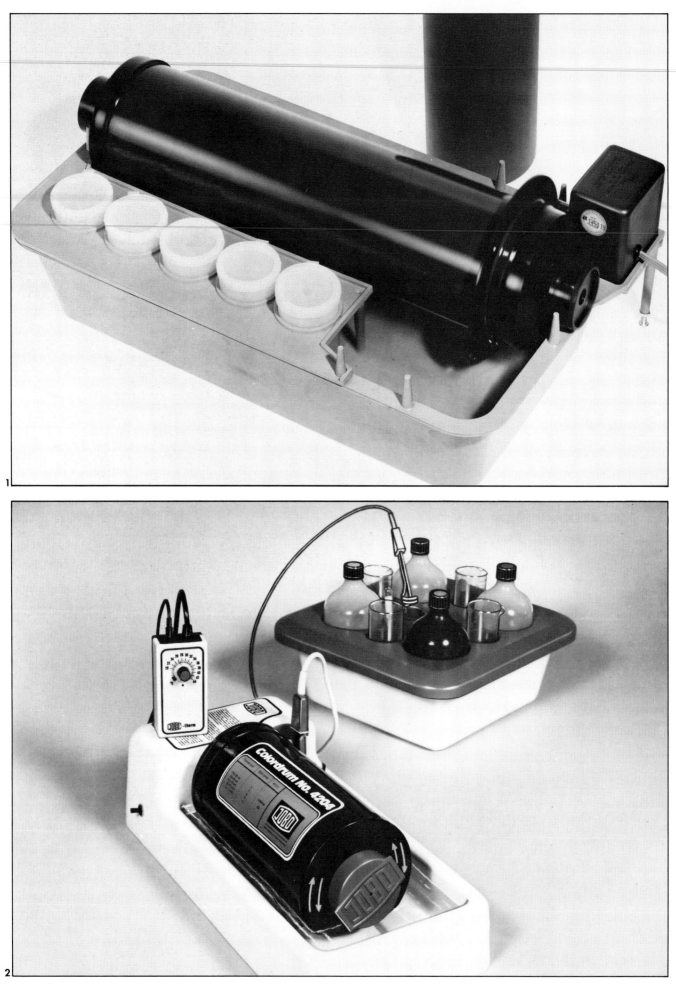

seen in the finished print will always be complementary to that of the filtered enlarger light—cyan filtration will produce a red print, etc. Changing the filtration will change the color, while altering the exposure will lighten or darken the print. Once exposed, your monochromatic print should be processed like any color print.

When changing exposure or filtration with this technique, make your changes considerable in degree, as the effect does not respond quickly to subtle ones. Should you find the filtration at your fingertips to be inadequate in a given color, use colored cellophane from an art store for even more dramatic punch. Variable-contrast filters used in black-and-white printing also produce interesting effects.

More control with this technique is offered by sandwiching the black-and-white negative with a blank piece of processed negative color film. By doing this, you "borrow" the orange mask from the negative and combine it with the black-and-white image. Use the recommended starting filter pack to make a print with you subtractive calculator; this locates a neutral gray patch and you can then change the filtration to suit your own taste.

TEXTURE SCREENS—These are used in black-and-white printing to add interest and hide negative defects; they can be used just as successfully in color printing. Using the large size screens which are placed directly on the paper will provide additional control. When the separate texture screen exposure given the paper requires a different filtration than the exposure made from the negative, the color and density of the texture pattern will be altered.

OTHER TECHNIQUES—You can also make photograms with color printing paper and colorful translucent objects; try various filtration schemes and exposures for a color blast. Using appropriate pieces of filter material for dodging or burning-in rather than the conventional tools will produce striking local areas of color control and provide effects virtually impossible to obtain in any other manner. Or make a negative print from a color slide for different images with complementary colors—changing filter packs here will also produce wild and dramatic visual effects.

FOR BETTER PRINTS—DON'T GET DISCOURAGED

At the outset of this discussion, I maintained that anyone who could

1-2. Modular print processing units are shown here from Spiratone (1) and Soligor/Jobo (2). These are virtually self-contained semiautomated home print processing systems.

3. For those who want the last word in convenience, the Durst RCP 20 roller processor is available. Feed the exposed sheet in at one end and seven minutes later, the finished print comes out at the other end—damp dry!

make a good black-and-white print could do the same in color—providing they know what they're doing and understand how things work and why. Don't let anyone sell you on color printing on the basis that it's an automatic "push the button—twist the dial" procedure, and that all you need to get good color prints is a box full of expensive equipment. If you don't *know* what you're doing, the results will *show* it—regardless of all the fancy

equipment you may own.

Let me leave you with one damper on your newly kindled enthusiasm for color printing. Just because you made a flawless print from negative A today does not necessarily mean that you'll be able to make another one exactly like it tomorrow or next week. Remember that I also mentioned the large number of variables to be controlled? Well, these will account for a high percentage of your color printing gremlins. If there's the slightest change (and there will be) in the time, temperature and agitation of the chemistry, the negative or the paper's emulsion batch, you'll have to return to Square A and begin all over again with a calibration print. So be prepared to *work*—just as you must in black-and-white printing—regardless of what the salesman tells you, and you'll not only enjoy color printing, you might even master it! □

20

Creative Darkroom Techniques

Once you have mastered the basics of negative development and enlarging, you may feel the urge to become creative under the safelight. It's only natural that you'll want to expand your darkroom capability beyond that involved in "straight" printing. While there are far more techniques of interest than we have space here to discuss, this chapter will serve to acquaint you with a few of the more interesting ways in which you can enjoy interpretative photography by using your darkroom as creatively as you do your camera. The particular techniques I've selected to include range from the simple to the complex, since this is the most appropriate way to demonstrate the wide range of effects possible.

The line that separates creative darkroom techniques from those used every day is somewhat fuzzy, and seems to depend primarily upon how an author chooses to define his terms. For my purposes, I consider standard control techniques such as negative reduction/intensification, dodging/burning-in, diffusion, distortion control, and the use of texture screens to be techniques that serious darkroom workers must count among their *basic* skills. You should be thoroughly conversant with such techniques, and how they are used, before attempting to achieve derivations from an original.

It's also important that you recognize that certain techniques work better with certain pictures; not every picture will possess the necessary attributes to work with every technique. For maximum visual impact, the picture must complement the technique, and vice-versa. Now let's begin our consideration with a look at one of the most popular and easiest techniques with which the beginner can work.

HIGH-CONTRAST DERIVATIONS

The litho process films used in this technique are designed primarily for line copy work, but they have the ability to produce needle-sharp black-and-white images when all gradations and half-tones are dropped. This results in a design that contains only the essential shapes within the picture, which is now made up primarily of pure blacks and whites. When applied to a suitable subject, the high-contrast technique increases visual impact far beyond that possessed by the original continuous-tone interpretation.

Since many high-contrast films are orthochromatic (not sensitive to red light), you can work with them under a red safelight. This is another advantage for the beginner, as it allows him to watch the film develop and see what he's doing at every step along the way. Negatives that are otherwise unusable due to negative damage, improper exposure or processing can often be salvaged by using them as the basis for a high-contrast derivation. The technique will also reduce a cluttered composition to one of utter simplicity, or allow you to create a totally new image from several lesser ones.

Since many high-contrast negatives will have to be retouched because of the tendency of the emulsion to pinhole, it's best to work with a larger-than-35mm negative. This allows you to easily touch up such defects, as well as making it easy to remove any distracting elements that might remain by simply painting them out with opaque. Working with the larger negative size means that you can often contact-print rather than enlarge, and this increases your total control over the end result with far less effort on your part. For example, you can cut two high-contrast negatives apart and recombine the elements in a different order, completely restructuring your composition in this way. Or you can print several small images on a single 4x5 sheet to create a single image.

Once you start to work with high contrast, you should perfect the technique if you intend to go on to other creative darkroom effects. High contrast is an elementary technique, to be sure, but it's one that is very important to master, since it is the foundation upon which numerous other creative darkroom processes are based. If you can make a good, clean high-contrast negative without difficulty, you'll find it far easier to work with posterization and other techniques.

The process of making a high-con-

trast derivation from your negative or color slide is exactly the same as that for making a regular enlargement, except that a red safelight should be used, and a sheet of litho film placed in the easel instead of enlarging paper. You should make a test strip to determine the correct exposure, and remember to develop the film for a minimum of 2½ minutes, or you may not get uniform tones. Underexposed litho film tends to develop pinholes to a greater extent, another reason for determining the correct exposure as accurately as possible.

Litho film processing uses a special two-solution developer which is mixed together just before use. The two stock solutions have a good shelf life by themselves, but once they are combined for use, the developer begins to chemically destroy itself. Since it exhausts itself rather rapidly when mixed, litho developer should be discarded after use.

Standard print developers such as Printol or Dektol can also be used, but since they are not designed for high-contrast work, it will be necessary to make several intermediate negatives in order to drop the half-tones completely. Of course, if your concept of the finished work includes the retention of some of the half-tones, this is the way in which they are kept.

Depending upon the final effect envisioned, you may have to repeat the process after the first generation lith has been washed and dried. Working from a negative will give a high-contrast positive, which prints to a negative image. A color slide will produce a litho negative, which prints to a positive image.

Now that you have your litho derivation, here's where the real fun begins. Apply opaque to a negative and the area covered will be white when printed; paint it on the positive and the area will print black. The high-contrast derivation can be combined with the original negative for printing, or it can be used with the slide for projection or further printing. You can add color to

A single image multiple print which began with Michael Parrish photographing a model on Kodak Tri-X against a black paper background. A Kodalith positive made from the camera negative was then used to make this spinoff print. Thirteen separate exposures were made, and the figures kept in registration by taping a sheet of clear acetate to the enlarging paper. The desired image positions were recorded on the acetate, which was moved out of the way during exposure, and then replaced to assist in repositioning the image for the next exposure.

litho film by using water-soluble dyes, or by taping a gelatin filter over it. You can combine the litho with texture screens, moire patterns, or continue on to make posterizations or other derivations. The choice is yours.

TONE-LINE DERIVATIONS

Quite popular among those starting out with high-contrast derivations, the tone-line process produces a print that seems to have all the qualities of a pen-and-ink drawing; many look more like a drawing than a photograph. Your choice of subject matter is very important with the tone-line process, as not every negative lends itself well to this interpretation. Because the process requires a considerable amount of experimentation to get the exposures correct in this multistage procedure, it's quite conceivable that you'll reach the end of the process before discovering that you're working with a negative that simply does not produce the desired impact.

Experience is the only real teacher with tone-line work, but as a general rule, it's safe to say that the negative should not be one that is extremely cluttered with fine detail. Try working with simple subjects at the outset, and progress to more complicated ones as your grasp of the technique becomes better. Whatever negative you choose, it must have a definite point of orientation, or you may lose your visual bearings with the final tone-line print. Should this happen, or if the result is excessively busy from a visual standpoint, the end result will be nothing more than a mass of fine lines with no real meaning.

If you like to create open-ended statements and let the viewer attempt to impose his own interpretation on the finished work, orientation may not matter to you, but it certainly will irritate those who attempt to make sense of what you've accomplished if they are unable to find a visual ''handle.'' The best way to determine whether or not you have succeeded is to hand a tone-line upside down to a good friend. If he turns it right side up to admire it, you're in. But if he begins discussing your work while still holding the print incorrectly, you've failed.

Making a tone-line is a somewhat involved procedure. Starting with your original negative, you print it onto a black-and-white film like Kodak Fine Grain Positive 7302, or Kodak Commercial 6127. Both are easy films to work with, because they can be handled under a safelight. The resulting

1-3. The traditional approach to high contrast derivations is shown in this sequence by Jeff Blackwell. To improve upon the original (3), Jeff printed his camera negative on Kodalith. The resulting positive gives a negative print (1). Printing the Kodalith positive on a second sheet of Kodalith results in a high contrast negative, which prints positive (2).

positive should possess a density and contrast as close to that of your negative as possible; if it doesn't, remake it.

Now sandwich your original negative and the positive together—back-to-back—and bring the images into perfect register. Tape the two sheets together along one edge to keep them in register. It's vital at this point that the films be placed back-to-back, as the tone-line process depends upon the space between the emulsion of the two films for its effect. If you have incorrectly registered them emulsion-to-emulsion, you'll get no tone-line effect.

Sandwich another sheet of high-contrast film with its emulsion side facing the emulsion side of the original negative, and place the three-piece sandwich in a printing frame. Position the printing frame on a turntable (a record player will do nicely) under a 100-watt frosted light bulb. The light should be placed three feet above and three feet to one side of the print frame so that its rays strike the film sandwich at a 45-degree angle. Rotate the turntable during the exposure, making at least one and preferably a minimum of three complete revolutions. If a turntable is not available, you can rotate the light over the printing frame instead by using an extension cord with a 100-watt frosted bulb, but it's more difficult to assure a proper exposure, since the

light must be held three feet above the frame while it is rotated in a six-foot circle above the frame.

The exact exposure required will depend upon your original and the high-contrast sandwich, and experimenting is the only way to arrive at it, but you might work with an 8-10-second exposure as a starting point. Remove the high-contrast film from the sandwich after the exposure has been completed and process it according to the directions under High-Contrast Derivations. When it has been processed, this sheet becomes your tone-line negative, and is printed just as any other negative.

PHOTO SKETCHING

Since Leonardo da Vinci occasionally cribbed and used the camera obscura to reproduce life with his paints, there's no reason why you can't put your enlarger to a similar use. With photo sketching procedures, you'll end up with various derivations of your negatives or slides, each of which appears to resemble a pencil etching or pen-and-ink drawing more than it does a photograph.

The basic tools required are a few soft lead pencils, a set of water colors, a supply of India ink, felt-tipped markers, etc. For hand-drawn prints, ordinary drawing paper or poster board will be required. Once the negative has been composed on your enlarger baseboard, tape the paper or poster board in place and shade in the light areas of the image with a soft lead pencil. Work slowly and don't apply too much pressure. Use a loose piece of paper for a hand rest; as the drawing progresses, you'll need this to avoid any smudges from the pressure of your hand as it

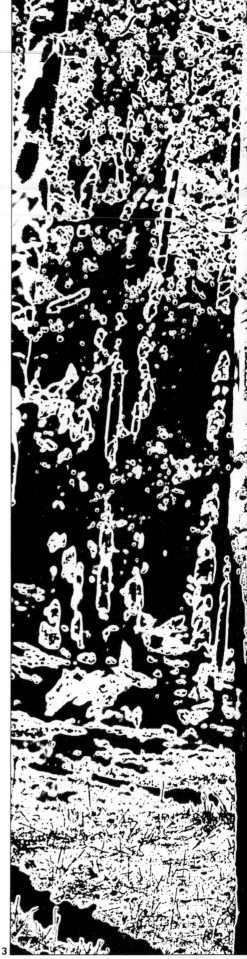

1-3. Tone-line prints are a popular form of high contrast derivation. Shirley I. Fisher made these examples as outlined in the text. The wealth of fine detail included in (1) gives the tone-line process a sensitivity unequalled by standard printing processes. Orientation in such abstractions is important; without the horizontal walk at the bottom of (2), the print would not be successful. A combination of fine detail contained within the gross outlines of the trees makes (3) an ideal tone line.

moves over areas which are already filled in with the soft lead. Since you're working with a negative image, remember to shade the light areas of the image the darkest.

Keep a small flashlight handy. As you complete more of the shading process, you'll find it helpful to occasionally flash the light on to see what remains to be done. If you use the room light instead, your eyes will be continually trying to readjust to the darkness, and the job will be that much more difficult. You can add to or delete from the subject as you wish, turning out an exact reproduction, or one that is modified. Here's where the artist in your soul really gets the opportunity to come forth.

When you're satisfied with the image you've created, turn off the enlarger and remove the drawing from the

baseboard. You're now free to embellish it with colors or with finer shading as you work with the India ink, felt-tipped pens or water colors. Once the picture has been completed to your satisfaction, try photographing it. From this camera negative, make a high-contrast positive and then print it for a negative effect, or use the high-contrast positive to make a high-contrast negative, and print that to a positive. Compare the results to a finished print of your original negative for an interesting surprise. You might even try using the litho derivations of your pencil sketch to make a bas-relief, the next technique we'll consider.

BAS-RELIEF PRINTS

The bas-relief process produces pictures with a distinct three-dimensional quality. The technique is sometimes called low-relief, since it is similar to what the artist can create with an etching, or the sculptor with stone. Forms of bas-relief have been around for cen-

turies, so you're working with a well-established technique. For our purposes, it's the variations in the technique that are of greatest interest.

Making a bas-relief print is really simplicity in itself, since all you do is print a negative and positive image slightly off register to obtain the effect. The technique itself thus requires very little to master, but obtaining the proper image values does require some skill and experience. Bas-relief works well with those subjects that contain a lot of fine detail, but not every such subject will make a good bas-relief. Flat frontal lighting should be avoided, as should strong backlighting, since neither will produce the desired off-register effect. The image used should contain moderate to high contrast, as the bas-relief process has a tendency to flatten tonal values, and the less contrast present at the outset, the less the effect in the finished print. A thin negative that contains good definition between the tonal values will work best for this process.

Depending upon the degree of the effect you desire in the final print, there are several different film stocks that can be used to make the positive from your negative. Kodak Commercial 6127, SO-015 Direct Duplicating film or Kodak Ektapan all work well for low-key bas-relief, but Fine Grain Positive is by far the most convenient emulsion to use. It has a contrast level equivalent to Grade No. 3 paper, can be handled under a red safelight, and can be processed in standard paper developer mixed 1:1.

1-2. A variation on sketching, Brenda Dean and Marvin Barre used color slides to make negative prints. Before placing the print in the developer, it was streaked with a flat head pen dipped in developer. The print was then developed for about two-thirds the normal time, giving the natural shaded and stroked effect. Brown toner was used to add color variations to the finished pictures.

Fine Grain Positive tends to be a bit more grainy than other emulsions but this factor should not interfere with its use for bas-relief derivations. You'll find an exposure of five seconds at f/16 to be about right for average negatives, with only 2½ minutes of development required. Since this is approximately one-third to one-half of the development required by other film types, it's a great time-saver when you're experimenting to find the right exposure to produce a positive of the proper contrast and density. You'll find the primary drawback to using Fine Grain Positive to be its thinner base, as it has a tendency to curl under some conditions.

The positive image used to make a bas-relief print is obtained by enlarging your negative onto a sheet of film placed in the easel. If you're working with a 4x5 or larger negative, you can make the positive by contact printing it on a same-size piece of film. For this discussion, assume that we are working with Fine Grain Positive film. Making a test strip will help you to establish the correct exposure. Try two-second increments with f/22 as a starting point for the test strip.

Once a proper exposure is deter-

mined, you can make the positive on the film, processing and drying it as usual. Work toward obtaining a positive that is thin but brilliant and contrasty. Having made a satisfactory positive, use it to contact-print a negative on Fine Grain Positive after making another test strip to determine the correct exposure for contact printing—try two-second intervals at f/8. After you've established the correct exposure that will give you a negative comparable to the positive in contrast and density, make the final negative from the positive. You now have both a negative and a positive image on Fine Grain Positive film, which can be sandwiched together to produce innumerable combinations.

If the two images are not quite equal in contrast and density, here's what you can expect from the final print. If one image is dense and the other is thin, the dense image will cancel out the thin one. As an example, if the positive is stronger than the negative, the final print will have a negative appearance. When the negative is stronger than the positive, the final print will be a positive. If this is not what you have in mind, but the thought of going through the process of making another set is also less than appealing at this point, try Farmer's Reducer on the denser image. Used with care, reduction can bring the stronger image back to a contrast-density level that is closer to that of the negative. Of course, if you over-reduce, you'll have to start back at the beginning.

A light box and a magnifier are handy items for use in making the final print on paper. Place the negative on the light box and sandwich the positive image to it slightly out of register. Use the magnifier if necessary to check the register, and when you arrive at a pleasing effect, tape the two together along one edge. Use a hard grade of paper for your print, as the superimposed images block each other out except for the outlines. Since this reduces values to middle tone grays, the contrasty paper will help to accentuate the remaining detail, and results in a picture that contains more snap.

Now that you have the basics under control, you can try making your images on high-contrast film. If you use one high-contrast image and one continuous-tone image, you'll arrive at a considerably different effect than that obtained with two continuous-tone images. By using high-contrast film for both images and printing them, you'll end up with a high-contrast bas-relief

3

1-3. The bas-relief process lends itself to subjects which contain a certain amount of bold lines. The sharp linear differentiation results from the use of a high contrast positive in these prints. The litho positive tends to hold back a muting of the tones found in bas-relief prints made from a continuous tone negative and positive. (Shirley I. Fisher.)

print, which can be visually intriguing, providing that your subject matter lends itself to the effect.

So far, we've only discussed working with negatives. For those who work with slides, the bas-relief technique can be used to produce interesting variations, and with far less effort. The original slide is contact-printed to create a negative image. High-contrast film works better with slides, since its effect is bolder and thus more noticeable. Continuous-tone film is a better choice when the subject is very soft by its nature, such as flowers, and you don't require a bold effect.

After printing, processing and drying, the negative image is sandwiched with the original slide between two slide glasses to form a bas-relief slide. The contrast and density of the negative image will determine the degree of effect, and just to be different, you might want to experiment in placing the two images back-to-back, as well as emulsion-to-emulsion.

POSTERIZATION

This technique is used to separate the normal tonal scale into distinct tonal ranges, each on a different piece of film. When the various films are combined with each other and printed in register, a sharp delineation of tones is produced. The end result contains the qualities of a poster, hence its name. Posterization is one of those techniques that seems to captivate the imagination completely when you initially come into contact with it. For this reason, its popularity is wavelike in that for a time, posterization is the rage, only to fade into the background once you've worked it out of your system.

But a few years later, it's high on the popularity poll of techniques as others who are new to creative darkroom techniques discover its visual potential. In this sense, it shares the same recurring popularity as solarization, which we'll also consider shortly.

A high-contrast print such as those discussed in the beginning of this chapter represents the most basic form of posterization, since it contains only two tones—black and white. A somewhat more complex form of posterization is represented by bas-relief, as it results in the use of three major tones—black, gray and white. But true posterization is a combination of graphic art and photographic techniques in which the continuous tonal scale of the photograph is broken into a number of tones that are both uniform and distinct. Since these separate one against the other and cannot merge, the most successful black-and-white posterization will contain only four tones—black, white, light gray and

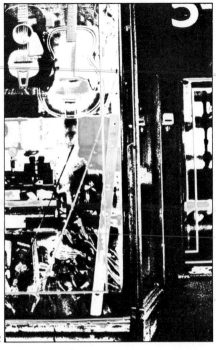

dark gray. Attempts to incorporate more than four tones seldom work well visually, as the more tones that are added to the posterization, the closer the end result approaches the original continuous-tone image.

With color posterizations, the number of variations obtainable is far greater because the tones are represented by different colors rather than shades of gray. As the number of hues, shades and color tones that can be produced and combined is more infinite, the end result of a color posterization can be far more striking visually, and infinitely more effective in conveying what the photographer had in mind.

Provided that you choose your subject with care, the posterization technique will result in pictures that are both dramatic and out of the ordinary. Simple patterns and/or strong visual designs usually can be counted on to produce the most effective results. There are far more possible variations in this technique than we can go into here, but a look at the basic procedure involved is in order.

Anything can be posterized—a print, negative or slide. But in addition to choosing the proper subject matter, you must also select your materials with care. When working from a color slide or color negative, you must use a panchromatic emulsion to create the tonal separations, as ortho films are not sensitive to red. This will mean working in the dark, instead of with the red safelight.

For best results, plan on working with sheets of litho film which are the same size as the final print you want.

3

4

1-3. Variations and modification of the posterization process are shown in these three renditions by Shirley I. Fisher. The original color slide was first printed to a continuous tone negative. This was used to make a continuous tone positive, which was then printed on Kodalith. Sandwiching the Kodalith negative and continuous tone positive resulted in (1). The sandwich was then printed on continuous tone film, which was sandwiched with the Kodalith negative to produce (2). By combining a Kodalith negative and Kodalith positive slightly out of register, (3) resulted.

4-5. For this example of the Sabattier Effect, Shirley I. Fisher printed the original on Kodalith to make a high contrast positive. This was printed on a second sheet of Kodalith, which was reexposed in development, producing the result shown in (4). The reexposed negative used in (4) was then printed on Kodalith once more, and that sheet was also reexposed in development to the effect shown in (5).

This is important, because the films must be printed in exact register, and for this, a punch and printing frame designed for pin registration should be employed.

The tonal separations are created by exposure. Normal or correct exposure will deliver the desired middle tones. To get the highlight tones, you must overexpose, and for the shadow tones, you underexpose. This will give you the three required separations. If you're working with a black-and-white negative, a black-and-white intermediate positive should be made on Fine Grain Positive film. This intermediate positive must be exposed to get a full tonal scale and slightly more contrast than the original negative. The intermediate positive is now contact-printed onto litho film to create the three separation negatives required.

Once you have the three high-contrast negatives with definite tonal separations, you're ready to begin printing. This is where the pin registration system comes in, since the negatives are printed *one at a time,* instead of being sandwiched together. This means that you will make three consecutive exposures of the same duration, each with a different separation negative. If you do not use a registration system, tape the negatives to the baseboard in register so that they can be flipped back and forth like the pages of a magazine.

Make your first exposure with the underexposed (shadow) negative, then follow with the normal (mid-tone) and overexposed (highlight) negatives. As exposure is cumulative (remember the test strip?), the shadow areas will become darker with each exposure. When all three exposures have been made, the shadow areas will be a dark gray or black, the highlights will be a light gray, and the rest, which received no exposure, will remain pure white. This divides the original continuous tonal scale into three highly defined density levels.

Working with a color posterization requires both high-contrast negatives and high-contrast positives. The positives are used as masks during printing and must be registered to do so. The first exposure is made with only the shadow negative. For the next exposure, the mid-tone negative and the shadow positive are used. The positive masks those areas already exposed through the shadow negative during the first exposure. This permits the second exposure to affect only the mid-tones. When the third exposure is made, the mid-tone mask is used to cover those areas which were exposed during the first and second exposures. Since you'll be printing through color filters, it's a good idea to preplan the composition so that you can use the correct filters to produce the desired colors in their appropriate tonal area. Until you have become fully familiar with the color posterization process, this is the best way to prevent disappointment, and avoid the time-consuming remakes necessary to get exactly what you want.

SOLARIZATION (THE SABATTIER EFFECT)

One of the most durable of the creative darkroom techniques, solarization is simply the partial reversal of an exposed negative or print. True solarization is caused by a chemical reaction brought on by gross overexposure, but with modern films, this image reversal by exposure alone is virtually impossible to achieve. The technique I'm about to describe is more properly known as the Sabattier Effect, named after the French photographer who discovered it in 1862, but still referred to by most photographers as solarization. The Sabattier Effect is a combination of negative and positive values within a single image, and is caused by reexposure to light during development. The technique owes much of its fascination to the unpredictable nature of the process—you can work with the same subject for days and not exhaust the potentially different effects.

You can use this technique to produce pictures with great impact in black-and-white, or highly futuristic images in color. The Sabattier Effect can be used with either negatives or prints, but you'll find it to your advantage to work with negatives when possible. Once you've achieved a suitable effect with which you're satisfied, it can be reproduced as often as you like. But when an effect is achieved with an individual print, duplicating it is a very difficult task for all but the most experienced, unless a copy negative is made and it is reproduced from this.

To solarize a print with the Sabattier Effect, make a normal enlargement and place the paper in the developer. As soon as it has developed sufficiently for the image to begin appearing, remove it from the developer, place on a flat surface and flash the white light on/off rapidly. After this brief reexposure, return the print to the developer and let the process continue until you are satisfied with the effect. By using a diluted developer and reexposing the print with a diffused white light when development is 50 percent complete, the process can be varied and you'll have more control over the end result.

You'll find the Sabattier Effect far more effective when used with negatives. The procedure is essentially the same as that used for solarizing prints, but you will not be able to follow the progress of development by safelight if

1-2. The Sabattier Effect produces considerably different results in these exposures by Shirley I. Fisher. The original negative was printed to a Kodalith positive. This was reprinted to a Kodalith negative and reexposed in development, resulting in (2). The process for (1) is identical, except that the Kodalith positive was reprinted on Fine Grain Positive, which was then reexposed in development.

you're working with original camera negatives. Because of the uncertainty involved, it's a good idea to shoot several frames of the scene if you plan to apply this technique during development. A better idea is to develop the original negative normally and then use it to make copies on Kodak Commercial 6127 film. These can be developed under the red safelight, which gives you a better idea of what you're doing. Once you've reexposed the negative, return it to the developer and agitate the film continuously for the remainder of the developing time. This applies to all emulsions except Kodalith, which should not be agitated while development is being completed. If you do agitate Kodalith, you'll end up with a mottled effect on the negative known as "bromide drag."

As the second phase of development is carried out, the sheet of film will turn very dark under the safelight, and there's a tendency on the part of newcomers to the technique to pull the film out of the solution ahead of time. Re-

sist this urge, as the excessive darkening of the film in a very short time is normal, and you really can't tell until after it has been fixed and cleared as to the degree of your success or failure. Since the resulting negative will contain a high fog level, make a print before attempting to judge whether or not the effect is successful. The results will be far more acceptable if you use a contrasty paper grade.

As you can see at this point, there are three distinct variables in the process: (1) when reexposure takes place, (2) the duration and intensity of reexposure, and (3) how long the negative or print is developed after reexposure. To obtain consistent results with the Sabattier Effect, you must standardize the size, location and intensity of illumination used for reexposure. You should also work with fresh developer and stop bath. The latter is especially important if you expect to halt the development action soon enough to retain the image as you want it.

When the Sabattier Effect is used with color film, the results are even more spectacular and intense. Not only is the image partially reversed, as in black-and-white work, the colors that are created by the reversal are both dramatic and brilliant, as well as totally different from what you would logically expect. Using white light for the reexposure will produce one set of vivid

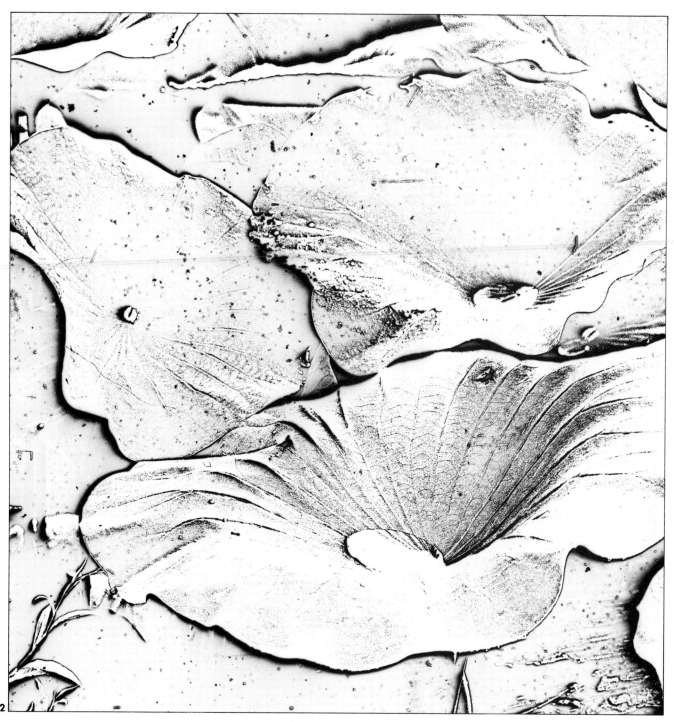

2

colors, while filtering the reexposure light with color printing filters will give another.

The combinations possible with the various filtration options are so wide-ranging that it's often difficult to select among the possibilities. It's also tricky to determine exactly what the result will be when you solarize a color print, since the color in the negative or slide being printed will act as a filter. The color that results from this printing exposure also serves as a filter during the reexposure step, which further complicates matters. Unless you're very good at calculating primary-to-complementary-to-primary colors, just forget

about the effect—go ahead and try it.

Don't overlook the possibility of adding wild colors to black-and-white images in this way. Start by printing your negative onto high-contrast film and use that positive as your original. Then make a print on color paper from the litho positive, using either white or filtered light for the printing exposure, and filtered light for the reexposure. The resulting pictures often take on a dimension you didn't expect, and like well-done posterizations, produce images that you're proud to display for your friends to admire.

MULTIPLE PRINTING

This term covers a multitude of sins,

from the simple use of two negatives to make a single print to the complex combination of several enlargers and a variety of continuous-tone and high-contrast negatives using control techniques. Most beginners find it best to start off with a simple technique, such as the negative sandwich.

NEGATIVE SANDWICH—This is the easiest form of multiple printing to master. Two negatives are placed emulsion-to-emulsion in the enlarger's negative carrier and exposed. The resulting print looks much like a double exposure at first, but once you learn to select negatives that overlap and blend to form a complementary image, you're

on your way. The negatives you select should contain simple subjects, and be somewhat thin in density, since you'll be exposing through two negatives instead of one. Excessive density caused by the combination of negatives will result in unattractive blank areas on the final print produced.

DOUBLE PRINTING—Suppose that you have a landscape which lacks clouds in the sky—the day you took the shot, the sky was barren. Since this area is overexposed relative to the rest of the picture, it detracts from the overall effect. If you can locate a negative that contains an appropriate cloud formation, you can use an elemental form of multiple printing to save the day. Just be certain that the two negatives are compatible; if the landscape is front-lighted and the clouds were backlighted, the effect will be visually disturbing. Here's how it works.

Place the scenic negative in the enlarger and adjust for image size and focus. Then place a sheet of white paper on the easel and sketch in the horizon line with a pencil. Remove the marked paper and insert your sensitized paper in the easel. Determine the correct exposure with a test print and then make a final print, holding back the sky if there's any detail present. Now mark the back of this exposed print to indicate which way the paper is to be replaced in the easel, and put it in a lighttight drawer or paper safe.

Replace the scenic negative with the one containing the cloud effect. Place the marked sheet with the horizon line back in the easel and use it to readjust the enlarger until the cloud formation is positioned above the horizon line. Make a test strip to determine the correct exposure for the clouds and then insert the previously exposed paper in the easel. Use a pair of scissors to cut the marked sheet along the horizon line and discard the sky portion, retaining the lower part to be used in dodging the second exposure. When you turn on the enlarger for the second exposure, hold the lower part of your mask in place a few inches above the easel and move it constantly. When you develop the print, you should have a suitable composite with nice clouds scattered through the previously empty sky above your landscape.

Shirley I. Fisher created this blend by dripping ink on a cleared sheet of film to make the starry night negative. The universe was a separate negative, as was the girl. All three were combined and printed on Fine Grain Positive to form a single negative used for this print.

You can use this technique in various ways—inserting faces in empty skies or behind clouds, creating dreamlike effects of a bride fantasizing about the groom in a wedding portrait, filling windows of a vacant house with recognizable objects—the list is virtually endless. While some are more complex to print than others, each is an example of a composite created by multiple printing.

SINGLE-IMAGE MULTIPLE PRINTING—In this variation on a theme, a high-contrast negative is used and its image reexposed several times across the surface of the paper. This creates an illusion of motion. The high-contrast picture of the pinwheel diver by Michael Parrish is an example of this technique that shows both form and motion. You can also vary the results by dragging the easel slowly across the projected negative's image during the exposure, or by making separate exposures with the enlarger positioned at different heights to produce different sizes of the images. In this way, one airplane on a negative can be turned into a formation, and perspective is artificially added to an otherwise static composition effect.

Single-image variations are also possible with continuous-tone negatives. A subject photographed against a very light or a white background can be printed on one half of the paper. The negative is then flipped end-for-end or top-to-bottom in the enlarger to produce the same image backward on the other half of the paper. The end result is two identical images facing in opposite directions. The same type of negative can be printed in a series across the diagonal of the paper, with each image successively larger.

MULTIPLE BLENDS

To this point, the various types of multiple printing discussed have involved only the use of a single enlarger. Multiple blends can also be accomplished with a single enlarger, but the time spent is lengthy and the results can be frustrating to achieve or to duplicate, as we're now going to combine selected portions of three or more negatives to produce the final print. The use of an enlarger for each negative to be printed permits you to prearrange and adjust each negative as desired.

Once you have the basic setup established, you simply move the easel from enlarger to enlarger to add each portion in the order desired. The advantages to such assembly-line printing are obvious; in addition to simplifying

the procedure considerably, you don't have to go back to square one and start juggling the enlarger up and down all over again if you should goof somewhere along the line. Even if you keep records on each enlarger adjustment for each negative, this can be a tiresome process to go through.

Obviously, none of us is going out and buy three, four or six enlargers to use this technique, but if you're involved with a photo club, school or public darkroom facility, you can often make arrangements to use several enlargers at a time when no one else is working with them. Shirley I. Fisher, who created the illustrations of this technique accompanying this chapter, is chairman of the Photography Department at DeAnza College in Cupertino, California, and has an entire darkroom facility at her disposal after school.

Beyond the spectacular effects that are possible, this technique represents the complex extreme of creative darkroom work, and challenges both your creativity and your imagination, but the end result can be worth the effort. To use it successfully, you must be able to visualize the effect you are seeking and then assemble the necessary negatives containing the various elements required. Assuming that you have reached this level of proficiency, or are striving toward that end, here's how a multiple blend is created.

Insert each negative from which you intend to use a portion in its enlarger in the order in which you wish to print. Compose and focus each negative in turn, adjusting the image size to correspond with what you have in mind. Now place a sheet of white paper in your easel and as you move from one enlarger to the next, sketch the arrangement of the portion of each negative to be used on the paper. When you have finished, you should have a completed pencil composite of the negatives to be printed. This is in effect a rough visualization of the finished print as you envision it.

You should now prepare a test strip for each negative segment in order to determine the most appropriate exposure for the desired effect. Pick a lens aperture that will provide a reasonable exposure duration in which to work—a five- or 10-second exposure can be far too brief to allow the manipulation necessary to successfully blend the images. Jot down your exposure recommendations in the sequence in which you will work and you're ready to begin. Starting with the basic segment in the first enlarger, refer to your sketch

2

1. **This combination of the Sabattier Effect, the technique of printing-in, and blending required five negatives to produce the final print, and is a good example of the use of multiple enlargers in multiple printing. (Shirley I. Fisher.)**
2. **Less mystical in approach, but just as complicated, this multiple print blend involves a negative flip. (Shirley I. Fisher.)**

as a guide and make your exposure. Since this technique will require considerable dodging and vignetting of each negative to print only the desired portions in their proper place, you'll find the use of a foot switch to control each enlarger to be invaluable. This frees your hands to hold back the light from those parts of the print other than the one with which you're working.

As soon as your first exposure is completed, move to the second enlarger, and using the red filter underneath the lens, position the easel according to your sketch for the second exposure. When you're ready to print, shut off the enlarger and swing the filter out of the way. Arrange your hands in their approximate position for the exposure and trip the foot switch, blending this negative in as desired during the exposure. Repeat this sequence with each succeeding negative until you have built up the entire image, then slip the paper into the developer and watch the fruits of your labor appear.

As you can see, if one portion of the exposure is incorrect, if the contrast of one segment does not match that of the rest of the print, or if you were unsuccessful in creating a satisfactory blend between areas, it's far easier to make a second print since everything is still intact. This is the major advantage of the assembly-line approach using several enlargers—you don't have to go back and repeat the entire process of aligning each negative as you make another exposure.

If you decide to try a multiple blend using just one enlarger, you'll have to run through the process of inserting each negative in the enlarger and adjusting it to make your composite sketch. At the same time, make your test strips to save an additional run through the process. When you're ready to print, start with the first negative and the sketch paper, using the red filter under the enlarger lens as your light control device. Once you're set to expose the paper, position one hand to start the blending process as soon as the light comes on, then swing the red filter out of the way gently. When the exposure is completed, turn off the enlarger lamp and change the negative. Move the red filter back in place under the lens and adjust the second image to match that as shown on your paper sketch. Repeat the first exposure procedure each time until you have completed the printing of all negatives involved in the blend.

IN PASSING

Unfortunately, it's time to terminate our all-too-brief look into what goes on in the darkroom of the creative photographer. As you probably realize by this time, creative darkroom techniques are integrally intwined with the graphic arts. But we've run out of space, and must now turn our attention to other equally pressing matters. It's possible to write a book or two (and some have) about the techniques there is not room to include here, as well as a further peek behind the curtain.

One of the most fascinating aspects of this kind of darkroom work is that while there *are* rules, virtually all can be bent, twisted or broken at will by the enterprising photographer with a purpose. The same negatives used with different processes will produce completely different artistic accomplishments. All you really need is something to say, and the urge to express it visually—the rest comes naturally. □

Shirley I. Fisher often works with a light box and several promising negatives to create her complex print-ins from a variety of differing elements.

21

Negative/Slide Storage Systems

When I first became seriously involved with photography some years ago, I thought that I had discovered the ideal way to manage my ever-growing "negative file." Tightly rolling up the 35mm negative strips, I simply stuck them back in the metal cans that were furnished with each cartridge of film. After fastening a label around the container for future identification, I dropped it into the nearest empty shoebox. After all, many "custom" labs of that day returned processed film to their customers in the same way. It just seemed logical to me that if custom labs used the system, I was in good company.

This went on month after month, as I accumulated shoebox after shoebox of film cans, all stuffed with tightly rolled strips of negatives. My first appreciation of the system's shortcomings came the first time I found it necessary to retrieve a particular negative. After searching through shoebox after shoebox, and innumerable cans of negatives, I finally found the strip of negatives I wanted—tightly wound and covered from one end to the other with a series of fine scratch lines. Naturally, the negative was unprintable, and I realized on the spot that I had successfully managed to destroy the value of my negatives in the misguided belief that I was preserving them. This realization brought me face-to-face with one of the most vexing problems to face any photographer—now that you have them, what do you do with them?

There are dozens of different "systems" which have been designed and promoted for negative and slide preservation, none of which are completely satisfactory, for reasons we'll examine. Since the techniques and systems dif-

fer, let's look first at what to do with negatives, and then turn our consideration to slides.

NEGATIVE PRESERVATION AND STORAGE

Probably the most important reasons for using any negative preservation system are the twin dangers of scratches and fingerprints. Either can change a prize-winning negative into a useless silver image on a piece of acetate with very little effort. A scratch across the lady's cheek, or a smudge that dims those sparkling eyes can mean hours spent at the retouching desk to set things right, and if you're not skilled at the art, forget it.

For some time now, manufacturers have been besieging us with various claims about the virtues of glassine, acetate-vinyl, and polyethylene preservation systems. While it may come as a surprise to some readers, the type of material used for negative preservers

1. The Bogen "See-Thru" file sheet has pockets on one side for the negatives, and a pocket on the other side for the proof sheet. You can proof through it and locate the exact negative needed by safelight illumination.
2. The Vue-All page has a frosted polyethylene preserver sheet attached to a reference card for binder filing.
3. The type of negative preserver you use will depend upon the filing system you select. Print-File preservers are optically clean polyethylene which allow proof printing without removing the negatives.

isn't all that important, unless you're into archival processing with the idea that your negatives should last forever. Far more important to the average photographer is how the negatives or negative strips are handled whenever they're out of the preserver.

If you (1) handle the negative only by its edges, (2) dust it carefully with a soft camel's hair brush, and (3) remove the negative carrier from your enlarger to open it fully when advancing the strip one frame, you've done about all that's humanly possible to prevent it from being scratched or covered with smudges from fingerprints. Of course, how you remove and replace the negative or strip into the preserver is also important. Dust and dirt on the surface of the negative or inside the preserver can do exactly what you've worked so hard to prevent, especially if you're rough in withdrawing and replacing the strip.

Regardless of which form of negative preserver you use, you're bound to find dust specks on the negatives when you pull them out for printing. It's one of those facts of life—dust has legs, or so it seems. No matter how hard you try to keep it out, the stuff somehow manages to get into closed

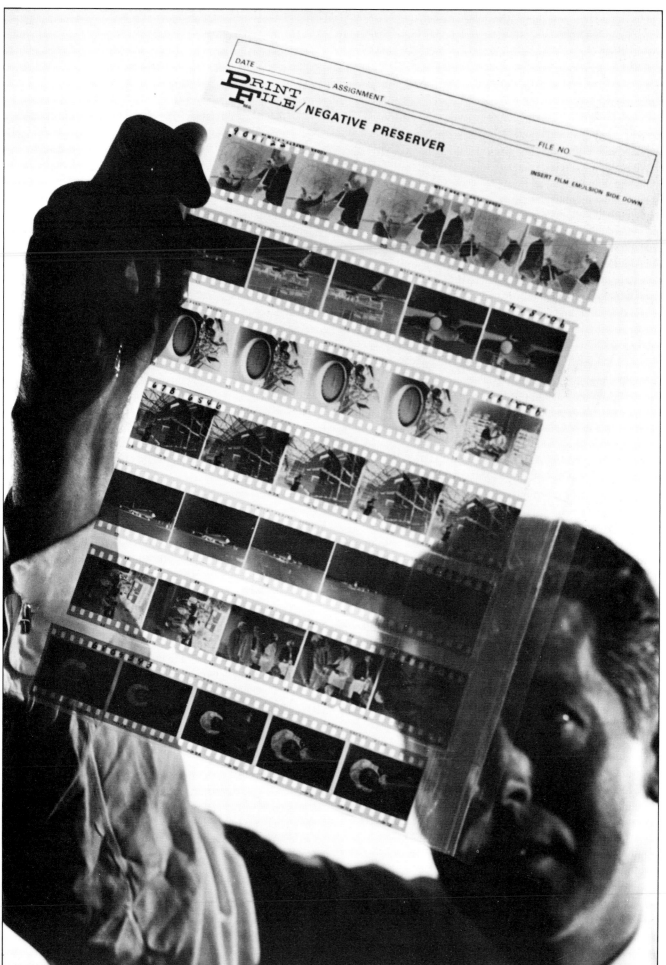

drawers and worm its way into the innermost recesses within. About all you can really hope for is to minimize the amount that collects.

Where you choose to store the negative preserver system you use will account for much of your battle against dust. Negative preservers left on a darkroom shelf or table are bound to accumulate dust, which somehow manages to penetrate the preserver. Storage in a negative album or file binder is one good way to reduce dust; storage in an album or binder which is then stored in a box and kept in a drawer or cabinet is even better, especially if you don't need or can't afford a specially designed filing cabinet, bringing us to another consideration.

The system you select will depend upon how extensive your negative collection really is, and how rapidly you add to it. Those who shoot only a handful of rolls a year will find little point in spending the money required by an elaborate, fail-safe negative preserver and storage system. A handful of glassines or a small negative file book will usually suffice in such cases. Either will offer as much protection for your negatives as the most expensive and complicated system.

But the larger your negative collection becomes, the more important the storage factor becomes. Thousands of loose glassines stored in an unused suitcase may be quite adequate for protection, but can you find the one you want without a full-scale negative hunt? The answer to this question is a compact and easily manipulated system that will lend itself well to quick negative retrieval with as little handling as possible, and that's where our next factor enters the picture.

The most efficient retrieval method means either that the proof sheet must be filed with the corresponding nega-

1. **Ben Parker offers negative preservation systems in album form. Matching print albums can be obtained.**
2. **The Pelican album from Portertown Products. Each page contains three glassine sleeves, space for matching proof strips, and blocks in which data describing each frame can be written.**
3. **From 20th Century Plastics, here is another proof-in-the-preserver. All of the plastic preservers are offered in sizes to hold all standard negatives.**
4. **Spiratone and others offer wallet style preservers in either glassine or polyethylene. These hold one 36-exposure roll of negatives and will also fold into easily filed units.**
5. **Vue-All offers its Film Saver, a corrugated cardboard box which contains 100 poly envelopes. Each has a plastic ziplock top and is able to hold several negative strips.**

tives, or that you maintain a separate proof sheet file which is accurately keyed to the negative file. Both are easy enough to accomplish, especially if you've adopted a binder system. But the real problem comes in identifying and cataloging your continually expanding negative file. For the sheet-film user, this is frustratingly simple. Each individual negative can be inserted in its own individual envelope with a proof sheet attached, and filed under its precise category.

Those who work with roll or 35mm film are not that fortunate. It's highly impractical to cut a roll of 36 negatives

into individual negatives—simply trying to print a single 35mm negative will convince you of that. If each roll of film you shot could be devoted to a single subject, say sunsets or candids of Jimmy, the task could be as delightfully simple as that enjoyed by the sheet-film user. Unfortunately, this is seldom the case—most of us mix and match all kinds of subjects on a single 36-exposure roll. Attempting to cut and file roll-film negatives strictly by subject matter can cause problems that I don't even care to bring up.

Once again, the size and type of your particular negative collection, as well as your own working preferences, will determine in large part the method you use to catalog your negatives for easy, safe storage and retrieval. You'll have maximum flexibility from a file that's cross-indexed. You can number each frame or each roll, date each frame or roll, etc., but whichever method you select should lend itself to cross-indexing, such as subject/date. The better and more accurately your file is cross-indexed, the easier it will be to locate exactly the negative desired with a minimum of trouble. But don't fool yourself—cross-indexing can become a monster all by itself, and you must be willing to devote the time and energy necessary to do it accurately and keep it up to date, or the system becomes a massive waste of time. Too many of us start out with good intentions, but gradually allow things to slide until the amount of indexing and filing to be done appears overwhelming. At that point, we generally throw up our hands and give in.

While you're trying to settle on the best system approach for your own requirements, protection and ease of retrieval should be kept uppermost on your list of factors the system must meet, but don't overlook convenience. Many 35mm negative preserver systems accept six-frame strips of negatives, while others are designed for five-frame negative strips, and a few accept only four-frame strips. A 20-exposure roll can be divided by five, giving you four strips, but when the five-frame strip preserver is used with 36-exposure rolls, you end up with one extra frame and no place to put it. A similar problem occurs with the six-frame strip—you get six full strips from a 36-exposure load, but only 3⅓ from the 20-exposure roll.

Those who use mainly 36-exposure rolls will find the five-frame system to be less than satisfactory, and those who work primarily with 20-exposure

3

4

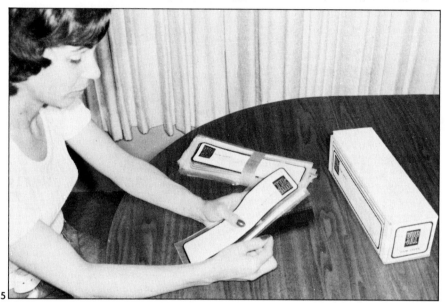

5

loads will not get the maximum benefit from a six-frame system. If you switch back and forth, using an equal number of 20- and 36-exposure rolls in the course of a year, I'd suggest that you change your habits, or you may end up adopting my old shoebox system out of sheer frustration. Fortunately, some manufacturers have started to recognize this problem, and are providing negative preservers like the Camrex No. 35, which will hold seven strips of 35mm negatives, each strip containing seven frames.

Readers who use 120 roll film have a choice of using three-frame or four-frame strips, either of which equally divide a 120/220 roll without problems. Their choice of negative preserver system may well revolve around the convenience factor alone.

Of equal importance to the factors already mentioned, the consideration of cost should not be overlooked. Will the system you select lend itself to easy storage and retrieval at an affordable cost, or will it end up bankrupting you? While we're on the subject of cost, let's relate it to the three basic types of materials used by manufacturers of negative preserver systems—glassine, acetate-vinyl, and polyethylene. The material chosen will be a determining factor in what your system will eventually cost you.

Glassine is the least expensive, lightest in weight, and the least durable of the three. Clear acetate or virgin vinyl is the toughest, but also the bulkiest material used, while the newer polyethylene combines the light weight and low cost factor of glassiness with the strength and durability of the acetate or vinyl preservers.

The most recent trend has been that of designing negative preservers in page form so that they can be used to make proof sheets without having to remove the negatives. You simply place the preserver on a sheet of 8x10 enlarging paper, cover with glass and print. This concept appeals to many as being a great time saver, and it does prevent the necessity of handling the negatives in order to make a proof sheet. But before committing your file to this concept, you should know that the frosted vinyls or polyethylenes require a somewhat longer exposure time than the clear vinyls, and have a tendency to produce a somewhat diffused proof. The clear vinyls occasionally contain a ripple or other manufacturing imperfection which will be visible on the proof sheet. But for the most part, the manufacturers' claims for proofing through the negative preserver systems are valid.

Whether you use preservers made of glassine, acetate or polyethylene is really academic, and of concern primarily to your budget; it's the system within which they are incorporated that is of greatest importance. Generally speaking, such systems can be described in three basic categories: singles, prebound files, and loose-leaf binders. It's fashionable these days to wrinkle your nose whenever single negative preservers are mentioned, but the companies which make individual glassines and polyethylene preservers have never enjoyed such fantastic business—someone out there continues to use a lot of them! These lend themselves nicely to small filing systems, such as my shoebox, a Nega-File, or some comparable home-devised cabinet. But attempting to file them with a corresponding proof sheet can prove a real headache.

Prebound book files come in an increasingly large variety of styles and sizes, ranging from the simple accordion-fold wallet pack, which accommodates one roll of negatives cut into equal length sections, to rather handsome albums that are stored in

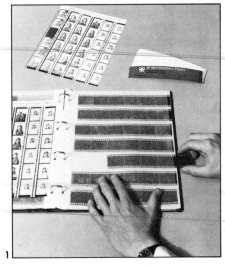

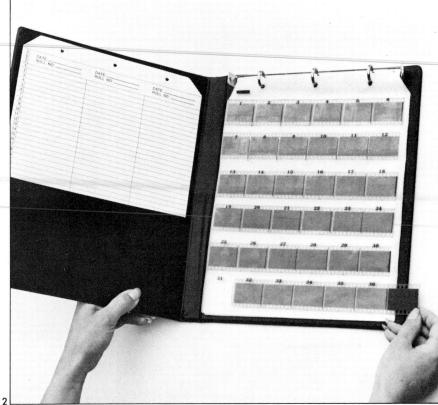

their own slipcovers. At least one of these can be converted into a handy self-contained filing unit to fit a standard file cabinet drawer. All have card pages or some other provision for incorporating descriptive data.

The most versatility is offered by a binder system, which allows you to file one roll of negatives in an individual preserver sheet. It also permits the incorporation of a proof sheet ahead of or behind the appropriate preserver page. Preserver pages and proof sheets are stored in a three- or four-ring binder cover. Note that I said three- or four-ring—this is important. American manufacturers have standardized on the three-hole punching, but file systems manufactured abroad and imported often use a four-hole style. Should you purchase a four-hole system and your local dealer discontinues stocking it at some future date, you could run into difficulty in acquiring additional preserver pages when required.

This inconvenience factor should be taken into account regardless of what system you embrace. It can result from the community in which you reside being outside the mainstream of distribution—dealers in rural Georgia will certainly not stock negative preserver systems to the same degree as New York City camera shops. It can also result from the manufacturer or importer going out of business because too few people embrace his system to make it worthwhile to continue. Nothing is more frustrating than to have to switch filing systems in midstream simply because your original choice is no longer available.

Does this mean that you should stick only to nationally known systems offered by manufacturers with a proven record of maintaining a product line? Not necessarily, as long as you recog-

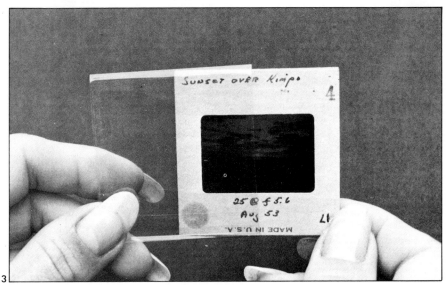

nize the risks inherent in settling on a lesser-known manufacturer's system. If you do find such a system that holds considerable appeal for you, it might be a good idea to lay in a stock of the sheets, pages or other components of the system in a quantity sufficient to handle your needs for some time to come. This is your best insurance that you'll be able to obtain more when necessary.

There are also a number of ''gimmick'' systems on the market, most of which are imported. Those who distribute such negative preservation and filing systems are primarily interested in unloading their stock and then finding

a newer gimmick to sell. You'll do well to stay away from such systems, regardless of how appealing their concept or price seems to be.

SLIDE FILING SYSTEMS

Those new to photography are likely to go through a multistage experience before finally concluding that there is no such thing as a perfect slide filing system. When you first discover color slides, you file them away in the boxes in which they are returned by the processor. But this is inconvenient for showing them, and so you purchase a slide projector. This locks you into a particular tray system, and so you ac-

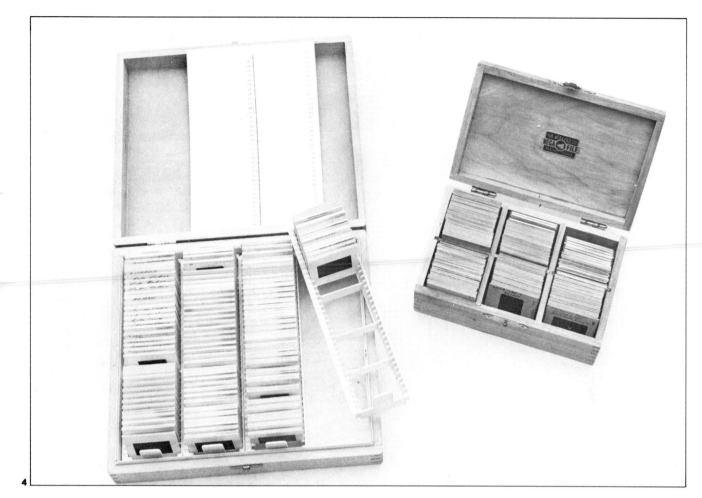

1. **The Paterson Negative File System is one of the oldest and best known. Proof sheets can be filed along with the corresponding negatives.**
2. **Capro imports this vinyl binder album. It comes complete with 10 proofable preserver sheets of polyethylene, and four numbered index sheets. Additional preservers are sold in packs of 10.**
3. **Individual Kimac acetate preservers are favored by some photographers, since they permit handling of the slides without the possibility of damaging their surface.**
4. **Traditional slide filing systems currently available are represented by this Rowi file with removable numbered plastic trays, and the Nega-File group file. Many different sizes are offered, and some are still made of metal.**
5. **LaGrange provides the answer to odd frames in their single sheet preserver which accommodates seven strips on each page.**

quire several trays as your needs grow. Only after you've made a substantial investment in trays do you discover that locating one of the 1200-odd slides you have stored in your 10 trays requires an evening of searching through them, one slide at a time.

At this point, you're likely to remove all of your slides from the trays and return to a more organized system of filing. This often involves purchasing one of the old-fashioned metal or wooden file boxes in which slides are stored by sequence or by category. After filling a couple of such boxes, and still not being able to locate the ones you want with any reasonable degree of efficiency, you'll probably move over to the use of plastic protector sheets. These hold 20 slides and are punched for use with three-ring binders. Now you have a dozen or so three-ring binders in the bookcase through which you can search. While you may not be able to put your fingers on that exact slide any quicker, at least you now get an opportunity to look at your slide collection as you examine each page during the search. Sound hopeless? For many, it is.

The most efficient system devised so far involves filing cabinets with individual drawers in which slides are filed by subject, but few of us have that kind of time, money and space to devote to our hobby. When you stop to consider all the effort that man has expended in devising organizational systems, you'd think that we could at least come up with an efficient slide storage and retrieval system that does not require a keeper of the file and two administrative assistants. Yet that seems to be one of the impossible dreams insofar as the amateur photographer is concerned. And so we suffer more or less in silence while continuing our search for that infernal slide.

Slide filing/storage systems do not offer the wide variety of exotic approaches comparable to those available for negative storage/preservation, for which I suppose we can be thankful. At least there's not as great a possibility of locking into a dead-end system, and discovering it only after it's too late to make an easy switchover. Since color film emulsions are softer than most black-and-white emulsions, protection is the primary concern, regardless of how you choose to store your slides. Some provision has to be made to keep them from the ravages

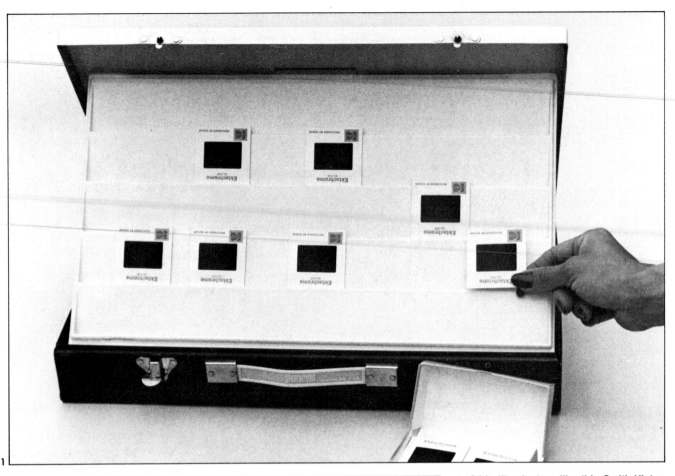

1

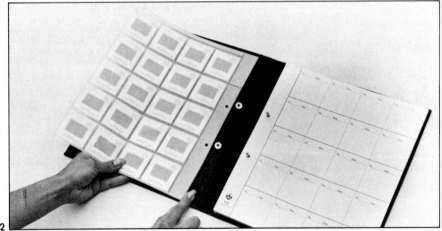

2

1. Slide illuminators like this Smith-Victor unit are helpful in evaluating your slides without the necessity of setting up the projector. When you're finished with it, the illuminator folds neatly into the metal carrying case for storage.

2. A variety of negative and slide filing systems constantly appear as close-out items in photo stores. This vinyl album has a snap-lock spine, and accommodates alternating frosted plastic sheets with file pages. Beware of such items; while many are nice designs, they may never be seen on the market again.

3. VPD offers a similar type of page complete with choice of binders. The 9x11 Skan-A-Page TM pages are designed to flex and fold into a single strip width for mailing, and are available with clear or frosted backs.

4. The newest slide binder concept is this "Slidekeeper" file box offered by La-Grange. Unlike other binder albums, this one forms a sealed box to keep out dust and dirt.

5. 20th Century Plastics provides plastic file pages for use in standard three-ring binders. These pages are offered in a variety of slide sizes, with the 35mm page holding 20 2x2 mounts.

of dust, dirt, accidental scrapes, and hasty handling. Repairing the damage done to a transparency by a scratch or scrape is far more complex than correcting the same damage done to a black-and-white negative.

At one time, it was highly recommended that you remove your slides from their cardboard mounts and remount them between two plates of glass, bound with cloth tape or fitted metal strips. While this approach still offers the maximum protection, it also involves a good deal of extra work, which many feel is unnecessary. Unlike earlier models, which had a tendency to occasionally fold a slide or two in half during projection, most modern

slide projectors will handle cardboard-mounted slides safely. The greatest problem with cardboard-mounted slides today is still in their handling—a misplaced thumbprint or a handful dropped during transfer from storage to slide projector.

This is one reason why the slide-tray filing systems caught on several years back. Once you've inserted the slides in a tray, they remain there ready for projection whenever you want them. From a protection standpoint, this is still the most foolproof system, but it also creates its own problems. Do you just stuff slides one after another into the tray until it's full, or do you try to separate them by subject or other

categories, fitting a few into this tray, and a few into that tray? The more sophisticated the slide arrangements, the more trays you'll have to buy and store. Yet in trying to hold down the number of trays involved in your system, you lose much filing flexibility.

The slide cube was designed to offer filing flexibility while requiring less stor-

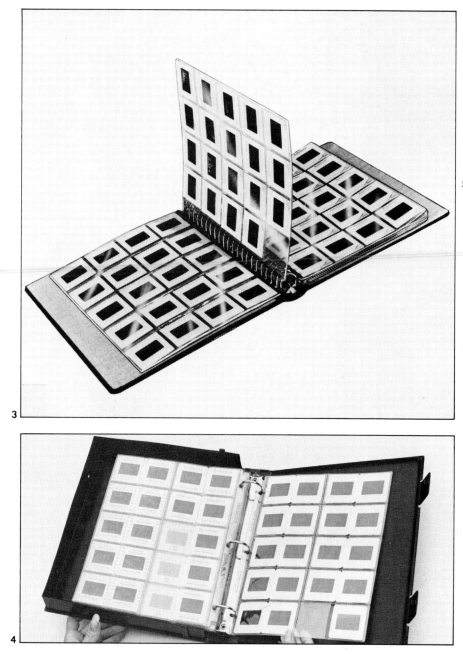

3

4

5

If you have not yet purchased a projector and are confused as to which type you should buy, I suggest that you visit a local photo shop that carries both systems. Take along some of your own slides and try them in both systems. The one which most appeals to you is the one to buy. Many users have strong feelings about the tray-cube controversy; for reasons I've never been able to fathom, it can be a strong emotional issue with photographers—almost like arguing one's political affiliation.

Personally, I do not care for either tray or cube, but prefer to project my slides manually with a push-pull slide carrier. But my projection requirements differ from those who work with slide shows, for example, a fact that emphasizes my primary point—you should select the system best suited to your own needs. We'll discuss this in greater detail in another chapter.

SLIDE FILES

Slide filing systems can be as simple as a small container designed to hold 100 or so slides (either individually or by groups), or as complex as a modular filing system with individual drawers that can be expanded to accommodate thousands of slides. Whether made of wood, plastic or metal, all files share one thing in common—they protect the slides from light, dust and damage equally well.

Intelligently selected and used, these can form the basis for a highly efficient retrieval system, allowing you to locate a given slide in a matter of seconds. Of course, to do so requires a cross-indexing system, and this takes both time and effort to maintain properly. The meticulous among us who chose this type of storage/filing system will probably want to encase each slide to be filed in its own individual acetate protector. This prevents fingerprints and other possible damage to slides being filed, withdrawn for use, or re-filed after use. The trade-off for this additional protection comes with the fact that such such protectors must be

age space. The cube design permits storage of a greater number of slides in a given space, and at the same time, it's possible to subdivide the slides into a larger number of categories. Which slide storage/filing system you embrace is partially dependent upon how you use your slides. Since table viewers are no longer in vogue, most of us view our slides with a projector, perhaps sneaking a preview glimpse with a hand viewer when they first return from the processor.

Those who treat their slides by subject grouping or chronological order may be inclined to use sequence files or trays for storage and filing. Others who mix and match their slides to create personalized slide shows suitable for a particular occasion, who are more interested in printing than projecting their slides, or who are attempting to sell their work in an effort to bridge the gap to professional status will probably find the plastic protector sheets more useful. Here's a quick rundown on the various types of slide storage/filing systems available, with a look at the advantages and the disadvantages of each.

TRAYS AND CUBES

If you enjoy projecting your slides, and storage space is not a problem, using your projector's trays or cubes for storage and filing is probably the safest way to treat your slides. Once it has been deposited in the tray or cube, the slide need not be touched by human hands—the projector will automatically remove and return it for viewing. The choice between trays or cubes is primarily one of philosophy, and the projection system used.

removed before the slides can be projected, and replaced before they are refiled.

SLIDE PROTECTOR SHEETS

Since they were first introduced about a decade ago, plastic protector sheets have become one of the most popular ways to protect and file slides. So many different companies offer such a wide variety of styles that it's difficult to catalog them all. Most are manufactured of a clear or frosted vinyl, containing 20 2x2 slip-in pockets of clear plastic, and are punched for storage in three-ring binders. The same type sheet is also offered for storing other film sizes.

These have proven popular for several reasons. Many find them to be the most versatile and economical way of handling their slides. You can insert an entire 20-exposure roll of slides in one sheet, and view all slides simultaneously for editing on a light box or slide illuminator. Since they can be folded or cut as desired, they are ideal for protection when shipping slides to friends, clients or potential customers. They also lend themselves nicely for portfolio use, and when stores in the loose-leaf binder for which they're designed, make an attractive filing system that doesn't have to be hidden.

The variety of storage binders offered to hold the sheets is almost as varied as the sheets themselves. Some are plain, others are plush and stamped with gold-leaf designs for bookcase filing. Until recently, all were open binders. Left in storage long enough, dust collects and filters down between the pages. For those who find this a matter of concern, Camrex (La Grange) has recently announced its "Slidekeeper," an enclosed type of three-ring binder that closes to form a plastic box.

As you might expect, the protector sheets do have their disadvantages. Because the slide is completely enclosed by plastic on both sides, air is unable to circulate. This promotes the formation of moisture traps within the individual pockets, which take the appearance of Newton's Rings. In some cases, the plastic is drawn into contact with the surface of the slide on one or both sides. While I have not heard of any serious problems resulting from this, it does make slide removal from the individual pocket difficult. There may be long-term chemical reactions between the plastic and the slide, but it's still too early to tell how this will affect their performance as archival storage units.

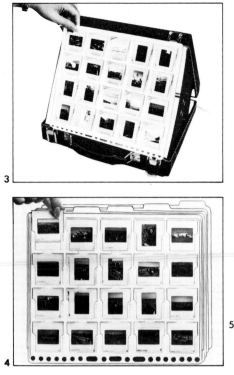

3

4

5

The protector sheet concept has continued to evolve. The most recent design is a rigid one of contour molded translucent white plastic. These contain 20 individually recessed 2x2 slots to hold the slides. The molded sheet has a matte diffusing backing which allows the slides to be inspected by holding the sheet up to any source of illumination. The molded design of the slide slot prevents contact with the slide surface on either side. This allows air to circulate and prevents moisture traps from forming. But there is a trade-off in that the open slide slots can allow dust to settle on the slides.

Molded sheets do have one filing advantage over the soft vinyl sheets. VPO Slide-Sho pages (manufactured by Joshua Meier Division, W. R. Grace, N. Bergen, N.J. 07047) can be purchased with one-fifth cut file tabs for use in standard filing cabinet drawers. You can color code or label the index tabs for quick identification and selection. Since they are also punched for binder use on the opposite edge, these pages can be used either way.

AND IF THE UNSPEAKABLE OCCURS

No system is perfect, regardless of how foolproof it seems. In spite of all the precautions you may take in storing and preserving your negatives or slides, suppose they become scratched, fingerprinted, or otherwise damaged/contaminated—what then? The answer depends upon the circumstances. Light scratches on the back of black-and-white negatives can usu-

1. The one-fifth cut tabs on VPD Slide-Sho pages make retrieval from a standard filing system a breeze. The tabs can be color-coded or identified with pressure-sensitive labels provided.
2. Those who use Slide Cube® cartridges will find the metal and plastic Kenco carrying case a practical way of filing and storing 18 cubes, or a total of 720 slides.
3. The Attache-Vue by VPD is a handy portable system for those photographers who need a slide portfolio. Up to 10 Slide-Sho pages can be carried in the desk-top attache viewer.
4. VPD Slide-Sho pages are available with or without index tabs. Each rigid translucent plastic page contains 20 molded slots for 2x2 mounts, and can be filed in binders or standard filing cabinets.
5. For those who couple their slide shows with sound narratives, Visual Horizons offers its "Media File." The Carousel tray locks into place and there's room for a sound cassette, as well as storage space for scripts, notes or other data.

ally be filled in with a thin layer of petroleum jelly for printing (see the chapter on enlarging). Spots caused by dirt and fingerprints can be minimized by rewashing the negative for several minutes in 68°F. water, and treating with a bath of Kodak Photo-Flo solution before drying.

If the rewash does not remove them completely, try a commercial film cleaner that specifies use with black-and-white film. But under no circumstances should you rub the negatives in an effort to hasten the process, as this will simply aggravate the problem in most cases. I've had good luck in removing stubborn spots with a solution of denatured alcohol, followed by a wash in water.

Cleaning color film calls for somewhat different procedures beyond the use of a rewash for removing dirt spots

and fingerprints. Scratches inevitably lead to retouching of the print, since you're dealing with a multilayered film. Light fingerprints or similar oily smudges can be removed with a sparing application of a good film cleaner, such as that offered by Kodak.

Many slides and color negatives are treated with a protective lacquer when processed. This makes general cleaning somewhat easier, and should minor damage occur, the lacquer can be removed. This will restore the surface, which is then recoated with a new application of lacquer. Kodak recommends two homemade solutions for lacquer removal. The first uses one level tablespoon of baking soda in eight ounces of water (60 to 70°F.). If Kodachrome transparencies are to be treated, 15ml of Kodak Formalin should also be used. The affected transparencies should be agitated in this solution for one minute (color negatives for four minutes), rinsed in water for one minute, and treated with a Kodak Photo-Flo bath for 30 seconds before drying in a dust-free place.

The other alternative (if the first does not work on a particular lacquer) uses a tablespoon of household ammonia added to eight ounces of denatured alcohol. This treatment should not exceed two minutes at room temperature, or color changes may occur in minimum density areas. Dry the film in a dust-free place. This method is recommended for slides or negatives suffering from fungus growth. Once the film is dry, it should be relacquered with Kodak Film Lacquer. Follow the direction on the label for proper application methods. □

22

Basic Retouching Techniques

Regardless of how hard you work to avoid the subject, a certain amount of retouching seems to be necessary, especially if you want your work to be the best possible. If you're presently involved in photography, it's quite likely that you've already discovered the need for at least a minimum of print spotting. No matter how carefully you try to banish dust, lint and the like from your camera, lenses and darkroom, there always seems to be a speck or two that insists on popping up at the wrong time. This chapter will introduce you to several remedies that will put the finishing touches on your prints, whether black-and-white or color.

Many are convinced that retouching is an art, and they're right. But that's no reason to avoid it. Like all other forms of artistry, retouching has various levels of accomplishment. A master retoucher can almost always improve the work of even the best of photographers. While I can't turn you into a master retoucher in the few pages we have to devote to the topic, there's no reason why you can't pick up the minimum skills needed to improve your own work.

Since there are certain corrections and improvements that can best be made only on the negative, almost all professional retouchers prefer to work directly on the original image. Once these corrections have been made, an unlimited number of prints can then be made with no further effort. But most amateurs will find working on the negative to be quite impractical for several reasons.

It's easy for the beginner to ruin a negative with one tiny slip. The only insurance against such a catastrophe

is lots of practice on old negatives before attempting work on a valuable one. To complicate matters, most of us use 35mm cameras, and the 24x36mm negative is far too small for any but the most skilled to work with. And even with talent, there's a limit to what can be accomplished on an image that small. These are a few of the reasons why our discussion of retouching techniques (except for the use of opaque) will be confined to working on prints. Let's begin with a look at the fine art of removing dust spots from your prints, a technique for which you'll probably find the most immediate use.

PRINT SPOTTING

When dust specks or lint are present on the negative or in the enlarger's optical system, they create white spots on the finished print. Judicious use of a negative brush and an aerosol can of compressed gas can reduce such print defects to a minimum. Negatives washed in contaminated water or dried in dusty areas are quite likely to be covered with tiny contaminant particles. These are often embedded in the emulsion and when the negatives are printed, the result looks like a misplaced dust storm landed on your easel. A water filter and a clean drying area can prevent the majority of such problems.

With such negatives, the best solution is to soak them in a warm water bath (75° F.) and then rewash thoroughly. This will remove some but not all of the particles. Don't try to remove the remainder by rubbing with your fingers or a squeegee. This mistake will turn a problem into a total disaster. At this point, your one salvation is print spotting. Naturally, the fewer the number of spots to be corrected on the print, the better the final job will look.

There are two ways in which prints can be spotted: with a graphite pencil or with a spotting brush and retouching dyes. The pencil method is best suited to correcting tiny spots, as it is both difficult and tiring to work a large spot or area to the desired uniform density. Beginners tend to assume that pencil retouching will rub off when it is touched, but it doesn't. Should you make a mistake, you'll need a tissue moistened with turpentine to remove the pencil marks.

Most print spotting is done with a sable brush and retouching dyes. Working with a brush is just as easy as working with the pencil. Since the dyes can be mixed to produce a near-perfect match with the tonal area being

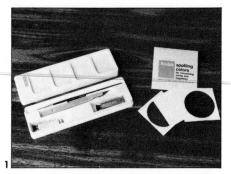

All technique demonstrations and retouching examples used as illustrations are by Anthony Takash.

1. Retouching equipment is not expensive. You can buy a basic set, such as this one offered by Paterson, and then add other dyes and materials as needed. The Kodak water colors are sold in a set of three basic colors, and have advantages over the dyes, as discussed in the text.
2-3. This copy of an oil painting (2) contains all the blemishes and defects of the original. With skillful print spotting, they can be eliminated to produce a better-than-the-original print (3).

spotted, the brush is far more flexible to use. Of course, working with retouching dyes requires a bit of practice in mixing and shading, but anyone can pick up the knack after a few tries.

Retouching dyes must be applied lightly, as they soak into the paper emulsion. The idea is to build up to the desired tone step by step. If you apply too much dye, you're in trouble, since dyes do not lend themselves easily to reduction. Pigments in the form of water colors hold a distinct advantage for the beginner. Since the pigment rests on top of the paper surface instead of soaking into it, it can be easily removed with a damp fingertip if applied too heavily.

Whether you're using dyes or pigments, the technique of print spotting with a brush is essentially the same. Mix a small quantity of the dye/pigment and let it dry. Moisten the brush slightly and twist it around on the dried color with a revolving motion. This will form the tip of the brush into a sharp point and pick up a sufficient amount of color at the same time. Don't wet the brush; if it's too moist, the tip will not deposit the color evenly on the desired area.

There are two schools of thought about applying the color to the print spot. Both require that you hold the brush perpendicular to the print surface. The difference is in the method of application. One school holds that you should touch the tip of the brush to the top of the spot. Stroke it lightly with a downward motion across the spot and remove the tip as soon as the

2

3

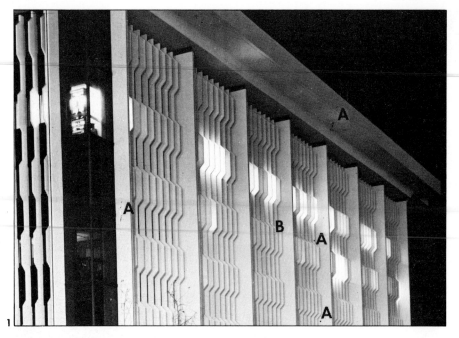

1

2

3

1,4. A combination of etching and spotting is required on this print (1). Done correctly, the blemishes are undetectable on the finished print (4).
2. To pick up color with the spotting brush, revolve it as shown. This forms the tip into a fine point without overloading the brush with color.
3. The brush should be held upright and the tip of the point used to apply color. Tony spotted this print with liquid dyes.

bottom of the spot is reached. The other suggests that it's best to touch the point of the brush gently on the spot to leave a tiny dot of color. This dotting motion should be repeated until the spot is completely filled in.

You might try both methods and see which one works best for you. Just remember to build up the color density slowly regardless of which method you use. More color can always be added to darken it, but if you apply too much initially, you've simply aggravated the problem. Small lint lines can also be removed in the same way. They respond best to the stroking motion, but it will take several treatments to fill in the line completely. Work carefully, keep your patience intact and don't hesitate to take a break in the middle of the line. This can help you relax, especially if you're in the habit of tensing up for fear of making a mistake.

When you're working with a white spot in an absolute black tone, you'll find that neither dye nor pigment is terribly effective. A black felt-tipped pen seems to be the best way to deal with this problem. Holding the pen perpendicular to a piece of blank paper, use it to form a series of dots. This will cause the ink to flow, and once it is flowing without pressure, move immediately to the print and lightly touch the center of the pen tip to the center of the spot. You should be able to cover up most tiny spots with only one touch; if the spot is not completely filled with a single touch, let it dry before repeating the procedure, or your second attempt will remove the ink already deposited. When you're finished, the spot should be invisible. If it isn't, your printing of black tones definitely needs to be improved.

Color prints are spotted in the same way. Tiny white spots can be covered with a gray water color of the proper density. Blue and brown/black dyes or pigments can also be mixed to obtain a neutral gray. For those who work larger areas or who work mainly in color, more versatility may be required. Kodak offers a variety of nine different colors for retouching Ektacolor RC/Ektachrome RC papers, and three dyes for working on transparencies. Just as

in oil coloring, the secret lies in mixing minute portions of colors until you get just the right tone.

PRINT ETCHING

Negative defects caused by air bubbles, pinholes, undissolved chemical particles and dirty processing equipment will appear as black spots on your prints. These can all be held to a minimum by proper processing techniques and cleanliness, but it's inevitable that such spots will appear from time to time despite your best efforts to avoid them. Such print defects can be treated by spotting them with a light color, but you'll seldom be satisfied with the result. Somehow, the end results seem to call attention to your remedial work rather than hiding it.

This is where the use of an etching knife comes in. Applied properly, it can reduce the density of the print emulsion sufficiently to remove the black spot. Depending upon where the spot is located on the print, and how skillfully you treat it with the knife, you may be inclined to finish the job with a pencil or spotting brush after etching the spot, but this urge should be avoided if at all possible. Further treatment beyond the knife blade is not recommended, except in extreme cases.

Notice that I referred to an etching knife—not an X-acto knife or a razor blade. Some amateurs work with the latter simply because they're readily available around the house, but to do the job properly, you need to work with the proper tools. An etching knife has several advantages over other blades. A good one is properly balanced, and has a finely honed blade that's as sharp as a surgeon's scalpel. Since you want to slice off the emulsion rather than scrape it off, blade sharpness is the major element in successful print etching. The X-acto or razor blade tends to dull rapidly. While a dull blade can be used, the end result is practically guaranteed to be more noticeable than the original spot was.

Hold the etching knife as you would a pen, but hold it loosely and at a slightly smaller angle from the paper. You want to work with the edge of the blade tip, not its point. Most beginners have a tendency to use the knife with a back-and-forth, or scraping motion. This is wrong, and will usually get you into greater trouble. Remove the print blemish by lightly stroking the knife—in one direction only. Use a wrist action, and avoid putting pressure on the knife; its own weight is usually sufficient to do the job.

Use the sound and feel of the knife

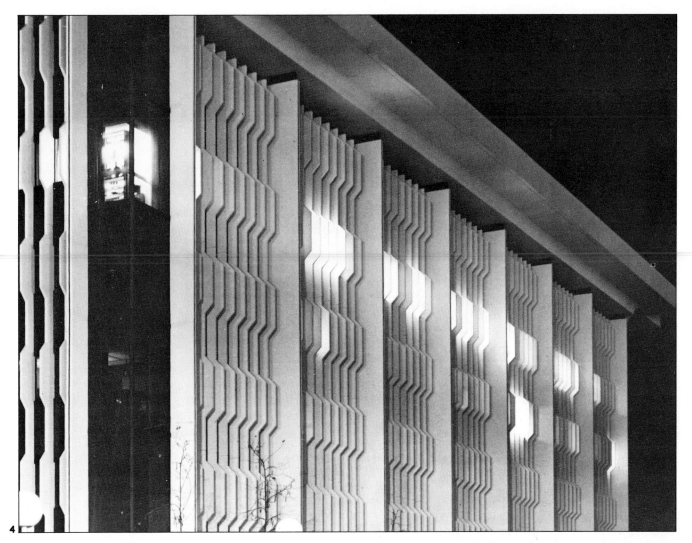

4

to determine how the etching is progressing. You should hear a slight scratching sound and see tiny fragments of the emulsion if you're using the knife correctly. A knife that slides across the paper is too dull; if it catches in the emulsion, you're applying excessive pressure.

Single-weight papers are more difficult to etch than heavier stock, and glossy surfaces require more care than matte papers. Etching a glossy print removes the glaze. This can often be restored by washing and redrying the print on a ferrotype plate or electric dryer. If that doesn't hide the spots that you've etched, or if you're working on an RC paper stock, try spraying the print with a coat of photographic print varnish when you're finished. This will give the print a permanent gloss and hide areas where etching was needed.

Incidentally, if you intend to apply oil colors or tints to the print, save your etching until after the color has been applied and has dried. If you etch a print before using oil colors, you'll have one or more spots where the emulsion is very thin or completely gone. When an oil color hits such a

spot, it's absorbed into the paper fibers. This causes the etched area to take on a greater intensity of color than the surrounding area. Not only will all the trouble involved in etching the print be wasted, the new spot will be virtually uncorrectable.

BLEACHING

Some retouchers prefer to bleach out black spots rather than etch them. This works fine in many cases, but it can be a bit tricky for beginners to work with, since overbleaching cannot be easily corrected. Several commercial products are sold in photo stores for print bleaching, but those new to the technique will find a 5-10-percent Clorox solution more adaptable to their needs. This is not only far less expensive than most commercial print bleaching solutions, it's also weaker.

Should you find that the 5-10-percent solution works a bit too fast for your level of skill in using it, you can add a bit more water to weaken the solution and thus slow down its effect. You should work close to a source of running water when bleaching. The back of a tray placed in a sink near

the water tap makes an ideal work space. When bleaching small areas or spots on a print, apply the solution with the tip of your retouching brush, just as you would retouching dye. To subdue larger areas by bleaching, use a cotton-tipped swab. Keep a wad of cotton or a cotton ball nearby. This is saturated with clean water to stop the bleaching action. Blot off any excess water with another cotton ball and let the print surface dry.

In cases where the bleaching solution goes a little too far in its effect, it may be possible to fill in the lightened area with diluted retouching dye to match the tones. As in all such cases, if you overdo the technique, you may find the results of the second corrective action to be less than satisfactory. The best approach, of course, is to work slowly, carefully and keep the technique under control at all times to avoid any excessive bleaching. Otherwise, you'll have to make another print and start all over again.

GRAPHITE TECHNIQUE

One of the most rewarding of the less-complex retouching techniques, working with graphite allows you to improve your printing. Unlike spotting or etching, which are both subtractive techniques used to correct print defects, graphite is an additive process that enhances what you might otherwise consider an acceptable print.

The most common use for this technique is in product photography, as shown in the accompanying illustrations, but it can be used to advantage with any subject where a stark background or light tone can be improved by deeper contrast, or when the contrast between light and dark tones really needs to be visually calmed down by the addition of intermediate tones. Graphite is especially valuable for the accentuation of detail, or for blending shades of gray into larger areas.

To work with this technique, you'll need sufficient table space where the print can be secured in place to prevent it from moving. The print itself should be a matte or semimatte rather than a glossy surface; you won't have much success trying to use graphite on a glossy print. If you must work with artificial lighting, use a small fluorescent table lamp. Since this illumination source more closely approximates the softness of daylight, you'll find it easier on the eyes than normal tungsten lighting. You'll need the following supplies: a small box of absorbent cotton, an art gum eraser, a number of cotton-tipped swab sticks, a pair of cotton retouching gloves, a bottle of Marshall's P.M. solution or turpentine, and graphite.

If you work with retouching pencils, you already have an ample supply of graphite at your disposal. The correct technique of sharpening a retouching lead uses an envelope about 4x5 inches in size that contains a folded piece of 00 sand or emery paper. Extend the retouching lead from the pencil holder and place it between the folded paper in the envelope. Move the holder up and down while rotating it to form the lead into a long tapered point. In the process, the graphite removed while forming the point is caught by the envelope. This dust is not thrown away, but should be saved for those occasions when you wish to use the graphite technique.

If you use a different envelope for sharpening each different grade of lead, you'll gradually accumulate various shades of graphite dust. With a selection of shades from which to choose, you can create almost any tonal effect you want. Incidentally, when the emery or sandpaper is worn, it will

3

4

5

sharpen the lead much faster than when it's new, so don't worry about changing it. Unless you do a good deal of pencil retouching, one piece of sandpaper should last for years. Those who don't work with pencil retouching will find small bottles of graphite dust in the retouching department of their local photo store, along with the other supplies they'll need.

You should clean the print thoroughly before setting to work. This is necessary to remove any fingerprints, as they'll show up vividly when graphite powder is used. The cotton retouching gloves will prevent your fingers from contaminating the print surface while you're working on it. The Marshall's P.M. solution not only cleans the print, it also gives the surface a ''tooth'' to which the graphite can adhere. If you don't have P. M. solution readily available, a good grade of turpentine can also be used. Wipe the picture with a cotton wad that has been moistened with P.M. or turpentine, and then dry it with a cleansing tissue.

How you apply the graphite will depend upon the size of the print area you're treating. For a large area, use a tightly wadded piece of cotton. Pick up some of the graphite dust with it and wipe the cotton repeatedly in a circular motion, starting from the outer edge of the area to be treated. As the paper surface gradually absorbs the dust, you can control the gradation as you wish. Continue wiping for lighter shades, add more graphite for darker

1,5. This wedding portrait suffers from negative contamination incurred during processing (1). By combining spotting with potassium ferricyanide bleaching (5), the distracting background is removed and a highly acceptable print is the final result.

2. Potassium ferricyanide works rapidly. Tony applies it with a wad of cotton, using long strokes to keep the bleaching action uniform.

3. You can purchase a single etching knife, or a set with various blade styles. Tony recommends this set by Hama. Notice how carefully he removes the blade to prevent damaging its edge.

4. The knife is held much like a pencil, but wrist action is used to control it. Don't apply pressure or you'll dig into the emulsion and cause problems.

gradations. Where highlights and contours require emphasis, use the art gum eraser to remove the graphite. You'll find it handy to have one edge of the eraser sharpened for working fine areas.

Smaller print areas should be shaded with a cotton-tipped swab stick. This is used in much the same manner as the cotton wad—move it in a continuous circular motion until you see the effect that you want. Don't overload the swab stick with graphite at the beginning; when a small area is being worked, a little of the dust will go a long way. It's better to build up density in stages than having to remove excessive

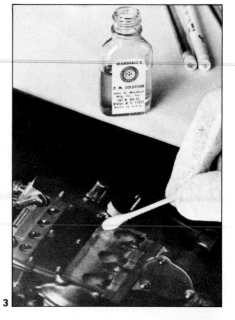

1

3

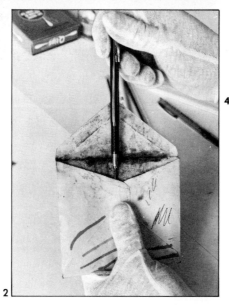

2

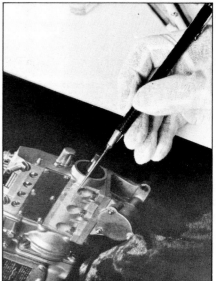

4

graphite by continued rubbing.

Once you're satisfied with the results, the print should be lightly sprayed with a protective coating. This will let you handle the print safely without smearing or marring it. The sheen of the coating also gives your finished work a crisp tonal effect. But what if you're not satisfied with the results? Simply moisten a wad of cotton with P.M. solution and remove the graphite from the print. Let the surface dry thoroughly, and you can start all over again. Bet you never thought that pencil dust could be so versatile!

USING OPAQUE

Opaque is a means of removing undesired backgrounds or other objects from a negative. It is applied directly on the negative and when used properly, results in a perfectly white background on the final print. This quality makes it an ideal tool in creating certain effects, such as a photo montage. Readers who are into creative darkroom techniques will easily find dozens of uses for this technique.

Since opaque is applied directly to the negative rather than to the print, those who work with camera formats smaller than 4x5 will find it necessary

in most cases to make a 4x5 copy negative of a good print. The opaque is then applied to the copy negative and new prints are made from it. If you wish, the opaque can be washed off to restore the negative to its original state once you're finished with it.

You'll need some form of retouching stand when working with opaque. This can be as sophisticated as you wish, or as simple as a light box. The impor-

tant thing is that the negative must be viewed by transmitted light while you're working on it. To avoid scratches and other possible damage to the negative surface, it's a good idea to use a mask made from a manila envelope. Cut out an area of the envelope somewhat larger than that portion of the negative to be opaqued, and insert the negative in the envelope before setting to work on it. Masking the negative in this way also minimizes distracting portions of the negative, allowing you to concentrate your attention on the area to be opaqued.

You'll also need some form of magnifier to view the negative by. I suggest that you consider the type that does not have to be hand-held. It's difficult enough for many simply to concentrate on retouching. If you constantly try to hold a magnifier at the correct distance in order to see what you're doing, the distraction can prove overwhelming. A

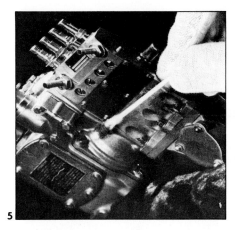

5

1,6. Graphite is extremely useful to those who work with product shots. It's difficult to photograph metals without picking up areas of uneven density because of the way in which the metal surface reflects light (1). By using a graphite treatment, such areas can be smoothed out for professional results (6).
2. Sharpen retouching leads as shown and save the resulting powder for graphite treatments.
3. The print surface must be cleaned and given a "tooth" to which the graphite can adhere. Marshall's P.M. solution or turpentine can be used.
4-5. Small areas can be worked with the pencil lead (4). For larger areas, use a cotton-tipped swab (5).

6

magnifying glass that can be attached to a gooseneck stand is one ideal method of negative viewing. Once this is properly positioned to suit both the negative size and your working distance, no further attention to it is necessary. Somewhat more expensive, but also more versatile, the type of magnifier that attaches to a headband is even better since it can be easily used with other hobbies, or for repairing small objects, etc. In this way, it does double duty and justifies the greater expenditure for the convenience that is enjoyed.

Opaque is a highly concentrated paste sold in small jars and available in either black or red. Since both colors block light from passing through the negative with equal efficiency, the color is important only insofar as identification of the opaqued area is necessary. For most applications, a small quantity of opaque is removed from the jar and mixed in a small container with a few drops of water until its consistency is free-flowing. Because opaque is applied with a retouching brush, its consistency is very important—you should be able to cover the negative area with only one or two brush strokes.

Once the opaque is mixed to a proper consistency, it is applied to the shiny side (back) of the negative with a 0 or 00 brush. Begin by carefully out-

lining the area to be opaqued. This requires a steady hand, but once the outline has been completed, the remainder of the area can be filled in with a large brush. If rather long straight lines are a part of the subject, you can save a lot of time and trouble by applying a strip of black or red Scotch tape instead of opaque. This makes the drawing of straight lines a breeze and the tape can be easily removed if desired. Simply fill in the rest of the area with opaque and you're done. It's a great time saver, as well as guaranteeing that a straight line will indeed turn out to be a straight line.

Suppose you slip while drawing the outline, what then? Start by wrapping a toothpick with a small piece of absorbent cotton. Moisten it with water and correct your mistake by working the line back into the area to be opaqued. With time and patience, you can usually correct the problem without having to remove all of the opaque and beginning over. Of course, if you really flub badly, a fresh start is the best ap-

proach. Somehow, gross errors never seem to lend themselves to perfect corrections, and the time wasted in such a futile attempt can often be better spent doing something else.

Once you've completely covered the area to be opaqued, let it dry thoroughly. It should then be inspected carefully for pinholes where the opaque did not adhere to the film. These are caused in part by using opaque whose consistency is too thick or too thin. If left uncorrected, the pinholes in the opaque will show up as black spots on the print, and this means a tedious etching job. It's better to check your work and apply a second coat of opaque where necessary to cover any pinholes.

Once you've made your final prints, it's really a simple process to remove the opaque from the negative if desired. Simply place the negative in a tray under running water and let it wash. When the opaque is gone, hang the negative up to dry and you're back where you began.

AIRBRUSHING

Probably the most versatile of all retouching tools, only your talent limits what can be done with an airbrush. The skillful airbrush technician is really an artist, and he can always make a good living plying his trade. But all artists have to begin somewhere. For those readers who have the pulse of airbrushing coursing through their veins, but are unaware of it, this introduction to its use may open up new avenues of expression.

Since the airbrush is so versatile, it's the ideal tool for those interested in the art of retouching. Unlike the other techniques discussed in this chapter, working with an airbrush will require a more substantial investment in equipment. A good etching knife will cost only a few dollars, but you can expect to spend upwards of $40 to $70 for a basic airbrush set, complete with tanks and connecting lines. The really fine units will cost you even more, but what's a hobby if you can't spend some money?

One way to economize is to use the small cans of freon gas sold as a power source for the airbrush. This is more expensive over the long run than the use of larger air tanks and/or a compressor, but for many photo enthusiasts, the small cans are sufficient for a session, and are thus more practical from a storage and investment standpoint. those who intend to do a lot of work with their airbrush will be more interested in the air tank/compressor arrangement.

Another economical way to get into the game is with a used airbrush. Check your local graphic arts supply store and you can occasionally find one in good condition, and at a rea-

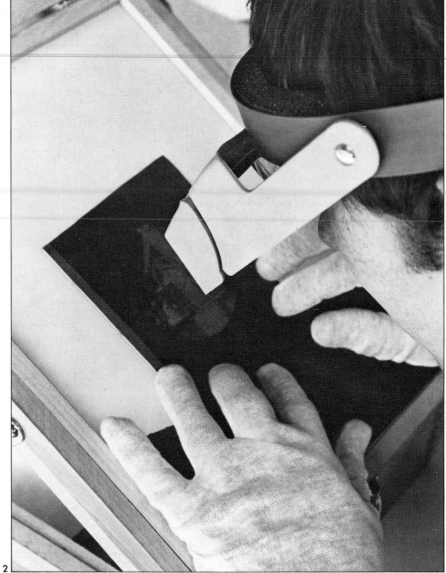

sonable price. This is a perfect low-budget way of starting out, and once you've got the knack of airbrushing, you can always trade up to a better model if you have the urge to expand your ability.

Exactly what can you do with an airbrush? Name it and the skilled user can do it. You can work on negatives, prints or transparencies with equal ease. You can restore old photos, create photo montages, or work at simple effects such as that demonstrated in the accompanying illustrations. When you're ready to handle complexity, you can remove, replace or alter portions of your subject. Unfortunately, there's not sufficient room in this chapter to extol the many uses of an airbrush, but those who are interested can acquire a copy of S. Ralph Maurelle's *Complete Airbrush Book* from most graphic art stores that carry airbrushes. This is virtually a complete self-instructional course, and will tell you everything you need or want to know about the topic.

1, 4. Some subjects simply cannot be photographed without a distracting background (1). Such backgrounds can be removed with opaque (4).
2. Tony adjusts his negative mask before setting to work. The adjustable retouching stand permits working at the correct angle. You can see the advantage of the visor magnifier over other types.
3. Liquid frisket is much easier to use where fine details are involved, and can easily be removed with a piece of sticky tape when the job is done.
5. Opaque is applied with a spotting brush to the back of the negative. When dried, it blocks light from passing through the negative.

Regardless of the nature of the retouching job, one of the great virtues of an airbrush is the speed with which it works. Opaquing and spotting can both be tedious, time-consuming chores when working by hand; a gentle squeeze of the trigger and the same job is done in a matter of seconds with an airbrush. For the exercise shown on these pages, a supply of rubber cement and masking frisket will be re-

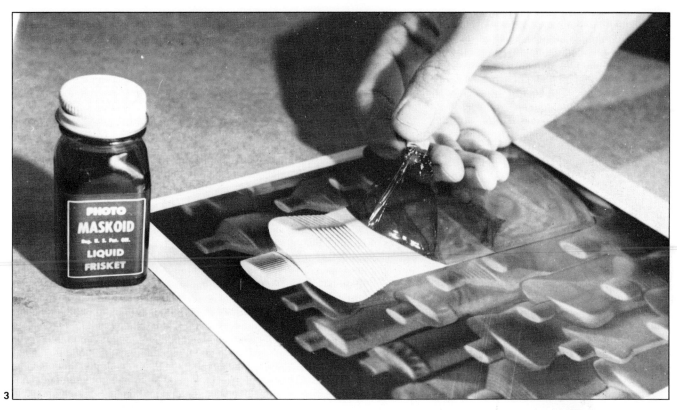

3

4

quired. The frisket is sold in sheets by most art supply stores, and is available in three weights—thin, medium and heavy. I'd suggest that you start out with the medium weight.

The frisket is rubber-cemented to the print surface and then that part covering the portion of the image to be airbrushed is trimmed away by careful cutting with a knife blade. After removing the frisket and the excess cement, the area is ready for airbrushing. The remaining frisket serves as a protective cover to catch any overspray. When it's removed, the image area under it is cleaned of any remaining cement, and your print is finished.

Those who do fine detail work will find liquid frisket easier with which to work. The best-known brand with

5

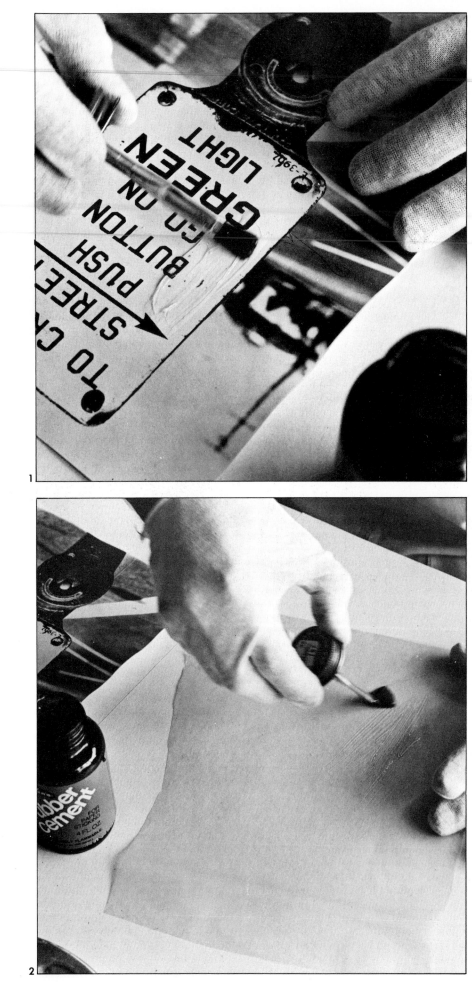

1. The entire print is then treated with a thin coat of rubber cement.

2. After cutting a piece of masking frisket large enough to cover the print, rubber cement is also applied. When both cemented surfaces are dry, the frisket is placed on the print.

3,8. A simple example in background removal (3), the use of an airbrush turns out a perfect job (8) with a minimum of time and effort.

4. Use a sharp knife blade to trim around the area which will not be airbrushed, and carefully remove the frisket from the rest of the print. Use a rubber cement eraser to clean off any remaining cement.

5. After preparing the dye to a spraying consistency, the airbrush is assembled by connecting the air hose to the tank and the paint supply to the body of the gun.

6. Spray the dye over the entire print surface until a uniform density is achieved.

7. After the dye has dried, remove the remaining frisket from the print surface, and the result is that shown in photo (8) on this page.

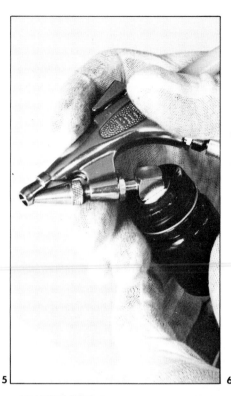

5

6

7

8

which I'm familiar is Photo Maskoid®. This can be applied with a No. 1 or No. 2 sable water color brush to the most minute details in a photo. Once it has dried (usually about five minutes), the Photo Maskoid has formed a thin, dry membrane that's impervious to dyes and chemicals used in airbrushing. After you finish, this type of frisket is removed by simply lifting it from the print surface with sticky tape.

As you can see, our example is an elemental use of the airbrush. But with a good airbrush unit, lots of practice, and a dash of imagination, you can work magic, or the closest thing to it, on your prints. Since that's what many of us attempt to do to our subjects with a camera, what's the harm of improving a little on nature and reality with the help of some of the oldest studio techniques in the business? □

23

Mounting & Display

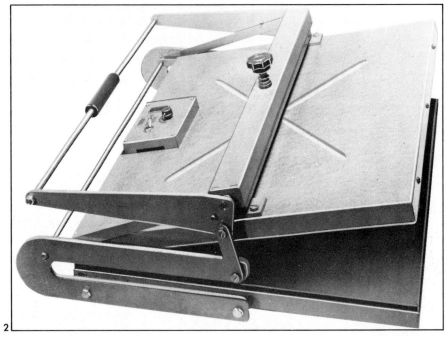

What happens to your prints once they're finished? Do you casually shove them in a handy drawer where they're soon forgotten, or are they allowed to accumulate in a box with the idea that someday you'll get around to putting them in an album or mounting them for wall display? The way in which you treat your finished work is, to some extent, a reflection of your self-image as a photographer and of your pride in your own creative work.

Granted, not every print that you make will be worthy of display, but certainly those that represent your best work should be visible for you and your friends to share and admire. If you feel your work suitable only for the dark recesses of a closet, or an empty corner in some cupboard, then it's very likely that you'd find greater enjoyment in some other hobby.

Those readers relatively new to photography may be unaware of the many options open to them in the mounting and display of their work. Others may not have kept abreast of the current trends, and although dissatisfied with the way in which they presently display their photographs, are looking for new and up-to-date ideas. Since that's the purpose of this chapter, let's start logically with the subject of print mounting, and then discuss display devices and techniques.

PRINT MOUNTING

Prints can be mounted on a wide variety of materials made for the purpose. These are available in many different sizes, shapes and colors. Most mounts you will use are a heavy, flat paper stock called mounting or mat board, although canvas, chip board, foam and other artificial materials are growing in acceptance as mounting materials. All are usually available in a number of colors and surfaces, allowing you to select the one that will best complement your picture.

Prints are secured to mounting boards by using some form of mounting tissue, cement or adhesive sheet. The traditional dry-mount tissue is a thin sheet of paper which has been coated with a dry adhesive on both sides. This melts under heat and bonds under pressure to form a permanent means of attaching your picture to the mount. Newer forms of mounting often use a self-sticking adhesive sheet or spray that does not require heat for effective bonding.

Cements are offered in liquid or aerosol spray forms. While rubber cement can be used with resin-coated papers, it isn't recommended for use with conventional paper stocks. Most such cements contain chemicals that

1. The Bogen Technal Roll-a-Mount combines the function of a tacking iron and dry mount press in one inexpensive unit, ideal for those who do occasional dry mounting of prints.
2. The Technal 550 represents the traditional soft bed dry mounting press design, with thermostatic heat control and adjustable platen pressure.
3. These samples from Photo Art Frames Inc. will give you an idea of the varied ways in which you might want to display your pictures.

will attack the print, eventually causing stains to appear on black-and-white papers and changing the colors in color prints. Those cements which are specifically recommended for photographic mounting, such as Kodak Rapid Mounting Cement, are chemically inert—they will not combine chemically to cause print deterioration.

The appearance of resin-coated pa-

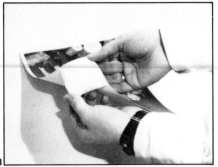

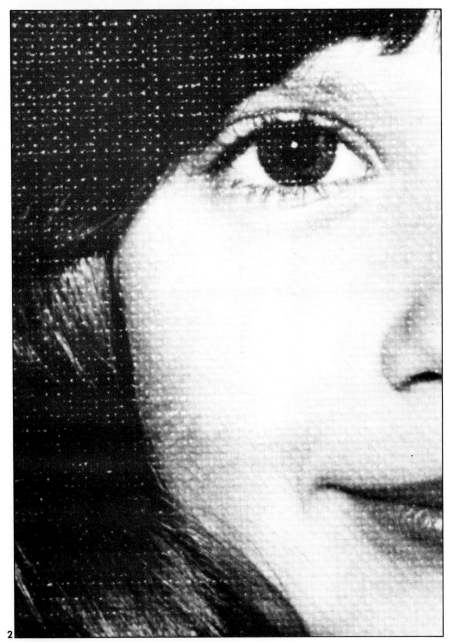

1. The Falcon Perma/Mount 2 is a double-adhesive covered card. Mounted to the back of the print, it provides adhesion to the mat board.
2. This small area of the finished print on canvas using the Ademco process shows close-up detail of the glossy surfaced canvas finish.
3. When using the Ademco canvas mounting process, the print emulsion must be separated from the resin-coated base.
4-6. To use the Falcon Positioner, place print in upper right corner of mount board and place positioner so number readings at points A and B are the same (4). Slide print flush against positioner and down to bottom. Note the reading on the large scale—C (5). Slide print up so numerical readings at C and D are identical (6).
7. To position your print correctly on a mat board without pencil marks, use the inexpensive Falcon Print Positioner.

pers some years ago brought about a major revolution in the methods, materials and techniques of print mounting. For years, the standard technique of mounting had been with dry-mounting tissue and a heat press, but the plactic-coated paper stock was not capable of withstanding the high temperatures required for a satisfactory bond with dry-mounting tissue. In addition, the back of a resin-coated print is not porous, and some mounting adhesives simply would not hold. Other forms of mounting were devised while the manufacturers of dry-mounting tissues revised their product to permit effective bonding at lower temperatures. Here's a rundown on the various methods and how they're used.

HEAT MOUNTING WITH DRY-MOUNT TISSUE—Dry-mount tissue is sold in precut sheets or in rolls. A very thin paper stock coated on each side with a dry cement that melts under heat, the tissue has a waxy feel to it. For the most effective mounting with this technique, the use of a dry-mount press and a tacking iron is recommended. To use dry-mount tissue successfully:

1—Cut a sheet slightly larger than the print to be mounted.

2—Tack the sheet of tissue to the back of the print. An X in the center of the print and tissue will do. If you do not have a tacking iron handy, an ordi-

place temporarily, and prevent it from moving on the mount when inserted in the press.

6—Prewarm the dry-mount press to the temperature specified by the tissue manufacturer (usually 175°F.). Place the mounting board with print attached between a double thickness of heavy kraft wrapping paper. This "package" is then inserted in the press, which should be closed for a minimum of 30 seconds. Remove the package, inspect your work and reinsert for another 15-30 seconds if necessary for complete bonding. Too long in the press and the print will scorch; too brief a period and it will not adhere uniformly.

7—When a mounting press is not available, the print can be mounted using a household iron at the lowest heat setting as specified under Step 2. Place the mounting board and print on a solid flat work surface and cover with the kraft paper. Starting in the center of the print, slowly move the iron toward the edges, running it back and forth over the print. Keep the iron moving, but don't use excessive pressure or the print surface may be marred.

Check your work after making several complete passes across the print. If necessary, replace the paper covering and continue "ironing" until all sections of the print adhere to the mount. This technique works well with prints up to 11x14; larger print sizes should definitely be mounted with a heat press for best results.

8—When mounting a resin-coated print with the recommended thermo-adhesive tissue, put it face down on a smooth, flat surface immediately after removing from the press. Place several weights on top and allow the print to cool naturally. This will increase the quality of adhesion over that achieved without pressure during cooling.

CANVAS MOUNTING WITH HEAT—Probably the best known canvas mounting system is that offered by Ademco. This process is used with resin-coated papers and requires the Ademco products listed below, as well as the use of a hardbed dry-mounting press. If you don't have access to the latter, cut top and bottom sheets of Masonite to fit your regular press. This will adapt it for use as a hardbed

nary household iron can be used. Set it at the lowest heat setting possible in the synthetic fabric range.

3—Trim the print and excess tissue.

4—Place the print with dry-mount tissue attached on the mounting board and position it as desired. This may be in the center, or with a wider space provided at top or bottom. (More on positioning in a minute.)

5—Holding the print in its desired position, lift one corner and tack the tissue to the mount. Repeat this step with each corner. This will hold the print in press. The end result of the Ademco canvas mounting process is a picture that transmits a distinct surface impression of the canvas on which it is mounted. This is laminated between two plastic films for protection. For canvas mounting using this technique, you will need the following Ademco materials:

Silicone Release Paper
Specialtex Heatseal Film
Dry Mount Film
Canvas (a special grade)
Overlay Foil
Ademco Foam Plastic
Multiwheel Piercing Tool

These are all obtainable from any photo store or graphic arts shop that handles the Ademco line, nationally distributed by EPOI, 623 Stewart Avenue, Garden City, New York 11530.

1—Cut the Specialtex Heatseal film to a size four inches larger than the print—an 8x10 will require a 12x14-inch sheet.

2—Run the Multiwheel piercing tool lightly over the face of the film from top to bottom, and from side to side.

3—Put your print on a piece of Silicone Release paper. Remove the Specialtex backing paper and smooth the film over the surface of the picture.

4—Cover the picture with the Ademco foam plastic and put in the press for two minutes at 185-205°F.

5—Remove the picture from the press, peeling it and the film from the Silicone Release paper.

6—Place the picture in cold water containing a few drops of wetting agent and let it soak for a minimum of 10 minutes.

7—Hold the print with its emulsion facing up and bend one corner back and forth until the resin-coated backing separates from the emulsion, then pull the Heatseal film with one hand while holding the paper base with the other.

8—Now cut a piece of dry-mount film (this is *not* dry-mount tissue) to provide a one-inch overlap on all sides, and run the piercing tool over it. With the print face down on a flat work surface, remove the paper backing from one side of the dry-mount film and smooth it over the back of the print.

9—Cut a piece of canvas with a two-inch overlap on all sides, remove the other backing paper from the film and place the picture on the canvas with the weave pattern aligned as desired.

10—If a glossy finish is desired, use the overlay foil on the face of the picture before covering with the foam plastic. No foil is required for a matte finish. Repeat Step 4 and you have a completed photographic canvas print.

COLD MOUNTING TECHNIQUES— Improvements over the past few years in double-surface, pressure-sensitive adhesives have made them increasingly popular as a means of mounting photographs to various surfaces. Several cold mounting systems are now available, the more popular of which are discussed here.

Falcon Perma/Mount 2—This is a double-faced, self-sticking adhesive card used for mounting pictures to mat boards or other such surfaces. Available in three different sizes, the cards can be easily trimmed to the exact size required. Their index-card thickness adheres easily, and prevents air bubbles from forming. The adhesive is inert and will not cause changes in color prints or stains with black-and-white pictures. To use Perma/Mount 2:

1—Peel the protective paper backing from one side of the adhesive card and apply it to the back of your print.

2—Trim the print and Perma/Mount to the desired proportion.

3—Peel the other protective backing from the Perma/Mount and apply the print to the mounting board surface, pressing firmly in place.

The Cold-Mount by Coda—This system offers the amateur the most extensive selection of mounting possibilities without the use of heat. Cold-Mount pressure-sensitive adhesive sheets are available individually for use as you

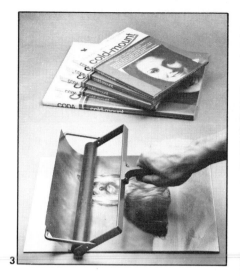

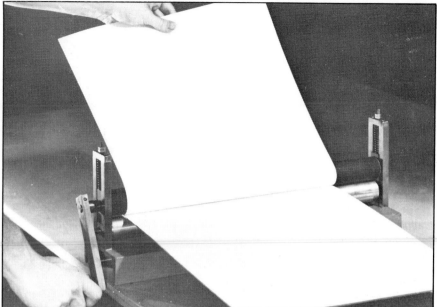

1. Most amateurs would have little use for a motor-driven Cold-Mount press, but with the ease of the Coda system, you could start a mounting service in your spare time and finance your hobby very well.

2. 3M Scotch brand Positionable Mounting Adhesive lets you align your print correctly regardless of how fumble-fingered you might be. But once this transfer-type adhesive is pressed with a roller, the bond is permanent.

3. Coda's hand roller press and Cold-Mount adhesive make print mounting a real breeze.

4. This table-mounted Coda press is perfect for salon and exhibition size prints. Simply hold the print over the roller and free of the adhesive surface as you turn the print handle—the rollers do the job.

5. The Coda press will handle mounts up to ⅛-inch hardboard and turns out wrinkle/bubble-free results every time.

wish, or already applied to top-quality mounting boards in single- or double-weight thicknesses. These have been precision-cut to popular sizes and so require no trimming. Since Cold-Mounts are also available in precut hardboard and foam materials, you have a wide choice of mounting materials available within the Cold-Mount system. The pressure-sensitive adhesive bonds permanently on contact at room temperatures, and can be safely used with all photographic papers including resin-coated and Cibachrome print materials.

While Cold-Mounts can be used by hand in much the same way as Falcon Perma/Mounts, Coda also offers a variety of inexpensive hand presses for those who do considerable mounting. These presses offer the advantage of maintaining the print's exact positioning on the mount without resulting in bubbles or wrinkles. When used without a press, Coda recommends that you peel back the protective paper backing about two inches and then position the print on the mount. Use finger pressure to tack the exposed

adhesive to the mounting surface and then peel the paper back another two inches. Smooth the print down on the exposed adhesive surface with finger pressure and continue repeating this step until the entire print has been mounted.

Scotch Mounting Adhesives—3M provides individual sheets of its Scotch-brand Positionable Mounting Adhesive #567 for mounting photographs to mat boards or other nonporous surfaces. This transfer-type adhesive allows you to move the picture around on the mount to achieve the correct positioning and alignment desired. Once the print is positioned where you want it, pressure applied by a hand roller or squeegee forms a permanent and high-strength bond.

3M also provides spray cans of adhesive which provide similar advan-

tages to the #567 sheets. Scotch Spra-Ment, Photomount and Spray Mounting adhesives all offer heat and moisture resistance without affecting the print. They differ primarily in the length of time that the print can be repositioned before the bond becomes permanent.

THE AESTHETICS OF MOUNTING PRINTS—Mounting boards can be used in a large variety of ways. All are correct, but some are more correct than others, as they will emphasize your prints and set them off to better visual advantage. The type, size, surface and color of the mounting board used is important, as well as the way in which the print is mounted.

In full-mounting, the board used is the same size as the print to be mounted. Prints may be full-mounted

with or without a border. With portraits and scenics, try darkening the corners and edges slightly by flashing during printing. When done correctly, this will help contain the eye within the print and on the center of interest.

With mat-mounting, the print is mounted on an oversized board, resulting in an add-on or mat border. Prints are usually trimmed of their own border or printed without a border when mat-mounting is intended. These are known as bleed prints.

Mounting materials are generally available in heavy cardboard, Masonite, paper-covered styrofoam board (foam-core), plywood and sheet aluminum. The size should be chosen to complement the size, shape and subject of the print. If you standardize on three basic sizes—8X10, 11X14 and 16X20—you can create long, tall or square mount sizes as the occasion requires. Smooth surfaces are best when the prints are on glossy paper, are full-mounted, or colored stock is used. The white or cream-colored pebbled surfaces work best when nonglossy prints are to be mat-mounted.

The color of the mount used is important with mat-mounted prints. If not tastefully chosen, it will detract from rather than complement your picture. Generally speaking, colored stock does not work well; an underlay created by mounting the print to a slightly larger size of colored board and then mounting this to a white, cream or ivory board will usually be more appropriate, as well as less expensive.

White mounting boards seem to work well with high-key subjects and prints that have been toned blue; cream is better with red or brown toned prints. Gray boards go well with a variety of subjects, especially portraits and scenics. A neutral gray is suggested for

1-2. Ben Parker albums represent much of the new thinking in the album industry. One style uses slip-in envelopes with spaces provided for writing captions (1), while another comes with double-adhesive tape strips for arranging your pictures in whatever manner you wish (2).

3. VPD albums using fold-up transparent acetate sleeves can be obtained for prints in various sizes.

4. There are an endless variety of ways in which you can display smaller prints. This Roto-Photo takes a tip from the office card file.

5. The VPD expandable concept uses acetate page protectors to hold prints in place. Since these are two-piece covers, additional pages can be inserted in any number desired.

6. Albums by Ben Parker feature special ring binders and personalized slip covers. These keep dust and dirt away from your prints, and prevent the edges of the pages from turning color.

7. Acetate album pages similar to those provided for negatives and slides are offered by 20th Century Plastics. Pages can be obtained with different slip-in pockets sizes, and turn any three-ring binder into a personal photo album.

color prints. Bleed mounting of low-key and warm-toned prints is most appropriate when using colored stock.

Choosing a mat width that works well visually is also important. For the most part, small prints will require a wider mat than large prints, but it should not be so wide as to overwhelm the picture (Figure A). A good practice with vertical prints is to have the top and sides of equal width, with the bottom slightly larger; with horizontal prints, the sides and bottom can be equal, with the top slightly smaller, as shown in Figure B.

Narrow gray mats work well with large, horizontal prints but most pictures, including portraits, look best when a wide mat is used, since it tends to enlarge and emphasize the subject matter. Bottom mats are used primarily for technical display, and will not work well visually with most general subjects. Remember, if the mounted print is used for display without a frame, the mat becomes the frame in effect, (Figure C.)

A natural question for beginners is where to place the print on the mat—should it always be centered or not? The answer here is called the dominant form and mood of the picture. The proportion of the mount and the mat placement/size should always be selected with the subject's dominant form in mind. Since the wide mat is used to emphasize space, it diminishes the image size. A narrow mat works in the opposite manner to compress space and increase the size of the image visually. By altering the mat width, the eye's attention will be forced to the center, as shown in Figure D.

The mat used must at least preserve and will hopefully accentuate the dominant mood within the picture. You may not always be successful in using the mat placement to these ends, but you should at least be aware that where and how the picture is placed on the mounting board will have a distinct effect on the picture's impact

There are no rules which state that the mat has to be a rectangle, although we seem to be forced into its use by negative format and enlarging paper sizes. When you add the cropping requirements often demanded by a particular subject to these established formats, you can end up with a huge headache by simply trying to be creative in an aesthetic manner.

Try various geometric shapes, as shown in Figure E. Ovals work well for portraits of women and children where intimate or soft effects are desired, as illustrated in the chapter on retouching.

Squares are O.K. when there is no other way to crop the picture. Circles have a tendency to focus attention, while parallelograms can be used to emphasize the dynamics of a subject. Keyholes are suggestive, etc. Use your imagination and try to match the shape to the subject in a way that makes use of its inherent potential.

PRINT DISPLAY

The state of the art has come a long way from Grandma's day when the prevailing concept of a picture automatically meant little black photo corners and an album that looked much like a child's scrapbook. Surprisingly enough, the photo frame/album industry has never really suffered a depression, although you might think that its products would be one of the first things people would cease to buy during the various periods of hard times that have come and gone in the past.

As a matter of fact, business has never been so good for manufacturers and sales outlets handling frames and albums, nor has there ever been such a diverse selection of these products available. These range all the way from the rather inexpensive plastic cube concepts for holding photofinisher-sized prints to the fine leather albums

designed for portfolio presentations. Somewhere in that large variety of display items, you'll find exactly what you need to suit your particular requirements and desires.

Albums have always been popular, and when most of us think in terms of what to do with our pictures, the album comes to mind first, probably because it's almost as much a family institution as the family Bible. But albums have come a long way from the old days when the coarse black paper pages held countless odd-shaped prints and newspaper clippings with those ugly little corner mounts, which incidentally are still with us.

1. Paper overmats can be used with frames such as this **Photo Art Frame** ® design to accentuate the subject and coordinate with the room decor.
2. The latest rage in the frame world, **Kraftique Placques** from **Kraft Color Lab** feature realistic wood detail and color. These are available for prints ranging up to 20x30 inches.
3-5. To assemble a **Photo Art Frame**®, carefully peel the protective paper from one side of the adhesive sheet included (3). Place it on the mount board and smooth out evenly, then trim the print to fit the frame exactly. Remove the other protective paper from the adhesive sheet on the mount board. Align the print on the board and smooth it out (4). Now apply glue to the inner edge of the frame (5). Place the mounted print in the frame and set it under a heavy book for five minutes.
6. **Photo Art Frames**® are sold with all the necessary materials in one package. Work with one of these, and you'll become an instant framing expert—you won't even have to look at what you're doing—it's that easy!

Many of us tend to think of albums as suitable only for storing snapshots, but that's not exactly true of today's albums; their use depends more upon album style and design than traditional concepts. Current offerings can be broken into two groups; those albums containing individual transparent acetate pockets that hold specific size prints, and those albums containing

3

4

5

6

large acetate page protectors to hold 8x10 or 11x14 prints individually, either with a black or white page backing, or no backing at all.

For photographers who are serious about their display albums, the newer trend is to provide a basic cover system that is designed to accommodate an un-limited number of pages—infinitely ex-pandable, as compared to the older al-bums with their rigid spine and fixed bindings, which held far too few pic-tures to make them a good investment. The loose-leaf binder concept has also been incorporated in album design. Such albums do have a limit as to the number of pages they will hold, but it's

surprising just how many can be put between a set of binder covers without overcrowding them.

Perhaps the most inviting aspect of the better albums is the use of the transparent acetate protective page concept. These hold your pictures in place regardless of size and without the use of glue, paste or corner, yet permit instant removal and replacement of any picture when necessary. Since the pictures can be rearranged at any time without problems, these albums lend themselves nicely to an ever-expanding picture file usage.

Individual pictures that have been singled out for display can be mounted on mat boards, enclosed between plexi-glass sheets, or inserted in the more traditional picture frame, of which an endless variety of styles is available. Regardless of which way you choose to treat your pictures, any of these can be mounted on the wall or placed on a convenient spot on a desk, end table, etc. However you choose to do it, you should be aware of a few of the basic

principles involved in exhibiting your photographs to their best advantage.

Prints to be hung look best on large empty walls, particularly if they are white or off-white in color. Pictures do not appear at their best when placed on paneled walls, especially those with grained patterns. Large horizontal prints are most effective on long walls, or over a sofa where their horizontal lines are complemented by the wall shape and furniture design. Vertical pictures go well in tighter spaces where lamps or other decorative items would interfere with a horizontal pic-ture. Try to arrange the pictures and furniture so that there are no obstruc-tions between the pictures and the viewer. Where color prints are in-volved, they should be in accord with the dominant color scheme of the room decor.

Small pictures look best when they are grouped together instead of being scattered around a room at random. Recognizing this, frame manufacturers have recently offered a wide variety of

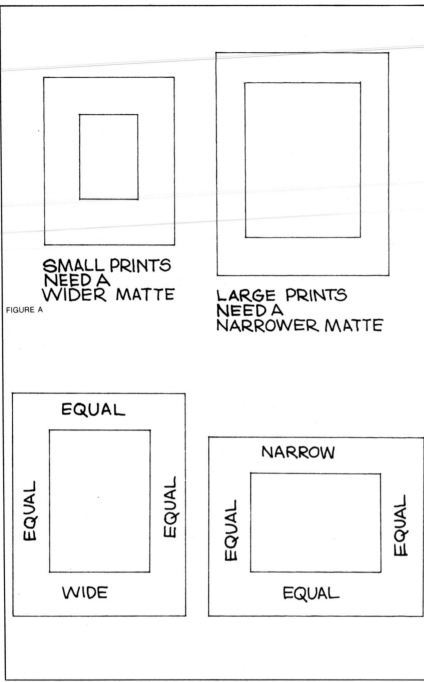

SMALL PRINTS
NEED A
WIDER MATTE

FIGURE A

LARGE PRINTS
NEED A
NARROWER MATTE

EQUAL

EQUAL

EQUAL

WIDE

NARROW

EQUAL

EQUAL

EQUAL

FIGURE B

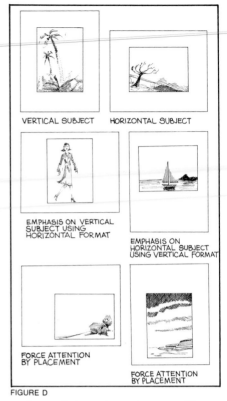

VERTICAL SUBJECT   HORIZONTAL SUBJECT

EMPHASIS ON VERTICAL
SUBJECT USING
HORIZONTAL FORMAT

EMPHASIS ON
HORIZONTAL SUBJECT
USING VERTICAL FORMAT

FORCE ATTENTION
BY PLACEMENT

FORCE ATTENTION
BY PLACEMENT

FIGURE D

three-dimensional montage kits for this purpose. These have become one of the latest crazes in print hanging, an aspect of decorating that tends to go through a new cycle every few years. The kits are sold with all the materials required to create the finished conversation piece, and while instructions are provided for arranging the individual elements in a structured form, you're free to revise the sequence in any way that you feel better suits the subject.

You may wish to frame your pictures for display. While some photographs can hang by themselves either flush or mat-mounted, the use of a frame to focus attention on the image within its boundaries is highly desirable. Since they are also decorator items, and sub-

ject to changing tastes according to whatever is "in" at the moment, the selection of the proper frame requires your close attention.

Because your pictures are two-dimensional and will hang on a two-dimensional surface, one major requirement of any frame is that it set the picture away from the wall or the other surroundings. Yet in doing so, it must not be overly decorative or garish in design, since this tends to visually detract from the image contained within, and focuses attention on the frame instead. If visitors compliment you on the frame, you know that you've selected the wrong one.

This idea of accentuating the picture's image has brought forth a large

variety of frameless frames. These range in style and design from simple plexiglass boxes, into which the photograph is inserted, to the more expensive and classic-looking style that uses a small plastic or metal lip surrounding the two pieces of plexiglass or glass. These give your picture the illusion of resting on a block and, used in contemporary settings with the correct choice of pictures, can be extremely effective.

Although you'll find all sorts and styles of wide frames ranging from highly ornate designs to simple shadow boxes, these are seldom satisfactory for what you wish to achieve. Strangely enough, the ornate designs seem best suited for use with oil-colored pictures, few of which you see these days.

Your best choice is undoubtedly a thin or narrow frame of metal or wood. Both are expensive, even those which are poorly manufactured and show it. Stay away from dime-store frames—you'll pay almost as much for one of those as you will for a good frame selected from a photo shop or art supply store. The high price of both metal and wood as frame materials has led to increasing use of plastic as a frame material. In many cases, the plastic frames look cheaper than their cost would indicate, but recent advances in molding techniques have led to some excellent wood replicas.

Whether you use frames of wood, metal or plastic, try to find the glassless design. If they come with glass,

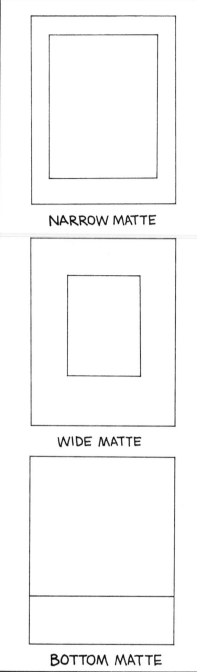

NARROW MATTE

WIDE MATTE

BOTTOM MATTE

FIGURE C

FIGURE E

don't use it, because glass has several disadvantages:

1—It causes glare. When glare-free glass is used, it tends to diffuse. Either results in poor viewing conditions.

2—It collects dust, can be scratched while being cleaned, and breaks if dropped.

3—It will eventually stick to the surface of your picture, making removal or replacement difficult.

4—It adds considerable weight to the framed picture, putting undue stress on the frame itself when it is hung. Unless the frame is of excellent construction, this extra stress can eventually lead to premature frame failure.

When it comes to choosing an appropriate frame color, you'll find that

black is most effective. Black has a universal quality in that it almost always projects the image it contains, while other colors are hit-and-miss in their effectiveness. Occasionally, you'll find that white or gray will work rather well with carefully selected subjects. Wood and metallic colors follow, with the colored, patterned and designs resting at the bottom—they will nearly always detract from the picture.

Metal frames are generally finished in a bright chrome or golden brass color. These can work well with contrasting subject matter, but are usually a source of distraction, especially since the less expensive ones tend to discolor rapidly. If you use metal frames, spray them lightly with a clear acrylic to stop discoloration from occurring.

There's also a wide variety of corner or edge clips used to hold a picture between two sheets of glass or plexiglass. These were quite popular when they first appeared a decade or so ago, but changing taste now considers their use as unprofessional, although you may find that they will serve your

purpose well.

Regardless of the manner in which you choose to display your photographic work, be sure to change it often. Don't leave the same prints where they can be seen month after month. Take a tip from the art and photo galleries, and change your display periodically. Granted, you may have certain prints that you never tire of looking at, but you should also have other work worthy of occupying the space.

For a wealth of ideas and concepts dealing with the mounting and display of your pictures, I refer you to a volume entitled "Photographic Print Display, Book X-6." Available from Royal Dossett, 2567 Commerce Boulevard, Mound, Minnesota 55364, this is perhaps the most complete and thorough treatment of the subject that has been compiled to date. You'll find it especially useful since it covers both the aesthetic and practical situations regarding the mounting, display, and lighting of photographic prints, as well as many handy hints for those who want to make their own frames. □

24

Mounting & Projecting Slides

Color slide users face a different set of problems in mounting and displaying their work. If you expect to fully enjoy your slides, you must pay the same attention to their presentation that you did while taking them. Regardless of how competent you are with your camera, or how dynamic your pictures, their ultimate worth and enjoyment (as well as your reputation with your friends) rests in the images you project on the screen. The world's best slides can be totally ruined by a bad projector, or one in poor condition—likewise, the best projector cannot cope with a poorly mounted slide either.

When transparency films are processed by commercial labs, they will be returned to you in cardboard mounts ready for projection. If your camera has a nonstandard format, as the Panon Widelux does, or if you wish to standardize on the use of a particular type of slide mount, you can request that the lab return your slides in an uncut roll. In this case, or if you process your own color film at home, you'll have to mount the slides for projection.

There are literally dozens of slide mounting systems available for those who wish to mount their own transparencies. They start with the ultrasimple heat-sealed or pressure-sensitive cardboard mounts, similar to those used by processors. At the other end of the range, transparencies can be mounted in a slide mask, placed between two cover glasses and bound with tape. In between these two options, you'll find snap-together plastic mounts much like the cardboard variety, plastic cover glasses that snap-lock into a thin metal frame, and virtually any other combination you can think of. Which one is

best for you? Or should you simply stick with the mounts used by the processors and forget it?

The answer will depend on two things—the slide projector you use, and you own particular philosophy concerning the best way in which you handle and store your slides. Slides that will be handled a considerable amount, as in a slide show you've assembled for repeated viewing, are best protected by a mount which encloses both sides of the film's surface. This prevents damage from fingerprints or accidents. Some photographers prefer to have duplicates made of their best slides, and use the dupes for everyday wear and tear, keeping the originals in reserve for use as masters in case other copies or prints may be needed.

Virtually every projector sold today incorporates some degree of automation in its slide changing mechanism. While great advances have been made in automatic advance systems over the past few years, there are still some projectors that will not work very well when slides are intermixed in a variety

1. Properly mounted and projected, your slide collection can provide many hours of enjoyment.
2. Manual slide projectors still exist in this age of automation, but the few remaining are small, portable models like this Prinz. Even so, it features a low-voltage lamp with built-in transformer.
3. The earliest slide projectors were little more than home movie projector lamphouses set on a base and fitted with slide carriers. This is the first Kodaslide model. (Courtesy Eastman Kodak Company.)

of different mounts. All projectors will function with a high degree of reliability when cardboard mounts are used, but slip a thicker mount of plastic or glass into the the slide tray, and you may have problems.

The cardboard mounts are quite satisfactory for projection purposes with modern projectors, but once in a blue moon, the machine may jam and fold a slide or two. This usually happens when the slide mount has been well-worn from repeated use, or when its corners are bent or dog-eared. To eliminate this possibility, the super-cautious among us who take no chances

2

3

will use a heavier mount. This means remounting those slides already in cardboard mounts, or mounting uncut rolls of film.

Regardless of the type of mount used, the procedure followed for mounting transparencies is essentially the same—the individual slides must be properly cut apart and inserted in the mounts. To do this, you'll need a clean workspace, a supply of mounts, a pair of sharp scissors, blunt-tipped tweezers, and a camel's hair brush. Slide-cutting jigs are available, but are a useful investment primarily for those who intend to do considerable mounting on a continuing basis. Whether you use scissors or a jig, a pair of cotton film-editing gloves are a definite asset. The transparencies should be handled only by their edges, and the use of gloves will prevent any damage should your fingers slip.

Cut and mount one frame at a time. Start by removing the leader from the roll of film. This should be cut between sprocket holes, as shown in Figure A. Figure A also shows where to cut between frames as you remove each transparency from the roll. Once the frame has been removed from the roll, use the tweezers to pick it up carefully by one edge. Dust gently on both sides with the camel's-hair brush and insert the transparency in the slide mount.

All frames should be mounted with the emulsion facing in the same direction. As an example, Kodak mounts all processed slides with the emulsion facing the side of the mount with the Kodak logo. Standardize on your procedure so that the emulsion always faces the same side of the mount. In this way, your slides can be easily identified for projection by the outside of the mount. This eliminates the necessity of checking each slide individually to make sure that the picture will not be reversed on screen.

Cleanliness is essential when mounting transparencies in a glass or plastic sandwich. Use the brush to remove any dust or lint from the transparency and cover glasses before sandwiching them together. Binding sandwiched slides with tape requires a little practice to do an even, smooth job. You'll find it easiest to manage if you precut your tape to 8¼-inch lengths for 2x2 mounts, or 11¼-inch lengths for 6x6.

To apply the tape correctly, start by holding a piece of tape in your right hand and the sandwich in your left. With the tape centered over the edge of the slide sandwich, press down as you turn the slide with your left hand.

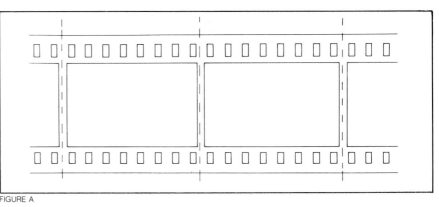

1

This lets you run the tape all the way around the slide without folding its sides down. Your tape will overlap about ¼ inch when you're finished. Now use the scissors or a single-edge razor blade to slit the corners on each side of the glass, then run your fingers along both edges of the slide to fold down the tape. This folds the tape under at each corner, and creates a corner cushion that helps to protect the slide glasses if they come in contact with other slides.

To assure that your slides are properly inserted into the tray or projector for screening, they should be marked with a thumbspot. Hold the slide upside down with the shiny side of the transparency facing you. Since this is the way in which it will be loaded into the tray or projector, mark the upper right hand corner. When you pick the slide up to insert it into the tray, your thumb will cover the mark, hence the designation "thumbspot." Just remember that your thumb must always cover the spot and you'll have no problems with upside-down or reversed pictures.

SLIDE VIEWERS

After World War II, hand and table slide viewers were very popular; a few of the table models even provided for

2

FIGURE A

automatic slide changing. The interest in such viewers has diminished considerably in recent years, since quality slide projectors are far less expensive now, and many can be used without completely darkening the room. But like the slide sorters discussed in the chapter on slide storage systems, a hand viewer is a very convenient way to sneak a peek at slides just back from the processor, and well worth the investment of a few dollars.

WHAT TO LOOK FOR IN A SLIDE PROJECTOR

The earliest slide projectors were nothing more than the lamphouse of a movie projector equipped with a push-pull slide carrier. This was fitted behind the lens to position the slide properly for projection on the screen. There was no forced cooling, automatic slide changing, or electronic focusing. In those days, a projector was selected primarily on the basis of how much light it would throw on the screen for the amount of money you could afford to spend. The maximum was 1000 watts, but since few amateurs could afford these so-called "auditorium" projectors, most settled for between 100 and 300 watts, and only dreamed of owning the more powerful models.

Until the early '60s, slide projectors used tungsten bulbs identical to those in home movie projectors of the era. Tungsten bulbs had several disadvantages—they gave off a great

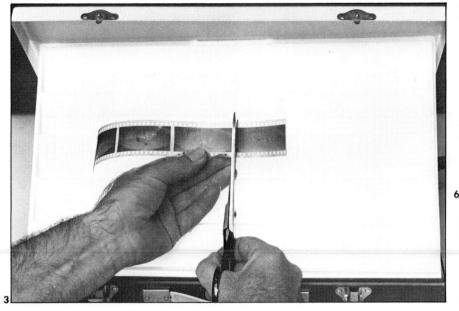

3.

6

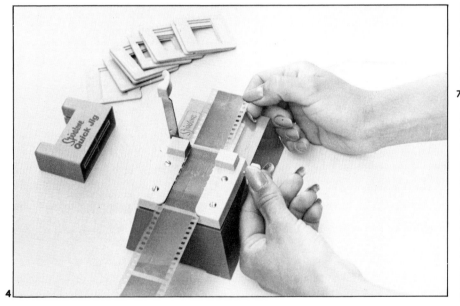

4

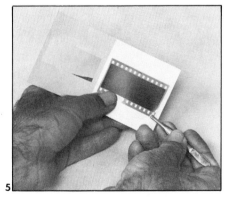

5

1. A small sampling of the hundreds of slide mounts available today. These range from the ordinary 2x2 cardboard mounts to the special Widelux 2¾ mount, and various special mask arrangements.
2. When cutting individual transparencies from the roll, cut between the sprocket holes as indicated, rather than through the holes.
3. You'll find a lightbox or slide illuminator useful in properly cutting film.
4. Spiratone offers an illuminated transparency cutter. To use, insert the film, turn the snubber until the frame line intersects the cutting platform and lower the cutting bar.
5. Because of its large size, the Panon Widelux transparency is easy to position and mount in its special pressure-sensitive cardboard mount.
6. When you're finished mounting, use a thumbspot as shown to indicate the proper positioning of the slide when inserted in the projector or tray.
7. The Spiratone Quick Jig and 2x2 mounts make an ideal mounting system. Insert a cut transparency in a mount and push into the jig. Pull the mount back out and the transparency is ready to project.

deal of heat and had a tendency to burn out long before their rated life was up, but even more annoying, the color of their light changed from white to a reddish-yellow with use. Projector design has certainly changed over the past 10-15 years, but in the process, choosing the right slide projector now involves far more than how many watts and how much it costs. Here are some

of the factors and considerations with which you should be acquainted before shopping for a slide projector.

LIGHT OUTPUT—The majority of today's projectors use a low-voltage, high-output, quartz-iodine or halogen bulb. Iodine or bromine crystals are used in the lamp to regenerate its filament. As a result, these are far more efficient than the old tungsten bulbs, yet deliver much less heat, have a longer life, and produce a more uniform intensity of illumination, with a color quality that's consistent for the life of the bulb.

Since the bulbs are more compact, they offer mechanical, optical and styling advantages. Low-profile machines have replaced the old upright designs required by the bigger bulbs. The screen image produced by projectors using low-voltage bulbs is sharper because their smaller filaments use only the center of the projection lens.

Some projectors allow you to select between full- and half-power illumination. The brighter picture on full power is often useful with slightly underexposed slides, while the reduced light output of the half-power position has a similar benefit with slightly overexposed slides. Projection lamps will last longer when used on the partial power position. To prevent thermal shock from destroying a cold filament, it's suggested that you turn the projector on with the switch set at half power. Once you

1. The Kodak Carousel is probably the world's most popular projector. When it first appeared, its gravity feed slide changer and circular tray made the older straight tray obsolete overnight.
2. The Carousel concept has been scaled down to produce the Kodak pocket Carousel projector for 110 slides.
3. The Bell & Howell Slide Cube projectors use the other major slide projection concept, utilizing plastic cubes which hold 40 slides each.
4. The Prinz 6x6 dual slide projector accommodates both 6x6 and 2x2 slides with an accessory kit. Powerful quartz-iodine lamp with high/low brightness control makes it a top quality projector for large-format fans.
5. The Leitz Pradovit C 2500, like the Leica camera, is regarded as the best of its kind, with unsurpassed optical performance and brightness.
6. The Pradovit concept has also been scaled down for a 110 projector, but the Color 110 uses a circular tray.
7. The Hanimex 110 projector uses a belt containing clips to hold and transport the slides. This design has been scaled *up* to produce a 35mm version.

have light on the screen, you can then switch to the full-power position if necessary for adequate screen brightness.

PROJECTION LENSES—The shorter the focal length, the larger the screen image. Although projection lenses are available in a number of different focal lengths, a four-inch lens is generally considered normal for a 35mm projector. Optional lenses range from 3-7 inches in focal length. Zoom lenses which vary the focal length from 4-6 inches are also offered for slide projectors. These permit adjustment of the image size on the screen without moving the projector and are regarded by many as a desired convenience.

With the inexpensive optics used in earlier slide projectors, the edges of the screen image tended to go soft when the center was sharply focused, and the center went soft if you brought the edges into sharp focus. Field-flatteners came into use, based on the idea that the lens was focusing on a flat surface—the slide. Because of the extreme amount of curvature present in the lenses previously used, the field-flattener was an improvement. But Kodak has determined that most slides seem to bow outward in the direction of the projection lamp, and now offers projection lenses with a curved field to compensate for this fact. These represent a step forward to some, but others are less impressed with the results, and there has been no industry-wide rush to replace current lenses with newer ones of the curved-field design. Try both types with the same slide in comparable machines to decide which of the two—flat- or curved-field lenses—seems to offer the best viewing advantages for you.

SLIDE-COOLING SYSTEMS—Blower

cooling is still necessary, even with the new lamps being used, but the reduced heat output of the low-voltage bulbs allows the use of a smaller fan. This reduces the overall size and weight dimensions of the projector. It also lowers the operational noise level, which can be an important factor where narration is used to accompany the slide presentation.

Blower design and operation are related to lamphouse ventilation. The fan's air stream should cool the slides as well as the lamp, and should also be directed away from the projector as it leaves the vent grille. Depending upon the efficiency of the fan's design, temperatures on the slides during projection can vary considerably. If the temperature is too great during projection, you'll have a problem with the slides "popping" in and out of focus.

This generally happens with cardboard-mounted slides. When the heat from the projection lamp strikes the cooler film, it causes the base to expand and buckle slightly. The result is a change in the film plane in the projector that throws the image on the screen out of focus. By the time you've readjusted the projector's focus, the slide has become acclimated

to the heat and may well pop back to its original plane, causing still another change of focus.

For this reason, some projectors use a "prewarming" chamber that exposes the slide to heat before it is projected. This is done to cause the popping or buckling of the transparency while it's in the chamber instead of during projection. Other designs direct heat over the entire slide magazine for the same purpose.

NOISE LEVEL—Some projector designs are noisy. In addition to the hum of the blower motor, their slide-changing mechanism will "clank-clank" its way through a tray of slides. The problem is usually found on lower-priced projectors where the mechanism is not properly dampened. Some users try to muffle the sound by placing their projector on a foam cushion or typewriter pad. This is fine if there are no ventilation slots in the base; if there are, the projector will quickly overheat as the pad or cushion used will obstruct the free flow of cooling air.

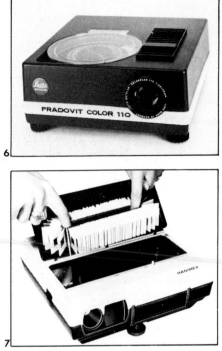

allow light to pass through again.

Stack loaders are available for some projectors that normally use trays. These attach to the projector like a tray, but are designed to let you screen a group or "stack" of slides without inserting them in a tray. Until the advent of the Kodak Carousel line some years ago, the straight tray was king. But virtually all current slide projectors now use a rotary tray. Exceptions to this are the Bell & Howell Slide Cube projectors, which use B&H's own cartridge design. Some Leitz and Rollei projectors also continue to use a straight tray that can be interchanged between the two projectors—Leitz trays will work with a Rollei projector, and vice versa.

To maximize the benefits of tray projection, the trays must be used for slide storage. For those who shoot slides on a frequent basis, this can not only require considerable storage space, it can become a sizable expense. Many users settle on a half-dozen trays, storing their slides in another manner and inserting them in the trays or a stack loader when they wish to screen them. While this extra handling increases the risk of physical damage to the slide (unless mounted in protective plastic or glass mounts), it does keep the cost of trays and storage space required to a minimum.

AUTOMATED FOCUSING—Remote focusing mechanisms have been in use for a number of years. This feature allows the user to control the projector focus from a distance without touching the machine. You simply depress a

SLIDE-CHANGING MECHANISMS—Those who long for the "good old days" of slide projection really haven't the slightest idea of what they missed, or they'd appreciate today's automatic slide projectors more. Slide presentations go far more smoothly with slides already prepared in their magazine, and your fingers never have to touch the slides, reducing the risk of finger damage by constant handling.

Instead of having to sit beside the projector to operate the slide carrier, you can sit at ease with your audience and change slides by remote control. Some machines also have a built-in timer that can be used to activate the slide-changing mechanism at preselected time intervals. Naturally, such features make the projector more complicated, increasing the possibility of a breakdown. But if the projector is properly maintained and your slides are in good condition, you'll experience little real trouble.

SLIDE TRAYS—Automatic slide projectors are designed to work with either a straight or a rotary slide tray. Each tray holds a specified number of slides in their own slots. As the projector is advanced, it returns the slide in the projector to the tray while a shutter blocks the light from reaching the screen. The tray is moved sufficiently to align the next slot with the changing mechanism, which extracts the slide from the tray, positioning it in the projector and removing the shutter to

Lens Focal Length	3″	4″	5″	6″	7″
Screen Size	Approximate Projection Distance In Feet—2×2 Slides				
30 × 30	5	7	9	10½	12¼
40 × 40	7	9	11¼	13½	16
50 × 50	8½	11 ½	14¼	17	20
60 × 60	10	14	18	21	24½

FIGURE B

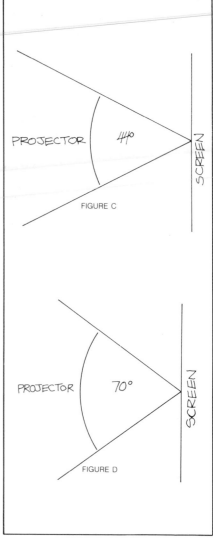

FIGURE C

FIGURE D

1

button on the remote focusing control unit and a small motor in the projector drives the lens forward or backward until you decide that the image is sharp and release the button.

A more recent improvement has been the addition of a system of servomotors and photocells, sometimes called automatic or electronic focusing. Once the image is brought into focus on the screen, this system takes over to maintain a constant distance between the slide and the lens. In this way, the image is kept in focus, even if the slide buckles due to projector heat.

BUYING A PROJECTOR

Slide projectors are best chosen on the basis of comparative shopping and store demonstrations; reading sales literature and specifications isn't really much help. It's hearing and seeing the machine in operation that tells you whether or not it fulfills your requirements, since a copywriter's idea of a quiet projector may not be the same as your idea.

Ask for a demonstration of the projector in which you're most interested, and take along a box of your own slides for this purpose. You may find the saleman a bit hesitant on this matter beyond plugging the machine into a wall socket, but if you can convince him that you're really in the market to buy a projector that meets your needs, he'll likely be happy to demonstrate the machine for you. It's a sad fact of life,

2

1. Kodak offers its slide clip concept for fumble-free use of a stack loader.
2. The Bell & Howell Slide Cube concept permits the storage of up to 720 slides in the same space required by a rotary tray.
3. Modern automatic projectors like the Rollei P350 Autofocus feature a convenient slide previewer.
4. The Kindermann AV100 is the only fully automatic daylight projector using a front-surface mirror and self-contained screen.
5. A molded projector case like this Kodak Model C will carry and protect everything you need for a slide presentation except the screen.

but many people use their camera shop for demonstrations and then walk around the corner to buy from a discount house, which does not provide the same service. You can't really blame the salesman if he's a bit leery of your motives, as he's probably been through this routine hundreds of times.

Turn the projector on, noting its noise level. Run a few slides through the changing mechanism. Try the controls and watch to see how the projec-

tor holds its focus over a two-three minute period. Compare the image sharpness from edge to center. If the projector has any drawbacks you consider serious, ask the saleman if any other designs are better in this respect. If he recommends another model, ask him to show you why it is better.

Don't be pressured into buying a machine that you really don't want, and resist all price reductions that may accompany the pressure. Projector manufacturers periodically discontinue a particular model and the dealer will be anxious to dispose of his stock. If the machine is satisfactory in all other respects, there's no reason to pass up a good buy just because the projector has been discontinued, but if it is not up to your requirements, there's little reason to buy it just because of the lower price.

PROJECTION SCREENS

Many treat the purchase of a projection screen in the same way they do a tripod—price is no object for the projector, but they find it difficult to spend the money for a good screen. Just as

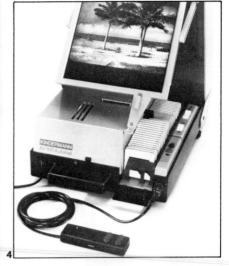

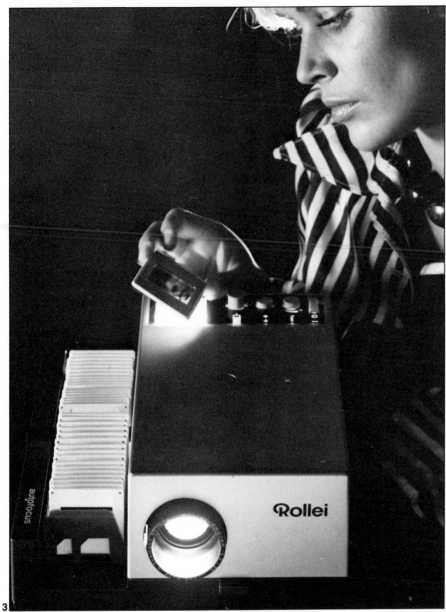

The screen surface interrupts the projection beam from the projector, sending the image back to your eyes. How efficiently it does this will affect the intensity and evenness of the image you see, as well as its color saturation and contrast. For this reason, the choice of screen surface is the most important factor in buying a screen. Three types of surfaces are generally available: beaded, matte and lenticular.

BEADED SCREENS—This surface contains thousands of small clear glass beads cemented or embedded on the white fabric. The beads reflect light back toward the projector at a relatively sharp angle (Figure C). Those seated close to the projection beam will see a very bright image, but brightness falls off rapidly as the audience spreads out.

Don't be fooled into thinking that the beaded fabric used with an economy screen is the same as that found in the more expensive models—beaded screen fabrics differ in quality. The least expensive use cemented beads, while the beads are actually embedded in the more expensive fabrics. Both types will lose a certain amount of

an economy tripod will compromise your pictures, projecting your slides on the wall or a bargain-basement screen defeats all the effort you put into selecting your projector.

Projection screens are sold in two general types. One hangs from the wall on brackets and the other is fitted with a tripod-type stand. In either case, the screen surface is attached to a spring-loaded roller and enclosed within a tubular case. For use, the screen surface is pulled from the case, and with tripod-mounted screens, is attached to a support rod above the case. Wall-mounted screens are pulled down from the case like a curtain.

The tripod-type screen offers portability, as it can be folded up for storage or carrying; the wall-mounted screen is usually designed for a fairly permanent installation. When selecting a tripod screen, consider the tripod and strut arrangment carefully. Is it

sufficiently sturdy? Can it be folded, unfolded and adjusted without difficulty? When the screen is set up, does its surface remain taut and wrinkle-free? This last consideration is of equal importance with wall screens, but a rod fastened to the end of the screen material combines with gravity to hold the surface flat with those screen sizes commonly used for home projection.

Screen size is another consideration. How large your projected image will be depends upon (1) the focal length of your projection lens, (2) the distance between projector and screen, (3) the light output of the projector and (4) the size of the slide being projected. Under most circumstances, you'll find a 50x50-inch screen sufficiently large for home projection. A 2x2 projector fitted with its normal four-inch lens must be placed 11½ feet away to fill this size screen (Figure B), making the combination good for most screenings.

beads with use, but the cheaper fabrics will lose many more much faster, resulting in the appearance of dark, blotchy spots on the screen's surface. For this reason, it is not advisable to attempt cleaning a beaded screen surface beyond a light dusting with a very soft brush.

MATTE SCREENS—A plain white surface, the matte screen diffuses light striking it evenly in all directions. This permits satisfactory viewing from a wider angle, as screen brightness is quite uniform regardless of where you sit. Since its surface is perfectly flat and white, it provides the sharpest picture of any screen material. Another considerable advantage over the beaded screen, the matte surface can be easily cleaned with a damp cloth.

LENTICULAR SCREENS—This screen surface contains a pattern embossed on a silver-coated vinyl surface. Although not apparent at viewing distances, the pattern is designed to control the reflection of light evenly over a wide area, usually 70 degrees (Figure D). But lenticular screen efficiency can be applied in many different ways. Some patterns provide wide viewing angles, while others restrict the angle

in favor of a far more brilliant picture than possible with a matte or beaded surface.

For home projection, this consideration becomes an important one only if the shape of the room in which the screen will be used is very long and narrow, or very wide and shallow. Since both are the exception, any lenticular screen should prove satisfactory for home use. If you plan on using your screen outside the home on many occasions, look for one that will give you the best results in the majority of places you intend to use it.

OTHER SCREENS—The Kodak Ektalite projection screen is a slightly concave frame with a surface of aluminum foil that has been treated to a special patterning process. The result is a screen approximately six times brighter than any of the other surfaces discussed. When positioned correctly, it can be used under normal room illumination, as its optical characteristic reflects ambient light away from the viewing area. These are expensive, nonportable and have rather limited application for home projection, unless you have a specific room devoted to your hobby where the screen could be mounted and left in place.

HOME SLIDE SHOWS

Like amateur movies, slide shows have a deserved reputation for being too long, and for boring audiences stiff. Too many of us seem unable to edit our slides to produce a briskly moving and interesting presentation. For some reason, we have an uncontrollable urge to show all seven of the views taken of the Washington Monu-

ment, rather than select the one good shot and leave the other six near-misses in the file.

If you're going to show your slides to friends or provide entertainment for a local church or service group with the pictures taken on your foreign trip, it should be done with a certain amount of professionalism and showmanship. The first slide to hit the screen should be impressive—its impact is important to move the audience off on a high pitch of interest. The last slide should top the first one, if possible. And those shown in between should be culled of all near-duplicates, second-rate and indifferent pictures. How many slide shows have you attended which were filled with under- and overexposed slides, accompanied by the rather lame excuse that the camera wasn't working correctly, or that the light meter failed every time it was used?

To avoid boring your audience and downgrading your own ability with a camera, follow a few simple rules and you can improve your presentations a hundredfold! Keep in mind that showing three shots of one particular subject is not better than showing just one. Limit the number of slides in your presentation. Any audience will enjoy watching 40-50 slides if the show moves along briskly—throwing 75-100 at them is guaranteed to bring you yawns and polite grumbles. Keep your family shots for family audiences—third-cousin Esther is of no interest to those who are not acquainted with her. Show only your best slides, and ones that are pertinent to the theme of your presentation.

Try to arrange sequences so that your slides are either all vertical or all horizontal. If you find it necessary to occasionally mix the formats, try masking one slide so that the format goes from horizontal to square to vertical. This helps to preserve the visual continuity of your presentation. Wherever possible, try to standardize on the type of transparency film used in the sequences. Unless you have a very good reason for doing so, it's not really visually appropriate to mix emulsions. The difference in grain and color bias between Kodachrome 25 and GAF 500 is all too apparent when one follows the other on the screen.

The easiest way to prepare your slide show is to use a light box or slide sorter unit. This technique allows you to see a number of slides at the same time, and helps you to plan the proper sequencing and continuity of presentation. While it's a bit like playing scrabble, you'll find it a big plus in helping you to properly intermix light and dark, vertical and horizontal, warm- and cool-tone slides for the most effective presentation.

Your equipment should be set up and adjusted ahead of time, with the first slide to be shown already in the projector so that it will appear when you turn on the projector lamp. You might want to use a blank slide instead, so that when the lights go down, you come up with a dark screen followed by your first slide. Make certain that your slides are all in the correct sequences, and will appear on the screen right side up. Nothing is more boring than a show that is constantly halted while the operator repositions the slides—by the time you have the slide correctly inserted and on the screen as it should have been, your audience has already figured out the

5

1. The Spiratone Pro/Show Director is a dissolve unit which provides a wide variety of staging effects for those who want to add a dash of showmanship to their slide presentations.
2. IAV Standard offers a synchronized sound system that can be installed in a Kodak Ektagraphic E-2 projector. This eliminates the need for a separate tape recorder.
3-4. Tripod-mounted screens (3) are the most popular for home use. When extended (4), the screen can be positioned wherever desired.
5. A tape deck can be used to provide narration and music for your slide show. Some projectors have a built-in capability to change slides upon command from the audio tape.

subject and probably couldn't care less about seeing it again, right side up or not. Keep a spare projection lamp handy—you never know when you'll need it. Be sure that the projector is

level, that everyone in the room can see properly, and that enough windows and doors are open to provide proper ventilation.

A carefully planned narrative can make your presentations far more interesting and effective. This can be prepared in script form for reading as the slides are projected, or prerecorded on tape to accompany the slides. For those who really want to add a touch of professionalism to their shows, dissolve devices are available, which use two projectors and blend the image from one into the other as the slides are changed. There's really no limit to how ingeniously you can prepare and present your slides to an audience—the main thing is that you have sufficient pride in your pictures to want them seen at their best. □

25

Collecting Photographica

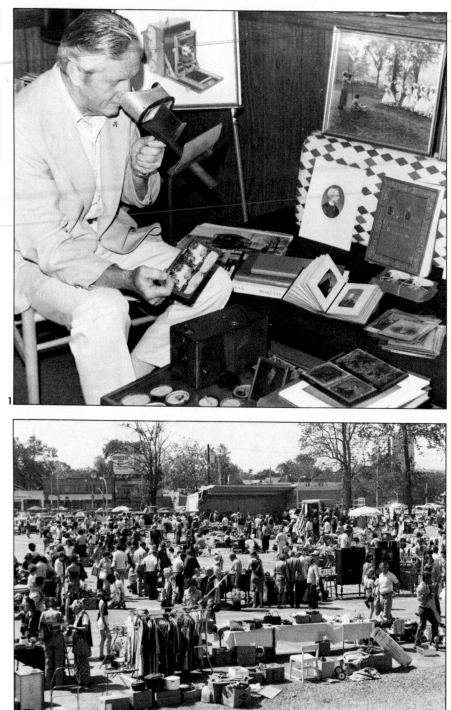

No current book on photography is complete without an introduction to the highly fascinating hobby of collecting photographic paraphernalia. Since it first caught on about a decade ago, the hobby has enjoyed a continuous growth, resulted in the publication of several fine books on the topic and led to the formation of national, state and regional historical associations devoted to the promotion of photography as an art form, as well as a field deserving of historical investigation and preservation.

For the most part, the general public has come in contact with the hobby of photographic collecting primarily through the publicity given to auctions, where exceptional and usually unrealistic prices have been paid for both old pictures and old cameras. Since your interest in photography is bound to bring you into contact with the collecting fraternity, this chapter is provided to give you a behind-the-scenes look, and to answer basic questions you might have. After all, there was a time not too long ago when you couldn't give old pictures or cameras away; now you'd be foolish to throw them out, regardless of the subject matter or condition. Why? What's it all about?

COLLECTING PHOTOGRAPHIC IMAGES

Within the last five or six years, serious attention has been focused on photographs for their value as ''art.'' Yet in spite of the large prices paid for exceptional prints, or images as they are called in the trade, many observers still doubt that photographs have any real value by themselves, especially when compared to the more traditional art objects, such as oil painting or sculptures. The primary problems that continue to hold back widespread acceptance of photography as a true art form are basic to the nature of the process itself—the ease of reproduction on a large scale, and the impermanent quality of the silver halide image.

Another problem is the same regardless of the art form considered—content. A walk through a modern photographic gallery can be appalling to the technical perfectionist. The search for ''meaning,'' or other artistic aspects demonstrated or claimed by a number of current popular photographic ''names'' escapes many viewers. How is one to know which, if any, of the current critics who comment on photography is right? And whether or not they are correct in their evaluations can have a distinct, lasting and most dramatic impact on the value of any collection you might start. Like the stock market, you buy on the informed advice of another person, who may or may not be correct in his approach.

Should you become interested in beginning a collection of photographs for their own sake, and not with the idea that you're going to collect photographic masterpieces which will outpace the rate of inflation, or greatly exceed the value of the declining dollar, then by all means do so. But if you're inclined to believe that moving

3.

modern materials, the resulting print is often undetectable when placed beside the original. Due to the inevitable variations in handmade prints, even an expert would have a difficult time in selecting a genuine print from among several copies. Such copying has been noted recently, even in nonpaper prints which involve techniques that have not been in use for generations.

Theft is a normal hazard faced by any collector, regardless of what he collects, but only recently have photographs attracted the attention of the thief. The George Eastman House reported over $20,000 worth of such thefts in 1976, a situation unheard of in the museum's history. When a Rembrandt painting was stolen from the same museum a few years back, not a single photograph was disturbed. Hearing of such thefts, you naturally wonder what the thieves do with the pictures. While there is no known black market for stolen pictures at the present, establishment of "market" values for photographs are certain to bring one into existence.

In the meantime, it is believed by most informed observers that such thefts occur more for the purpose of enhancing private collections than for the profit motive. Since few worthwhile pictures are one-of-a-kind prints which cannot be easily replaced, the detection of a stolen photograph is equally frustrating as the detection of a fraudulent one. Law enforcement agencies and galleries have yet to devise a technique that can be used with certainty to determine that a recovered photograph is the one that was stolen, much less make their case stand up in a court of law. While a painting can be x-rayed, dated by paint samples, or by the canvas itself, photographs are not susceptible to any such known ways of testing.

Regardless of the popularity of image collecting, the basic question remains—are photographs worthy of classification as art? To which I can only respond, would you consider a painting of a soup can or a papier-mâché dummy to be a work of art? The answer, of course, is that art is what we make it. The more traditional art has tended to involve the more traditional media, or at least variations of traditional media—paint, pencil, or other materials that can be manipulated on a one-time basis. But photography is the instantaneous freezing of image on film, using materials that are far more limited in the degree of manipulation possible. Photographs are flat in

in on the ground floor now will assure you of a prosperous retirement later, it might be well to reconsider your decision to invest. Few of those who are madly assembling collections at this time will have anything of lasting value, and unless you have money to burn, it's a very risky proposition. Here are some reasons why:

Photographs are comparable to lithographs in terms of their reproducibility. For the collector, it may be important to know who actually made the print, and whether or not it is signed. Like lithographers, many of the popular living photographers no longer make their own prints. The printing is done instead by assistants, supposedly under the direction of the photographer. To futher complicate matters, original prints that required a considerable amount of darkroom manipulation can be copied to produce a fairly "straight" negative, which can be

1. Dick Casey, a Rochester, New York camera dealer and collector, with a small part of his image/hardware collection— tintypes, Daguerreotypes, Ambrotypes, photo books, old display items and his stereoscope, the standard parlor item of the 1880's. Such a collection reflects a life-long hobby.
2. Photographic collectors of all kinds find flea markets like this one in Rochester, New York, to be a prime source of collectibles.
3. Old portraits are particular favorites with many image collectors, despite the fact that they seldom know who is pictured or anything else about the subject.

printed to reproduce the desired quality. This permits quantity reproduction at a rapid rate, and even applying the signature is a chore that can be done by a clever assistant once he has mastered the photographer's scrawl.

Unfortunately there are two other factors that are beginning to emerge as trends in the collecting of images— fraud and theft. It's a fairly easy procedure to copy a photograph and with

tion than from genuine recognition by the art world.

One indicator of this is the fact that relatively few buyers actually seem to exist for "rare" pictures. While the sales of such pictures are widely publicized, the publicity comes from a small number of sources and tends to be on an organized basis. There's a good deal of trading among a small number of people, for example, which reminds one of the exchange of two $500 cats for a $1000 dog. You seldom read or hear of actual amounts of money being exchanged, or whether the "estimated values" of rare finds really attract any buyers at such prices. ·

Whenever such follow-up accounts are noted, they frequently report the disappointing receipts from the actual sale. All this should serve as a warning to the potential buyer of photography. Collecting anything where an extraordinary value is attached is not as easy as the get-rich theories or stories would have you believe.

BEGINNING AN IMAGE COLLECTION—
One of the encouraging things about collecting pictures is that it can be simple, satisfying, and often free—if you're wise and stay out of the galleries. Remember, any dealer is there to make a profit. He may or may not be knowledgeable; there is even a remote possibility that he may not be reputable. But he is certainly there for his ultimate benefit, not yours. This may seem a hard attitude to adopt toward dealers, but it's a realistic one. As for collecting photographic images, there seems to be little need at present for dealers on an organized scale.

This lack of a need for dealers lies in the fact that there are literally billions

their basic form, and usually three-dimensional only by way of complicated or cumbersome viewing apparatus.

For these and various other reasons, photography has never fully received the honor of being considered a genuine art form—anyone can take a picture, but not everyone can sculpt a piece of stone. The fact that it offers the opportunity for expression and the possibility for infinite variation does not seem to have made a lasting impression on critics. And perhaps more than any other reason, the fact that silver images seem to have a less-than-lasting quality when compared to other art forms has caused the photograph to be regarded as more temporary in na-

ture. As one critic noted, "Photographs are more comparable to cloth fences than is a painting—a fleeting 'art form,' but of doubtful lasting value."

Whether or not you agree with this statement, there's an interesting observation to be made about photography. Now in the latter part of its second century of development, it seems strange that photography should suddenly be accepted as "pure" and embraced as such by its former detractors. The fact is that it *has not* been embraced by the *majority* of them, and to a large extent, the present spate of collecting and the resulting high prices have come more from shrewd promo-

4

1. **Swap meets are another way in which the collector can further his hobby at small expense.**

2. **These card-mounted prints of someone's long-departed relatives are typical of the images available at swap meets. Some collectors search for pictures by a particular photographer, studio or from certain locations. Most of these were made in Canada.**

3. **Collecting photographic books, catalogues, magazines, camera instruction manuals, etc. is a popular alternative to collecting images and equipment. Like all printed matter, the value varies from nothing to thousands of dollars. Since relatively few copies of many photographic books were printed, those of lasting interest gain value rapidly once out of print.**

4. **Stereoptican cards are in great demand among collectors, along with albums and individual prints. (Dick Casey Collection.)**

of interesting (if not always quality) photographs available, many of which are free for the asking. Since people have not tended to regard pictures other than those of family members as having much value, many photographs of interest to others have been relegated to storage or the garbage can. Collections of pictures have often been donated to libraries, who generally discard all but scenes; others have been donated to charity organizations, usually to get rid of them. These also tend to be discarded, unless they have some unusual quality, like a good frame that can be salvaged. Even tintypes, Daguerreotypes and other such processes have not fared much better. Many adults can recall a parent or grandparent tossing out dozens of tintypes of unknown relatives. Even so, vast quantities of such material remain to be found by those interested in the search. But how to separate the wheat from the chaff?

WHERE TO BEGIN—A good way to start your collection is to look in the attic, especially those belonging to older relatives. Then pay a visit to the local Salvation Army, Disabled Veterans, Goodwill or other such thrift stores. It's not uncommon to find albums of old pictures in general ''junk'' or salvage stores. These are usually priced on the basis of the album rather than its contents. Another fairly obvious source is an antique shop. Dealers are usually well informed about current collecting interests, but their customers are not always interested in what they have available. If your interest in old pictures is not equally shared by the shop's established clientele, you might be able to strike a decent bargain with the owner for what you'd like.

Experience has shown that like the junk store, the antique shop has a tendency to emphasize the value of the album, not its contents. You might even be able to obtain certain pictures from the album without buying the whole thing. If you're not accustomed to the ways of antique dealers, there are certain facts with which you should become acquainted:

1—Most antique dealers plan on at least doubling their money.

2—Many items like photo albums are obtained as a part of a larger group of materials. For this reason, the dealer may have little or nothing invested in them, so the price may be extremely arbitrary.

3—There is *no* established technique for evaluating a photograph, regardless of what the dealer tells you.

4—Since most dealers expect you to deal, they seldom expect to get their initial asking price.

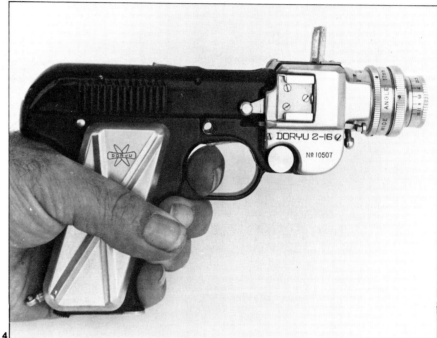

5—Most antique dealers are interested in moving their stock and will accept reasonable offers for such items.

6—If you look interested, the price may well double. Few experienced collectors tip their hands as to what they are most interested in, unless they know the dealer, or fail to see anything of interest on display

7—Becoming a ''dealer'' yourself will often get you an automatic discount without having to haggle. This can be accomplished as easily as having a business card printed.

Stay away from auctions—they can be dangerous places for any collectors. In most cases, you can assume that the stock has been carefully appraised and evaluated prior to the auction, and in some cases, anything valuable has been set aside for private sale. Even the best auction houses are primarily interested in their commissions. Informal local auctions are often fun and interesting, but you may easily get caught up in the euphoria of the moment and end up bidding far more than the item is really worth to you.

What about acquiring serial-numbered prints? These are usually ''limited edition'' photos made from a fa-

mous negative. They are often sold either mounted or framed, and are usually signed by the photographer, if he's still living. In virtually all cases, there is supposedly only a limited number made to retain the value. In most cases, there is no reason to believe otherwise, but I've never heard of a case in which the negative was actually destroyed after the prints were made up, and so the possibility always remains that duplicates or an additional serial run may be made at a later date. Like lithographs, the price may or may not be worth what you get.

Actual prints rather than photoengraved copies have come and gone at various times over the years. Today, they sell in the general range of $10 to $15 per print. Since these are usually

1. Collectors like Dick Casey are fond of using their cameras rather than simply displaying them.
2. Probably the only box camera of real value, the first Kodak (1888) has inspired replicas which are also of value. (Courtesy, Eastman Kodak Company.)
3. Many early cameras like this Kodak were fitted with pneumatic shutters. These were largely replaced with shutters using cable releases. In rare cases, you'll come across one which still has the original rubber ball attached, which may still be soft and usable.
4. Cameras come in all sizes and shapes. Unusual ones like this gun camera fascinate collectors. This one uses 16mm film, has a movie camera lens and originally fired magnesium flares which enabled one to take night pictures.
5. Using one of his cameras aboard the Gallia in 1890, George Eastman was photographed by another. The circular print format was typical of Kodaks of that era. (Courtesy, Eastman Kodak Company.)

5

machine-made by the hundreds or thousands, they should be purchased only if you would like to hang the picture on your wall. Such prints should not be deposited in your collection with the intention that they will increase in their value.

Daguerreotypes, ambrotypes and tintypes are all distinctively different processes, and all are increasingly popular as collectible images. Many people value the cases in which the Daguerreotypes and ambrotypes are mounted more than the pictures they contain. Since tintypes were considered the poor man's Daguerreotype, few were handled with much care. As a result, they are often in poor condition, a factor which greatly affects their value.

All of these techniques are being duplicated today, even to the cases. Those new to the hobby of image collecting have occasionally found to their great surprise that the 1877 vintage image they bought is really a product of 1977—and I'm certain that just as many more haven't discovered yet that they've been ''taken.'' Some of my wealthier acquaintances have found to their dismay that even a dusty, somewhat-worn case is not a guarantee of the genuine item; counterfeiters are a crafty lot regardless of the product. Actually, fraud in photographic collecting is not widespread, but it is increasing in frequency. Even clothing styles and the facial hair styles

(beards) worn today tend to give recent pictures an air of antiquity. So check Figure A carefully if your interests lie in these areas, as it will help you to tell how one process can be determined from another, and provides hints for determining age.

COLLECTING PHOTOGRAPHIC HARDWARE

Cameras are the most popular subject for collectors of photographic hardware, and are usually collected according to type (35mm, folding, subminiature, box, etc.), brand name (Leica, Contax, etc.), or features (built-in automatic film wind, special shutters, etc.). Other collections are composed of accessories, lenses, and photo-

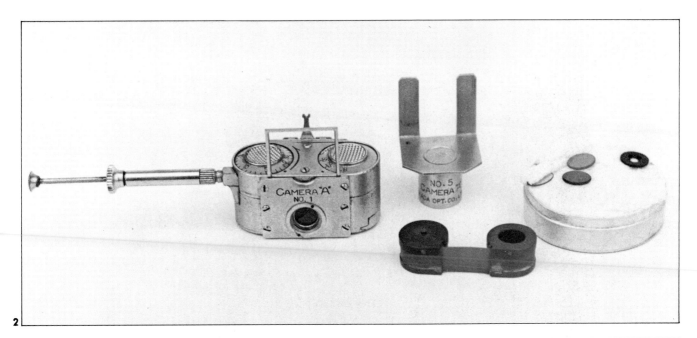

1. With its square corners, the No. 2 Folding Autographic Kodak was one of the many variations Kodak offered during the years after World War I. Printed around the lens was the camera's most outstanding feature—one of the most complicated exposure guide systems.

2. Perhaps the most fascinating of the Japanese subminiature cameras, the Camera "A" No. 1 was a product of Tokyo's Okada Optical Company. Designed about 1950, the camera used a cassette load of 8mm film and came complete with tripod adapter, glass filters and close-up lens. The camera is valued at several hundred dollars.

3. Once the pride of Rochester's Folmer and Schwing division of Kodak, the basic Graflex cameras never changed. This one includes a clever film storage container on its left front side.

4. Shown here with its semisoft pouch case, the original Argus Model A made 35mm photography a popular hobby in America. One of the first produced, this example looks almost exactly as it would have been seen on a dealer's shelf way back in 1936.

graphically oriented materials such as bottles, advertising and other such items. To a lesser extent, there are active collections of darkroom and projection equipment. Of all the areas, those involving smaller equipment and specific brands seem the most popular. This is partly due to space limitations required for a large collection of Graphic cameras, for example. Press/view cameras fall into the same category, with motion picture equipment probably the least popular of all. There are some collectors of professional motion picture equipment, but physical size of the collection is a limitation most collectors cannot overcome.

While the prices of rare items like Daguerreotype cameras have skyrocketed over the last few years, most cameras have stabilized at rather reasonable values. The Daguerreotype and similar cameras are primarily museum pieces. These were often exquisitely crafted, and since their original production was highly limited in comparison to today's mass-production runs, they are most desirable to those who can afford them. Most of the best-known examples of such cameras are already in the hands of well-known collectors, many of whom are also dealers. As long as there is a select few willing to pay the premium for rarity, their prices, like those of certain Leica cameras, will continue to increase.

Prices of old cameras have taken two divergent paths in recent years. The genuine antiques—those nearing the magic 100-year-old mark—are of immense value, primarily due to their scarcity. A genuine Daguerreotype camera would bring upwards of $4000 at some auctions, but few exist on the open market. On the other hand, those cameras which are common, such as the Kodak folders, have gained little in value, and in some cases, have actually lowered their worth due to a lack of demand—and demand is the key word in any form of collecting, whether it's cameras, cars or what have you.

The demand for extremely rare cameras is rather small, but then their availability is so limited that even the small demand results in high prices. In the case of Leicas, which are probably the best investment camera for collectors, the demand is actually relatively small but the publicity about collection of the marque has been such that the prices continue to rise unassisted.

WHAT TO COLLECT?

Those new to the urge to accumulate displays of photographic equipment may well be at a loss to determine where their true interests lie. An accurate count of camera manufacturers and the various names they placed on their products would number into the thousands. Of the total figure, only a very small percentage were major manufacturers like Kodak, E. Leitz and Ansco; the vast majority were small companies, many of which are virtually unknown or forgotten today. At the same time, the photographic industry has not been adequately chronicled over the years, and its products and their historical significance have been completely ignored by all but the die-hard collectors. For these reasons, it's possible to find an astonishing number of cameras that are not listed in any of the admittedly scanty reference works available to the collector. Since the companies themselves have long disappeared and those employed by it are no longer among the living, the only remains of their existence is the occasional camera resurrected from some forgotten attic.

To help you get started in determining what is of interest to you, I've broken the history of photography into seven rather distinct eras insofar as

hardware is concerned. Admittedly, the capsule descriptions below are an oversimplification, but they should serve to clarify a general breakdown of hardware availability in your mind, and then we'll take a look at some specific brands, types and kinds of equipment that can make up extremely fascinating collections.

ERA ONE: PRE-1840—Few of the cameras from the pioneers of photography —Niepce, Fox Talbot, etc.—remain, and those are usually in museums. Such

cameras are not likely to be found in the United States and it's doubtful that many more will be uncovered. Photography was not exactly a toy of the general public during this period. Unless you're wealthy, patient and persevering, you can forget about this one.

ERA TWO: 1840 TO 1880—Daguerreotype cameras were produced in Europe during this period. Basically two boxes, one of which slides into the other, the cameras have signed oval nameplates which state that they are

1. When Kodak purchased the Nagel Company in Germany, Nagel cameras changed their name to become Kodak cameras. Collectors try to find both version of models like the Pupile. As many original Nagel cameras were fitted with Leitz lenses, they have great appeal for Leica collectors.

2. Extremely popular and versatile, this Kodak Recomar took both sheet film and roll film, with an adapter. This and other cut film cameras like it are still excellent performers, offering compact flexibility with such features as rising/shifting fronts, multifilm formats, and very sturdy construction.

3. Ever popular with many collectors, the Kodak Retina series is a good one for the beginning collector to cut his teeth on. Plentiful, reasonable in price, and extremely attractive performers, the Retina remains one of Kodak's finest hours.

4-5. Box cameras hold a unique fascination for many collectors. This wooden model by Scovill and Adams dates to 1888 (4), while the Six-20 Brownie E by Kodak Ltd. (England) represents the end of the era, comes complete with flash sync contacts (5).

genuine. Considering their age, there are a surprising number of these camera around, but the majority are well-known and in museums such as the George Eastman House. Their value is usually estimated at between $1500 and $4000, depending upon condition.

ERA THREE: 1880-1900—Wet-plate cameras were often sold as complete kits, since it was necessary for the photographer to carry a darkroom and all of its chemicals with him. A camera complete with such a kit is of great value to collectors. Almost all are well-made of hardwoods; lenses are often in brass mounts with "cap" shutters and a revolving disc containing the diaphragm openings (Waterhouse stops). A tripod is usually part of the kit. While many of these cameras have survived,

they are still considered "rare." The manufacturer's name is relatively unimportant, so their value depends upon condition, completeness and the salesmanship of the current owner, but you could expect to part with $100 and even more.

ERA FOUR: 1880-1900—This was also the era of high craftsmanship in the art of wooden cameras. Probably the most beautiful cameras to emerge from any era, these attract lovers of fine natural woods such as polished mahogany or cherry. While the time period coincides with that of the wet-plate camera, it was also the one in which dry plates first became available. The cameras thus became more important than the accessory equipment required to produce a picture.

Most of these cameras are fitted with red leather bellows, some of which are still in a remarkable state of preservation. The corners of the bellows are often 90 degree cutoff (modern bellows cameras use 135 degree) and few cameras will have shutters. Those which do are either very late models, or the shutters were added later. Price depends upon condition and to a great extent, upon eye appeal. Large num-

bers of these cameras are available, and prices vary with size, uniqueness, and condition more than with brand names. As a rule, the large sizes are less desirable than those 4x5 or less. Not surprisingly, the very large studio cameras of this type are relatively inexpensive, but then what do you do with it? One popular use is to place a glass top over the camera for use as a coffee table.

ERA FIVE: 1890-1920—Flexible film brought with it the era of shutters and smaller cameras. The most valuable remnants of this era seem to be the so-called "detective" cameras, which were usually made in the form of books, guns, walking sticks and even vests in an attempt to disguise the actual purpose of the user. It's difficult today to imagine a gun camera in use without someone being curious as to its true intent.

To a great extent, cameras became less the captive of the woodworker and more a product of the machinist and the instrument maker. Shutters, many of which were operated by air pistons and rubber bulbs, enabled the photographer to more accurately time his exposures. Shutters tended to be made by instrument makers such as Bausch and Lomb, and form the basis for several well-known collections around the country. The use of Japanned metal, chrome and polished brass make them visual treats for those who love intricate mechanical devices.

With the exception of a few famous names, such as Kodak, Ensign, Zeiss, Voightlander, et al, manufacturers' names are still of less importance than the uniqueness of the particular camera in question. Original cameras such as the No. 1 Kodak are relatively rare and command prices in the area of $750, but there are known copies that could well be mistaken for the genuine thing, and even the copies have considerable value when well-done.

For the most part, cameras from this era are relatively plentiful and prices reasonable, but film is no longer available for the roll-film sizes popular during their period of use. Toward the end of this era, the Kodak Autographic models were introduced. These came in many sizes and it was even possible to convert some older cameras to the Autographic feature by purchasing a new back. Since Autographics are still very plentiful, they have little value but can be made into a very nice pair of bookends.

ERA SIX: 1920-41—This period covers those years that saw vast advances in

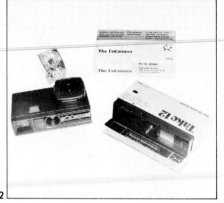

1. The unusual scissor-strut system used on this 1A Folding Pocket Kodak makes it a more-than-average folding camera to the collector.

2. The collector of disposable cameras has the most hectic life of all—here today and gone tomorrow. In the case of the Take-12—never was and never will be. The one shown here is one of the few prototypes remaining, as the company went bankrupt before the camera got to the market.

3. This early Autographic 1A Series III folder shows how the first Autographic "windows" were sealed with a sliding door. Later models used a flip-up door. The writing stylus is at the back of the camera near the handle; later models carried it inside the camera on the lens mount, or attached to the flip-up door.

4. Those captivated by the art deco of the thirties find these Jiffy Kodak cameras desirable collectibles. Collecting such models in their various sizes as well as designs can form the basis of some unique displays.

the development of mechanical and optical qualities leading to the appearance of the first production 35mm camera, which would so captivate the camera-buying public as to make it a legend in its own time—the Leica. The use of wood declined in favor of metal and some plastics as the period advanced. Not only did cameras become smaller and more precise in their construction and operation, but automatic exposure, synchronized flash and high-speed lenses became both possible and popular. Film emulsions became faster and finer grained and color films emerged. For each such development, there seemed to be a series of new manufacturers, a few of whom would become household words.

Because of the proliferation of cameras in this period, collectors find it easy to specialize in film size, camera types or brand names. The value of cameras from this era is dependent on age, condition, scarcity, and to a les-

ser extent, the original price or quality range. Late models of this period can be distinguished from look-alikes produced after World War II by the lack of a coated lens on most (coated lenses usually have a bluish cast), the lack of built-in flash and the use of nickel rather than a chrome finish.

ERA SEVEN: 1941 TO DATE—Camera production was suspended for the most part during World War II, except for those manufactured for use by the military in the warring countries. These are generally of greater value than their civilian counterparts, especially those of German and Japanese manufacture. Immediate postwar camera design was virtually identical to the prewar models with the exception of built-in flash synchronization and coated optics, but new designs and concepts began to emerge in the late '40s. This era has seen the 35mm single-lens reflex triumph in popularity over folding cameras, twin-lens reflex models and

the rangefinder 35mm. For this reason, there are some excellent buys in cameras that are not only prime collectibles, but are practical investments, since they can still be used to take excellent pictures. Such cameras command high prices today, and some models are sufficiently popular with photographers to bring a price almost equal to their original cost when new.

While this period offers relatively few cameras that could be classified as extremely rare, there are several short-lived brands such as Kardon, Fotochrome, Fotron, and others that failed to achieve popular acceptance. These have more than passing interest for the collector since they usually feature some innovation that did not catch on with the camera-buying public. A large variety of simple box-type models, including the 126 and more recent 110 cartridge-loading cameras, offer inexpensive starting points for younger collectors of cameras.

Of special interest to a growing number are the disposable or "throw-

3

away'' cameras, as well as the premium cameras. The latter are usually based on a low-priced model from a major company like Kodak. They are generally offered for a small sum of money and several product labels or box tops. While the same basic mold will be used for a variety of premium cameras, each one differs cosmetically. Your soup label camera is really the same as your chewing gum label camera, but the exterior appearance is changed from one offer to another. Collecting such variations is a quite popular and inexpensive pastime for many people.

WHAT TO LOOK FOR

One of the interesting aspects of camera collecting as a hobby is the casual manner in which many find themselves ''hooked'' as collectors. It usually starts when a friend or relative passes along a camera for which he no longer has any use. Others are compulsive thrift shop or flea market ''shoppers'' who find such bargains irresistible. Before they realize it, they have acquired a collection of several cameras at reasonable prices, and decide to continue collecting.

A surgeon at a local hospital bought all of my duplicate models at a collec-

4

tors' trade fair some years back. Curious as to why he would buy such a diverse group of cameras, I inquired about his collection, only to have him point to the cameras he had just bought from me. It seems that he wanted to become a camera collector, but couldn't find time from his hospital duties to search out what was available, so he decided to buy mine,

which put him into the hobby as an ''instant'' collector. For those in a similar quandry as to what to collect, here are a few hints and tips about the more interesting names you'll find.

ANSCO—America's oldest camera manufacturer made several models that interest collectors, of which the 35mm Memo is perhaps the most popular.

1. While Anthony and Scovill preceded George Eastman in the camera business, their Ansco line never posed much of a threat. This Ansco Junior Model A (1906) represents their turn-of-the-century handi-craft quite well.

2. For those interested in variations on a theme, these tiny 16mm cameras were produced in innumerable variations, and appeal to many collectors. Whether or not they really take pictures can be debated.

3. This Ansco folding camera from 1926 may not look different to the casual ob-server, but a collector knows that it has a spring-wound film transport—an early forerunner of today's motor drive.

4. The Kodak No. 2 Stereo Brownie is one of the few American stereo cameras prior to 1946. Stereo was far more popular abroad, thus the more desirable collec-tors' items are prewar foreign stereo plate cameras. (Courtesy, Eastman Kodak.)

The early Anthony & Scoville models were primarily wet- and dry-plate cam-eras. Later models offered were Agfa cameras imported from Germany and had little real impact on the market. The Ansco Automatic Reflex was its last attempt at a quality camera, and this twin-lens reflex from the immediate postwar years is neither rare nor too expensive.

ARGUS—The father of the inexpensive modern 35mm camera, Argus pro-duced a series of collectible cameras in that film size, as well as numerous interesting accessories, such as a con-version to turn the camera into an en-larger. The Argus A originally sold for under $10, and one in good condition will cost you only slightly more today. The Argus line was so varied and the production of each model so great (ov-er three million C-3s were made) that both prices and supplies are reason-able and steady. This is a good choice for a single-brand collection.

AGFA—The products of one of the world's older camera makers were nev-er as popular in this country as abroad. Agfa owned Ansco for some years before World War II, and many prewar models were marked Agfa-Ansco. With the exception of the Memo models of the '20s and '30s, there is not a very great demand for these folding cameras, which makes them a good buy for single-brand col-

lectors who want something different at a reasonable price.

BLAIR CAMERA COMPANY—This early camera maker later became a part of Eastman Kodak. Its cameras were pri-marily those of the plate and early roll-film era, and those made before Blair became a part of Eastman have a higher value. Condition and appear-ance will dictate the price of these fair-ly common cameras.

BURKE & JAMES—The name goes way back, and is found primarily on view, plate and sheet-film cameras, none of which is currently popular.

CANDID CAMERA CORPORATION—Candid manufactured the medium-priced 35mm Perfex cameras common in the immediate prewar and postwar years. These cameras are interesting primarily as a page in the history of the American 35mm, and can be easily lo-cated at reasonable prices.

CANON CAMERA COMPANY—Its ear-lier rangefinder cameras were Leica copies, which makes them interesting and highly desirable collectibles. Like the Leica, there were numerous run-ning changes made during the produc-tion life of each model, and this fact alone makes rangefinder Canon cam-eras a favorite. Most models are fully usable and thus have the added

4

advantage of being more than just a display item. Except for the very early models, you'll find them relatively easy to locate and fairly priced for what you acquire.

CIRO CAMERAS—Ciro manufactured the Ciroflex (five versions) and Ciro 35, which later became the Graphic 35 when Ciro threw in the towel. All are available at reasonable prices.

CONLEY CAMERA COMPANY—A view-camera manufacturer owned by Sears, Roebuck in the early days, Conley made cameras that were originally inexpensive models, and they're not the highest examples of the art, but do make nice fillers. You'll find them in fairly abundant quantities at medium price levels.

EASTMAN KODAK COMPANY—As the largest American camera manufacturer, Kodak has produced umpteen millions of cameras within specific types and series names, such as the Instamatics. Although few Kodak cameras are really rare, several such as the Bantam Special, Ektra and Super 620 are sufficiently unique to command premium

1. For something different, try a collection of early flash guns. This powder-and-bulb arrangement was an early thirties' innovation of Ralph Baird, a Denver Post photographer. (Courtesy, Honeywell Photo Products.)

2. A $9.95 camera, 30-cent film and 15-cent processing made you a movie mogul during the thirties. This first UniveX was fitted with a "fast" f/5.6 lens, but the advent of color film made it somewhat less desirable, even at the price. The UniveX line took special 8mm film and could not use color emulsions available at the time. This is a collectible novelty, but not widely popular with collectors generally.

3. This Expo watch camera shown with its film magazine was a popular seller before World War I, and is prized by collectors today. The Expo's lens is in the stem and protected by the stem cap when it is not being used.

4. Not all collectible cameras look like cameras. This Mick-O-Matic used 126 film cartridges, and is coveted by collectors.

prices. Other than these three, the most desirable models or series seem to be the original roll-film cameras and special models like the Boy Scout and Girl Scout cameras. You can assemble a good collection of certain series like the Kodak 35s or the 3A folders without working too hard or spending too much. The 3A folders make ideal book-

ends, a use that dismays the true collector to no end.

FRANKE & HEIDECKE—One of Germany's best manufacturers (Rolleiflex, Rolleicord), but due to the declining popularity of twin-lens reflex cameras, the cameras are reasonable and readily available, with the exception of the very earliest models. Certain special cameras are expensive, but only the Heidoscope, a stereo camera, is really very rare.

GRAFLEX—The majority of cameras from this company were large and so pose a storage problem for the average collector, but if you have the space, they are available at reasonable prices in a wide variety. The company as well as its products began to get smaller in its declining years, and many cameras of the early '60s were imported from Japan and Germany with the Graflex nameplate. Its 35mm cameras and the smaller reflex models, like the National Graflex, are desirable collectors' items. Graflex-Graphic cameras are almost always in working order and if not, they can be repaired quite easily.

IHAGEE—Its most famous product was the Exakta, made in countless models which all look very much alike. Exakta variations make a collection that is virtually open-ended, but the only ones of value are those produced before World War II, particularly the Model B, which used 127 film.

E. LEITZ—The most famous name in 35s is also the most collectible and valuable. Early models command premium prices, with those manufactured after World War II worth somewhat less, except for current models. Like the Canon cameras, almost all Leicas are usable and thus are more than simply display pieces. All but the rarest Leicas are readily available and at reasonable prices for those in the later series like the IIIf. Leica imitations offer another aspect of collecting and can be indulged in by those who do not feel like investing in the genuine item. Late-model Leicas like the now-discontinued M5 are prime targets for speculators, since the production run was not as great as previous models, and younger collectors see them increasing in value a few years from now at a rate faster than inflation is destroying the value of the dollar. There's always a handful of Leicas around that com-

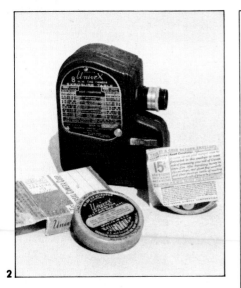

2

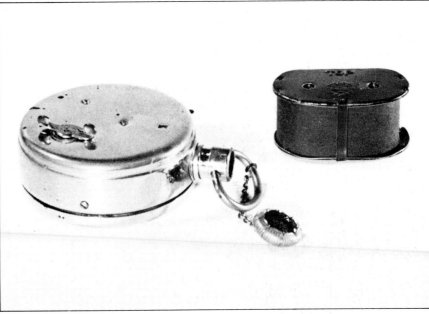

3

mand premium prices; the latest R3 is assembled in Portugal and the cameras are so stamped, but a few were assembled in Germany and marked to that effect, which automatically guarantees that they will bring a higher price from the true Leicaphile.

RUSSIAN CAMERAS—Relatively few Russian cameras are available in this country, but when they can be located, you'll find them fairly inexpensive and great conversation pieces, if nothing else. Most of the demand for Fed and Zorki models comes from those who collect Leica and Contax imitations.

MINOLTA—Although this is an old-line Japanese manufacturer, almost all of the Minolta models you'll locate will be post-World War II vintage. Those brought back by GIs during the Korean War are the most desirable.

POLAROID—Since few people collect Polaroid cameras, the prices are often ridiculously low. As a result, almost all Polaroid models are readily available. The Model 95 is long overdue in receiving its recognition as a classic and collectible camera.

ROCHESTER OPTICAL COMPANY—Although later a part of Kodak, this company once made view and box cameras under its own name. Like Conley cameras, they are fairly abundant and quite reasonable in price.

UNIVERSAL CAMERA COMPANY—Its most famous product was the UniveX Mercury (prewar) and Mercury II (postwar). Universal did not manufacture a wide variety of cameras, but did offer something in almost every type. Its prewar cameras are all unique in that they used a special film size (00) manufac-

4

tured only by Universal. The tiny plastic box cameras that launched the Universal line in the early '30s were sold in large quantities and still appear regularly at fairly reasonable prices. Other cameras that used their unique film size have less appeal, although the tiny folding models are of interest. The UniveX movie line also used a special film load. Many UniveX cameras will still contain a spool of film, as if their owners stopped using them in mid-roll, and this makes the cameras all the more interesting.

UTILITY MANUFACTURING COMPANY —These cameras generally carried the Falcon nameplate and formed the basis for the later Spartus line. Manufactured of inexpensive plastic, most were either 127 or 35mm and often used as premium items under their own and various

other names. Such cameras and their many variations make interesting and usually inexpensive collections.

VOIGHTLANDER—Never widely distributed in this country, cameras from this respected German firm probably command less attention here than in Europe. The very earliest models are rare, but even so, are in very little demand. Even the later models do not hold a high value for U.S. collectors.

ZEISS-IKON—Once a close competitor in sales to the Leica, its Contax has not developed the same intense following among collectors, although prices for those in good condition are beginning to climb. Zeiss also offered dozens of Ikonta folders and Ikoflex twinlens reflex cameras, but with the exception of the Contarex 35 and the Super Ikonta BX, few are avidly sought.

Type	Approximate Dating*	Size	Material	Description
Daguerreotype	1839 to the 1860s	Usually 2¾ × 3¼ or smaller	Metal (copper)	Silver or brown tone image is negative, but because of the mirrorlike silver image, it appears positive in reflected light. These are usually in a case with a glass cover to protect the image which is usually sharp and clear.
Ambrotype	1854 to the 1870s	Same as Daguerreotypes	Glass	The image is made on glass, the back of which is either painted or bound with a dark backing. Since it is really a collodion negative, it appears to be a positive with the backing. Usually found in cases, like the Daguerreotype, with sharp and clear images; more commonly found in the United States than Daguerreotypes.
Tintype Ferrotype Melainotype	1854 to turn of the century	Various sizes, often in odd or uneven shapes	Iron (sheet)	These have negative images, as in the other processes, but a collodion emulsion was applied to japanned (black painted) metal. The dark background makes the image appear positive. These usually are sharp but the images are somewhat dull.
Cartes De Visite	1860 to 1880s	Various sizes	Paper cards	These appear much like modern prints. They were made from glass negatives, often with multiple-lens cameras which produced several images on a single plate.
Early Eastman Prints	1884 to WWI	Circular images 2½ or 3½''	Paper mounted on cards	Paper prints made in the early Eastman (Kodak) cameras, such as the No. 1 Kodak.
Other Early Prints		Various sizes	Often mounted	The exact dates of early pictures are often difficult to determine except through subject matter dress or objects in the picture. Most made in the early period (1860-1900) were mounted on card stock, often with the photographer's name on the mount. This practice continued with studio pictures into the early 20s, but "snapshot" (unmounted) prints taken with roll-film cameras by amateurs began to be popular shortly after 1900. Most such pictures are fairly sharp, since they were contact prints. Large "postcard" prints were also popular.

MOVIE CAMERAS—Few collections of movie cameras have been assembled; for some reason, neither 8mm nor 16mm models seem to have much of a following. This may seem rather strange, since there are virtually hundreds of different 8mm, super 8 and 16mm cameras sitting on dealers' shelves and available for a pittance. A fine collection tracing the history of home movies can be assembled at a very small cost.

Movie projectors also fail to attract the attention of collectors. Although they are not as easy to come by, there have been many interesting designs from well-known companies no longer in the business. Perhaps it's the very ease with which movie equipment can be located that has prevented the various cameras and projectors from becoming desirable collectibles.

DIFFERENT APPROACHES TO COLLECTIONS

There are several ways to approach a collection of photographica other than to collect cameras by brand name. Some collectors restrict their activities to particular features, such as cameras containing a built-in power-driven film wind, while others concentrate on the various subminiature and spy-type cameras, or the disposable, mail-in-for-processing models that are usually obtained as premiums. Here are a few collection possibilities you might consider:

STEREO CAMERAS—There are two types of buyers for stereo equipment. Those who buy the 35mm models like the Stereo Realist, Kodak Stereo, Revere Stereo, etc. do so primarily to use in taking pictures. The older and generally European models using odd-sized plates are collectibles and are of interest primarily to stereo fans who also happen to collect cameras. For this reason, all but the cheaply made plastic stereo cameras and oddballs like the Linex Stereo command a premium price.

1. A well-known collector and authority on early shutters, William Carroll has won innumerable awards for his collection of restored shutters.
2. These 127 cameras preceded the Kodak Instamatic line. Since millions were made, they are an easy-to-acquire collection. The automatic model at left front is one of the more desirable, as it was one of the first automatic exposure cameras.
3. Just another movie camera? Nope, just another toy gun! When the "exposure lever" is pulled, the front pops out and you have a submachine gun.

FOLDING CAMERAS—Few of these have much value for other than the beginning collector. The ones that are of interest generally have unique features—rangefinders, interesting or novel strut designs, advanced shutters/lenses—somthing that sets them apart from the run-of-the-mill variety. Folding cameras like the Zeiss Ikontas are in demand primarily by those who want to use them for picture-taking, rather than to display in a collection. One possibility for the novice collector is to assemble the variations of a single series. For example, the Kodak 3A cameras were made over a period of many years, gradually changing until the last production run bore only a passing resemblance to the original design. A collection of this nature might not be of great investment value, but the historical value is

2

3

considerable, and with the current low interest in such cameras, is not difficult to assemble. Another decade and it may well be impossible to do so.

NOVELTY CAMERAS—Over the years, an almost endless array of novelty cameras has been produced. Some actually look like cameras while others relate to photography in different ways. Cigarette lighters, whiskey flasks in the shape of a camera, key chains, and hundreds of other items have been and are still manufactured to promote photography in one way or another.

ACESSORIES—Photographic accessories arrived almost before the camera, and have ranged from tents to cable releases to candles designed for use in the darkroom. The list is endless and if you think that they're not still around, consider the lowly screw-base flash bulb manufactured by such companies as Wabash Electric. These have not been in use or sold for two decades, yet you'd be surprised at how many photo stores have one or more cases of the old foil-filled bulbs on hand. While the cartons are naturally faded from the years, the bulbs only await an electrical charge to set them off—anyone for a collection of flash bulbs or exposure meters?

STEREO CARDS—Popular as soon as prints became possible, the stereo parlor viewer was widely available, and millions of cards were produced. The pictures were generally of historical scenes, tragedies and famous people. They exist today in the form of the View-Master reel, which by itself makes a fascinating collection, and a rather large one at that. The interest in images has increased the price of stereo cards found in antique shops, but there still seems to be a sufficient number available for most of those who are interested. Viewers are relatively inexpensive, but recent trends have noted a price increase.

MISCELLANEOUS—People collect almost anything, and many of the items being collected today were regarded as throw-aways yesterday. For example, I know of one collector who collects photographic bottles only, another who is into film boxes, one who seeks out old shutters and lens caps, and still others who favor flash attachments—the older the better. The possibilities are endless and the desire to be unique is always present among the collecting fraternity. If you can come up with something no one else has started collecting, your collection will be unique too.

WHERE TO FIND THEM

As with photographic images, the best place to look for collectible cameras is right around you. Once you've taken stock of your friends, relatives and neighbors, any of whom may either have something of interest, or know of someone who has, check in with the thrift shops, junk stores and other such establishments in your neighborhood. While it's unlikely that you'll find any truly rare cameras in such places, you can never tell for certain. One collector friend of mine recently bought a Stereo Realist with carrying case, instruction manual and warranty card packed in the original factory box—all for $7.50, and in a Palm Springs thrift shop, of all places! Since the camera appears to be brand new and carries a low serial number, he has a prime collectible worth 10 times what he paid for it.

Other good locations are church-related sales; auctions, particularly of households and farms; old stores, especially drug and variety stores; and the most likely of all—small camera shops. Camera repair shops occasionally offer unusual bargains, particularly in cameras that are not worth the re-pair bill, but still make good additions for display in a collection. Garage sales and flea markets have opened up a wide new avenue of finding real values, but antique shops are not as good possibilities as one might think. And many pawnshops, once prime sources for the collector, have taken their cue from the antique shops and turned into dealing in collectibles themselves. This limits their variety, with prices excessively high in most cases.

One of the best ways to keep in touch with what's happening in the collecting field on a national level, as well as learning the going price for specific items, is to subscribe to *Shutterbug Ads,* P. O. Box 730, Titusville, Florida 32780. This 40-page monthly newspaper from Patch Publishing Company serves as a national forum for those who wish to buy, sell or trade collectibles, as well as current photographic equipment. The average issue contains over 2000 different advertisements—fascinating reading even for those not interested specifically in collecting.

Shutterbug Ads also carries news of upcoming events sponsored by local, regional and national collectors' societies and associations. This will put you in touch with other collectors in your geographic area who share similar interests, as well as keep you informed about the increasing number and frequency of photographic trade fairs and swap meets being sponsored around the country by collectors. The paper's large readership (in excess of 10,000 subscribers) is proud of its collective reputation for honesty in its transactions, and you can deal by mail without fear of being exploited or duped.

If you should become interested in collecting photographica as a hobby, you'll find that it can be both interesting and educational. You'll meet a lot of like-minded people, and learn a good deal more about photography, its history and its influence as a communicative art. And you just may end up with a collection that's worth more than you invested.

Having covered the topics necessary in a book of this nature, let me now call your attention in closing to the final page, where you will find a complete listing of all the titles in the Petersen PhotoGraphic Library. These 80-page books provide an in-depth treatment of their subject matter, and further information on virtually any subject treated within the pages of this book can be found in one or more of the smaller volumes. □

If you would like to learn more about the basic subjects discussed in this book, or would like to learn about more advanced subjects, the following books are available from Petersen Publishing Company:

BASIC GUIDE TO PHOTOGRAPHY—This introductory guide clearly presents methods and techniques for beginners to give a comprehensive working knowledge of photography. 144 pages.

PHOTOGRAPHIC'S BLUEPRINT SERIES—A collection of concise, expertly written chapters, each dealing with a specific problem or technique. 80 pages.

BASIC DARKROOM—All the information necessary to begin developing and printing your own film. 80 pages.

PHOTOGRAPHING CHILDREN—The psychology and photo techniques of working with children to assure effective pictures. 80 pages.

SPECIAL EFFECTS—How to achieve many intriguing special effects without expensive and elaborate equipment. 80 pages.

PHOTO FILTERS—How to use the many filters available to improve your photos, and a discussion of light and color and how both affect films. 80 pages.

POCKET CAMERA PHOTOGRAPHY—Advantages, accessories and operating features of pocket cameras plus an evaluation of their strengths and weaknesses. 80 pages.

NIKON SYSTEM—A concise, up-to-date handbook that completely explains the system and how to get the most out of it and includes a section on creative techniques. 80 pages.

110 FORMAT PHOTOGRAPHY—A book to assure the photographer of getting maximum use and versatility from the new miniature cameras and their accessories. 80 pages.

INTERCHANGEABLE LENSES—The complete range of lenses available to the photographer is described along with how to use each different focal length and what can be achieved with each. 80 pages.

WIDE-ANGLE PHOTOGRAPHY—The gamut of wide-angle lenses, from fisheye through near-normal focal length, is covered in detail. Which focal length(s) are best for what, and how to put them to best use. 80 pages.

TELEPHOTO PHOTOGRAPHY—Companion volume to *Wide-Angle Photography*, this one tells all the whys and wherefores of the longer focal lengths, from portrait telephoto through super-long mirror optics. 80 pages.

PHOTOGRAPHIC MODELING—A book for both the photographer and the model with individual sections directed to each by the operator of a modeling agency. 80 pages.

PHOTO EQUIPMENT YOU CAN MAKE—Tells how to construct equipment inexpensively in just a few hours of spare time. Step-by-step illustrated instructions explain each project. 80 pages.

PHOTO EQUIPMENT YOU CAN MAKE, VOL. 2—Eleven more projects are explained and illustrated for the photo do-it-yourselfer. 80 pages.

CREATIVE DARKROOM TECHNIQUES—Basic information and techniques for achieving special photographic effects and producing creative pieces of photography inexpensively. 80 pages.

PHOTO LIGHTING TECHNIQUES—Teaches how to use light in very deliberate ways as a basic tool to create moods, effects and specific qualities. Fully illustrated. 80 pages.

AVAILABLE LIGHT—How to get the most out of the light that exists at your scene, how to improve upon it, and how to deal with low light levels. 80 pages.

PHOTOGRAPHICS—Methods for achieving consistent and predictable results with such advanced darkroom techniques as color posterization, line and multiple-line effects and others. 80 pages.

FIGURE PHOTOGRAPHY—The definitive book on the photography of the female form—includes the use of props and costumes, equipment, lighting and film. 80 pages.

SMALL-CAMERA PORTRAITURE—This book is a how-to description of photographic portraiture using today's most popular cameras combined with those contemporary tools and techniques most suited to the cameras' characteristics. 80 pages.

FREE-LANCE PHOTOGRAPHY—Discusses the subject of free-lance photography thoroughly, including developing a portfolio, markets available, methods of obtaining business. 80 pages.

ARCHITECTURAL PHOTOGRAPHY—Explores the challenging and lucrative field of architectural photography—exteriors and interiors. Detailed instructions are given for using the necessary equipment. 80 pages.

ELECTRONIC FLASH PHOTOGRAPHY—Everything you wanted to know about using electronic flash, from miniature camera-mount units to multiple-strobe studio setups. 80 pages.

COLOR PRINTING—Tells about recent advances in technology which have made processing a color print as easy as processing black-and-white prints. 80 pages.

CLOSE-UP PHOTOGRAPHY—This book covers the whole range of close-up equipment, describing each item and how to use it. It discusses extension tubes, bellows units, slide copiers and other equipment. 80 pages.

GUIDE TO MOVIE MAKING—A unique approach to making movies, which includes how the camera works, types of cameras and sound systems, film formats, how projectors work, tips on scripts and editing. 80 pages.

GUIDE TO 16mm MOVIE MAKING—A basic introduction to 16mm photography—how the camera works, how to utilize its special features, how to select and care for film, with a guide to advanced cinematic techniques. 80 pages.

FILM MAKING—How to make home movies the Hollywood way. Professional film making techniques and how the amateur movie maker can put them to good use are fully explained. 80 pages.

VIDEO TAPE RECORDING—All the information necessary to obtain professional results from small-format video tape systems, with complete instuctions for operating all types of video tape equipment. 80 pages.

FUNDAMENTAL PHOTOGRAPHY—An introduction to cameras, lenses, filters, exposure, composition, darkroom work and more. 96 pages.

HOW TO ENTER AND WIN PHOTO CONTESTS—Everything the beginner and advanced photographer needs to know about contests and producing winning photos, including a section on how to protect his interests. 96 pages.